NATIONALITIES OF THE SOVIET EAST PUBLICATIONS AND WRITING SYSTEMS

A Bibliographical Directory and Transliteration Tables for Iranian- and Turkic-Language Publications, 1818-1945, located in U.S. Libraries By *EDWARD ALLWORTH*

New York and London · Columbia University Press · 1971

THE MODERN MIDDLE EAST SERIES
No. 3

Sponsored by
The Middle East Institute
Columbia University, New York

SBN: 231–03274–9
Library of Congress Catalog Card Number: 73–110143
Printed in the United States of America

Бу китобни азиз Жаннат хонимга бағишлайман

FOREWORD

The compilation of this Bibliographical Directory, begun as a scholar's personal search for sources with which to support a small specialized study, ended as a large work in itself, expanded greatly with the realization that knowledge should be shared about the existence and location of what are surely rare publications in the West, and, one has good reason to believe, often in the East as well. A second motivation behind extending the bibliographical effort stemmed from a recognition that the time has almost passed when these scarce materials—too many of which are disintegrating into dust, disappearing into refuse barrels, or being pilfered—can be preserved.

Hopefully, scholars and curators will find this Bibliographical Directory a useful aid in selecting for filming, or other methods of copying, the valuable books and serials which may otherwise elude a promising new generation of American students capable of probing all aspects of society, politics, and the humanities in the Soviet East.

In both these broader aims the School of International Affairs, with the Middle East and Russian Institutes at Columbia University, concurred, generously providing support for the purpose of completing the compilation and preparing the Directory for publication. This volume now becomes the second in a series of such directories, the first, by the same author, being entitled *Central Asian Publishing and the Rise of Nationalism* (1965). A third contribution, listing bibliographies pertaining to the Soviet East, is well on its way toward completion.

The other major part of the present study, comprised by the Transliteration Tables, was generated by the first portion when it became clear that, to present the data required to identify each publication, some sort of transliteration would have to be provided. Our plans to print all titles in the original alphabets had proved to be slow and far too expensive. By the time the compiling ended, no fewer than eighty-six alphabets spread through almost half a dozen writing systems had to be dealt with. It was obvious that the informality with which the task of transliterating had first been approached would have to be abandoned in favor of something much more systematic. Consequently, the Transliteration Tables were worked out with the help of many of the publications included in the Bibliographical Directory which are devoted to the alphabets in the Soviet East. The tables serve a dual purpose, making possible the reproduction of this list and at the same time supplying in themselves a convenient guide for persons seeking information about the development of modern writing systems and alphabets of the Soviet East.

In conducting the research for the Bibliographical Directory we examined every publication, or a photocopy of it, named in the Directory. Since one of our primary aims consisted of registering particularly those titles which exist in peripheral collections but find no place in the general catalogs of the principal American research libraries, the compilers concentrated upon finding such publications. The search inevitably led, however, also to those cataloged materials, held in the same libraries, which fall within our bibliographical framework. No guarantee can be given that all such treasures have been discovered. Details about the method employed in that process will be described in the section introducing the Directory.

A work of this magnitude could not have been prepared without a huge amount of assistance and advice from qualified persons, and it is one of the pleasures of soliciting counsel from colleagues that the receiving of it not only educates the questioner but provides an opportunity to express one's gratitude to wise, generous people, surely making this one of academic society's most satisfying and civilized interactions. Thus, to Professors John R. Krueger and Ilya Gershevitch as well as Mr. Mustafa R. Bucak, who gave their time graciously in clarifying special problems relating to the Chuvash, Yakut, Ossetic, and Kurd titles in the Directory, sincere thanks. Neither they nor any others mentioned here of course are accountable for mistakes which may have crept into this study. Within the Department of Middle East Languages and Cultures at

Columbia University I am particularly indebted to Dr. William Hanaway, Jr., and to Professors John Badeau, Karl H. Menges, Isaac Barzilay, and Maan Madina. Dean Schuyler Wallace gave the effort a sympathetic nudge at its inception.

Special mention deserve those who shared with me the labor of compiling the several thousand titles listed below: Azamat Altay, Dr. Leon Kassin, Professor Edward Keenen, Dr. Aman B. Murat, Dr. David Nissman, and Professor Andreas Tietze. Many who contributed in a variety of ways to benefit the general effort were Professors Salo Baron, Sakine Berengian, Alexandre Bennigsen, Dr. Gustave Burbiel, Dr. Chantal Lemercier-Quelquejay, Garip Sultan, Malihe Sattarzade, Saniye Altay, Helly Barzilay, Izzudeen Essa'id, Shafiq Kazzaz, Eleanor Buist, Eugene Sheehy and John Waddell. At several of the libraries surveyed we enjoyed the helpful cooperation of Ibraham Pourhadi (Library of Congress), Dr. Viktor Koresaar (New York Public Library), Arline Paul (Hoover Library), Donald Anthony and Robert Karlowich (Columbia University), and Dr. Simon Cohen (Hebrew Union College).

Joan McQuary, at Columbia University Press, edited the unruly material into good order after the very difficult manuscript was typed and retyped in large part by Janet Allworth, Azamat Altay, Ellen Ervin, and Halime Shahmay. There must be more creditors, and to them also goes sincere appreciation in repayment, if possible, for kind assistance rendered on a thousand different days.

Edward Allworth

New York
March, 1970

CONTENTS

A NEW PHASE IN AMERICAN RESEARCH ON NATIONALITIES OF THE SOVIET EAST

A NEW PHASE IN AMERICAN RESEARCH ON NATIONALITIES OF THE SOVIET EAST

The peculiar social and political complexity which characterizes the Soviet East today, quite aside from the great natural ethnic and linguistic diversity, has resulted to a large extent from the manipulation of outsiders. An extraordinary flux marking the progress of Eastern nationality affairs now increasingly attracts the attention of American scholars, and can be traced directly through conflicting but politically inspired tendencies within the area. Throughout recent history the Eastern territory and population, annexed by the Czarist and then the Soviet regime, have served as a laboratory accommodating zealots eager to test their formulas for unifying the widely disparate nationalities into one homogeneous mass.

As Russia invaded the East in centuries past, Orthodox missionaries mixed with or followed Czarist soldiers moving into the Asian expanse, driven on by a fervor for uniting heathens and heretics alike with Russia through the teachings of the church. (This effort reflects itself noticeably, for example, in the cultural history of the Chuvash, Kreshen Tatars, Yakuts, and smaller groups whose writing systems and publications are recorded below.)

After Christianity ceased to provide the official faith in 1917, new ideologies brewing in what St. Petersburg had called "indivisible" Russia claimed the same right to universal popular allegiance as religion had before. Communism has likewise devoted a substantial part of its energies for fifty years to the purpose of binding together the nationalities, a considerable proportion of them (about 40 percent of the over 100 million non-Russians in 1959) inhabiting the Soviet East. Paradoxically, while the new regime was attempting to reunify all the nationalities around a novel, Marxist (nonnationality) core, it was simultaneously endeavouring to divide these Eastern populations administratively and culturally down to the smallest (nationality) denominator. Thus, the Russian government in power since 1917, like the one which preceded it, has worked indefatigably to mold a citizenry out of the more than five dozen Eastern nationalities which would regard itself, along with the Russians, as uniform from Moscow to Yakutsk. But the astonishing degree to which heterogeneity has resisted the government's campaign for unity, after all the effort expended, seriously affects the picture which outsiders acquire through cursory examination of Soviet Eastern affairs.

This latent disunity, plus a Marxist compulsion to rewrite history, added to the paucity of appropriate sources, makes accurate interpretation of data concerning that massive area and its millions of people not only more challenging than investigating an open society but much more risky, for the distance between recorded Soviet policy, official history, and actual reality, like the expanse of the Soviet East, is immense. These considerations, together with factors related to the pattern of development in American academic training on the USSR—formerly dominated by an almost exclusive interest in Slavic Russia alone—had until fairly recently delayed inquiry into many vital questions concerning the Soviet East. Since World War II, however, that preoccupation has been significantly modified by American historians, political scientists, and literary and other scholars who have turned their minds to the why and how of developments among the nationalities of the Transcaucasus, Turkistan, Kazakhstan, and comparable parts of the Eastern USSR. The appearance of these valuable studies demarks a second stage, the first having been largely linguistic and archaeological, in American scholarship on the area. Important examples are Firuz Kazemzade's *The Struggle for Transcaucasia, 1917–1921* (1951), Alexander Park's *Bolshevism in Turkestan, 1917–1927* (1957), Thomas Winner's *The Oral Art and Literature of the Kazakhs of Russian Central Asia* (1958), Richard Pierce's *Russian Central Asia, 1867–1917* (1960), Serge Zenkovsky's *Pan-Turkism and Islam in Russia* (1960), and Lawrence Krader's *Peoples of Central Asia* (1963).

Especially following Stalin's death in 1953 and perhaps thanks to it the Soviet East has been gradually reopened by Russian authorities to travel by foreigners. During the same period the flow of local-language publications abroad, interrupted for the most part between 1937 and 1955, has resumed. Now, a promising quantity of new journals, newspapers, books, and pamphlets in those languages may be found in most major research libraries in the United States. Without a doubt this change, combined with widening realization in America that the Soviet East was to acquire crucial importance in the postwar era of de-colonization in Asia and Africa, helped to stimulate the rise of a different sort of scholar in this country, committed to deeper study of the Soviet East.

Superficially, the new scholar may be identified through his preoccupation with social science or humanities disciplines other than pure linguistic study. But at the same time, his work acquires a special character by employing, in addition to Russian and the usual European languages, those from among the Iranian, Turkic, or other Soviet Eastern families which serve his research needs. It is a notable achievement that, almost without exception, this new scholar has been trained by the European linguist-philologists who have contributed so much to preparing American graduate students for this evolution to studies of the East which are focused outside of linguistics. In addition, among the younger scholars in this field, there has been a noticeable tendency to replace the former concern with antiquities for greater concentration upon the recent past or the contemporary scene. Interest in modernization nevertheless seems to be grounded upon a fundamental sensitivity to preparatory developments of the past.

Notwithstanding laudable attempts by some American students of the Soviet East to employ local-language sources in their work, it cannot be proved that by itself this technique comprises more than a beginning. Scholarship in this new phase has as its indispensible ingredient a unique orientation toward the problems under scrutiny. More and more, such questions are necessarily being viewed from the inside of the target area, so to speak, rather than from Moscow, Leningrad, or the academic capitals of the West. The major difficulty underlying this kind of inquiry is plainly the need to perfect a method of studying the Soviet East in this country which may be freed in large measure from dependence upon secondary, generally Russian, materials which are often weighted with their pervasive biases and methodology. Up to now, perhaps too great credence has been granted Russian recapitulations of occurrences in the recent decades. The new type of American social scientist or humanist focusing upon the Soviet East is endeavoring to initiate his own, distinctive approach to the subjects of research in that world. He will consequently succeed in avoiding the kind of imbalance resulting from the play of ethnocentricities and other prejudices which has sometimes caused the Soviet Easterner to be treated merely as a curious ethnographic specimen or an uncultured "native." The new phase in scholarship is typified by more than its conservative caution, however. An affirmative drive which propels the research embodies a desire to grasp and to interpret the picture of the personal and public world of the Soviet Easterner much as he himself has viewed it at significant junctures in current or earlier history, politics, literature, sociology, art, and other rewarding fields. New emphasis is being placed, therefore, not so much upon what outsiders see, or what happens to the Tajik or Tatar, or what the regime wants to happen, as to understanding the local citizen's attitude toward what was transpiring in his own cultural, social, and political milieu.

Nearly everyone will agree, most likely, that for a pioneer on this frontier to employ Iranian- or Turkic-language publications definitely moves him toward those distant goals, but it is also clear that merely scrutinizing the local-language press, though it will often alter the viewpoint of the scholar, cannot guarantee that he has found a safe way to detour around every pitfall dug by distortion, subjectivity, and ideology in the past or present. Local material is, nevertheless, susceptible to careful analysis, whether it was published in earlier times or the present. But there is a pointed difference between works issued, for example between 1900 and 1935 and those coming out today. Now, contemporary local writers and scholars in the Soviet East rely a great deal upon what are apparently ideologically secure Russian secondary sources for guidance in their own work. This was true to a much smaller degree in the 1920s and early 1930s, and before those decades it was generally not very often a highly significant element in forming local attitudes towards the milieu of the Soviet Easterner.

Equipped with an understanding of all these complications, the new scholar, through deepening his approach to such research, has quite naturally developed an appetite for extensive amounts of materials issued in the languages of the nationalities indigenous to the Caucasus and Transcaucasus, Central Asia (including Kazakhstan), the Crimea, Asian regions of the Urals, Siberia and the Volga Basin, and some other parts of the Czarist or Soviet East. Among the steps which he may take to clarify the confusions and organize his evidence is to systematize records of sources and bibliography. This method, besides bringing the available materials under control, provides a graphic manner of verifying the patterns of tremendous diversity, coupled with relevant similarities, in people, languages, and ways of thinking, all dynamically on the move constantly throughout the Soviet East.

The following Bibliographical Directory (a name used here to designate what American librarians call a "union list"—showing the location of publications in one or more libraries), prepared for the use of the new scholars, attempts to achieve progress along these channels, in codified form, simultaneously illustrating important features and effects of Russian nationality policies. The main purpose of issuing this Bibliographical Directory is to facilitate direct study of local-language materials from the Soviet East in order to support the growing tendencies in American scholarship already described. Beyond that primary objective lies the goal of encouraging all branches of scholarship in the United States to take cognizance of the fruits beginning to mature in this still-neglected area in Western research. Examples of these new studies are starting to appear in history, literature, and politics.

Fortunately for the announced aims of this bibliographical effort, the Directory—through no design on the part of its author—exhibits by far its greatest strength in publications issued during the transition period of the 1920s or earlier, rather than in the late 1930s and early 1940s when Russian Communist dominance became so apparent in most printed material and the nationalities virtually lost their true voices. The Directory lists, in addition to works originated by local authors, agencies, or institutions, many translations from European languages and Russian into Soviet Eastern tongues. Those translations provide clues to the range of outside influences to which the Soviet Easterner was potentially exposed. Some works available here in translation may also well be rarities in the original Russian, for many authors have since become un-persons in Russian politics. Other translations attain significance more by reason of the identity of the translator—often the most prominent nationalists in the Soviet East engaged in this traditionally respected activity—than from their own content. Among the translations, besides ideological and other tracts, may be found masterpieces by writers as well known as Gogol and Pushkin, along with writings of Western literary figures, which have been taken into Crimean Tatar, Tajik, and related languages by outstanding poets or scholars in the Soviet East. For a sampling, see Nos. 1160, 1164, 1616, and 2482 in the Bibliographical Directory. Although the new research into problems of the Soviet East emphasizes fields other than linguistics, the Bibliographical Directory registers many titles useful for the analysis of language.

The period covered by the Directory has been terminated with 1945 for several reasons: back from 1946 extends the era of most acute shortage in American source materials for these studies; at the same time, for many scholars interested in the affairs of the 1960s and later, this period preceding 1946 constitutes an essential watershed for the understanding of later developments. Other reasons include drawing attention to the need for preservation of the rare older publications, many seriously deteriorating; dividing the post-World War II atomic decades from the preceding distinct periods in Soviet Eastern development while embracing publications issued in all writing systems and alphabets published up to the present; limiting the bibliographical research effort as well as the bulk of the Directory to manageable size. There is still a great need for preparation of a sequel to this volume covering a suitable portion, say twenty years, of the following period. Hopefully, someone with sufficient resources, patience, and time will undertake the altruistic task—bibliographies are published for the benefit of persons other than their authors or compilers.

Dates and Numbers of Publications

The Bibliographical Directory's more than 3,350 entries for journals, newspapers, books, and pamphlets in twenty-six Iranian and Turkic languages of the Soviet East—which have been located in various university or public libraries in the United States—are supplemented in the file upon which this bibliography is based with cards reporting another 536 titles of works in the fields of science and technology.

These, as well as those in the main file, may be consulted by arrangement with the author. They include works in sixteen of the languages represented by the Bibliographical Directory; the largest group, Uzbek, is spread among agriculture (70 titles), technology (5), medicine (10), and science (13). Smallest is Khakass with 1 agricultural title. Other relatively large numbers of titles located in these fields are made up of the Kazakh (91), Volga Tatar (86), Azerbaijanian (79), and Chuvash (59).

Besides the publications singled out in previous passages because they are especially germane to the problem of nationalities in the Soviet East, this Directory lists diverse subject and discipline offerings spread over a publishing period of nearly a century and a half. The list cannot be taken as a reliable mirror of the publishing activity in that area, since the method of distributing and preserving publications in that period must be regarded as quite haphazard. Nevertheless, in the earliest local printing and lithographing in a few of these languages—a nineteenth-century phenomenon for some, a later one for the others—this bibliography reveals clusters which often roughly correspond to the peaks of such publishing activity. In this respect, the Bibliographical Directory goes beyond its essential function as a guide to specific works in definite fields to tell the scholar a little about the development of publishing among the people of the Soviet East. Table 1 provides statistics about publishing in this area between 1913 and 1928.

Chuvash, Karaim, Kreshen and Volga Tatar, and Yakut works had been published in their languages no later than the early nineteenth century.[1] Many of these books were, however, either

---

[1]P. V. Popov, "Kratkaia istoriia razvitiia iakutskogo pis'ma," in L. N. Kharitonov, *Sovremennyi iakutskii iazyk. Chast' pervaia: Fonetika i morfologiia* (Yakutsk: Gosizdat IaASSR, 1947), pp. 286–87; Edward Allworth, *Central Asian Publishing and the Rise of Nationalism* (New York: New York Public Library, 1965), pp. 10, 34; Alexandre Bennigsen and Chantal Lemercier-Quelquejay, *La Presse et le Mouvement national chez les Musulmans de Russie avant 1920* (Paris: Mouton, 1964), pp. 21–33; and Vasiliĭ Sboev, "Zamietki o Chuvashakh," *Izsliedovaniia ob inorodtsakh kazanskoi gubernii* (Kazan: Izdanie Knigoprodavtsa Dubrovina, 1856), pp. 55–56.

TABLE 1

*Book Publishing in Iranian and Turkic Languages**

LANGUAGE	TITLES 1913	TITLES 1927	TITLES 1928	COPIES 1913	COPIES 1927	COPIES 1928
Altay (Oyrot)		26	23		34,550	32,381
Azeri (Tiurkskii)	95	473	525	111,540	1,387,750	1,801,236
Bashkir		87	118		205,450	282,890
Bukharan Jewish			3			9,000
Chuvash	57	83	115	106,900	278,800	464,272
Crimean Tatar } Volga Tatar	267	88	103	1,052,100	220,600	225,650
		374	428		1,518,602	1,806,030
Karachay-Balkar		10	15		26,000	29,750
Kazakh } Kirgiz	37	291	300	156,300	1,139,323	1,792,571
Khakass		3	18		5,500	27,500
Kumyk		42	34		65,570	62,190
Noghay		5	2		11,000	2,500
Ossetic	4	19	28	2,270	28,300	51,200
Tajik	5	56	54	15,000	227,205	269,499
Tat		2	11		4,000	17,570
Turkmen		85	94		219,091	298,720
Uyghur		3	2		6,500	3,000
Uzbek	36	424	402	85,300	1,596,465	1,973,614
Yakut	1	20	33	1,614	54,140	60,300

**Natsional'naia politika VKP (b) v tsifrakh* (Moscow: Izdatel'stvo Kommunisticheskoi Akademii, 1930), pp. 299–300. The source overlooks Karaim, Karakalpak, Kreshen Tatar, Kurd, Nagaybak, Shor, and probably other languages (Tuvan?) in which Czarist and Soviet Eastern books appeared during 1913, 1927, or 1928. See Nos. 1749, 1750, 1851 in this Bibliographical Directory. None the less, it is one of the few available reports concerning the publishing in this period.

issued by Russian Orthodox missionaries for religious proselyting or were texts recorded by Russian linguists and philologists. Genuine local publishing flourished in most of those cases only after 1850. This Bibliographical Directory lists but 14 titles dating before that year; 8 of them fall under the category of Philosophy and Religion. Through 1889 another 21 titles appear here, 9 of them in Language, 4 in History, 4 in Philosophy and Religion, 3 from Literature, and 1 under General (Newspapers and Periodicals). That final item may stand out as one of the most interesting and valuable in the collections for it refers to the first periodical issued in a local Turkic language in the Czarist East by and for an indigenous nationality. This is the Azerbaijanian *Äkinchi* (No. 30) published in Baku, 1875–1877. From 1890 through 1916 more frequent examples from the local press are to be found here, continuing as before to stress the fields of Language, Literature, and Philosophy and Religion, with a few now turning up in Education, and from 1905 on a surprising 25 entries appear under the heading General (Newspapers and Periodicals). In all, as Table 2 shows, the Bibliographical Directory records 140 titles distributed before 1917 in languages of the nationalities of the Czarist East. Of these, periodicals or newspapers, a number of which ran well beyond one year of publication, comprised 27.

Holdings surveyed in American libraries begin to grow rapidly only in the early 1920s, when the Soviet government, in its effort to propagandize developments under the new regime, took pains to disseminate materials in Soviet Eastern languages rather widely. The reflection of this policy can be discerned easily in Table 2, where the composite totals for publications in all disciplines beginning in 1920 starts at 6 titles but quickly jumps to 12 in 1921, 33 in 1922, 53 in 1923, and 167 for 1924. Thereafter, the totals rise successively to the peak year in 1927 (584 titles, including 26 periodicals), and remain at a high level through 1930. The sudden drop from 417 titles in 1930 to 27 in 1932 probably reflects a drying up of the export flow due to the hotter political climate in the USSR as suspicion toward foreigners became a fetish in Moscow and domestic purges intensified.

Not until the final year of World War II, as Table 2 reveals, does the bibliography record a return to the annual number of titles

TABLE 2

Number of Titles in the Bibliographical Directory, by Date and Discipline

	1818–1871	1875	1878	1883	1884	1885	1890	1892	1
General: Books									
General: Serials		1		1					
Anthropology									
Economics									
Education									
Geography									
Government	1								
History	5					1			
Law									
Social Organization									
Art, Architecture									
Language	7	1	1	1				1	
Literature	4						1		
Music									
Philosophy, Religion	11				1		1		
Total	28	2	1	2	1	1	2	1	

	1907	1908	1909	1910	1911	1912	1913	1914	1
General: Books									
General: Serials	2	3		1	2		1	3	
Anthropology									
Economics									
Education							1		
Geography									
Government					1				
History								1	
Law									
Social Organization									
Art, Architecture									
Language						2			
Literature			3	1	1	1	1	3	
Music									
Philosophy, Religion								1	
Total	2	3	3	2	4	3	3	8	

	4	1895	1897	1898	1899	1900	1901	1902	1903	1904	1905	1906
											1	6
	1			1	1							
										1		
										2	1	
										1		
	2	1	1	1	4	2				2		1
	1		1	1		3	1	2	1	2		
	1	1	1	2	1	2	1	1	1			
	5	2	3	5	6	7	2	3	2	8	2	7

	6	1917	1918	1919	1920	1921	1922	1923	1924	1925	1926	1927
									1		3	9
	1			1			3	1	1	12	13	35
											2	2
						2	1	6	7	11	36	54
					3	1	7	7	23	47	67	78
						1			2	4	2	7
		1	2		3	1	1	12	44	69	100	156
			1					1	20	16	16	22
								1	2	3	3	21
						2	1	3	9	14	37	45
												3
							3		3	3	13	9
	1	4	1			5	17	22	50	72	90	132
												1
									5	5	1	10
	2	5	4	1	6	12	33	53	167	256	383	584

Continued on following pages

TABLE 2 (continued)

Number of Titles in the Bibliographical Directory, by Date and Discipline

	1928	1929	1930	1931	1932	1933	1934	1935
General: Books	6	5	5					
General: Serials	26	26	17	2	1		1	2
Anthropology			1					
Economics	53	71	90	8	3			
Education	76	91	64	8	7	1		1
Geography	2	1						
Government	120	92	78		4	1		
History	11	13	10	1				1
Law	11	7	15	6	1			
Social Organization	40	47	44		1			
Art, Architecture	3	3						
Language	7	5	8	2	1		1	3
Literature	79	80	72		3	1	1	3
Music		1						
Philosophy, Religion	12	11	12					
Total	446	453	416	27	21	3	3	10

*Statistical work for this table was carried out by Aman B. Murat, Ph.D candidate at Columbia University. Statistics do not include No. 229a Azeri Government, Nos. 1799a, 1799b, 1801a Kurd Education, No. 1180a Crimean Tatar Literature, No. 1656 Khakass Literature, No. 1781a Kumyk Social Organization, No. 1886a Tajik History, Nos. 1915a, 1915b, 1915c Tajik Literature, No. 2502a Uzbek Philosophy and Religion, No. 2791a Volga Tatar Government, and No. 3171a Volga Tatar Literature.

reached as early as 1923. If a similar bibliographical guide is one day prepared to list available publications from the Soviet East issued after 1945, the record very likely will evidence the periodic opening and closing of the outside doors from the Soviet Union. On this basis, one could expect the years 1946–1953 to be rather poorly represented in American libraries, with an upswing since the death of Stalin, and particularly following the renewal of active tourist travel and cultural exchanges in and with that area.

1938	1939	1940	1941	1942	1943	1944	1945	n.d.	*Total** 1818–1945
									29
1	2					1	3	2	178
									5
	4			1			1	21	373
1		1					11	12	516
							1	1	21
1	13	11	3	2	3	6	6	27	760
	2	1	4		3	2	1	3	138
3	3	2	2			1	3	4	88
	1						1	8	253
									10
1	5	1	2	1		2	2		101
1	2	16	19	7	5	12	29	11	770
									3
	2							3	96
8	34	32	30	11	11	24	58	92	3341*

Subject Fields and Disciplines

Anyone referring to the Bibliographical Directory should be aware that in the search for information to be registered by this Directory the compilers generally approached the libraries to be surveyed without preconceptions respecting the exact nature of published material in Soviet Eastern languages which might be found. Only Karaim publications were sought specifically—at the libraries of the Hebrew Union College in Cincinnati and the Jewish Theological Seminary in New York. Other language groups would also have been treated individually had there been promising leads available suggesting that separate public collections for languages such as Ossetic, Volga Tatar, or Uzbek existed somewhere in the United States. As a result, the list, organized conventionally on the basis of materials actually located, provides data for separate publications, periodicals, and newspapers dated before 1946 in these three major categories: General reference, Social

Sciences, and Humanities, the last two divided into subcategories:

General

(Includes bibliography and catalogs; calendars; newspapers, listed individually; periodicals, listed individually; press and publishing)

Social Sciences

- Anthropology
- Economics
- Education
- Geography
- Government (Political Science)
- History
- Law
- Social Organization

Humanities

- Art and Architecture
- Language
- Literature
- Music
- Philosophy and Religion

Within this broad system the difficult decisions which were required to choose proper subclassifications appropriate for some publications in a few instances are worth mentioning. Such problems arise mainly out of the peculiarities of Soviet classifications and terminology. The study of "Marxism–Leninism," "Communism," "dialectical materialism," or "class struggle" for example, fall under their conception of philosophy.[2] That procedure has not been followed here. The first three subjects appear in this directory under Government, and the study of "class struggle" along with class structure is subordinated to Social Organization.

Economics includes, in addition to statistical and economic studies, materials relating to agricultural and industrial development, cotton- and tea-raising and processing, irrigation and water problems, factories, cooperatives, kolkhozes and collectivization, and labor and labor union matters. Education embraces the usual ingredients relating to instruction and schooling plus textbooks in

[2] *Knizhnaia letopis'*, No. 1 (Moscow, 1969), p. 77.

whatever field, the alphabet question and orthography, intellectuals, and illiteracy. Government, besides structure, administration, and elections, combines all party political affairs in addition to war, peace and military matters, study of the nationality question, political indoctrination, revolution, foreign affairs, and the works and tenets of Marx, Engels, Lenin, Stalin, and other ideologists. Social Organization subsumes materials regarding human groups, women, children, family, youth, adults, farmers, factory workers, the village, urban problems, and public health. Literature has in it, besides poetry and prose, criticism, literary history, oral art, sayings and proverbs, drama and theater. Literature and language each include texts in Soviet Eastern tongues issued by Russian and other foreign linguists. These publications, as well as a number of dictionaries, have been added to the Directory occasionally, but no systematic attempt was made to exhaust this category. The category of Philosophy and Religion embraces antireligious propaganda and atheism as well as religious books.

By organizing the bibliography's entries according to various recognized disciplines it has been intended to accommodate any scholar or bibliographer who may refer to this work. This conventional approach should be construed not so much as an endorsement of academic custom in this respect as an invitation to innovation by persons with an interest in crossing disciplinary lines to integrate their findings. For them, the extensive subject index should be particularly useful.

Students of government and of literature have at their disposal the largest fund of publications from the Soviet East recorded in the Bibliographical Directory, each discipline by chance totaling around 760 titles. This surprising coincidence will serve one useful purpose if it dispels the notion common among those aware of the Soviet Eastern collections around the country that such publications consist only of literary and linguistic materials (see Table 3). In fact, the disciplines best represented, after government and literature, are education (515), economics (373), social organization (253), and history (139). Periodicals and newspapers numbering 178 touch a variety of fields. Not counting this last category, the social sciences as a group numerically outweigh the humanities (2,183 against 980). Furthermore, the preeminence,

*TABLE 3 Number of Titles, by Language and Discipline**

Language	General	Anthropology	Economics	Education	Geography	Government	History	Law	Social Organization	Art, Architecture	Language	Literature	Music	Philosophy, Religion	Total
Altay			2	5		5		3	2		2	6		1	26
Azeri	49	3	47	58	3	138	11	20	54		19	183		14	599
Bashkir	21		29	23	1	40	5	4	8		5	25		3	164
Chuvash	16	1	22	27	3	80	11	3	25		5	60	1	15	269
Crimean Tatar	9	1	14	32		10	8	3	15	1	1	45		3	142
Karachay-Balkar			1	5		11	1		6			7			31
Karaim						2					4	3		11	20
Karakalpak			1			1	2								4
Kazakh	20		67	47		111	11	10	28	1	13	75		3	386
Khakass			2	3		2			5		3			1	16
Kirgiz	3		16	15	1	29	2	3	5	1	3	13			91
Kreshen Tatar				1			1								2
Krymchak														1	1
Kumyk	1		4	10		10	1	3	6			7		1	43
Kurd	1		1	7		1	3					1			14
Nagaybak														1	1
Noghay				1		1		1	1			1		1	6
Ossetic	2		1	5		8			6		3	8		2	35
Shor				1											1
Tajik	1		6	11	2	14	5	2	4	1	2	22			70
Tat			1						1						2
Turkmen	5		13	20	1	17	4	2	4		2	14			82
Uyghur				1								3			4
Uzbek	30		80	88	3	100	27	28	22		20	86	2	7	493
Volga Tatar	45		60	147	7	175	45	6	55	6	17	204		29	796
Yakut	4		6	8		5	2		6		2	7		3	43
Total	207	5	373	515	21	760	139	88	253	10	101	770	3	96	3341

*Statistical work for this table was carried out by Aman B. Murat, Ph.D candidate at Columbia University. Statistics do not include 229a Azeri Government, 1180a Crimean Tatar Literature, 1656 Khakass Literature, 1781a Kumyk Social Organization, 1799a, 1799b, 1801a Kurd Education, 1886a Tajik History, Nos. 1915a, 1915b, 1915c Tajik Literature, No. 2502a Uzbek Philosophy and Religion, 2791a Volga Tatar Government, and 3171a Volga Tatar Literature.

for this bibliography, of the year 1927 in the entire chronology of publishing held true to some extent within the individual disciplines as well. The strongest publishing period in this collection for the categories of Government, Literature, History, and General (including Newspapers and Periodicals) remained exactly 1927. For Education and Social Organization, however, it was 1929; for Economics, 1930. In summary, the numerical superiority among holdings in American libraries of publications in languages of the Soviet East for the period up through 1945 lies clearly within the range 1924-1930. Thus, the scholar seeking the widest selection of available material within the framework outlined will have the greatest choice if he looks to the output of the mid-1920s to early 1930s.

Quite apart from the quantitative measurement of the entries included in the Bibliographical Directory, it shows that the collections offer many works and serial publications which deserve recognition because of their extremely small edition, their unique content, the fact that they have been banned in their homeland and their authors liquidated, that the publisher issued very few titles, or for other reasons are rare items in any library, whether Soviet or non-Soviet. Among these, nearly all of the serial publications circulated from the 1920s and earlier present unrivalled opportunities for research into the ideological controversies or social and intellectual currents of their day. Most of such publications simultaneously also shed light upon developments in the particular subject fields or disciplines. For example, the Uzbek journal *Pakhta üchün küräsh* (No. 2031) provides a rare chance to study from original material of the mid-1930s not only the drive to improve cotton production in Central Asia and the attendant drastic effect upon the economy of the area, but to investigate the political significance of a very controversial corollary issue in that territory: whether to deemphasize cotton-raising and keep the region self-sustaining in food production or to make Central Asia dependent upon central Russia for provisions and thus subject to direct pressure in a most sensitive, vital sector of the economy. This journal, taken in conjunction with many other listed publications emanating from Tashkent in the late 1920s and early- to mid-1930s, may supply an excellent selection of sources not only relevant to the economy and politics of Uzbekistan, but for all cotton-growing sections of Central Asia.

In the intellectual and ideological sphere no question could be more volatile than that of religion in the Soviet East. Of the nationalities represented in the Bibliographical Directory, the Altays, Chuvash, Karaims, Khakass, Kreshen Tatars, Krymchaks, Nagaybaks, some Ossets, Shors, Tats (Mountain Jews), and Yakuts, altogether comprising nearly half of the nationalities represented on our list, were not Muslims. This fact supports one of the pertinent arguments against lumping the people of the Soviet East only under the rubric "Muslims." A second difficulty created by attempting to apply "Muslim" to the Soviet East becomes more evident with each passing year: as the older generations pass away, the younger men and women can hardly be considered religious in any sense. Therefore, besides the "Muslim" approach, today's study of the "Soviet East" may be equally fitting. It would be particularly revealing, nevertheless, to study the problem of religion among one of the formerly Muslim nationalities of the Soviet East in order to pursue the course of the ideological conflict connected with this issue. American libraries possess several publications especially relevant to such research if it were directed toward the situation among the Volga Tatars, for instance: *al-Din va' l-Adab* (No. 2511) is a substantial pre-Soviet periodical in this field from the early twentieth century. *Fän häm din* (No. 2512) focuses upon similar problems in the framework of the late 1920s and early 1930s. These journals can be supported by nearly thirty books and pamphlets (Nos. 3270–3298), also in Volga Tatar, concerning problems of religion in the nineteenth and early twentieth centuries, a promising compilation for any investigator. Additional materials regarding the same problem among other nationalities of the Soviet East are also registered in this Bibliographical Directory.

Certain language groups included in this Directory show up much more strongly than any others with respect to materials from specific subject fields or disciplines. Volga Tatar, in the example just given, seems to be the leader in publications concerning philosophy and religion. Volga Tatar likewise heads the list in the overall number of titles located in American libraries, with above 800 entries, including periodicals for which many issues are available over a period of years. Table 3 shows that after the Volga Tatars the most numerous collections represented in the Bibliographical Directory represent the Azeris (Azerbaijanians) with just 600 titles, including many periodicals, and Uzbek, of which American libraries hold almost 500 separate and serial publications from the period covered. At the numerical bottom of the language list stand Krymchak, Nagaybak, Shor, Kreshen Tatar, Tat, Karakalpak, and Uyghur, each with 4 or fewer. Though they are not great in quantity, among the most significant holdings, perhaps, should be considered those publications in the Crimean Tatar language, for that group had virtually ceased its national existence after it was evicted from the Crimea in 1944, until 1967, so far as the Russian authorities were concerned. Even now, the Crimean Tatars have no distinct administrative status within the USSR, their scanty publishing being handled in Central Asia for the present. It is doubtful, even though the Crimeans have been "rehabilitated," that Russia will find it necessary to reinstate a recalcitrant nationality that has once been removed from its own territory and from the list of special oblasts or republics.

Turkic nationalities belong to the most populous indigenous language family of the Soviet East. Altogether, publications from those nationalities far outnumber all others from the Soviet East issued between 1818 and 1945 and located in U.S. libraries. This superiority can be explained not only by the fact that the Turkic population exceeds that of any other Eastern people in the area, but also because the Azerbaijanians, Kirgiz, Yakuts, and their kinsmen underwent administrative-political organization into at least sixteen union, autonomous, and peoples Soviet republics at one time or another during the period studied. Most of them possessed their own publishing establishments. Iranian nationalities entered into several of these Soviet republics with their Turkic neighbors. Iranian cultural or religious patterns and those of these Turkic people have born noticeable resemblance in many instances. Interplay between their languages and civilizations in the past continues today. These and other factors led to the decision to concentrate in this Bibliographical Directory upon the Iranian and Turkic-language material from the Soviet East.

Besides the publishing undertaken by them, books and periodicals from many local nationalities outside the Iranian and Turkic groups of the Soviet East can also be found in the libraries of the United States. Like the publications registered in this volume, those of the Buriats and Kalmyks, Maris and Komis, Adiges and Chechens, and more, remain generally uncatalogued and uncared for. To bring them one step out of such obscurity, the same type of bibliographical information and notation of where they may be consulted has also been compiled for around 1000 such publications in the course of this research. Simple card files are maintained for each. The most extensive of these collections include Mordvin (203 entries), Komi (196), Mari (173), Udmurt (72), and Chechen (65). In the present effort plans are under way to issue lists of only those in Mongolian languages.

Entries in the Directory and Index

The aim in the preceding section has been to give a broad survey of the contents of the Bibliographical Directory while highlighting a few of the subject fields and disciplines for which American libraries can give research special meaning with their holdings. These mixed library collections have been rearranged here alphabetically by author–title according to language for the convenience of scholars and others, the primary division of the material beginning with Altay and proceeding to Yakut. Disciplines provide the next subdivisions, and a key for both, along with subtopics, authors, and places is indicated in the Index. Such publications are identified in the Index under the subject or other heading by the entry number, followed by an indication of the language of the publication involved (Alt for Altay, Az for Azeri, and so on).

In each entry shown by the Bibliographical Directory, the following information will be provided if it is known:

1. Author, or compiler, or editor (for separate publications)
2. Title of the publication, or titles if changed, in the case of a serial
3. Place of publication (given in accepted American form)
4. Publisher (for separate publications)
5. Date or dates of publication

6. Numbers of the issues for newspapers or journals (numbers with slash, e.g., 3/4, indicate one issue bearing two numbers; the form 3–4 indicates consecutive issues)
7. Number of pages (for separate publications)
8. Size of the edition (for separate publications)
9. Code letters and numbers indicating the alphabet from which the entry has been transliterated (see section entitled Transliteration Tables). [Special Cyr] signifies that the publication so marked has been printed in one of the Russian missionary or academy alphabets
10. Code letters for the libraries in which the publications have been located. These include:

CLU	University of California at Los Angeles
CStH	The Hoover Institution for War, Revolution and Peace
CtY	Yale University
DLC	The Library of Congress
MH	Harvard University
NN	The New York Public Library
NNC	Columbia University
NNJ	Jewish Theological Seminary
OCH	Hebrew Union College

BIBLIOGRAPHICAL DIRECTORY

ALTAY Social Sciences

Economics

Avinovitskiy, Ya. L. *Biskë juu kërëk jok udurlazharga bëlën turubïs.* Ulala: Oyrot Oblastïng VKP(b) Obkomi Chïgargan, 1927, 20 pp., 1500 cop. [Alt 1 Cyr; NN] 1

Koopërativ dëgëni nëmë, anang kandïy tuza bolgodïy. Moscow: Tsentral'noe Izdatel'stvo Narodov SSSR, 1926, 36 pp., 3000 cop. [Alt 1 Cyr; NN] 2

Education

Kalanakov, N. A. *Bisting shkol: Oodosh boldar üürener tangmalïk.* Moscow: SSSR-de Jatkan Jüzün Jüür Uktu Albatïga Bichik Chigarïp Bazïb Jatkang Tsentizdat, 1930, 48 pp., 12000 cop. [Alt 2 Lat; NN] 3

Kalanakov, N. A. *Ömölik joktuga arga: Jaan ulustïng üürepeten tangmaligï.* Moscow: SSSR-de Jatkan Jüzün Jüür Uktu Albatïga Bichik Chigarïp Bazïbjasatkan Tsentrizdat, 1930, 128 pp., 12000 cop. [Alt 2 Lat; NN] 4

Likpunktïng programazï. Ulala: Oyrot Oblastïng Polit Prosvet Chïgargan, 1930, 48 pp., 5000 cop. [Alt 2 Lat; NN] 5

Mundus-Ëdokov, M. V. *Oyrot shkola: Bashtapkï kïchïrar bichik.* Moscow: Tsentral'noe Izdatel'stvo Narodov SSSR, 1924, 83 pp., 3000 cop. [Alt 1 Cyr; CStH, NN] 6

Vishnevskiy, G. *Arifmeticheskii zadachnik: Jangï üürëngën baldardï toogo üürëdër bichik.* Moscow: Izdanie Oyratskoi Perevodcheskoi Komissii, 1924, 71 pp., 2500 cop. [Alt. 1 Cyr; NN] 7

Government

Lenin-la partiya. Moscow: SSSR Kalïktï Bichiktërin Büdürüp Turgan, 1926, 35 pp., 3000 cop. [Alt 1 Cyr; NN] 8

Nënïn uchun Angliyanïn kapitalistarï SSSR-dï öshtön turgan? Ulala: Oyrot Oblastïng Litkollegiyazï Chïgargan, 1927, 37 pp., 1500 cop. [Alt 1 Cyr; NN] 9

Ochi-Mikhailov, I. N. *Oyrot ulustï kïzïl cherügë kïchïrarï*. Ulala: Oyrot Oblastïng VKP(b)-nïng Komitedi Chïgargan, 1928, 20 pp., 1061 cop. [Alt 1 Cyr; NN] 10

Rossëyding kommunist partiyanïng (bol.) 13-chi juunïnda büdurgën rezolyutsiyazïla postanovleniya bichigi. Moscow: Tsentral'noe Izdatel'stvo Narodov SSSR, 1924, 111 pp., 1000 cop. [Alt 1 Cyr: CStH] 11

Zorin. *Kïzïl cherüüding küchi nëëindë?* Ulala: Oyrot Oblastïng VKP(b) Obkomi Chigargan. Izd. Tipograficheskoe Ob'edinenie "Oyrotskii Krai," 1927, 32 pp., 1500 cop. [Alt 1 Cyr; NN] 12

Law

Batraktar-la mal küdüüchilerding izhing korïïr kereginde chïgargan zakondordïng juuntï-bichigi. n.p.: Oyrot Oblastïng Sovet-Komitedi Chïgargan, 1929, 40 pp., 200 cop. [Alt 1 Cyr; NN] 13

Gurov, P. Ya. *R.S.F.S.R-ding jër kërëgin bashkarar kodeks-zakonïng uchurïn surap ukkanï, karuuzïn aytkanï.* Ulala: Oyrot Oblastïng Otdel Narodnïy Obrazovaniyada Turgan Literaturnïy Kollegiyanïng Chïgarganï, 1926, 76 pp., 2000 cop. [Alt 1 Cyr; NN] 14

Sovet bashkaruudïng bütkeni-le konstitutsiya. Ulala: Oyrot Oblastïng Tipografiyazï, 1927, 20 pp., 1050 cop. [Alt 1 Cyr; NN] 15

Social Organization

Altay delegatkalardïng juundarïnïng programmazï. n.p.: Oyrot Oblastïnïng VKP(b) Obkomi Chïgargan, 1929, 43 pp., 300 cop. [Alt 1 Cyr; NN] 16

Sovet zakonïnda üy kizhining jürër jürümi. Ulala: Oyrot Oblastïng Tipografiyazï, 1927, 23 pp., n.c. [Alt 1 Cyr; NN] 17

ALTAY Humanities

Language

Grammatika altaiskago iazyka. Kazan: Universitet, 1869, 298 and 289 pp., n.c. [Special Cyr; CtY] 18

Language

Starchevskii, A. V. *Sibirskii perevodchik po linii stroiushcheisia sibirskoi i ussuriiskoi zh.-d.* St. Petersburg: Parovaia Skoropechatnia A. V. Pozharovoi, 1893, 414 pp., n.c. [Special Cyr; MH] 19

Literature

Akulova, Yek. *Ëmëënder kul ëmes.* Ulala: Oyrot Oblastïng Litkollegiyazï Chïgargan, 1927, 24 pp., 1500 cop. [Alt 1 Cyr; NN] 20

Kalanakov, N. A. *Ishmëkchilërding jaan üyzü aydagï bayramï.* Ulala: Oyrot Oblastïng Litkollegiyazï Chïgargan, 1928, 12 pp., 1000 cop. [Alt 1 Cyr; NN] 21

Kosh-Agach, S. *Jangï jürüm.* Ulala: Oyrot Oblastïng Litkollegiyazï Chïgargan, 1927, 24 pp., 1000 cop. [Alt 1 Cyr; NN] 22

Kuchiyak, Pavel. *Altayda.* Oyrot-tura: Oyrotskiy Oblastïng Natsional'nïy Izdatel'stvozï, 1945, 117 pp., 3000 cop. [Alt 3 Cyr; DLC] 23

Mundus-Ëdokov. *Jarïtkïsh.* n.p.: Oyrot Oblastïng Politprosvet Chïgargan, 1929, 42 pp., 1000 cop. [Alt. 1 Cyr; NN] 24

Ulagashev, N. *Malchï-mergen.* Chörchöktör. Oyrot-tura: Oyrotskiy Oblast'tïng Natsional'nïy Izdatel'stvozï, 1945, 152 pp., 3000 cop. [Alt 3 Cyr; DLC] 25

Philosophy and Religion

Jër-tëlëkëydë në bolup turganïnïng uchuri. Ulala: Oyrat Oblastïng Politprosvet Chïgargan, 1929, 32 pp., n.c. [Alt 1 Cyr; NN] 26

Adhärbayjan (Baku) 1919: Dec. 17. [Az 1 & 2 Arab; NNC] 27

Adhärbayjan ishji kändli mükhbiri (Baku) n.d.: 9/10. [Az 1 & 2 Arab; NN] 28

Adhärbayjan mätbü'atnïn älli iligi: Ekinchi (1875–1925). Baku: Qomonist Ghäzetäsinin Näshriyatï, 1926, 48 pp., 5000 cop. [Az 1 & 2 Arab; NN] 29

Äkinchi (Baku) 1875: 2–12; 1876: 1–24; 1877: 1–20. [Az 1 & 2; NNC*] 30

Azärbayjan devlät näshriyyatï bulleteni (Baku) 1929: 4. [Az 4 Lat; CStH, NN] 31

Azärbayjan dovlät qitab palatasïnda olan qitablarïn siyahisi; ⟨from 1927⟩ *Azärbayjan dövlät qitab palatasïnïn qitabiyyatï;* ⟨from 1928⟩ *Azärbayjan mätbuat kitabiyyatï* (Baku) 1926: 1–5; 1927: 1–4 [DLC, MH, NN, NNC], 5/6 [DLC, NN, NNC]; 1928: 1–7, 9–12; 1929: 1–12; 1930: 1–3 [DLC, NN, NNC], 4 [NN], 5–12; 1931: 1–12; 1932: 3–5 [DLC, NN, NNC], 4 [NN], 5 [DLC, NN, NNC], 6 [NN], 7 [DLC, NN, NNC], 8–9 [NN], 10–12; 1933: 1–6 [DLC, NN, NNC], 9–12; 1934: 1–3 [DLC, NNC], 4 [DLC, NN, NNC]; 1935: 1–12 [NN]. [Az 1 & 2 Arab, 3 Lat, 4 Lat] 32

Azärbayjan Sosiyalist Shüra Jumhüriyäti ishchi qäntli höqümätinin kanün vä kärardadlar mäjmüäsi (n.p.) 1928: 3. [Az 3 Lat; NN] 33

Baba-i ämir (Baku) 1915: 2–30; 1916: 1–29. [Az 1 & 2 Arab; NNC*] 34

Bählül (Baku) 1907: 2–9. [Az 1 & 2 Arab; NNC*] 35

Bäṣirät (Baku) 1914: 1–35; 1915: 36–63, 65–73; 1916: 74–127, 129, 131; 1917: 132–140, 142–149, 151–152, 154–168, 173, 175. [Az 1 & 2 Arab; NNC*] 36

Bokharin, N. *Ishchi vä känd mükhbiri ḥaqïndä mäqalä vä niṭqlär*. Baku: Adhärnäshr, 1927, 88 pp., 3000 cop. [Az 1 & 2 Arab; NN] 37

Bolshävik (Baku) 1926: 9/10; 1927: 8/9; 1928: 3/4 [Az 1 & 2 Arab, 3 Lat; NN] 38

Däbistan (Baku) 1906: 1, 3–5, ⟨numbering repeated⟩ 4–5, 8–9. [Az 1 & 2 Arab; NNC*] 39

---

*Microfilm

Füyuzat (Baku) 1906: 1–6; 1907: 7–15 [CLU, NNC*], 16 [CLU], 17–32 [CLU, NNC*]. [Az 1 & 2 Arab] 40

Hämkarlar ittifaqï (Baku) 1927: 22. [Az 1 & 2 Arab, 3 Lat; NN] 41

Ibrahimof, ʿAli Sättär. *Täblighatchiyä rähbär*. Baku: Adhärnäshr, 1927, 71 pp., 3000 cop. [Az 1 & 2 Arab; NN] 42

Iqtiṣadï khäbärlär (Baku) 1925: 3, 6 [DLC]; 1927: 14 [NN]. [Az 1 & 2 Arab] 43

Irshad (Baku) 1906: 21, 102–122, 124–140, 142–143, 145–153, 155–159, 161–171, 173–179, 182–186, 188–195, 197–205, 207–220, 224–232, 234–252, 254–256, 259–281, 283–294, 296. [Az 1 & 2 Arab; NNC*] 44

Ittifaq (Baku) 1908: 3–25; 1909: 1–226. [Az 1 & 2 Arab; NNC*] 45

Kanünlar ve emrleri qulliyyatï (Moscow) 1928: ⟨index⟩, 15, 18; 1929: 1–76; 1930: 8, 18–37, 39–60. [Az 3 Lat; NN] 46

Kononenko, Y. *Qäntdä gäzetä ilä nejä ishlämäli*. Baku: Azärnäshr, 1929, 44 pp., 2000 cop. [Az 3 Lat; NN] 47

Läbädäf. *Vaqtï nä ichon yëni täqvim uzärä ḥesablamalïdïr?* Baku: Adhärnäshr, 1927, 46 pp., 2500 cop. [Az 1 & 2 Arab; NN] 48

Mäʿarif ishchisi (Baku) 1927: 9, 12. [Az 1 & 2 Arab; NN] 49

Mäʿarif vä mädäniyyät (Baku) 1926: 1–6 [DLC]; 1927: 1/2, 4–12 [NN]. [Az 1 & 2 Arab] 50

Mäktäb (Baku) 1911: 1–3; 1912: 4–22; 1913: 1–7, 9–17, 19–22; 1914: 1–7, 9–20; 1915: 1–15; 1916: 1–8, 11. [Az 1 & 2 Arab; NNC*] 51

Mätbüat ghunu: Mäʿrüzä uchun materyal. Baku: Azärnäshr, 1928, 40 pp., 1500 cop. [Az 3 Lat; NN] 52

Mäzäli (Baku) 1914: 1; 1915: 1–26, 28–30, 32–35, 37–38, 40–41. [Az 1 & 2 Arab; NNC*] 53

Molla Näsräddin (Tiflis) 1906: 1–39; 1907: 1–48; 1908: 1–52; 1909: 1–52; 1910: 1–42; 1911: 1–11, 13–47; 1912: 1–9; 1914: 1–25; 1917: 2, 21 [NNC*]; n.d.: 32 [NN]. [Az 1 & 2 Arab] 54

Muällimä qömäq (Baku) 1930: 1. [Az 4 Lat; NN] 55

Mukhtariyyätli Daghïstan SShCh ishji-kändli hukumätinin qanun vä qärarläri (Makhachkala) 1930: 2. [Az 4 Lat; NN] 56

Övraq-i näfisä (Baku) 1916: 1–6 [MH]; 1919: 2–6; n.d.: 1 [DLC]. [Az 1 & 2 Arab] 57

Pioner (Baku) 1927: 9–11. [Az 1 & 2 Arab, 3 Lat; NN] 58

---

*Microfilm

Qanon vä boyroqlar mäjmu'äsi; ⟨title varies⟩ *Qanon vä qärarlar mäjmu'äsi* (Makhachkala) 1926: 1–2; 1927: 3; 1928: 4, 8. [Az 1 & 2 Arab; DLC] 59
Qomsomol (Baku) 1926: 1; 1927: 12. [Az 1 & 2 Arab, 3 Lat; NN] 60
Rähbär (Baku) 1906: 1–3; 1907: 5. [Az 1 & 2 Arab; NNC*] 61
SSRI Elmlär Aqademiyasï Azärbayjan filialï khäbärläri (Baku) 1938: 1–3, 6; 1939: 3–4. [Az 4 Lat; NN] 62
Shälalä (Baku) 1913: 1–22 [NNC*], 23–33 [CStH, NNC*], 34–47; 1914: 1–9 [NNC*]. [Az 1 & 2 Arab] 63
Shärk fäkültänin khäbärläri (Baku) 1926: 1 [NN, NNC], 2 [NNC], 3–4 [NN, NNC]. [Az 3 Lat] 64
Ṣon khäbär (Baku) 1915: 1–32, 34–35; 1916: 36–37. [Az 1 & 2 Arab; NNC*] 65
Täräqqi (Baku) 1908: 4–8, 11–20, 22–38, 42, 46–76, 80–112, 114–125, 128–129, 131–139; 1909: 1–97, 99–196, 198–225. [Az 1 & 2 Arab; NNC*] 66
Tazä ḥäyat (Baku) 1907: 4–12, 14–29, 31–114, 116–136, 139–141, 143–146, 148–168, 170–176, 178–209, 210 ⟨*sic*⟩; 1908: 2–7, 9–36, 38–111, 113–230. [Az 1 & 2 Arab; NNC*] 67
Türani. *Pioner damgasï "Leninchi."* Baku: Azärnäshr, 1930, 73 pp., 3000 cop. [Az 4 Lat; NN] 68
Ṭuṭi (Baku) 1914: 1; 1915: 28–45; 1916: 1–24; 1917: 1–10, 12–13, 15–21. [Az 1 & 2 Arab; NNC*] 69
Ŭlyanova, M. I.; Yaroslavsqi. *Ishchi-qäntli mukhbirinin rolü.* Baku: Azärnäshr, 1929, 41 pp., 1500 cop. [Az 3 Lat; NN] 70
Yeñi füyuẕat (Baku) 1910: 1, 3–11; 1911: 1–10. [Az 1 & 2 Arab; NNC*] 71
Yeñi iqbal (Baku) 1915: 1–196; 1916: 197–388, 390–470, 472–493; 1917: 570–579, 581–586, 588, 591–592, 594, 596–597, 599–605, 608–609, 611, 613–655, 658–662. [Az 1 & 2 Arab; NNC*] 72
Yeñi iqdam (Baku) 1915: 1–25, 27, 29–40, 42–45, 47–103, 105–106, 108–138, 140–154. [Az 1 & 2 Arab; NNC*] 73
Yeñi irshad (Baku) 1911: 1–83, 85–100. [Az 1 & 2 Arab; NNC*] 74
Yeñi mäktäb (Baku) 1926: 7/8; 1927: 1, 5–8. [Az 1 & 2 Arab, 3 Lat; NN] 75

---

*Microfilm

AZERI Social Sciences

Anthropology

Da'standä qan doshmanlighi vä onun ilä mubaräzä. Makhachkala: Da'stan 'Adliyä Qomisarlighi, 1926, 20 pp., 1000 cop. [Az 1 & 2 Arab; NN] 76

Nansän, F. *Ozaq shimalda.* Baku: Adhärnäshr, 1927, 84 pp., 3000 cop. [Az 1 & 2 Arab; NN] 77

Nansen, F. *Üzak shimalda: Esqimoslarïn yashayïshï.* Baku: Azärnäshr, 1927, 69 pp., 2000 cop. [Az 3 Lat; NN] 78

Economics

A.Kh.T.Sh. Azärbayjan Dävläti inshaat trestinin S.Sh.J.I. inshaat ishchiläri ittifakïnïn Azärbayjan märqäzi idäräsi ilä äkd etdighi mushtäräq mukavilä. Baku: n.p., 1928, 36 pp., 100 cop. [Az 3 Lat; NN] 79

Äliyev, T. *Qänt täsärrufat verghisinda yunghulluqlär.* Baku. Äzärnäshr, 1929, 22 pp., 5000 cop. [Az 4 Lat; NN] 80

Baqï qänd sänaye' trestinin S.Sh.J.I. ärzak vä tä'm sänayei ishchiläri ittifakïnïn umüm Azärbayjan komitäsi ilä äkd etdighi mushtäräq mukavilä. Baku: n.p., 1928, 53 pp., n.c. [Az 3 Lat; NN] 81

Baratof, M. *Ishchi vä qäntli ittifakï nä uchun lazïmdïr?* Baku: "Baqï Ishchisi" Kooperatif Näshriyyatï, 1926, 34 pp., 4000 cop. [Az 3 Lat; NN) 82

1928–29nji yil känd täṣärrufatï vergisi dhatlarini ḥesaba almaq ishini kechirmäk barädä tä'limat. Baku: Bakpolighrafun Qïzïl Shärq Mäṭbäsi, 1928, 22 pp., 1400 cop. [Az 1 & 2 Arab; NN] 83

Bunyadzada, D. *Shüralar ittifakï toküma sänayeinin kharijdän ghätirilän pambükdan asïlï olmamasï ügründa mubaräzä.* Baku: Azärnäshr, 1929, 107 pp., 5000 cop. [Az 4 Lat; NN] 84

Chirdansof, P. *Qabaq vä indi.* Makhachkala: Daghstan Sho'bäsinin Näshriyatï, 1927, 40 pp., 1100 cop. [Az 1 & 2 Arab; NN] 85

Drozdov, V. P. *Qäntli öz täsärrufatïnda nejä hesab aparmalïdür?* Baku: Azärnäshr, 1929, 54 pp., 2000 cop. [Az 4 Lat; NN] 86

Friq, L. *1920–1927nji yillärdä shüralï adhärbayjanda hämkarlar ittifaqï ḥäräkatï tarikhïndan parchalar.* Baku: Hämkarlar Ittifaqlarï Adhärbayjan Shürasïnïn "Näshriyat Müdiriyyäti" Shö'bäsi Näshriyatï, 1927, 73 pp., 1000 cop. [Az 1 & 2 Arab; NN] 87

Gavrilov, V. V. *Süyü nejä ölchmäli?* Baku: Azärnäshr, 1930, 40 pp., 2000 cop. [Az 4 Lat; NN] 88

Güzik, K. O. *Zakafkaziyanïn iktisadi jografiyasï.* Baku: Azärnäshr, 1930, 174 pp., 3800 cop. [Az 4 Lat; NN] 89

Hämkarlar ḥäräkatï mäktäbi. Baku: Adhärnäshr, 1927, 166 pp., 3000 cop. [Az 1 & 2 Arab; NN] 90

Istiqraz bizä lazïmmïdïr? Makhachkala: Daghnäshr, 1930, 13 pp., 560 cop. [Az 4 Lat; NN] 91

Kalinin, M. I.; Yenüqidze, A. Ye. *Bashdan-basha kollektivläshmä vä Shüralarïn väzifäläri.* Baku: Azärnäshr, 1930, 48 pp., 3000 cop. [Az 4 Lat; NN] 92

Karaghichev. *Pambükchülar agrominimüm baräsindä nä bilmälidurlär?* Baku: Azärnäshr, 1930, 20 pp., 5000 cop. [Az 4 Lat; NN] 93

Karaghözov, A. *Qährizlärinizi korüyünüz.* Baku: Azärnäshr, 1930, 11 pp., 3000 cop. [Az 4 Lat; NN] 94

Karayev, Äsäd. *Azärbayjan qäntlärindä shürä täsärrufatlarï nä ish ghörmälidurlär?* Baku: Azärnäshr, 1930, 8 pp., 2000 cop. [Az 4 Lat; NN] 95

Karayev, Äsäd. *Mirab vä jüarlar näyi bilmälidurlär?* Baku: Azärnäshr, 1930, 14 pp., 5000 cop. [Az 4 Lat; NN] 96

Kautsqï, Karl. *Karl Marksïn iktisad näzariyyäsi.* Baku: Azärnäshr, 1928, 230 pp., 3000 cop. [Az 3 Lat; NN] 97

Khaubüdagov, Ä. *Kredit shirqätläri vä äqïn kampaniyasï.* Baku: Azärnäshr, 1930, 31 pp., 5000 cop. [Az 4 Lat; NN] 98

Khuṣüṣi bodjätlari olmiyan D.I.Sh.J. känd shoralarindä kargudharlïq, hesabä almaq vä ḥü-ḥesabat ishläri tä'limatï. Makhachkala: D.I.Sh.J. Merkezi Neshri, 1929, 28 pp., 200 cop. [Az 1 & 2 Arab; NN] 99

Kolkhozchülara verilän ghuzäshtlär. Baku. Azärnäshr, 1930, 80 pp., 4000 cop. [Az 4 Lat; NN] 100

Krzhizhanovsqi, G. *Üshaklara besh illiq plan hakkïnda mä'lümat.* Baku: Azärnäshr, 1930, 35 pp., 3000 cop. [Az 4 Lat; NN] 101

Leontiyev, A. *Siyasi iktisad: Ibtidai mä'lümat.* Baku: Azärnäshr, 1928, 161 pp., 3000 cop. [Az 3 Lat; NN] 102

Livof, V. *Chay.* Baku: Adhärnäshr, 1927, 59 pp., 3000 cop. [Az 1 & 2 Arab; NN] 103

Lvof, V. *Chay.* Baku: Azärnäshr, 1927, 49 pp., 3000 cop. [Az 3 Lat; NN] 104

M.I.Sh.J. *Känd täṣarrufat vä mishä ishchiläri ittifaqïniñ adhärbayjan märkäzi idaräsi, vä zaqafqasya pamboq qomitäsiniñ adhärbayjan shö'bäsi ilä 'äqd edilmish müshtäräk muqavilänamä.* Baku: n.p., 1928, 33 pp., 300 cop. [Az 1 & 2 Arab; NN] 105

Mähämmädov, Äli (Shirvansqi). *Qäntliyä pambük älberishlidur ya takhïl?* Baku: Azärnäshr, 1930, 20 pp., 5000 cop [Az 4 Lat; NN] 106

Mal-mätaḥ: Natura fondlar kitabi. Makhachkala: D.M.I.Sh. Jumhüriyyäti, 1929, n.pp., n.c. [Az 1 & 2 Arab; NN] 107

Melkümyan, V. *Qäntli täsärrufatïnda töräyän zähmät iddialarï nejä häll olünür?* Baku: Azärnäshr, 1930, 36 pp., 3000 cop. [Az 4 Lat; NN] 108

Molochnïy, D. *Müzdürlarïn vä chobanlarïn ijtimai sïgortasï.* Baku: Azärnäshr, 1929, 28 pp., 2000 cop. [Az 4 Lat; NN] 109

Mosesov, P; Mochalov, N. *Besh illighin uchunju ili vä Baqï istehlaq kooperasiyasïnïn väzifäläri.* Baku: Azärnäshr, 1930, 48 pp., 2000 cop. [Az 4 Lat; NN] 110

Osipov, M. *Qäntdä ghönullu verghi.* Baku: Azärbayjan Devlät Näshriyyatï, 1929, 54 pp., 2000 cop. [Az 3 Lat; NN] 111

Öz-özunä värgi mäs'äläsi Rähbärligi. Makhachkala: Daghneshr, 1929, 26 pp., 350 cop. [Az 4 Lat; NN] 112

Pambuq tarlasïnï ishletmäk, tukhum sepmek, mehsuluyïghmaq, saqlamaq vä täslim etmäk barädä tapshïrïq-tä'limat. Makhachkala: n.p., 1930, 22 pp., 2000 cop. [Az 4 Lat; NN] 113

Panofqa, M. *Dävläti istiqraz baredä aktävistä rähbärlik.* Makhachkala: Daghneshr, 1930, 44 pp., 2060 cop. [Az 4 Lat; NN] 114

Plotnisghi, V. *Azärbayjanda toprak mäsäläsi.* Baku: "Baqï Ishchisi" Kooperatif Näshriyyatï, 1926, 52 pp., 2000 cop. [Az 3 Lat; NN] 115

Qänt täsärrufat mashïn kooperativ shirqäti nizamnamasï. Baku: Azärnäshr, 1929, 26 pp., 3000 cop. [Az 3 Lat; NN] 116

Qaragichäf. *Känd täṣärrufatï gelirini.* Baku: Adhärnäshr, 1927, 29 pp., 3000 cop. [Az 1 & 2 Arab; NN] 117

Qaragichäf. *Pamboq.* Baku: Adhärnäshr, 1927, 29 pp., 3000 cop. [Az 1 & 2 Arab; CStH, NN] 118

Räjäbli, Ä. *Azärbayjanda tutunchuluq.* Baku: Azärnäshr, 1930 2d ed. 16 pp., 3000 cop. [Az 4 Lat; NN] 119

Säkkizinji boton adhärbayjan qoroltayida ittifaq märkäzi idaräsiniñ mä'rüẕäsi üzärinä chiqilan qärarlar. Baku: Inshaat Ishläri (Adhr) Näshriyyatï, 1926, 32 pp., 500 cop. [Az 1 & 2 Arab; NN] 120

Segal, B. M. *Besh illiq planda sänayä.* Baku: Azärnäshr, 1929, 74 pp., 3000 cop. [Az 4 Lat; NN] 121

Shüralar jumhüriyätläri inshaat ishchiläri ittifaqïnïñ adhärbayjan märkäzi idaräsilä adhärbayjan devlät 'ali khalq täṣärrufatïnïñ inshaat vä täḥniki qanṭorasï aralarïnda baghlanmïsh müshtäräk muqavilä. Baku: n.p., 1927, 40 pp., 200 cop. [Az 1 & 2 Arab; NN] 122

Sviridov, Iv. *Kollektivläshdirmä vä mähsül ghunu.* Baku: Azärnäshr, 1929, 24 pp., 5000 cop. [Az 4 Lat; NN] 123

Tarshis, P. *Müzdür vä müzdür dütanïarïn shärtläri.* n.p.: "Baqï Ishchisi" Kooperatif Näshriyyatï, 1926, 47 pp., 4000 cop. [Az 3 Lat; NN] 124

Vassirman, I. S. *Daghstanda pamboqchïlïq täṣärrufatï naṣïl yorodïlmälidir?* Makhachkala: Bash Pamboq Qomitäsi, Daghstan Müväkkillikinin Idaräsi, 1929, 27 pp., 1000 cop. [Az 1 & 2 Arab; NN] 125

Education

Äfändizada, Huseyn. *Beshinji il.* Baku: Azärnäshr, 1930, 234 pp., 10000 cop. [Az 4 Lat; NN] 126

Agazada, F.; Äliyev, Y.; Sanïlï, H. Q. *Zähmät mäqtäbi.* 2nji il. Baku: Azärnäshr, 1928, iii and 159 pp., 25000 cop. [Az 3 Lat; NN] 127

Äläkbärli, G. *Azärbayjan dili särf vä yazï gaydalarï kolkhoz qänjläri mäktäbi üchün.* Baku: Azärnäshr, 1945, 216 pp., 15000 cop. [Az 5 Cyr; MH] 128

Äläkbärli, M. K. *Yeni älifba vä orfoghrafiya.* Makhachkala: Daghïstan Yeni Älifba Qomitäsi Näshriyyatï, 1929, 55 pp., 1000 cop. [Az 4 Lat; NN] 129

Alqadarskiy, A. K. *Hisab mäsʾäläläri.* 1inchi il ichin. Makhachkala: "Dagh-Älif" Komitäsi Täräfindän Chap Olundu, 1928, 111 pp., 3000 cop. [Az 3 Lat; NN] 130

Alqadarskiy, A. K. *Yeni Türk älifba vä ilk qïraät.* Makhachkala: "Dagh-Älif" Komitasï Täräfindän Chap Olunmïshdur, 1928, 80 pp., 6100 cop. [Az 3 Lat; NN] 131

Astryab, A. M. *Täjribi händäsä mäsäläläri mäjmüäsï.* Baku: Azärnäshr, 1927, 182 pp., 5000 cop. [Az 3 Lat; NN] 132

Azärbayjanda khalk mäarifi, 1920–27. Baku: ASShJ KhMK Näshriyyatï, 1928., 179 pp., 500 cop. [Az 3 Lat; DLC] 133

Babazadä, Ä. *Türk dili: Ghrammatiqa vä yazï qaydalarï ibtidai mäktäbin üchünjü sinifi üchün.* Baku: AShShJ KhMQ Täräfindän Täsdiq Edilmishdir; Tädris-Pedaghozhi Shöbäsi, 1936, 107 pp., 75000 cop. [Az 4 Lat; MH] 134

Bachinski. *Fiziq mäsäʾlä vä miṣallarï.* Baku: Adhärnäshr, 1927, 266 pp., 3000 cop. [Az 1 & 2 Arab; NN] 135

Bachinsqï, A. *Fizik mäsälä vä misallarï.* Baku: Azärnäshr, 1927, 227 pp., 3000 cop. [Az 3 Lat; CStH, NN] 136

Bachinsqi, A. *Fizika.* Baku: Azärnäshr, 1930, 209 pp., 5000 cop. [Az 4 Lat; NN] 137

Bachinsqi, A. *Fizika.* Baku: Azärnäshr, 1930, 284 pp., 5000 cop. [Az 4 Lat; NN] 138

Bachinsqi, A. *Fizikadan ish qitabï.* Baku: Azärnäshr, 1930, 296 pp., 8000 cop. [Az 4 Lat; NN] 139

Berg, M. F.; Znamensqiy, M. A.; Popov, G. N.; Slüdsqiy, I. F.; Khvostov, N. P.; Shshentinin, N. I. *Riyaziyyatdan ish qitabï.* Baku: Azärnäshr, 1929, 276 pp., 6000 cop. [Az 4 Lat; NN] 140

Berg, M. F.; Znamensqiy, M. A.; Popov, G. N.; Slüdsqiy, I. F.; Khvostov, N. P.; Shshetinin, N. I. *Riyaziyyatdan ish qitabï.* Baku: Azärnäshr, 1930, 239 pp., 6000 cop. [Az 4 Lat; NN] 141

Binyadof; Shaʾiq; Shamilof; Väyslof. *Dordinji il.* Baku: Adhärnäshr, 1927, 158 pp., 5000 cop. [Az 1 & 2 Arab; CStH, NN] 142

Birinji däräjä mäktäbin proghramlarï: Khalq mäʿarif qomisarlighi bash ijtimaʿi tärbiyä daʾiräsi. Baku: Azärnäshr, 1926, 84 pp., 2000 cop. [Az 1 & 2 Arab; NN] 143

1nji däräjäli känd mäktäbinin 1nji, 2nji, vä 3nji sänälärinä ʿaʾid ghos proghramï. Baku: Adhärnäshr, 1927, 69 pp., 1500 cop. [Az 1 & 2 Arab; NN] 144

Bochin, L. *Sözlä deyil—ishlä.* Baku: Azärnäshr, 1930, 52 pp., 1500 cop. [Az 4 Lat; NN] 145

Eminbäyli, Ibr.; Sanïlï, H. Q. *Iqinji il.* Baku: Azärnäshr, 1927, 119 pp., 20000 cop. [Az 3 Lat; NN] 146

Filippof, S. *Käraät qümasïnïn mäʿlumat ishläri.* Baku: Azärbayjan Ali Siyasi Mäarif Komitäsi Näshriyyatï, 1927, 32 pp., 1000 cop. [Az 3 Lat; NN] 147

Gasïmzadä, F. *Ädäbiyyat müntäkhäbatï.* Orta mäktäbin 8-ji sinfi üchün. Baku: Azärnäshr. Tädris–Pedagozhi Shöʿbäsi, 1945, 406 pp., 9000 cop. [Az 5 Cyr; MH] 148

Gratsiansqi; Kavün, I. *Riyaziyyat mäsälä vä misallarï: Shähär mäqtäblärindä 3-ju tädris ili uchun ish qitabï.* Baku: Azärnäshr, 1929, 91 pp., 5000 cop. [Az 4 Lat; NN] 149

Istalin, I. *Shärq khalqlarï daralfunününiñ siyasi mäqṣädläri ḥaqqïndä.* Moscow: SSSR Khalqlariniñ Märkäz Näshriyatï, 1925, 30 pp., 3000 cop. [Az 1 & 2 Arab; NN] 150

Ivanof. *Jografiya.* I hissä. Baku: Azärnäshr, 1928, 159 pp., 12000 cop. [Az 3 Lat; NN] 151

Jäbrayilbäyli, J. *Akvariüm vä terrariüm.* Baku: Azärnäshr, 1930, 69 pp., 2000 cop. [Az 4 Lat; NN] 152

Känd ähalïsï arasïnda mätro uṣülini täblighat yapan mäʿrüẓächilärä mätod yaddashtï Baku: Zaqafqasya Beynalmoʾssat Mätro Qomisyonï Näshriyatï, 1928, 10 pp., 2000 cop. [Az 1 & 2 Arab; NN] 153

Kazachkov, A. *Khäritä vä planlardan nejä istifadä etmälidur.* Baku: Azärnäshr, 1929, 62 pp., 3000 cop. [Az 3 Lat; NN] 154

Khalq maʿarifi vä shora ḥukometi. Buinaksk: Daghstan Ijtimaʿi Shora Jumhoriyati Ḥukometinin Näshriyatï, 1921, 8 pp., 2000 cop. [Az 1 & 2 Arab; CStH] 155

Komarovski, V. V. *Pedagozhinin umümi äsaslarï.* Baku: Azärnäshr, 1930, 64 pp., 2300 cop. [Az 4 Lat; NN] 156

Kovanko, A. S. *Ali riyaziyyata mädkhäl.* Baku: Azärnäshr, 1930, 14 pp., 3200 cop. [Az 4 Lat; NN] 157

Krüpskaya, N. *Qutubkhana ügründa hujüma qechälim.* Baku: Azärnäshr, 1930, 19 pp., 5000 cop. [Az 4 Lat; NN] 158

Lankov, A. V. *Jäbr mäsäläläri.* II hissä. Baku: Azärnäshr, 1928, 151 pp., 5000 cop. [Az 3 Lat; NN] 159

Mäqtäbä kädär tärbiyä baräsindä metodiq mäqtüblar. Dördunju mäqtüb. Baku: Azärnäshr, 1927, 26 pp., 1500 cop. [Az 3 Lat; NN] 160

Mäqtäbä kädär tärbiyäyä dayir metodiq mäqtüblar. Beshinji mäqtüb. Baku: Azärnäshr, 1927, 21 pp., 1500 cop. [Az 3 Lat; NN] 161

Mäqtäbä kädär tärbiyäyä dayir metodiq mäqtüblar. Uchunju mäqtüb Baku: Azärnäshr, 1927, 16 pp., 1500 cop. [Az 3 Lat; NN] 162

Mendelson, A. L., *Agïl ämäghinin hifzi-sihhäsi.* Baku: Azärnäshr, 1930, 24 pp., 3000 cop. [Az 4 Lat; NN] 163

Milkovich, N. *Yerin häyat vä tarikhi.* Baku: Azärnäshr, 1929, 284 pp., 3000 cop. [Az 3 Lat; NN] 164

Petrov, N. *Yayda shakhsi tähsil ishläri.* Baku: Azärnäshr, 1929, 32 pp., 2000 cop. [Az 4 Lat; NN] 165

Pinkävich, A. P. *Pädaghozhiyä medkhal.* Baku: Adhärnäshr, 1928, 142 pp., 25000 cop. [Az 1 & 2 Arab; NN] 166

Qäntli ghänjlär mäqtäbläri vä qänt täsärrufatïnïn kollektivläshdirilmäsi. Baku: Azärnäshr, 1930, 32 pp., 3000 cop. [Az 4 Lat; NN] 167

Qimya programï. Baku: Azärnäshr, 1930, 32 pp., 3200 cop. [Az 4 Lat; NN] 168

Räjäbli, Ä. *Qänt täsärrufatï därsläri.* Baku: Azärnäshr, 1929, 117 pp., 3000 cop. [Az 4 Lat; NN] 169

Räshad, Gafür, *Jografiya.* I hissä. Baku: Azärnäshr, 1926, 176 pp., 5000 cop. [Az 3 Lat; NN] 170

Rashefsqi; Qamil, M. *Händäsä rähbäri.* Stereometriya. II hissä. Baku: Azärnäshr, 1927, 100 pp., 3000 cop. [Az 3 Lat; NN] 171

Rasülov, M. *Mäqtäblärdä öz-özunu idarä.* Baku: Azärnäshr, 1930, 42 pp., 3000 cop. [Az 4 Lat; NN] 172

Ribkin. *Muṣällaṣat.* Baku: Adhärnäshr, 1926, 246 pp., 5000 cop. [Az 1 & 2 Arab; NN] 173

Sanïlï; Neʿmanzadä; Akhündof, H. *Uchunju il.* Baku: Azärnäshr, 1927, 118 pp., 15000 cop. [Az 3 Lat; NN] 174

Sanïlï; Neʿmanzadä, F.; Akhündof, H. Ä. *Uchunju il: Devläti Elmi shüra täräfindän bir däräjäli mäqtäblärin 3-ju gürüpünda okümäk uchun täsdik vä täsvib edilmishdur.* Baku: Azärnäshr, 1928, 130 pp., 25000 cop. [Az 3 Lat; NN] 175

Sanïlï, H. A. *Turq älifbasï.* Baku: Azärnäshr, 1927, 92 pp., 40000 cop. [Az 3 Lat; NN] 176

Sanïlï, H. A. *Turq älifbasï: Säs usülü ilä.* Baku: Azärnäshr, 1929, 147 pp., 6000 cop. [Az 4 Lat; NN] 17

Sazonof; Verkhofsqï. *Qimya: Geyri-uzvi.* Baku: Azärnäshr, 1927, 190 pp., 2000 cop. [Az 3 Lat; NN] 17

Shayik; Shamilov; Müstafazada. *Dördunju il.* Baku: Azärnäshr, 1928, 161 pp., 10000 cop. [Az 3 Lat; NN] 17

Sokolov, S. N.; Belavin, A. F.; Üvarov, P. P.; Kamenetsqi, V. A. *Mäqtäblär uchun jografiya atlasï.* Moscow, S.Sh.J.I. Ähalisinin Märqäzi Näshriyyatï, 1928, 24 pp., 3000 cop. [Az 4 Lat; NN] 18

Üippl, G. M. *Faydalï chalishmak yollarï.* Baku: Azärnäshr, 1927, 36 pp., 3000 cop. [Az 3 Lat; CStH, NN] 18

Uippl, Gh. M. *Faydali chalishmaq yollarï.* Baku: Adhärnäshr, 1927, 46 pp., 2000 cop. [Az 1 & 2 Arab; NN] 18

Zeynalov, Yu; Garfarli, Ä. M. *Älifba.* Baku: Azärnäshr, 1945, 92 pp., 30000 cop. [Az 5 Cyr; DLC] 18

Geography

Arzhanof, S. P. *Joghrafyaya medkhal.* Baku: Adhärnäshr, 1927, 116 pp., 3000 cop. [Az. 1 & 2 Arab; CStH, NN] 18

Bähärli, Muḥämmäd Ḥasan. *Adhärbayjan: Joghrafi-ṭabiʿi, ätnoghrafik vä iqtiṣadi mulaḥaẓat.* Baku: Birinji Ḥökümät Maṭbʿäsi, 1921, 306 pp., n.c. [Az 1 & 2 Arab; CLU] 18

Pimänof, Ä. *Quṭb yollarïnda.* Baku: Adhärnäshr, 1927, 112 pp., 3000 cop. [Az 1 & 2 Arab; NN] 18

Government

A.K.(b)F. Baqï komitasïnïn tabligat-täshvikat kabinäsi materyallarï. Baku: Azärnäshr, 1928, 49 pp., 3000 cop. [Az 3 Lat; NN] 18

A.K.(b)F. märqäzi komitäsinin 1929 dekabrïndaqï plenümünün kärarlarï. Baku: Azärnäshr, 1930, 72 pp., 3000 cop. [Az 4 Lat; NN] 18

A.L.Q.K. ittifaqïnïn ikinji adhärbayjan qonfransïnïn qärar vä qäṭʿnamäläri. Baku: Adhärnäshr, 1927, 54 pp., 2500 cop. [Az 1 & 2 Arab; NN] 18

A.Q.(b)F. *Qäṭʿnamä.* Baku: 3nji Intrnasyonal Mäṭbäsi, 1927, 22 pp., 400 cop. [Az 1 & 2 Arab; NN] 190

Abäzgha'oz; Protasof. *Firqä savadï.* Baku: Baku Ishchisi Qo'opäratif Näshriyatï, 1926, 52 pp., 1000 cop. [Az 1 & 2 Arab; NN] 191

Aläksinski, M. *Müdafʿä häftäsi.* Baku: Adhärnäshr, 1927, 32 pp., 3000 cop. [Az 1 & 2 Arab; NN] 192

Aläqsäyif, M. *Bolshäviqlär.* Baku: Adhärnäshr, 1927, 290 pp., 3000 cop. [Az 1 & 2 Arab; NN] 193

Aleksandrov, A. *Äl bombalarï nädur vä charpïshma zamanï bünlardan nejä istifade etmäli.* Baku: Azärnäshr, 1929, 40 pp., 3000 cop. [Az 3 Lat; NN] 194

Alekseyef, M. *Balsheviqlär.* Baku: Azärnäshr, 1927, 223 pp., 2000 cop. [Az 3 Lat; NN] 195

Baghïrov, M. J. *Baki vä Azärbayjan bolshevik täshkilatïnïn tarikhindän.* Baku: Azärnäshr, 1945, 172 pp., 10000 cop. [Az 5 Cyr; DLC] 196

Böyuk oqtyabrïn 6 nji senä' devriyyäsinä ittiḥaf edilmish mäjmüʿä. Moscow: Tsentral'noe Vostochnoe Izdatel'stvo pri N.K.N., 1917–1923, 38 pp., 2300 cop. [Az 1 & 2 Arab; NN] 197

Bükharin, N. *Kommünist internasyonalï VI-kongrasïnïn yäqünlarï.* Baku: Azärnäshr, 1928, 62 pp., 3000 cop. [Az 3 Lat; NN] 198

Bükharin, N. *Kommünist internasyonalï ijraiyyä komitäsi plenümünün yeqünlarï.* Baku: Azärnäshr, 1927, 75 pp., 2000 cop. [Az 3 Lat; CStH, NN] 199

Bükharin, N. *Komsomolün jarï vazifäläri.* Baku: Azärnäshr, 1928, 72 pp., 3000 cop. [Az 3 Lat; NN] 200

Bükharin, N. I. *Beynälkhalk väziyyat hakkïnda.* Baku: Azärnäshr, 1927, 96 pp., 2000 cop. [Az 3 Lat; NN] 201

Bükharin, N. I. *Beynälkhalk väziyyät vä kominternin väzifäläri.* Baku: Azärnäshr, 1928, 93 pp., 2000 cop. [Az 3 Lat; NN] 202

Bükharin, N. I. *Komintern ijraiyyä komitäsindäqi UIK(b) firkäsi numayändäliyinin XV firkä kürültayïna atchotü.* Baku: Azärnäshr, 1928, 184 pp., 2000 cop. [Az 3 Lat; NN] 203

Bükharin, N. I. *UIK(b)F. M.K. vä Märqäzi Kontrol Komisyasï plenümünün yeqünlarï.* Baku: Azärnäshr, 1927, 65 pp., 2000 cop. [Az 3 Lat; NN] 204

Burokratizmlä mubaräzänin yäqünü vä än yakïn mäsäläläri. Baku: Azärnäshr, 1929, 82 pp., 5000 cop. [Az 4 Lat; NN] 205

Butun dunya devlätläri. Äsas mä'lümat. Baku: Azärnäshr, 1930, 202 pp., 3000 cop. [Az 4 Lat; NN] 206

Chïn mäsäläsi inghiltärädäqï väz'iyyät vä mukhaliflär hakkïnda kärarlar. Baku: Azärnäshr, 1927, 45 pp., 2000 cop. [Az 3 Lat; NN] 207

Davïdov, A. *Säfärbärliq nädur?* Baku: Azärnäshr, 1930, 34 pp., 6000 cop. [Az 4 Lat; NN] 208

Döghushchi vä manga ichin 60 döghush mäshkläri. Baku: Azärbayjan Härbiyyä Mäqtäbinin Hey'ät Tähririyyäsi Täräfinden Rüschadan Tärjumä Edilmishdir, 1926, 78 pp., 1000 cop. [Az 3 Lat; NN] 209

Dübrovsqï; Gürev. *Leninizm älifbasi.* Baku: Azärnäshr, 1928, 247 pp., 3000 cop. [Az 3 Lat; NN] 210

Düshak, A. *Firkä mäarifinin kürülüsh vä metodikasï.* Baku: Azärnäshr, 1930, 194 pp., 2000 cop. [Az 4 Lat; NN] 211

El kömäk chämiyätlärindä muäyyän mäqsäd üjün üzvülük haqqï almaq barädä tä'limat. Makhachkala: Dag. Giz., n.d., 9 pp., 410 cop. [Az 4 Lat; NN] 212

Enghels, Fridrikh. *Sosializmin ütopiyadan elmä dogrü inqishafï.* Baku: Azärnäshr, 1930, 137 pp., 3000 cop. [Az 4 Lat; NN] 213

Estoniya vä onün ordüsu. Baku: Azärnäshr, 1928, 13 pp., 2000 cop. [Az 3 Lat; NN] 214

Fä'alläh kändchi qïrmïzï ordü 'äskär vä matros nümayändäläri baku shürasinïñ 27–28 il mähälli bodjäsi. Baku: Baku Shürasï Äkhbarïnïñ Näshriyatï, 1927, 32 pp., 700 cop. [Az 1 & 2 Arab; NN] 215

Finlanda vä onün ordüsü. Baku: Azärnäshr, 1928, 13 pp., 2000 cop. [Az 3 Lat; NN] 216

Firkä täshqïlatlarï hakkïnda nizamnamä. Baku: A.K.(b)F. Baqï Komitäsi, 1928, 14 pp., 1000 cop. [Az 3 Lat; NN] 217

Ghrishin, M. I. *Länin yolilä.* Ikinji qïsïm. Baku: Baku Ishchisi Qo'opäratif Näshriyatï, n.d., 79 pp., 1000 cop. [Az 1 & 2 Arab; NN] 218

Glaübaüf, F. *Kominternin III: Kongrasï.* Baku: Azärnäshr, 1930, 64 pp., 2000 cop. [Az 4 Lat; NN] 219

Grishin, M. I. *Lenin yolü ilä: Shähär normal siyasi savad*

mäqtäbläri vä shäkhsi biliyini artïrmak uchun tädris qitabïdïr. Baku: "Baqï Ishchisi" Kooperatif Näshriyyatï, 1926, 536 pp., 2000 cop. [Az 3 Lat; NN] 220

Grishin, M. I. *Lenin yolü ilä: Shähar normal siyasi savad mäqtäbläri vä shäkhsi biliyini artïrmak uchun tädris qitabïdïr.* Baku: "Baqï Ishchisi" Kooperatif Näshriyyatï, 1926, 72 pp., 750 cop. [Az 3 Lat; NN] 221

Grishin, M. I. *Lenin yolü ilä: Shähär normal siyasi savad mäqtäbläri vä shäkhsi biliyini artïrmak uchun tadris qïtabïdïr.* 4 kism. Baku: "Baqï Ishchisi" Kooperatif Näshriyyatï, 1926, 127 pp., 750 cop. [Az 3 Lat; NN] 222

Härbi tekhnika dähshätlimidir? Baku: Azärnäshr, 1928, 14 pp., 3000 cop. [Az 3 Lat; NN] 223

I.Q.K.O. muväkkät intizamnamasï. Baku: Azärbayjan Härbi Näshriyyat Komisiyonü, 1926, 33 pp., 1000 cop. [Az 3 Lat; NN] 224

Ibtidai firkä mäqtäblärinin 1930–31-ji il uchun programï. Baku: Azärnäshr, 1930, 46 pp., 3000 cop. [Az 4 Lat; NN] 225

Jäbhä arqasï polchänyasïnda qulluq etmäk mäjbüriyyätindä olanïñ shähadätnamäsi. n.p.: Krasnyi Vostok, n.d., 12 pp., 2030 cop. [Az 1 & 2 Arab; NN] 226

Jäfärov, Jäfär. *Jäbhä geydläri.* Baku: Azärneshr, 1943, 33 pp., 5000 cop. [Az 5 Cyr; DLC] 227

Kalachensqi, N. *Chin.* Baku: Azärnäshr, 1930, 51 pp., 4000 cop. [Az 4 Lat; NN] 228

Kamenef, S; Mekhonoshin, K. *Ähalïnïn härbi hazirlïgï.* Baku: Azärnäshr, 1927, 42 pp., 2000 cop. [Az 3 Lat; NN] 229

Kand shuralarï ḥaqïnda vaẕʿiyet iẕaḥatli ve qanuni matäryallar. Makhachkala: Daghstan Merkezi Ijraʾiä Qomitäsining Neshriyatidir, 1929, 331 pp., 400 cop. [Az 1 and 2 Arab; NN] 229a

Kazakov, A. *Bolsheviq firkäsi müzdürün mänafeini nejä mudafää ädir.* Baku: Azärnäshr, 1928, 41 pp., 4000 cop [Az 3 Lat; NN] 230

Kitayghorodskï, P.; Porätski, B. *Jäzaʾir, märakäsh, tunis istïqlaliyat mubaräzäsi oghorïnda.* Baku: Adhärnäshr, 1927, 119 pp., 3000 cop. [Az 1 & 2 Arab; NN] 231

Kommünist internasyonalïnïn 10 illighi. Baku: Azärbayjan Devlät Näshriyyatï, 1929, 48 pp., 1000 cop. [Az 3 Lat; NN] 232

Kosarev, A. *Komsomol sïnïfï charpïshmalar meydanïnda.* Baku: Azärnäshr, 1929, 110 pp., 1000 cop. [Az 4 Lat; NN] 233

Kosarev, A. *U.I.L.K.Gh.I. VIII kürültayï vä komsomol mäsäläläri.* Baku: Azärnäshr, 1928, 61 pp., 2000 cop. [Az 3 Lat; NN] 234

Koy birligi 1925–26nji senäsiniñ: Ikinji ʿämäliyyat senäsi. Ḥaqqḥesabï. Baku: Koy Birligi, 1927, 37 pp., 300 cop. [Az 1 & 2 Arab; NN] 235

Krüpskaya, N. K. *Shüra kürülüshü ilä mämläqätin sänayeʿläshdirilmäsinin siyasi mäarif ishlärinä täʾsiri.* Baku: Azärnäshr, 1928, 39 pp., 2000 cop. [Az 3 Lat; NN] 236

Küliyef, Müstafa. *Azärbayjanda oktyabr düshmanlarï.* Baku: Azärnäshr, 1927, 55 pp., 2000 cop. [Az 3 Lat; CStH, NN] 237

Kürella, A. *Ghänjlär kominterni tarikhi kïsa khulasäsi.* Baku: Azärnäshr, 1927, 92 pp., 3000 cop. [Az 3 Lat; NN] 238

Länin. *Länin vä ishchi-kändli ittifaqï.* Baku: Adhärnäshr, 1927, 31 pp., 3000 cop. [Az 1 & 2 Arab; NN] 239

Länin. *Topraq vä kändli ḥaqqïndä.* Baku: Baku Ishchisi Qoʾopäratif Näshriyatï, 1927, 48 pp., 5000 cop. [Az 1 & 2 Arab; NN] 240

Ledo, Ameriko. *Arzhentina.* Baku: Azärnäshr, 1930, 19 pp., 3000 cop. [Az 4 Lat; NN] 241

Lenin, N. (V. I. Ülyanof). *Imperyalizm kapitalizmin än yäni devri gibi.* Baku: Azärnäshr, 1927, 99 pp., 2000 cop. [Az 3 Lat; NN] 242

Lenin, V. *Musabäkäni nä jur täshqil etmäli?* Baku: Azärnäshr, 1929. 19 pp., 5000 cop. [Az 4 Lat; NN] 243

Lenin, V. I.; Stalin, I. V. *ÜIQ(b)P tarikhinin öyränilmäsinä dair.* Baku: Azärnäshr, 1939, 110 pp., 10000 cop. [Az 4 Lat; DLC] 244

Lenin vä kïzïl ordü. Baku: Dövläti Härbi Näshriyyatï Sïfarïshïla Maskov Sähmdaran Nashriyyat Jämiyyäti Tärafindän Näshr Olünmüshdür, 1926, 33 pp., 2100 cop. [Az 3 Lat; NN] 245

Lizyükov, A. *Tanklar vä onlar ilä mubaräzä hakkïnda söhbät.* Baku: Azärnäshr, 1929, 35 pp., 3000 cop. [Az 3 Lat; NN] 246

Marks, Karl. *Lüi Bonapartïn 18 Brumeri.* Baku: Azärnäshr, 1929, 142 pp., 3000 cop. [Az 4 Lat; NN] 247

Marksizm vä milli mäsälä. Baku: Azärnäshr, 1930, 304 pp., 3000 cop. [Az 4 Lat; NN] 248

Maydinov, D. *18 mart—MOPR ghununu nä jur qächirmälidur?* Baku: Azärnäshr, 1930, 38 pp., 5000 cop. [Az 4 Lat; NN] 249

Melkümov. *Qänt yoksüllarï arasïnda firkänin ishi.* Baku: Azärnäshr, 1929, 53 pp., 3000 cop. [Az 3 Lat; NN] 250

Mirzoyan, L. *Chin inklabï.* Baku: Azärnäshr, 1927, 52 pp., 2000 cop. [Az 3 Lat; NN] 251
Mirzoyan, L. *Chin inqïlabï.* Baku: Adhärnäshr, 1927, 68 pp., 2000 cop. [Az 1 & 2 Arab; NN] 252
Molotov, V. *UIK(b)F märqäzi komitäsinin noyabr plenümü yäqünlarï.* Baku: Azärnäshr. 1929, 41 pp., 1000 cop. [Az 3 Lat; NN] 253
Molotov yoldashïn U.I.K.(b) firkäsinin komintern ijraiyyä komitäsindäqï hey'ätinin XVI-kürültayda hakhesabï uzrä mä'rüzäsi, son sözu vä hak-hesab uzrä kärar. Baku: Azärnäshr, 1930, 109 pp., 8000 cop. [Az 4 Lat; NN] 254
Moyrova, V. *Komintern programïnda kadïn mäsäläsi.* Baku: Azärnäshr, 1930, 54 pp., 2000 cop. [Az 4 Lat; NN] 255
Müsabäyov, G. *Iqi yol.* Baku: Azärnäshr, 1930, 156 pp., 30000 cop. [Az 4 Lat; NN] 256
Musabekof, Gh. *Oqtyabr inqilabï vä adhärbayjannda shüra ḥökumätinin äsas nä'iliyyätläri.* Baku: Adhärnäshr, 1927, 71 pp., 3000 cop. [Az 1 & 2 Arab; CStH, NN] 257
Naqiyof, Jähangir. *Homindan.* Baku: Adhärnäshr, 1928, 117 pp., 2000 cop. [Az 1 & 2 Arab; NN] 258
Narimanof, N. *Länin vä shärq.* Moscow: SSSR Khalqlarïnïñ Märkäz Näshriyatï, 1924, 19 pp., 4000 cop. [Az 1 & 2 Arab; NN] 259
Niqitin, I.; Näzärli. *Yakhshi atïsh achmagï näjä öghränmäli?* Baku: Azärnäshr, 1926, 30 pp., 3000 cop. [Az 3 Lat; NN] 260
Noyabr plenümünün yäqünlarï. Baku: Azärnäshr, 1929, 74 pp., 3000 cop. [Az 4 Lat; NN] 261
Nyurina, F. *Ämäqchi kadïnlar shüralar ittifakïnïn mudafääsïndä.* Baku: Azärbayjan Devlät Näshriyyatï, 1929, 23 pp., 1500 cop. [Az 3 Lat; NN] 262
Orjoniqidze, G. *Firkänin bash khätti vä sag tämayul.* Baku: Azärnäshr, 1930, 24 pp., 5000 cop. [Az 4 Lat; NN] 263
Pavlovich, M.; Ghorqo, V.; Qurbazhin; Rasqolniqof, Q. *Torkiyä ïstïqlal mubaräzäsi oghurïnda.* Baku: Adhärnäshr, 1927, 180 pp., 3000 cop. [Az 1 & 2 Arab; NN] 264
Pioner dästäbashïsï nä bilmälidur? Baku: Azärnäshr, 1930; Books V, VI, VIII, XI, XII, each 32 pp., each 2500 cop. [Az 4 Lat; NN] 265
Plekhanov, Gh. *Marksizmin äsas mäsäläläri.* Baku: Azärnäshr, 1928, 117 pp., 3000 cop. [Az 3 Lat; NN] 266

Polsha vä onün ordüsü. Baku: Azärnäshr, 1928, 13 pp., 2000 cop. [Az 3 Lat; NN] 267
Qitaygorodsqi, P. *Turqiyä.* Baku: Azärnäshr, 1930, 36 pp., 4000 cop. [Az 4 Lat; NN] 268
Qomsomolïn qira'ät komalarïnda ishläri. Baku: Adhärnäshr, 1927, 134 pp., 3000 cop. [Az 1 & 2 Arab; NN] 269
Quliyef, Muṣṭafa. *Adhärbayjanda oqtyabr doshmanlarï.* Baku: Adhärnäshr Mäṭb'äsindä Basïldï, 1927, 70 pp., 3000 cop. [Az 1 & 2 Arab:; CStH, NN] 270
Quzmin, V. *Ilich.* Baku: Adhärnäshr, 1926, 92 pp., 3000 cop. [Az 1 & 2 Arab; NN] 271
Ramirets, M. *Meksika.* Baku: Azärnäshr, 1930, 30 pp., 3000 cop. [Az 4 Lat; NN] 272
Ratghaozär, Y. *Kändli mäs'äläsindä läninizm vä mükhalifät.* Baku: n.p., 1927, 24 pp., 1000 cop. [Az 1 & 2 Arab; NN] 273
Rayäfski, A. *Ingliz "dostlar" vä müsavatchi "väṭänpärvärlär."* Baku: Adhärnäshr, 1927, 93 pp., 3000 cop. [Az 1 & 2 Arab; CStH, NN] 274
Räzvoshkin, Ya. *Känddä qomsomol ta'limin nä jur täshkil etmäli?* Baku: Baku Ishchisi Qo'opäratif Näshriyatï, 1927, 70 pp., 1100 cop. [Az 1 & 2 Arab; NN] 275
Räzvoshkin, Ya. *Känddä qomsomolïn siyasi-ma'ärif ishläri.* Baku: Adhärnäshr, 1927, 176 pp., 3000 cop. [Az 1 & 2 Arab; NN] 276
Rikof, A. I. *U.I.K(b)F MK vä MKK-nün muttähid plenümü yäghunlarï hakkïnda.* Baku: Azärnäshr, 1927, 87 pp., 2000 cop. [Az 3 Lat; NN] 277
Rudi, A. *Qomsomol nä dir?* Baku: Adhärnäshr, 1927, 62 pp., 3000 cop. [Az 1 & 2 Arab; NN] 278
Ryefsqi, A. *Inghilis "dostlar" vä müsavat "vätänpärvärlär."* Baku: Azärnäshr, 1927, 74 pp., 2000 cop. [Az 3 Lat; NN] 279
SSRI Ali Sovetinin onunju sessiasï: Stenografik hesabat. n.p.: SSRI Ali Sovetinin Näshriyyatï, 1944, 350 pp., n.c. [Az 5 Cyr; DLC] 280
SSRI Bash Sovetinin altïnjï sessiyasï: Stengrafik hesabat. Moscow: SSRI Bash Sovetinin Näshriyyatï, 1940, 611 pp., 4000 cop. [Az 5 Cyr; DLC] 281
SSRI Bash Sovetinin yeddinji sessiyasï: Stenografik hesabat. Moscow: SSRI Bash Sovetinin Näshriyyatï, 1940, 224 pp., 3000 cop. [Az 5 Cyr; DLC] 282

SSR Ittifagï Ali Soveti serqilärinä dair äsasnamä. Baku: Azärnäshr, 1945, 27 pp., 50000 cop. [Az 5 Cyr; DLC] 283

Sag-"sol" bloka karshï. Baku: Azärnäshr, 1930, 78 pp., 8000 cop. [Az 4 Lat; NN] 284

Satanävich, V. *Känd qomsomol özäkiniñ täshkilat ishläri.* Baku: Adhärnäshr, 1927, 104 pp., 3000 cop. [Az 1 & 2 Arab; NN] 285

Savelyev, A. P. *Hava vä qimiya hijümlarïnda zärardidä olanlara ilq yardïm.* Baku: Azärbayjan Hilal Ähmär Jämiyyätinin Bash Idaräsi Näshriyyatïndan, 1927, 42 pp., 5000 cop. [Az 3 Lat; NN] 286

Sef. *Balsheviqlär 1917–18-inji illärdä Baqï dayiräsinde haqimiyyät bashïna nejä ghäldilär?* Baku: Azärnäshr, 1927, 61 pp., 2000 cop. [Az 3 Lat; NN] 287

Sef, Semyon. *Shämgir hadisäläri hakkïnda dogrü mäʿlümat.* Baku: Azärnäshr, 1927, 66 pp., 3000 cop. [Az 3 Lat; NN] 288

Shähär komsomol siyasi mäqtäbläri uchun därs qitabï. Baku: Azärnäshr, 1929, 156 pp., 5000 cop. [Az 4 Lat; NN] 289

Shatsqin, L. *Nosqenin ghözläri önundä.* Baku: Azärnäshr, 1930, 50 pp., 1500 cop. [Az 4 Lat; NN] 290

Shokhin, A. *Oktyabr inkilabïnda ishchi qäntli ghänjlär.* Baku: Azärnäshr, 1927, 110 pp., 2000 cop. [Az 3 Lat; NN] 291

Shulghin, V. N.; Shamlli, S. *Marqs vä ängälsiñ pädghozhïq mülaḥiẓäläri.* Baku: Adhärbayjan Devlät Näshriyatï, 1926, 91 pp., 3000 cop. [Az 1 & 2 Arab; NN] 292

Shüralarïn yeni väzifäläri. Baku: Azärnäshr, 1930, 7 pp., 6500 cop. [Az 4 Lat; NN] 293

Simqin, Iv. *Azärbayjan komsomolünün gechdighi yol.* Baku: Azärnäshr, 1930, 47 pp., 1500 cop. [Az 4 Lat; NN] 294

Siyasi savad. Baku: "Baqï Ishchisi" Kooperatif Näshriyyatï, 1926, 62 pp., 2500 cop. [Az 3 Lat; NN] 295

Siyasi savad: Känd säyyar-siyasi savad mäktäbläri ichün tädris kitabidur. Baku: "Baku Ishchisi" Qo'opäratif Näshriyatï, 1926, 72 pp., 6000 cop. [Az 1 & 2 Arab; NN] 296

Smolyarof, I. *Pionär qolobi.* Baku: Baku Ishchisi Qo'opäratif Näshriyatï, 1926, 16 pp., 4000 cop. [Az 1 & 2 Arab; NN] 297

Spiring, M. *Dushmän karshïsïnda piyadanïn sänghärlänmäsi.* Baku: Azärnäshr, 1929, 47 pp., 3000 cop. [Az 4 Lat; NN] 298

Stalin; Kosior, S. *Märqäzi komitänin UIK(b) firkäsinin XV kürültäyïnä ätchotü.* Baku: Azärnäshr, 1928, 126 pp., 2000 cop. [Az 3 Lat; NN] 299

Stalin, I. *Böyuq dönush ili.* Baku: Azärnäshr, 1929, 20 pp., 1500 cop. [Az 4 Lat; CStH, NN] 300

Stalin, I. *Dialektik vä tarikhi materializm haggïnda.* Baku: Azärnäshr, 1945, 34 pp., 10000 cop. [Az 5 Cyr; DLC] 301

Stalin, I. *Lenin vä ortabablar ilä ittifak mäsäläsi.* Baku: Azärnäshr, 1928, 19 pp., 2000 cop. [Az 3 Lat; NN] 302

Stalin, I. V. *Firqämizdäki sosyal-dämoqrat tämayulï ḥaqqïndä.* Baku: Adhärnäshr, 1927, 184 pp., 2000 cop. [Az 1 & 2 Arab; CStH, NN] 303

Stalin yoldashïn UIK(b) firkäsinin XVI kürultayïna märqäzi komitänin hak-hesabï uzrä 1930-jü il iyünda mäʿrüzäsi vä son sözu märqäzi komitänin hak-hesabï uzrä XVI kürültayïn kätʿnamasï. Baku: Azärnäshr, 1930, 176 pp., 20000 cop. [Az 4 Lat; NN] 304

Sültanzada. *Iran.* Baku: Azärnäshr, 1930, 36 pp., 4000 cop. [Az 4 Lat; NN] 305

Tal, B. *Qïzïl ordü tarikhi.* Baku: Adhärnäshr, 1927, 264 pp., 3000 cop. [Az 1 & 2 Arab; CStH, NN] 306

Tayshin, M. I. *Siyasi savad.* Baku: Adhärnäshr, 1928, 216 pp., 5000 cop. [Az 1 & 2 Arab; NN] 307

Tayshin, M. I. *Siyasi savad.* II hissä. Baku, Azärnäshr, 1928, 191 pp., 3000 cop. [Az 3 Lat; NN] 308

Tayshin, M. I.; Kozlof, F. F. *Siyasï savad.* Baku: "Baqï Ishchisi" Kooperatif Näshriyyatï, 1926, 102 pp., 2500 cop. [Az 3 Lat; NN] 309

Ṭomski. *Oqtyabr inqïlabï ishjilärä nä verdi?* Moscow, SSSR Khalqlarnïñ Märkäz Näshriyatï, 1928, 55 pp., 1500 cop. [Az 1 & 2 Arab; NN] 310

U.I.K(b)F. XV konfransï kararlarï. Baku: Azärnäshr, 1927, 92 pp., 1500 cop. [Az 3 Lat; NN] 311

U.I.K.(b)F. sïralarïnïn umümi tämizlänmä vä yoklanïlmasïnï duzäldib qechirmäq uchun täʿlimat. Baku: Azärnäshr, 1929, 24 pp., 3000 cop. [Az 4 Lat; NN] 312

UIK(b) firkasïnïn program vä nizamnamasï. Baku: Azärnäshr, 1930, 94 pp., 8000 cop. [Az 4 Lat; NN] 313

Ü.I.Q.(b)F. Daghïstan qomitäsi 3-nchü plenomunun qararlarï. Makhachkala: Daghnäshr, 1930, 52 pp., 500 cop. [Az 4 Lat; NN] 314
U.I.Q.(b)F. Daghïstan qomitäsinin firqe özäk burolarïnï sejmäk haqqïnda mürachäetnamäsi. Makhachkala: Daghnäshr, 1929, 19 pp., 300 cop. [Az 4 Lat; NN] 315
'U.I.Q.(b)F.M.Q. vä M.Q.Q. muttaḥid plänomi qärarlarï. Baku: Adhärnäshr, 1927, 82 pp., 3000 cop. [Az 1 & 2 Arab; NN] 316
Uchuta alïnmasï ichun müväqqäti rähbär. n.p.: Ishji Kändli Qïzïl Ordü Bash Idarä Toplama Idaräsiniñ Näshriyatï, 1926, 80 pp., 400 cop. [Az 1 & 2 Arab; NN] 317
Umüm ittifak Lenin Kommünist ghänjlär ittifakïnïn program vä nizamnamasï. Baku: Azärnäshr, 192?, 86 pp., 3000 cop. [Az 4 Lat; NN] 318
'Umüm ittifaq L.Q.K.I. 5nji 'umüm ittifaq qonfransinin qärar vä qäṭ'namäläri. Baku: Adhärnäshr, 1927, 81 pp., 2000 cop. [Az 1 & 2 Arab; NN] 319
'Umüm ittifaq qommonist (b) firqäsinin XV-nji qoroltay: Stalin yoldashïn mä'rüẕäsi. Baku: Adhär. Qom. Firqäsi Märkäzi Qomitänin Näshriyatï, 1927, 54 pp., 3000 cop. [Az 1 & 2 Arab; NN] 320
'Umüm ittifaq qommonist (b) firqäsi XV qonfransï: N. i. boḥarïn, a. i. rikhof, m. p. tomski, vä i. v. stalin yoldashlarïñ mä'rüẕäsi uzrä qärarlarï. Baku: Adhärnäshr, 1927, 119 pp., 2000 cop. [Az 1 & 2 Arab; NN] 321
Val, V. *Hava donanmasï dostlarï jäm'iyyäti: Hava donanmasï bizä nä ichin lazïmdur?* Baku: n.p., 1925, 15 pp., n.c. [Az 1 & 2 Arab; NN] 322
Viktorov, R. *Ilich vä Komsomol.* Baku: Azärnäshr, 1930, 46 pp., 2000 cop. [Az 4 Lat; NN] 323
Yakovlev. *UIK(b)F XVI kürültayïnda kolkhoz häräqatï vä qänt täsärrufatïnïn yuqsälishi hakkïnda mä'rüzä.* Baku: Azärnäshr, 1930, 92 pp., 15000 cop. [Az 4 Lat; NN] 324
Yakovlev, A. *Oktyabr.* Baku: Azärnäshr, 1930, 157 pp., 3000 cop. [Az 4 Lat; NN] 325
Yaraslavski, Em. *Firqäni tämizlämäk mäs'äläsinä Lenin nä jür baqïrdï?* Makhachkala: Daghïstan Dävlät Näshriyyäti, 1929, 32 pp., 850 cop. [Az 4 Lat; NN] 326

History

Agamalï oglü. *Iqï mädäniyyät.* Baku: Azärnäshr, 1928, 48 pp., 2000 cop. [Az 3 Lat; NN] 327

Fridliyand, S.; Slütsqi, A. *Gärbi Avropa inkilab häräqatï tarikhi, 1789–1914.* Khristomatiya. Baku: Azärnäshr, 1929, 304 pp., 5000 cop. [Az 4 Lat; NN] 328

Husäynof, T. *Adhärbayjanda oqtyabr.* Baku: Adhärnäshr, 1927, 32 pp., 3000 cop. [Az 1 & 2 Arab; NN] 329

Huseynof, T. *Azärbayjanda oktyabr.* Baku: Azärnäshr, 1927, 25 pp., 2000 cop. [Az 3 Lat; NN] 330

Lenin Vladimir Ilich: Häyat vä fäaliyyätinin gïsa khülasäsi. Baku: Azärneshr, 1944, 344 pp., 10000 cop. [Az 5 Cyr; DLC] 331

Pelka, V. *Dag aüllarïnda.* Baku: Azärnäshr, 1930, 43 pp., 3000 cop. [Az 4 Lat; NN] 332

Popof, N. N. *Umüm ittifak kommünist (b) firkäsï tarihi.* Baku: Azärnäshr, 1927, 524 pp., 3000 cop. [Az 3 Lat; NN] 333

Popof, N. N. *ʿUmüm ittifaq qommonist (b) firqäsi tarikhi.* Baku: Adhärnäshr, 1927, 691 pp., 5000 cop. [Az 1 & 2 Arab; NN] 334

Rid, Jon. *Dunyanï sarsïdan 10 gun.* Baku: Adhärnäshr, 1927, 313 pp., 5000 cop. [Az 1 & 2 Arab; NN] 335

Valles, Zhul. *Kanlï häftä.* Baku: Azärnäshr, 1928, 46 pp., 3000 cop. [Az 3 Lat; NN] 336

Voloshin. *Ishchi ghänjlär tarïhïnïn khulasäläri.* Baku: Azärnäshr, 1927, 75 pp., 2000 cop. [Az 3 Lat; NN] 337

Law

A. D. *A.S.Sh. jumhüriyyätindä mähqämälär nejä kürulmüsh vä nejä ishläyirlär.* Baku: Azärnäshr, 1929, 32 pp., 2000 cop. [Az 4 Lat; NN] 338

Adhärbayjan ijtimaʿi shüra jumhüriyäti märkäzi ijraʾiä qomitäsi: Känd shüralarï ijmam vä bolmälär ḥaqïndä niẓamnamä. Baku: A.M.I. Qomitäsinin Täshkilat Shöʿbäsi Näshriyatï, 1927, 21 pp., 5000 cop. [Az 1 & 2 Arab; NN] 339

Adhärbayjan sosyalist shüra jumhüriyäti: Qanon äsasisi. Baku: A.M.I. Qomitäsiniñ Näshriyatï, 1927, 23 pp., 8000 cop. [Az 1 & 2 Arab; NN] 340

Ghrämyatskï, M. *Qadïm insanlarda täkhniqa.* Baku: Baku Ishchisi Qo'opäratïf Näshriyatï, 1926, 59 pp., 4000 cop. [Az 1 & 2 Arab; NN] 370

Ghrinbärgh, M. *Üshaghïñ yüqüsini mühafizä ediñiz!* Baku: Adhärnäshr, 1928, 33 pp., 3000 cop. [Az 1 & 2 Arab; NN] 371

Grigoryev, A. *Hali-hazïrda ghänjlärin sïnfi tärbiyäsi.* Baku: Azärnäshr, 1929, 75 pp., 2000 cop. [Az 4 Lat; NN] 372

Ijtimaiyyatdan ish qitabï. Baku: Azärnäshr, 1929, 430 pp., 6000 cop. [Az 4 Lat; NN] 373

Isma'ïl zadä, Ibrahim. *Sifilis vä 'a'ilä.* Baku: Adhärnäshr, 1927, 38 pp., 3000 cop. [Az 1 & 2 Arab; NN] 374

Kalinin, M. I. *Qänt ilä mädäni rabitä yollarï.* Baku, Azärnäshr, 1928, 17 pp., 2000 cop. [Az 3 Lat; NN] 375

Kanel, L. V. *Zöhräri khästäliqlär hakkïnda süal-javablï on söhbät.* Baku: Azärnäshr, 1930, 130 pp., 3000 cop. [Az 4 Lat; NN] 376

Kharitonova-Ostrovskaya, R. *Kommünist chajüklar häräqatï vä mäqtäbä kädär tärbiyä.* Baku: Azärbayjan Devlät Näshriyyatï, 1929, 52 pp., 1500 cop. [Az 3 Lat; NN] 377

Khüdadov, V. N.; Demidov, G. V. *Ghurju kadïnï.* Baku: Azärnäshr, 1928, 38 pp., 2000 cop. [Az 3 Lat; NN] 378

Korshün, S. *Küdüzlük.* Baku: Azärnäshr, 1927, 40 pp., 3000 cop. [Az 3 Lat; NN] 379

Kotelnikov, M. V. *Elliqlä toprak bejärmäq shirqäti.* Baku: Azärbayjan Devlät Näshriyyatï, 1929, 32 pp., 2000 cop. [Az 3 Lat; NN] 380

Külikof, V. *Choban vä uakhïrchïnï mudafää.* Baku: "Baqï Ishchisi" Kooperatif Näshriyyatï, 1926, 48 pp., 4000 cop. [Az 3 Lat; NN] 381

Küliyev, M. *Turq kadïnïnïn yolü.* Baku: Azärnäshr, 1930, 46 pp., 5000 cop. [Az 4 Lat; NN] 382

Küznetsov, A.; Tsvetkov, D. *Qänt özäghi mänsül ügründa yurushu nejä täshqil etmälidur?* Baku: Azärnäshr, 1930, 80 pp., 2000 cop. [Az 4 Lat; NN] 383

Molotov, V. *Kolkhoz häräqatïna dogrü.* Baku: Azärnäshr, 1930, 23 pp., 5000 cop. [Az 4 Lat; NN] 384

Nükhrat, A. *Shärkdä 8 mart ghunu.* Baku: Azärnäshr, 1929, 32 pp., 2000 cop. [Az 3 Lat; NN] 385

Oleshshük, F. *Kolchomak vä molla müzdürün dushmänidur.* Baku: Azärnäshr, 1929, 42 pp., 2000 cop. [Az 4 Lat; NN] 386

Paläpa, Gh. A. *Inqilabï oyünlar—äliñi chäk!* Baku: Adhärnäshr, 1928, 20 pp., 3000 cop. [Az 1 & 2 Arab; NN] 387

Paläpa. Gh. A. *Inqilabï oyünlar: Mopr.* Baku: Adhärnäshr, 1928, 22 pp., 3000 cop. [Az 1 & 2 Arab; NN] 388

Paläpa, Gh. A. *Inqilabï oyünlar—värsal ṣulḥ.* Baku: Adhärnäshr, 1928, 19 pp., 3000 cop. [Az 1 & 2 Arab; NN] 389

Paläpa, Gh. A. *Yoq olsun äsarät zänjirläri.* Baku: Adhärnäshr, 1926, 30 pp., 3000 cop. [Az 1 & 2 Arab; NN] 390

Palepa, G. A. *Kïzïl yardïm jämʿiyyäti.* Baku: "Azärnäshr," 1926, 29 pp., 3000 cop. [Az 3 Lat; NN] 391

Pribilof, I., *Qäntdä pionerlärin bädän tärbiyäsi.* Baku: Azärnäshr, 1927, 73 pp., 2500 cop. [Az 3 Lat; NN] 392

Qadïnlarïn ḥalï shimdi vä geläjekdä. Buinaksk: Daghstan Ijtimaʿi Shura Jumhoriyati Ḥukomatinin Nashriyatï, 1921, 18 pp., 1000 cop. [Az 1 & 2 Arab; CStH] 393

Qändi sosializm äsaslarï uzärindä yenidän kürmak hakkïnda. Baku: Azärnäshr, 1930, 160 pp., 3000 cop. [Az 4 Lat; NN] 394

Qänt muällimäsi ijtimaï ishdä. Baku: Azärnäshr, 1928, 44 pp., 2000 cop. [Az 3 Lat; NN] 395

Qänt täsärrufat artellärinin dakhili kaydalarï. Baku: Azärbayjan Devlät Näshriyyatï, 1929, 19 pp., 2000 cop. [Az 3 Lat; NN] 396

Qänt täsärrufat kollektivlärinin birinji umüm ittifak kürültayïnïn kärarlarï. Baku: Azärnäshr, 1929, 52 pp., 2000 cop. [Az 3 Lat; NN] 397

Qerzhentsef, P. M. *Öz-özunu täshqil et!* Baku: Azärnäshr, 1928, 103 pp., 2000 cop. [Az 3 Lat; NN] 398

Qonyus, Ä. M. *Üshaghï nä jur saqlamalïdur?* Baku: Baku Ishchisi Qoʾopäratïf Näshriyatï, 1926, 49 pp., 5000 cop. [Az 1 & 2 Arab; NN] 399

Qorshun, S. V. *Quduzluq.* Baku: Baku Ishchisi Qoʾopäratïf Näshriyatï, 1926, 50 pp., 3000 cop. [Az 1 & 2 Arab; NN] 400

Razümova, A. *Beynälkhalk kadïnlar ghunu vä MOPR.* Baku: Azärnäshr, 1930, 34 pp., 5000 cop. [Az 4 Lat; NN] 401

Rozänblyum, Gh. *Evlänmäk vä onïn ähämiyäti.* Baku: Adhärnäshr, 1927, 97 pp., 3000 cop. [Az 1 & 2 Arab; NN] 402

Säryudkin, T. *Känddä bädän tarbiyäsi.* Baku: Adhärnäshr, 1927, 61 pp., 3000 cop. [Az 1 & 2 Arab; NN] 403

Seryadqïn, N. *Qäntdä bädän tärbiyäsi.* Baku: Azärnäshr, 1927, 44 pp., 3000 cop. [Az 3 Lat; NN] 404
Shibayev, A. *Kadïn därraqäsi.* Baku: Azärnäshr, 1930, 40 pp., 3000 cop. [Az 4 Lat; NN] 405
Sviridov, I. *Shüra-yoksül-ortabab aktivin täshqilatchïsïdür.* Baku: Azärnäshr, 1930, 34 pp., 3000 cop. [Az 3 Lat; NN] 406
Uspänski, A. *Vaqtïndan ävväl tänasül ʿälaqälarïnïn zäräri.* Baku: Adhärnäshr, 1927, 60 pp., 3000 cop. [Az 1 & 2 Arab; NN] 407
Vezir, Yusuf. *Arvadlarïmïzïn ḥalï.* Baku: Adhärnäshr, 1928, 37 pp., 3000 cop. [Az 1 & 2 Arab; NN] 408
Vishnevsqi, A. *Ämäli zhimnastiq.* Baku: Azärnäshr, 1930, 41 pp., 5000 cop. [Az 4 Lat; NN] 409
Zorin, V.; Nahid, H. *54 ghun gärb pionerläri arasïnda.* Baku: Azärnäshr, 192?, 70 pp., 2000 cop. [Az 3 Lat; NN] 410
Zorin, V.; Nahid, H. *54 gun ghärb pionärläri arasïnda.* Baku: Adhärnäshr, 1927, 82 pp., 3000 cop. [Az 1 & 2 Arab; NN] 411

AZERI Humanities

Language

Abdullayev, M. *Fiziqa terminläri.* Kitab 7. Baku: SShJI Elmlär Aqademiyasï, Azärbayjan Shöʿbäsi Näshriyyatï, 1935, 302 pp., 2000 cop. [Az 4 Lat; DLC, NN] 412
Akhündov, R. (ed.). *Rüsja–Turqjä lugät.* 2 vols. Baku: Azärnäshr, 1928–1929, I 320 pp., II 305 pp., 10400 cop. [Az 1 & 2 Arab, 3 Lat; NNC] 413
Äli zadä, A. *Geologiya terminläri.* Kitab 8. Baku: SShJI Elmlär Aqademiyasïnïn Azärbayjan Filial Näshriyyatï, 1935, 146 pp., 2000 cop. [Az 4 Lat; NN] 414
Alizade, M.; Askerli, M. R.; Ganbarov, A.; Mirbabaev, Yu. *Rusja–farsja–azärbayjanja mükhtäsär lüghät.* Baku: Izdatel'stvo Azerbaidzhanskogo Filiala Akademii Nauk SSSR, 1944, n.pp., 1000 cop. [Az 1 & 2 Arab, 5 Cyr; MH] 415
Azärbayjan Turq khalq shiväläri lugäti: Rüsja, almanja tärjumälärilä. 2 vols. Baku: A.D.E.T.I. Näshriyatï, 1930–1931, I 250 pp., II 260 pp., n.c. [Az 4 Lat; NN] 416

Chobanzadä. *Qumuq dili vä ädäbiyyatï tädqiqläri*. Baku: Adhärbayjanï Tädqiq vä Tätäbbü' Jäm'iyyat Näshriyatï, 1926, 105 pp., 1000 cop. [Az 1 & 2 Arab; CStH, NN, NNC*] 417

Chobanzadä, B. *Turk-tatar diyaläktolozhisï*. Girish. Baku: Adhärbayjan Tädqiq vä Tätäbbu' Jäm'iyyatïnïn Näshriyatï, 1927, 133 pp., 1000 cop. [Az 1 & 2 Arab; CStH, NNC] 418

Ghanï zadä, Sulṭan Mäjid. *Lughät-i turki vä rusi*. Baku: Tipografiia 1-ago Tipograficheskago Tovarishchestva, 1904, 164 pp., n.c. [Az 1 & 2 Arab; MH] 419

Hüseynov, H. *Azärbayjanja–rusja lüghät*. Baku: SSR Elmlär Aqademiyasï Azärbayjan Filialïnïn Näshriyatï, 1939, 318 pp., 10000 cop. [Az 4 Lat; NN] 420

Hüseynov, H. *Rusja–azärbayjanja lüghät*. Baku: Izdatel'stvo Azerbaidzhanskogo Filiala Akademiia Nauk SSSR, 1939, 317 pp., 10000 cop. [Az 4 Lat; NN] 421

Hüseynov, H. (ed.). *Azärbayjanja–rusja lüghät*. Baku: SSRI Elmlär Akademiyasï Azärbayjan Filialïnïn Näshriyyatï, 1941, 381 pp., 30000 cop. [Az 5 Cyr; DLC] 422

Hüseynov, H. (ed.) *Rusja–azärbayjanja lüghät*. Baku: Ensiqlopediya vä Lüghätlär Institutu Näshriyyatï, 1939, 747 pp., 10000 cop. [Az 4 Lat: NN, NNC] 423

Mirbabaev, Yu. *Mükhtäsär farsja–rüsja–azärbayjanja lüghät*. Baku: Izdatel'stvo AN Azerbaidzhanskoi SSR, 1945, 339 pp., 2000 cop. [Az 1 & 2 Arab, 5 Cyr; NNC] 424

Mohämmäd-zadä, J. *Turqjä oyrädän*. Baku: Azärnäshr, 1928, 155 pp., 5000 cop. [Az 3 Lat; NN] 425

Näzäri mekhaniqdän istilab lugäti. Baku: ADETI Näshriyyatï, 1930, 52 pp., n.c. [Az 4 Lat; NN] 426

Sa'id, Khalid. *'Othmanlï ozbek qazaq dillärinïn muqayäsäli ṣärfi*. Baku: Adhär. Tädqiq vä Tätäbbu' Jäm'iyyatï Näshriyatï, 1926, 110 pp., 1000 cop. [Az 1 & 2 Arab; CStH, NN] 427

Zifeldt-Simünyagi, A. R. *Turqolozhï etyüdlarï*. Seriia "Uralo-Altaica." Kn. II, vyp. 1; *Izvestiia* No. 1. Baku: Azerbaidzhan Gos. Issled. Institut. Otd. Iazyka, Lit., i Iskusstv, 1930, 28 pp., 1000 cop. [Az 4 Lat; NN] 428

---

*Microfilm

Adhärbayjan Prolätar Yazïchïlar Jäm'iyatï. *Oqtabr alavlarï.* Baku: Adhärnäshr, 1927, 172 pp., 5000 cop. [Az 1 & 2 Arab; NN] 429
Akhundzadä, Mirzä Fäth 'Ali. *Särgudhäsht-i märd-i khasis vä murafa'ä väkillärininñ ḥikayäti.* Baku: Adhärnäshr, 1942, 184 pp., n.c. [Az 1 & 2 Arab; CLU] 430
Akhunzadä, Mirza Fäth 'Ali. *Tämthilat.* Tiflis: Serkar Äshräf Ämjäd Janïshïn Qafqazïn Basmakhanäsindä Mäṭbu'a Olunubdur, A.H. 1277/A.D. 1861, 286 pp., n.c. [Az 1 & 2 Arab; NNC*] 431
Alazan. *Yolda.* Roman. Baku: Azärnäshr, 1930, 109 pp., 3000 cop. [Az 4 Lat; NN] 432
'Äliyof, A. 'Omär khayam vä ruba'iyatï. Moscow: Märkäzi Shärq Näshriyatï, 1924, 84 pp., 5000 cop. [Az 1 & 2 Arab; CStH, NN] 433
'Älizadä, Hümmät (ed.). *Kor oghli.* Baku: Adhärnäshr, 1941, 167 pp., n.c. [Az 1 & 2 Arab; NN] 434
Älizadä, Hümmät (ed.). *Koroglü.* Baku: Azärnäshr, 1941, 226 pp., 9000 cop. [Az 5 Cyr; DLC] 435
Amnüel, A. *Marat.* Bir pärdäli piyes. Baku: Azärnäshr, 1927, 26 pp., 3000 cop. [Az 3 Lat; CStH, NN] 436
Amundsän, Roal. *Qanaqlar üzärindä buzlar ölkäsinä.* Baku: Adhärnäshr, 1927, 88 pp., 3000 cop. [Az 1 & 2 Arab; NN] 437
Anaṭollï, Aḥmäd. *Ajï ḥaqïqat.* Qopletler. Tiflis: n.p., 1926, 32 pp., 1000 cop. [Az 1 & 2 Arab; NN] 438
Andräyäf. *Loghalar.* Baku: Adhärnäshr, 1928, 11 pp., 5000 cop. [Az 1 & 2 Arab; NN] 439
Aprel alavlarï: Proletar yazïjïlarïndan numünälär. Baku: Azärnäshr, 1930, 95 pp., 3000 cop. [Az 4 Lat; NN] 440
Arborä-Rallï, I. *Li'u-changh-yangh.* Baku: Baku Ishchisi Qo'opäratif Näshriyatï, 1926, 67 pp., 5000 cop. [Az 1 & 2 Arab; NN] 441
Armen, Mikirtich. *Sona.* Baku: Azärnäshr, 1930, 28 pp., 2000 cop. [Az 4 Lat; NN] 442
Ashïghïn säsi. Baku: EAAzF Näshriyyatï, 1939, 162 pp., 3000 cop. [Az 4 Lat; DLC] 443

---

*Microfilm

Äzimzadä, Yusif. *Ilk qörüsh.* Baku: Azärnäshr, 1945, 118 pp., 5000 cop. [Az 5 Cyr; DLC] 444

Bakünts, Aksel. *Ivan bäy.* Heqayä. Baku: Azärnäshr, 1930, 31 pp., 3000 cop. [Az 4 Lat; NN] 445

Chekhov, A. P. *Vishnä bagï.* 4 pärdäli komediya. Baku: Azärnäshr, 1930, 98 pp., 3000 cop. [Az 4 Lat; NN] 446

Choghoryan, Arutiyon. *Chadonïn bakhtï yoqsulluk ḥalï.* Baku: Adhärnäshr, 1927, 56 pp., 3000 cop. [Az 1 & 2 Arab; NN] 447

Divan-bäy oglü, Ä. B. *Jan yangïsi.* Heqayä. Baku: Azärnäshr, 1927, 43 pp., 3000 cop. [Az 3 Lat; NN] 448

Dmitriyeva, V. *Mayna-vira: Endir-kaldïr.* Baku: Azärnäshr, 1930, 46 pp., 2000 cop. [Az 4 Lat; NN] 449

Dorokhov, P. *Bolsheviq oglü.* Baku: Azärnäshr, 1930, 42 pp., 3000 cop. [Az 4 Lat; NN] 450

Farük, A. *Ufuklär kïzaranda.* Sheirlär. Baku: Azärnäshr, 1929, 42 pp., 2000 cop. [Az 4 Lat; NN] 451

Feridun Bek Kochärli. *Adhärbayjan ädäbiyatï tarikhi materyallarï.* Birinji jild, ikinji hiṣṣä. Baku: Adhärnäshr, 1925, 625 pp., n.c. [Az 1 & 2 Arab; CLU] 452

Fevzi, Ä., *Irmaklar.* Baku: Azärnäshr, 1930, 121 pp., 3000 cop. [Az 4 Lat; NN] 453

Fevzi, Ä. *Kadïn intikamï.* Heqayälär. Baku: Azärnäshr, 1930, 71 pp., 3000 cop. [Az 4 Lat; NN] 454

Fikret, Tevfiq. *Müntäkhäb parchälär.* Moscow: Märkäzi Shärq Näshriyatï, 1923, 112 pp., 5000 cop. [Az 1 & 2 Arab; CStH, NN] 455

Fürmanov, D. *Isyan.* Baku: Azärnäshr, 1930, 414 pp., 3000 cop. [Az 4 Lat; NN] 456

Füzuli. *Äsärläri.* I jild. Baku: EAAzF Näshriyyatï, 1944, 419 pp., 4000 cop. [Az 5 Cyr; MH] 457

Füzuli. *Leyli vä mäjnün: Sechilmish äsärläri.* II jild. Baku: Azärnäshr, 1940, 232 pp., 8000 cop. [Az 5 Cyr; DLC] 458

Gänizade, H. A. *Ütanïram.* Heqayälär. Baku: Azärnäshr, 1930, 60 pp., 3000 cop. [Az 4 Lat; NN] 459

Gorki, Maksim. *Ushaglar.* Baku: Azär. LKKI MK, 1945, 16 pp., 10000 cop. [Az 5 Cyr; DLC] 460

Gorqi, M. *Mänin darulfunünlarïm.* Baku: Azärbayjan Devlät Näshriyyatï, 1929, 211 pp., 2000 cop. [Az 3 Lat; NN] 461

Hagverdiev, Ä. *Äsärläri.* III jild: proza. Baku: EAAzF Näshriyyatï, 1941, 320 pp., 5000 cop. [Az 5 Cyr; DLC] 462
Hajjibekof, ʿÜzeyirbek. *Arshin mal alan.* 4 shäkilli bir opärättadur. Baku: Orujof Qardashlarïnïñ Eliqtriq Mäṭbʿäsindä Täbʿ Olïndï, A.H.1335/A.D.1917 3d ed., 53 pp., n.c. [Az 1 & 2 Arab; NN, NNC] 463
Hakverdiyef, Ä. *Marallarïm.* Qichiq heqayälär. Baku: Azärnäshr, 1927, 86 pp., 2000 cop. [Az 3 Lat; NN] 464
Hamsün, Knüt. *Ajlïk.* Roman. Baku: Azärnäshr, 1930, 167 pp., 3000 cop. [Az 4 Lat; NN] 465
Ḥaqverdiyof, ʿA. *Köhnä dudman.* Piyäsa. Baku: Adhärnäshr, 1927, 99 pp., 3000 cop. [Az 1 & 2 Arab; NN] 466
Ḥaqverdof, A. *Maralarïm.* Küchük ḥikayälär. Baku: Adhärnäshr, 1927, 108 pp., 4000 cop. [Az 1 & 2 Arab; NN] 467
Ḥaqverdof, ʿAbdalrahimbek. *Bakhtsïz javan.* Baku: Adhärnäshr, 1926, 64 pp., 5000 cop. [Az 1 & 2 Arab; NN] 468
Ḥikmät, Naẓim. *Gunäshi ichenlärïñ türkisi.* Baku: Adhärnäshr, 1928, 104 pp., 3000 cop. [Az 1 & 2 Arab; NN] 469
Hugho, V. *Gulän adam.* Baku: Adhärnäshr, 1927, 419 pp., 5000 cop. [Az 1 & 2 Arab; NN] 470
Hüseynov, Heydär. *M. F. Akhundovun fälsäfi görüshläri.* Baku: EAAzF Näshriyyatï, 1938, 74 pp., 2000 cop. [Az 4 Lat; NN] 471
Ibrahimof, ʿAlïmjan. *Adamlar.* Ḥikayä. Baku: Adhärnäshr, 1927, 65 pp., 3000 cop. [Az 1 & 2 Arab; NN] 472
Ilyas, Ä. *Aydïnlïg qejälär.* Baku: Azärnäshr, 1945, 115 pp., 5000 cop. [Az 5 Cyr; DLC] 473
Ingliz khanïmï. Roman. Baku: Adhärnäshr, 1927, 262 pp., 3000 cop. [Az 1 & 2 Arab; NN] 474
Irkütov, A. *Qichiq mubarizlär: Amerika khalk mäqtäbi häyatïndan.* Baku: Azärnäshr, 1930, 172 pp., 3000 cop. [Az 4 Lat; NN] 475
Ivanov, Vsevolod. *Partizanlar.* Heqayä. Baku: Azärnäshr, 1929, 79 pp., 2000 cop. [Az 4 Lat; NN] 476
Jäbrayïlbäyli, Jämo. *Gäribä hekayälär.* Baku: Azär LKKI MK Üshag vä Qänjlar Ädäbiyyatï Näshriyatï, 1945, 72 pp., 10000 cop. [Az 5 Cyr; DLC] 477
Jälal, Mir. *Füzulinin poetik khüsüsiyyätläri.* Baku: EAAzF Näshriyyatï, 1940, 94 pp., 3000 cop. [Az 5 Cyr; DLC] 478

Jälal, Mir. *Häyat hekayäläri*. Baku: Azär. LKKI MK, 1945, 156 pp., 10000 cop. [Az 5 Cyr; DLC] 479
Javad, A. *Qoshma*. Baku: "Achiq Soz" Mäṭb'äsi, A.H. 1335/A.D. 1916, 60 pp., n.c. [Az 1 & 2 Arab; CLU] 480
Javid, Ḥüseyn. *Iblis*. 4 pärdäli faj'iä. Baku: Adhärnäshr, 1927, 115 pp., 5000 cop. [Az 1 & 2 Arab; NN] 481
Javid, Ḥüseyn. *Iblis*. Faj'iä, 4 pärdä. Baku: Adhärbayjan Devlät Näshriyatï, 1924, 109 pp., 5000 cop. [Az 1 & 2 Arab; NNC] 482
Javid, Ḥüseyn. *Peyghämbär*. 4 pärdäli mänẓum dram. Baku: Adhärnäshr, 1926, 147 pp., 5000 cop. [Az 1 & 2 Arab; NN] 483
Ji'ovani'oli. *Spartak*. Roman. Baku: Adhärnäshr, 1928, 457 pp., 4000 cop. [Az 1 & 2 Arab; NN] 484
Kamanin, F. *Shishä fabriqindä*. Häqayälär. Baku: Azärnäshr, 1930, 85 pp., 3000 cop. [Az 4 Lat; NN] 485
Kataev, I. *Kälb*. Häqayä. Baku: Azärnäshr, 1930, 116 pp., 3000 cop. [Az 4 Lat; NN] 486
Kemal, Sami. *Qira'ät därsläri*. Baku: Adhärnäshr, 1926, 170 pp., 6000 cop. [Az 1 & 2 Arab; NN] 487
Khalidbek, Ṣabri Begzadä. *Zähärli chichäklär*. Baku: "Qaspi" Mätb'äsindä Täb' vä Tämthil Olunmushdur, Izdanie Isa-bek Ashurbekova, A.H.1331/A.D.1913, 62 pp., n.c. [Az 1 & 2 Arab; CLU] 488
Khändan, Jäfär. *Sabir—häyat vä yaradïjïlïghï*. Baku: EAAzF Näshriyyatï, 1940, 167 pp., 3000 cop. [Az 5 Cyr; DLC] 489
Khülüflü, V. *Kor oghlï*. Baku: Adhär. Orgränän Jäm'iyatïn Näshriyatï, 1927, 165 pp., 1000 cop. [Az 1 & 2 Arab; NN] 490
Khülüflü, V. *Tapmajalar*. Baku: Azärbayjanï Öyränän Jämiyyätin Näshriyyatï, 1928, 130 pp., 1000 cop. [Az 3 Lat; NN] 491
Khülüflü, Väli (comp.). *El ashiqlarï*. Baku: Adhär. Ögränän Jäm'iyatïn Näshriyatï, 1927, 101 pp., 1000 cop. [Az 1 & 2 Arab; NN] 492
Korolenko, V. G. *Bir lähzä*. Baku: Azärnäshr, 1930, 18 pp., 3000 cop. [Az 4 Lat; NN] 493
Korolenko, V. G. *Ghejä*. Baku: Azärnäshr, 1930, 52 pp., 3000 cop. [Az 4 Lat; NN] 494
Korolenko, V. G. *Khülya vä häyat*. Baku: Azärnäshr, 1930, 30 pp., 3000 cop. [Az 4 Lat; NN] 495
Labünskaya, G. V. *Shäkhsi fääliyyätli dram därnäghindä sähnä,*

dekarasiya vä kostümlar. Baku: Azärnäshr, 1930, 91 pp., 2000 cop. [Az 4 Lat; NN] 496
Lahutï. *Krämäl.* Moscow: Märkäzi Shärq Näshriyatï, 1923, 32 pp., 3000 cop. [Az 1 & 2 Arab; NN] 497
Lavrenev, B. *Kïrk birinji.* Heqäyä. Baku: Azärnäshr, 1930, 88 pp., 3000 cop. [Az 4 Lat; NN] 498
Lermontov, M. Y. *Zämanämizin qährämanï.* Baku: Azärbayjan Devlät Näshriyyatï, 1937, 237 pp., 5000 cop. [Az 4 Lat; NN] 499
London, Jäq. *Adamdan ävväl.* Ḥikayä. Baku: Baku Ishchisi Qo'opäratif Näshriyatï, 1926, 116 pp., 7000 cop. [Az 1 & 2 Arab; NN] 500
London, Jäq. *Agh dish.* Baku: Adhärnäshr, 1927, 191 pp., 4000 cop. [Az 1 & 2 Arab; NN] 501
London, Jäq. *Smoq vä balaja.* Baku: Adhärnäshr, 1928, 127 pp., 3000 cop. [Az 1 & 2 Arab; NN] 502
London, Jek. *Kan säsi.* Heqayä. Baku: Azärnäshr, 1927, 83 pp., 3000 cop. [Az 3 Lat; NN] 503
Lopatin. *Böyuq yalanchï.* Qino. Baku: Azärnäshr, 1927, 47 pp., 3000 cop. [Az 3 Lat; NN] 504
Mamin-Sibiryak, D. *Avchï Häsän.* Baku: Azärnäshr, 1928, 19 pp., 3000 cop. [Az 3 Lat; CStH] 505
Mamin-Sibiryak, D. N. *Üldüz.* Baku: Azärnäshr, 1930, 36 pp., 4000 cop. [Az 4 Lat; NN] 506
Mämmäd-Külüzada, Jälil. *Ölulär.* Komediya 4 mäjlisdä. Baku: Azärnäshr, 1929, 78 pp., 3000 cop. [Az 3 Lat; NN] 507
Mandälshtam. *Mäṭbäkh.* Baku: Adhärnäshr, 1927, 10 pp., 5000 cop. [Az 1 & 2 Arab; NN] 508
Mehdi, H. *Tärlan.* Baku: Azärnäshr, 1940, 261 pp., 6000 cop. [Az 5 Cyr; DLC] 509
Meliqyan, Novik. *Tünel ügründa.* Heqayä. Baku: Azärnäshr, 1929, 16 pp., 3000 cop. [Az 4 Lat; NN] 510
Moskvada Azärbayjan ädäbiyyatï dekadasï. Baku: Azärnäshr, 1940, 322 pp., 3000 cop. [Az 5 Cyr; DLC] 511
Muḥammäd zadä, 'Ali Näẓmi. *Sizhim qolï namä.* Ash'ar mäjmu'äsi. Baku: Adhärnäshr, 1927, 508 pp., 5000 cop. [Az 1 & 2 Arab; NN] 512
Mumtaz, Salman. *Adhärbayjan ädäbiyatï: Aqa mäsiḥ shirvanï.* Ṣayï 1. Baku: "Qommonist" Ghazitäsi Näshriyatï, 1925, 48 pp., 4000 cop. [Az 1 & 2 Arab; CLU, NN] 513

Mumtaz, Salman. *Adhärbayjan ädäbiyatï: ʿAshiq ʿabdallä*. Baku: Adhärnäshr, 1927, 71 pp., 3000 cop. [Az 1 & 2 Arab; NN] 514
Mumtaz, Salman. *Adhärbayjan ädäbiyatï: Bababek shakir*. Baku: Adhärnäshr, 1927, 34 pp., 3000 cop. [Az 1 & 2 Arab; NN] 515
Mumtaz, Salman. *Adhärbayjan ädäbiyatï: El shaʿïrlarï*. Baku: Adhärnäshr, 1927, 397 pp., 3000 cop. [Az 1 & 2 Arab; NN] 516
Mumtaz, Salman. *Adhärbayjan ädäbiyatï. Kärbälayï älli ʿarif*. Ṣayï 6. n.p.: Qommonist Näshriyyatï, 1925, 18 pp., 4000 cop. [Az 1 & 2 Arab; NN, NNC] 517
Mumtaz, Salman. *Adhärbayjan ädäbiyatï: Mirza näṣrallä bek didä*. Baku: Adhärnäshr, 1928, 88 pp., 3000 cop. [Az 1 & 2 Arab; NN] 518
Mumtaz, Salman. *Adhärbayjan ädäbiyatï: Mirza shäfiʿ vaẕïh*. Baku: Qommonist Näshriyyatï, 1926, 30 pp., 4000 cop. [Az 1 & 2 Arab; NNC] 519
Mumtaz, Salman. *Adhärbayjan ädäbiyatï: Molla pänä vaqïf*. Ṣayï 2. Baku: Uchunju Beynälmiläl Devläti Mäṭbuʿäsi, 1925, 128 pp., 4000 cop. [Az 1 & 2 Arab; NNC] 520
Mumtaz, Salman. *Adhärbayjan ädäbiyatï: Muḥämmäd hüseyn khan mushtaq*. Ṣayï 4. n.p.: Qommonist Näshriyatï, 1925, 48 pp., 4000 cop. [Az 1 & 2 Arab; NNC] 521
Mumtaz, Salman. *Adhärbayjan ädäbiyatï: Näshaṭ shirvanï*. Ṣayï 3. Baku: Qommonist Ghazitäsi, 1925, 72 pp., 4000 cop. [Az 1 & 2 Arab; CLU, NN, NNC] 522
Mumtaz, Salman. *Adhärbayjan ädäbiyatï: Nuṭqi shirvanshah*. Ṣayï 7. Baku: Qommonist Näshriyyatï, 1925, 24 pp., 4000 cop. [Az 1 & 2 Arab; NNC] 523
Mumtaz, Salman. *Adhärbayjan ädäbiyyatï: Qasïmbek dhakïr*. Ṣayï 8. Baku: Qommonist Näshriyyatï, 1925, 374 pp., 4000 cop. [Az 1 & 2 Arab; NNC] 524
Mumtaz, Salman. *Adhärbayjan ädäbiyyatï: Qavsï*. Ṣayï 5. n.p.: Qommonist Näshriyatï, 1925, 79 pp., 4000 cop. [Az 1 & 2 Arab; NNC] 525
Mumtaz, Salman. *Adhärbayjan ädäbiyyatï: Säyyid ʿïmadadin "näsimi."* Ṣayï 10. Baku: Qommonist Näshriyatï, 1926, 251 pp., 3000 cop. [Az 1 & 2 Arab; NNC] 526
Mushfik, M. *Quläqlär*. Sheirlär. Baku: Azärnäshr, 1930, 121 pp., 2000 cop. [Az 4 Lat; NN] 527

Muznib, Äli-Abbas. *Molla Näsräddin lätifäläri.* Baku: Azärnäshr, 1927, 135 pp., 3000 cop. [Az 3 Lat; NN] 528

Naghïllar. Baku: Azärbayjan LKKI MK Ushag vä Qänjlär Ädäbiyyatï Näshriyyatï, 1941, 256 pp., 10000 cop. [Az 5 Cyr; DLC] 529

Nakam. *Sä'chmä parchalarï.* Baku: Adhärnäshr, 1928, 105 pp., 3000 cop. [Az 1 & 2 Arab; NN] 530

Närimanof, Näriman. *Nadïr shah.* 4 mäjlis vä 7 pärdäli drama. Baku: Azärnäshr, 1927, 55 pp., 3000 cop. [Az 3 Lat; NN] 531

Nasimovich, A. *Senya Kalüghin: Bir pionerin särghuzäshti heqayä.* Baku: Azärnäshr, 1930, 24 pp., 3000 cop. [Az 4 Lat; NN] 532

Näzärli, H. *Ölulär räks edärqän.* Heqayälär. Baku: Azärnäshr, 1930, 86 pp., 3000 cop. [Az 4 Lat; NN] 533

Näzärli, H. *Satkïn.* Heqayälär. Baku: Azärnäshr, 1930, 95 pp., 2000 cop. [Az 4 Lat; NN] 534

Neverof, A. *Chöräqlï Dashqänt.* Heqayä. Baku, Azärnäshr, 1927, 105 pp., 3000 cop. [Az 3 Lat; NN] 535

Neverov, A. *Bolsheviq Marya.* Heqayälär. Baku: Azärnäshr, 1928, 76 pp., 3000 cop. [Az 3 Lat; NN] 536

Niqiforov, Gheorghi. *Fanar ïshïgïnda.* Roman. Baku: Azärnäshr, 1929, 249 pp., 3000 cop. [Az 4 Lat; NN] 537

Nizami. Birinji kitab. Baku: Azärnäshr. Bädii Ädäbiyyat Shö'bäsi, 1940, 264 pp., 6000 cop. [Az 5 Cyr; NNC] 538

Nizami. Ikinji kitab. Baku: Azärnäshr. Bädii Ädäbiyyat Shö'bäsi, 1940, 214 pp., 6000 cop. [Az 5 Cyr; NNC] 539

Nizami. Üchünjü kitab. Baku: Azärnäshr. Bädii Ädäbiyyat Shö'bäsi, 1941, 258 pp., 6000 cop. [Az 5 Cyr; NNC] 540

Nizami Qänjävi. *Fitnä.* Ushaglar üchün. Baku: Azär. Lenin Kommunist Qänjläk Ittifagi Märkäzi Komiteti, 1941, 15 pp., 20000 cop. [Az 5 Cyr; DLC] 541

Nizami Qänjävi. *Iskändärnamä—"Shäräfnamä."* I hissä. Baku: Azernäshr, 1940, 125 pp., 6000 cop. [Az 5 Cyr; DLC] 542

Nizami Qänjävi. *Iskändärnamä: Igbalnamä.* II. Baku: Azärbayjan Dövlät Näshriyyatï, 1941, 256 pp., 6000 cop. [Az 5 Cyr; NNC] 543

Nizami Qänjävi. *Iskändärnamä: Shäräfnamä.* I. Baku: Azärbayjan Dövlät Näshriyyatï, 1941, 439 pp., 6000 cop. [Az 5 Cyr; DLC, MH, NNC] 544

Nizami Qänjävi. *Khosrov vä Shirin.* Baku: Azärnäshr, 1940, 112 pp., 6000 cop. [Az 5 Cyr; DLC] 545
Nizami Qänjävi. *Leyli vä Mäjnün.* Baku: Azärbayjan Dövlät Näshriyyatï, 1942, 321 pp., 6000 cop. [Az 5 Cyr; NNC] 546
Nizami Qänjävi. *Yeddi qözäl.* Baku: Azärbayjan Dövlät Näshriyyatï, 1941, 312 pp., 6000 cop. [Az 5 Cyr; NNC] 547
Nizami Qänjävi. *Yeddi qözäl.* Näsrlä. Baku: Azärnäshr, 1941, 150 pp., 8000 cop. [Az 5 Cyr; DLC] 548
Nizaminin müasirläri. Baku: Azärnäshr, 1940, 80 pp., 3100 cop. [Az 5 Cyr; DLC] 549
Ordübadi, M. S. *Mänim sheirlärim.* Baku: Azärnäshr, 1930, 60 pp., 2000 cop. [Az 4 Lat; NN] 550
Ordübadi, M. S. *Mollanïn yüküsü: Din äleyhinä.* Baku: Azärbayjan Devlät Näshriyyatï, 1929, 60 pp., 3000 cop. [Az 3 Lat; NN] 551
Ordubadi, Mämmäd Säid. *Qizli Baki.* Baku: Azärnäshr, 1940, 328 pp., 8000 cop. [Az 5 Cyr; DLC] 552
Pushkin, A. S. *Qapitan qïzï.* Baku: Adhärnäshr, 1928, 174 pp., 3000 cop. [Az 1 & 2 Arab; NN] 553
Püshqin. *Kïzïl balïk.* Baku: Azärnäshr, 1927, 21 pp., 5000 cop. [Az 3 Lat; NN] 554
Püshqin, A. *Böyuq Petronün äräbi.* Baku: Azärnäshr, 1929, 58 pp., 3000 cop. [Az 4 Lat; NN] 555
Püshqin, A. S. *Belqinin heqayäläri.* Baku: Azärnäshr, 1930, 109 pp., 3000 cop. [Az 4 Lat; NN] 556
Püshqin, A. S. *Karachïlar.* Baku: Azärnäshr, 1930, 30 pp., 3000 cop. [Az 4 Lat; NN] 557
Qoläsniqof, L. *Uch näsl.* Baku: Adhärnäshr, 1927, 62 pp., 3000 cop. [Az 1 & 2 Arab; NN] 558
Räfili, Miq. *Liriq sheirlär* (*1927–1929*). Baku: Azärnäshr, 1930, 59 pp., 2000 cop. [Az 4 Lat; NN] 559
Rahim, M. *Arzïlar.* Sheirlär. Baku: Azärnäshr, 1930, 72 pp., 2000 cop. [Az 4 Lat; NN] 560
Rähimov, Süleyman. *Sachlï.* I. Baku: Azärnäshr, 1943, 358 pp., 3000 cop. [Az 5 Cyr; DLC] 561
Rähimov, Süleyman. *Shamo.* I. Baku: Azärnäshr, 1940, 501 pp., 8000 cop. [Az 5 Cyr; DLC] 562
Rakhmanin, S. *Väkshï kohümlar.* Baku: Azärnäshr, 1927, 12 pp., 5000 cop. [Az 3 Lat; NN] 563

Roni, Böyuq. *Od ügründa mubaräzä.* Baku: Azärnäshr, 1930, 211 pp., 3000 cop. [Az 4 Lat; NN] 564

Rübaqïn, N. A. *Nühün tüfanï.* Baku: Azärnäshr, 1927, 36 pp., 3000 cop. [Az 3 Lat; NN] 565

Rustäm, Suleyman. *Addïmlar.* Baku: Azärnäshr, 1930, 66 pp., 2000 cop. [Az 4 Lat; NN] 566

Sabir, M. Ä. *Sheirläri mäjmüäsi.* Baku: Azärnäshr, 1929, 278 pp., 3000 cop. [Az 4 Lat; NN] 567

Ṣabïr, Mirza ʻAli Äkbar. *Mäktäb ushaqlarïna tuḥfä.* Baku: Adhärbayjan Länin Qommonist Gänjlär Ittifaqï Märkäzi Qomitäsi Ushaq vä Gänjlär Ädäbiyatï Näshriyatï, 1942, 53 pp., n.c. [Az 1 & 2 Arab; CLU] 568

Saḥḥat, ʻAbbas. *Müntäkhäbat.* Baku: Khariji Dillärdä Ädäbiyat Näshriyatï, 1945, 96 pp., 4200 cop. [Az 1 & 2 Arab; MH] 569

Säid Zadä, Ä. Ä. (Zaqï). *Ghänjäli böyuq mutäfäqqir vä shair Mirzä Säfi "Vazeh."* Yashayïsh vä yaradïchïlïgï, 9 namätlü mänzümäläriilä. Ghänjä: A.K.(b)F. Ghänjä Okrük Komitäsinin Täbligat vä Täshvikat Shöʻbäsinin Näshriyyatï, 1929, 16 pp., 1000 cop. [Az 3 Lat; NN] 570

Säid Zadä, Ä. Ä. (Zaqï). *Mirzä Shäfi (Vazih).* Mirzä Shäfi Vazihin yashayïsh vä yaradïjïlïgïnï arkhiv materiallarïna ghörä öyränish täjribäsi. Baku: Azärbayjan Märqäzi Ijraiyyä Komitäsi Yanïnda Azärbayjan Elmi Tädkikat Institünün Näshriyyatï, 1929, 22 pp., 275 cop. [Az 4 Lat; NN] 571

Sämyonof, A. *Bir varaq kaghïdhïñ tarikhi.* Baku: Adhärnäshr, 1927, 53 pp., 3000 cop. [Az 1 & 2 Arab; CStH, NN] 572

Sanili. *Däli öquz.* Baku: Azärnäshr, 1927, n.pp., 5000 cop. [Az 3 Lat; NN] 573

Sänt-Ilär. *Bayqosh naghïlï.* Baku: Adhärnäshr, 1927, 23 pp., 3000 cop. [Az 1 & 2 Arab; NN) 574

Sarabsqi, H. *Bir aktyorün khatiräläri.* Baku: Azärnäshr, 1930, 72 pp., 2000 cop. [Az 4 Lat; NN] 575

Sattar oghli, Mirshid. *Kitab gejäsi.* Baku: ʻAli Siyasi Mäʻarif Idaräsi Näshriyatï, 1926, 101 pp., 1000 cop. [Az 1 & 2 Arab; NN] 576

Sattar oghli, Mirshid. *Savad ardïnjä.* Baku: ʻAli Siyasi Mäʻarif Idaräsi Näshriyatï, 1926, 45 pp., 1000 cop. [Az 1 & 2 Arab; NN] 577

Serafimovich, A. *Kïz küshü vä bashka heqayälär*. Baku: Azärnäshr, 1927, 48 pp., 3000 cop. [Az 3 Lat; NN] 578

Seyidzadä, M. *Gorkhmaz*. Baku: Azär. LKKI MK Ushag vä Qänjlär Ädäbiyyatï Näshriyatï, 1945, 68 pp., 10000 cop. [Az 5 Cyr; DLC] 579

Shaig, A. *Ovchu mästan*. Baku: Azär. LKKI MK, 1945, 19 pp., 15000 cop. [Az 5 Cyr; DLC] 580

Shaik, Abdülla. *Tulqu häjjä ghedir*. Baku: Azärnäshr, 1927, 63 pp., 3000 cop. [Az 3 Lat; NN] 581

Shayik, Abdülla. *Yïldïrïm*. 5 pärdäli dram. Baku: Azärnäshr, 1927, 77 pp., 2000 cop. [Az 3 Lat; NN] 582

Shayiq, ʿAbdallä. *Ana bajï*. Baku: Adhärnäshr, 1926, 22 pp., 5000 cop. [Az 1 & 2 Arab; NN] 583

Shayiq, ʿAbdallä. *Mäktüb yätishmädi: Aghlashma*. Baku: Adhärnäshr, 1926, 22 pp., 5000 cop. [Az 1 & 2 Arab; NN] 584

Shirindilli. *Tevbä*. Heqayälär. Baku: Azärnäshr, 1930, 61 pp., 3000 cop. [Az 4 Lat; NN] 585

Shirvanzada. *Khaos*. II vä III hissä. Baku: Azärnäshr, 1929, 168 pp., 2000 cop. [Az 3 Lat; NN] 586

Sinkler, Epton. *Yuz fayiz*. Baku: Azärnäshr, 1930, 171 pp., 3000 cop. [Az 4 Lat; NN] 587

Sveyg, Stefan. *Korkü*. Baku: Azärnäshr, 1930, 70 pp., 2000 cop. [Az 4 Lat; NN] 588

Sviridof, I. *Kejmishiñ kölkäläri*. Baku: Adhärnäshr, 1927, 62 pp., 3000 cop. [Az 1 & 2 Lat; NN] 589

Täl'ät, Ä. *Anam toprag*. Baku: Azärnäshr, 1945, 64 pp., 3000 cop. [Az 5 Cyr; DLC] 590

Talïblï, B. A. *Diräq*. Baku: Azärnäshr, 1930, 74 pp., 2000 cop. [Az 4 Lat; NN] 591

Ṭalïblï, Böyük Agha. *Ärkäk tükäzban*. Baku: Baku Ishchisi Qo'opäratif Näshriyatï, 1926, 20 pp., 4000 cop. [Az 1 & 2 Arab; NN] 592

Ṭalïblï, Böyük Agha. *Qïrq zärpa*. Baku: Adhärnäshr, 1927, 12 pp., 3000 cop. [Az 1 & 2 Arab; NN] 593

Tevfiq Efendi zadä, ʿA. *Agoy qich*. Baku: Näshriyat-ï Mäktäb, 1914, 12 pp., n.c. [Az 1 & 2 Arab; NNC*] 594

---

*Microfilm

Thanïlï. *Kändimiz vä aran kochi.* Baku: Adhärnäshr, 1927, 63 pp., 5000 cop. [Az 1 & 2 Arab; NN] 595

Thanïlï, Ḥ. K. "*Namüs*" *dä'vasï.* Baku: Adhärnäshr, 1927, 59 pp., 3000 cop. [Az 1 & 2 Arab; NN] 596

Thanïlï; Maḥzun, 'A. *Meymün vä ilan.* Baku: Adhärnäshr, 1927, 8 pp., 5000 cop. [Az 1 & 2 Arab; NN] 597

Tulki vä qurt. Chojuq na'ïlï. Baku: Baku Ishchisi Qo'opäratif Näshriyatï, 1926, 16 pp., 3000 cop. [Az 1 & 2 Arab; NN] 598

Tumanyan, Avanäs. *Bir damjï bal vä gïkor.* Baku: Baku Ishchisi Qo'opäratif Näshriyatï, 1926, 50 pp., 3000 cop. [Az 1 & 2 Arab; NN] 599

Türanlï, Hilal. *Krakadil.* Baku: Azärnäshr, 1927, 31 pp., 3000 cop. [Az 3 Lat; NN] 600

Vahid, A. *Gäzällär.* Baku: Azärnäshr, 1944, 127 pp., 5000 cop. [Az 5 Cyr; DLC] 601

Vaḥid, 'Ali Aqa. *Ghäzallar.* Baku: Khariji Dillärdä Ädäbiyat Näshriyatï, 1945, 70 pp., 10200 cop. [Az 1 & 2 Arab; DLC] 602

Väliev, Äli. *Gähräman.* Baku: Azärnäshr, 1941, 289 pp., 6000 cop. [Az 5 Cyr; DLC] 603

Väzir, Yüsif. *Jännätïn käbzi.* Heqayä. Baku: Azärnäshr, 1927, 27 pp., 3000 cop. [Az 3 Lat; NN] 604

Väzirov, Näjäf bäy. *Yagïshdan chïkhdïkh, yagmïcha dushduq.* Komediya. Baku: Azärnäshr, 1929, 58 pp., 3000 cop. [Az 4 Lat; NN] 605

Zaydan, Jurji. *Armanusät.* Baku: n.p., A.H.1329/A.D.1911, 471 pp., n.c. [Az 1 & 2 Arab; CLU] 606

Zaydan, Jurji. *Kitab: On yeddi ramaẓan.* Baku: Mäṭb'ä-i Brädäran Orojof, A.H.1328/A.D.1909, 374 pp., n.c. [Az. 1 & 2 Arab; CLU] 607

Zeynallï, Ḥ. *Azärbayjan atalar sözi.* Baku: Adhärbayjanï Tädqiq vä Tätäbbu' Jäm'iyatï Näshriyatï, 1926, 234 pp., 1000 cop. [Az 1 & 2 Arab; NN] 608

Zeynallï, Hänäfi; Hiqmät, Ismayïl; Shayïk, Abdülla; Müsakhanlï, Atababa. *Ädäbiyyat därsläri.* Iqinji qitab. Baku: Azärnäshr, 1927, 279 pp., 3000 cop. [Az 3 Lat; NN] 609

Zeynallï, Ḥänäfi; Sha'iq, 'Abdallä; Ḥikmät, Isma'il; Müsakhanlï, Atababa. *Ädäbiyat därsläri.* Birinji kitab—altinji il. Baku: Adhärnäshr, 1928, 350 pp., 6000 cop. [Az 1 & 2 Arab; NN] 610

Zolya, Ämil. *Qazmachïlar*. Baku: Adhärnäshr, 1927, 214 pp., 3000 cop. [Az 1 & 2 Arab; CStH, NN] 611

Philosophy and Religion

Amosov, N. *Allahsïz chojüklar yetishdirmäq ügründa*. Baku: Azärnäshr, 1930, 32 pp., 3000 cop. [Az 4 Lat; NN] 612

Ishchi allahsïzlar därnäghi uchun därs qitabï. Baku: Azärnäshr, 1929, 228 pp., 3000 cop. [Az 4 Lat; NN] 613

J. Ḥ. *Movhümat vä din ʿäleyhinä*. Baku: Adhärnäshr, 1927, 58 pp., 3000 cop. [Az 1 & 2 Arab; NN] 614

J. H. *Movhümat vä din äleyhinä*. Baku: Azärnäshr, 1927, 50 pp., 3000 cop. [Az 3 Lat; NN] 615

Khülüflü, V. *Pan islamizm impäryalizm vä rüḥaniyyät*. Baku: Adhärnäshr, 1928, 47 pp., 2000 cop. [Az 1 & 2 Arab; NN] 616

Khülüflü, V. *Panislamizm imperiyalizm vä rühaniyyät*. Baku: Azärbayjan Devlät Näshriyyatï, 1929, 40 pp., 2000 cop. [Az 3 Lat; NN] 617

Ordübadi, M. S. *Kürban qäsmäq häkkïnda*. Baku: Azärnäshr, 1930, 30 pp., 5000 cop. [Az 4 Lat; NN] 618

Ordübadi, M. S. *Muhärrämlïq vä mädäni inkilab*. Baku: Azärnäshr, 1929, 25 pp., 3000 cop. [Az 4 Lat; NN] 619

P. G. *Imam Riza bästi*. Baku: Azärnäshr, 1927, 44 pp., 3000 cop. [Az 3 Lat; NN] 620

P. Gh. *Imam riẕa bästi*. Baku: Adhärnäshr, 1927, 56 pp., 3000 cop. [Az 1 & 2 Arab; NN] 621

Rizayev, B. *Bähayilär qimlärdur?* Baku: Azärnäshr, 1930, 27 pp., 5000 cop. [Az 4 Lat; NN] 622

Stäpanof, I. *Dini eʿtiqadlarïn inkishafï*. Baku: Adhärnäshr, 1927, 46 pp., 3000 cop. [Az 1 & 2 Arab; NN] 623

Väliyov, Ä. *Allahïn säyahäti*. Baku: Azärnäshr, 1930, 20 pp., 3000 cop. [Az 4 Lat; NN] 624

Zanqof, L. V. *Insanïn vä ḥayvanlarïn ruhi varmï?* Baku: Adhärnäshr, 1928, 66 pp., 3000 cop. [Az 1 & 2 Arab; NN] 625

BASHKIR General (including periodicals)

Allasiz (*Allahïdh*) (Ufa) 1929: 2, 6, 9. [Bash 2 Arab, 3 Lat; NN] 626
Aymaq (n.p.) 1931: 1 (7). [Bash 3 Lat; NN] 627
Bashqürt aymaghï (Ufa) 1925: 1; 1926: 2 [NN]; 1927: 4 [MH]; 1928: 5–6; 1929: 7 [NN]. [Bash 2 Arab] 628
Belem (Ufa) 1927: 6 (42) [MH]; 1928: 10; 1929: 4–7, 12; 1930: 1, 7 [NN]. [Bash 2 Arab, 3 Lat] 629
Byüllitini (Ufa) 1927: 10/11. [Bash 2 Arab; NN] 630
Dehri (Ufa) 1928: 4/5. [Bash 2 Arab, 3 Lat; NN] 631
Dïyanat (Ufa) 1928: 6. [Bash 2 Arab; NN] 632
Fän häm din (Moscow) 1929: 1, 4, 6, 13–15. [Bash 2 Arab, 3 Lat; NN] 633
Haban (Ufa) 1927: 9; 1928: 1, 3–4, 8–10, 12. [Bash 2 Arab; NN] 634
Islam mejlesi (Ufa) 1926: 4 (17). [Bash 2 Arab; NN] 635
Kerpe (Ufa) 1929: 2–5. [Bash 3 Lat; NN] 636
Khidmeti (Sterlitamak) 1922: 1. [Bash 1 Arab; NN] 637
Linin yüli (Ufa) 1928: 1; 1929: 8/9, 11. [Bash 2 Arab; NN] 638
Peyanir (Ufa) 1930: 4. [Bash 3 Lat; NN] 639
Sänäk (Ufa) 1927: 9, 11–12; 1928: 2; 1929: 2–3, 6; 1930: 8/9. [Bash 2 Arab, 3 Lat; NN] 640
Säsän (Ufa) 1928: 4/5; 1929: 10, 12. [Bash 2 Arab, 3 Lat; NN] 641
Traktïr (Ufa) 1929: 1, 4–5; 1930: 3, 6, 15/16. [Bash 2 Arab, 3 Lat; NN] 642
Üktäber (Ufa) 1930: 2, 5/6. [Bash 3 Lat; NN] 643
Üktäber balasï (n.p.) 1930: 7/8. [Bash 3 Lat; NN] 644
Yangïlïq (Ufa) 1928: 3–6, 9/10; 1929: 1, 2, 5/6, 8–14. [Bash 2 Arab, 3 Lat; NN] 645
Zakün hem büyrüqtar (n.p.) 1928: 1, 8–11; 1929: 7/8/9. [Bash 2 Arab; NN] 646

BASHKIR Social Sciences

Economics

Abarin, A. *Sheher hem aülda prafsayüz ishlerï.* Ufa: Bashprafsavit Neshri, 1928, 53 pp., 1000 cop. [Bash 2 Arab; NN] 647

Ämirïf, Khälim. *Haqlïq aqsa yïynav aylïghï kampanyahï.* Ufa: Bashqortostan Maleyä Khalïq Kamisarlïghï Näshere, 1930, 26 pp., 2000 cop. [Bash 3 Lat; NN] 648

Ämirïf, Khälim. *Saqlïq aqcha jiu aylïghï kampaniäse.* Ufa: Bashqrtstan Maliä Khalq Kamisarlïghï Näshere, 1930, 26 pp., 2000 cop. [Bash 3 Lat; NN] 649

Bashkoopkhlibsayuz. *Kantraktatseyä ney öson häm nisek udhgharïla.* Ufa: Badhtïrïvsïhï Bashkoopkhlibsayuz, 1930, 7 pp., 2000 cop. [Bash 3 Lat; NN] 650

Bashqortostan dävlät aksïyalï tödhöv jämgheyäte "Bashïstïruy" dhïng kümäk höyläshmähä. Ufa: n.p., 1929, 43 pp., 100 cop. [Bash 3 Lat; NN] 651

Bashqörtöstan ölke istraḥ kassahïnïng 1924–25 nsi ïsh yïlïnan ḥisab. Ufa: Istraḥ Kassanïng Bashqörtöstan Ülke Kemitetï Neshri, 1926, 52 pp., 1000 cop. [Bash 2 Arab; DLC] 652

Bashqörtüstan üzek basqürmahi hem ḥalïq kamïsarnar sävitïnïng 1929–30 nsï yïlda bïrïkken aöïl ḥüzhalïghï nalügï ütkerïü ḥaqïndaghï palazhinyanï tesdyïq iytïü türahïndaghï qararï. Ufa: n.p., n.d., 51 pp., 7000 cop. [Bash 2 Arab; NN] 653

Baylïqtï erem eytmegïdh-segïlerdhï yïyïp hatïghïdh. Ufa: R.A.T.Ü. 1929, 16 pp., 1000 cop. [Bash 2 Arab; NN] 654

1930–1931 nsï yïlda bïrlestïrïlgen avïl ḥüzhalïghï nalügi ütkerïü tertibi türahïnda ïyinstrüksiye. Ufa: Bashnarkamfïn Neshri, 1930, 114 pp., 1000 cop. [Bash 2 Arab; NN] 655

1930–1931nsï yïlgha aöïl ḥüzhalïghï nalügï hem istraḥavasi tülevdher tülevsïlerdhïng litsïvüy eshchüttarïn yörïtü hem kirgen sümmalarnï üchütqa alïü qaghideleri. Ufa: Bashnarkamfin Neshri, 1930, 13 pp., 1000 cop. [Bash 2 Arab; NN] 656

1930–1931 nsï yïlgha bïrleshtïrïlgen avïl ḥüzhalïghï nalügï. Ufa: Bashnarkamfïn Neshïrï, n.d., 51 pp., 1000 cop. [Bash 2 Arab; NN] 657

Beynealmilel kapirasiya köni. Ufa: "Okt. Natisk," n.d., 4 pp., 2000 cop. [Bash 2 Arab; NN] 658

Bikbay, N. *Ḥisab yörötütür ahïnda qïqasa angghartmalar.* Ufa: Bash Üdhek Tïl Kemisiyehi, 1927, 35 pp., 1000 cop. [Bash 2 Arab; NN] 659

Bikbulat, M. *Kalkhuzdar tödhölöshö turahïnda.* Ufa: Bashnäsher, 1930, 50 pp., 5000 cop. [Bash 3 Lat; NN] 660

"*Bish yillïqtï-dürt yïlda*" *zayïmï*. Ufa: Bashnarkamfin, 1930, 28 pp., 5000 cop. [Bash 2 Arab; NN] 661

Bötegantün krethtïyen kemitetterïne, izhtimaghi e'minat vekilderïne, vülis hem avïl krethtïyen yardham kemitetterïne. Ufa: Tipo-Litografiya "Okt. Natisk," n.d., 17 pp., 1500 cop. [Bash 2 Arab; NN] 662

Ghabbas, Gh. *Kalkhuzdar tödhölöshö linin yulï*. Ufa: Bashgiz, 1930, 19 pp., 5000 cop. [Bash 3 Lat; NN] 663

Ghabbasïf, Gh. *Nïy ösön bïdhge 3 nsö eyndostrïye zayïmï kerek*. Ufa: V.K.P.(b). Ölke Kemitetïnïng Agitprobï, 1929, 30 pp., 5000 cop. [Bash 2 Arab; NN] 664

Ghabbasïf, Gh. *Totosh kalkhuzdar oyoshtorabïdh-kulaktïng tamïrïn aqtarabïdh*. Ufa: Bashgiz, 1930, 13 pp., 6000 cop. [Bash 3 Lat; NN] 665

Gribüf, P. *Batrakting ḥidhmet dügüvrï*. Ufa: Bashqörtöstan Avïl Ḥüzhalïghi, 1928, 61 pp., 1000 cop. [Bash 2 Arab; NN] 666

Grigureyef, V. *Nindäy kalkhuzdar bula häm ular nisek tödölälär*. Ufa: Bashnäsher, 1930, 61 pp., 3000 cop. [Bash 3 Lat; NN] 667

Gurin, A. *Ere kumäk khuzhalïqtargha taban, algha*. Ufa: Bashnäsher, 1930, 74 pp., 3000 cop. [Bash 3 Lat; NN] 668

Ḥalïq ḥüjalïghïn tözü ishlerïnde devlet zayümlarïnïng ehemmïyetï. Ufa: Bashqörtöstan Malïye Ḥalïq Kamisarlïghï Neshïrï, 1929, 39 pp., 5000 cop. [Bash 2 Arab; NN] 669

Ishmidt, V. *Ish kanflikteri niden kilib sïgha hem alar nisek ḥel iytleler*. Ufa: Bashprafsavit Neshrï, 1928, 43 pp., 1000 cop. [Bash 2 Arab; NN] 670

Kepiretif lafkahïnïng tödholishï. Moscow: SSSR Ḥalqtarïnïng Üdhek Neshriyatï, 1928, 27 pp., 1000 cop. [Bash 2 Arab; NN] 671

Kepiretif maln telef iytüsïler ḥiyanetsïler minen nisk köreshirge. Moscow: Sintr Izdat, 1928, 27 pp., 4000 cop. [Bash 2 Arab; NN] 672

Prafsayüzlarnïng VIII nchï bashqrtstan isyizdïnïng qerarlarï. Ufa: Bashprsavit Neshri, 1928, 48 pp., 1000 cop. [Bash 2 Arab; NN] 673

Shalimïf, S. *Aftanümiyalï bashqörtöstan satsiyal sevitter yömhüriyetïnïng iqtisad hem maliye ishterï*. Ufa: Bashsavnarküm Neshrï, 1927, 163 pp., 1000 cop. [Bash 2 Arab; MH] 674

Yähudin, Gh. *Bish yïlleqtï durt yïlda*. Ufa: Bashgiz, 1930, 18 pp., 5000 cop. [Bash 3 Lat; NN] 675

Education

Ayukhan, Z.; Khosnötdinof, U. *Yangïlïq.* 1 bathqïs esh mäktäptärdheng 1 törkömdhäre ösön uqu kitabï. Moscow: Tsentïrizdat, 1928, 76 pp., 3000 cop. [Bash 3 Lat; NN] 676

Bayïsh, Tahir. *Ḥesen hem fen.* Ufa: Bashknige, 1928, 23 pp., 2000 cop. [Bash 2 Arab; NN] 677

Birinchi basqïch mektebler üchön mattimatike mitüdikese. Ufa: Bashknige, n.d., 101 pp., 3000 cop. [Bash 2 Arab; NN] 678

Dhürdhar ösödh bashqörtsa elifba. Ufa: Vserossiiskaia Chrezvychainaia Kommissiia po Likvidatsii Bezgramotnosti, 1924, 48 pp., 80000 cop. [Bash 2 Arab; DLC] 679

Ghimran, Ä.; Tahir, Kh. *Yangï yul: Ololar ösön bashqortsa älifba.* Ufa: "Bashkenägä," 1929, 43 pp., 12000 cop. [Bash 3 Lat; NN] 680

Ghismeti, Gh.; Bilal, M. *Yangï avïl.* Moscow: SSSR Ḥalqtarïnïng Üdhek Neshriyati, 1928, 156 pp., 2500 cop. [Bash 2 Arab; NN] 681

Ghömdä. *Berense bathqïs mäktäptä äsä tele uqïtïvsïlargha yetäkse.* II kithäk. Ufa: Bashgiz, 1930, 52 pp., 3000 cop. [Bash 3 Lat; NN] 682

Källiktif. *Äsä telenän. Esh kitabï.* Ufa: Bashgiz, 1930, 145 pp., 9000 cop. [Bash 3 Lat: NN] 683

Kalliktif. *Tebighiyghat habaqtari.* 3 nsi synyftari üsün. Ufa: Bashnarkamprüs, 1928, 310 pp., 5000 cop. [Bash 2 Arab; NN] 684

Kalliktif. *Yäsh bïvïn.* Bashqortsa durtense uqïv kitabï. Ufa: Udhäk Bashqort Yangï Älep Kämitäte häm "Bashkenägä" Näshere, 1928, 447 pp., 4000 cop. [Bash 3 Lat; NN] 685

Källiktif. *Yäsh bïvïn.* Berense bathqïs mäktäptärdheng III nsö törkömdäre ösön. Ufa: Bashqort Udhäk Yangïälep Kämitäte häm "Bashkenägä" Näshere, 1929, 325 pp., 1067 cop. [Bash 3 Lat; NN] 686

Kalliktif. *Yesh biüin.* II. Ufa: Bashnarkamprüs, 1928, 172 pp. 5000 cop. [Bash 2 Arab; NN] 687

Kalliktif. *Yesh biüin.* IV. Ufa: Bashnarkamprüs, 1928, 357 pp., 4000 cop. [Bash 2 Arab; NN] 688

Kelliktif. *Yesh bïüïn.* III. Ufa: Bashnarkampïrüs Hem "Bashknege" Neshïrï, 1928, 280 pp., 5000 cop. [Bash 2 Arab; NN] 689

Krilüf, G. *Mektepte ḥidhmettï fen büyïnsa öyïshtïrü mes'elelerï.* Ufa: Bashnarkamprüs Neshri, 1929, 80 pp., 1500 cop. [Bash 2 Arab; NN] 690

Education

Megharif ishchïlerïnïng kvalyfykatsyasin küterü hem ikstirnlar öchön tözlgen prakrammalar. 1nchi kisek-tebyghiyat. Ufa: Bashknige, 1927, 143 pp., 1500 cop. [Bash 2 Arab; NN] 691

Razumïf. *Mäktäp ergähendäge yer uchasakahï häm unda eshläv.* Ufa: Bashnarkamprus Näshere, 1930, 51 pp., 1500 cop. [Bash 3 Lat; NN] 692

Shakiref, Z.; Churayïf, Sh. *Ghämäli Bashqort ele däreslege.* Ufa: Udhäk Bashqort Yangï Älep Kämitäte häm "Bashkenäge" Näshere, 1928, 96 pp., 4000 cop. [Bash 3 Lat; NN] 693

Sünchelei, Sherif; Vaḥidïf, Ghebbas. *Yangi mektab.* Ufa: "Bashknige," 1927, 215 pp., 5000 cop. [Bash 2 Arab; NN] 694

Üktebïr 10 yillïghï. Ufa: Bashnarkamprüs Neshrï, n.d., 16 pp., 1500 cop. [Bash 2 Arab; NN] 695

Ülkender elifbahi. Moscow: RSFSR Megharif Kamisariyatïnïng Ang Bilïm Taratü Bülimi Qashïnda Tüdhülgen Ghedetten Tash Kemisiye Neshri, 1927, 64 pp., 25000 cop. [Bash 2 Arab; NN] 696

Ülkender elifbahi. Moscow: RSFSR Megharif Kamisariyatïnïng Ang Bilim Taratü Bülimi Qashïnda Tüdhülgen Ghedetden Tash Kemisiye Neshri, 1928, 64 pp., 10000 cop. [Bash 2 Arab; NN] 697

Üqü yeshïndegï balalarnï ḥisapqa alü mes'elesi. n.p.: "Bïlïm Iydaresi" Neshri, n.d., 8 pp., n.c. [Bash 2 Arab; NN] 698

Geography

Feḥrtdinïf, Gh. *Bashqörtöstan yeghrefiyehï.* Ufa: Bashknige, 1927, 152 pp., 4000 cop. [Bash 2 Arab; NN] 699

Government

VI nchï chaqïrma bashqörtöstan üdhek bashqarmasïnïng III nchï sisïyesï qerarlarï (1928). Ufa: Bashqörtöstan Üdhek Bashqarmasï Neshrï, n.d., 67 pp., 800 cop. [Bash 2 Arab; NN] 700

Avïl sevitlerinde iseb hem ish yörtu türinda instrüksiye. Ufa: Bashqörd Tïlin ghemelge Qüyü Üdhek Kemisiyesi, 1927, 79 pp., 550 cop. [Bash 2 Arab; NN] 701

Avïl, ütar hem bashqa shündi sevitlerde iseb hem ḥisab ishlerin yörtü öchön instrüksiye. Ufa: Bashqört Tïlin ghemelge Qüyü Merkez Kemisiyesï Neshrï, 1927, 32 pp., 500 cop. [Bash 2 Arab; NN] 702

Avïl, ütar hem öshölar minen ber tigedh sevit terdhe iteb hem ḥisab ishterin yörtü ösön instrüksiye (1927–28). Ufa: Bashqört Tïlin ghemelge Qüyü Üdhek Kemisiyehi Neshrï, 1928, 32 pp., 600 cop. [Bash 2 Arab; NN] 703

Bashqörtöstan aftanümïyalï satsïyal sevitter yömhöriyetïnïng VII nsï yübeley ïsyïzï qararshari. Ufa: Bashqörtöstan Üdhek Basqarma Kemiteti, 1929, 112 pp., 1000 cop. [Bash 2 Arab; NN] 704

Bashqortostan häm Tatarïstan peyanir oyoshmalarï häm narkamprustarï arahïnda tödholgän satseyalizem yarïshïnïng dugïvr ithtälege. Ufa: Bashgiz, 1930, 25 pp., 20000 cop. [Bash 3 Lat; NN] 705

Bashqortostan häm Tatarstan kamsamul oyoshmalarï arahïnda satseyalizem yarïshï dugïvïrï. Ufa: VLKSMding Bashabkumï Näshere, 1930, 26 pp., 2500 cop. [Bash 3 Lat; NN] 706

Bashqörtstan asa avyaḥiminïng II nchï ïsyïzï chïgharghan qararlar. Ufa: Bash. Asa Avyaḥim Neshri, 1929, 55 pp., 400 cop. [Bash 2 Arab; NN] 707

V nsï saqrilish bashqörtöstan üdhek bashqarmahi hem ḥalq kamisardharï sevitïnïng ishmekerlïgï türahïnda itheb 1925–mart 1927 yïl. Ufa: Tipo-Litografiia "Oktiabr'skii Natisk," 1927, 87 pp., 3500 cop. [Bash 2 Arab; MH] 708

Börhan; Ishimghöl. *Qidhl armiye könï.* Ufa: Bashknige, 1928, 61 pp., 2000 cop. [Bash 2 Arab; NN] 709

Börhan, S.; Ishimghöl, B. *Qanlï yekshembï: 22 nsï ghinvari.* Moscow: SSSR Ḥalqtarïnïng Üdhek Neshriyatï, 1927, 40 pp., 2000 cop. [Bash 2 Arab: NN] 710

Borhan, Safa; Ishemghol, Bulat. *Parizh kammunahï.* Ufa: Udhäk Bashqort Yangï Älep Kämitäte häm "Bashkenägä" Näshere, 1928, 39 pp., 2000 cop. [Bash 3 Lat; NN] 711

Börḥan, Safa; Ishimghöl, Bülat. *Fivral rivalütsiyehi: 12 nsi mart.* Moscow: SSSR Ḥalqtarïnïng Üdhek Neshriyati, 1927, 24 pp., 2000 cop. [Bash 2 Arab; NN] 712

Börhan, Safa; Ishimghöl, Bülat. *Parizh kammünahi.* Moscow: SSSR Ḥalqtarïnïng Üdhek Neshriyatï, 1927, 43 pp., 2000 cop. [Bash 2 Arab; NN] 713

Böte bashqörtöstan sevitterining 6 nsi isyizi qarardhar. Ufa: n.p., 1927, 35 pp., 2000 cop. [Bash 2 Arab; NN] 714

Böte erasey üdhek bashqarmahï hem R.S.F.S.R. ḥalïqka bisardhar sevitining döyöm devlet zadanyalarïn hem pïlandarïn böyömgha ashïrïügha yardham itïv tekkelïnde avïl sevitterining ḥöqüqtarïn kingeytïü türahñdaghï 1929 yïl 28 nsï iyün qararïn qüllanïö ösön instïrüksïye. Ufa: Bashglavlit., 1920, 10 pp., 500 cop. [Bash 2 Arab; NN] 715

Bötöb bashqörtstan ishsï krestyen mem qdhïl ghesker savittaïning 4nsï isiyizd pritaküldarï. Ufa: Tipo-Litografiia Bashproma "Oktiabr'skii Natisk," 1924, 187 pp., 250 cop. [Bash 2 Arab; MH] 716

Chirnüḥa, P. *Kamsamülding avïldaghï medeni terbiye ishterï.* Ufa: Bashknige, 1928, 36 pp., 1500 cop. [Bash 2 Arab; NN] 717

Ghöbäy, R. *Kamsamul urazhaydhï kütärevdhä pakhutqa.* Ufa: Bashnäsher, 1930, 75 pp., 5000 cop. [Bash 3 Lat; NN] 718

Ghozäyäref, Gh. *Kalkhuz tödhölöshö häm kamsamul.* Ufa: Bashgiz, 1930, 54 pp., 5000 cop. [Bash 3 Lat; NN] 719

Izakuf, B. *Üktebïr batraktargha neme birdï.* n.p.: Bashprafsavit Neshri, 1928, 47 pp., 1000 cop. [Bash 2 Arab; NN] 720

Kirzhintsif, P.; Lïyuntïyif, A. *Lininizm elïpbiyi.* Ufa: Bashknige Neshri, 1928, 291 pp., 3000 cop. [Bash 2 Arab; NN] 721

Kiselguf, Z. *Satseyalizem mägharifse tödhölöshöndä.* Ufa: n.p., 1930, 42 pp., 1500 cop. [Bash 3 Lat; NN] 722

Mansürif, Lötfi. *Vülis bashqarmalarïning kidhüdhegï bürstaryï.* Ufa: Bashknige, 1928, 31 pp., 2000 cop. [Bash 2 Arab; NN] 723

Müḥtaiyatli bashqirdstan satsyal shüralar jümhüriyetining 3 nchï shüralar isyizdi. Ufa: Tip-Litografiia "Oktiabr'skii Natisk," 1923, 32 and 45 and 46 and 20 and 17 pp., 200 cop. [Bash 1 Arab; MH] 724

Partïya tadhalïghï yülïnda. Ufa: V.K.P.(b)ning Bashqörtöstan Ölke Kemitetï Neshrï, 1929, 55 pp., 3000 cop. [Bash 2 Arab; NN] 725

Qïdhïl ärmeyestär ösön uqïv kitabï. Ufa: Bashgiz, 1930, vi and 288 pp., 4000 cop. [Bash 3 Lat; NN] 726

Rivalyütsiye hem bashqörtöstan. Ufa: Bash'abkümding Partiya Tariḥï Bülïgï Neshrï, n.d., 130 pp., 1000 cop. [Bash 2 Arab; NN] 727

SSSR Verkhovnïy Sovetining altïnsï sessiahï: Stenografik otchot. n.p.: SSSR Verkhovnïy Sovetining Izdaniehe, 1940, 562 pp., 3000 cop. [Bash 3 Lat: DLC] 728

Sakalüf I. *Daprizivnik üdhïnïng havlïghï türahinda neme bilirgetiysh.* Ufa: Bashnarkamzdraf hem "Bashknige" Neshrï, 1928, 63 pp., 2000 cop. [Bash 2 Arab; CStH, NN] 729

Tayshin, M. I. *Palitgramïta: Seyasi bilïm kitabi.* Ufa: Bashknige, 1927, iv and 304 pp., 3000 cop. [Bash 2 Arab; NN] 730

XII nsï bashqörtöstan ölke partiya kanfirinsiyehïnïng qerardharï. Ufa: V.K.P.(b)nïng Bashqörtüstan Ülke Kemiteti Neshrï, 1928, 79 pp., 1000 cop. [Bash 2 Arab; NN] 731

Ün yïl. Ufa: Bashqürtstan Üzek Bashqarmasïnïng Neshri, 1928, 315 pp., 3000 cop. [Bash 2 Arab; NN] 732

V.K.P.(b)nïng böte kantün, vülis kemitetterïne hem yecheykelerïne. Ufa: n.p., n.d., 9 pp., n.c. [Bash 2 Arab; NN] 733

V.K.P.(b)nïng bötïn kantün vülist kemititlerïne. Ufa: Tipo-Litografiia "Okt. Natisk," n.d., 9 pp., n.c. [Bash 2 Arab; NN] 734

V.K.P.(b)nïng XVI nsï böte sayüz kenfirinsïyehïnïng qarardharï. Ufa: Bashknige, 1929, 99 pp., 2000 cop. [Bash 2 Arab; NN] 735

Vezmin, G. A. *Seyasi ang-bïlim ishsïlerïne yülbashsï.* Ufa: Bashknige, 1928, 131 pp., 2000 cop. [Bash 2 Arab; NN] 736

Vülis bashqarmalarinda iseb hem ish yörtü türinda instrükssiye. Ufa: Bashqird Tilin ghemelge Qüyü Üzek Kemisiyesï Neshrï, 1927, 53 pp., 150 cop. [Bash 2 Arab; NN] 737

Yenebi, Töḥfet. *Partiya hem avïl yarlïlari.* Ufa: Bashknyge, 1928, 43 pp., 1000 cop. [Bash 2 Arab; NN] 738

Zinüvyif, Gh. *Armiya hem ḥalq.* Ufa: Bashknige, 1925, 48 pp., 2000 cop. [Bash 2 Arab; NN] 739

History

Börhan; Ishimghöl. *Lina bölalarï.* Moscow: SSSR Ḥalqtarïnïng Üdhek Neshriyati, 1927, 20 pp., 2000 cop. [Bash 2 Arab; NN] 740

Feḥritdinïf, Gh.; Miras, S. *Bashqört tariḥï.* Ufa: "Bashknige" mnen Bashnarkamprüs Nashrï, 1927, iii and 156 pp., 5000 cop. [Bash 2 Arab; CStH, NN] 741

Ismaghil ibtesh sültanïf. Ufa: Bashtsïk hem Bashknige, 1928, 55 pp., 1000 cop. [Bash 2 Arab; NN] 742

Krasnüf, V. *Iki yödh yillïq köresh.* Moscow: SSSR Ḥalqtarïnïng Üdhek Neshriyatï, 1926, 55 pp., 3000 cop. [Bash 2 Arab; NN] 743

History

Krupïskaya, N. K. *Mineng tormoshom.* Ufa: Bashnäsher, 1929, 18 pp., 2000 cop. [Bash 3 Lat; NN] 744

Law

Bashqortostan avtonomiyalï sovet sotsialistik respublikahïnïng konstitutsiyahï: Töp zakonï. Ufa: n.p., 1940, 23 pp., 7200 cop. [Bash 4 Cyr; DLC] 745

Bashqürtöstan yömhüriyetïnïng böte kantün yört hem avïl krethtiyen üdh ara yardham kemitetterïne teghlïmat. Ufa: "Okt. Natisk," n.d., 10 pp., 1000 cop. [Bash 2 Arab; NN] 746

R.S.F.S.R. mölket küdiksï. Ufa: Bashknige, 1928, 350 pp., 1000 cop. [Bash 2 Arab; NN] 747

R.S.F.S.R. myilk ishtern yörötü küdikïsï. Ufa: Bashknige, 1928, 96 pp., 500 cop. [Bash 2 Arab; NN] 748

Social Organization

Börhan, Safa; Ishimghöl, Bülat. *8 mart.* Moscow: SSSR Ḥalqtarïnïng Üdhek Neshriyatï, 1927, 32 pp., 2000 cop. [Bash 2 Arab; NN] 749

Bürhan; Iyshïmghül. *Yeshter könï.* Ufa: "Bashknige," 1928, 37 pp., 2000 cop. [Bash 2 Arab; NN] 750

Ghözäyeref, Gh. *Yangï keshe: Yangï keshe ösön köräsh häm yäshtär.* Ufa: Bashnäsher, 1930, 76 pp., 3000 cop. [Bash 3 Lat; NN] 751

Kanüküf. *Yir ïshï ertilderï hem kammünalar.* Moscow: SSSR Ḥalqtarïnïng Üdhek Neshryyatï, 1925, 72 pp., 3000 cop. [Bash 2 Arab; NN] 752

Kaskin, L. *Bise-qidhdhargha keeriktï zakündar.* 1nsï kithek. Moscow: SSSR Ḥalqtarïnïng Üdhek Neshriyatï, 1925, 44 pp., 3000 cop. [Bash 2 Arab: NN] 753

Sazhin, I. V. *Ispirtlï ismlikter havliqqa qalay te'thir iteler.* Ufa: Bashknige, 1927, 41 pp., 2000 cop. [Bash 2 Arab: NN] 754

Varansufskey, G. M. *Öydhä tadha hava ney ösön käräk.* Ufa: Bashgiz, 1930, 20 pp., 3000 cop. [Bash 3 Lat; NN] 755

Yaralï ürta ḥellï hem külak türahïnda. Moscow: SSSR Ḥalqtarïnïng Üdhek Neshriyatï, 1926, 42 pp., 4000 cop. [Bash 2 Arab; NN] 756

BASHKIR Humanities

Language

Bashqört tele tirmindäre hüdhlege. Sotseyal–ikanumik–fälsäfi tirmindär. 1 kithäk. Ufa: Bashgiz, 1931, 72 pp., 3000 cop. [Bash 3 Lat; NN] 757

Bashqort telen boyomgha atqarïv turahïndagï zakundar qozamahï. Ufa: Bashgiz, 1930, 78 pp., 3000 cop. [Bash 3 Lat; NN] 758

Dävlätshin, Ghabbas. *Bashqort tele häm unï döröth yadhïv qaghidhäläre.* Ufa: B.Ü.Y.K. häm "Bashkenägä" Näshere, 1929, 61 pp., 12000 cop. [Bash 3 Lat; NN] 759

Katarinskii, Vasilii Vladimirovich. *Bashkirsko–russkii slovar'.* Orenburg: Tip.-Lit. B. Breslina, 1899, 237 pp., n.c. [Special Cyr; MH, NN] 760

Khimeyä tirmindäre. 1 kithäk. Ufa: Bashqort Telendä Tirmindär Tödöv Kämiseyähe, 1932, 35 pp., 3000 cop. [Bash 3 Lat; NN] 761

Literature

Agish, S. *Adhghïn malay: Balalar ösön köylö khikäyä.* Ufa: Bashgiz, 1930, 13 pp., 3000 cop. [Bash 3 Lat; NN] 762

Agish, S. *Qüsh töyme.* Ufa: Bashknige, 1928, 35 pp., 2000 cop. [Bash 2 Arab; NN] 763

Baghdanïf, Gh. *Qïr öyräge, qïr tavïgï.* Ufa: Udhäk Bashqort Yangalep Kämitäte häm "Bashkenägä" Näshere, 1928, 18 pp., 2000 cop. [Bash 3 Lat; NN] 764

Baghdanof, Gh. *Qart särek ike qara bashlï turgay.* Ufa: Udhäk Bashqort Yangalep Kämitäte häm "Bashkenägä" Näshere, 1928, 31 pp., 2000 cop. [Bash 3 Lat; NN] 765

Börünghilarding hödhdheri. Moscow: Merkez Sherq Neshriyati, 1924, 48 pp., 3000 cop. [Bash 2 Arab; NN] 766

Chanïsh, Ä. *Yulda.* Khikäyä. Ufa: Bashnäsher, 1930, 48 pp., 5000 cop. [Bash 3 Lat; NN] 767

Gadilov, A. *Aqbay balalarï.* Ufa: Bash. Narkampros hem "Bashknige" Neshrï, 1928, 22 pp., 1500 cop. [Bash 2 Arab; NN] 768

Ghabidïf, Ḥabiballe. *Bashqird müngliri.* 2nchi ktab. Orenburg: "Ṭülqün" Üyüshmasi Neshriyatindin, 1918, 36 pp., n.c. [Bash 1 Arab; CStH] 769

Ghabidïf, Ḥebibülla. *Iniïqay mnen yüldïqay*. Taryḥi pyese, 4 aktta. Moscow: SSSR Ḥalqtarïnïng Üdhek Neshriyati, 1926, 104 pp., 3000 cop. [Bash 2 Arab; NN] 770

Ghabidïf, Ḥebibülla. *Ural yirdhari*. Ufa: Bashqrdstan Neshriyat hem Kitab Sevdesi Shirketi, 1923, v and 66 pp., 2000 cop. [Bash 1 Arab; CStH] 771

Ghömär, Gharif. *Ber qïdhïl galïstuktïng kürgändäre*. Ufa: Üdhäk Bashqort Yangï Älep Kämitäte häm "Bashkenägä" Näshere, 1928, 29 pp., 2000 cop. [Bash 3 Lat; NN] 772

Gorki, Maksim. *Keshe*. Ufa: Üdhäk Bashqort Yangalep Kämitäte häm "Bashkenägä" Näshere, 1928, 13 pp., 2000 cop. [Bash 3 Lat; NN] 773

Karalinkö, V. *Yir athti balalarï*. Ufa: Bashknige, 1927, 38 pp., 1500 cop. [Bash 2 Arab; NN] 774

Khalq ädäbeyatïnan mäqäldär häm yomaqtar. Ufa: Bashnäsher, 1930, 81 pp., 2000 cop. [Bash 3 Lat; NN] 775

Kudash, Säyfi. *Bötä yöräktän*. Ufa: Bashgosizdat, 1943, 124 pp., 3000 cop. [Bash 4 Cyr; DLC] 776

Mehdiyif, M. *Uyïn hem süz tiḥnikesï*. Ufa: Bashknige, 1928, 56 pp., 2000 cop. [Bash 2 Arab; NN] 777

Mirath, Seghid. *Salavat batir*. Moscow: SSSR Ḥalqlari Üzek Neshriyati, 1924, 59 pp., 3000 cop. [Bash 1 Arab; NN] 778

Nasïyri, Imam. *Göldär*. Ruman. Ufa: Bashnäsher, 1930, 121 pp., 2000 cop. [Bash 3 Lat; NN] 779

Pokrovskii, Ivan. *Sbornik bashkirskikh i tatarskikh pesen'*. Kazan: Tipografiia Universiteta, 1870, 78 pp., n.c. [Bash 1 Arab; MH] 780

Qudash, Säyfi. *Kümäk tormosh. Balalar ädäbeyäte*. Ufa: Bashgiz, 1930, 29 pp., 3000 cop. [Bash 3 Lat; NN] 781

Tahir, Ebü. *Ayü ekiyetï*. Resmli. Ufa: Bashknige, 1926, 15 pp., 2000 cop. [Bash 2 Arab; NN] 782

Vildanïf, Gh. *Bashqört yömaqtarï*. Moscow: SSSR Ḥalqtarïnïng Üdhek Neshriyatï, 1927, 40 pp., 2000 cop. [Bash 2 Arab; CStH, NN] 783

Yänäbi, Tökhfät. *Bormalï yuldar*. Paimalar. Ufa: Bashnäsher, 1930, 64 pp., 3000 cop. [Bash 3 Lat; NN] 784

Yenebi. *Yadh bülegï*. Ufa: Bashknige, 1928, 27 pp., 3000 cop. [Bash 2 Arab; NN] 785

Yultïy, Davït. *Avïl töpkölöndä.* Paimalar, shigïrdhar, bäyläme. Ufa: "Bashknägä" häm B.Y.Ö.K. Näshere, 1929, 39 pp., 3000 cop. [Bash 3 Lat; NN] 786

Philosophy and Religion

Ishemghulïf, Bulat. *Urïth samadirzhaveyähe häm mösölman dineyä nazaratï.* Ufa: Bashnäsher, 1930, 52 pp., 3000 cop. [Bash 3 Lat; NN] 787

Maganük, A. *Balalar naydän yuq-bargha ïshanïvsan bulïp.* Ufa: Bashgiz, 1930, 16 pp., 3000 cop. [Bash 3 Lat; NN] 788

Sharit al-'iman. Ufa: Muṭi' Allah al-Ghaṭa'i, 1928, 24 pp., 10000 cop. [Bash 1 Arab; NN] 789

Ës'khërarämë (Cheboksary) 1928: 1; 1929: 2, 4–7, 9–10, 12. [Chu 1 Cyr; NN] 790

Es'lekensen sassi (Cheboksary) 1925: 1–2. [Chu 1 Cyr; NN] 791

Ivanov-Tal'. *Tirpe käs'atä tuma vërenessi.* Cheboksary: Tchävash Këneki Uyrämë, 1927, 66 pp., 3000 cop. [Chu 1 Cyr; CStH, NN] 792

Kapkän (Cheboksary) n.d.: 2; 1929: 3; n.d.: 11; 1930: 16. [Chu 1 Cyr; NN] 793

Khaläkha vërentes ës' (Cheboksary) 1928: 1; 1929: 5, 9–10. [Chu 1 Cyr; NN] 794

Khatër pul (Cheboksary) 1929: 9–10; 1930: 2–3, 5–7. [Chu 1 Cyr; NN] 795

Kochedïk (shëshlë) (n.p.) 1929: 11–13. [Chu. 1 Cyr; NN] 796

Markkovnikkäv, V. S. *S'ampäksen pitchetchëpe s'amkorsen yukhämë.* Cheboksary: Tchävash Këneki Uyrämë, 1929, 40 pp., 3000 cop. [Chu 1 Cyr; NN] 797

Sakkun khïparë tchävashsen akhtonomlä sotsialisämpa sovet respuplëkëntchi ës'lekensemle khrestchensen, tata khërlë saltak tepputatchësen sovetchën ës' tävakan komittetchë kälarat' (Cheboksary) 1925: 1–2 [DLC], 3–4; 1926: 5–8, 11–16, 19/20 [DLC, MH], 21/22 [DLC], 23–26 [DLC, MH], 27 [MH]; 1927: 30 [DLC, MH], 31 [MH], 32/33 [DLC, MH]. [Chu 1 Cyr] 798

Sakkunsempe khushusem tchävash respuplëk pravittëlstvi, tata SSR soyusëpe RFSSR pravittëlstvisem yïshännä pallärakh tekretsempe postanovlenisem (Cheboksary) 1927: 1–3; 1928: 4–10; 1929: 11–13, ⟨new series⟩ 1–7 [MH], 8 [MH, NN], 9; 1930: 10–20, 22–26, 28–30, 32–34; 1931: 1 [MH]. [Chu 1 Cyr] 799

Suntal (Cheboksary) 1927: 6; 1928: 2, 7, 10, 12; 1930: 6–9. [Chu 1 Cyr; NN] 800

Tchävash këneki uyrätë kälarnä kënekesem. Cheboksary: n.p., 1928, 24 pp., 500 cop. [Chu 1 Cyr; NN] 801

Tchävash respuplëk pravittëlstvi kälarnä sakkunsempe khushusem, SSR soyusëpe RFSSR pravittëlstvi yïshännä pallärakh tekretsempe postanovlenisem (Cheboksary) 1927: 1–3; 1928: 7–9; 1929: 2–4, ⟨second series⟩ 1–9; 1930: 10–18, 22, 24–33; 1931: 4. [Chu 1 Cyr; DLC] 802

CHUVASH General

Tchävash yalë (Cheboksary) 1928: 1–3, 5, 11/12; 1929: 4, 7–9, 12–13; 1930: 1, 13. [Chu 1 Cyr; NN] 803

Tchävashla kälentar. Cheboksary: Tchävash Këneki Uyrämë, 1930, 112 pp., 5000 cop. [Chu 1 Cyr; NN] 804

Yalkor (Cheboksary) 1930: 3–4, 7, 10. [Chu 1 Cyr; NN] 805

CHUVASH Social Sciences

Anthropology

Gornostaev, F. Z. *Kilkepe-vëren yavma vërener!* Cheboksary: Tchävash Këneki Uyrämë, 1926, 75 pp., 3000 cop. [Chu 1 Cyr; NN] 806

Economics

Antonov, M. *Ës'khaläkhne sotsialisämla ämärtäva khutshäntarar.* Moscow: SSSR-ti Khalakhsen Tëp Istattëlstvipe Tchentrosoyus, 1929, 48 pp., 3000 cop. [Chu 1 Cyr; NN] 807

Bogdanov, A. *Ïytusem s'ine kalasa s'ïrna polittikällä ekkonomi.* Cheboksary: Tchävash Këneki Uyrämë, 1924, 209 pp., 6000 cop. [Chu 1 Cyr; NN] 808

Ezerskiy, P. *Potrepkopperatsin s'uraki kamppanintchi ës'esem.* Moscow: SSSR-ti Khaläkhsen Tëp Istattëlstvipe Tchentrosoyus, 1930, 39 pp., 10000 cop. [Chu 1 Cyr; NN] 809

Kaganovich, A. S. *Pashaläkh sapomësem s'intchen mën pëlmelle.* Moscow: SSSR-ti Khaläkhsen Tëp Istattëlstvi, 1929, 38 pp., 3000 cop. [Chu 1 Cyr; NN] 810

Kopperatsi uks'ine purläkhne salatakansempe yeple kereshmelle. Moscow: SSSR-ti Khaläkhsen Tëp Istattëlstvipe Tchentrosoyus, 1928, 31 pp., 6000 cop. [Chu 1 Cyr; NN] 811

Lenin kopperatsi s'intchen. Moscow: SSSR-ti Khaläkhsen Tëp Istattëlstvipe Tchentrosoyus, 1929, 22 pp., 3000 cop. [Chu 1 Cyr; NN] 812

Merkkuryëv, I. *Patraksempe këtüs'sen, sotsial'ni strakhkhovani s'intchen mën asratïtsa tämalla.* Cheboksary: Tchävash Strakhkassä Kälarnä, 1930, 30 pp., 1100 cop. [Chu 1 Cyr; NN] 813

Mikkolenko, Y. *Talkkäshpe kolkhosa kus'assin ustave.* Cheboksary: Tchävash Këneki Uprämë, 1930, 66 pp., 11000 cop. [Chu 1 Cyr; NN] 814

Neppomn'äshtchin, N. P. *SSSR-tchi yalkhus'aläkhpa värman ës'ëntche ës'lekensen profsoyusë yelpe yërkelense, tata mën tusa tärät.* Cheboksary: Yalkhus'aläkhpa Värman Ës'entche Ës'lekensen Soyusën Tchävash Papë Kälarnä, 1928, 58 pp., 3000 cop. [Chu 1 Cyr; NN] 815

Nikitinskiy, I. *Khamär tavrari s'uts'antaläk.* Moscow: SSSR-ti Khaläkhsen Tëp Istattëlstvi, 1927, 102 pp., 3000 cop. [Chu 1 Cyr; NN] 816

Nikitinskiy, I. I. *Khamär tavrari s'uts'antaläk.* Moscow: Tsentral'noe Izdatel'stvo Narodov SSSR, 1926, 70 pp., 5000 cop. [Chu 1 Cyr; NN] 817

Nikitinskiy, I. I. *Khamär tavrari s'uts'antaläk.* Moscow: SSSR-ti Khaläkhsen Tëp Istattëlstvi, 1929, 88 pp., 4000 cop. [Chu 1 Cyr; NN] 818

Orlov, I. *Kopperatsi.* Moscow: Tsentral'noe Izdatel'stvo Narodov SSSR, 1925, 18 pp., 3000 cop. [Chu 1 Cyr; NN] 819

Orlov, I. *Kretit tovarishchëstvisem.* Moscow: Tsentral'noe Izdatel'stvo Narodov SSSR, 1925, 27 pp., 3000 cop. [Chu 1 Cyr; NN] 820

Patshaläkh raskhutchësempë takhkhutchësem. Moscow SSSR-ti Khaläkhsen Tëp Istattëlstvi, 1927, 27 pp., 5000 cop. [Chu 1 Cyr; NN] 821

Pereket kassi-shanäs'lä yentchëk. Cheboksary: Tchavash Respuplëkëntchi Tëp Pereket Kassi No. 60, 1929, 16 pp., 5000 cop. [Chu 1 Cyr; NN] 822

Radomskiy, S. G. *Mayän 1-mëshë tëntcheri prolettariatan s'ënterü uyavë.* Moscow: SSSR-ti Khalakhsen Tep Istattëlstvi, 1930, 45 pp., 3000 cop. [Chu 1 Cyr; NN] 823

S'ërës'ne përleshse ës'lemelli kopperattivlä yultashläkhsen ustavë. n.p., "Kanash" Khas'atna Kolkhossen S'eksiye Kälarnä, n.d., n.pp., 4000 cop. [Chu 1 Cyr; NN] 824

Strakhkassä patraksene mën parat? Cheboksary: Tchävashstrakhkassa, 1929, 10 pp., 4000 cop. [Chu 1 Cyr; NN] 825

Tchävash ASS Respuplëkëntchi yalkhus'aystvi, kubs'enlëkh tata tërlë promïsla kopperattivsen soyusë "Tchävashproisvotsoyus" pus'lannipe unän ës'ësem. Cheboksary: Tchävashproisvotsoyus Kälarnä, 1928, 17 pp., 2060 cop. [Chu 1 Cyr; NN] 826

Tmitriyev, V. T. *Ushkänlä khus'aläkhsen.* Cheboksary: Khalakh S'utes' Komissariatche, 1929, 48 pp., 3000 cop. [Chu 1 Cyr; NN] 827

Tsingovatov, I. A. *Khamär kopperattiv ustavëntchen mën pëlmelle.* Moscow: SSSR-ti Khaläkhsen Tëp Istattëlstvipe Tchentrosoyus, 1929, 32 pp., 2000 cop. [Chu 1 Cyr; NN] 828

Education

Agapov, S.; Kamenetskiy, V; Kashchenko, B.; Sokolov, S. *S'amräk keokräf.* Moscow: Tsentral'noe Izdatel'stvo Narodov SSSR, 1927, 109 pp., 4000 cop. [Chu 1 Cyr; NN] 829

Akhtonomlä tchävash opläs'ë shkulra ta, kilte te vulama yuräkhlä këneke. Cheboksary: Respuplikkäri Tchävash Kënekine Kälarakan Uyräm, 1923, 181 pp., 5000 cop. [Chu 1 Cyr; NN] 830

Antonov, A. *Piren soyus: Tvattämesh kruppära verenmelli këneke.* Moscow: SSSR-ti Khalakhsen Tëp Istattelstvi, 1930, 608 pp., 30000 cop. [Chu 1 Cyr; NN] 831

Antonov, A. *Vërener: Khuta sakhal pëlekensene vërenteken shkulta ës'lemelli këneke.* Moscow: SSSR-ti Khaläkhsen Tëp Istattëlstvi, 1930, vi and 322 pp., 30000 cop. [Chu 1 Cyr; NN] 832

Antonov, A.; Ozerov, P. *Prokrammä: Khuta natchar pëlnine peteresshen ës'leken shkulsempe krushoksem val'l'i.* Moscow: SSSR-ti Khälakhsen Tëp Istattëlstvi, 1929, 49 pp., 2000 cop. [Chu 1 Cyr; NN] 833

Isaev, I. V. *Vulamalli s'urtra khas'at-kënekepe mënle es'lemelle.* Moscow: SSSR-ti Khaläkhsen Tëp Istattëlstvi, 1929, 42 pp., 1500 cop. [Chu 1 Cyr; NN] 834

Ivanov, P. I. *Yalti shkulsentche tävattämäshla pillëkëmëm s'ul vërenmelli satatch këneki.* Cheboksary: Tchävash Opläs'ëntchi Këneke Kälarakan Uyräm, 1925, 96 pp., 5000 cop. [Chu 1 Cyr; NN] 835

Ivanov, P. I. *Yalti shkulsentche vis'emesh s'ulta vërenmelli satatch këneki.* Cheboksary: Tchävash Respuplëkentchi Këneke Kälarakan Uyräm, 1926, 124 pp., 6000 cop. [Chu 1 Cyr; NN] 836

Kol'tsovä, S. I. *S'ënë yal: S'itënnisene vërentmelli këneke.* Moscow: SSSR-ti Khaläkhsen Tëp Istattëlstvi, 1929, 96 pp., 30000 cop. [Chu 1 Cyr; NN] 837

Kol'tsovä, S. I. *S'ënë yal: Üsse s'itnisene vërentmelli pukvar.* Moscow: SSSR-ti Khaläkhsen Tep Istattëlstvi, 1930, 71 pp., 150000 cop. [Chu 1 Cyr; NN] 838

Krikorpëvä, A. *Shkul s'ulentchen irtnë s'amräksene vërentessi.* Cheboksary: Tchävash Respupl. S'utës' Khaläkh Komissariatchë, 1929, 14 pp., 600 cop. [Chu 1 Cyr; NN] 839

Krupskaya, N. *Lenin khaläkha s'utta kälares es' s'intchen vërentni.* Moscow: Tsentral'noe Izdatel'stvo Narodov Soiuza SSR, 1925, 32 pp., 3000 cop. [Chu 1 Cyr; NN] 840

Ozerov, P. *Krayevetenipe Tchävash shkulë.* Moscow: SSSR-ti Khaläkhsen Tëp Istattëlstvi, 1927, 62 pp., 2000 cop. [Chu 1 Cyr; NN] 841

Perremesh sïpäklä shkulsentche verentmelli prokrammä. Cheboksary: Khalakh S'utes' Komissariatchë Kalarna, 1928, 57 pp., 2000 cop. [Chu 1 Cyr; NN] 842

Pervonachal'nyi uchebnik russkago iazyka dlia Chuvash. Kazan: Prav. Miss. Obshch. Tip. Imp. Universiteta, 1893 2d ed., 131 pp., n.c. [Chu 1 Cyr; MH] 843

Pëtchik atchasene päkhsa üsteressi. Moscow: SSSR-ti Khaläkhsen Tëp Istattëlstvi, 1928, 32 pp., 2000 cop. [Chu 1 Cyr; NN] 844

Petrov, M. P. *Tchëmpërti Tchävash shkulëpe Ivan Yakkältch Yakkävlëv s'intchen kesken kalasa kätartni.* Cheboksary: Khalakh S'utes' Komissariatchë Kälarnä, 1928, 95 pp., 4000 cop. [Chu 1 Cyr; NN] 845

Petrov, M. P. *Yalti shkulsentche maltankhi s'ul vërenmelli satatch këneki.* Cheboksary: Tchävash Këneki Uyrämë, 1926, 112 pp., 20000 cop. [Chu 1 Cyr; CStH, NN] 846

Shatrënpa, S. K.; Kol'tsova, S. I. *S'itënnisene vërentmelli mettotek.* Moscow: SSSR-ti Khaläkhsen Tëp Istattelstvi, 1929, 112 pp., 6000 cop. [Chu 1 Cyr; NN] 847

S'uttalla: Ikkëmësh s'ul vulamalli këneke. Cheboksary: Tchävash Këneki Uyrämë, 1929, 95 pp., 10000 cop. [Chu 1 Cyr; NN] 848

S'uttalla: Pukvar khïs's'än vulamalli ikkëmësh këneke. Cheboksary: Tchävash Këneki Uyrämë, 1926, 184 pp., 20000 cop. [Chu 1 Cyr; NN] 849

Vanerkke. *Tchävash chëlkhiyën orfokrafi slovarë.* Cheboksary: Tchävash Këneki Uyrämë, 1926, 135 pp., 6000 cop. [Chu 1 Cyr; CStH] 850

Vanerkke, E. *S'ulpus'ë tchävash s'ïrune verenmelli këneke.* Cheboksary: Tchävash Këneke Uyrämë, 1926, 68 pp., 50000 cop. [Chu 1 Cyr; NN] 851

Vanerkke, N. *Khrestchen pukvarë.* Moscow: Tsentral'noe Izdatel'stvo Narodov SSSR, 1927, 64 pp., 25000 cop. [Chu 1 Cyr; CStH, NN] 852

Vas's'ilyëv, S. V. *Maltankhi shkulra vërenmelli fis'ikkä.* Cheboksary: Tchävash Respuplëkentchi Këneke Kälarakan Uyräm, 1925, 139 pp., 10000 cop. [Chu 1 Cyr; NN] 853

Zarovnyadnïy, N. *Kharpar khäy tëllën verenmelli s'intchen.* Moscow: Tsentral'noe Izdatel'stvo Narodov SSSR, 1925, ii and 70 pp., 2000 cop. [Chu 1 Cyr; CStH, NN] 854

Zorin, G.; Antonov, A.; Yurkin, P.; Efimov, M. *Ës' këneki. Vis's'ëmësh kruppära vulasa es'lemelli këneke.* Moscow: SSSR-ti Khaläkhsen Tëp Istattëlstvi, 1928, vi and 289 pp., 4000 cop. [Chu 1 Cyr; NN] 855

Geography

Keokrafi atläsë 17 taplitsä. Moscow: SSSR-ti Khaläkhsen Tëp Istattelstvi Kälarnä, n.d., 16 pp., 5000 cop. [Chu 1 Cyr; NN] 856

Krupër, A.; Krikoriëv, S.; Parkkäv, A.; Tchekhranäv, S. *Pus'lamäshëntche vërenmelli keokrakhvi.* Cheboksary: Tchäväsh Opläs'entchi Këneke Kälarakan Uyräm, 1924, 144 pp., 10000 cop. [Chu 1 Cyr; NN] 857

Petrov, M. P. *S'ürevs'ësem vësem s'ürenisem s'intchen kësken kalasa pani.* Cheboksary: Tchävash Këneki Uyrämë, 1927, 73 pp., 5000 cop. [Chu 1 Cyr; NN] 858

Government

Alentey, K. T. *1905 s'ulti revol'utsi.* Cheboksary: Tchävash Respuplëkëntchi Këneke Kälarakan Uyräm, 1925, 98 pp., 3000 cop. [Chu 1 Cyr; NN] 859

Avinovitski, Yak. *Prottivokassem, vësene mënle tunä tata mënle tïtkalamalla.* Cheboksary: Osoaviakhim Tchävash Sovetche Kälarnä, 1929, 59 pp., 3000 cop. [Chu 1 Cyr; NN] 860

Borzov, L. *Komsomol vërenü lëkhshën këreshhes es're.* Moscow: SSSR-ti Khaläkhsen Tëp Istattelstvi, 1930, 38 pp., 8000 cop. [Chu 1 Cyr; NN] 861

Dimanshteyn, S. *Parttin XV-mësh syesë tunä ës'sem s'intchen.* Moscow: SSSR-ti Khaläkhsen Tëp Istattëlstvi, 1928, 82 pp., 3000 cop. [Chu 1 Cyr; NN] 862

Ekhlin, N.; S'erkeyëva, A. *Tchävash khërarämë sovet sërshïvne sïkhlama khatërlen.* Cheboksary: Tchävash Këneke Uyrämë, 1929, 28 pp., 3000 cop. [Chu 1 Cyr; NN] 863

Kaganovich, L. M. *Pëtëm soyusri komunissen parttiyë.* Moscow: SSSR-ti Khaläkhsen Tëp Istattëlstvi, 1928, 88 pp., 250 cop. [Chu 1 Cyr; NN] 864

Kakanovitch, L.; Timanshteyn, S. *Parttipe sovetsen suylavë.* Moscow: SSSR-ti Khaläkhsen Tëp Istattëlstvi, 1928, 54 pp., 3500 cop. [Chu 1 Cyr; NN] 865

Kamenev, L. B. *Leninpa unän parttiyë.* Cheboksary: Tchavash Respuplëkëntchi Këneke Kälarakan Uyräm, 1925, 48 pp., 5000 cop. [Chu 1 Cyr; NN] 866

Khaykkevitch, A. *Komsomol pïtansa ës'lenë tchukhne.* Cheboksary: Tchävash Këneki Uyrämë, 1928, 94 pp., 3000 cop. [Chu 1 Cyr; NN] 867

Khrestchensem! S'er pirki tchenttärta tukhmalli s'ak s'ënë sakkun proyektine väkhätä per täsmasar pukhusentche teplen sütse yavsa, "kanash" khas'at urlä s'ïrsa pëlterër. Cheboksary: Tchävash Tëpës'tavkom Pres'itiumë, 1928, 12 pp., 3900 cop. [Chu 1 Cyr; NN] 868

Komsomol tchavash opkomën 6-mesh plenämën resol'utsiyesem. Cheboksary: Komsomol Tchävashopkomë Kälarnä, 1929, 15 pp., 1000 cop. [Chu 1 Cyr; NN] 869

Komsomolän khërlë s'arta ës'lemelli polosheni. Cheboksary: Tchävash Terrupravleniye Kälarna, 1929, 20 pp., 2100 cop. [Chu 1 Cyr; NN] 870

Komunissen internatsionale. Cheboksary: Tchavash Keneki Uyrämë, 1929, 88 pp., 3000 cop. [Chu 1 Cyr; NN] 871

Korläv, A. *Yalti komsomolësän politkramatti.* Cheboksary:

Tchävash Respuplëkentchi Këneke Kälarakan Uyräm, 1925, 176 pp., 10000 cop. [Chu 1 Cyr; NN] 872

Korrenkkä, L.; S'mirnov, V. *Pionera shkulta yertse pïrakanni.* Cheboksary: Tchävash Këneki Uyrämë, 1926, 30 pp., 2000 cop. [Chu 1 Cyr; NN) 873

Kosarev, A. *Komsomol partii s'ul-yërëshën këreshne s'ërte.* Moscow: SSSR-ti Khaläkhsen Tëp Istattëlstvi, 1930, 46 pp., 3000 cop. [Chu 1 Cyr; NN] 874

Kovalenko, P. *Politkramota këneki.* Moscow: RKP Tëp Komittetchë S'umentchi S'eksiyë Kälarnä, 1923, 47 pp., 5000 cop. [Chu 1 Cyr; DLC, NN] 875

Krasnov, V. I. *Epir värs'asshän mar, antchakh khamär s'ër-shïva sïkhlama khatër.* Moscow: SSSR-ti Khaläkhsen Tëp Istattëlstvi, 1927, 33 pp., 2000 cop. [Chu 1 Cyr; NN] 876

Krasnov, V. I. *Lenin s'ulë.* Cheboksary: Tchävash Respupl. Këneke Kälarakan Uyräm, 1925, 20 pp., 4000 cop. [Chu 1 Cyr; NN] 877

Krasnov, V. I. *Vus'ë revol'utsi.* Cheboksary: Tchävash Këneki Uyrämë, 1926, 64 pp., 6000 cop. [Chu 1 Cyr; NN] 878

Krupskaya, N. K. *Natsi kul'tturëpë internatsionalla kul'ttur s'intchen.* Cheboksary: Tchävash Këneki Uyrämë, 1929, 20 pp., 3000 cop. [Chu 1 Cyr; NN] 879

Kutyăshov, S. *Tëne khirës' proppakantä tävassi.* Moscow: SSSR-ti Khaläkhsen Tëp Istattelstvi, 1928, 51 pp., 1000 cop. [Chu 1 Cyr; CStH] 880

L'ava, Plattunë. *Khërlë s'ar istoriye.* Cheboksary: Tchävash Respuplëkën Këneke Kälarakan Uyrämë, 1927, 90 pp., 2000 cop. [Chu 1 Cyr; NN] 881

Lenin, V. I. *Ekkonomëkkän s'ënë polittëkë s'intchen.* Cheboksary: Tchävash Këneki Uyrämë, 1926, 52 pp., 3000 cop. [Chu 1 Cyr; NN] 882

Lenin, V. I. *Khaläkha s'utta kalarassi s'intchen.* Cheboksary: Tchävash Këneki Uyrämë, 1928, 72 pp., 5000 cop. [Chu 1 Cyr; NN] 883

Lenin, V. I. *Khëraräm s'intchen vërentni.* Cheboksary: Tchävash Këneki Uyrämë, 1927, 44 pp., 3000 cop. [Chu 1 Cyr; NN] 884

Lenin, V. I. *Khrestchenpë s'ër s'intchen.* Cheboksary: Tchävash Këneki Uyrämë, 1927, 64 pp., 3000 cop. [Chu 1 Cyr; NN] 885

Lenin, V. I. *Kopperatsi s'intchen kalani.* Cheboksary: Tchävash Këneki Uyrämë, 1926, 51 pp., 5000 cop. [Chu 1 Cyr; NN] 886
Lenin, V. I. *Okt'apërti revol'utsi s'intchen.* Cheboksary: Tchävash Këneki Uyräme, 1927, 72 pp., 5000 cop. [Chu 1 Cyr; NN] 887
Lenin, V. I. *Sovet patshaläkhë s'intchen.* Cheboksary: Tchävash Këneki Uyrämë, 1927, 63 pp., 5000 cop. [Chu 1 Cyr; NN] 888
Levkur. *Komsomolësän tumalli ës'ësem.* Cheboksary: Tchävash Respuplëkëntchi Këneke Kälarakan Uyräm, 1926, 47 pp., 3000 cop. [Chu 1 Cyr; NN] 889
Manifesë: Sovet soyusëntchi tëp ës' tävakan komittet. Moscow: SSSR-ti Khaläkhsen Tëp Istattëlstvi, 1927, 29 pp., 2000 cop. [Chu 1 Cyr; NN] 890
Molättäv, V. M. *Parttin yalti tchukhänsem khushshintche ës'lessi.* Cheboksary: Tchävash Këneki Uyrämë, 1926, 30 pp., 2000 cop. [Chu 1 Cyr; NN] 891
Novakovskiy, I. *Vunä s'ul.* Moscow: SSSR-ti Khaläkhsen Tëp Istattelstvi, 1927, 93 pp., 3000 cop. [Chu 1 Cyr; NN] 892
Oleynikov, N. "*Vlas' pirën alära.*" Moscow: SSSR-ti Khaläkhsen Tëp Istattëlstvi, 1928, 44 pp., 2000 cop. [Chu 1 Cyr; NN] 893
PSK(p) Parttin tchävash orkanisatsin 12-mësh konferentsiyën resol'utsipe postanovlenisem. Cheboksary: PSK(p) P. Tchävashopkomë Kälarna, 1927, 102 pp., 1000 cop. [Chu 1 Cyr; NN] 894
PSK(p)P-in khërlë s'arti yatcheykkisem ës'lemelli s'intchen kälarnä instruksi. Cheboksary: Tchävash Terrupravleniye Kälarnä, 1929, 30 pp., 2100 cop. [Chu 1 Cyr; NN] 895
Partti ëretchësene tërësles'e tasatassi s'intchen. Cheboksary: PSK(p) Parttin Tchävash Opkomë Kälarnä, 1929, 44 pp., 2000 cop. [Chu 1 Cyr; NN] 896
Parttin tchävash orkanisatsin XIII-mësh konferentsiyë. Cheboksary: Tchävash Këneki Uyrämë Kälarnä, 1929, 51 pp., 2000 cop. [Chu 1 Cyr; NN] 897
Pavlov, I. *Tchävash s'amräkësene komsomolan VIII-mesh syese s'intchen.* Moscow: SSSR-ti Khaläkhsen Tëp Istattëlstvi, 1928, 64 pp., 2000 cop. [Chu. 1 Cyr; NN] 898
Pavlov, I. *Yalti komsomolës ës' s'ule.* Moscow: SSSR-ti Khaläkhsen Tëp Istattëlstvi, 1929, 100 pp., 3000 cop. [Chu 1 Cyr; NN] 899
Pëtëm soyusri komun. (pol'sh.) part. Tchävash respuplëkëntchi

komittetchën 6-mësh plenämen ës'ësem. Cheboksary: PSK(p)P. Tchävash Respuplëk. Komittetche, 1926, 38 pp., 3000 cop. [Chu 1 Cyr; NN] 900

Petrov, S. *Pëtëm soyusri komunissen (p) parttiyën 15-mesh konferentsi ës'ësem*. Cheboksary: Tchävash Opkomën Orkpaye, 1926, 56 pp., 2000 cop. [Chu 1 Cyr; NN] 901

Petrov, S'. P. *Pëtëm soyusri komunissen (pol'sheviksen) parttin XV-mesh syesënës'ësem*. Cheboksary: PSK(p)P-in Tchävash Opkomë Kälarnä, 1928, 59 pp., 2000 cop. [Chu 1 Cyr; NN] 902

Petrova, V. *Yut s'ër-shïvsem tärähh*. Moscow: SSSR-ti Khalakhsen Tëp Istattelstvi, 1930, 80 pp., 5000 cop. [Chu 1 Cyr; NN] 903

Pionersen s'urakintchi ës'ësem. Cheboksary; Tchävash Këneki Uyrämë, 1930, 23 pp., 6000 cop. [Chu 1 Cyr; NN] 904

Pirën khrestchensen germani revolyütsiyë s'intchen pelse tämalla. Moscow: Tsentral'noe Vostochnoe Izdatel'stvo Pri NKN, 1923, 26 pp., 2000 cop. [Chu 1 Cyr; CStH, DLC, NN] 905

Pol'shshäpa unan s'apë. Cheboksary: Tchävash Këneke Uyrämë, 1928, 18 pp., 1500 cop. [Chu 1 Cyr; NN] 906

Puläshu komittetchësen suylavësem s'intchen RFSSR puläshu khaläkh komissariatchëpe tëp puläshkom kälarnä instruksi no: 54/20. Cheboksary: Tchävash Respupl. Pulashu Khaläkh Komissariatchë, 1929, 12 pp., 1500 cop. [Chu 1 Cyr; NN] 907

Ras's'eyri komunissen (pol'sheviksen) parttin vunvis's'ëmësh syesë yïshännä resol'utsisem. Moscow: Tsentral'noe Izdatel'stvo Narodov SSSR, 1924, 92 pp. 3000 cop. [Chu 1 Cyr; NN] 908

Rïkov, A. I. *Sovet soyusëpe kapitalisäm tentchi*. Moscow: SSSR-ti Khaläkhsen Tëp Istattëlstvi, 1929, 48 pp., 3000 cop. [Chu 1 Cyr; NN] 909

Rubakin, N. A. *Tërlë khaläkhsem kharpär khäy n'ëlkhipe khäs'an tata ieple kalas'ta vërennë*. Moscow: Tsentral'noe Izdatel'stvo Narodov SSSR, 1924, 60 pp., 2000 cop. [Chu 1 Cyr; CStH, NN] 910

SSR soyusin ës' tävakan tëp komittetchë kälarnä mänakhvis. Leningrad: n.p., 1927, 17 pp., 1000 cop. [Chu 1 Cyr; NN] 911

S'ar slushpi sakkunë. Cheboksary: Tchävash Tëpës'tävkomë Kälarnä, 1926, n.pp., 2500 cop. [Chu 1 Cyr; DLC] 912

Sattanevitch, V. *PSS'LKS yalti yatchtcheykkin orkanisatsillë ës'e*. Cheboksary: Tchävash Këneki Uyrämë, 1926, 82 pp., 3000 cop. [Chu 1 Cyr; NN] 913

S'emenäv, T. S'. *Sovet soyusne täshmansentchen sïkhlama khatër pul!* Cheboksary: Tchävash Këneki Uyräme, 1927, ii and 74 pp., 3000 cop. [Chu 1 Cyr; NN] 914

S'emenë, Khumma. *Komsomol kalavësem.* Cheboksary: Tchävash Respuplëkëntchi Këneke Kälarakan Uyräm, 1926, 59 pp., 5000 cop. [Chu 1 Cyr; NN] 915

S'ereprovskipe, I.; Lepëtev, M. *Stanoklä pulemet tata unän värs'äri ës'ë.* Cheboksary: Tchävash Terupravleniye Kälarnä, 1930, 29 pp., 2100 cop. [Chu 1 Cyr; NN] 916

Shipaylo, K. I. *PSK(p) parttin XV-mësh syese yalta ës'lessi s'intchen mën kalarë.* Moscow: SSSR-ti Khaläkhsen Tëp Istattëlstvi, 1928, 58 pp., 3000 cop. [Chu 1 Cyr; NN] 917

Sïltäsh suläntchäkpa, tata kilështerekensempe këresher. Moscow: SSSR-ti Khaläkhsen Tëp Istattëlstvi, 1929, 68 pp., 2000 cop. [Chu 1 Cyr; NN] 918

Sotsialisäm tävakan s'amräksem. Moscow: SSSR-ti Khaläkhsen Tëp Istattëlstvi, 1930, 107 pp., 3000 cop. [Chu 1 Cyr; NN] 919

Sovet soyusentchi tëp ës' tävakan komittet manifesë. Moscow: SSSR-ti Khaläkhsen Tëp Istattëlstvi, 1927, 29 pp., 2000 cop. [Chu 1 Cyr; CStH] 920

Stalin, I. *Leninpa leninisäm s'intchen.* Cheboksary: Tchävash Këneki Uyrämë, 1926, 123 pp., 5000 cop. [Chu 1 Cyr; NN] 921

S'teppanäv, F. S.; Oryëv, K. K. *Yalti komsomolëssen pus'lasa polittëke vërenmelli këneke.* Cheboksary: Tchävash Këneke Uyrämë, 1928, 112 pp., 3000 cop. [Chu 1 Cyr; NN] 922

Sterlin, S. *Värs'ä väkhätën'tchë ës'khalakh khërlë s'ara mënpe puläshma pultarat.* Moscow: SSSR-ti Khaläkhsen Tëp Istattëlstvi, 1929, 32 pp., 3000 cop. [Chu 1 Cyr; NN] 923

Tchävash respuplëkënn'i sovetsen 111(8)-mësh syesë iïmännä postanovlenisem. Cheboksary: Izdanie TsIKa ChASSR, 1929, 53 pp., 4000 cop. [Chu 1 Cyr; NN] 924

Trotskisäm s'intchen. Cheboksary: Tchävash Respuplëkëntchi Këneke Kälarakan Uyräm, 1926, 40 pp., 4000 cop. [Chu 1 Cyr; NN] 925

Tsïpin, G. *Oktaperen 13-mësh s'ule.* Moscow: SSSR-ti Khaläkhsen Tëp Istattëlstvi, 1930, 29 pp., 3000 cop. [Chu 1 Cyr; NN] 926

Tümër, Viktärë. *Tchävashsem khushshintche 1905–1907-mësh s'ulsentche pulnä revol'utsille palkhavsem.* Cheboksary: Tchävash

Respuplëkentchi Këneke Kälarakan Uyräm, 1926, ii and 82 pp., 5000 cop. [Chu 1 Cyr; NN] 927

VKP-n XV-mesh syesë yïshännä resol'utsisem. Moscow: SSSR-ti Khalakhsen Tëp Istattëlstvi, 1928, 110 pp., 3000 cop. [Chu 1 Cyr; NN) 928

Vasil'ev, B. *Komunisla internatsionalän VI-mësh konkresën ës'ësempe reshsheniyësem.* Moscow: SSSR-ti Khaläkhsen Tëp Istattëlstvi, 1929, 80 pp., 2000 cop. [Chu 1 Cyr; NN] 929

Virganskiy, V. *Komsomolän polittik këneki.* Moscow: SSSR-ti Khaläkhsen Tëp Istattelstvi, 1927, 75 pp., 3000 cop. [Chu 1 Cyr; NN] 930

Vlatimëräv, T. *Yalti komsomolëssene parttin 14-mësh syesë s'intchen.* Cheboksary: Tchävash Respup. Këneke Kälarakan Uyräm, 1926, 27 pp. 3000 cop. [Chu 1 Cyr; CStH, NN] 931

Volkkäv, A. *Pionerän kilyïshëntchi ës'ësem.* Cheboksary: Tchävash Këneke Uyrämë, 1927, 24 pp., 2000 cop. [Chu 1 Cyr; NN] 932

Volkkäv, A. *Yalti pionersene puläsh.* Cheboksary: Tchävash Këneke Uyrämë, 1927, 19 pp., 2000 cop. [Chu 1 Cyr; CStH, NN] 933

Yăroslavskiy, Em. *Teoripë ës'ri opportunisämän s'ënë khurmisem s'intchen.* Moscow: SSSR-ti Khaläkhsen Tëp Istattëlstvi, 1930, 46 pp., 4000 cop. [Chu 1 Cyr; NN] 934

Yuman, M. *Irëklëkh s'ulë.* Moscow: Tsentral'noe Izdatel'stvo Narodov SSSR, 1924, 97 pp., 2000 cop. [Chu 1 Cyr; NN] 935

Yuman, M. (D. P. Petrov). *1905-mësh s'ul: Tchävashsen khushshintche pulnä ës'sene asanni.* Cheboksary: Tchävash Opläs'ëntchi Këneke Kälarakan Uyräm, 1925, ii and 118 pp., 3000 cop. [Chu 1 Cyr; NN] 936

Zaytsev, E. *Komsomol yalkhus'aystvintche ës'lessi.* Moscow: SSSR-ti Khaläkhsen Tëp Istattëlstvi, 1928, 65 pp., 2000 cop. [Chu 1 Cyr; NN] 937

Zorin, B. *Kherlë s'arän vaye mënre.* Moscow: SSSR-ti Khaläkhsen Tëp Istattëlstvi, 1928, 36 pp., 2000 cop. [Chu 1 Cyr; NN] 938

History

Anutchtchän, T. N. *Etem yäkhë ieple pus'lansa kayni.* Cheboksary: Tchävash Opläs'entchi Këneke Kälarakan Uyräm, 1925, 108 pp., 6000 cop. [Chu 1 Cyr; NN] 939

History

Gremyăttskiy, M. *S'ïn mashshinä.* Moscow: SSSR-ti Khaläkhsen Tëp Istattëlstvi, 1927, 95 pp., 3000 cop. [Chu 1 Cyr; CStH, NN] 940

Kovalenski, M. N. *Ras's'ëy istoriyë.* Cheboksary: Tchävash Respuplëkëntchi Këneke Kälarakan Uyräm, 1926, 119 pp., 5000 cop. [Chu 1 Cyr; NN] 941

Kudryăvskiy, L'. *Maltankhi s'ïnsem yeple purănni.* Cheboksary: Tchävash Opläs'ëntchi Këneke Kälarakan Uyräm, 1925, 89 pp., 6000 cop. [Chu 1 Cyr; NN] 942

Lenin s'intchen: Unän purănas'ëne ës'ësene shkulta asänsa irtterni. Cheboksary: Tchävash Këneki Uyrämë, 1927, 63 pp., 6000 cop. [Chu 1 Cyr; NN] 943

M. V. Frunze. Moscow: SSSR-ti Khaläkhsen Tëp Istattëlstvi, 1925, 24 pp., 2000 cop. [Chu 1 Cyr; NN] 944

Mikhail Pavlovitch Tomski. n.p., Izdanie Chuvashprofsoveta, 1928, 21 pp., 3000 cop. [Chu 1 Cyr; NN] 945

Stalin. Moscow: SSSR-ti Khaläkhsen Tëp Istattëlstvi, 1930, 95 pp., 3000 cop. [Chu 1 Cyr; NN] 946

Vartin, I. *Ras's'eyri komunissen parttin këske istoriyë.* Cheboksary: Tchävash Oplas'ëntchi Këneke Kälarakan Uyräm, 1925, 36 pp., 3000 cop. [Chu 1 Cyr; NN] 947

Volosevich, V. *Pëtëm soyusri komunissen (pol'sheviksen) parttin tchi këske istoriyë.* Moscow: SSSR-ti Khalakhsen Tëp Istattelstvi, 1929, 195 pp., 4000 cop. [Chu 1 Cyr; NN] 948

Zinov'ev, G. *Ras's'eyri komunissen (pol'sheviksen) parttin istoriyë.* Moscow: Tsentral'noe Izdatel'stvo Narodov, SSSR, 1924, 154 pp., 3000 cop. [Chu 1 Cyr; CStH, NN] 949

Law

Gurov, P. Yă.; Lyŭtovskiy, N. A. *Värman sakkupë.* Moscow: n.p., 1924, 48 pp., 2000 cop. [Chu 1 Cyr; NN] 950

Mukhitdinova, E. *Sovet vlas'ë yäla tëlëshpe pulakan ayäplakhsempe mënle këreshet.* Moscow: SSSR-ti Khaläkhsen Tëp Istattelstvi, 1930, 63 pp., 3000 cop. [Chu 1 Cyr; NN) 951

RSFSR 1926-mësh s'ulta kälarnä ukolovnäy koteks. Cheboksary: Tchävash Respuplëkën Yus'titsi Khaläkh Komissariatchë Kälarna, 1928, 86 pp., 3000 cop. [Chu 1 Cyr; NN] 952

Social Organization

Akakkäv, Leonit. *"Volont't'or" komunän purnäs'ë*. Cheboksary: Tchävash Këneki Uyrämë, 1930, 15 pp., 10000 cop. [Chu 1 Cyr; NN] 953
Akkimäv, V. *Khërlë khëres yal khushshintche*. Cheboksary: RKhKh Ushkänën Tchävash Komittetchë, 1929, 30 pp., 1100 cop. [Chu 1 Cyr; NN] 954
Anisov, Tukhtar. *Yas'lësempe konsul'tatsisem*. Cheboksary: Tchävash Këneki Uyrämë, 1926, 24 pp., 3000 cop. [Chu 1 Cyr; NN] 955
Fateyëva, A. *Tchëtchë atchine pakhsa üsteressi s'intchen*. Cheboksary: Tchävash Respuplëkëntchi Këneke Kälarakan Uyräm, 1926, 29 pp., 5000 cop [Chu 1 Cyr; NN] 956
Geshelina, L. *Atchana s'ïvläkhlä apat s'iterër*: Moscow: SSSR-ti Khaläkhsen Tëp Istattëlstvi, 1929, 22 pp., 2000 cop. [Chu 1 Cyr; NN] 957
Israilit, E. *Atchapätcha väyyipe ës'ë*. Cheboksary: S'utës' Komissariatche, 1929, 20 pp., 2000 cop. [Chu 1 Cyr; NN] 958
Khëraräm telekatchësen pukhavësene irttermelli plan-prokrammä. Cheboksary: Tchävash Këneki Uyrämë, 1926, 52 pp., 3000 cop. [Chu 1 Cyr; NN] 959
Khrestchen irëklëkhëshen: Pansempe khrestchensem. Cheboksary: Tchävash Respuplëkëntchi Këneke Kälarakan Uyräm, 1926, 58 pp., 3000 cop. [Chu 1 Cyr; NN] 960
Kolkhossentchi s'ullakhi yas'lësem. Cheboksary: Tchävash Këneki Uyrämë, 1930, 80 pp., 3100 cop. [Chu 1 Cyr; NN] 961
Koptev, N. *Kulaksene klasë pëkh pëteressi s'intchen mën pëlmelle*. Moscow: SSSR-ti Khaläkhsen Tëp Istattëlstvi, 1930, 38 pp., 5000 cop. [Chu 1 Cyr; NN] 962
Korokhkhäv, K. *Khëraräma tchuraläkhran khätarassi*. Cheboksary: Tchävash Këneki Uyrämë, 1926, 59 pp., 5000 cop. [Chu 1 Cyr; NN] 963
Kulisher-Buntsel'man, N. *Atchasene mënshën khëneme vars'ma, iatlama yuramast'*. Moscow: SSSR-ti Khaläkhsen Tëp Istattëlstvi, n.d., 22 pp., 2000 cop. [Chu 1 Cyr; NN] 964
Lipilin, I. P. *Sovet vlas'ë s'ënë puränäs' yeple tavat*. Moscow:

SSSR-ti Khaläkhsen Tëp Istattëlstvi, 1928, iv and 148 pp., 3000 cop. [Chu 1 Cyr; NN] 965

Mayzel', I. *Atchasene tchirsentchen yeple sïkhlamalla.* Moscow: SSSR-ti Khaläkhsen Tëp Istattëlstvi, 1929, 25 pp., 2000 cop. [Chu 1 Cyr; NN] 966

Romanova, E. *Sïvläkha sïkhlassi.* Cheboksary: Tchävash Respup. Këneke Kälarakan Uyräm, 1926, 80 pp., 10000 cop. [Chu 1 Cyr; NN] 967

S'amräk natturalissempe vësen ës'ësem. Moscow: SSSR-ti Khaläkhsen Tëp Istattëlstvi, 1929, 53 pp., 2000 cop. [Chu 1 Cyr; NN] 968

Sergeev, F. N. *Klassen këreshëvën istoriyë.* Moscow: SSSR-ti Khaläkhsen Tëp Istattelstvi, 1929, iv and 276 pp., 2000 cop. [Chu 1 Cyr; NN] 969

Sifëlëspe tchirle s'ïnän men astumalla. Cheboksary: Khaläkh Sïvläkh Komissariatche, n.d., 8 pp., 10000 cop. [Chu 1 Cyr; NN] 970

Surovtsev, A. *Atcha ploshtchatki mën väl, äna mënle tumalla.* Moscow: SSSR-ti Khaläkhsen Tëp Istattëlstvi, 1928, 7 pp., 2000 cop. [Chu 1 Cyr; NN] 971

Suyev, Këterni. *Khërarä̈m puläshu komittetëntche.* Cheboksary: Tchävash Këneki Uyrämë, 1926, 56 pp., 3000 cop. [Chu 1 Cyr; NN] 972

Tchävash khërarä̈me ës'lë viränsentche. Cheboksary: Tchävash Këneki Uyrämë, 1927, 43 pp., 2000 cop. [Chu 1 Cyr; NN] 973

Tchertantsëv, P. *Patraksempe këtüs'ësen ëlëkkhipe khal'khi purnäs'ë.* Cheboksary: Yalkhus'aläkhne Värman Ës'ëntche Ës'lekensen Soyusën Tchävash Paye Kälarnä, 1929, 60 pp., 3000 cop. [Chu 1 Cyr; NN] 974

Yal sovetne suylanä khërarämän mën ës'lese tämalla? Kazan: Izdanie Orgotdela TTsIKa, 1927, 32 pp., 500 cop. [Chu 1 Cyr; NN] 975

Zinov'ev, G. *Ës'lekensempe khrestchensem.* Moscow: Tsentral'noe Izdatel'stvo Narodov Soiuza SSR, 1925, 52 pp., 3000 cop. [Chu 1 Cyr; NN] 976

Zorina, A. *Atcha pakhtchi mën väl, äna mënle tumalla.* Moscow: SSSR-ti Khaläkhsen Tëp Istattëlstvi, 1928, 14 pp., 2000 cop. [Chu 1 Cyr; NN] 977

Language

Ashmarin, N. I. *Tchävash sämakhësen këneki.* 14 vols. Cheboksary: Chuvashkoe Gosudarstvennoe Izdatel'stvo, 1928–1937, I 335 pp., II iv and 230 pp., III 363 pp., IV 352 pp. [CtY, NN], V 420 pp. [CStH, CtY, NN], VI 320 pp., VII 335 pp., VIII 355 pp., IX 319 pp., X 296 pp., XI 343 pp., XII 320 pp., XIII 320 pp., XIV 335 pp. [NN], each 3100 cop. [Chu 1 Cyr] 978

Vanerkkë. *Chävash chëlkhiyën orfokrafi slovarë.* Cheboksary: Tchävash Këneki Uyrämë, 1926, 135 pp., 6000 cop. [Chu 1 Cyr; NN] 979

Vanerkke, N. *Tchävashla s'ïrassi: Pravëläsempe orfokrafi slovarë.* Cheboksary: Tchävash Këneki Uyrämë, 1929, 167 pp., 6000 cop. [Chu 1 Cyr; NN] 980

Vanerkke. *Yut tchëlkhesentchen khutshännä sämakhsen petchek slovarë.* Cheboksary: Tchävash Këneki Uyrämë, 1924, 112 pp., 6000 cop. [Chu 1 Cyr; NN] 981

Zolotnitskii, N. I. *Kornevoi chuvashsko-russkii slovar'.* Kazan: Imperatorskii Universitet, 1875, 279 pp., n.c. [Chu 1 Cyr; CtY] 982

Literature

Alentey. *Pirën sävä.* Cheboksary: Tchävash Pisatëlësen "Kanash" Soyuse, 1925, 31 pp., 2000 cop. [Chu 1 Cyr; NN] 983

⟨Andersen⟩. *Kävak mäy shaptchak yurri.* Cheboksary: Respuplëkri Tchävash Këneki Kälarakan Uyräm, 1924, 26 pp., 3000 cop. [Chu 1 Cyr; NN] 984

Ashmarin, N. K. *Vattisem kalanä sämakhsem.* Cheboksary: Tchävash Oplas'entchi Këneke Kälarakan Uyräm, 1925, 56 pp., 3000 cop. [Chu 1 Cyr; NN] 985

Auslentër. *Vët-shaksem: Pëtchek atchasem val'l'i s'ïrnä kalavsem.* Cheboksary: Tchävash Këneki Uyrämë, 1927, 38 pp., 3000 cop. [Chu 1 Cyr; NN] 986

Chekhov, A. P. *Khäravs'ä pal'l'a: Khula khïs'ëntche, tëttëmlëkh pëteret.* Cheboksary: Respuplëkri Tchävash Këneki Kälarakan Uyräm, 1924, 43 pp., 3000 cop. [Chu 1 Cyr; NN] 987

Chekhov, A. P. *Tipë s'ïrmara*. Cheboksary: Tchävash Respuplëkëntchi Këneke Kälarakan Uyram, 1926, 74 pp., 3000 cop. [Chu 1 Cyr; NN] 988
Danilov, M. (Tchaltun). *Kalavsem*. Moscow: SSSR-ti Khaläkhsen Tëp Istattëlstvi, 1930, 88 pp., 3000 cop. [Chu 1 Cyr; NN] 989
Danilov, M. *Taykara*. 4 paylä, 5 karttinlä tramä. Moscow: SSSR-ti Khaläkhsen Tëp Istattëlstvi, 1929, 22 pp., 2000 cop. [Chu 1 Cyr; NN] 990
Garin, N. G. (Mikhaylovskiy). *Sarpike*. Väyä kalavë. Cheboksary: Tchävash Opläs'ëntchi Këneke Kälarakan Uyram, 1924, 59 pp., 3000 cop. [Chu 1 Cyr; NN] 991
Goryăchii, A. *Khëraräm s'ënterëve*. Cheboksary: Tchävash Respuplëkëntchi Këneke Kälarakan Uyräm, 1926, 44 pp., 5000 cop. [Chu 1 Cyr; NN] 992
Inti tchikkintche. Cheboksary: Tchävash Këneki Uyrämë, 1929, 47 pp., 2000 cop. [Chu 1 Cyr; NN] 993
Khutar. *Khura tar*. Säväsem. Moscow: SSSR-ti Khaläkhsen Tëp Istattëlstvi, 1930, 27 pp., 3000 cop. [Chu 1 Cyr; NN] 994
Korkki, M. *S'amräk ëmërëm*. Cheboksary: Tchävash Këneki Uyrämë, 1929, 166 pp., 5000 cop. [Chu 1 Cyr; NN] 995
Kor'kki, Maks'ämë. *Tchëlkash*. Kalav. Cheboksary: Tchävash Këneki Uyrämë, 1924, 80 pp., 3000 cop. [Chu 1 Cyr; NN] 996
Küko, Viktär. *93-mësh s'ul*. Roman. Cheboksary: Tchavash Respuplëkëntchi Këneke Kälarakan Uyräm, 1926, 80 pp., 3000 cop. [Chu 1 Cyr; NN] 997
Kutyina, V. M. *Viruk komuniskä*. Cheboksary: Tchävash Respuplëkëntchi Këneke Kälarakan Uyräm, 1926, 67 pp., 3000 cop. [Chu 1 Cyr; NN] 998
Lashman. *Savni yentchëkë*. Poemä. Cheboksary: Tchävash Këneki Uyrämë, 1926, 19 pp., 3000 cop. [Chu 1 Cyr; NN] 999
Leventti, Shus'. *Yüs's'i takäntartchë*. Tävatä aktällä tramä. Cheboksary: Tchävash Këneki Uyrämë, 1927, 72 pp., 1500 cop. [Chu 1 Cyr; NN] 1000
Lippinä, N. *Minkkä kurpunë*. Kalav. Cheboksary: Tchävash Këneki Uyrämë, 1927, 47 pp., 3000 cop. [Chu 1 Cyr; NN] 1001
Lunkkevetch, V. *Aslatipe s'is'ëm*. Cheboksary: Tchävash Opläs'ëntchi Këneke Kälarakan Uyräm, 1923, 39 pp., 3000 cop. [Chu 1 Cyr; NN] 1002

Maksimov, S. *Revol'utsi yurrisem.* Moscow: Tsentral'noe Izdatel'stvo Narodov SSSR, 1926, 34 pp., 4000 cop. [Chu 1 Cyr; NN] 1003

Maksimov, S. M. *Tchävash këvvisem.* Moscow: Tsentral'noe Izdatel'stvo Narodov SSSR, 1924, 87 pp., 4000 cop. [Chu 1 Cyr; CStH, NN] 1004

Maksimov-Koshkinskiy, I. S. 1. *Uy-tchüka.* Prolokla, 4 paylä tramä. 2. *Yutra.* 1 paylä kometi. Moscow: SSSR-ti Khaläkhsen Tëp Istattëlstvi, 1928, 77 pp., 2000 cop. [Chu 1 Cyr; NN] 1005

Mësken Antun. Cheboksary: Tchävash Opläs'ëntchi Këneke Kälarakan Uyräm, 1924, 124 pp., 3000 cop. [Chu 1 Cyr; CStH, NN] 1006

Neveräv, A. *Tashkent khuli tulakh khula.* Kalav. Cheboksary: Tchävash Këneke Uyrämë, 1927, 79 pp., 3000 cop. [Chu 1 Cyr; NN] 1007

Neverov, A. *Pëtchik atchasem val'l'i s'ïrna kalavsem.* Moscow: SSSR-ti Khaläkhsen Tëp Istattelstvi, n.d., 31 pp., 3000 cop. [Chu 1 Cyr; CStH, NN] 1008

Perovskaia, L. *Mishka.* Moscow: SSSR-ti Khaläkhsen Tëp Istattëlstvi, 1928, 28 pp., 2000 cop. [Chu 1 Cyr; NN] 1009

Petrov, F.; Tsvetkov, M. *Tëne khirës'.* Ufa: Bashgiz, 1930, 85 pp., 2000 cop. [Chu 1 Cyr; NN] 1010

Polonskayă, Elizaveta. *Tchassi.* Moscow: SSSR-ti Khaläkhsen Tëp Istattëlstvi, 1928, 24 pp., 2000 cop. [Chu 1 Cyr; NN] 1011

Polorussäv, N. *Kushakpa avtan.* Atcha-patcha väyyi. Cheboksary: Tchävash Respuplëkëntchi Këneke Kälarakan Uyräm, 1926, 19 pp., 3000 cop. [Chu 1 Cyr; NN] 1012

Polorussov, N. I. *Shelepi sävvisem.* 1mësh tom. Cheboksary: Tchävash Këneki Uyrame, 1926, 167 pp., 3000 cop. [Chu 1 Cyr; NN] 1013

Potyatchtchëv, S. *Vïs'äkhakansem.* Cheboksary: Tchävash Respuplëkentchi Këneke Kälarakan Uyram, 1926, 28 pp., 3000 cop. [Chu 1 Cyr; NN] 1014

Samoyskiy, P. *Ulput salamatchë.* Cheboksary: Tchävash Këneke Uyrämë, 1926, 55 pp., 3000 cop. [Chu 1 Cyr; NN] 1015

S'emenäv, L. *Tchärsär t'ikha tëplë khres'tchen.* Cheboksary: Tchavash Opläs'entchi Këneke Kälarakan Uyräm, 1924, 36 pp., 3000 cop. [Chu 1 Cyr; NN] 1016

Semenov, T. S. *Mänastirte.* Ikë paylä kometi. Moscow: SSSR-ti Khaläkhsen Tëp Istattëlstvi, 1927, 46 pp., 1000 cop. [Chu 1 Cyr; NN] 1017

S'ënë khunav. Kalavsen pukhkhi. Cheboksary: Tchavash Keneke Uyrämë, 1929, 194 pp., 3000 cop. [Chu 1 Cyr; NN] 1018

S'ënë yuräsem. Cheboksary: Khaläkhän S'utes' Komissariatche Kälarnä, 1927, 35 pp., 3000 cop. [Chu 1 Cyr; NN] 1019

S'ër s'intchi turäsem. Cheboksary: Tchävash Opläs'entchi Këneke Kälarakan Uyräm, 1925, 82 pp., 3000 cop. [Chu 1 Cyr; NN] 1020

Serafimovich. *Khëraram yale.* Cheboksary: Tchävash Respuplëkëntchi Këneke Kälarakan Uyram, 1925, 15 pp., 3000 cop. [Chu 1 Cyr; CStH, NN] 1021

Shchedrin, S. *Për mushik: petchtchen ikë kënerala tarantarsa usrani s'intchen kalani: Äslä ïrash petri.* Cheboksary: Respuplëkri Tchävash Këneki Kälarakan Uyram, 1924, 38 pp., 3000 cop. [Chu 1 Cyr; NN] 1022

Shelepi s'ïrnisen pukhkhi. Cheboksary: Tchävash Këneki Uyrämë, 1928, 70 pp., 2000 cop. [Chu 1 Cyr; NN] 1023

Sivatchtchev, M. *Sarä shuyttan.* Poves'. Cheboksary: Tchävash Respuplëkentchi Këneke Kälarakan Uyräm, 1926, 231 pp., 5000 cop. [Chu 1 Cyr; NN] 1024

Timukhkha, Khëvetërë; Timofeev, F. T. *Tchävash s'ïrassi.* Cheboksary: Tchävash Këneki Uyrämë, 1926, 43 pp., 5000 cop. [Chu 1 Cyr; NN] 1025

Tisker kayaksem khushshintche. Upa. Cheboksary: Respuplëkri Tchävash Këneki Kälarakan Uyrämë, 1924, 96 pp., 3000 cop. [Chu 1 Cyr; NN] 1026

Torokhkhäv, P. *Pet'uk ilyitch patne kayni.* Cheboksary: Tchävash Këneki Uyrämë, 1926, 51 pp., 3000 cop. [Chu 1 Cyr; NN] 1027

Torokhkhäv, Paväle. *S'ënë puränäs'.* Kalav. Moscow: SSSR-ti Khaläkhsen Tep Istattëlstvi, 1927, 22 pp., 4000 cop. [Chu 1 Cyr; CStH, NN] 1028

Trubina, M. *Khërlë kalstuk.* Atchasem val'l'i kalav. Cheboksary: Tchävash Respup. Këneke Kälarakan Uyram, 1925, 23 pp., 3000 cop. [Chu 1 Cyr; NN] 1029

Trupina, M. *Atchasem valli s'ïrnä yumakhsem.* Cheboksary: Tchävash Respuplëkëntchi Këneke Kälarakan Uyräm, 1925, 32 pp., 3000 cop. [Chu 1 Cyr; NN] 1030

Trupina, Markhvi. *Marine*. Kalav. Cheboksary: Tchävash Këneki Uyrämë, 1929, 24 pp., 3000 cop. [Chu 1 Cyr; NN] 1031

Tümër, V. V. *Pus'lamësh 1905–6 s'*. 3 paylä piessä. Cheboksary: Tchävash Respuplekentchi Këneke Kälarakan Uyräm, 1926, 40 pp., 3000 cop. [Chu 1 Cyr; NN] 1032

Ulittën, M. N. *Vis'ë-pussa sut tuni*. Për paylä pyessä. Cheboksary: Tchävash Respuplëkëntchi Këneke Kälarakan Uyram, 1925, 91 pp., 4000 cop. [Chu 1 Cyr; NN] 1033

Värman khalapë. Cheboksary: Tchävash Respuplëkëntchi Këneke Kälarakan Uyräm, 1925, 19 pp., 3000 cop. [Chu 1 Cyr; NN] 1034

Vas'ankka, N. *Khastarläkh: Komsomol yurri-sävvisem*. Cheboksary: Tchävash Këneke Uyrämë, 1926, 56 pp., 3000 cop. [Chu 1 Cyr; NN] 1035

Veresayëv, V. V. *Khïpalantchäk*. Cheboksary: Tchävash Respuplëkëntchi Këneke Kälarakan Uyram, 1926, 11 pp., 3000 cop. [Chu 1 Cyr; NN] 1036

Viktorov, I. *Yalti këvësam*. Moscow: Tsentral'noe Izdatel'stvo Narodov SSSR, 1925, 39 pp., 3000 cop. [Chu 1 Cyr; NN] 1037

Vladimirskiy, V. *Savät atchi mikul*. Moscow: SSSR-ti Khaläkhsen Tëp Istattëlstvi, 1927, 27 pp., 4000 cop. [Chu 1 Cyr; NN] 1038

Volkkäv, M. A. *S'ënë tchirkü*. Cheboksary: Tchävash Respuplëkëntchi Këneke Kälarakan Uyräm, 1926, 18 pp., 5000 cop. [Chu 1 Cyr; NN] 1039

Yevkrafäva, P. N. *Irtnë kunsem*. Cheboksary: Tchävash Këneki Uyrämë, 1929, 127 pp., 3000 cop. [Chu 1 Cyr; NN] 1040

Yuman, M. *Ukaltcha kassi*. 4 paylä tramä. Cheboksary: Tchavash Këneke Uyrämë, 1927, 96 pp., 3000 cop. [Chu 1 Cyr; NN] 1041

Yurkkin, P. *Vërenteken*. 3 paylä, 4 karttinällä eppiläklä tramä. Cheboksary: Tchävash Këneki Uyrämë, 1928, 48 pp., 3000 cop. [Chu 1 Cyr; NN] 1042

Music

Khorovyia tserkovnye piesnopieniia na chuvashkom iazykie. Vyp I: *Liturgiia, molebnyia pieniia, vienchaniia i panikhida*. Kazan: Prav. Miss. Obshch. Tip. Imp. Universiteta, 1893, 40 pp., n.c. [Chu 1 Cyr; MH] 1043

Bïstrov, K. *Tchävash khushshintche tëne khirës' propakantä tavakan krushoksem val'l'i s'ïrnä prokrammä.* Moscow: SSSR-ti Khaläkhsen Tëp Istattëlstvi, 1927, 22 pp., 1500 cop. [Chu 1 Cyr; CStH, NN] 1044

Bïstrov, K. *Tura pur-i, s'uk-i?* I. Moscow: Tsentral'noe Izdatel'stvo Narodov SSSR, 1925, 46 pp., 3000 cop. [Chu 1 Cyr; NN] 1045

Bïstrov, K. *Turä pur-i, s'uk-i?* II. Moscow: Tsentral'noe Izdatel'stvo Narodov SSSR, 1925, 30 pp., 3000 cop. [Chu 1 Cyr; NN] 1046

Bïstrov, K. *Turä pur-i, s'uk-i?* III. Moscow: Tsentral'noe Izdatel'stvo Narodov SSSR, 1925, 63 pp., 3000 cop. [Chu 1 Cyr; NN] 1047

Ey turä, s'ïläkhämshën esë mana ku tëntcherekh asaplanter lutchtchë. Kazan: Prav. Miss. Obshch., Tip. Imp. Universiteta, 1893, 12 pp., n.c. [Chu 1 Cyr; MH] 1048

Gorev, Mikh. *Molepën-i traktär-i?* Moscow: SSSR-ti Khaläkhsen Tëp Istattëlstvi, 1930, 14 pp., 4000 cop. [Chu 1 Cyr; NN] 1049

Innokentïy. *Ukazanïe puti v tsarstvïe nebesnoe.* 1. *Tsarstvo nebesnoe, na chuvashkom iazykie,* 18 pp.; 2. *Zhizn' i stradanyia Ïisusa Khrista, na chuvashskom iazykie,* 16 pp. Kazan: Prav. Miss. Obshch. Tip. Imp. Universiteta, 1893, n.c. [Chu 1 Cyr; MH] 1050

Ioganson, O. *Atcha mënshën tëshmëmlenet.* Moscow: SSSR-ti Khaläkhsen Tëp Istattëlstvi, 1930, 22 pp., 3000 cop. [Chu 1 Cyr; NN] 1051

Kutyăshov, S. *Tëne khirës' proppakantä tävassi.* Moscow: SSSR-ti Khaläkhsen Tëp Istattëlstvi, 1928, 52 pp., 1000 cop. [Chu 1 Cyr; NN] 1052

Mukhtav yurrisen këneki. Simbirsk: Tip. I. S. Khapkova, 1901, 155 pp., n.c. [Chu 1 Cyr; MH] 1053

Nastavlenie o khristïanskom vospitanïi dietey. Kazan: Prav. Miss. Obshch., Tip. Imper. Universiteta, 1893, 23 pp., n.c. [Chu 1 Cyr; MH] 1054

Tchukhän puränakan s'ïnta khäyne s'ïväkh s'ïnsene ïräläkh tuma pultarat'. Kazan: Izdanie Pravoslavnago Missionerskago Obshchestva, 1897, 15 pp., n.c. [Chu 1 Cyr; DLC] 1055

Tëne khirës' vëreneken krushoksen këneki. Moscow: SSSR-ti Khaläkhsen Tëp Istattëlstvi, 1929, 244 pp., 3000 cop. [Chu 1 Cyr; NN] 1056

Tri poucheniia iz tvorenii izhe vo sviatykh ottsa nashego tikhona zadonskago na chuvashskom iazykie. Kazan: Prav. Miss. Obshch., Tip. Imp. Universiteta, 1893, 15 pp., n.c. [Chu 1 Cyr; MH] 1057

Yaroslavskiy, Em. *Pipli këneki ënenekensempë enenmennisem valli.* Cheboksary: Tchavash Oplas'entchi Keneke Kälärkan Uyräm, 1925, 87 pp., 5000 cop. [Chu 1 Cyr; NN] 1058

Ileri (Simferopol) 1926: 4; 1927: 11–12; 1928: 2, 5, 13/14/15, 33/34/35; 1929: 1, 3, 5, 7, 9, 17; 1930: 2–4. [Crim 2 Arab, 3 Lat; NN] 1059

Köz aydïn: Yangï elifba mefkuresïnï neshr eden haftalïq zhurnal (n.p.) 1928: 7, 9, 12, 15, 19, 22, 26–27, 35, 40; 1929: 2, 6, 8; 1930: 1–2, 4, 14/15. [Crim 3 Lat; NN] 1060

Oqu ishleri (Aq Mesjid) 1926: 6/7 [CStH]; 1927: 2/3; 1928: 2, 5, 8; 1929: 8/9/10 [NN]. [Crim 2 Arab, 3 Lat] 1061

Qïrïm töpraq ishleri khalq komisarlïghï Qïrïm nebatatï qorchalar ülke stansiyasïnïng khaberleri (n.p.) 1930: 7. [Crim 3 Lat; NN] 1062

Qrim mukhtariyetli sosyalist shuralar jümhuriyeti merkezi ijra qomitesi byulleteni (Aq Mesjid) 1928: 2 ⟨supplement⟩, 3. [Crim 2 Arab; NN] 1063

Qrïm mukhtariyetli sotsialist shuralar jümhuriyeti ishchi köylü hukümetining qanunnama ve emrleri jïyïntïghï (Aq Mesjid) 1929: 1. [Crim 3 Lat; DLC] 1064

Qutub-Zada, V. A. *Kolkhoz dïvar gazetalarïna yardamchï.* Simferopol: Qïrïm Devlet Neshriyatï, 1930, 39 pp., 1500 cop. [Crim 3 Lat; NN] 1065

Tatarja kitablarïng qataloghï. Ikinji qatalugh. Aq Mesjid: Qrim Devlet Neshriyatï, 1928, 20 pp., 1500 cop. [Crim 2 Arab; NN] 1066

Terjuman (Bakhchisarai) 1883: 1; 1894: 1–48; 1895: 2–50; 1901: 1–13, 15–42, 45–48; 1902: 1, 3–5, 7–44, 46–49; 1903: 1–50; 1904: 1–80, 82–104; 1905: 1–6, 9–11, 13–15, 17–18, 21–22, 25–28, 30–31, 38–39, 41, 43–78, 80–83, 85–104, 106–110; 1906: 1–11, 13–52, 54–62, 66–70, 72–77, 79–90, 92–94, 96–101, 108–127, 129–132, 136–138; 1907: 23, 31–33, 35–47, 50–62, 64–75; 1908: 3–6, 9–22, 64–65, 67–71, 74–76, 78–79; 1909: 1–2, 4–5, 9–11, 13–16, 18–20, 22–48, 50–52; 1912: 8, 24, 41, 43; 1913: 6–8, 32–34, 36–40, 52, 55, 57–59, 61–62, 66, 68, 72–74, 76–78, 81–82, 85–87, 89–96, 104–135, 137–139, 141, 143–144, 150–154, 157–163, 171, 173–174, 179–208, 225, 227–228, 232–252, 254–256, 262–265, 268–270, 272–273, 278–281;

CRIMEAN TATAR General

1914: 1–2, 4–9, 15–18, 24–25, 48–58, 60–64, 66–68, 70–73, 75–78, 80–85, 87–88, 80, 92–105, 107–108, 110–113, 115, 117–122, 129–133, 135–137, 139–152, 160–163; 1915: 124–128, 184–189, 198–202. [Crim 1 Arab; NNC*] 1067

CRIMEAN TATAR Social Sciences

Anthropology

Il'in, M. *Evingizning sizleri: Ev ichinde kezinti.* Simferopol: Qïrïm Devlet Neshriyatï, 1930, 48 pp., 3000 cop. [Crim 3 Lat; NN] 1068

Economics

Besh yïllïqnïng uchinji senesi ichun kureshge. 1. *V.K.P.(b)M.K.ning murajiatnamesi.* 2. *Qïrïm oblast kömitetining qararï.* 3. *V.S.S.P.S.-nïng qararï.* 4. *K.S.P.S.-nïng murajiatnamesi.* 5. *V.S.S.P.S.-nïng udarnik küni haqqïnda qararï.* Simferopol: Qïrïm Devlet Neshriyatï, 1930, 35 pp., 3000 cop. [Crim 3 Lat; NN] 1069

Grinko, G. *Besh seneden songra shuralar ittifaqï.* Simferopol: Qïrïm Devlet Neshriyatï, n.d., 68 pp., 2000 cop. [Crim 3 Lat; NN] 1070

Kolkhozlarda idare ishleri ve emekni teshkil etüv esas qaideleri. Simferopol: Qrïm Kolkhozsayuzlar Sayuzïnïng Neshri, 1929, 45 pp., 3000 cop. [Crim 3 Lat; NN] 1071

Murtaza, Lutfi. *Mektebde balalar qo'operatifi teshkili ichun yol kosterkich.* n.p.: Baghcha Saray Huner ve Sanai' Mektebi Basma Khanesi, 1925, 24 pp., 1000 cop. [Crim 2 Arab; NN] 1072

Qasaba (poselok) koy khuzaystvasï istihsal zakhire tovarishestvasïnïng nizamnamesi. n.p.: n.p., n.d., 6 pp., 1000 cop. [Crim 3 Lat; NN] 1073

Qrïmi okrenmek ichun ish kitabï. Aq Mesjid: Qrïm Devlet Neshriyatï, 1927, 295 pp., 2500 cop. [Crim 2 Arab; NN] 107

---

*Microfilm

Economics

Qrïmnïng istatistigh ve iqtiṣadi atlasï. Vïpusk 1. Simferopol: Izdanie Krïmstat Upravleniia i Krïmizdata, 1922, 50 pp., n.c. [Crim. 2 Arab; NNC] 1075

Reyzin; Pakhomov; Kudrof. *Kolkhozjï-teshkilatjïgha yol köstergich.* Simferopol: Qrïm Devlet Neshriyatï, 1930, 105 pp., 2000 cop. [Crim 3 Lat; NN] 1076

SSSR Khalq maliye komisarlïghïndan "Besh senelïknï-dört yïlda" zayomïnï dargatuv kampaniyasï ichün köy shuralarïna pamiyatka. Simferopol: n.p., 1930, 5 pp., 2000 cop. [Crim 3 Lat; NN] 1077

Shutyayef, P. *Yangï köy ichün yangï köy khozaystvasï naloghï.* Simferopol: Qrïm Devlet Neshriyatï, n.p., 100 pp., 3000 cop. [Crim 3 Lat; NN] 1078

Sosiyalizm müsabaqasï haqqïnda. Simferopol: Qrïm Devlet Neshriyatï, 1929, 35 pp., 5000 cop. [Crim 3 Lat; NN] 1079

Toropchï, ʿA. *Köyli azbarï ve topraq taqsïmï.* Simferopol: Qrïm Devlet Neshriyatï, 1928, 50 pp., 2000 cop. [Crim 2 Arab; NN] 1080

Troyanovski, A. A. *Bir turli köyli virkisi nichün kerekdir ve av ishbu 1926–27 senesi qrïmda nasli ulajaq?* Aq Mesjid: Qrïm Ḥukumet Neshriyatï, 1926, 44 pp., 1500 cop. [Crim 2 Arab; NN] 1081

Varonin. *Köyü sosiyalizm esasïnda yangïdan quruv.* Simferopol: Qrïm Devlet Neshriyatï, 1929, 34 pp., 2000 cop. [Crim 3 Lat; NN] 1082

Education

ʿAbdulla, Meḥmed. *Tabiʿat dersleri.* Üchinji kitab. Aq Mesjid: Qrïm Ḥükumet Neshriyatï, 1926, 151 pp., 4000 cop. 1083 [Crim 2 Arab; NN]

ʿAbdulla, Meḥmed. *Tabiʿat derslerining usul tedrisi ḥaqqïnda: Fenni kezintiler ve laboratorya isherli.* Aq Mesjid: Qrïm Ḥükumet Neshriyatï, 1925, 83 pp., 1000 cop. [Crim 2 Arab; NN] 1084

ʿAbdulla, Raḥmed. *Tabiʿat dersleri.* Birinji kitab. Aq Mesjid: Qïrïm Meʿarïf Qomisarlïghï Tarafïndan Basdïrïlmïshdïr, 1926, 178 pp., 5000 cop. [Crim 2 Arab; CStH] 1085

ʿAbdulla, Raḥmed. *Tabiʿat dersleri.* Ikinji kitab. Aq Mesjid: *Qrïm* Ḥükumet Neshriyatï, 1926, 141 pp., 4000 cop. [Crim 2 Arab; CStH] 1086

ʿAbdulla, Raḥmed. *Tabiʿat dersleri.* Üchinji kitab. Aq Mesjid: *Qrïm* Ḥükumet Neshriyatï, 1926, 151 pp., 4000 cop. [Crim 2 Arab; CStH] 1087

Abdurahim, S.; Abdullayef, M. *1nji basmaq mekteblernïng 5nji yïlï ichün oquv ve ish kitabï.* Simferopol: Qrïm Devlet Neshriyatï, 1930, 219 pp., 3000 cop. [Crim 3 Lat; NN] 1088

Bayburtli, Yaḥya'aji. *Elifba.* Bakhchisarai: Hüner ve Sanayïʿ Nefise Teḥnikumi Basmaḥanesi, 1926, 60 pp., n.c. [Crim 2 Arab; NN] 1089

Bayrashevski, ʿUmer. *Mekteb ḥifẓ ṣiḥḥasini.* Aq Mesjid: Qrïm Ḥükumet Neshriyatï, 1920, 82 pp., 1500 cop. [Crim 2 Arab; NN] 1090

Belayef, Y. M.; Lakidi, K. Y.; Levchenko, V. V. *Tabiat-bilgisi haqqïnda ish kitabï VII-nji gruppalar ichün.* Simferopol: Qïrïm Devlet Neshriyatï, 1930, 200 pp., 3000 cop. [Crim 3 Lat; NN] 1091

Berg, M.; Znamenskiy, M.; Popof, J.; Sludskiy, I.; Khvostof, N.; Shchetinin, H. *Riyaziyat ish kitabï altïnjï gruplara makhsus.* Aq Mesjid: Qrïm Devlet Neshriyatï, 1929, 168 pp., 2000 cop. [Crim 3 Lat; NN] 1092

Büyüklerge umumiy bilgi verüv mektebleri (az öqur-yazarlar mektebleri) ichün programma ve usuliy mektüb: Köy ve sheher mektebleri ichün II-nchi qïsïm. Simferopol: Qrïm Devlet Neshriyatï, 1929, 67 pp., 2000 cop. [Crim 3 Lat; NN] 1093

Fradkin, G. A. *Mektebde beynelmilel terbiye.* Simferopol: Qrïm Devlet Neshriyatï, 1929, 89 pp., 2000 cop. [Crim 3 Lat; NN] 1094

Gratsiyanskiy, I. *Riyazïyat derslerinden ish kitabï.* Aq Mesjid: Qrïm Devlet Neshriyatï, 1929, 172 pp., 3000 cop. [Crim 3 Lat; NN] 1095

Ḥasan, ʿÜmer Ḥaji. *Elifbe oqutu usullarï.* Bakhchisarai: Khalq Meʿarïf Qomisarlïghï Neshri, 1926, 70 pp., 2000 cop. [Crim 2 Arab; NN] 109[illegible]

Ignatyef, V.; Okünkof, A.; Sokolof, S. *1-nji dereje tatar mekteblerining II-nji ve III-nji gruplarï ichün tabiat derslerinde yapïlajaq ishler.* Simferopol: Qrïm Devlet Neshriyatï, 1929, 46 pp., 5000 cop. [Crim 3 Lat; NN] 109[illegible]

Jemil, K.; Seit-Khalil, T. *Matematikadan ish kitabï.* Simferopol: Qïrïm Devlet Neshriyatï, 1931, 181 pp., 3000 cop. [Crim 3 Lat; DLC] 109[illegible]

Köylü alifbasï. Ikinji tabʿï. Aq Mesjid: Qrïm Ḥükumet Neshriyatï, 1926, 71 pp., 1000 cop. [Crim 2 Arab; CStH] 109[illegible]

Kurkchi, ʿAbdulla. *Riyaziyat dersleri.* 1nji kitab. Aq Mesjid: Qrïm Ḥükumet Neshriyatï, 1927, 92 pp., 12000 cop. [Crim 2 Arab; NN] 1100

Kurkchi, ʿAbdulla. *Riyaziyat dersleri.* 2nji kitab. Aq Mesjid: Qrïm Ḥükumet Neshriyatï, 1927, 82 pp., 8000 cop. [Crim 2 Arab; CStH] 1101

Kurkchi, ʿAbdulla. *Riyaziyat dersleri.* 3nchi kitab. Aq Mesjid: Qrïm Devlet Neshriyatï, 1927, 78 pp., 8000 cop. [Crim 2 Arab; NN] 1102

Lebedef, P. P. *Khimiya ish kitabï: Sheher Tatar yedi yïllïq mekteblerining 5-nji ve 6-nji oquv yïllar ichün.* Birïnji daire. Simferopol: Qrïm Devlet Neshriyatï, 1929, 133 pp., 3000 cop. [Crim 3 Lat; NN] 1103

Odabash, Ḥ.; Ḥasan, ʿA. Ḥaji. *Turk-tatar tili.* Birinji kitab. Aq Mesjid: Qrïm Ḥükumet Neshriyatï, 1925, 240 pp., 10000 cop. [Crim 2 Arab; CStH] 1104

Obadash, Ḥ.; Khasan, ʿA. Khaji. *Turk-Tatar tili.* Aq Mesjid: Qrïm Meʿarïf Qomisarlïghï Neshri, 1926, 264 pp., 8000 cop. [Crim 2 Arab; NN] 1105

Oktabr bakhshïsï: Rus mekteblerining V-nji gruplarïna makhsus tatar dili ish kitabï. Simferopol: Qrïm Devlet Neshriyatï, 1929, 56 pp., 10000 cop. [Crim 3 Lat; NN] 1106

Shamilef, A. *1-nji basamaq tatar mekteblerining 1-nji senelerïne makhsus til alïshghanlïqlarï ish kitabï.* Simferopol: Qïrïm Devlet Neshriyatï, 1930, 48 pp., 10000 cop. [Crim 3 Lat; NN] 1107

Sheykh Zade, N.; Yunusof, U. *Ilki adïm.* Simferopol: Qïrïm Devlet Neshriyatï, 1930, 72 pp., 15000 cop. [Crim 3 Lat; NN] 1108

Sheykh Zade, N.; Yunusof, Ü. *Ilki adïm elifbesini oqutuvgha makhsus usuliy yol kostergich.* Simferopol: Qïrïm Devlet Neshriyatï, 1930, 33 pp., 1000 cop. [Crim 3 Lat; NN] 1109

Sheykh Zade, N.; Yunusof, U. *Oqu yaz: Ishchi ve köyli elifbasï.* Simferopol: Qrïm Devlet Neshriyatï, 1929, 104 pp., 20000 cop. [Crim 3 Lat; NN] 1110

Sheykh Zade, N.; Yunusof, U. *Yangï adïm.* Simferopol: Qrïm Devlet Neshriyatï, 1928, 100 pp., 25000 cop. [Crim 3 Lat; NN] 1111

Sheykh Zade, N.; Yunusof, U. *Yangï yol.* Simferopol: Qïrïm Devlet Neshriyatï, 1930, 120 pp., 10000 cop. [Crim 3 Lat; NN] 1112

Speranski. Gh. *Köylü ananïng elifbesi.* Aq Mesjid: Qrïm Ḥükumet Neshriyatï, 1920, 31 pp., 3000 cop. [Crim 2 Arab; NN] 1113

Vsevyatskiy, B. V.; Vuchetich, V. N.; Isayef, S. I.; Mikelson, K. M.; Smolin, P. P.; Flörova, E. A.; Yakhontof, A. A. *Tabiat derslerinden ish kitabï.* Simferopol: Qrïm Devlet Neshriyatï, 1929, 170 pp., 3000 cop. [Crim 3 Lat; NN] 1114

Government

Bizim qïzil ordumïz. Aq Mesjid: Qrïm Ḥükumet Neshriyatï, 1926, 52 pp., 3000 cop. [Crim 2 Arab; CStH] 1115

Kerzhentsef, P.; Leontyef. *Leninizem elifbesi. Sheher fïrqa mektebleri ve öz bashïna oquv ichün yardïm.* Aq Mesjid: Qrïm Devlet Neshriyatï, 1928, 278 pp., 3000 cop. [Crim 3 Lat; NN] 1116

Lenin. *Ishche ve köylü birligi.* Simferopol: Qrïm Devlet Neshriyatï, 1929, 76 pp., 2000 cop. [Crim 3 Lat; NN] 1117

Makarof, P. V. *Qrïmda qïzïl partizanlar hareketi.* Simferopol: Qrïm Devlet Neshriyatï, 1928, 53 pp., 2000 cop. [Crim 3 Lat; NN] 1118

Partiyanïng XVI-jï siyezdining qabul etgen qararlarï. Simferopol: Qïrïm Devlet Neshriyatï, 1930, 76 pp., 2000 cop. [Crim 3 Lat; NN] 1119

Punga, Kh. *Muharebe khavfï ve gharb qomshularïmïz.* Aq Mesjid: Qrïm Devlet Neshriyatï, 1928, 24 pp., 3000 cop. [Crim 3 Lat; NN] 1120

Qozlof, F.; Nikolikhin, Ya. *Siyasi bilgi.* Simferopol: Qrïm Devlet Neshriyatï, 1928, 412 pp., 3000 cop. [Crim 2 Arab; NN] 1121

Smirnof, A. *Köy qomsomollarïnïng siyasi qira'at derslerine yardem.* Birinchi kitab. Aq Mesjid: Qrïm Ḥükumet Neshriyatï, 1925, 45 pp., 2000 cop. [Crim 2 Arab; NN] 1122

Smirnof, A. *Köy qomsomollarïnïng siyasi qira'at derslerine yardem.* Ikinji kitab. Aq Mesjid: Qrïm Ḥükumet Neshriyatï, 1925, 38 pp., 2000 cop. [Crim 2 Arab; CStH] 1123

Yelagïn, V. *Inqilab yïllarïnda qrïm tatarlarïnïng milli khayallarï.* Aq Mesjid: Qrïm Ḥükumet Neshriyatï, 1920, 90 pp., 2000 cop. [Crim 2 Arab; NN] 1124

History

Arnu, A. *Kommuna qurbanlarï.* Simferopol: Qrïm Devlet Neshriyatï, 1929, 24 pp., 3000 cop. [Crim 3 Lat; NN] 1125
Bakhanovskaya, Ye. *Khristofor Kolumb.* Simferopol: Qrïm Devlet Neshriyatï, 1929, 36 pp., 3000 cop. [Crim 3 Lat; NN] 1126
Balïch, Ḥ. *Qrïm tatar milli medeniyetining tarikhi muqedderatï.* Bakhchisarai: Baghchasaray Hüner ve Sanayïʻ Nefise Tekhnikumi Basmaḥanesi, 1926, 54 pp., 250 cop. [Crim 2 Arab; NN] 1127
Feliche, Art. *Jems Uatt.* Simferopol: Qïrïm Devlet Neshriyatï, 1930, 60 pp., 3000 cop. [Crim 3 Lat; NN] 1128
Nikolski, P. V. *Baghchasaray medeni tarikhi ekskursiyalar.* Aq Mesjid: Qrïm Khalq Maʻarïf Qomisarlïghïnïng Neshriyatï, 1924, 64 pp., n.c. [Crim 2 Arab; NN] 1129
Ozenbashlï, Aḥmed. *Charlïq ḥakimiyetinde qrïm fajiʻasï yakhud tatar hijretleri.* Aq Mesjid: n.p., 1925, 119 and 30 pp., 4000 cop. [Crim 2 Arab; CStH] 1130
Ulyanova, A. *V. I. Leninning balalïq ve oquv seneleri.* Simferopol: Qrïm Devlet Neshriyatï, n.d., 23 pp., 3000 cop. [Crim 3 Lat; NN] 1131
Vel'iaminov-Zernov, V. V. (ed.). *Qrim yurtina wa ul taraflargha dair bolghan yarligh wa khaṭlar.* St. Petersburg: Akademiia Nauk, 1864, ix and 941 pp., n.c. [Crim 1 Arab; NNC] 1132

Law

Bekirof, ʻA. Zeki. *Khalq maḥkemesi ve proqurorlïq.* Aq Mesjid: Qrïm Ḥükumet Neshriyatï, 1927, 40 pp., 2000 cop. [Crim 2 Arab; DLC] 1133
Mukhtarof, Yaya. *Ehaliye ḥuquqi yardim.* Aq Mesjid: Qrïm Devlet Neshriyatï, 1927, 30 pp., 2000 cop. [Crim 2 Arab; DLC] 1134
Qrïm avtonomiyalï sovet sotsialist respublikasïnïng konstitutsiyasï: Ësas zakonï. Simferopol: Qrïm ASSR Devlet Neshriyatï, 1940, 43 pp., 3000 cop. [Crim 4 Cyr; DLC] 1135

Social Organization

Beden terbiyesi oyunlarï. Aq Mesjid: Qrïm Devlet Neshriyatï, 1928, 40 pp., 1000 cop. [Crim 3 Lat; NN] 1136

Bochagof, A. K. *Deghri yol ayle yaḥud: Faqïr orta ḥalli köyli ve qulak ḥaqqïnda.* Simferopol: Qrïm Devlet Neshriyatï, 1927, 50 pp., 2000 cop. [Crim 2 Arab; NN] 1137

Chapchaqchi, Ḥ.; Mu'edin, Bekir. *Tenasul aghzalarï khastalïqlarï yakhud zohrevi khastalïqlar.* Aq Mesjid: Qrïm Ḥükumet Neshriyatï, 1926, 43 pp., 3000 cop. [Crim 2 Arab; NN] 1138

Kalinin, M.; Krupskaya, N. *Kitlening öz ishküzarlïghïnï qüvvetleshdiriyik.* Simferopol: Qrïm Devlet Neshriyatï, n.d., 20 pp., 2000 cop. [Crim 3 Lat; NN] 1139

Köy qadïnlarï delaghat sabranyalarïnïng proghramlï praktik ʿameli ishlerine da'ir materyalar ve usuli taʿlïmatlar. Simferopol: Qrïm Ḥükumet Neshriyatï, 1929, 115 pp., 600 cop. [Crim 2 Arab; NN] 1140

Köyni yangïdan quru yolïnda: Qrïm köy khazaystvasï qo'operatsyasïnïng esasi vazifeleri. Simferopol: Qrïm Devlet Neshriyatï, 1929, 41 pp., 1000 cop. [Crim 2 Arab; NN] 1141

Kurkchi, Umer. *Abört ve oning qadïngha teisiri.* Simferopol: Qrïm Devlet Neshriyatï, 1930, 26 pp., 2000 cop. [Crim 3 Lat; NN] 1142

Levin, R. S. *Ḥastalïqdan baqïnmaq ichün mullaghamï, ïrimjiʿami yoqsa hekimgemi varmaq kerek.* Simferopol: Qrïm Devlet Neshriyatï, 1928, 27 pp., 2500 cop. [Crim 2 Arab; NN] 1143

Lübimova, S. *Qadïn täshkilatjïsï Natasha Kotova.* Simferopol: Qrïm Devlet Neshriyatï, n.d., 38 pp., 2000 cop. [Crim 3 Lat; NN] 1144

Myuns, F. V. *Qo'operatsya ve qadïnlïq.* Simferopol: Qrïm Devlet Neshriyatï, 1928, 44 pp., 1500 cop. [Crim 2 Arab: NN) 1145

Ne ichün 18 mart mopr kunüdr. Simferopol: Neshr Eden Qrïm Mopr, 1928, 19 pp., 3000 cop. [Crim 3 Lat; NN] 1146

Nukhrad, A. *Oktabir ve sharq qadïnï.* Aq Mesjid: Qrïm Devlet Neshriyatï, 1927, 83 pp., 1500 cop. [Crim 2 Arab; NN] 1147

Petrupavlufskaya kechmish ve shïmdiki zamanlarda qadïnlïq. Simferopol: Qïrïm Izdat ve Qomite Firqasï Qadïnlar Sho'besining Neshri, 1926, 47 pp., 3000 cop. [Crim 2 Arab; NN] 1148

Tarakanova, S. *Köyli qadïn mopr sïralarïna.* Simferopol: Qrïm Devlet Neshriyatï, n.d., 15 pp., 3000 cop. [Crim 3 Lat; NN] 1149

Volghin, F. *Sheherning köy ile birleshmesi ne ichün kerekdir.* Simferopol: Qrïm Devlet Neshriyatï, 1928, 44 pp., 2000 cop. [Crim 2 Arab; NN] 1150

CRIMEAN TATAR Humanities

Architecture

Zelzeleden yïqlamamaq ichün qrïmda köy evlerini nasïl yapmalïdïr? Aq Mesjid: Qrïm-Plan Idaresi, 1928, 19 pp., 1000 cop. [Crim 2 Arab; NN] 1151

Language

Lazarev, L. M. *Turetsko-tatarsko-russkii slovar'—nariechii osmanskago krymskago i kavkazskago.* Moscow: Lazarevskii Institut Vostochnykh Iazykov, 1864, 336 pp., n.c. [Crim 1 Arab; CtY, NN] 1152

Literature

Amp, Pyer. *Shampanskiy.* Simferopol: Qrïm Devlet Neshriyatï, 1929, 96 pp., 3000 cop. [Crim 3 Lat; NN] 1153

Barbüs, Hanri. *Atesh ichinde.* Simferopol: Qrïm Devlet Neshriyatï, n.d., 148 pp., 3000 cop. [Crim 3 Lat; NN] 1154

Bekirof, ʻUsman. *Qzïl oktabïr.* Aq Mesjid: Qrïm Ḥükumet Neshriyetï, 1927, 30 pp., 2000 cop. [Crim 2 Arab; NN] 1155

Beren, M. *Insanïng tabiatle küreshi haqqïnda hikayeler: Insanlar mesafeyi nasïl maghlüb etdiler.* 2nji kitab. Simferopol: Qrïm Devlet Neshriyatï, 1929, 39 pp., 2000 cop. [Crim 3 Lat; NN] 1156

Bianki, Vitaliy. *Izlar boyïnja.* 1. *Izlar boyïnja.* 2. *Anütkanïng papiyi.* 3. *Deli qush.* 4. *Fomka haydud.* 5. *Qïzïlbash torghaynïng seyahatï.* Simferopol: Qïrïm Devlet Neshriyatï, 1930, 51 pp., 3000 cop. [Crim 3 Lat; NN] 1157

Bret-Gart. *Qïtay balasï.* Simferopol: Qrïm Devlet Neshriyatï, 1929, 20 pp., 3000 cop. [Crim 3 Lat; NN] 1158

Burgel, Bruno. *Yïldïzlargha doghru hey'etshinas olghan bir ishchining kendi balalïghï, genjligi haqqïnda khatïralar.* Simferopol: Qrïm Devlet Neshriyatï, n.d., 83 pp., 3000 cop. [Crim 3 Lat; NN] 1159

Chekhof, A. P. *Apaylar*. Hikaye. Simferopol: Qrïm Devlet Neshriyatï, 1929, 20 pp., 3000 cop. [Crim 3 Lat; NN] 1160

Chobanzade, B. *Song devr qrïm tatar ëdebiyatï*. Aq Mesjid: Neshr Iden Ileri Zhurnali Idaresi, 1928, 102 pp., n.c. [Crim 2 Arab; NNC] 1161

Ferskhofen. *Qashqïr Fenris*. Maliy hikaye. Simferopol: Qrïm Devlet Neshriyatï, n.d., 80 pp., 3000 cop. [Crim 3 Lat; NN] 1162

Furmanov. *Chapayef. D. Furmanof romanï üzerine Y. N. Vinogradskaya tarafïndan ishlendi*. Simferopol: Qrïm Devlet Neshriyatï, n.d., 72 pp., 3000 cop. [Crim 3 Lat; NN] 1163

Ghogol. *Evlenmek*. Qomidya. Iki perdede. St. Petersburg: Tipo-Litografiia I. Boragonskago i K., 1903, 64 pp., n.c. [Crim 1 Arab; NN] 1164

Görkiy, M. *Izergil qart*. Simferopol: Qrïm Devlet Neshriyatï, 1928, 28 pp., 2000 cop. [Crim 3 Lat; NN] 1165

Görkiy, M. *Khan ve onung oghlï: Opcha meselesi*. Simferopol: Qrïm Devlet Neshriyatï, 1928, 24 pp., 2000 cop. [Crim 3 Lat; NN] 1166

Görkiy, M. *Sheytan haqqïnda*. Simferopol: Qrïm Devlet Neshriyatï, 1928, 24 pp., 2000 cop. [Crim 3 Lat; NN] 1167

Görkiy, Maksim. *Men nasïl oqudïm*. Aq Mesjid: Qrïm Devlet Neshriyatï, 1929, 15 pp., 3000 cop. [Crim 3 Lat; NN] 1168

Ipchi, ʻUmer. *Azad ḥalq*. Bir pralugh ve uch perdeli pyesi. Aq Mesjid: Qrïm Devlet Neshriyatï, 1927, 55 pp., 1000 cop. [Crim 2 Arab; NN] 1169

Ipchi, ʻUmer. *Faḥishe yaḥud: Bir köylining bashïna kelenler*. Aq Mesjid: Qrïm Ḥükumet Neshriyatï, 1926, 52 pp., 2000 cop. [Crim 2 Arab; NN] 1170

Ipek. Simferopol: Qïrïm Devlet Neshriyatï, 1934, 15 pp., 5000 cop. [Crim 3 Lat; DLC] 1171

Kenche, J. *Urluqdan aq pamuq—pamuqdan urbalïq*. Simferopol: Qïrïm Devlet Neshriyatï, 1932, 14 pp., 10000 cop. [Crim 3 Lat; DLC] 1172

Keraibai, ʻA. E. *Kuchuk ḥikayechikler: Qurtchïqlarnïng yashayïshïndan*. Aq Mesjid: Qrïm Ḥükumet Neshriyatï, 1927, 20 pp., 3000 cop. [Crim 2 Arab; CStH] 1173

Latif Zade, A. *Yangï saz*. 1 kitab. Aq Mesjid: Qrïm Merkezi Yangï Elifbe Qomitesi Neshri, 1928, 54 pp., 3000 cop. [Crim 3 Lat; NN] 1174

Lepskiy, V. L. *Ishchi yemelyanof*. Hikaye. Simferopol: Qrïm Devlet Neshriyatï, n.d., 29 pp., 3000 cop. [Crim 3 Lat; NN] 1175

Menli Ghaziz, Z. (Javtubeli). *Inqilabï shi'irlar: Yashlar ichün*. Simferopol: Qrïm Ḥükumet Neshriyatï, 1927, 62 pp., 2000 cop. [Crim 2 Arab; CStH] 1176

Nemirovich-Danchenko, V. *Onlar besh kishi ediler*. Simferopol: Qrïm Devlet Neshriyatï, n.d., 26 pp., 3000 cop. [Crim 3 Lat; NN] 1177

Olesnitskii, Aleksei. *Pesni krymskikh turok*. Moscow: Tipografiia N-v Gattsuka, 1910, 147 and 10 pp., n.c. [Special Cyr; MH] 1178

Podyachef, S. *Ishchiler arasïnda*. Hikaye. Simferopol: Qrïm Devlet Neshriyatï, n.d., 106 pp., 3000 cop. [Crim 3 Lat; NN] 1179

Qrïm tatar masallarï ve legendalarï. Simferopol: Qrïm ASSR Devlet Neshriyatï, 1937, 379 pp., 7100 cop. [Crim 3 Lat; NN] 1180

Radlov, V. V. *Obraztsy narodnoi literatury sievernykh tiurkskikh plemen*. Chast' VII: Nariechïia krymskago poluostrova. St. Petersburg: Tïpografïia Imperatorskoi Akademïi Nauk, 1896, 408 and 527 pp., n.c. [Special Cyr, Karai 1 Heb; NNC] 1180a

Rubakin, B. *Nuhïng tufanï*. Simferopol: Qrïm Devlet Neshriyatï, 1929, 45 pp., 2000 cop. [Crim 3 Lat; NN] 1181

Safron arqadash. Dört perdelik drama. Simferopol: Qrïm Devlet Neshriyatï, 1930, 41 pp., 1000 cop. [Crim 3 Lat; NN] 1182

Salka, Mate. *Char oghrïnda*. Hikaye. Simferopol: Qrïm Devlet Neshriyatï, 1929, 27 pp., 3000 cop. [Crim 3 Lat; NN] 1183

Serafimovich, A. *Furtïnda*. Hikaye. Simferopol: Qïrïm Devlet Neshriyatï, 1930, 24 pp., 3000 cop. [Crim 3 Lat; NN] 1184

Servantes, M. *Don-Kikhot Lomanchskiy*. Simferopol: Qïrïm Devlet Neshriyatï, 1930, 72 pp., 3000 cop. [Crim 3 Lat; NN] 1185

Shtangey, V. *Batrachka: Ïrghat qïz*. Simferopol: Qrïm Devlet Neshriyatï, 1929, 38 pp., 3000 cop. [Crim 3 Lat; NN] 1186

Sinkler, Epton. *Jüngli*. Simferopol: Qïrïm Devlet Neshriyatï, 1930, 111 pp., 3000 cop. [Crim 3 Lat; NN] 1187

Tïyncherof, R. *Yash ezgiler*. Shiïrlar. Aq Mesjid: Qrïm Devlet Neshriyatï, 1928, 38 pp., 2000 cop. [Crim 3 Lat; NN] 1188

Tompson, Seton. *Ayuv balasï jonni*. Simferopol: Qrïm Devlet Neshriyatï, 1929, 27 pp., 3000 cop. [Crim 3 Lat; NN] 1189

Troshin, Nikolay; Deyneko, Ölga. *Ekmek zavodï*. Simferopol: Qr. MSSJ Neshriyatï, 1933, 10 pp., 10000 cop. [Crim 3 Lat; DLC] 1190

Uyda. *Nello ve Patrash*. Simferopol: Qrïm Devlet Neshriyatï, 1929, 16 pp., 3000 cop. [Crim 3 Lat; NN] 1191

Vladimirskiy, Vl. *Chïraq-shergit kolyajïq*. Simferopol: Qïrïm Devlet Neshriyatï, 1930, 19 pp., 3000 cop. [Crim 3 Lat; NN] 1192

Vladimirskiy, Vl. *Zumrud maidenï*. Hikaye. Simferopol: Qïrïm Devlet Neshriyatï, 1930, 79 pp., 3000 cop. [Crim 3 Lat; NN] 1193

Volnof, I., *Vasya Pazukhin*. Hikaye. Simferopol: Qrïm Devlet Neshriyatï, n.d., 54 pp., 3000 cop. [Crim 3 Lat; NN] 1194

Zhitkof, Boris. *Emjechigim*. Aq Mesjid; Qrïm Devlet Neshriyatï, 1929, 16 pp., 3000 cop. [Crim 3 Lat; NN] 1195

Zhitkof, Boris. *Maymunchïq haqqïnda*. Simferopol: Qïrïm Devlet Neshriyatï, 1930, 19 pp., 3000 cop. [Crim 3 Lat; NN] 1196

Zola, Emil. *Kömür qazïjïlar*. Simferopol: Qrïm Devlet Neshriyatï, 1929, 176 pp., 3000 cop. [Crim 3 Lat; NN] 1197

Philosophy and Religion

Aziz, Ya.; Shteynbakh. *Dinge qarshï köyli oquv kitabï*. Simferopol: Qïrïm Devlet Neshriyatï, 1930, 172 pp., 3000 cop. [Crim 3 Lat; NN] 1198

Chobanzade, B. *Dini islaḥat ve medeni inqïlab*. Aq Mesjid: Qrïm Devlet Neshriyatï, 1927, 91 pp., 1000 cop. [Crim 2 Arab; NN] 1199

Menliaziz, Z. (Javtöbeli). *Orazagha qarshï sefer*. Simferopol: Qrïm Devlet Neshriyatï, n.d., 34 pp., n.c. [Crim 3 Lat; NN] 1200

KARACHAY–BALKAR Social Sciences

Economics

El-mülk nalog: 1930-chü jïlda 23-chü fevralda jïqghan el-mülk nalognu zakonu bla 1930-chü jïl 15-chi martola SSSR-nï akhcha komisariyatïnï inistruksiyasï. Nalchik: n.p., 1930, 40 pp., 250 cop. [Kar–Bal 2 Lat; NN] 1201

Education

Abaylanï, U. M.; Aqbaylanï, U. *Bizni küchübüz bizni jeribizd.* Moscow: SSSRni Milletlerini ara Basmasï, 1926, 46 pp., 15000 cop. [Kar–Bal 2 Lat; NN] 1202

Alilanï, Umar. *Jangngï qarachay-malqar elible.* Kislovodsk: Izdanie Oblastnogo Karachaevskogo Izdatel'stva, 1929 3d ed., 64 pp., 5000 cop. [Kar–Bal 2 Lat; NN] 1203

Lankof. *Ekinchi jïlgha tergev kitab.* Moscow: SSSR-ni Milletlerini ara Basmasï, 1927, 112 pp., 4000 cop. [Kar–Bal 2 Lat; NN] 1204

Lankof, A. *Birinchi jïlgha tergev kitab.* Moscow: SSSR-ni Milletlerini ara Basmasï, 1926, 110 pp., 15000 cop [Kar–Bal 2 Lat; NN] 1205

Qarakotlanï, Ismail. *El shkollanï 1-chi bölümlerine programma.* Rostov-on-Don: Izdanie Obl. Ono KAO i Obl. Koma NTA Krainatsizdat, 1928, 12 pp., 250 cop. [Kar–Bal 2 Lat; NN] 1206

Government

Artemenko, N. *Askerge barïrdan alghïn quralmaqlïq emda anï maghanasï.* Kislovodsk: Izdanie Karachaevskogo Oblastnogo Izdatel'stva, 1930, 30 pp., 1000 cop. [Kar–Bal 2 Lat; NN] 1207

Bolkof, A. *Pioner üydegide.* Moscow–Rostov-on-Don: Kraynatsizdat (Sentrizdatnï Shimal Kaf. Butaghï), 1928, 23 pp., 3000 cop. [Kar–Bal 2 Lat; NN] 1208

Dedov, S.; Potapov, N. *Elde pioner ishi.* Kislovodsk: Izdanie Karachaevskogo Oblastnogo Izdatel'stva, 1930, 41 pp., 1000 cop. [Kar–Bal 2 Lat; NN] 1209

Freydin, S. I. *Shimal kavkazda khalqlanï qïzïl askerge chaqïrïlmaqlïqlarï.* Rostov-on-Don: Izdanie Ch.-K. Kraipolitprosveta i Kraikoma N.T.A. Krainatsizdat, 1928, 16 pp., 1500 cop. [Kar–Bal 2 Lat; NN] 1210

Grazhdan qazavatda biz nek khorladïq. Kislovodsk: Izd. Karachaevskogo Oblastnogo Izdatel'stva, 1930, 11 pp., 1000 cop. [Kar–Bal 2 Lat; NN] 1211

Köualenkö, P. *Siyasi bĭlĭm kĭtabi.* Moscow: Tsentral'noe Vostochnoe Izdatel'stvo, 1923, 112 pp., 2000 cop. [Kar–Bal 1 Arab; NN] 1212

SSSR ni qoruvlavgha emda anï aviasion khimiya quruluvuna bolushghan qaumlanï yacheykasï. Kislovodsk: Izdanie Karachaevskogo Oblosoaviakhima, 1929, 20 pp., 1500 cop. [Kar–Bal 2 Lat; NN] 1213

Tambilani, Islam. *Kengesh khukumat ve milletler mes'elesi.* Rostov-on-Don: Kraynasizdat, 1928, 43 pp., 1500 cop. [Kar–Bal 2 Lat; NN] 1214

Tayshin. *Sharq üchün qïskhartïlghan politgramota.* Moscow–Rostov-on-Don: Kraynasizdat [Sentrizdatnï Shimal Kafkazda Butaghï), 1928, 117 pp., 2000 cop. [Kar–Bal 2 Lat; CStH, NN] 1215

Toltururgha boyunlarïnda ishleri OSO-Aviyakhimni ellede yacheykalarïnï jaz bashïnda urluq chachkhan zamanda. Nalchik: Kab. Malq. Ortalïq Oblastïnda OSO-Aviyakhimin Soveti, 1929, 20 pp., 50 cop. [Kar–Bal 2 Lat; NN] 1216

Trotski. *Qabarti bla malqarnï aftonomï oblastlarï bla anï nezat eterge kerekliy bolghanïnï khaqïndan.* Moscow: SSSRni Mĭlletlerĭni ara Basmasi, 1925, 35 pp., 2000 cop. [Kar–Bal 1 Arab; CStH, NN] 1217

History

Neuski, V. I. *Uladĭmĭr ĭlyĭch lenĭn (ulyanuf).* Moscow: SSSR Mĭlletlerĭni ara Basmasi, n.d., 75 pp., 2000 cop. [Kar–Bal 1 Arab; CStH, NN] 1218

Social Organization

Begeulov, A. *Shimal kavkaznï avtonom oblastlarïnda jarlïlanï ichlerinde etilgen ish.* Rostov-on-Don: Izdanie Oblastnogo Karachaevskogo, Izdatel'stva, 1929, 35 pp., 2000 cop. [Kar–Bal 2 Lat; NN] 1219

Bronner, B. *Uyatlïq avruvla.* Moscow–Rostov-on-Don: Kraynatsizdat (Sentrizdatnï Shimal Kafkazda Butaghï), 1928, 59 pp., 3000 cop. [Kar–Bal 2 Lat; CStH, NN] 1220
Dĭkshteyn, A. *Kĭm ne bla jashaydï.* Moscow: Mĭlletler Ĭshleri Khalq Kamĭsaryatnï Janïndaghï Orta Sharq Basmasi, 1923, 48 pp., 1000 cop. [Kar–Bal 1 Arab; CStH, NN] 1221
Kravchenko, E. *Kolkhozgha kirmekligi elli tĭshĭrïvgha nek khayïrlïdï.* Kislovodsk: Izdanie Karachaevskogo Oblastnogo Izdatel'stva, 1930, 61 pp., 1000 cop. [Kar–Bal 2 Lat; NN] 1222
Mayzel, I. E. *Sabiyleni avruvladan qalay saqlargha bolluqdu.* Kislovodsk: Izdanie Oblastnogo Karachaevskogo Nats. Izdatel'stva, 1929, 23 pp., 1500 cop. [Kar–Bal 2 Lat; NN] 1223
Qorqmazlanï, I. *Bunt.* Kislovodsk: Izdanie Oblastnogo Karachaevskogo Izdatel'stva, 1928, 27 pp., 2000 cop. [Kar–Bal 2 Lat; NN] 1224

KARACHAY–BALKAR Humanities

Literature

Bianki, Bitali. *Cheget üychükle.* Moscow: SSSR-in Milletlerini ara Basmasï, 1927, 20 pp., 1500 cop. [Kar–Bal 2 Lat; CStH, NN] 1225
Mamin-Sibiryak. *Aqboz at.* Qïrghïz khapar. Moscow–Rostov-on-Don: Kraynatsizdat (Sentrizdatnï Shimal Kafkazda Butaghï), 1928, 36 pp., 3500 cop. [Kar–Bal 2 Lat; NN] 1226
Örtenleni, Azret. *Erkinlik jiltinleri.* 2chi kitab. n.p.: Qarachay Millet Basma Khanada Basïldï, 1929, 72 pp., 5000 cop. [Kar–Bal 2 Lat; NN] 1227
Qarachay fol'klor. Mikoyan-shakhar: Qarachay Oblastnï Natsional'nïy Izdatel'stvosu, 1940, 239 pp., 3000 cop. [Kar–Bal 3 Cyr; DLC] 1228
Qaraködlani, Ĭssa. "*Jangï shĭ'ïrle*". Moscow: SSSR Mĭlletlerĭni ara Basmasi, 1924, 23 pp., 1000 cop. [Kar–Bal 1 Arab; NN] 1229
Sakharov, Iv. *Ach börüleni khaparlarï.* Kislovodsk: Izdanie Karachaevskogo Oblastnogo Izdatel'stva, 1930, 12 pp., 1000 cop. [Kar–Bal 2 Lat; NN] 1230
Verga, Jiovanni. *Tamghalï sarï: Italiyada ishchi sabïyleni jashaundan.* Kislovodsk: Izdanie Oblastnogo Karachaevskogo Natsional'nogo Izdatel'stva, 1929, 23 pp., 2000 cop. [Kar–Bal 2 Lat; NN] 1231

KARAIM Social Sciences

Government

Lutsqi, Yosef Shelomo ben Moshe. *'Iggeret teshu'at yisra'el.* Eupatoria: n.p., 5588*/1841, 60 and 38 pp., n.c. [Karai 1 Heb; NNC, NNJ] 1232

History

Pigiṭ, Shemu'el ben Shemaria. *Vedabar be'itto.* Warsaw: Hatstsefira, 5564*/1904, 42 pp., n.c. [Karai 1 Heb; DLC, NN, NNJ] 1233

KARAIM Humanities

Language

⟨Firkovits, 'Abraham(?)⟩ *Kelale haddiqduq.* ⟨Eupatoria (Gozlava): n.p., 5592*/1832⟩, 64 pp., n.c. [Karai 1 Heb; DLC, NNJ] 1234

Kowalski, Tadeusz. *Karaimische Texte im Dialekt von Troki.* Cracow: Nakładem Polskiej Akademji Umiejętności, 1929, 302 pp., n.c. [Karai 1 Heb, 2 Lat; NNC, NNJ] 1235

Mardkowicz, Aleksander. *Karay sez-bitigi.* Lutsk: n.p., 1935, 71 pp., n.c. [Karai 2 Lat; DLC, NNC] 1236

Qazaz, 'Eliyahu. *Leregel hayyeladim.* Odessa: M. Beilinson, 5629*/1869, 294 and 152 and 160 pp., n.c. [Karai 1 Heb; DLC, MH, NN, NNJ] 1237

Literature

Ḥannah veshib'a baneha. Eupatoria: 'Abraham Firkovich, 5595*/1835, 7 pp., n.c. [Karai 1 Heb; NNJ] 1238

---

*anno Hebraico

Meshalim ʾumaʿasiyot. Eupatoria: ʾAbraham Firkovich, 5595*/1835, 67 pp., n.c. [Karai 1 Heb; DLC, NN] 1239
Pigiṭ, Shemuʾel ben Shemaria. *Dabar dabur.* Warsaw: Hatstsefira, 5664*/1904, 254 and 42 pp., n.c. [Karai 1 Heb; DLC, MH, NN, NNJ] 1240

Philosophy and Religion

Begi, M. *Dalet ṭurim beʿinyan shabbat.* Eupatoria: n.p., 5594*/1834 12 pp., n.c. [Karai 1 Heb; DLC, NN, NNC, NNJ] 1241
Dubinski, Simḥa ben Ḥilqiyahu. *Tsaqun laḥash.* Vilna: Haʾalmana Vehaʾaḥim, Ram, 5655*/1895, 73 pp., n.c. [Karai 1 Heb; NNJ] 1242
Firkovits, Moshe ben Yaʿaqob. *Kichik tefillah: Qeṭoret tamid. . .* Odessa: M. B. Beilenson, 5629*/1868–69, 3 pp., n.c. [Karai 1 Heb; OCH] 1243
Firkovits, Yaʿaqob ben Abraham. *Nasiʿaṭe ʾadam. . .* ⟨Eupatoria: n.p., 5601*/1841⟩, 8 pp., n.c. [Karai 1 Heb; NNJ] 1244
Malitski, Pineḥas ben ʾAharon. *Ronne falleṭ.* Vilna: Yudah Leb Mats, 5650*/1890, 39 pp., n.c. [Karai 1 Heb; DLC, NNJ] 1245
Pigiṭ, Shemaria ben Shemuʾel. *ʾIggeret nidḥe shemuʾel.* St. Petersburg: Behrman; Rabinowits, 5654*/1894, 226 pp., n.c. [Karai 1 Heb; DLC, MH, NN, NNJ] 1246
Qazaz, Mordekhai ben Shelomo. *Tsuf debash.* Eupatoria: ʾAbraham Firkovich, 5595*/1835, 42 and 26 and 67 pp., n.c. [Karai 1 Heb; DLC, NN, NNJ] 1247
Qazaz, Mordekhai ben Shelomo. *Ṭub ṭaʿam.* Eupatoria: ʾAbraham Firkovich, 5595*/1835, 26 pp., n.c. [Karai 1 Heb; DLC, NN, NNJ] 1248
Tirgum hallel haqqaṭan. ⟨Eupatoria: n.p., 183?⟩, 13 pp., n.c. [Karai 1 Heb; OCH] 1249
⟨*Tirgum ketubim*⟩. Eupatoria: n.p., 5602*/1841, 215 and 52 pp., n.c. [Karai 1 Heb; NN] 1250
Yitsḥaq ben Shelomo. *Pinnat yiqrat.* Eupatoria: n.p., 5594*/1834, 32 and 20 and 12 and 14 and 10 pp., n.c. [Karai 1 Heb; DLC, NN, NNC, NNJ] 1251

---

*anno Hebraico

KARAKALPAK Social Sciences

Economics

Avïl-charïvachïlïq ärtelining ülgi-ustabï. Törtkül: n.p., 1930, 13 pp., 2000 cop. [Kar 3 Lat; NN] 1252

Government

ÖzSSR joqarghï sovetining birinshi sessiyasï. Tashkent: ÖzSSR Joqarghï Sovetining Baspasï, 1939, 110 pp., 1000 cop. [Kar 3 Lat; DLC] 1253

History

Baranskiy, N.; Pospelov, P. (eds.). *Bizing turghan el*. Törtkül–Tashkent: Qaraqalpaq Mämleket Baspasï, 1939, 96 pp., 10000 cop. [Kar 3 Lat; DLC] 1254

Lebedep, N. K. *Eng ädep jerdi aylanïp shïghuv: Magellannïng sayaqatï*. Moscow: Mämleketlik Oquv–Pedagogiyke Baspasï, 1935, 47 pp., 1000 cop. [Kar 3 Lat; DLC] 1255

Ayel tengdigi (Kzil Orda) 1926: 5/6; 1927: 12; 1928: 3; 1929: 1. [Kaz 3 Arab; NN] 1256

Den savlïq jolï (n.p.) 1930: 4–5. [Kaz 4 Lat; NN] 1257

Janga adebiyat (Kzil Orda) 1928: 5/6, 10; 1929: 1–4, 7, 9. [Kaz 3 Arab; NN] 1258

Janga mekteb (Kzil Orda) 1925: 2; 1926: 3–8; 1927: 6–8, 10–12; 1929: 7, 9–10; 1930: 4, 6–7. [Kaz 3 Arab, 4 Lat; NN] 1259

Kaqobskiy. *Qabïrgha gazeti men tilshiler uyirmesi.* Kzil Orda: Qazaghïstan Kesibshiler Odaghï Kengeshi men Memleket Basbasï, 1927, 41 pp., 2000 cop. [Kaz 3 Arab; DLC] 1260

Kedey aynasï (Tashkent) 1928–1929: 45. [Kaz 3 Arab, DLC] 1261

Qazaghïstan olkelik partiya kamitetinin böleteni (Kzil Orda–Alma Ata) 1928: 1; 1929: 5–6; 1930: 1–3. [Kaz 3 Arab, 4 Lat; NN] 1262

Qazaghïstan satsïyal kengesshil respublikesining jumïskerqarashariva ukimetining zang jïynaghï (Kzil Orda) 1927: 13–19, 21/24. [Kaz 3 Arab; DLC, MH] 1263

Qazaghïstandïq kesibshiler odaqtarï kengesining maghlïvmat jiynaghï (Kzil Orda) 1927: 9–11; 1928: 3. [Kaz 3 Arab; NN] 1264

Qazaghïstandïq sïrtan oqïtatïn kenges partiya mektebi: Sharuvashïlïq jaghrapiyä (Kzil Orda) 1930: 6. [Kaz 4 Lat; NN] 1265

Qazaq (Orenburg) 1915: 127–131, 144, 146–147. [Kaz 1 Arab; NNC*] 1266

Qazaq S.S.R. Ghïlïm Akademiyasïnïng khabarlarï. Fililogiyälïq seriyä (Alma Ata) 1945: 3. [Kaz 5 Cyr; MH] 1267

Qazaq–tatar kitabtarïnïng tizimi. Semipalatinsk: Semeyding Okiriktik Tutinivsïlar Kaperetibining Sayozï, 1928, 13 pp., n.c. [Kaz 3 Arab; NN] 1268

Qazaq tilinde basïlghan kitabtardï körsetkish. Kizil Orda: Qaz. Mamleket Basbasï, 1926, 112 pp., 2000 cop. [Kaz 2 Arab; NN] 1269

Qazaq tilinde basïlghan kitabtardï körsetkish. Kzil Orda: Qaz. Memleket Basbasï, 1927, 53 pp., 3000 cop. [Kaz 3 Arab; NN] 1270

Qïzïl qazaghïstan (Kzil Orda, Alma Ata, Orenburg, Tashkent) 1922: 9; 1924: 7/9; 1925: 3/5; 1926: 11–18 [NN]; 1927: 3/4 [DLC], 8–9; 1928: 3–7, 11–12; 1929: 7/8 [NN]. [Kaz 2, 3 Arab] 1271

*Microfilm

KAZAKH General

Sana (Tashkent) 1923: January. [Kaz 2 Arab; NN] 1272

Sïrttan oqïtatïn olkelik kenges partiya mektebi (Kzil Orda) 1929: 2; 1930: 1–5. [Kaz 3 Arab; NN] 1273

Sotsialistik Kazakstan (Alma Ata) 1945: 138, 158–164, 166–197, 201, 203, 205–208, 210–217, 219–224, 226–230, 232–244, 250–251, 253–263. [Kaz 5 Cyr; CStH] 1274

Tarbiye, bilim, adebiyet janïndaghï maqalalardan terme. Tashkent: Qaz. Memleket Basbasïnïng Künshïghïsh Bölimi, 1925, 143 pp., 3000 cop. [Kaz 2 Arab; NN] 1275

KAZAKH Social Sciences

Economics

Avïl kaperetibterin oyïmdastïrïvshïlar taqïrïbtï ereje. Kzil Orda: Azïq Jomïstarï Bas Mekemesi, 1929, 16 pp., 2000 cop. [Kaz 3 Arab; NN] 1276

Avïl sharïvashïlïq kaperetib negizindegi mal ösiriv seriktigining ustabï. Semipalatinsk: Semeyding Gübernelik Basbasï, 1928, 24 pp., 2000 cop. [Kaz 3 Arab; NN] 1277

Balïq sharïvasï tuvralï anggime. Astrakhan: Izdanie Okrshtaba Agrorïbpokhoda, 1929, 125 pp., 3000 cop. [Kaz 3 Arab; NN] 1278

Baqïraq, M.; Omar ulï, Ïlïyas. *Qazaghïstanda 1930–31 inshi jïldïng bir ïngghay avïl sharuva salïghï.* Kzil Orda: Qazaghïstan Baspasï, 1930, 40 pp., 10000 cop. [Kaz 4 Lat; NN] 1279

Barjaqsï olï. *Totïnïv dökenining isin qalay jörgiziv kerek.* Moscow: Kenges Odaghïndaghï Elderding Kindik Basbasï, 1927, 36 pp., 4000 cop. [Kaz 3 Arab; NN] 1280

Berezansky, L. *Öndïrs majilisi.* Kzil Orda: Izdanie KSPS i Kazgiza, 1927, 48 pp., 2000 cop. [Kaz 3 Arab; NN] 1281

Bir ingghay avïl sharuva salïghï tuvralï ereje. Alma Ata: 1930, 18 pp., 5000 cop. [Kaz 4 Lat; NN] 1282

1930–31 inshi jïlghï sharïva salïghï ügit navqanmïn jürgizivding tartibi. Alma Ata: Qazaghïstannïng Aqsha Kamiysariyatï, 1930, 57 pp., 5000 cop. [Kaz 3 Arab; NN] 1283

Birlestik sharttï uvade. Kzil Orda: Qazaghïstan Ken Jumïskerlerining Ortalïq Basqarmasï, 1927, 51 pp., 1000 cop. [Kaz 3 Arab; DLC] 1284

Debatob, M. *Kesibshilder odaqtarï jana kengesterdi qayda saylav.* Kzil Orda: Qaz. Kesibshiler Kengesi, 1928, 20 pp., 3000 cop. [Kaz 3 Arab; NN] 1285

Duken kemesiyesi degen ne? Moscow: Kenges Odaghïndaghï Elderding Kindik Basbasï, 1927, 40 pp., 4000 cop. [Kaz 3 Arab; NN] 1286

Elen olï, J. *Kengester odaghïnda kesibshiler qozghalïsïnïng tarïyqï.* Kzil Orda: Qaz. Kesibshiler Kengesi, 1928, 130 pp., 3000 cop. [Kaz 3 Arab; NN] 1287

Eshshenkï, N. *Jabayï jol men (artel-kammïvnlarda birlesib jer ongdev serikterinde) avïl-sharïvashïlïq kalektibterinde eseb jörgizïv tartibi.* Kzil Orda: Qazaghstan Basbasï, 1929, 79 pp., 3000 cop. [Kaz 3 Arab; NN] 1288

Gosrebtirestding bataghalarïndaghï baldïqtï oqsatïv, jïynav jöninde kelisib isteletdin qïzïmetterding erkekter men ayelderding qaqï Astrakhan: n.p., 1930, 90 pp., 1000 cop. [Kaz 3 Arab; NN] 1289

Jalpï shart qaghaz: Jalpï odaqtïq üy-jurt, jol salïvshï jumïskerler odaghïnïng qazaghïstandïq basqarmasïnïng turkistan-sibir temir jolïn salïvshï basqarma men 1928-jïlghï aprelding 1 inen 1929-jïlghï marttïng 1 ine deyingi uvaqïtqa jasasqanï. n.p.: Semeyding Guberinelik Baspasï "Gubizdat" Basbaqanasï, 1928, 81 pp., 1000 cop. [Kaz 3 Arab; NN] 1290

Jarnashilardïng jïyïlïshï-totïnïvshïlardïng oyïmshasïnïng qojasï. Moscow: Kenges Odaghïndaghï Elderding Kindik Basbasï, 1927, 16 pp., 10000 cop. [Kaz 3 Arab; NN] 1291

Kalqozdargha kömek. Semipalatinsk: Semeydïng Okïrïktïk Baspasï, 1930, 47 pp., 1500 cop. [Kaz 3 Arab; NN] 1292

Kanatshïykob, S. *Jumïskorler men qarasharïvalar odaghïnïng kuzetinde.* Orenburg: Qazaghïstan Memleket Basbasï, 1925, 16 pp., 5000 cop. [Kaz 2 Arab; CStH] 1293

Kenges qorïlïsï tovralï bolghan 1-qazaghïstandïq majilisting qararlarï. n.p.: n.p., 7 pp., n.c. [Kaz 3 Arab; NN] 1294

Keperetip tovralï lenin ne dedi. Moscow: Kenges Odaghïndaghï Elderding Kindik Basbasï, 1927, 16 pp., 5000 cop. [Kaz 3 Arab; NN] 1295

Kepiretib dökenining qorïlïsï. Moscow: Kenges Odaghïndaghï Elderding Kindik Basbasï, 1928, 33 pp., 2000 cop. [Kaz 3 Arab; NN] 1296

Kesibshi odaqtarïnïng bastï-bastï mïndetteri. Kzil Orda: Kazgiz, 1928, 103 pp., 1500 cop. [Kaz 3 Arab; NN] 1297

Kesibshiler odaghïnïng moshesine serik. Kzil Orda: Qaz. Mamleket Basbasï, 1926, 54 pp., 5000 cop. [Kaz 2 Arab; NN] 1298

Kezektegi mindetter: Jappay kälektip bolghan avdandarda, partïya jurtshïlïghï jäne batïraq, kedeyler, arasïnda jumïs istev tuvralï ölkelik partiya kämiytätining derektibi men ortalïq partïya kämiytätining qavlïlarï. Kzil Orda: Qazaghïstan Baspasï 1930, 44 pp., 15000 cop. [Kaz 4 Lat; NN] 1299

Konko, B. M. *Avïldïq totïnïvshï qoghamdarïnda tavardï soribtav satïb alïv jane baghalav.* Moscow: Kenges Odaghïndaghï Elderding Kindik Basbasï, 1929, 102 pp., 5000 cop. [Kaz 3 Arab; NN] 1300

Konuvkof, I. A. *Qarz serktigi onïng qara sharvagha paydasï.* Moscow: Sabet Odaghïndaghï Ḥalqdardïng Kindik Basbasï, 1925, 88 pp., 4000 cop. [Kaz 3 Arab; NN] 1301

Kosob, A. *Kalqozdardïng jer shigin qalay uyumdastïrïv kerek.* Moscow: Maqtagershilik jäne Maqta Öndirisining Jalpï Odaqtïq Ayïlïm Zeritev Ünisteti (NIQI), 1932, 11 pp., 3000 cop. [Kaz 4 Lat; NN] 1302

Lenin jana sharïva qurïlïsï. Orenburg–Kzil Orda: Qazaqstan Memleket Basbasï, 1925, 68 pp., 5000 cop. [Kaz 2 Arab; CStH] 1303

Lorïya; Savosiyn. *Ïstïroiytelding mavsïmdï jomïsïnda jurgen jumïsshïlardï qamsïzdandïrïv jabdïghï.* Kzil Orda: Qaz. Engbek Kemesereti, 1928, 21 pp., 1000 cop. [Kaz 3 Arab; NN] 1304

Lötsenko, M. *Käsibshiler odaghï, partïya jäne kenges ökimeti.* Moscow: Kenges Odaghïndaghï Elderding Kindik Basbasï, 1929, 42 pp., 3000 cop. [Kaz 4 Lat; NN] 1305

Matbeenko, A. *Jer suvlandïrïv tuvralï maqtagerler ne bilivleri kerek.* Tashkent: Maqtagershilik jäne Maqta Öndirisining Jalpï Odaqtïq Ayïlïm-Zertev Ünisteti (NYQY), 1931, 13 pp., 6500 cop. [Kaz 4 Lat; NN] 1306

Mushelïk kïtabsha, nomïrï. . . . avïl sharïvashïlyq qarïzgha koshbeli sharïvalar serïktïgï. Uralsk: Oral Okïrïktïk Avïl Sharïvashïlïq Qarïz Serïktïgï, 1929, 29 and 38 pp., 3000 cop. [Kaz 3 Arab; NN] 1307

Oktabr özgerisi ham janga önem sayasatï. Orenburg: Qaz. Mamleket Basba Söz Bölimi, 1924, 55 pp., 2500 cop. [Kaz 2 Arab; NN] 1308

Pedolïb, M. B. *Kaperetibting qavïpsïzdandïrïv tovralï anggime.* Moscow: Sayoz Sayozïptïng Ulttar Boyrasï, 1929, 48 pp., 3000 cop. [Kaz 3 Arab: NN] 1309

Piyn, Ya. *Kasïbshiler odaghïning köbshilik jomïsï.* Kzil Orda: Qaz. Kesibshiler Odaqtarïnïng Kengesi, 1929, 63 pp., 3000 cop. [Kaz 3 Arab; NN] 1310

Pomiytsky olï, Pil. *Jaqsï da jaman koperetib jayïnan.* Moscow: Kenges Odaghïndaghï Elderding Kindik Basbasï, 1929, 36 pp., 5000 cop. [Kaz 3 Arab; NN] 1311

Qara sharïva saqtïq qamïnïng omirdi qavïpsïzdendïrïv erejesi. Kzil Orda: Resey Memleketting Saqtïq Basqarmasïnïng Qazaghïstandaghï Vakili, 1927, 14 pp., 10000 cop. [Kaz 3 Arab; NN] 1312

Qazaghïstan kerek–jaraq kaperatib orïndarïnda saylav navqanïn jorgïzïv tovralï jïynaqtar. Kzil Orda: Qaz. Olkelik Kerek–Jaraq Kaperatib Odaghï, 1929, 52 pp., 2500 cop. [Kaz 3 Arab; NN] 1313

Qazaghïstan kesibshilder odaghïnïng 2-jïldïq jomïsï. Kzil Orda: Olkelik Kesibshilder Kengesi, 1929, 44 pp., 1000 cop. [Kaz 3 Arab; NN] 1314

Qazaghïstanda 1928–1929 inshi jïldïng sharïva salïghï. Kzil Orda: Qaz. Aqsha Kemesereti, 1928, 72 pp., 8000 cop. [Kaz 3 Arab; NN] 1315

Qazaghïstanda 1930–31 inshi jïldïng birïngqay avïl-sharïva salïghï. Moscow: Odaqtïq Kenges Respoblikelerining Qalïq Aqsha Kemeseriyeti, 1930, 83 pp., 7000 cop. [Kaz 3 Arab; NN] 1316

Qazaghïstannïng el sharïvalarïna qarïz bereton qavïmnïng (selqoz bankening) basqarmasï. 1928. Kzil Orda: Kazgosizdat, n.d., 8 pp., 600 cop. [Kaz 3 Arab; NN] 1317

Qazaghïstannïng ong töstikindegi ongdev (sov) seriktikterining esebin jorgïzïv joninde tabsïrïv. Kzil Orda: Ongdev Oyistïrïv Boyrosï, 1929, 34 pp., 500 cop. [Kaz 3 Arab; NN] 1318

Qazaqïstan kengesti respivblikesining ortalïq atqarïv kamïyteti qasïnda kenges qorïlïsï tovralï shaqïrïlghan majlisining bolletenderi. Kzil Orda: Qaz. Ortalïq Atqarïv Kamitetining Basbasï, 1925, 33 pp., 1000 cop. [Kaz 2 Arab; NN] 1319

Qol önershiler käsip ärteli degen ne? Kzil Orda: Kazizdat, 1930, 68 pp., 5000 cop. [Kaz 4 Lat; NN] 1320

Qolmogorskiy, B. *Mal sharïvashïlïghïnïng keperetsiyesi*. Moscow: Qazagh. Memleket Basbasïnïng Konshïghïs Bolimi, 1926, 40 pp., 3000 cop. [Kaz 2 Arab; NN] 1321

Rïsqol olï, Torar. *Torkistan–sibir temir jolï*. Moscow: Kengester Odaghïndaghï Elderding Kindik Basbasï, 1930, 76 pp., 2000 cop. [Kaz 3 Arab; NN] 1322

Säköliskiy, A. *Engbek qorghav jäne onï iske asïrïv*. Moscow: Kenges Odaghïndaghï Elderding Kindik Basbasï, 1929, 51 pp., 2500 cop. [Kaz 4 Lat; NN] 1323

Salïm tuvralï qara sharvalar men anggime: Surav men javab. Moscow: Rosselbanïk, 1928, 19 pp., 10000 cop. [Kaz 3 Arab; NN] 1324

Saluvshlar odaghïnïng Qazaghïstan men Qïrghïzstan ortalïq bashqarmasï men Türkistan–Sibir temir jolïn saluv basqarmasï arasïndaghï jasaghan birlestik shart qaghazï. Kzil Orda: n.p., 1930, 47 pp., 3000 cop. [Kaz 4 Lat; NN] 1325

Saparbek olï, Sadïqbek. *Kanpeske qortïndïsï*. Kzil Orda: Qazaghïstan Basbasï, 1929, 36 pp., 3000 cop. [Kaz 3 Arab; NN] 1326

Senivshkin, P. *Kesibshiler odaghïndïng madeniy aghartïv jomïsï*. Kzil Orda: Qaz. Mamleket Basbasï, 1926, 90 pp., 3000 cop. [Kaz 3 Arab; NN] 1327

Sharïva qarïzï. Orenburg: Qazaqïstan Aqsha Kemeserïyetï, 1925, 15 pp., 20000 cop. [Kaz 2 Arab; NN] 1328

Sharïva salïghï tovralï ogit navqanïna tezis. Kzil Orda: n.p., n.d., 6 pp., 6000 cop. [Kaz 2 Arab; NN] 1329

Shövliykib, M. *Engbek aqï jana jomïsshïlardïng tormïs tilegin orindav maseleleri*. Kzil Orda: Qaz. Ortalïk Kesibshiler Kengesi, 1928, 38 pp., 3000 cop. [Kaz 3 Arab; NN] 1330

Shüvlikip, M. *Käliktip shartnama jäne onï jasav ireti*. Moscow: Kenges Odaghïndaghï Elderding Kindik Basbasï, 1929, 55 pp., 3000 cop. [Kaz 4 Lat; NN] 1331

Siymanup, N. V. *Maqtagha jol ashïlsïn*. Kzil Orda: Qazaqstan Baspasï, 1930, 61 pp., 4000 cop. [Kaz 4 Lat; NN] 1332

Sviderski, B. *Engbek hem kapital*. Orenburg: Kirgiz. Gosud. Izdatel'., 1923, 40 pp., 2000 cop. [Kaz 2 Arab; NN] 1333

Tav jomïsshïlarï odaghïnïng semey avdandïq kamiyteti men odaqtïq altïn mekemesining shïghïs qazaghstandïq kenderining jogharghï basqarmasï arasïnda jasalghan birlestik shart qaghaz. Semipalatinsk: Semeyding Okïrïktïk Baspasï, 1929, 82 pp., 660 cop. [Kaz 3 Arab; NN] 1334

Tomiskiy, M. *Respobliykeler odaghïnïng VI-kesibshiler siyezining qorïtïndïsï.* Kzil Orda: Qazaq Memleket Basbasï, 1925, 56 pp., 4000 cop. [Kaz 2 Arab; NN] 1335

Tomski, M. *Kasibshilder odaghï janga jolda.* Orenburg: Qaz. Memleket Basba Soz Bolimi, 1923, 56 pp., 3000 cop. [Kaz 2 Arab; NN] 1336

Toqtïbayïf. *Türkistan.* Tashkent: Türkistan Rïspublïkasïnïng Basba Asdern Basqarov Maḥkemesi, 1923, 54 pp., n.c. [Kaz 1 Arab; NN] 1337

Tovïlshïnïsky, S. *Totiniv kaperetibining aghartïv jumïsï.* Kzil Orda: Qaz. Olkelik Totiniv Kaperetib Odaghï, 1928, 52 pp., 3000 cop. [Kaz 3 Arab; NN] 1338

Tutïnivshiler qoghamïnïng basqarmasïne nosqav. Moscow: Kenges Odaghïndaghï Elderding Kindik Basbasï, 1927, 40 pp., 2000 cop. [Kaz 3 Arab; NN] 1339

Yanïshebski, N. A. *Suv paydalanïvdïng on tasili.* n.p.: Ortaazye Suv Sharïvlïghïnïng Neshriyatï, 1929, 27 pp., 553 cop. [Kaz 3 Arab; DLC] 1340

Yïzepobish, L. *Sholdï suvarïvdï koyeytïv.* Moscow: Kenges Odaghïndaghï Elderding Kindik Basbasï, 1926, 21 pp., 5000 cop. [Kaz 2 Arab; NN] 1341

Zivbrïlïn, A. A. *Qaytkende qara chekbender charïvasïn jondevge boladï.* Moscow: SSSR Ḥalqdarïnïng Kindik Basbasï, 1924, 20 pp., 4000 cop. [Kaz 2 Arab; NN] 1342

Education

Äbdïraqman; Ghabit. *Qïzïl äsker älipbesi.* Kzil Orda: Qazaghïstan Basbasï, 1929, 143 pp., 10000 cop. [Kaz 4 Lat; NN] 1343

Avïlda kokoshbeli mektebterding jïyïlïstardïng kuristening 26–27 jïlqï sayasï savat ashïv jumïsïnïng pïrogïrammasï. Kzil Orda–Tashkent: Qazaghïstan Memleket Basbasï, 1927, 22 pp., n.c. [Kaz 3 Arab; DLC] 1344

Baidïlda ulï, A. 1. *Janga alïbbe tuvralï.* 2. *Janga alïbbe sabaghï.* n.p.:

Kazizdat. Ispolneno po Zakazu VUKNTA, 1928, 35 pp., n.c. [Kaz 4 Lat; NN] 1345

Balalar! Mekteb kitabqanasïnan jengil, uvaq kïtabshalar alïb oqïngdar. n.p.: Qazaqïstan Memleket Basbasï, n.d., n.pp., n.c. [Kaz 3 Arab; CStH] 1346

Barlamob, P. *Pozner oqïv qoralïn tosindirgishi.* Kzil Orda: Qaz. Memleket Basbasï, 1926, 96 pp., 5000 cop. [Kaz 2 Arab; NN] 1347

Baydïlda olï, Abdïraqman. 1. *Janga alïbbe tuvralï.* 2. *Janga alïbbe sabaghï.* Kzil Orda: Qaz. Janga Alïbbe Kamïyteti, 1928, 166 and 35 pp., 5000 cop. [Kaz 3 Arab, 4 Lat; NN] 1348

Baytursïn olï, Aqïmet. *Alïb-bïy: Janga qoral.* Kzil Orda: Kazizdat, 1927 2d ed., 116 pp., 50000 cop. [Kaz 3 Arab; DLC, NN] 1349

Baytursïn ulï, Aqïmet. *Alïb-bïy: Janga qoral.* Kzil Orda: Kazizdat, 1928 3d ed., 116 pp., 2000 cop. [Kaz 3 Arab; NN] 1350

Baytursïn ulï, Aqïmet. *Alïb-bïy: Janga qural.* Kzil Orda: Qazaqstan Mamleket Basbasï, 1926, 116 pp., 10500 cop. [Kaz 2 Arab; CStH] 1351

Baytursunïf, A. *Oquv quralï.* Birinchi jïldïq kitab. Tashkent: Turkestan. Gosud. Izdat., 1922, 95 pp., 40000 cop. [Kaz 2 Arab; NN] 1352

Begäli uli. *Esep quralï.* Birinshi jïldïq. Kzil Orda: Qazaghïstan Baspasï, 1929, 75 pp., 45000 cop. [Kaz 4 Lat; NN] 1353

Bereza, G. *Qazaghïstanda jappay bastavïsh oqïtuv jumïsï.* Alma Ata: Izdanie Gosplana Kazakskoi ASSR, 1930, 34 pp., 3000 cop. [Kaz 4 Lat; NN] 1354

Dos-muqambet ulï, Qalel. *Oqïvshïnïng savlïghïn saqtav.* Tashkent: Qazaghstan Memleket Basbasïnïng Künshïghïs Bölimï, 1925 2d. ed., 23 pp., 5000 cop. [Kaz 2 Arab; NN] 1355

Dovlat olï, Mirjaqïb. *Eseb qoralï.* Orenburg: Kirgizskoe Gosudar. Izdat. 1925 4th ed., 76 pp., 15000 cop. [Kaz 2 Aarb; NN] 1356

Dovlat olï, Mirjaqïb. *Eseb quralï.* Kzil Orda: Kazizdat, 1926 5th ed., 76 pp., 10000 cop. [Kaz 2 Arab; NN] 1357

Ïstalïn, Jusub. *Shïghïs engbekshïlerï onïbersïtetnïng sayasï mïndetterï taqïrïbtï.* Moscow: Kenges Odaghïndaghï Olderdïng Kïndïk Basbasï, 1925, 32 pp., 5000 cop [Kaz 2 Arab; CStH] 1358

Ïybanïp, G. *Bastavïsh jaghïrapya.* n.p.: Qazaghïstan Memleket Basbasï, 1927, 210 pp., 10000 cop. [Kaz 3 Arab; NN] 1359

Ïybanop, G. Y.; Ïybanop, G. G. *Bastavïsh jaghïrapïya men aymaq tanuv*. Kzil Orda: Qazaghïstan Baspasï, 1929, 148 pp., 10000 cop. [Kaz 4 Lat; NN] 1360

Ïymash ulï, T. *Janga älïb sabatï*. Astrakhan: Ashtarqan Ökiriktik Sabatsïzdïq ben Shala Sabatsïzdïqtï Joyatïn Ädeyi Kämesiye, 1929, 63 pp., 13000 cop. [Kaz 4 Lat; NN] 1361

Jazuga üiretenin knege. Kazan: Tip. Imp Universiteta, 1894, 44 pp., n.c. [Special Cyr; MH] 1362

Joldïbay ulï, M.; Shonan ulï, T. *Janga arna*. Kzil Orda: Qazaghïstan Baspasï, 1929, v and 150 pp., 25000 cop. [Kaz 4 Lat; NN] 1363

Jomabay ulï, Maghjan. *Savattï bol!* Moscow: SSSR Qalïqtarïnïng Kindik Basbasï, 1926, 63 pp., 20000 cop. [Kaz 2 Arab; NN] 1364

Jomabay ulï, Maghjan. *Savattï bol!* Moscow: Kenges Odaghïndaghï Elderding Kindik Basbasï, 1928, 96 pp., 36000 cop. [Kaz 3 Arab, 4 Lat; NN] 1365

Jumabay ulï, Maghjan. *Savattï bol*. Moscow: Kenges Odaghïndaghï Elderding Kindik Basbasï, 1929, 95 pp., 50000 cop. [Kaz 4 Lat; NN] 1366

Jusïb-bek. *Janjuyesi men oner tangdav*. n.p.: Qazaqstan Memleket Basbasïnïng Kun-shïghïs Bolïmi, 1926, 80 pp., 3000 cop. [Kaz 2 Arab; NN] 1367

Kenges respoblikeleri odaghïndaghï moghallimderding birinshi tobïnïng qavlïlarï. Moscow: Qalïq Aghartïv Qayratkerlerining Basbasï, 1925, 48 pp., 1000 cop. [Kaz 2 Arab; NN] 1368

Kïrovbïskaya, N. K. *Qalïqtï aghartïv tovralï leninning osïyeti*. Moscow: Kenges Odaghïndaghï Elderding Kindik Basbasï, 1925, 56 pp., 10000 cop. [Kaz 2 Arab; NN] 1369

Mägniytskiy, S. D. *Qara sharuvalar avïl sharuvashïlïq kitaptarïn qalay oquv kerek*. Alma Ata: Qazaghïstan Baspasï, 1930, 45 pp., 10000 cop. [Kaz 4 Lat; NN] 1370

Maldïbay olï, Biylal. *Qazaghïstandaghï jogharghï, orta darejeli mektebter*. Kzil Orda: Engbekshi Qazaq, 1926, 39 pp., 5000 cop. [Kaz 2 Arab; NN] 1371

Maler, Larïssa. *Avïlgha tazalïq kerek*. Kzil Orda: Qaz Basbasï, 1928, 58 pp., 3000 cop. [Kaz 3 Arab; NN] 1372

Maylï olï, Beyimbet. *Shala savattar öshin oqïv kitabï*. Moscow: Kenges Odaghïnïng Kindik Basbasï, 1928, 196 pp., 6000 cop. [Kaz 3 Arab; NN] 1373

Maylï olï, Beyimbet. *Shala savattïlar öshin oquv kitabï*. Moscow: Kenges Odaghïndaghï Elderding Kindiri Basbasï, 1929 2d ed., 196 pp., 20000 cop. [Kaz 3 Arab; NN] 1374

Qasim ulï, Älmaghambet. *II-jïldïq esep quralï*. n.p.: Qazaghïstan Baspasï, 1930, 74 pp., 5000 cop. [Kaz 4 Lat; NN] 1375

Qasïm uli, Älmäghambet. *III-jïldïq esep quralï*. Kzil Orda: Qazaghïstan Baspasï, 1929 4th ed., 59 pp., 10000 cop. [Kaz 4 Lat; NN] 1376

Qasïm ulï, Älmaghambet. *III-jïldïq esep quralï*. Kzil Orda: Qazaghïstan Baspasï, 1930 5th ed., 59 pp., 30000 cop. [Kaz 4 Lat; NN] 1377

Qazaq bilimpazdarïnïng tongghïsh siyezi. Orenburg: Kirgizgosizdatel'., 1925, 120 pp., 2000 cop. [Kaz 2 Arab; NN] 1378

Qazaq janga emlesi. Kzil Orda: Kazizdat, 1929, 40 pp., 5000 cop. [Kaz 4 Lat; NN] 1379

Qoljanova, N. *Mektebden borunghï tarbiya*. Orenburg: Qaz. Memleket Basba Soz Bolimi, 1923, 36 pp., 4000 cop. [Kaz 2 Arab; NN] 1380

Saparbek olï, Sadïqbek. *Madeniyet maydanïndaghï mindetterimiz*. Kzil Orda: Qaz. Qalïq Sharïvasïnïng Ortalïq Kengesining Basbaqanasï, 1928, 78 pp., 6000 cop. [Kaz 3 Arab; NN] 1381

Shonan olï, T.; Joldibay olï, M. *Janga arna: Alghashqï jïldïq oqïv qoralï*. Kzil Orda: Qazaqïstan Memleket Basbasï, 1927, 188 pp., 50000 cop. [Kaz 3 Arab; NN] 1382

Shonan ulï, T. *Savattan*. Kzil Orda: Kazizdat, 1929 4th ed., 32 pp., 100000 cop. [Kaz 4 Lat; NN] 1383

Shonan ulï, T. *Savattan*. Kzil Orda: Qazaghïstan Baspasï, 1930 6th ed., 48 pp., 100000 cop. [Kaz 4 Lat; NN) 1384

Shonan ulï, Teljan. *Jangalïq: Alippe*. Kzil Orda: Kazizdat, 1929, 72 pp., 25000 cop [Kaz 4 Lat; NN] 1385

Shonan ulï, Teljan. *Jangalïq: Alippe*. Kzil Orda: Kazizdat, 1930 5th ed., 73 pp., 150000 cop. [Kaz 4 Lat; NN] 1386

Sïdïq ulï, Ä. *Savatsïzdardï oqïtuv metödiykesi*. Kzil Orda: Qazaq Jangalip Kämiyteti, 1930, 78 pp., 5000 cop. [Kaz 4 Lat; NN] 1387

Sïrttan oqïtatïn mughalïm körisi. 2inshi kitap. Kzil Orda: Kazizdat, 1930, 137 pp., 2000 cop. [Kaz 4 Lat; NN] 1388

Education

Toräqul, Nazïr. *Janga alïb-bi nägä käräk?* Moscow: Säbät Odaghïndaghï Qalqdardïng Kindik Basbasï, 1924, 88 pp., 3000 cop. [Kaz 2 Arab; CStH, NN] 1389

Government

VI syezde saylanghan semey göbirnelik atqarïv kamïytetining III pilenumï shïgarghan qavlïlar. n.p.: Semeyding Gubernelik Atqarïv Kamiteti, 1928, 26 pp., 180 cop. [Kaz 3 Arab; NN] 1390

Aso-abïyaqïym qoghamïnïng oyasï. Kzil Orda: Qazaghïstandaghï Aso-abïyaqïym, Qoghamï 1928, 32 pp., 3000 cop. [Kaz 2 Arab; NN] 1391

Avdandïq partïya kamïytetterïne, partïya uyalarïna. Qazaghïstan partïya uyïmïnïng moshelerïne. Alma Ata: Olkelik Partïyya Kamïytetï, 1930, 12 pp., 3000 cop. [Kaz 3 Arab; NN] 1392

Avïlda jïynalïb sayasat sabaghïn oqïvdïng porghïramï. Kzil Orda: Kazkraikom VKP(b), 1927, 42 pp., 2000 cop. [Kaz 2 Arab; NN] 1393

Avïldaghï askerlik jomïs. Kzil Orda: Qaz. Asker Kemeseriyetiyning Sayasat Bölimi, n.d., 34 pp., 3000 cop. [Kaz 2 Arab; NN] 1394

Avïldïq, qïstaqtïq usaq kengester üshin eseb qïsab jayïndaghï nusqav. Kzil Orda: Qazaghïstan Memleket Basbasï, 1927, 23 pp., 2000 cop. [Kaz 2 Arab; NN] 1395

Balasebish, B. *Odaqtïq kamonis partiyasïnïng qïsqasha tariyqï:* Moscow: Kenges Odaghïndaghï Elderding Kindik Basbasï, 1927, 263 pp., 4000 cop. [Kaz 2 Arab; NN] 1396

Barashïylïp, K. Y. *Soghïs bolama?* Kzil Orda: Qazaghïstan Baspasï, 1930, 19 pp., 25000 cop. [Kaz 4 Lat; NN] 1397

Baydïlda, olï, Abdïraqman. *Aldïmïzdaghï maqsattarïmïz.* Kzil Orda: Qaz. Memleket Basbasï, 1926, 49 pp., 3000 cop. [Kaz 2 Arab; NN] 1398

Berdniykop, A.; Sibetlop, P. *Kamones partiyasïna kirivshi ar bir engbekshi ne bilivge tiyis?* n.p.: Qaz. Memleket Basbasï, 1925, vi and 110 pp., 5000 cop. [Kaz 2 Arab; NN] 1399

Bereshshegin. *Bizdi kim biyleb otïr.* Moscow: Kenges Odaghïndaghï Elderding Kindik Basbasï, 1929, 58 pp., 5000 cop. [Kaz 2 Arab; NN] 1400

Bereshshegin, G. *SSSR (Sosïyalshïl kenges irespoblikelarïnïng odaghï)*. Moscow: Kenges Odaghïndaghï Elderding Kindik Basbasï, 1927, 72 pp., 5000 cop. [Kaz 2 Arab; NN] 1401

1925 inshi jïl, oktabïrding biri keshki majilis. n.p.: n.p., n.d., 13 pp., n.c. [Kaz 2 Arab; NN] 1402

1925 inshi jïl 30-inshi sentabir keshki majilis. n.p.: n.p., n.d., 16 pp., n.c. [Kaz 2 Arab; NN] 1403

1925 inshi jïldïng 2-inshi oktabirinde keshki majilis. n.p.: n.p., n.d., 19 pp., n.c. [Kaz 2 Arab; NN] 1404

1925 jïl oktabirding 3-i keshki majilis. n.p.: n.p., n.d., 6 pp., n.c. [Kaz 2 Arab; NN] 1405

1929 inshi jïldïng egis navqanïna kamsamoldardïng qatïnasi tuvralï qazaghïstan kamsamoldari olkelik kamiytetining nusqav qatï. Kzil Orda: n.p., 1929, 23 pp., 7000 cop. [Kaz 3 Arab; NN] 1406

Bironin, Ya. *Lenin men qïzïl saya*. Moscow: Kenges Odaghïndaghï Elderding Kindik Basbasï, 1925, 48 pp., 4000 cop. [Kaz 2 Arab; NN] 1407

Bizding ghaniy: Ghaniygha arnalghan maqalalar jïyïntïghï. Moscow: Kenges Odaghïndaghï Elderding Kindik Basbasï, 1925, 184 pp., 4000 cop. [Kaz 2 Arab; CStH, NN] 1408

Blonina, E. *Intrnatsïynaldaghï jumïsker ayelder*. Orenburg: Qazaqstan Memleket Basba Söz Bölimi, 1924, 65 pp., 3500 cop. [Kaz 2 Arab; NN] 1409

Bovbnof. *Resey ortaqshïl partiyasïnïng östinen ötkizken davrleri*. Orenburg: Qazaqïstan Memleket Basba Söz Bölimi, 1924, 57 pp., 4000 cop. [Kaz 3 Arab; NN] 1410

Buykip, A. *Soghïstïng baghasï*. Alma Ata: Qazaghïstan Baspasï, 1929, 44 pp., 10000 cop. [Kaz 4 Lat; NN] 1411

Deminshteyn. *Dünye soghïsïna on jïl boldï*. Moscow: SSSR Ḥalqdarïnïng Kindik Basbasï, 1924, 62 pp., 4000 cop. [Kaz 2 Arab; NN] 1412

2-oktabïr konï tang ertegi majïlïs. n.p.: n.p., n.d., 18 pp., n.c. [Kaz 3 Arab; NN] 1413

Elezarïp. *Partiyanïng körsetken jolï*. Moscow: Kenges Odaghïndaghï Elderding Kindik Basbasï, 1926, 60 pp., 5000 cop. [Kaz 2 Arab; NN] 1414

Esip. *May mayramï*. Moscow: Kenges Odaghïndaghï Elderding Kindik Basbasï, 1927, 59 pp., 5000 cop. [Kaz 3 Arab; NN] 1415

Estrḥan okrogïnda savïtlarnïng ḥïsab biru-saylau kampaniyalarïn ötkeroge ḥezïrlïq üshin matïrïyallar. Astrakhan: Izdatel' Okrispolkoma, 1929, 8 pp., 200 cop [Kaz 3 Arab; NN] 1416

Ïnsertof; Zaqarïf. *Sayasï savattïqdïng kitabshasï*. Tashkent: Torkistan Rïspoblikasïnïng Basba Söz Taratov Bölimi, 1923, 96 pp., 5000 cop. [Kaz 3 Arab; NN] 1417

Ïstalin, I. *Kamsamol tovralï*. Kzil Orda: Gos. Izdat. KSSR, 1926, 30 pp., 5000 cop. [Kaz 2 Arab; NN] 1418

Ïstalin, I. *Partiyanïng avïldaghï kezektï isteri tuvralï*. Orenburg: Qazaqstan Memleket Basbasï, 1925, 21 pp., 1000 cop. [Kaz 2 Arab; DLC] 1419

Ïydelson, L. *Engbekshïlerdïng askerlïk mïndetterï*. Kzil Orda: Qaz. Sayasï Aghartïv Mekemesï, 1927, 34 pp., 3000 cop. [Kaz 2 Arab; NN] 1420

Jalpï odaqtïq kamenes partïyasïnïng XI-inshi, XIV-inshi sïyezderi shïgharghan qararlar. Kzil Orda–Tashkent: Qaz. Memleket Basbasï, 1926, 47 pp., 5000 cop. [Kaz 2 Arab; NN] 1421

Jalpï odaqtïq kamonïs partiyasïnïng XV-sïyezi. Moscow: Kenges Odaghïndaghï Elderding Kindik Basbasï, 1928, 144 pp., 5000 cop. [Kaz 3 Arab; NN] 1422

Jalpï reseylik ortalïq atqarüv kamïyteti men resey quramasïnïng qalïq kamiysarlarï kengesining qavlïsï. n.p.: Semokrizdat, 1929, 8 pp., 1000 cop. [Kaz 3 Arab; NN] 1423

29-jïl noyabir ayïnda bolghan ortalïq partiya kämiyetining pilenümi. Kzil Orda: Qazaghïstan Baspasï, 1930, 139 pp., 5000 cop. [Kaz 4 Lat; NN] 1424

Jol baschï: Qazaghïstan respivblikesindegi bolstïq atqarïv kamiytetderinde is jürgiziv tïvralï. Orenburg: n.p., 1924, 53 pp., 1000 cop. [Kaz 2 Arab; NN] 1425

Kälektip qurïlïsïnda partïya jolï buzïlmasïn. Moscow: Kengester Odaghïndaghï Elderding Kindik Basbasï, 1930, 29 pp., 15000 cop. [Kaz 4 Lat; NN] 1426

Kamenïp, L. B. *Lenin jana onïng partïyasï*. Kzil Orda: Qaz. Memleket Basbasï, 1925, 140 pp., 5000 cop. [Kaz 2 Arab; NN] 1427

Kamonis enternasïyanalïnïng seksiyesi jalpï odaqtïq kamonis: Balshebek partiyasïnïng ostabï. Kzil Orda: Qazaqnïng Memleket Basbasï, 1928, 63 pp., 20000 cop. [Kaz 3 Arab; NN] 1428

Kamsomoldardïng avïldaghï oyalarïna ovaqïtsha joba. Kzil Orda:

Qazaghïstan J.Sh.K. Memleketting Basbaqanasï, 1928, 42 pp., 1500 cop. [Kaz 3 Arab; NN] 1429

Kasabolatof, E. *Kommïvnist partïyasïnïng 10–12 inshi tobdarïnda joldas ïstalïnnïng ult maselesi tuvralï jasaghan bayandamasï ham syezding shigharghan qararlarï.* Orenburg: Qazaqstannïng Mamleket Basba Söz Bölimi, 1924, 59 pp., 3000 cop. [Kaz 2 Arab; NN] 1430

Katokop, V. *Qazaghïstandaghï ult askerning qurïlïsï.* Alma Ata: Qazaghïstan 10 Jïldïq Toyïn Ötkizüvshi Kemesiye Baspasï, 1930, 40 pp., 10000 cop. [Kaz 3 Arab; NN] 1431

Kemenger ulï, Q. *Burïnghï ezilgen ultdar.* Moscow: Sabet Odaghïndaghï Elderding Kindik Basbasï, 1925, 127 pp., 4000 cop. [Kaz 2 Arab; CStH, NN] 1432

Kengester respübliykesin qorghav qorïn jasayïq. Alma Ata: Qazaghïstan Asabïyaqïm Qoghamï, 1929, 16 pp., 15000 cop. [Kaz 4 Lat; NN] 1433

Kengester saylav aldï jana saylav navqanïn otkïzïv jayay materïyaldar. Astrakhan: Izdatel' Okrispolkoma, 1929, 8 pp., 300 cop. [Kaz 3 Arab; NN] 1434

Khelq kingeshchïysïge ïysïleme. Tashkent: Qazaghïstan Memleket Basbasï, 1926, 11 pp., 1000 cop. [Kaz 2 Arab; DLC] 1435

Kirïvpïskaya, N. K. *Olttïq jana enternatsiyonaldïq madeniyet tovralï.* Kzil Orda: Qaz. Basbasï, 1928, 40 pp., 2000 cop. [Kaz 2 Arab; NN] 1436

Koloshokiyn, P. I. *Qazaghstannïng oktabïr merekesïndegi küni.* Kzil Orda: Qaz. Memleket Basbasï, 1927, 39 pp., 2000 cop. [Kaz 2 Arab; NN] 1437

Kolshiyre. *Ayel er men qashan tengelmek.* Moscow: Kenges Odaghïndaghï Elderding Kindik Basbasï, 1927, 56 pp., 6000 cop. [Kaz 3 Arab; NN] 1438

Lebgor. *Ortaqshïl jastar odaghï qalaysha shïghïb ösib öndi.* Moscow: Kenges Odaghïndaghï Elderding Kindik Basbasï, 1925, 43 pp., 6000 cop. [Kaz 2 Arab; NN] 1439

Lenin, N. *1905.* Moscow: Kenges Odaghïndaghï Elderding Kindik Basbasï, 1926, 280 pp., 5000 cop. [Kaz 2 Arab; NN] 1440

Lenin, N. *1905 töngkerisi.* Kzil Orda: Qaz. Memleket Basbasï, 1926, 44 pp., 5000 cop. [Kaz 2 Arab; NN] 1441

Lenin, N. *Janbardïng toghïzï*. Moscow: Kenges Odaghïndaghï Elderding Basbasï, 1926, 40 pp., 5000 cop. [Kaz 2 Arab; NN] 1442

Lenin, N. *Parij kamoni*. Moscow: Kenges Odaghïndaghï Elderding Kindik Basbasï, 1925, 62 pp., 3000 cop. [Kaz 2 Arab; CStH, NN] 1443

Lenin, N. *Qara sharïva tovralï*. Moscow: Kenges Odaghïndaghï, Elderding Kindik Basbasï, 1927, 130 pp., 8000 cop. [Kaz 3 Arab; NN] 1444

Lenin N. *Rosïyadaghï sayasï partïyalar*. Moscow: Kenges Odaghïndaghï Elderding Kindik Basbasï, 1926, 94 pp., 5000 cop. [Kaz 2 Arab; NN] 1445

Lenin, N. *Sözderi men maqalalarï*. II. Kzil Orda–Tashkent: Qaz. Memleket Basbasï, 1926, 122 pp., 3000 cop. [Kaz 2 Arab; NN] 1446

Lenin, N. *Sözderi men maqalalarï*. Kzil Orda: Qazaghïstan Memleket Basbasï, 1926, 31 pp., 3000 cop. [Kaz 2 Arab; CStH] 1447

Lenin, V. I. (Ulaynïv). *Jastar uymïnïng maqsatï*. Moscow: Sabet Odaghïndaghï Elderding Kindik Basbasï, 1925, 44 pp., 6000 cop. [Kaz 2 Arab; NN] 1448

Lenin jolï (öktebïrding 10 jïldïq merekesine). Kzil Jar: n.p., 1927, 39 pp., 1000 cop. [Kaz 3 Arab; NN] 1449

Leninning ult maselesi taqïrbiti sözderi. Kzil Orda: Gosudarstvennoe Izdatel'stvo KSSR, 1926, 304 pp., 3000 cop. [Kaz 2 Arab; NN] 1450

Metïropanïb, A. *Avïldaghï partiya oyïmdarïnïng kallektib qorïlïsï iretindegi maqsattarï*. Kzil Orda: n.p., 1929, 64 pp., 3000 cop. [Kaz 3 Arab; NN] 1451

Mindetti askerlik qïzmeti tovralï zang. Kzil Orda: Qaz. Ortalïq Kenges Kamiyteti, 1928, 80 pp., 5000 cop. [Kaz 3 Arab; NN] 1452

Mopr ne? Moscow: Moprdïng Kindik Kamiteti, 1924, 48 pp., 3000 cop. [Kaz 2 Arab; NN] 1453

Mostapa. *Jïldïq jomïsïmïz jane aldïmïzdaghï maqsattarïmïz*. Chimkent: Sïrdarïya Gobïrnalïq Partiya Kamïyteti, 1928, 51 pp., 500 cop. [Kaz 3 Arab; NN] 1454

Oktabïrdïng 1-indegi keshgi majïlïs. n.p.: n.p., n.d., 8 pp., n.c. [Kaz 3 Arab; NN] 1455

Oral jem avdanïndaghï munay kasbïnïng memleketdik uyïmdastrïvshïsï, tiresti emba neptining, qïzmetterining ishki tartibteri. Gur'ev: Ural. Gub. Tipografiia, n.d., 38 pp., 2000 cop. [Kaz 2 Arab; NN] 1456

Orïsshïldïq, ultshïldiq pen küresüv tuvralï ölkelik partïya kämiyteti men ölkelik baqïlav kämesiyesining qatï. Alma Ata: n.p., n.d., 7 pp., 7000 cop. [Kaz 4 Lat; NN] 1457

Ortalïq partïya kamiytetining 1929-jïl noyabir pilenumining qorïtïndïsï. Semipalatinsk: Semeyding Okriktik Partïya Kameyteti, 1930, 100 pp., n.c. [Kaz 3 Arab; NN] 1458

Otar men olt sayasatï maseleleri jana III-intirnatsïyanal. Kzil Orda: Qazaghïstan Memleket Basbasï, 1925, 77 pp., 3000 cop. [Kaz 2 Arab; NN] 1459

Partïya mektebi men avïldaghï sayasïy oqïvdïng pïraghïramï. Semipalatinsk: Qazaghïstan Memleket Baspasï, 1928, 40 pp., 6000 cop. [Kaz 3 Arab; NN] 1460

Partïya oqïvï pïroghramdarïnïng jiynaghï. Kzil Orda: Kazizdat, 1929, 275 pp., 3000 cop. [Kaz 3 Arab; NN] 1461

Popob, N. N.; Yakoblep, Ya. A. *Lenninning ömiri men leninshildik.* Kzil Orda: Qazmemleket Basbasï, 1925, 186 pp., 5000 cop. [Kaz 2 Arab; NN] 1462

Qazaghïstan aymaqïtïq kommunist partïya kamïytetining II inshi plenomï (moshelerining jalpï jïylïsï) shïqarghan qavlïsï em qararlarï. Orenburg: Qaz. Memleket Basbaqanasï, 1924, 42 pp., 500 cop. [Kaz 2 Arab; NN] 1463

Qazaghïstan olkelik kamsamoldar kamiytetining III-pilenimining qavlïlarï. Kzil Orda: Olkelik Kamsamoldar Kamiyteti, 1929, 54 pp., 2000 cop. [Kaz 3 Arab; NN] 1464

⟨1⟩ *Qazaghïstan ortalïq atqarïv kamïyteti men kameserïyetderining istegen isderi taqrïbïtï bayandama*, 67 pp.; ⟨2⟩ *Qazaqstan qalq komisarlar kengesi*, 28 pp.; ⟨3⟩ *El bileytun qalq komisariyatdarï*, 90 pp.; ⟨4⟩ *Qarj, kasb ham avïl charvasï*, 202 pp.; ⟨5⟩ *Madani-qalq aghartïv komisarïyatdarï*, 156 pp. Orenburg: Qaz. Memleket Basba Söz Bölimi, 1923, 850 cop. [Kaz 2 Arab; NN] 1465

Qazaghïstan tovralï ortalïq partiya kamiytetining qavlïsï. Kzil Orda: "Engbekshi Qazaq," 1928, 38 pp., 12000 cop. [Kaz 3 Arab; NN] 1466

Qazaqïb, A. *Balshebekter partïyasï jalshï-batïraqtïng modesin qalay qorghaydï.* Moscow: Kenges Odaghïndaghï Elderding Kindik Basbasï, 1929, 48 pp., 2000 cop. [Kaz 3 Arab; NN] 1467

Qazaqïstan respüblikesi ükimetining 5 inshi jalpï kengester siyezine arnalghan esebi. Aq Mesjid–Orenburg: Qazaqstan Memleket Basbasï, 1925, 156 pp., 1000 cop. [Kaz 2 Arab; NN] 1468

Qazaqstan aymaqtïq kommivnist partïyasïnïng IV inshi kanferensiyasïnda shïgharïlghan "qavlï em qararlarï." Orenburg: Qazaqstan Memleket Basbaḥanasï, 1924, 64 pp., 1500 cop. [Kaz 2 Arab; NN] 1469

Qazaqstan ortalïq kenges kamiytetining 4 inshi jalpï jïylisdan keyngi III-sessiyesi. Orenburg: Qaz. Memleket Basbasï, 1924, 84 pp., 350 cop. [Kaz 2 Arab; NN] 1470

Qïzïl askerden avïl engbekshilerine. Kzil Orda: Qazaghstan Osoabïyaqïm Kengesi, 1928, 7 pp., 10000 cop. [Kaz 2 Arab; NN] 1471

Qostanay ökiriktik partïya kemiytetining IV pilenumïnïng qavlï qararlarï. Kustanai: Qostanaydïng Ökiriktik Partïya Kemiyteti, 1930, 60 pp., 500 cop. [Kaz 3 Arab; NN] 1472

Rabïynop, D. *Ondïrïs jana mekemedegi ishki tartïb tovralï jomïsshi men qïzmetker ne bilivi kerek.* Kzil Orda: Qaz. Kesibshilder Kengesi, 1928, 31 pp., 3000 cop. [Kaz 3 Arab; NN] 1473

Radek, K. *Tongkeris kösemi.* Orenburg: Qaz. Memleket Basbasï, 1925, 18 pp., 5000 cop. [Kaz 2 Arab; NN] 1474

Radnebish. *1927 inshi jïlï qazaghïstanda kengester men kenges kamiytetterining saylavï qalay ötti.* Kzil Orda: Qaz. Ortalïq Kenges Kamiyteti, 1927, 58 pp., 3500 cop. [Kaz 2 Arab; NN] 1475

Resey leninshil ortaqshïl jastar uyïmïnïng pïroghramasï men ustabï. Orenburg: Kirgizskoe Gosud. Izdat., 1924, 51 pp., 8000 cop. [Kaz 2 Arab; NN] 1476

Resey ortalïq kenges kamïytet pïrezïdomïnïng avdandïq kenges siyezderi men avdandïq atqarïv kamiytetteri tovralï 1928-jïlï, 18-uiyondegi bekitken erejesi. Alma Ata: Qazaghstan Ortalïq Kenges Kamiyteti, 1929, 32 pp., 1500 cop. [Kaz 3 Arab; NN] 1477

Rezböshkin. *Kamsamol ne?* Moscow: Kenges Odaghïndaghï Elderding Kindik Basbasï, 1926, 68 pp., 5000 cop. [Kaz 2 Arab; NN] 1478

Riumin, E. *Mekteptegy P.V.O. oquï.* Alma Ata: Qazaqtïng Byrykken Memlekettyk Baspasï, 1941, 60 pp., 10000 cop. [Kaz 4 Lat; DLC] 1479

Rodïnebish, B. *Osoabiyaqïym degen ne? Jana ar bir engbekshi oghan nege müshe bolïv kerek.* Kzil Orda: Osoabiyaqïymnïng Qazaghïstandïq Qoghamï, 1928, 14 pp., 15000 cop. [Kaz 3 Arab; NN] 1480

Rovsïya ortaqshïl partïyasïnïng on öshinshi siyezi qavlïlar. Tashkent:

Orta Azïya Basba Söz Taratïvshï Mekemesi, 1924, 111 pp., 1000 cop. [Kaz 2 Arab; NN] 1481

SSSR ulï sovetynyng altïnshï sessiasï stenografialïq otshot. n.p.: SSSR Ulï Sovety, 1940, 555 pp., 3000 cop. [Kaz 4 Lat; DLC] 1482

SSSR ulï sovetynyng jetynshy sessiasï: Stenografialïq otshot. Moscow: SSSR Ulï Sovety, 1940, 202 pp., 3000 cop. [Kaz 4 Lat; DLC] 1483

Semenniyköp, A. *Qalqoz tobïnïng jumïsï tuvralï piyänerlerge!* Kzil Orda: Qazaghïstan Baspasï, 1930, 27 pp., 3000 cop. [Kaz 4 Lat; NN] 1484

Semey okïrïgindegi barlïq avdandïq partïya kamïytetteri men uyalarïna okïriktegi kalqozdar qozghalïsïna basshïlïq istev mindetteri tuvralï. n.p.: Semeyding Okïrïktik Partïya Kamiyteti, 1929, 16 pp., n.c. [Kaz 3 Arab; NN] 1485

Sentabir 30 ïndaghï tang ertenggi majilis. n.p.: n.p., 15 pp., n.c. [Kaz 2 Arab; NN] 1486

Shïyshob, M. *Qïzïl asker nege kerek.* Kzil Orda: Qaz. Memleket Basbasï, 1926, 27 pp., 3000 cop. [Kaz 2 Arab; NN] 1487

Shornïy, B. *Avïl belsendilerin tarbiyelevding jolï.* Kzil Orda: Qaz. Memleket Basbasï, 1927, 54 pp., 3000 cop. [Kaz 3 Arab; NN] 1488

Sïrdariya göbirnelik IV inshi partïya kanperensesining qavïlï-qararlarï. Chimkent: GOMKh, 1927, 54 pp., 500 cop. [Kaz 3 Arab; NN] 1489

Sïrdariya okïriktik kamiytetining ekinshi pilenumïnïng qararlarï. Chimkent: Sïrdariya Okïriktik Partïya Kamïytetining Shigharmasï, 1929, 29 pp., 500 cop. [Kaz 3 Arab; NN] 1490

Smirnob; Alibekob. *Avïldaghï partïya oïyalarïnïng el sharïvasï jönindegi jomïstarï.* Orenburg: Kirg. Gosud. Izdatel'stvo, 1925, 36 pp., 3000 cop. [Kaz 2 Arab; NN] 1491

Soghïs önerindegi jangalïqtar tovralï. Kzil Orda: Qaz. Avekeme Dostïghïnïng Qoghamï, 1928, 23 pp., 15000 cop. [Kaz 3 Arab; NN] 1492

Sopya. *Qïzïl otav.* Kzil Orda: Kazak. Gos. Izdat, 1927, 72 pp., 2000 cop. [Kaz 3 Arab; DLC] 1493

Tayïshïn, M. Y. *Sayasat tanïv.* Moscow: Kenges Odaghïndaghï Elderding Kindik Basbasï, 1927, 361 pp., 5000 cop. [Kaz 3 Arab; NN] 1494

Government

Tïrotïskiy, L. *Lenin olt kösemi sïyaqtï.* Kzil Orda–Orenburg: Qaz. Memleket Basbasï, 1925, 12 pp., 5000 cop. [Kaz 2 Arab; NN] 1495

Tomiskiy. *Oktabir tongkerisi jomïsshïlar tabïna ne berdi.* Moscow: Kenges Odaghïndaghï Elderding Kindik Basbasï, 1927, 48 pp., 2500 cop. [Kaz 3 Arab; NN] 1496

3-oktabir köni ertenggi majïlïs. n.p.: n.p., n.d., 12 pp., n.c. [Kaz 2 Arab; NN] 1497

Yaroslawïskïy, Em. *Lenin qoraldï köterilisting qïysïnshïlï jana tajïrïybashïlï.* Orenburg: Qaz. Memleket Basbasï, 1925, 24 pp., 5000 cop. [Kaz 2 Arab; NN] 1498

Yushkop, A. *Joriqta.* Kzil Orda: Qazaghïstan Baspasï, 1930, 56 pp., 15000 cop. [Kaz 4 Lat; NN] 1499

Zinovyef, G. *Öchinchi ortaqchïldar biy-bavrmaldïq oyïmdarï.* Orenburg: Qaz. Memleket Basbasï, 1923. 40 pp., 3000 cop. [Kaz 2 Arab; NN] 1500

History

Dorïqav, Pavïl. *Balshebek balasï.* Moscow: Kenges Odaghïndaghï Elderding Kindik Basbasï, 1927, 40 pp., 4000 cop. [Kaz 2 Arab; NN] 1501

Gorïp. *Marks ben lenin.* Moscow: Kenges Odaghïndaghï Elderding Kindik Basbasï, 1926, 76 pp., 3000 cop. [Kaz 2 Arab; NN] 1502

Kemenger ulï, Q. *Qazaq tarïkhïnan.* Moscow: SSSR Ḥalqdarïnïng Kindik Basbasï, 1924, 72 pp., 4000 cop. [Kaz 2 Arab; NN] 1503

Kengester odaghïnïng tengiz askerï men jay asker ïsïnïng qalïq kemeseri jana tongkerisshil asker kengesining toraghasï. Moscow: Kenges Odaghïndaghï Elderding Kindik Basbasï, 1925, 36 pp., 3000 cop. [Kaz 2 Arab; NN] 1504

Kodïrebsky, D. *Arghï madanïyat.* Tashkent: Turk. Gosud. Izdatel'stvo, 1924, 205 pp., 10000 cop. [Kaz 2 Arab; NN] 1505

Lïlïna, Z. *Leninning adamgershiligi.* Orenburg: Qazaqstan Mamleket Basbasï, 1925, 20 pp., 5000 cop. [Kaz 2 Arab; CStH] 1506

Lïlïna, Z. *Ustatïmïz lenin.* Moscow: Sabet Odaghïndaghï Elderding Kindik Basbasï, 1925, 24 pp., 6000 cop. Kaz 2 Arab; NN] 1507

Nurmaq ulï, Nïghmet. *Qazaghïstan qurïlïsï.* Kzil Orda: Qazagh. Memleket Basbasï, 1929, 93 pp., 1000 cop. [Kaz 3 Arab; DLC] 1508

Pokïrovïskïy. *Reseyding 19, 20-y ghasïrlardaghï tongkeris qozghalïstarï.* Kzil Orda–Tashkent: Qazaqstan Memleket Basbasï, 1926, 313 pp., 3000 cop. [Kaz 2 Arab; NN] 1509

Särsek ulï, Jumaghalïy. *Qazaghïstannïng tarïyqï tabïstarï.* Qarqaralï: Qarqaralï Ökiriktik Partïya Kämiytetining Mädeniyet Nasïyqat Bölimi, 1930, 18 pp., 10000 cop. [Kaz 4 Lat; NN] 1510

Shonan olï, Tel-jan. *Qazaq jeri maselesining tarïyqï.* Kzil Orda–Tashkent: Kazizdat, 1926, 224 pp., 3000 cop. [Kaz 2 Arab; NN] 1511

Law

Ali Qaydar olï, Shakïr. *1922-jïlï shïgharïlghan engbek zangdarï.* Kzil Orda: Qaz. Memleket Basbaqanasï, 1928, 128 pp., 5000 cop. [Kaz 3 Arab; NN] 1512

Arïstanbek ulï, T. *Kenges sotï.* Kzil Orda: Qazaghïstan Baspasï, 1930, 82 pp., 3000 cop. [Kaz 4 Lat; NN] 1513

Engbek khaqïndaghï 1922 jïldïng zangdarï. Orenburg: Gosud. Izdatel'stvo KSSR, 1923, 68 pp., 3000 cop. [Kaz 1 Arab; NN] 1514

Jer zangï. Kzil Orda–Tashkent: Qazaghïstan Memleket Basbasï, 1927, 82 pp., 10000 cop. [Kaz 2 Arab; NN] 1515

Jer zangïnïng 28–38 inshi ïstatïylarïna tösinis berib jön körsetiv iretinde engbekti jerlerdi jalgha berivding tartibi tovralï qazaghstan qalïq jer kamïysarïyatï shïgharghan ereje. Alma Ata: Jetisuv Göbernelik Jer Basqarmasï, 1927, 13 and 11 pp., 1000 cop. [Kaz 2 Arab; NN] 1516

Kïrasüvkop, B. *Malïng bolsa mal därigerligining zangïn bil.* Kzil Orda: Qazaghïstan Baspasï, 1930, 26 pp., 4000 cop. [Kaz 4 Lat; NN] 1517

Mugedekterge, asïravshïysïnan ayïrïlghandargha alevmet qavïpsïzdandïrïv iretinde pensiye beriv tovralï janga zangdar. Kzil Orda: Qazaghïstan Ölkelik Qavïpsïzdandïrïv Kassesi, 1929, 132 pp., 3000 cop. [Kaz 3 Arab; NN] 1518

Qïlmïs zangï. Kzil Orda: Kazak. Gosud. Izdatel'stvo, 1925, 83 pp., 5000 cop. [Kaz 2 Arab; NN] 1519

Resey respivilikesining engbek arqïlï totqïn tüzev zangï. Kzil Orda: Qaz. Ïshkï Ister Kemeseriyeti, 1925, 59 pp., 1000 cop. [Kaz 2 Arab; NN] 1520

Law

Satsïyaldïq kenges respüvbliykeleri odaghï men resey satsïyaldïq qurama kenges respüvbliykelerining negizgi zangï: Könistiytüvtsiya. Kzil Orda: Qazaghïstan Basbasï, 1930, 79 pp., 4000 cop. [Kaz 4 Lat; NN] 1521

Social Organization

Arïstan olï, Josïb bek. *Janga tormïs jolïnda.* Moscow: Kenges Odaghïndaghï Elderding Kindik Basbasï, 1925, 103 pp., 5000 cop. [Kaz 2 Arab; NN] 1522

Avïl sharïvashïlïghï artelining ülgili ustabï. n.p.: n.p., 1930, 14 pp., 7000 cop. [Kaz 3 Arab; NN] 1523

Avïl sharïvashïlïghï artelining ustabï. Semipalatinsk: Qazaghïstan Avïl Sharïvashïlïq Kalektib Odaghï, 1929, 29 pp., 300 cop. [Kaz 3 Arab; NN] 1524

Aynala jarïs. Kzil Orda: Kazak. Gosud. Izdatel'stvo, 1926, 24 pp., 2000 cop. [Kaz 2 Arab; NN] 1525

Balïqshïlar ärtelining ülgili ostabï. Astrakhan: Balïqshïlar Qalqozïnïng Ashtarqandaghï Odaghï, 1930, 9 and 8 pp., 10000 cop. [Kaz 3 Arab, 4 Lat; NN] 1526

Baylar ökömetderining törmeleri. Orenburg: Orenburg. Gubern. Otdel. MOPR, 1924, 34 pp., 5000 cop. [Kaz 2 Arab; NN] 1527

Besenebïskiy, A. Y. *Qazaqtar üshin dene tärbiyesi oyïndarï.* Alma Ata: n.p., 1930, 64 pp., 6000 cop. [Kaz 4 Lat; NN] 1528

Bïkhovski, N. I. *Qavïbsïzdendiruv kassilarï degen ne?* Orenburg: Kirgiz Gosud. Izdatel'stvo, 1924, 48 pp., 1000 cop. [Kaz 2 Arab; NN] 1529

Dägüt. *Pabrnïng-zavït kamitäti.* Kzil Orda: Qazaqstan Mämläkät Basbasï, 1926, 145 pp., 2000 cop. [Kaz 2 Arab; NN] 1530

Dikshteyn. *Jurt ne men tirshilik qïladï?* Moscow: Oltdar Komisariyatï Janïndaghï Künshïghïs Basba Sözi, 1923, 38 pp., 5000 cop. [Kaz 2 Arab; NN] 1531

Es qïzï, Sara. *Marttïng 8-i.* Kzil Orda: Kaz. Gos. Izdat., 1926, 24 pp., 2000 cop. [Kaz 2 Arab; NN] 1532

Ïsmaghïl. *Jastar men anggime.* Orenburg: Kirgiz. Gosud. Izdatel'stvo, 1925, 53 pp., 5000 cop. [Kaz 3 Arab; NN] 1533

Jamiyle. *Jomïsshï ayelge zangnan ne biliv kerek?* Moscow: Kenges Odaghïndaghï Elderding Kindik Basbasï, 1927, 62 pp., 3000 cop. [Kaz 3 Arab; NN] 1534

Kedey, batïraqtardïng arasïndaghï jumïsï tuvralï. n.p.: n.p., 1929, 8 pp., 1000 cop. [Kaz 3 Arab; NN] 1535

Konuvkof, Y. A. *Engbekshi qara sharvanïng artelderi men kammunderi.* Moscow: Sebet Odaghïndaghï Ḥalqdardïng Kindik Basbasï, 1925, 72 pp., 4000 cop. [Kaz 3 Arab; CStH, NN] 1536

Lenin, N. *Kenges ökimeti jane ayelder jayï.* Moscow: Kenges Odaghïndaghï Elderding Kindik Basbasï, 1926, 20 pp., 4000 cop. [Kaz 2 Arab; NN] 1537

Lepisky, E. M. *Analïq pen balalïqtï qorghav ne.* Kzil Orda: Qazaghïstan Savlïq Saqtav Kemeseriyetining Tazalïq Aghartïv Bölimi, 1926, 54 pp., 2047 cop. [Kaz 2 Arab; DLC] 1538

Molkob, A. B. *Sovï taza avïl-sav boladï.* Tashkent–Samarkand: Öz. Deulet Neshryatï, 1926, 20 pp., 1047 cop. [Kaz 2 Arab; NN] 1539

Ökil ayel eskeritkishi. Orenburg: Kirgiz. Gos. Izdatel'., 1924, 20 pp., 2200 cop. [Kaz 2 Arab; NN] 1540

Ostïrovskaya, N. *Engbekshi ayelge kaperatsiya ne üshin kerek.* Orenburg: Kirgiz. Gosud. Izdat., 1925, 42 pp., 1500 cop. [Kaz 2 Arab; NN] 1541

Pïrotoklïtub, S. *Qara-sharïva ayelderine—besik üyi kerekpe.* Kzil Orda–Tashkent: Öz. Devlet Neshriyeti, 1927, 20 pp., 1047 cop. [Kaz 3 Arab; DLC, NN] 1542

Pïrtïn, E. A. *Den savlïqtïng eng ongay jolïdene shïnïqtïrïv.* Kzil Orda: Qaz. Kesibshileri Odaqtarïnïng Kengesi, 1928, 75 pp., 2000 cop. [Kaz 3 Arab; NN] 1543

QSSR avïl sharïvashïlïq artelining ülgili ostabï. Kzil Orda: Avtonom. Sektsiia, 1930, 27 pp., 1300 cop. [Kaz 3 Arab; NN] 1544

Qazaq ayelderining tengdik meyramï. Kzil Orda: Kaz. Gos. Izdat., 1926, 55 pp., 4000 cop. [Kaz 2 Arab; NN] 1545

Qazaq ayeli ham kenges khükümeti. Orenburg: Qazaqstan Memleket Basba Söz Bölimi, 1924, 44 pp., 3000 cop. [Kaz 2 Arab; NN] 1546

Qoghamdasqan eginshilik seriktigi. n.p.: Semokrizdat, 1929, 12 pp., 500 cop. [Kaz 3 Arab; NN] 1547

Täshtiyt ulï, Qaysar. "*Kedey*" *uyïmï jäne kedey batïraqtar arasindaghï jumïs.* Kzil Orda: Qazaghïstan Baspasï, 1930, 21 pp., 4000 cop. [Kaz 4 Lat; NN] 1548

Social Organization

Toghjan olï, Ghabbas. *Janga jortshïlïq.* Kzil Orda: Qaz. Memleket Basbasï, 1925, 75 pp., 1000 cop. [Kaz 2 Arab; NN] 1549

KAZAKH Humanities

Art and Architecture

Yazbetskiy, B. *Öyding tariyqï.* Moscow: Kenges Odaghïndaghï Elderding Kindik Basbasï, 1927, 36 pp., 4000 cop. [Kaz 3 Arab; NN] 1550

Language

Baytorsïn olï, Aḥmet. *Til-qoral.* Orenburg: Kirgizskoe Gosud. Izdat., 1924 5th ed., 46 pp., 5000 cop. [Kaz 2 Arab; NN] 1551

Baytorsïn olï, Aqïmet. *Til-qoral.* II. Kzil Orda: Kazizdat, 1925, 119 pp., 10000 cop. [Kaz 2 Arab; NN] 1552

Baytorsïn olï, Aqïmet. *Til-qoral.* II. n.p.: Gosudarstvennoe Izdatel'stvo KASSR., 1927, 121 pp., 15000 cop. [Kaz 3 Arab; NN] 1553

Baytursïn ulï, Aqmet. *Til jumsar.* I. Kzil Orda: Qazaghstan Jogharghï Sharïvashïlïq Kengesining Memlekettik Basbaqanasï. 1928, 46 pp., 3000 cop. [Kaz 3 Arab; NN] 1554

Baytursunïf, A. *Til-qoral.* II. Tashkent: Turkestan. Gosud. Izdat., 1922, 96 pp., 25000 cop. [Kaz 1 Arab; NN] 1555

Baytursunïf, A. *Til-qural.* Tashkent: Turkestan. Gos. Izdat., 1922, 90 pp., 35000 cop. [Kaz 1 Arab; NN] 1556

Bukin, Ish Mukhammed. *Russko-kirgizskii i kirgizsko-russkii slovar'.* Tashkent: Tipo-Litografiia S. I., Lakhtina, 1883, 363 pp., n.c. [Rus Cyr, Kaz 1 Arab; NN] 1557

Il'minskii, N. "*Materialy k izucheniiu kirgizskago nariechiia.*" Kazan: n.p., 1861, 196 pp., n.c. [Kaz 1 Arab; MH, NNC] 1558

Katarinskii, Vasilii Vladimirovich. *Kirgizsko-russkii slovar'.* Orenburg: Tipo-Litografiia B. A. Breslina, 1897, 243 pp., n.c. [Special Cyr; NN] 1559

⟨Katarinskii, V. V.⟩ *Grammatika kirgizskago iazyka: Fonetika, etimologiia i sintaksis.* Orenburg: Turgaiskaia Oblastnaia Tip., 1906, 217 pp., n.c. [Special Cyr; MH] 1560

Kemenger ulï. *Qazaqsha–russha tilmash.* Moscow: Turkestanskie Kursy Vostokovedeniia RKKA, 1925, 224 pp., 10000 cop. [Kaz 2 Arab; NN] 1561

Laptev, I. *Materialy po kazak–kirgizskomu iazyku. . .* Moscow: Trudy po Vostokovedeniiu Izdavaemye Lazarevskim Institutom Vostochnykh Iazykov, 1900, 148 pp., n.c. [Special Cyr; MH, NNC] 1562

Melïoranskïi, P. M. *Kratkaia grammatika kazak–kirgizskago iazyka: Chast' 1, fonetika i morf.* St. Petersburg: Tip. Imp. Ak. Nauk, 1894, 72 pp., n.c. [Special Cyr; MH] 1563

Literature

Abay. *Ibray Qunanbay ulï.* Tashkent: Turkistan Rispöblikesining Basba Söz Taratuvshï Mekhkemesi, 1922 3d ed., 293 pp., 3000 cop. [Kaz 1 Arab; NN] 1564

Abay (Ibrahim) Qunanbaev. *Shïgharmalarïnïng tolïq jïynaghï.* Alma Ata: Qazaqtïng Bïrïkken Memleket Baspasï, 1945, 504 pp., 10200 cop. [Kaz 5 Cyr; DLC] 1565

Abdïqadïr olï, Qalmaqan. *Jalshï.* Tangdamalï ölengder. Kzil Orda: Kazgiz, 1928, 63 pp., 5000 cop. [Kaz 3 Arab; NN] 1566

Aghjan. *Josob qan.* Moscow: Kenges Odaghïndaghï Elderding Kindik Basbasï, 1928, 18 pp., n.c. [Kaz 3 Arab; NN] 1567

Anop, N. *Merezden qotqardï.* Kzil Orda: Kaznarkomzdrav, 1926, 39 pp., 2000 cop. [Kaz 2 Arab; NN] 1568

Asqar. *Qïzïl äsker ölengderi.* Kzil Orda: Qazaghïstan Baspasï, 1929, 56 pp., 5000 cop. [Kaz 4 Lat; NN] 1569

Aymautïf, J. *Slang qïz.* Orenburg: Kazgosizdat, 1922, 24 pp., 3000 cop. [Kaz 1 Arab; NN] 1570

Aymavït ulï, Jusïpbek. *Qartqoja.* Kzil Orda: Kazakstanskoe Gosudarstvennoe Izdatel'stvo, 1926, 209 pp., 5000 cop. [Kaz 2 Arab; NN] 1571

Barbïvs, Anri. *Mayli köye.* Uralsk: Qazaghstan Basbasï, 1929, 99 pp., 3000 cop. [Kaz 3 Arab; NN] 157

Barjaqsï balasï, Akhmet. *Ming bir maqal.* Moscow: Konchïghïs Basbasï, 1923, 58 pp., 10000 cop. [Kaz 1 Arab; NN] 157

Basïghara olï, Jusïb-bik. *Kün kürkirev min tayzaghay.* Tashkent: Turkistan Riyspoblikesining Söz Taratuvshï Makhkemesi, 1923, 44 pp., 5000 cop. [Kaz 1 Arab; NN] 1574

Bayghoja ulï, Saypolla. *Pediyeshil moldalar.* Kzil Orda: Qazaghstan Memleket Basbasï, 1927, 35 pp., 3000 cop. [Kaz 2 Arab; DLC] 1575

Bayzaq olï, Ïysa. *Qoralay solïv.* Kzil Orda: Kazizdat, 1926, 50 pp. 3000 cop. [Kaz 2 Arab; NN] 1576

Beyimbet. *Saghïndïq.* Kzil Orda: Qaz. Memleket Basbasï, 1927, 34 pp., 4000 cop. [Kaz 2 Arab; NN] 1577

Beyimbet. *Soyqandï sodïrlar.* Kzil Orda: Qaz. Qalïq Sharïvasïnïng Ortalïq Kengesining Basbaqanbasï, 1928, 151 pp., 6000 cop. [Kaz 3 Arab; NN] 1578

Beymbet. *El mektebi.* Kzil Orda: Kazak. Gos. Izdat., 1926, 16 pp., 3000 cop. [Kaz 2 Arab; NN] 1579

Chaykh Islam ulï, Jusibbek. *Qïz jibek.* Tashkent: Turkistan Respoblikasïnïng Basba Soz Taratov Maḥkamesi, 1923, 130 pp., 5000 cop. [Kaz 2 Arab; NN] 1580

Divaev, A. A. *Kirgizskaia bylina o Biket-batyrie.* Kazan: Tipo-litografiia Imperatorskago Universiteta, 1897, 72 pp., n.c. [Kaz 1 Arab, Russ Cyr; MH] 1581

Divayïf, Abubikir. *Batïrlar.* 1. *Qoblandï baṭïr*, 158 pp.; 2. *Nark ughlï chora*, 23 pp.; 3. *Bikat baṭir*, 27 pp.; 4. *Qambar baṭïr* 39 pp.; 5. *Shora baṭïr*, 59 pp.; 6. *Alpamïs baṭïr*, 56 pp.; 7. *Mirza idege baṭïr*, 24 pp. Tashkent: Turkistan Rispöblikasïnïng Basba Söz Chïgharuvchï Mahkamasï, 1922, 10000 cop. [Kaz 1 Arab; NN] 1582

Divayïf, Abuv-Bakir. *Kene-sarï: Navrïzbay.* Tashkent: Turkistan Respöblikensining Basba Söz Taratuchï Makhkemesi, 1923, 111 pp., 5000 cop. [Kaz 1 Arab; NN] 1583

Dosmuqambet ulï, Qalel. *Ïsatay-maqambet.* Tashkent: Qazaghstan Memleket Basbasïnïng Künshïghïs Bölimi, 1925, 161 pp., 3000 cop. [Kaz 2 Arab; NN] 1584

Emeliyanov, N. *Sïrlï kürke.* Orenburg: Qazaqïstan Memleket Basbasï, 1925, 16 pp., 5000 cop. [Kaz 2 Arab; CStH] 1585

Er sayïn. Moscow: Konchighis Basbasï, 1923, 95 pp., 6000 cop. [Kaz 1 Arab; NN] 1586

Gorïnïp. *Sakko men bansetti.* Kzil Orda: Qaz. Basbasï, 1929, 48 pp., 3000 cop. [Kaz 3 Arab; NN] 1587

Gorki, Maksim. *Sungqar jïrï.* Moscow: SSSR Khalqdarïnïng Kindik Basbasï, 44 pp., 1924, 4000 cop. [Kaz 2 Arab; NN] 1588
Ïsmaghïl. *Ult tiyatïrï tovralï.* Kzil Orda: Engbekshi Qazaq, 1926, 30 pp., 5000 cop. [Kaz 2 Arab; NN] 1589
Ïybanïb, Pse-Bolot. *Tört anggime.* Moscow: Kenges Odaghïndaghï Elderding Kindik Basbasï, 1927, 64 pp., 5000 cop. [Kaz 2 Arab; NN] 1590
Ïybanob, Bsebolot. *Temir talqan.* Kzil Orda: Qazaghïstan Baspasï, 1929, 63 pp., 3000 cop. [Kaz 3 Arab; NN] 1591
Jansogor olï, Ileyas. *Ötirik.* Moscow: Kenges Odaghïndaghï Elderding Kindik Basbasï, 1927, 94 pp., 4500 cop. [Kaz 2 Arab; NN] 1592
Jansügir ulï, Iliyas. *Odaq.* n.p.: Qazaghstan Basbasï, 1929, 14 pp., 5000 cop. [Kaz 4 Lat; DLC] 1593
Jansügür ulï, Iliyas. *Jumbaq.* Kzil Orda: Qazaghïstan Baspasï, 1930, 35 pp., 5000 cop. [Kaz 4 Lat; NN] 1594
Josïb-bek olï, Qamza. "*Qarsaqbay.*" Kzil Orda: Gos. Izdat. KSSR, 1928, 56 pp., 3000 cop. [Kaz 3 Arab; NN] 1595
Kïrolenko. *Maqardïng tüsï.* Moscow: Tsentr. Vost. Izd. pri NKN, 1923, 39 pp., 3000 cop. [Kaz 1 Arab; NN] 1596
London, Jek. *Eki änggime: Moyïngha aluv, shïda.* Kzil Orda: Qazaghïstan Baspasï, 1930, 36 pp., 3000 cop. [Kaz 3 Arab, 4 Lat; NN] 1597
Maghjan. *Aq boz at.* Moscow: Qazaghïstan Memleket Basbasï, 1925, 31 pp., 3000 cop. [Kaz 2 Arab; NN] 1598
Mamin-Sibirek. 1. *Baymaqan.* 2. *Özi.* Moscow: Kenges Odaghïndagï Elderding Kindik Basbasï, 1927, 47 pp., 3000 cop. [Kaz 2 Arab; NN] 1599
Marabay. *Er targhïn.* Moscow: Künchïghïs Basbasï, 1923, 72 pp., 10000 cop. [Kaz 1 Arab; NN] 1600
Materialy po kazak-kirgizskomu iazyku, sobrannye I. Laptevym. Moscow: Tipografiia Varvary Gattsuk, 1900, 148 pp., n.c. [Kaz 1 Arab, Russ Cyr; NN] 1601
Maylï olï, Beyimbet. *Kolpash.* Kzil Orda: Kazak. Gos. Izdat., 1926, 61 pp., 3000 cop. [Kaz 2 Arab; NN] 1602
Maylï olï, Beyimbet. *Neke qïyar.* Kzil Orda: Qaz. Memleket Basbasï, 1927, 40 pp., 4000 cop. [Kaz 2 Arab; NN] 1603

Maylï olï, Beyimbet. *Shoghanïng belgisi.* Jana basqa anggimeler. Moscow: Tsent. Izdat. Nar. SSSR, 1926, 75 pp., 5000 cop. [Kaz 2 Arab; NN] 1604

Moqan olï, Sabïyt. *Ölengder jïnaghï.* I–III iret. Kzil Orda: Qaz. Memleket Basbasï, 1927, 182 pp., 3000 cop. [Kaz 2 Arab; NN] 1605

Morat. *Morat aqïnnïng sözderi.* Tashkent: Orta Aziya Memleket Basbasï, 1924, 152 pp., 1000 cop. [Kaz 2 Arab; NN] 1606

Mosireb olï, Ghabiyt. *Amirqan biydayïghï.* Kzil Orda: Kazizdat., 1928, 64 pp., 5000 cop. [Kaz 3 Arab; NN] 1607

Mostapa olï, Seyit Battal. *Sherniyaz aqïn.* Moscow: Kenges Odaghïndaghï Elderding Kindik Basbasï, 1925, 32 pp., 5000 cop. [Kaz 2 Arab; NN] 1608

Naqïmjan olï, Amze. *Ush kezeng.* Uralsk: Qazaghïstan Basbasï, 1929, 132 pp., 3000 cop. [Kaz 3 Arab; NN] 1609

Neberob, A. *Men omirge jerikbin.* Moscow: Kenges Odaghïndaghï Elderding Kindik Basbasï, 1927, 23 pp., 4000 cop. [Kaz 3 Arab; NN] 1610

Nïsambay. *Kenesarï-navrïzbay.* Moscow: Könchïghïs Basbasï, 1923, 72 pp., 6000 cop. [Kaz 2 Arab; NN] 1611

Nïsambay. *Kene-sarï-navrïzbay.* Moscow: Tsent. Vostoch. Izdatel'., 1924, 72 pp., 6000 cop. [Kaz 2 Arab; NN] 1612

Nurjan. Bir pirdelik istaq. Tashkent: Izdanie Turkestanskogo Gosudarstvennogo Izdatel'stvo, 1922, 11 pp., 5000 cop. [Kaz. 1 Arab; NN] 1613

Olï kon: "Kedey" gazetining tilshilerining oktabirdïng tutïna arnaghan ölengi. Akmolinsk: "Kedey" Gazeti, 1927, 32 pp., 1500 cop. [Kaz 2 Arab; NN] 1614

Pantusov, Nikolai. *Obraztsy kirgizskoi narodnoi literatury.* 1. *Irtegilar.* 2. *Her türli tajrïybe sozdar.* 3. *Alghïs qarghïs sozdarï.* 4. *Ṣaylav ṭurasïnde bir aulang.* Kazan: Daralghïlïm va Alfïnun Matbaghasï, 1909, 55 and 54 pp., n.c. [Kaz 1 Arab; MH] 1615

Povshkin. *Tas mïyman.* Kzil Orda: Qazaghïstan Memleket Basbasï, 1926, 55 pp., 1000 cop. [Kaz 2 Arab; NN] 1616

Qanïsh. *Er edige.* Moscow: Kenges Odaghïndaghï Elderding Kindik Basbasï, 1927, 98 pp., 3000 cop. [Kaz 2 Arab; NN] 1617

Radlof, V. V. (ed.). *Qozï-körpesh-bayan.* Moscow: SSSR Ḥalqdarïnïng Kindik Basbasï, 1924, 60 pp., 5000 cop. [Kaz 1 Arab; NN] 1618

Seypolda olï, Sadoïvaqas. *Oyïmdasïv jana engbek shart jalshïlar qorghanï.* Kzil Orda: Qaz. Memleket Basbasï, 1926, 44 pp., 5000 cop. [Kaz 2 Arab; DLC, NN] 1619

Shana ulï, Atïghay; Bäyseyit ulï, Qana-bek. *Zävre.* Kzil Orda: Qazaghïstan Baspasï, 1930, 47 pp., 4000 cop. [Kaz 4 Lat; NN] 1620

Sholpannïng ölengderi. Kzil Orda: Qaz. Mamleket Basbasï, 1927, 50 pp., 4000 cop. [Kaz 2 Arab; NN] 1621

Sifalle olï, Saduaqas. *Bakht jolïna.* Orenburg: Kirgosizdat., 1922, 36 pp., 5000 cop. [Kaz 1 Arab; NN] 1622

Sïzdïq olï, Jaqan. *Engbek jemisteri.* Kzil Orda: Qaz. Memleket Basbasï, 1929, 177 pp., 3000 cop. [Kaz 3 Arab; NN] 1623

Stalin tuvralï jïr. Alma Ata: Qazaghïstan Körkem Ädebiyet Baspasï, 1937, 28 pp., 35150 cop. [Kaz 4 Lat; NNC] 1624

Tang ölengderi. Moscow: Kenges Odaghïndaghï Elderding Kindik Basbasï, 1925, 115 pp., 4000 cop. [Kaz 2 Arab; CStH] 1625

Tav elindegi oqïya. Tashkent: Kazak. Gosud. Izdat., 1925, 78 pp., 3000 cop. [Kaz 2 Arab; NN] 1626

Tolstoy, L. N. 1. *Kafkaz tutqïnï.* 2. *Jumïrtqaday bïday.* 3. *Jeti qarashï.* Moscow: Sebet Odaghïndaghï Qalqdardïng Kindik Basbasï, 1925, 56 pp., 5000 cop. [Kaz 2 Arab; NN] 1627

Tolstoy, L. N. *Khajï murat.* Moscow: Kunchïghïs mam Kunbatïs Basbasïnïng Qazaq Bolïmï, 1924, 179 pp., 4000 cop. [Kaz 1 Arab; CStH, NN] 1628

Toqmagambetov, Asqar. *Tangdamalï shïgharmalarï.* Alma Ata: Qazaqtïng Bïrikken Memleket Baspasï, 1945, 222 pp., 10000 cop. [Kaz 5 Cyr; DLC] 1629

Tormanjan olï, Ötebay (ed.). *Tang ölengderi.* Moscow: Kenges Odaghïndaghï Elderding Kindik Basbasï, 1925, 115 pp., 4000 cop. [Kaz 2 Arab; NN] 1630

Vagner, Yu. *Ava tovralï anggimeler.* Tashkent: Turk. Gosud. Izdatel'stvo, 1924, 77 pp., 10000 cop. [Kaz 2 Arab; NN] 1631

Vagner, Yu. *Denemizding tözelivi men jomïs qïlïvï tovralï anggimeler.* Tashkent: Turk. Gosud. Izdatel'stvo, 1924, 126 pp., 10000 cop. [Kaz 2 Arab; NN] 1632

Vagner, Yu. *Janïvarlar tovralï anggimeler.* Tashkent: Turk. Gosud. Izdatel'stvo, 1924, 126 pp., 10000 cop. [Kaz 2 Arab; NN] 1633

Vagner, Yu. *Jerding jaratïlïsï jayïndaghï anggïmeler.* Tashkent:

Turk. Gosud. Izdatel'stvo, 1924, 96 pp., 10000 cop. [Kaz 2 Arab; NN] 1634

Vagner, Yu. *Ösimdikderding tiriychiligi men tozelivi tovralï anggimeler*. Tashkent: Turk. Gosud. Izdatel'stvo, 1924, 102 pp., 10000 cop. [Kaz 2 Arab; NN] 1635

Vagner, Yu. *Suv khaqïnda anggïmelar*. Tashkent: Turk. Gosud. Izdatel'stvo, 1924, 90 pp., 10000 cop. [Kaz 2 Arab; NN] 1636

Vasil'ev, A. V. *Obraztsy kirgizskoi narodnoi slovesnosti*. Orenburg: Tipo-Litografiia B. A. Breslina, 1898, 89 pp., n.c. [Special Cyr; NN] 1637

Yansugur ulï, Ïlïias. *Yangqa*. Kzil Orda: Qazaq Yanga Alïpbe Kïndïq Kamïitetï, 1929, 60 pp., 5000 cop. [Kaz 4 Lat; NN] 1638

Philosophy and Religion

Sviashchennaia istoriia vetkhago i novago zaveta na kirgizskom iazykie. Kazan: Prav. Miss Obshch. Tip. M. A. Chirkovoi, 1893, 301 pp., n.c. [Special Cyr; MH] 1639

Yisus khristostïng aytkan mïsaldarï. Kazan: Prav. Miss. Obshch., 1893, 26 pp., n.c. [Special Cyr; MH] 1640

Yisus khristostïng etken küdretteri. Kazan: Prav. Miss. Obshch., Tip. M. A. Chirkovoi, 1893, 31 pp., n.c. [Special Cyr; MH] 1641

KHAKASS Social Sciences

Economics

Soboläf, V. *Chon sadi kopäratsa TKP(b) XVI sïyächïnïng püdürgängïndä.* Moscow: SSRS Chonïnïng Säntïr Izdatelïstïvazï, 1930, 15 pp., 2000 cop. [Khak 2 Lat; NN] 1642

Ülüschü. *San pirerïneng khatap tapchang togista: Ir, ipchï kresen argistar.* n.p.: Mingostip, 1928, 7 pp., 2000 cop. [Khak 1 Cyr; NN] 1643

Education

Khakasstïng shkolazï pastaga khorar pichik. Moscow: Tsentral'noe Izdatel'stvo Narodov SSSR, 1926, 48 pp., 3000 cop. [Khak 1 Cyr; NN] 1644

Samrin, K. *Naa chol: Khakas shkolazïnïng bukvarï.* Moscow: SSRS Chonïnïng Säntïr Izdatälstïvazï, 1930, 48 pp., 4000 cop. [Khak 2 Lat; NN] 1645

Togïshev, K. *Khakasstïng ing pastap ügrener pichi.* Moscow: Tsentral'noe Izdatel'stvo Narodov SSSR, 1926, 92 pp., 3000 cop. [Khak 1 Cyr; NN] 1646

Government

Krivolapov, N. *Partiyă, komsomol paza pioner.* Moscow: Khakaskay Okrugtïng Ügregïz Pölinïng Tïlbeschï Komissiyazï, 1928, 29 pp., 1000 cop. [Khak 1 Cyr; NN] 1647

Topang, A. M. *Chöpter ülgüzü.* Moscow: Khakas Okrugïnïng Pïchïk Sïgaryang Kolegïyezï, 1928, 81 pp., 1000 cop. [Khak 1 Cyr; NN] 1648

Social Organization

Falïkner, V. N. *Khazïg küstüg polangar.* Ikinchi chardïchï. Moscow: Khakas Okrugïnïng Pïchïk Sïgaryang Kolägïyezi Agban-Piltïri, 1928, 52 pp., 2000 cop. [Khak 1 Cyr; CStH, NN] 1649

Falïkner, V. N. *Khazïg küstüg polangar pastagï chardïchï.* Moscow:

Khakas Okrugïnïng Pïchïk Sïgaryang Kolegïyezï Agban-Piltïrï, 1928, 70 pp., 2000 cop. [Khak 1 Cyr; NN] 1650

Noga alganni sogïy chaltandïrarga charabas. Moscow: Khakas Okrugïnïng Pïchïk Püdüryeng Kollegiyazï, 1928, 28 pp., 2000 cop. [Khak 1 Cyr; NN] 1651

Spirin, A. *Ipchïlärbïnäng khaang aynïng 8-jï künü.* Moscow: SSRP Chonïnïng Säntr Ïzdatälïstvazï, 1930, 34 pp., 1000 cop. [Khak 2 Lat; NN] 1652

Zalkind, I. *Palanï arïgha ügrädïnger.* Moscow: SSRP Chonïnïng Säntr Ïzdatälïstvazï, 1929, 20 pp., 2000 cop. [Khak 2 Lat; NN] 1653

KHAKASS Humanities

Language

Katanov, N. *Khakastïng orus tïllerïnïng sös pïchïgï.* Moscow: Khakas Okrughïnïng Ügregïgh Pölinïng Pïchïk Püdüryeng Kollegiyazï Agban Piltïrï, 1928, 47 pp., 2000 cop. [Khak 1 Cyr; NN] 1654

Khakas tïlïne alïlgan naa sösternïng pichïgï. Minusinsk: Khakas Okrugïnïng Pïchïk Sïgaryang Kollegiyazï, 1929, 46 pp., n.c. [Khak 1 Cyr; NN] 1655

Literature

Radlov, V. *Obraztsy narodnoi literatury tiurkskikh plemen.* Chast' IX: Nariechïia uriankhaitsev (Soiotov), abakanskikh Tatar i Karagasov. Teksty, sobrannye i perevedennye N.Th. Katanovym. Teksty. St. Petersburg: Napechatano po rasporiazhenïiu Imperatorskoi Akademïi Nauk, 1907, xlviii and 668 pp., n.c. [Special Cyr; NNC] 1656

Spirin, I. M. *Talas.* Moscow: SSRP Chonïnïng Sentr Ïzdatelïstvazï, 1930, 35 pp., 2000 cop. [Khak 2 Lat; NN] 1656a

Philosophy and Religion

Topang, A. M. *Noga olgan tayma sagïstïg polparcha.* Moscow: Khakastïng Pïchïk Püdüryeng Kollegiyazï, 1928, 21 pp., 2000 cop. [Khak 1 Cyr; CStH, NN] 1657

KIRGIZ General (periodicals)

Dïyqan (Frunze) 1929: 1, 5–7; 1930: 1/2. [Kir 1 Arab, 2 Lat; NN] 1658
Jangï madanïyat jolunda (Frunze) 1929: 2–5, 8/9. [Kir 2 Lat; NN] 1659
Kemonos (Frunze) 1927: 10/11; 1928: 3/4. [Kir 1 Arab; NN] 1660

KIRGIZ Social Sciences

Economics

Ayïlcharba nologu tuuralu jangï mïyzam. Frunze: Qïr. Aqcha Kemiyseriyeti, 1929, 10 pp., 5000 cop. [Kir 1 Arab; NN] 1661
Dïyqan charbasïn nïghayta torghan otosh zayïmï tooralo. Frunze: Kirgosizdat, n.d., 4 pp., 4000 cop. [Kir 1 Arab; NN] 1662
El aralïq keperetib künü. Frunze: Kirgosizdat, 10 pp., n.d., 10000 cop. [Kir 1 Arab; NN] 1663
Kerek jaraq qoomdorunun teksherüü kemesiyesinin nusqasï. Moscow: Kengesh Sayuzundaghï Elderdin Borbor Basmasï, 1928, 59 pp., 1000 cop. [Kir 1 Arab; NN] 1664
Kerek-jaraq qoomunun bashqarmasïnïn birinchï arïshï. Moscow: Kengesh Sayuzundaghï Elderdin Borbor Basmasï, 1928, 63 pp., 1000 cop. [Kir 1 Arab; CStH, NN] 1665
Khanin, B. F. *1.1 gektar jerden 6739 kïloghïram, (411 pul 15 qadaq) asïl alïp qalqozchu Moolon Palban Abdughapar uulunun bïrïghadï qanday qïlïp baqtanïn asïlïn mïnchalïq joghoru kötördü.* Tashkent: Baqtachïlïq Jana Baqta Önör Jaylarï Jönünön Jalpï Sayuzduq Ilim Teksherüü Inistüti (NIKhI], 1931, 14 pp., 5000 cop. [Kir 2 Lat; NN] 1666
Konko, B. M. *Ayïl-qïshlaq, kerek-jaraq keperetibine kerek maldardï ïlghab baa qoyub satïb aluu.* Moscow: Kengesh Sayuzundaghï Elderdin Borbor Basmasï, n.d., 98 pp., 2000 cop. [Kir 1 Arab; NN] 1667
Matbeenko, Y. *Sugharuu jönünön paqta egüüchülör emine bilishi kerek.* Tashkent: Baqtachïlïq jana Baqta Önör Jaylarïnïng Jalpï Sayuzduq Ilim Izildöö Inistüti (NIKhI], 1931, 10 pp., 6500 cop. [Kir 2 Lat; NN] 1668
Memleket qarïzïnïn paydasï. Frunze: Qïrghïzïstan Memleket Basmasï, 1929, 42 pp., 2000 cop. [Kir 1 Arab; NN] 1669

Economics

Molochnïy, D. *Jalchï-malaylardï qamsïzdandïruu*. Moscow: Sayuzdaghï Elder menen Memleket Basmasï, 1929, 37 pp., 3000 cop. [Kir 1 Arab; NN] 1670

Qïrghïzïstanda özara salïq saluu tuuralu. Frunze: Qïrghïzstan A.Q.S.K.R. Aqcha Kemiyseriyeti, 1929, 36 pp., 1500 cop. [Kir 1 Arab; NN] 1671

SKRSnïn el charbasïn ündüstürlöshtürö turghan 3-memilekettik ichki utush zayïmïnïn ablighatsiyasïn ayïl jerlerinde satuu shertteri tuuralu ayïl kengeshteri üchün bolghon nosghoo. Frunze: Kirgosizdat, n.d. 41 pp., 800 cop. [Kir 1 Arab; NN] 1672

Semenob, A. S. *Jündön kiyim-kiyiz jasoo önürüsh jayï*. Moscow: Kengesh Sayuzundaghï Elderdin Borbor Basmasï, 1929, 54 pp., 2000 cop. [Kir 1 Arab; NN] 1673

Shimonopskaya. *Birikme charbasïnïn öndürüsh pïlanï*. Tashkent: Baqtachïlïq jana Baqta Önör Jaylarï Jönünön Jalpï Sayuzduq Ilim Teksherüü Inistitüti (NIKhI), 1931, 17 pp., 2000 cop. [Kir 2 Lat; NN] 1674

Shubayup, K. *Batïraqtar jana birikmeleshtirüü*. Moscow: SSSR Elinin Borborduq Basmasï jana Qïrghïz Memleket Basmasï, 1930, 36 pp., 3000 cop. [Kir 2 Lat; NN] 1675

Zabavin, A. N. *1930-31-jïlda birimdik ayïl charba nalogü*. Frunze: Qïrghïzïstan Memleket Basmasï, 1930, 76 pp., 10000 cop. [Kir 2 Lat; NN] 1676

Education

Aghartuu kemesiyasï. Tashkent: Orto-Azïya Kesibchiler Buyrosu, 1927, 17 pp., 500 cop. [Kir 1 Arab; DLC] 1677

Arabay uulu. *Jazuu jolunda saamalïq*. Moscow: Maskudogu Borbor Khalq Basmakhanasïnda, 1925, 23 pp., 10000 cop. [Kir 1 Arab; NN] 1678

Birinchi basqïch el maktabterine arnalghan eseb kitabï. Moscow: SSSR Qalqïnïn Borbor Basmasï Meḥkemesi, 1925, 68 pp., 10000 cop. [Kir 1 Arab; NN] 1679

Ghratsïyanskey, I.; Kevun, I. *Esep kitebi*. III. Frunze: Qïrghïzïstan Memleket Basmasï, 1928, 105 pp., 7000 cop. [Kir 2 Lat; NN] 1680

Ïybanob, G. Ï. *Bashtooch jaghrabiya.* II. Moscow: Qïr Memleket Basmasï, 1928, 224 pp., 6500 cop. [Kir 1 Arab; NN] 1681

Ïybanov, G. Ï.; Ïybanov, G. G. *Birinchi basqïch jaarapïya jana ölkö taanuu.* Frunze: Qïrghïzstan Memleket Basmasï, n.d., 130 pp., 7000 cop. [Kir 2 Lat; NN] 1682

Ïyvanof, G. Ï. *Joorapïyanïn bashqï darsï.* I. Moscow: SSSR Qalqtarïnïn Borbor Basma Maḥkemesi, 1925, 154 pp., 5300 cop. [Kir 1 Arab; NN] 1683

Jalenof, K. *Bashtooch maktebte eseb üyrötüünün jolu.* Moscow: SSSR Qalqtarïnïn Borbor Basma Maḥkemesi, 1925, 16 pp., 3000 cop. [Kir 1 Arab; CStH, NN] 1684

Jangïbay uulu, M. *Qïrghïz tilinin oquu kitebi.* I. Frunze: Qïrghïzïstan Memleket Basmasï, 1930, 64 pp., 15000 cop. [Kir 2 Lat; NN] 1685

Jantösh uulu, Q. *Oquu kitebi.* I. Frunze: Qïrghïzïstan Memleket Basmasï, 1930, 126 pp., 26000 cop. [Kir 2 Lat; NN] 1686

Jumabay uulu, M. *Bashtooch maktebte ana tilin oquutu jönü.* Moscow: SSSR Qalqtarïnïn Borbor Basma Maḥkamasï, 1925, 27 pp., 3000 cop. [Kir 1 Arab; CStH, NN] 1687

Naamat uulu, S.; Ajïyman. *Tungghuch: Ayaldar üchün oquu kitebi.* Frunze: Qïrghïzïstan Memleket Basmasï, 1929, ii and 37 pp., 5000 cop. [Kir 2 Lat; NN] 1688

Qïrghïzdïn jangï alïp-beesinin qïsqacha tarïghï. Frunze: Qïrghïzïstandïn Basma Söz Taratuu Mekemesi, 1927, 11 and 5 pp., 3000 cop. [Kir 1 Arab; NN] 1689

Qïzïl burchok. Tashkent: Orto-Azïya Kesibchiler Buyrosu, 1927, 8 pp., 500 cop. [Kir 1 Arab; DLC] 1690

Tïnïstan uulu, Qasïm. *Oquu-jazuu bil.* Moscow: Kengesh Sayozondaghï Elderdin Borbor Basmasï, 1927, 48 pp., 10000 cop. [Kir 1 Arab; NN] 1691

Geography

Ïyvanov, G. Ï. *Satsïyaldïq kengeshter respoblikeler sayuzunun jaarapïyasï.* Frunze: Qïrghïzïstan Memleket Basmasï, 1928, 145 pp., 2500 cop. [Kir 2 Lat; NN] 1692

Ayïl kengeshterinde eseb aluu eseb qïsab ötkörüü jana ish jörgözö jaghïnan bolghon jöndöö. Frunze: Kirgosizdat, 1928, 85 pp., 500 cop. [Kir 1 Arab; NN] 1693

Balïydob, Ark. *Qïzïl armiyanïn köchö eminede.* Frunze: Qïr. Memleket Basmasï, 1928, 38 pp., 2000 cop. [Kir 1 Arab; NN] 1694

Balshabekter partïyasï jardï-jalchïlardïn suroosun qantib qorghoyt. Moscow: SSSRdïn Ayïl-Charba jana Toqoy Jumushchular Kemiteti, n.d., 28 pp., 1500 cop. [Kir 1 Arab; NN] 1695

Bereshegin, G. *SSSR degen emine.* Moscow: Kengesh Sayozondaghï Elderdin Borbor Basmasï, 1927, 46 pp., 2500 cop. [Kir 1 Arab; NN] 1696

Birgeniskiy, B. *Ayïl kemonos jashtarï öchön sayasï oqoo kitebi.* Moscow: Kengesh Sayozondaghï Elderdin Borbor Basmasï, 1927, 80 pp., 3000 cop. [Kir 1 Arab; NN] 1697

Boloshtoq jana ïrayondoq atqaroo kemitetterinin eseb jörgözöö jana eseb-qïsab ötköröö jaghïnan bolghon jönidöösö: Instiröksiyasï. Frunze: Kirgosizdat, 1927, 52 pp., 250 cop. [Kir 1 Arab; NN] 1698

Buloton: B.K.Pnïn orto-azïyalïq büyrosunun jumushchu dïyqan ayaldar bölömü. Kezeksiz chïgharma. 1927/28 jïlï jumushchu dïyqan ayaldarïnïn ökülün qayta shayloo tuuralo materiyaldarï. Tashkent: B.K.P nïn Orto-Azïyalïq Büyrosunun Jumushchu, Dïyqan Ayaldar Bölümünün Basmasï, n.d., 48 pp., 1000 cop. [Kir 1 Arab; NN] 1699

Eriktöö qïrghïzïstan sasïyalchïl kengeshter respüblikesinin qurulushu: Frunze: E.Q.O. Oblostuq Atqaruu Kemiteti, 1927, 78 pp., 1053 cop. [Kir 1 Arab; DLC] 1700

Eriktöö qïrghïzïstan sasïyalchïl kengeshter respüblikesinin qurulushu: Matïrïyal jana dakomentter. Frunze: E.Q.O. Oblostuq Atqaruu Kemiteti, 1927, 102 pp., 1053 cop. [Kir 1 Arab; NN] 1701

Jalpï sayuzduq kemunus (b) partïyasïnïn pïroghram jana ustabï. Frunze: Qïrghïzïstan Memleket Basmasï, 1927, 148 pp., 3000 cop. [Kir 1 Arab; NN] 1702

Kamonostor intirnatsanalïnïn pirghiramï. Frunze: Qïrghïzïstan Memleket Basmasï, 1929, 100 pp., 2000 cop. [Kir 1 Arab; NN] 1703

Kamunus partïyasïnïn Qïrghïzïstan uyumun tazaloo jana teksherüünün jïyïntïghï. n.p.: Qïrghïzïstan Oblustuq Partïya Kemiyteti, 1930, 31 pp., 1000 cop. [Kir 2 Lat; NN] 1704

Kerpinski, O. *Jardï-jalchï dïyqandar jolbashchïsï*. Moscow: SSSR Qalqtarïnïn Borbor Basma Meḥkamesi, 1925, 12 pp., 5000 cop. [Kir 1 Arab; NN] 1705

Lenin, B. I. *Jalchïlardïn üstömdügü jana kengeshter ökümötü*. Frunze: n.p., 1928, 80 pp., 3000 cop. [Kir 1 Arab; NN] 1706

N. Sh. *Dünöyü jüzündügü joldoshtorubuz*. Moscow: Kengesh Sayozondaghï Elderdin Borbor Basmasï, 1927, 72 pp., 3000 cop. [Kir 1 Arab; NN] 1707

Nodel, B. V. *XV-jalpï sayuzduq part kenperensïya tuuralu kemünüster emine bilöö kerek*. n.p.: Orto Azïya Basmaqanasï, 1927, 55 pp., 2000 cop. [Kir 1 Arab; DLC, NN] 1708

Oblustuq partïya kemitetinin 5-kenperensiyesinin jïyïyntïqtarïna qarata. Frunze: Qïrghïzïstan Memleket Basmasï, 1929, 66 pp., 2000 cop. [Kir 1 Arab; NN] 1709

Ongcholdoqqa jana kelishööchölökkö qarshï matïrïyaldar jïynaghï. Frunze: Qïrghïzïstan Memleket Basmasï, 1929, 56 pp., 2000 cop. [Kir 1 Arab; NN] 1710

Orusïya kemönister partïyasïnïn ustabï. Pishpek: Qïrghïz. Oblostoq Partïya Kemitetinin Ogot-Nasïyat Bölümü, 1925, 28 pp., 1000 cop. [Kir 1 Arab; NN] 1711

Özgörüsh jolonda köröshööchölörgö jardam böröö el aralïq oyomonon mildeti menen ishi. Frunze: Qïrghïz. Oblostoq Mopor Kemiyteti, 1928, 39 pp., 3000 cop. [Kir 1 Arab; NN] 1712

Qamït. *Piyenerler menen anggeme*. Moscow: Kengesh Sayozondaghï Elderdin Borbor Basmasï, 1927, 64 pp., 2000 cop. [Kir 1 Arab; NN] 1713

Qatïndar vakilderinin jïyïlïshïnda qoldonu üchün jïyïntïq buyumdar. Moscow: SSSR Qalqtarïnïn Borbor Basmasï, 1925, 223 pp., 3000 cop. [Kir 1 Arab; NN] 1714

Qïrghïzstan respublikesinin borborduq atqaru kemiytetinin II-sessïyasïnïn chïgharghan toqtomdoru. Frunze: Qïrmembas, 1932, 46 and 2 pp., 3000 cop. [Kir 2 Lat; DLC] 1715

Qïrghïzïstandïn III oblustoq partïya kenperensiyasïnïn qarardarï jana toqtomdoro. Frunze: J.S.K.(b) Partïyasïnïn Qïrghïzïstan Oblostoq Kemiteti, 1927, 48 pp., 500 cop. [Kir 1 Arab; NN] 1716

SSSR jogorku sovetine shayloolor tuuralu jobo. Frunze: Kïrgïzmambas, 1945, 69 pp., 50190 cop. [Kir 3 Cyr; DLC] 1717

Government

SSSR jogorku sovetinin onunchu sessiyasï. 28-yanvar'–1-fevral' 1944-jïl: Stenografiyalïq otchyöt. Moscow: SSSR Jogorku Sovetinin Bastïruusu, 1944, 364 pp., n.c. [Kir 3 Cyr; DLC, NNC] 1718

Sebestiyenib, I. *Lenin menen dïyqandar.* Moscow: SSSR Qalqtarïnïn Borbor Basmasï, 1925, 55 pp., 3000 cop. [Kir 1 Arab; NN] 1719

Tayshin, M. *Sayasat taanuu.* I. Moscow: Kengesh Sayuzundaghï Elderdin Borbor Basmasï, 1928, 184 pp., 2000 cop. [Kir 1 Arab; NN] 1720

Tayshin, M. I. *Sayasat taanoo.* II. Moscow: Kengesh Sayozondoghï Elderdin Borbor Basmasï, 1928, 312 pp., 4000 cop. [Kir 1 Arab; NN] 1721

History

Kamenop, L. B. *Lenin ham anïn partiyasï.* Moscow: SSSR Qalïqtarïnïn Borbor Basmasï, 1926, 71 pp., 3000 cop. [Kir 1 Arab; NN] 1722

Kudryavski, D. *Bayïrqï madanïyat tarihi.* Moscow: SSSR Qalqtarïnïn Borbor Basmasï, 1925, 116 pp., 3000 cop. [Kir 1 Arab; NN] 1723

Law

Jumushchu dïyqan Qïzïl Armïyasïnïn askerdik qïzmatchïlarï jana askerdik mildettüülörü jana alardïn bülölörü üchün jengildikter tuuraluu mïyzamdar jïynaghï. Frunze: Qïrghïzïstan Memleket Basmasï, 1930, 35 pp., 3000 cop. [Kir 2 Lat; NN] 1724

Sovettik sotsialistik respublikalar soyuzunun konstituttsiyasï: Negizki zakonu. Frunze: Kïrgïzmambas, 1945, 26 pp., 20170 cop. [Kir 3 Cyr; DLC] 1725

Tüb mïyzamï: Kenistitötsiyasï. Frunze: Orgotdel TsIK'a Kir. ASSR, 1927, 29 pp., 1000 cop. [Kir 1 Arab; NN] 1726

Social Organization

Ayïl charba toqoy jömöshkerlerinin sayozo, batïraqtar menen mal qaytaroocholardïn qïzïghïn qan-etib saqtayt. Tashkent: Ayïlcharba

Toqoy Jömöshkerler Sayozonon Orta Azïyalïq Böyrösönön Borbor Kamiteti, 1927, 48 pp., 1000 cop. [Kir 1 Arab; DLC, NN] 1727

Dene tarbïyasï. Tashkent: Orto-Azïya Kesibchiler Büyrösü, 1927, 15 pp., 500 cop. [Kir 1 Arab; DLC] 1728

Dikshteyn. *Ar kim öz enbegi men tora-ma?* Orenburg: Kirgiz. Gosud. Izdatel'., 1923, 37 pp., 2000 cop. [Kaz 1 Arab; NN] 1729

Dïyqan ayal birikmeleshüügö bet alsïn. Frunze: Qïrghïzïstan Memleket Basmasï, 1930, 38 pp., 3000 cop. [Kir 2 Lat; NN] 1730

Izrailit, E. *Bala emine üchün oynob emgektenüügö tiyish.* Frunze: Qïrghïzïstan Memleket Basmasï, 1930, 22 pp., 3000 cop. [Kir 2 Lat; NN] 1731

KIRGIZ Humanities

Art and Architecture

Yazbitiskiy, Beleriy. *Adamzattïn öyöyön tarïqï.* Moscow: Kengash Sayozondaghï Elderdin Borbor Basmasï, 1927, 26 pp., 3000 cop. [Kir 1 Arab; NN] 1732

Language

Cholponqulov, J. *Adamdïn anatomiya jana fiziologiyasï terminderinin oruscha–qïrghïzcha sözdügü.* Frunze–Kazan: Qïrghïzstan Mamlekettik Basmasï, 1939, 34 pp., 1140 cop. [Kir 2 Lat; DLC] 1733

Iudakhin, Konstantin Kuz'mich. *Kirgizsko–russkii slovar'.* Moscow: Goz. Izdat. Inostrannykh i Natsional'nykh Slovarei, 1940, 576 pp., 7000 cop. [Kir 2 Lat; NN] 1734

Tïnïstan uulu, Qasïm. *Ene tilibiz.* Frunze: Qïrghïzïstan Memleket Basmasï, 1930 3d ed., 51 pp., 15000 cop. [Kir 2 Lat; NN] 1735

Literature

Bayalinov, K. *Anggemeler jïynagï.* Frunze: Kïrgïzmambas, 1945, 135 pp., 5170 cop. [Kir 3 Cyr; DLC] 1736

Chïngghïsh uulu, A. *Menim baldarïm ayantchada.* Frunze: Qïrghïzïstan Memleket Basmasï, 1929, 14 pp., 2000 cop. [Kir 2 Lat; NN] 1737

Qarach uulu, S. *Tör agha zeyneb.* Frunze: Qïrghïzïstan Memleket Basmasï, 1929, 32 pp., 2000 cop. [Kir 1 Arab; NN] 1738

Qarach uulu, Sïdïq. *Eriksiz köndördö.* Frunze: Qïrghïzïstan Memleket Basmasï, 1928, 101 pp., 3000 cop. [Kir 1 Arab; NN] 1739

Satïbaldï. 1. *Jöjölör.* 2. *Moldo sasïq.* Frunze: Qïrghïzïstan Memleket Basmasï, 1929, 28 pp., 3000 cop. [Kir 2 Lat; NN] 1740

Seketbay. Moscow: Masködögü Borbor Khalq Basmakhanasïnda, 1925, 59 pp., 5000 cop. [Kir 1 Arab; NN] 1741

Surnay jana dobulbas. Frunze: Qïrghïzïstan Memleket Basmasï, 1929, 21 pp., 5000 cop. [Kir 2 Lat; NN] 1742

Tamsilder. Moscow: SSSR Qalqtarïnïn Borbor Basma Maḫkemesi, 1925, 80 pp., 10000 cop. [Kir 1 Arab; CStH, NN] 1743

Tanin qïzï, Mïskine. *Jetïlgen jetïmder.* Frunze: Qïrghïzïstan Memleket Basmasï, 1928, 48 pp., 3000 cop. [Kir 1 Arab; NN] 1744

Tïnïstan uulu, Qasïm. *Qasïm ïrlarïnïn jïyïnaghï.* Moscow: SSSR Qalqtarïnïn Borbor Basma Maḫkamasï, 1925, 111 pp., 10000 cop. [Kir 1 Arab; MH, NN] 1745

Toqchoro (comp.). *Qïzïl kül.* Moscow: Kengesh Sayuzundaghï Elderdin Borbor Basmasï, 1927, 100 pp., 2000 cop. [Kir 1 Arab; NN] 1746

Toqombay uulu, Aalï. *Lenin tuuralu.* n.p.: Orto-Azïya Basmaqanasï, 1927, 73 pp., 2500 cop. [Kir 1 Arab; DLC, NN] 1747

Toqombayev, Aalï (Balqa). *Qanduu jïldar* (*1916-jïl*). Roman. Frunze–Kazan: Qïrghïzïstan Memleket Basmasï, 1937 2d ed., 296 pp., 6125 cop. [Kir 2 Lat; NN] 1748

KRESHEN TATAR Social Sciences

Education

Grigor'ev, A. N. *Kryäshennyär arasïnda "Yängalif" myäsyälyäse.* Kazan: Izdatel'stvo "Ianalif," 1927, 30 pp., 2000 cop. [Kresh 1 Cyr; NN] 1749

History

Vladimir Il'ich Ul'yänov-Lenin tormosho, anïn ëshlägän ëshläre. Moscow: Tsentral'noe Izdatel'stvo Narodov SSSR, 1927, 40 pp., 2000 cop. [Kresh 1 Cyr; NN] 1750

KRYMCHAK Humanities

Philosophy and Religion

ʾAshkenazi, Nissim ʾAbraham. *ʾAbne miqdash*. Cracow: Yosef Fisher, 5663*/1903, 24 pp., n.c. [Karai 1 Heb; NNJ] 1751

* anno Hebraico

KUMYK General (including periodicals)

Mä'arif yuli (Makhachkala) 1928: 7/8; 1929: 8/9.
[Kum 2 Arab; NN) 1752

KUMYK Social Sciences

Economics

Daghïstan Satsialist Savet Jumhuriyatnï yurt savetlerine, rayon ispolkomlarïna va maliya idaralarïna özlege salaghan nalognu yürütmegine instruksiya. Makhachkala: DSSJ-nï Maliya Kamisarlïghïnï Nashriyatï, 1929, 38 pp., 500 cop.
[Kum 3 Lat; NN] 1753

Istihlak jam'iyatlarini tuntiv kamisiyalarina ta'limat. Makhachkala: Dagh. Sayuznï Nashriyatï, 1928, 62 pp., 450 cop.
[Kum 2 Arab; NN] 1754

Pachalïq zayomlar bizge tarïqmï. Makhachkala: Dag Giz, 1930, 13 pp., 560 cop. [Kum 3 Lat; NN] 1755

Vassirman. *Daghstanda mamuqchuluq khazaystu isin nächik yurutmägä gäräk.* Makhachkala: Bash Mamuq Kamitätini Daghïstan Vakilligi Idarasini Nashri, 1929, 25 pp., 2000 cop.
[Kum 2 Arab; NN] 1756

Education

Alqadarski, A. Q. *Hesab mas'alalari.* 1nchi yïl ïchun. Makhachkala: Yanghï Daghïstan Alifba Komitesini Nashriyyatï, 1929, 104 pp., 4000 cop. [Kum 3 Lat; NN] 1757

Daghïstan ijtimai shura jumhuriyatda umumi okuv. Makhachkala: Daghïstan Khalq Maarif Qomisarlighï Neshriyyati, 1929, 69 pp., 1500 cop. [Kum 3 Lat; NN] 1758

Dibirof, Muhammad. *Qumuq alifba.* Makhachkala: Daghïstan Yanghï Alifba Qomitetinï Nashriyyati, 1928, 72 pp., 3000 cop.
[Kum 3 Lat; NN] 1759

Gäräyuf, Yusuf. *Sabanchïlanï harishinä bärilägän arzalanï va tiläv kaghïzlanï yazaghan kuyun kürsätgän kitab.* Makhachkala: Dagh. Dulat Näshriyatï, 1928, 319 pp., 1600 cop. [Kum 2 Arab; NN] 1760

Education

Likpunktlarda okhutmaq ichün pragramma. Makhachkala: Daghnashr, 1929, 18 pp., 200 cop. [Kum 3 Lat; NN] 1761
Majlislärdä chï'ïb daklad itmak uchün matiryal. Buinaksk: Dagsovnarkhoz, n.d., 48 pp., 300 cop. [Kum 1 Arab; CStH] 1762
Shuri ḥukumati vä khalq ma'arifi. Buinaksk: Izdanie Daggosizdata, n.d., 29 pp., 2000 cop. [Kum 1 Arab; CStH] 1763
Temirkhanof, M. *Ullular ichün qumuq alifba.* Makhachkala: Daghïstan Hukumat Nashriyatïnïng Basmasï, 1930, 92 pp., 32060 cop. [Kum 3 Lat; NN] 1764
Yashlanï dünyasï. Buinaksk: Daghstan Ijtima'i Shura Jumhuriyatï Ḥukumatini Maṭbu'at Idaräsini Näshriyatï, 1922, 195 pp., 10000 cop. [Kum 1 Arab; CStH] 1765
Zaḥmat maktabi. Buinaksk: Daggosizdat, n.d., 56 pp., 1000 cop. [Kum 1 Arab; CStH] 1766

Government

Atayuf, Abumuslim. *Daghïstanda milli 'askär va majburi 'askär qulluq bizgä nä uchun tarïqlï.* Makhachkala: Dagh. Tärri Turbyasï Idaräsi, 1928, 44 pp., 1065 cop. [Kum 2 Arab; NN] 1767
Bütün sayuz kammunist partiyasïnï Daghistan kamitetini III-nchü plenumunu qararlarï. Makhachkala: Daghïstan Hukumat Nashriyyatï, 1930, 49 pp., 1000 cop. [Kum 3 Lat; NN] 1768
D.S.Sh.J. *1905 nji yïlda daghistan.* Buinaksk: Ma'arif Qomisarlïghï, 1926, 36 pp., 850 cop. [Kum 2 Arab; NN] 1769
Izakuf. *Butun dunyadaghï qazaq turaghanlanï birläshdirmäkni yulunda.* Makhachkala: Yurt Khazaystva Nashri, 1928, 52 pp., 1260 cop. [Kum 2 Arab; NN] 1770
Kun, Fäliks. *Yanghï davnu qurqunchlughu.* Makhachkala: Dagh. Ḥukumat Nashriyatï, 1927, 35 pp., 1075 cop. [Kum 2 Arab; NN] 1771
Länin, V. I. *1905 nji yïlnï inqilabï ḥaqïnda.* Buinaksk: Ma'arif Qumisarlïghï, 1925, 24 pp., 1000 cop. [Kum 2 Arab; NN] 1772
Sabanchïlanï kümäk kamitätlärini tintuv (rävizkum) kamisiyalarini ishin nächik gutärmägä gäräk. Buinaksk: Buynaqskïdä Ḥukumat Nashriyatï, 1926, 14 pp., 1060 cop. [Kum 2 Arab; NN] 1773
Tughuzunchu daghistan ublast partiya kanfäränsiyasïnï qararlarï. Makhachkala: Dagh. Partiya Kamitätini Matbu'atï, 1928, 23 pp., 1100 cop. [Kum 2 Arab; NN] 1774

'Umumi shura jumhuriyatlanï kummunist(b) partiyasïnï yachäykalanï nizamnamäsi. Makhachkala: "Daghnashr," 1928, 41 pp., 1100 cop. [Kum 2 Arab; NN] 1775

Utkäs, D. *Yurtlardaghï mopranï yachaykasï.* Makhachkala: Daghkom Mopranï Nashriyatï, 1929, 18 pp., 3000 cop. [Kum 2 Arab; NN] 1776

History

Nävski, V. I. *Vladimir iliyich länin: Uliyanuf.* Moscow: SSSRni Millätlärini ara Basmasï, 1926, 70 pp., 3000 cop. [Kum 2 Arab; NN] 1777

Law

Batraklanï zahmatlarïn saqlav va ikhtiyarlarïn yaqlav zakonlarï. Makhachkala: Daghïstan Hukumat Nashriyyatï, 1930, 55 pp., 235 cop. [Kum 3 Lat; NN] 1778

Gäräyuf, Yusuf. *Abzar ahlu abzarïn-paylamaqnï ḥaqïndan.* Makhachkala: Dagh. Dulat Nashriyatï, 1928, 23 pp., 2100 cop. [Kum 2 Arab; NN] 1779

Sovet Sotsialist Respublikalanï Soyuzunu Konstitutsiyasï: Aslu zakonu. Makhachkala: Daggosizdat, 1940, 54 pp., 1000 cop. [Kum 4 Cyr; DLC] 1780

Social Organization

Butun daghstan kumäk jamiyatlarïnï II nchi siyäzini qararlarï Makhachkala: Dagh. M.A. Kumäkläshiv Kamitätni Nashri, 1929, 27 pp., 500 cop. [Kum 2 Arab; NN] 1781

Dikshtein, A. *Har kim oz qiyini bolan yashai.* Buinaksk: Daggosizdatel'stvo, n.d., 68 pp., 1000 cop. [Kum 2 Arab; CStH] 1781a

Kiriskomlarda belgili murat uchun maya jïymaq haqïnda instruksiya. Makhachkala: Daghïstan Hukumat Nashriyyatï, 1930, 10 pp., 460 cop. [Kum 3 Lat; NN] 1782

Social Organization

Läbädäv, G. *Kammunist partiyanï 15 nchi siyäzdini ḥukmularïnï ḥaqïndan kulaklar bulan nächik yabushma gäräk va yarlï sabanchïlagha nächik kumäk ätmä gäräk.* Buinaksk: "Sabanchïnï" Nashriyatï, 1928, 31 pp., 1100 cop. [Kum 2 Arab; NN] 1783

Länin, V. I. *Ishchi va sabanchïlanï arasïndaghï birlik yuruqlashunu ḥaqïndan.* Makhachkala: Dagh. Ḥukumat Nashriyatï, 1927, 35 pp., 1000 cop. [Kum 2 Arab; NN] 1784

Qaragïshïzadä, Muharrem. *Daghstan qatunlarï va yanghï yashau.* Buinaksk: Ḥukumat Nashriyatï, 1926, 71 pp., 1560 cop. [Kum 2 Arab; NN] 1785

Qatunlanï ḥalï. Buinaksk: Daghïstan Ijtimaʿi Shura Jumhuriyyatï Ḥukumatïnïng Nashriyyatï, 1921, 60 pp., 1000 cop. [Kum 1 Arab; CStH] 1786

KUMYK Humanities

Literature

Bashiruf, ʿA. *Yashlar adabiyatï.* Makhachkala: Daghistan Dulat Nashriyatï, 1928, 27 pp., 1060 cop. [Kum 2 Arab; NN] 1787

Baṭïrmurza, ʿAbdalʿaẕïm. *Muritlär.* 2-pärdäli. Makhachkala: Dagh. Ḥukumat Nashriyatï, 1929, 48 pp., 1000 cop. [Kum 2 Arab; NN] 1788

Gärayuf, Yusuf. *Mulla nasurutdïnnï safar yuldashï.* Makhachkala: Dagh. Ḥukumat Nashriyatï, 1927, 64 pp., 1600 cop. [Kum 2 Arab; NN] 1789

Lärmuntuf. *Ismaʿilbäy.* Moscow: SSSR Millätlärini ara Basmasï, 1925, 64 pp., 3000 cop. [Kum 2 Arab; NN] 1790

Qafqasya esiri. Ḥikayä. n.p.: Daghstan Shura Jumhuriyatïnï Maṭbuʿat Idaräsini Nashriyatï, 1922, 95 pp., 1000 cop. [Kum 1 Arab; CStH] 1791

Qarakhanïm. Ḥikayä. Buinaksk: Daghstan Shura Jumhuriyatï Ḥukumatïnï Maṭbuʿat Idaräsini Nashriyatï, 1922, 77 pp., 1000 cop. [Kum 1 Arab; CStH] 1792

Vagnär, Yu. *Birin qarqalabïznï qurulmaqlïghïnï va unu ishläygän qaʿidäsini ḥaqïndan suyläygän khabarlar.* n.p.: Buynaqsïndägi Maʿarif Kamïsarlïghïnï Basmakhanäsi, 1926, 64 pp., 1000 cop. [Kum 2 Arab; NN] 1793

KUMYK Humanities

Philosophy and Religion

Sitin, Aläksandr. *Alläni gäzivläri.* Makhachkala: Daghnashr, 1927, 70 pp., 1075 cop. [Kum 2 Arab; NN] 179

KURD General (including periodicals)

Rya t'äzä (n.p.) 1931: 5, 7. [Kur 2 Lat; NN] 1795

KURD Social Sciences

Economics

K'ara kolkhoza gündyara. Erivan: Näshra Däwläta Shewre Ermänistane, 1930, 34 pp., 2000 cop. [Kur 2 Lat; NN] 1796

Education

Drambyan, R. *Bär bï ämre t'äzä: K'teba khwändïne zmane Kurmanjï.* Erivan: Näshra Däwläta Shewre Ermänistane, 1931, 213 pp., 5000 cop. [Kur 2 Lat; NN] 1797

Faleyev, Gr. *K'ït'abe khäbat'a fizike (Bona mäk't'äbed häft' sali u tekhnikuma kürmanja): Sala V semestra dïduya.* Erivan: Näshra Hükmata Shewre Ermänistane, 1931, 129 pp., 2000 cop. [Kur 2 Lat; NN] 1798

Kolkhoznike därbdar: K'tebe därse bona koma III. Erivan: Näshra Hükmata Shewre Ermänistane, 1931, 215 pp., 2000 cop. [Kur 2 Lat; NN] 1799

Kolkhoznike därbdar: K'teba zmane kürmanji bona k'oma IV. Erivan: Näshra Hükmat'a Shevre Ermänistane, 1932, 105 pp., 1000 cop. [Kur 2 Lat; NN] 1799a

K't'eba zmane kürmanji bona k'oma chara. Erivan: Näshra Hükümata Shewra Fïlïstane, 1933, 174 pp., 2000 cop. [Kur 2 Lat; NN] 1799b

Marogulov, I.; Drambyan, R. *Renjbäre sor: K'teba khwändïne zmane kurmanji säbä mäzïna.* Erivan: Näshra Däwläta Shewre Ermänistane, 1930, 150 pp., 3500 cop. [Kur 2 Lat; NN] 1800

Nuri. *Ülme t'ä'byäte: K'tada khäbate bona mäktäba koljahela tekhnikuma.* Erivan: Näshirata Hük'mate, 1932, 163 pp., n.c. [Kur 2 Lat; NN] 1801

Salibegyan, S.; Khachatryan, H. *K't'eba mat'ematikaye sala penja küandïne.* Erivan: Näshra Hük'mata Shewra Ermänistane, 1932, 196 pp., 1000 cop. [Kur 2 Lat; NN] 1801a

KURD Social Sciences: Education

T'.J.Sh.S. zanbuna dïnyaye ktaba khäbate bona mäktäbe koljahela u tekhnikuma. Erivan: Näshra Hük'mate, 1932, 205 pp., 700 cop. [Kur 2 Lat; NN] 180

Zanbuna dïnyaye: Kteba khäbate bona mäktäbe däräja 1 k'ome sïsea u chare. Erivan: Näshra Hükmate, 1933, 155 pp., 1500 cop. [Kur 2 Lat; NN] 180

Government

Khanjyan, A. *Bï rya shär krïne u alt'kïrïneva.* Erivan: Näshra Fïrqe-Sektsia Kïtebe Kurmanja, 1933, 48 pp., 1500 cop. [Kur 2 Lat; NN] 180

History

Ä'rsham. *Ämre Lenin.* Erivan: Näshra Däwläta Shewre Ermänistane, 1930, 20 pp., 2000 cop. [Kurd 2 Lat; NN] 180

T'ariqa inglaba Oktyabre. Erivan: Näshra Däwläta Shäwre Ermänistane, 1931, 70 pp., 2000 cop. [Kurd 2 Lat; NN] 180

Vladimir ilij Uiyanov Lenin zindane u srgunede. Erivan: Neshra Däwläta Shäwre Ermänistane, 1930, 22 pp., 2000 cop. [Kurd 2 Lat; NN] 180

KURD Humanities

Literature

Shamilov, Äräb. *K'ochäke däräwin: T'äqlid krna sut chknavar.* Pyesa dü fälsa säzdä sïfäta. Erivan: Näshra Däwläta Shewre Ermänistane, 1930, vi and 32 pp., 2000 cop. [Kurd 2 Lat; NN] 180

NAGAYBAK Humanities

Philosophy and Religion

Ioganson, P. *Neylektän bala jukka ïshana torgan bula.* Moscow: Tsentrizdat, 1929, 16 pp., 1000 cop. [Nag 1 Cyr; NN] 1809

NOGHAY Social Sciences

Education

Ibräyimip, Äliy. *Üykönner ushun Noghay elippesi.* Moscow: SSSR Orta Basbasï, 1929, 80 pp., 5000 cop. [Nogh 3 Lat; NN] 181

Government

Ibrayimif, Ghäli. *Qatin-qazlar arasinda sayasi ang-bilim jörtlarïnïng islärï.* Moscow: SSSR Ellerïning Orta Basbasï, 1928, 30 pp., 1500 cop. [Nogh 2 Arab; NN] 181

Law

Sovetskiy sotsialisticheskiy respublikalar soyuzïnïng konstitutsiyasï: Tüp zakonï. Piatigorsk: Ordzhonikidzevskii Krai Izdat., 1939, 40 pp., 3000 cop. [Nogh 4 Cyr; DLC] 181

Social Organization

Noghaylï, N. *8-mart—jangghï ämïl.* Moscow: SSSR Ellerïning Orta Basbasï, 1927, 87 pp., 3000 cop. [Nogh 2 Arab; NN] 18

NOGHAY Humanities

Literature

Noghay äl ädäbïyäti: Qaraydar minan qizil kül. Moscow: SSSR Ellerïning Orta Basbasï, 1928, 26 pp., 1000 cop. [Nogh 2 Arab; NN] 18

Philosophy and Religion

Injïl al-muqaddes. Astrakhan: n.p., 1825, 588 pp., n.c. [Nogh 1 Arab; MH] 18

OSSETIC General

Älbortü, B. *Nä fütstsag mükhuürgond iron chinügäy nog khabärttä.* Dzäujüqäu: n.p., 1929, 9 pp., 1300 cop. [Oss 3 Lat; NN] 1816

"*Rästdzinadü*" *magazinü chinguütü katalog.* Dzäujüqäu: n.p., 1928, 11 pp., 1000 cop. [Oss 3 Lat; NN] 1817

OSSETIC Social Sciences

Economics

Saveton tsädisü TsÄK-ü prezidiumü ämä kavkazü krayü äkhkhästkomü III plenumü uünaffätä: Savettü nog khästü tükhkhäy qäuuon khädzaradü iuguür kollektivizatsitä, gäsgä. Dzäujüqäu: "Rästdzinad," 1930, 21 pp., 500 cop. [Oss 3 Lat; NN] 1818

Education

Älbortü, B. *Iron füstü damühätä.* Dzäujüqäu: n.p., 1929, 22 pp., 1300 cop. [Oss 3 Lat; NN] 1819

Brüthyatü, Sozürüqo. *Metron (däsgay) baräntä.* Rostov-on-Don: Nog (Latinag) Alfavitü Tsädat Kavkazaü Komitetü Rauahd, 1928, iv and 163 pp., 3000 cop. [Oss 3 Lat; NN] 1820

Guriati, Gagudz; Gadiati, Tsomaq. *Akhuyradi rokhs.* Dzäujüqäu: Tsäg. Iristoni Kiunuguadzän "Rästdzinad," 1929 2d ed., 75 pp., 2000 cop. [Oss 3 Lat; NN] 1821

Qotsiti, Bidzina. *Rokhs fändag: Fitdzag kiunugä raidayän kiunugi fäste.* Dzäujüqäu: n.p., 1929, 235 pp., 3500 cop. [Oss 3 Lat; NN] 1822

Qotsütü, Bidzina. *Rukhs fändag: Füddzaü tsinüg damhuatü bästä.* Dzäujüqäu: Mükhuürgond u Nog Latinag Alfavitü Tsentron Komitetü Dzürdmä Gäsgä, 1928, 237 pp., 7000 cop. [Oss 3 Lat; NN] 1823

Government

ÄK(b)P tsentron kämitetü plenum: 1929 azü noyabrü may 10–17 bon. Dzäujüqäu: "Rästdzinadü" Chinüguadzän, 1930, 104 pp., 2000 cop. [Oss 3 Lat; NN] 1824

Äppättsädison kämmuniston partiyü (bälsäviktü) program ämä uagävär. Dzäujüqäu: "Rästdzinad," 1929, 131 pp., n.c. [Oss 3 Lat; NN] 182

Baraqtü, Gino. *Fälloygänäg adäm ämä Lenin.* Moscow: SSSR-ü Adämtü Tsentrizdat, 1928, 280 pp., 2000 cop. [Oss 3 Lat; NN] 182

Dimansteyn. *Leninü akhuür.* Dzäujüqäu: "Rästdzinad," 1929, 210 pp., 4000 cop. [Oss 3 Lat; NN] 182

Gagloytü, Mukhtar. *Ävzong pionerü chinüg.* Moscow: SSRTs Adämtü Chinüguadzän, 1926, 43 pp., 3000 cop. [Oss 3 Lat; NN] 182

Oktyabrü revolyutsiyül däs arü ratsäünü tükhkhäy Soveton tsädisü tsentron äkhkhästgänäg komitetü manifest. Dzäujüqäu: "Rästdzinad," 1927, 25 pp., 500 cop. [Oss 3 Lat; NN] 182

Plitü, Aron. *Politakhuradü chinüg.* Moscow: SSR Tsädisü Adämtü Chinüguadzän, 1926, 242 pp., 3000 cop. [Oss 3 Lat; NN] 183

Qäutü komfäsivädü politikon kästütän chinüg. Dzäujüqäu: "Rästdzinad," 1930, 138 pp., 5000 cop. [Oss 3 Lat; CStH, NN] 183

Social Organization

Gozümtü, G. *8-äm Marthi.* Dzäujüqäu: Tsägat Irüstonü Partüu Bästkomü Sülgoymägtü Äkhsän Kusäg Khayad, 1929, 43 pp., 1000 cop. [Oss 3 Lat; NN] 18

Kravchenko, Elena. *Kolkhoztäu tsäuün tsämän u payda zäkhkusäg sülgoymagän.* Dzäujüqäu: "Rästdzinad," 1930, 53 pp., 5000 cop. [Oss 3 Lat; NN] 18

Lunchenkov, I. *Äkhsänü khaltsü quüdtajü äräst büdürü.* Dzäujüqäu: Rästdzinad Kraynatsizdat, 1930, 40 pp., 2000 cop. [Oss 3 Lat; NN] 18

"*Näkhi tsästütäy fedtam.*" Dzäujüqäu: "Rästdzinadü" Chinüguadzän, 1930, 75 pp., 5000 cop. [Oss 3 Lat; NN] 18

Qäuuon khädzaradü artelü midtsardü ähdäudtä. Dzäujüqäu: "Rästdzinad," 1930, 34 pp., 4000 cop. [Oss 3 Lat; NN] 18

Qäuuon khädzaradü artelü uagäväird. Dzäujüqäu: "Rästdzinad," 1930, 39 pp., 4000 cop. [Oss 3 Lat; NN] 18

Language

Älbortü, B. Ä. *Iron ävzajü tsübür grammatikä.* Dzäujüqäu: Tsentroizdatü Uahd, 1925, 156 pp., 5000 cop. [Oss 3 Lat; NN] 1838
Miller, V. F. *Osetinsko-russko-nemetskii slovar'.* 3 vols. Leningrad: Izdatel'stvo Akademii Nauk SSSR, 1927–1934, I 618 pp., II 557 pp., III 552 pp., 1050 cop. [Oss 3 Lat; NN, NNC] 1839
Schiefner, Franz A. *Osetinskie teksty.* St. Petersburg: A. Shifner, 1868, 104 pp., n.c. [Special Cyr; NNC] 1840

Literature

Bolayü, Fürt. *Chermen.* Moscow: SSSR-ü Säyraq Politrukhsadü, Khudozhnikon Khayad, 1928, 208 pp., 2000 cop. [Oss 3 Lat; NN] 1841
Bolayü, Furt. *Khäs.* Moscow: SSSR-ü Adämtü Tsentrizdat, 1928, 67 pp., 1000 cop. [Oss 3 Lat; NN] 1842
Bolayü, Fürt. *Oktyabrü skhuüddzägtä.* Moscow: USSR'ü Chusül Natsitü Uünaffädon, 1928, 28 pp., 1000 cop. [Oss 3 Lat; NN] 1843
Kotsoytü, Arsen. *Radzürdtä.* Moscow: USSR Chüsül Natsitü Uünaffädon, 1927 2d ed. 83 pp., 1000 cop. [Oss 3 Lat; NN] 1844
Miller, Vsev. *Digorskiia skazaniia.* Moscow: Tipografiia Varvary Gattsuk, 1902, 148 pp., n.c. [Special Cyr; NN] 1845
Neverov, Aleksandr. *Taskent—khorjün sakhar.* Dzäujüqäu: "Rästdzinad," 1929, 149 pp., 2500 cop. [Oss 3 Lat; NN] 1846
Protsenko, N. *Znaggadgänjütä.* Radzürd. Dzäujüqäu: n.p., 1927, 22 pp., 1000 cop. [Oss 3 Lat; NN] 1847
Yaltsev, P. *Susäg kusjütä.* Fondz arkhaydü pyesea. Dzäujüqäu: "Rästdzinad," 1928, 60 pp., 800 cop. [Oss 3 Lat; NN] 1848

Philosophy and Religion

Änäkhuütsäudtü khord. Dzäujüqäu: "Rästdzinad," 1927, 11 pp., 1000 cop. [Oss 3 Lat; NN] 1849
Dadus, G. *Kuüd rav zhärdüstü dintä.* Moscow: Kraynatsizdat, 1928, 36 pp., 1500 cop. [Oss 3 Lat; NN] 1850

OYROT, see *ALTAY*

QARAIM, see *KARAIM*

SHOR Social Sciences

Education

Tel'gerekov, Ya.; Totïshev, A. *Karashkïdan shïgar: Shorlardïng pashtapkï urgencheng bukvar'ï.* Moscow: Tsentral'noe Izdatel'stvo Narodov SSSR, 1927, 48 pp., 3000 cop. [Shor 1 Cyr; NN] 1851

TAJIK General (including periodicals)

Rahbar-i dānish (Tashkent) 1927: 2–3; 1928: 4–10; 1929: 1–12; 1930: 2–6, 8/9. [Taj 1 & 2 Arab, 3 Lat; DLC] 1852

TAJIK Social Sciences

Economics

Barobari J.SH.S. Toj. soli 1932 shamai. Tashkent: Izdanie Upr. Upol. NK Trudy SSSR v Srednei Azii i NK Trudy Tadzh. SSR, 1932, 27 pp., 2050 cop. [Taj 3 Lat; DLC] 1853

Dastūr al-ʿamal: tartīb-i godharāndan-i andāz-i yigāne-yi khājagī-yi dihāt be sāl-i 1927–28-m: Dar jumhūrīyyat-i uzbakistān be zabān-i tājikī. Samarkand: Nashr-i Shuʿbe-yi Malīyye-yi Uzbakistān, 1927, 114 pp., 630 cop. [Taj 1 & 2 Arab; NN] 1854

Ṣāḥeb-i kārkhānehā-yi davlatī kīst? Tashkent–Dushanbe: Nashrīyyāt-i Davlatī-yi Tājīkistān, 1928, 24 pp., 2000 cop. [Taj 1 & 2 Arab; DLC] 1855

Shelfer, M. *Qarẕ be khājagī-yi dihāt.* Samarkand: Bānk-i Khājagī-yi Dihāt, 1927, 47 pp., 1053 cop. [Taj 1 & 2 Arab; DLC] 1856

Tartībnāme-yi ḥesābhā-yi jārī-yi sūdnāk-i bānk-i khājagī-yi dihāt-i jumhūrīyyat-i ijtimāʿī-yi shuravīyye-yi uzbakistān. Samarkand: n.p., n.d., 9 and 4 pp., 1000 cop. [Taj 1 & 2 Arab; NN] 1857

Varga, Ye. *Resurshoi Germaniya ado shuda istodaand.* Stalinabad: Nashriyoti Davlatii Tojikiston, 1942, 35 pp., 2800 cop. [Taj 4 Cyr; DLC] 1858

Education

Alīzāde-yi Samarqandī, Sayyid Riẕā. *Ṣarf-u naḥv-i tājīkī.* Samarkand–Dushanbe: Nashrīyyāt-i Davlatī-yi Tājīkistān, 1927, 84 pp., 5000 cop. [Taj 1 & 2 Arab; DLC] 1859

Gretsyanskī; Kavon. *Majmūʿe-yi masʾalehā-yi ḥesāb.* Jild yakum. Samarkand–Dushanbe: Nashrīyyāt-i Davlatī-yi Tājīkistān, 1927, 52 pp., 10000 cop. [Taj 1 & 2 Arab; DLC] 1860

Gretsyanskī, A. A. *Majmūʿe-yi masʾalehā-yi ḥesāb.* Jeld III. Samarkand–Dushanbe: Nashrīyyāt-i Davlatī-yi Tājīkistān, 1927, 144 pp., 6070 cop. [Taj 1 & 2 Arab; DLC] 186

Hoshim, Rahim (Mim). *Jihoni nav—kitabi qaroatī baroyi maktabhoyi savod.* Tashkent: Nashriyati Davlatiyi Tojikiston, 1929, vi and 260 pp., 9000 cop. [Taj 3 Lat; DLC] 186

Ivānof. *Jughrāfīyā-yi ibtidāʾī.* Samarkand–Dushanbe: Nashrīyyāt-i Davlatī-yi Tājīkistān, 1927, 120 pp., 10000 cop. [Taj 1 & 2 Arab; DLC] 186

Ivānof, G. I. *Ḥeṣṣe-yi sivvum. Jughrāfīyā-yi ibtidāʾī: Avrūpā.* Samarkand–Dushanbe: Nashrīyyāt-i Davlatī-yi Tājīkistān, 1927, 222 pp., 5000 cop. [Taj 1 & 2 Arab; DLC] 186

Kollektif. *Soli avval.* Tashkent: Nashriyati Davlatiyi Tojikiston, 1929, 80 pp., 30000 cop. [Taj 3 Lat; DLC] 186

Lankāf, A. V. *Masʾale-yi ḥesāb.* Samarkand: Nashrīyyāt-i Davlatī-yi Tājīkistān, 1927, 117 pp., 4000 cop. [Taj 1 & 2 Arab; DLC] 186

Maḥmūdī, V.; Dhihnī. *Kitāb-i qirāʾat.* I. Samarkand–Dushanbe: Nashrīyyāt-i Davlatī-yi Tājīkistān, 1927, vi and 107 pp., 8000 cop. [Taj 1 & 2 Arab; DLC] 186

Manāfzāde, Thābat. *Kilīd-i dānish: Barā-yi ṣinf-i duvvum-i maktabhā-yi daraje-yi avval-i tājīkān.* Samarkand: Nashrīyyāt-i Davlatī-yi Tājīkistān, 1926, 147 pp., 13047 cop. [Taj 1 & 2 Arab; NN] 186

Sokhārīvā. *Nabātāt: az ṭaraf-i shurā-yi ʿelmī-yi tājīkān barā-yi ṣinf-i chahārum-i maktabhā-yi ibtidāʾī monāsib dīde shude ast.* Samarkand: Nashrīyyāt-i Davlatī-yi Tājīkistān, 1927, 130 pp., 5000 cop. [Taj 1 & 2 Arab; DLC, NN] 186

Geography

Ivānof, G. I. *Jughrāfīyā-yi mukhtaṣar.* Samarkand: Nashrīyyāt-i Davlatī-yi Tājīkistān, 1927, 266 pp., 7000 cop. [Taj 1 & 2 Arab; DLC] 187

Ivānof, V. I. *Davre-yi ibtidaʾī jughrāfīyā-yi āsiyā: Az ṭaraf-i shurā-yi ʿelmī-yi tājīkān be tabʿash ijāzat dāde shud.* Samarkand: Nashrīyyāt-i Davlatī-yi Tājīkistān, 1927, 104 pp., 6000 cop. [Taj 1 & 2 Arab; DLC, NN] 187

Alipof, S. A. *Kānfrīns-i pānzdahum-i firqe-yi kommūnīst-i tamām-i ittifāq che mas'ale hārā hall namūd.* Samarkand: Nashrīyyāt-i Davlatī-yi Tājīkistān, 1927, 55 pp., 3000 cop. [Taj 1 & 2 Arab; NN] 1872
Baghdādbikof, Jalīl. *Lenīn va millithā-yi sharq.* Tashkent–Stalinabad: Nashrīyyāt-i Davlatī-yi Tājīkistān, 1929, 12 pp., 1000 cop. [Taj 1 & 2 Arab; DLC] 1873
Firqe-yi komūnīst fāide-yi mardikārān (bātrākhā)rā chegūne muḥāfiẓe mikunad. Samarkand: Nashrīyyāt-i Davlatī-yi Tājīkistān, 1928, 39 pp., 2000 cop. [Taj 1 & 2 Arab; DLC] 1874
Ghlagholof, A. *Be che jahat har fard-i dihāqīn bāyad ʿuẓv-i "Jamʿīyyat-i ṭarafdārān-i flut-i havāʿī" bāshand.* Moscow: Az Ṭaraf-i Jamʿīyyat-i Shuʿbe-yi Vasaṭī-Sharqī-yi Ṭarafdārān-i Flut-i Havāʿī, 1925, 24 pp., 10000 cop. [Taj 1 & 2 Arab; NN] 1875
Istālīn, I. *Mavqeʿhā-yi millet dar sakhtimān-i firqe va davlat.* Samarkand–Dushanbe: Nashrīyyāt-i Davlatī-yi Tājīkistān, 1927, 48 pp., 3050 cop. [Taj 1 & 2 Arab; DLC] 1876
Kāgānovīch, M. L. *Firqe-yi kāmmūnīstān-i ittifāq chegūne bar pā shude ast?* Samarkand–Dushanbe: Nashrīyyāt-i Davlatī-yi Tājīkistān, 1927, 62 pp., 3000 cop. [Taj 1 & 2 Arab; DLC] 1877
Lenīn, N. *Darbāre-yi davlat.* Tashkent–Samarkand: Nashr-i Tājīk, 1929, 29 pp., 2000 cop. [Taj 1 & 2 Arab; DLC] 1878
Lenin, V. I. *Kasalin bachagonai "Chapchigī" dar kommunizm.* Stalinabad: Nashriyoti Davlatii Tojikiston, 1941, 131 pp., 5150 cop. [Taj 4 Cyr; DLC] 1879
Nikolikhin. *Sīyāsat-i firqe dar dihāt.* Samarkand–Dushanbe: Nashrīyyāt-i Davlatī-yi Tājīkistān, 1927, 66 pp., 3000 cop. [Taj 1 & 2 Arab; DLC] 1880
Prāgrām: Marāmnāme. Samarkand–Dushanbe: Nashrīyyāt-i Davlatī-yi Tājīkistān, 1927, 62 pp., 3000 cop. [Taj 1 & 2 Arab; DLC] 1881
Solts, A. A. *Dar khuṣūṣ-i akhlāq-i firqe.* Tashkent: Nashr-i Tājīk, 1930, 24 pp., 1500 cop. [Taj 1 & 2 Arab; NN] 1882
Virishaqin, I. Q. *Ittiḥād-i jumhūrīyyathā-yi shuravī-yi susyālīst chīst?* Moscow: Dar Maṭbaʿe-yi Nashrīyyāt-i Markazī-yi Milal-i Jumhūrīyyathā-yi Shuravī, 1926, 72 pp., 2000 cop. [Taj 1 & 2 Arab; NN] 1883

Yaroslavskiy, Yem. *Taqdiri batanamon dar dasti armiyai surkh meboshad.* Stalinabad: Nashriyoti Davlatii Tojikiston, 1942, 19 pp., 3000 cop. [Taj 4 Cyr; DLC] 1884

Yilizarof. *Anjuman-i chahārdahum.* Samarkand–Dushanbe: Nashrīyyāt-i Davlatī-yi Tājīkistān, 1927, 96 pp., 3000 cop. [Taj 1 & 2 Arab; DLC] 188

History

Aynī, S. *Shaykhurraīs Abūlalī Sīno.* Stalinabad: Nashriyoti Davlatii Tojikiston, 1941, 83 pp., 4200 cop. [Taj 4 Cyr; DLC] 188

Bukhārī, Mīrzā Shems. "Bayān-i ba'ẓ-i ḥavādithāt-i bukhārā va khvāqand va kāshghar. Taṣnīf-i mīrzā shams-i bukhārī," (Kazan) *Uchenyia zapiski* izdavaemyia Imperatorskĭm Kazanskĭm Universitetom. Knizhka I (1861), pp. 3–129. [Taj 1 Arab; MH, NN, NNC] 188

Dimitriyef, S. *Dar beshahoyi Hinduston.* Tashkent–Stalinabad: Nashriyoti Davlatiyi Tajikiston, 1930, 77 pp., 3000 cop. [Taj 3 Lat; DLC] 188

Khadaraviski, I. *Vlādīmīr īlīch lenīn.* Samarkand–Dushanbe: Nashrīyyāt-i Davlatī-yi Tājīkistān, 1927, 47 pp., 4000 cop. [Taj 1 & 2 Arab; DLC] 188

Mollā Nīyāz Moḥammad ibn Mollā 'Ashūr Moḥammad Khoqandī. *Tarīkh-e shahrokhī.* Kazan: Ṭab'khāna-ye Madrasa-ye al-Kubrā, A.H. 1303/A.D. 1885, 333 pp., n.c. [Taj 1 & 2 Arab; NNC] 188

Narshakhī, Abū Bakr Muḥammad ibn Ja'far. *Nuskhe-yi marghūbe-yi nādire-yi asandīde-yi zā'irān al-musammā be mullāzāde va tārīkh-i narshakhī.* Bukhara: Maṭba'e-yi Kāgān. A.H.1322/A.D.1904, 72 pp., n.c. [Taj 1 & 2 Arab; NNC] 189

Law

Konstitutsiyai (qonuni asosii) respublikai sovetii sotsialistii tojikiston. Stalinabad: Nashriyoti Davlatii Tojikiston Shū"bai Adabiyoti Politikī, 1941, 37 pp., 6150 cop. [Taj 4 Cyr; DLC] 189

Qānūn-i asāsī: Jumhūrīyyat-i ijtimā'ī-yi shurā'ī-yi uzbekstān. Faṣl-i avval. Samarkand: n.p., n.d., 39 pp., 300 cop. [Taj 1 & 2 Arab; DLC, NN] 189

Social Organization

Glavadski, Ā. A. *Kārgarān-i ittifāq va be dihqānān-i tājīkistān "chegūne" yārmandī midihand.* Samarkand: Nashrīyyāt-i Davlatī-yi Tājīkistān, 1927, 55 pp., 3000 cop. [Taj 1 & 2 Arab; DLC, NN] 1893

Marāmnāme-yi ittifāq-i khājagī-yi dihāt va toqāy dar jumhūrīyyat-i ittifāq-i shurā'i. Tashkent: Byūrā-yi Qumīte-yi Markazī-yi Ittifāq-i Khājagī-yi Dihāt va Toqāy-yi Asyā-yi Mīyāne dar Jumhūrīyyat-i Ittifāq-i Shorā'i, 1927, 52 pp., 1000 cop. [Taj 1 & 2 Arab; NN] 1894

Simeshkā, N. E. *Kasal-i kambaghalān.* Samarkand–Dushanbe: Nashrīyyāt-i Davlatī-yi Tājīkistān, 1927, 54 pp., 4070 cop. [Taj 1 & 2 Arab; DLC] 1895

Zakhm: Sīflīs. Samarkand–Dushanbe: Nashrīyyāt-i Davlatī-yi Tājīkistān, 1927, 29 pp., 4070 cop. [Taj 1 & 2 Arab; DLC] 1896

TAJIK Humanities

Art and Architecture

Abū Ṭāhir Valad Qāẕi Abū Sa'yyīd Samarqandī. *Samarīyye.* St. Petersburg: Chābkhāne-yi Ilyās Mīrzā Borāghānskī va Shurakāyish, A.H.1322/A.D.1904, xii and 81 pp., n.c. [Taj 1 & 2 Arab; NNC] 1897

Language

Maḥmūd, V. *Dastūr-i 'amalī-qā'idehā-yi zabān barā-yi ṣinf-i duvvum.* Samarkand–Dushanbe: Nashrīyyāt-i Davlatī-yi Tājīkistān, 1927, 132 pp., 7000 cop. [Taj 1 & 2 Arab; DLC] 1898

Semenov, A. *Materialy dlia izucheniia nariechiia gornykh Tadzhikov tsentral'noi Azii.* Chast' I–II: grammaticheskii ocherk i pamiatniki narodnago tvorchestva. Moscow: O. O. Gerbek, 1900–1901, 56 and 75 pp., n.c. [Special Cyr; NNC] 1899

Literature

ʿAynī, Ṣ. *Sargudhasht-i yak tājīk-i kambaghal yāke ādīne.* Samarkand–Dushanbe: Nashrīyyāt-i Davlatī-yi Tājīkistān, 1927, 141 pp., 3000 cop. [Taj 1 & 2 Arab; DLC] 1900

Aynī, Ṣadr al-Dīn. *Namūne-yi adabīyāt-i tājīk ha (1200–1300).* Moscow: Chāpkhāne-yi Nashrīyyāt-i Markazī-yi Khalq-i Ittihād-i Jamāhīr Shuravī-yi Susyalīstī, 1927, 189 pp., 5000 cop. [Taj 1 & 2 Arab; DLC, NJP] 1901

Buzurzoda, L.; Jalilov, R. *In"ikosi shūrishi Vose" dar folʹklor.* Stalinabad–Leningrad: Nashriyoti Davlatii Tojikiston, 1941, 130 pp., 4200 cop. [Taj 4 Cyr; DLC] 1902

Dhihnī, Maḥmūd. *Bakhsh-i nakhustīn az adabīyyāt-i bachchagāne-yi tājīkī: tarānehā-yi kūdakān.* Samarkand: Nashrīyyāt-i Davlatī-yi Tājīkistān, 1927, 35 pp., 3000 cop. [Taj 1 & 2 Arab; DLC, NN] 1903

⟨Ferdovsi⟩ *Dastani chänd äz shahnamäye Ferdovsi.* Ashkhabad: Näshriyyate Dovlätiye Torkmänästan, 1935, xlviii and 194 pp., 2000 cop. [Taj 3 Lat; DLC] 1904

⟨Hiravī, Nāẓim⟩ *Yūsuf-i zulaykhā-yi nāẓim-i hiravī.* Tashkent: Maṭbaʿe-yi Pūr-Ṣaf, A.H.1322/A.D.1904, 192 pp., n.c. [Taj 1 & 2 Arab; NNC] 1905

Ismati, Obidi (ed.). *Sabzayi navkhez.* Tashkent–Stalinabad: Nashriyoti Davlatiyi Tojikiston, 1930, 76 pp., 2000 cop. [Taj 3 Lat; DLC] 1906

Jangar (Jahongir). Stalinabad: Nashriyoti Davlatii Tojikiston, 1941, 16 pp., 5000 cop. [Taj 4 Cyr; DLC] 1907

Kataev, V. *Toqa yak badbon tobon ast.* Stalinabad: Nashriyoti Davlatii Tojikiston, 1941, 278 pp., 2000 cop. [Taj 4 Cyr; DLC] 1908

Kullīyāt-i tīmūr nāme-yi fārsī. Tashkent: Maṭbaʿ-i Mullā Ghulām Ḥasan, A.H. 1331/A.D. 1912, 441 pp., n.c. [Taj 1 & 2 Arab; NNC] 1909

Lāhūtī. *Adabīyāt-i surkh.* Samarkand: Nashrīyyāt-i Davlatī-yi Tājīkistān, 1927, 144 pp., 5000 cop. [Taj 1 & 2 Arab; NN] 1910

Lāhūtī. *Kriml va rubāʿīyāt.* Samarkand–Dushanbe: Nashrīyyāt-i Davlatī-yi Tājīkistān, 1927, 53 pp., 3000 cop. [Taj 1 & 2 Arab; DLC] 1911

Lāhūtī. *Kriml va rubāʿīyāt*. Samarkand: Nashrīyyāt-i Davlatī-yi Tājīkistān, 1927 2d ed., 59 pp., 3000 cop. [Taj 1 & 2 Arab; DLC, NNC] 1912

Lāhūtī. *Rubāʿīyāt*. Moscow: Nashrīyyāt-i Markazī-yi Milal-i Jūmhūrīhā-yi Muttahide-yi Ijtimāʿī va Shuravī, 1924, 40 pp., 1000 cop. [Taj 1 & 2 Arab; CStH, NN] 1913

Lāhūtī. *Tā chand Kunī girye bar masnad-i nūshravān, Dar qaṣt-i Kriml, ay dil, astrār-i nahān bar khwān!* Moscow: Markazī Sharq Nashrīyātī, 1923, 32 pp., 3000 cop. [Taj 1 & 2 Arab; CStH] 1914

Lohuti. *Adabiyoti surkh. Majmuayi sheʿrho.* Stalinabad: Nashriyoti Davlatiyi Tojikiston, 1932/1933 2d ed., 170 pp., 5000 cop. [Taj 3 Lat; NNC] 1915

⟨Lohutī⟩ *Devoni Lohutī.* II (1933–1939). Stalinabad–Leningrad: Nashriyoti Davlatiyi Tojikiston, 1940, 272 pp., 3500 cop. [Taj 3 Lat; NNC] 1915a

Lohutī. *Zūri kollektiv.* Stalinabad–Leningrad: Nashriyyoti Davlatiyi Tojikiston, 1935, 44 pp., 5000 cop. [Taj 3 Lat; NNC] 1915b

Lohutī, A. *Kovayi ohangar.* Libretto baroyi opera dar 6 namoyish. Stalinabad–Leningrad: Nashriyoti Davlatiyi Tojikiston. Shubayi Adabiyoti Badei, 1940, 72 pp., 5000 cop. [Taj 3 Lat; NNC] 1915c

Lutfī, Obidkhojaev. *Najminiso.* Stalinabad: Nashriyoti Davlatii Tojikiston, 1941, 65 pp., 3150 cop. [Taj 4 Cyr; DLC] 1916

Maktub ba jangovaroni tojik az khalqi tojik. Stalinabad: Nashriyoti Davlatii Tojikiston, 1943, 16 pp., 10000 cop. [Taj 4 Cyr; DLC] 1917

Namunahoyi adabiyoti tojik. Stalinabad: Gosudarstvennoe Izdatel'stvo Tadzhikskoi SSR, 1940, 604 pp., 10000 cop. [Taj 3 Lat; DLC] 1918

Tolstoy, L. N. *Hojī Murod.* Stalinabad: Nashriyoti Davlatii nazdi SKKh RSS Tojikiston, 1945, 180 pp., 5000 cop. [Taj 4 Cyr; DLC] 1919

Vagnir, Yu. *Nabātāt che ṭavr sākhte shude ast va ānhā che ṭavr ḥayāt migodharānand?* Samarkand: Nashrīyyāt-i Davlatī-yi Tājīkistān, 1928, 104 pp., 3000 cop. [Taj 1 & 2 Arab; NN] 1920

de Vega, Lope. *Fuente ovekhuna.* Chashmai gūsfandon. Stalinabad: Nashriyoti Davlatii Tojikiston, 1942, 95 pp., 3000 cop. [Taj 4 Cyr; DLC] 1921

TAT Social Sciences

Economics

Skomorokhov, A. *Dorit ḥäyvuhorä äz yulukhmä h'äzorho.* Makhachkala: Däfuskhonäy Ḥükümät, 1930, 16 pp., 1000 cop. [Tat 2 Lat; NN] 1922

Social Organization

Spläranskiy, G. N. *Chü gäräki eri t'änüsdä däädrd.* Makhachkala: Dofuskhonäy Ḥükümät, 1930, 24 pp., 1060 cop. [Tat 2 Lat; NN] 1923

TATAR, see *CRIMEAN TATAR; KRESHEN TATAR; VOLGA TATAR*

TURKMEN General (including periodicals)

Sovet Turkmenistanï (Ashkhabad) 1945: 143, 145–146, 150–158, 160–165, 168–182, 185–218, 221–223, 226–241, 244–260. [Tur 4 Cyr; CStH] 1924

TSShJ Halq Komisarlar shurasï Ish dolandïrïjïlïghï tayïndan yayradïlmalï TSShJ Ishchi-Dayhan Hökumeti Qarar Buyrïqlarïnïng Yïghïndïsï, ⟨see number 1927⟩.

Torkmänistan mätboʿat kitabiyatï (Ashkhabad) 1930: 1. [Tur 2 Arab; DLC, NN] 1925

Torkmänistan satsyalist shoralar jomhoriyätindä ishchi vä dayḥan ḥokomätining qada-qanonlar yïghïndïsï ⟨by 1928 title changed to⟩ *Türkmenistaan Jemhuuriyeti Iishchi, Dayhaan Hökimedining Qaada ve Qanuunlar Yïghïndïsï* (Ashkhabad) 1926: 1–19, 21–22 [MH]; 1928: 1–4; 1929: 5–30 [NNC]; 1930: 1 [DLC, MH, NNC], 2 [DLC, MH], 3–11 [DLC, MH, NNC], 12–13 [MH, NNC], 14–18 [NNC]; 1931: 1–2 [MH, NNC], 4–7 [MH, NNC] 1926

⟨in 1932 title changed to⟩ *TSShJ Halq Komisarlar Shurasï Ish dolandïrïjïlïghï tayïndan yayradïlmalï TSShJ Ishchi-Dayhan Hökumeti Qarar Buyrïqlarïnïng Yïghïndïsï* ⟨and by July 1, 1932, to⟩ *Türkmenistan SShJ Ishchi-Dayhan Hökimedining chïqaran Qarar ve Buyrïqlarïnïng Yïghïndïsï* (Ashkhabad) 1932: 1–7 [MH, NNC], 8–9 [DLC, MH, NNC]; 1933: 1–8, 10; 1935: 2–6 [MH]; 1936: 1–6 [DLC, MH], 7–9 [MH], 10–11 [DLC, MH], 12–19; 1937: 1–10 [MH]. [Tur 2 Arab, 3 Lat] 1927

Türkmenistan metbughat kitabïyatï (Ashkhabad) 1930, 3; 1932: 5. [Tur 3 Lat; NN] 1928

TURKMEN Social Sciences

Economics

Aazïq iishchileri sayuuzï bilen devlet baqlïq senaaghatï tresti aarasïnda baaghlanan zehmet shertnaamasï. Ashkhabad: Türkmenbaalïq, 1929, 74 pp., 200 cop. [Tur 3 Lat; DLC] 1929

Alochï birläshik pravläniyanïng birinji adïmï. Moscow: SSSR Ḥalqlarïnïng Doyib Näshriyatï, 1928, 56 pp., 1000 cop. [Tur 2 Arab; NN] 1930

Aytaqof, N. *Shura turkmänistanning bir yilï*. Ashkhabad: Turkmänistan Däolät Näshriyatï, 1926, 20 pp., 2000 cop. [Tur 2 Arab; NN) 1931

Fomitski, V. *Yaḥshi vä yaman koparatïb ḥaqinda*. Moscow: SSSR Ḥalqlarïnïng Doyïb Näshriyatï, 1929, 40 pp., 2000 cop. [Tur 2 Arab; NN] 1932

Matveyenko, A. *Suvarma ishleri haqïda her bir paghtakesh dayhan näme bilmelidir*. Tashkent: N.I.Kh.I. Nashrïyatï, 1931, 14 pp., 12500 cop. [Tur 3 Lat; NN] 1933

Milonïf, Yo. *Bizin käsäbä sayuzlarïmïzïng nakhïla ishlämäläri lazïm*. n.p.: Bütün SSSR Käsäbä Sayuzlar Märkäzi Shorasïnïng Orta Asiya Byürasï, n.d., 106 pp., 1000 cop. [Tur 2 Arab; DLC] 1934

Namä säbäbdän oz qoparatibing shärtnamasïnï bilmäk käräk. Moscow: SSSR Ḥalqlarïnïng Doyïb Näshriyatï, 1929, 38 pp., 2000 cop. [Tur 2 Arab; NN] 1935

Paskotski, N. *Turkmänistan ḥojalïghïn nakhïlï ayagha ghaldïrmalï*. Ashkhabad: Turkmänistan Dävlät Näshriyatï, 1926, 28 pp., 2000 cop. [Tur 2 Arab; NN] 1936

Platof. *Tot aghaji*. Tashkent: Orta Asiya Hissälik Jäm'iyäti "Torksholk" nïng Näshri, 1927, 28 pp., 2050 cop. [Tur 2 Arab; NN] 1937

Qovachanï hachan ve nenengsi suvarmalïdïr. Tashkent–Moscow: Dövlet Birlegen Neshriyatïng Orto-Azïya Bölimi, 1931, 36 pp., 5000 cop. [Tur 3 Lat; NN] 1938

Saḥatmiradof; Atabayif. *Torkmänistanda yär-su räformasï*. Ashkhabad: Turkmänistan Däolät Näshriyatï, 1926, 64 pp., 5000 cop. [Tur 2 Arab; DLC, NN] 1939

Shamurat oghli, Murat. *Yupäkchilik*. Ashkhabad: Turkmänistan Däolät Näshriyatï, 1926, ii and 115 pp., 3000 cop. [Tur 2 Arab; NN] 1940

Yopäk fabrikindä ishliyan ishchiläring vazipalarï. n.p.: Tork Yopeking Yayïradanï, 1928, 35 pp., 160 cop. [Tur 2 Arab; DLC] 1941

Education

Aliyif, A. *Ävrädoji yigiding yoldashï*. Tashkent: Orta-Aziya Ḥokomät Kitab Basdïrojï Divanḥanäsi, 1924, 8 pp., 1000 cop. [Tur 2 Arab; NN] 1942

ʻAliyif, A. *Muṣavvar ikinchi yïl turkmän dili.* Tashkent: Turkestanskoe Gosudarstvennoe Izdatel'stvo, 1922, 72 pp., 30000 cop. [Tur 1 Arab; NN] 1943

Altï aylïq savatsïzlïghï bitirmäk ochin oqïdlïghalarda oqlïyan sapaqnïng programmasï. Tashkent: Torkistan Däolät Näshriyatï, 1923, 16 pp., 1000 cop. [Tur 1 Arab; NN] 1944

Ang-bilim qamisiyasï. Tashkent: Sr.-Az. Biuro VTsSPS, 1927, 53 pp., 5000 cop. [Tur 2 Arab; DLC] 1945

Gäldiyif, M. *Mäktäbä chänli tärbiyä.* Ashkhabad: Turkmänistan Dävlät Näshriyatï, 1925, 43 pp., 4000 cop. [Tur 2 Arab; DLC, NN) 1946

Gäldiyif, M.; Alparïf, Gh. *Elipbi.* Poltoratsk: Turkmänistan Däolät Näshriyatï, 1926, 94 pp., 25000 cop. [Tur 2 Arab; DLC] 1947

Gäldiyif, M.; Alparïf, Gh. *Ulïlara oqu-jazu ogrätmäk uchin sapaqlïq.* Poltoratsk: Torkmänistan Dävlät Nashri, 1926, 117 pp., 15000 cop. [Tur 2 Arab; DLC] 1948

Ivanov. *Joghrafiyä.* Ashkhabad: Turkmänistan Dävlät Nashriyatï, 1926, 119 pp., 10000 cop. [Tur 2 Arab; DLC] 1949

Lanqof. *Ḥasab mäsälälär yighindisi.* Ashkhabad: Torkmänistan Däolät Näshriyatï, 1925, iii and 115 pp., 15000 cop. [Tur 2 Arab; DLC] 1950

Mädäni ishlär qamisiyasï Tashkent: Hämmä Orsiyät Doyïb Frafsayozlar Maslaḥatnïng Orta Asiyada Bolan Biyorosïnïng Näshriyatï, 1927, 16 pp., 500 cop. [Tur 2 Arab; NN] 1951

Oba mäktäbläri ichon qompläks asasindä dozbilän proghramma. Ashkhabad: Turkmenskoe Gosudarstvennoe Izdatel'stvo, 1928, 43 pp., 650 cop. [Tur 2 Arab; DLC] 1952

Potseluyevskiy, A. P. *Turkmen edebi dili orfografiyasïnïng reformasï.* Ashkhabad: Turkmendövletnesir, 1936, 24 pp., 300 cop. [Tur 3 Lat; MH] 1953

Qaraḥanïf, Allaqolï. *Änä dilimiz.* Tashkent: Turkestanskoe Gosudarstvennoe Izdatel'stvo, 1923, 71 pp., 5000 cop. [Tur 2 Arab; NN] 1954

"*Qïzïl borch.*" Tashkent: Hämmä Orsïyät Doyïb Frafsayozlar Maslaḥatïnïng Orta Asiyada Bolan Byorosïnïng Näshriyatï, 1927, 8 pp., 500 cop. [Tur 2 Arab; NN] 1955

Education

Sävad mäktäbläridä kättälärni oqish tärtibi ochon programma. Tashkent: Torkistan Hokomät Näshriyatï, 1923, 14 pp., 1000 cop. [Tur 1 Arab; NN] 1956

Usulï yol görkezmeklikde mugallïmlara kömekche. Ashkhabad: Türkmendövletneshir, 1935, 215 pp., 6000 cop. [Tur 3 Lat; DLC] 1957

Vagnär, Yu. *Hava ḥaqïnda.* Tashkent: Turkistan Ḥukomätining Kitab Basdïrojï Devankhanasï, 1924, 109 pp., 5000 cop. [Tur 2 Arab; NN] 1958

Vagnär, Yu. *Su ḥaqinda.* Tashkent: Turkistan Dävlätining Kitab Basdïrochï Divankhanasï, 1924, 105 pp., 5000 cop. [Tur 2 Arab; NN] 1959

Vagnär, Yuu. *Bizim andammïzïng naḥïl pasalandïghï häm ishlishi doghrïsïnda gurringlär.* Ashkhabad: Turkmänistan Jämḥoriyätining Däolät Näshriyatï, 1925, 179 pp., 5000 cop. [Tur 2 Arab; DLC, NN] 1960

Vagnär, Yuu. *Yär ḥaqinda.* Ashkhabad: Turkmänistan Däolät Näshriyatï 1925, 119 pp., 5000 cop. [Tur 2 Arab; DLC, NN] 1961

Geography

Gäyki, A. *Täbighi joghrafiyä.* Ashkhabad: Turkmänistan Dävlät Näshriyatï, 1926, 181 pp., 5000 cop. [Tur 2 Arab; DLC, NN] 1962

Government

Bäyik särdar. Ashkhabad: Torkmänistan Dävlät Näshri, 1926, 26 pp., 5000 cop. [Tur 2 Arab; DLC] 1963

Länin, V. I. *Qomsomolïng nichik bolmaghï gäräk.* Moscow: SSSR Khalqlarïnïng Doyïb Näshriyatï, 1925, 27 pp., 2000 cop. [Tur 2 Arab; NN] 1964

Nasïrlï, I. (Il oghlï). *Yoqsullar ïnqlabïnïng 9 inji yïlï oqtyabrï.* Ashkhabad: Turkmänistan Dävlät Nashriyatï, 1926, 65 pp., 3000 cop. [Tur 2 Arab: DLC] 1965

Nodäl, V. *Här bir qammonist namä bilmäli.* Ashkhabad: Torkmänistan Däolät Näshriyatï, 1925, 51 pp., 5000 cop. [Turk 2 Arab; NN] 1966

Qamänyäf, L. B. *Linin vä onïng partiyasï.* Ashkhabad: Torkmänistan Däolät Näshriyatï, 1925, 166 pp., 5000 cop. [Tur 2 Arab; DLC] 1967

Qovalinko, P. *Torkmän dilindä siyasi sooad kitabï.* Tashkent: Torkistan Däolät Näshriyatï, 1923, 61 pp., 3000 cop. [Tur 1 Arab; NN] 1968

Radïk, Qarl. *Linin—ïnqïlab yolbashchïsï.* Poltoratsk: Torkmänistan Däolät Näshriyatï, 1925, 22 pp., 5000 cop. [Tur 2 Arab; DLC] 1969

Rosiyä länin yash qommonïstlar sayozïnïng proghrammasï häm ustabï. Ashkhabad: Torkmänistan Dävlät Nashriyat, 1925, 34 pp., 3000 cop. [Tur 2 Arab; DLC] 1970

Rosiyät qammonïst (balshäoilär) partiyasïnïng praghrammasï. Ashkhabad: Torkmälistan Dolät Näshriyatï, 1925, 100 pp., 2000 cop. [Tur 2 Arab; NN] 1971

SSSR yokarï sovetining mejlisining stenografigi khasabatï. Moscow: SSSR Yokarï Sovetining Neshiri, 1942, 58 pp., n.c. [Tur 4 Cyr; DLC] 1972

Shästaqof, A. V. *Oktabr ïnqïlabï daykhanlara namä bärdi.* Moscow: SSSR Ḥalqlarïnïng Doyïb Näshriyatï, 1926, 36 pp., 3000 cop. [Tur 2 Arab; NN] 1973

Siyasi sooat kitabï. 2 boläk. Ashkhabad: Torkmänistan Däolät Näshriyatï, 1927, 236 pp., 3080 cop. [Tur 2 Arab; DLC] 1974

T.A.Sh. jämhoriyätindä admïnïstratsïya bolinishi. Ashkhabad: Märkäzi Ijraaiyä Qommitäsi vä Ḥalq Qamisarlar Shorasï, 1926, 179 pp., 1000 cop. [Tur 2 Arab; DLC] 1975

Vïrganskï, B. *Obalar qomsomollarïndan otïrï siyasi oqo kitabï.* Moscow: SSSR Ḥalqïnïng Doyïb Näshriyatï, 1927, 79 pp., 3000 cop. [Tur 2 Arab; NN] 1976

Yaraslavskï. *Länin daykhanlar vä qamonistlär partiyasï.* Ashkhabad: Turkmänistan Dävlät Näshriyatï, 1926, 61 pp., 5000 cop. [Tur 2 Arab; NN] 1977

Yaroslauskï, Yäm. *Länin häm yash qommonïstlar sayozï-oyoshmäsi. (Qomsomol).* Ashkhabad: Turkmänistan Jämḥoriyätining Däolät Näshriyatï, 1925, 40 pp., 5000 cop. [Tur 2 Arab; NN] 1978

Zaytsäf, A. *Daykhan gozäranchïlïghï ḥaqïnda pirqanïng zäror qararlarï.* Moscow: SSSR Ḥalqlarïnïng Doyïb Näshriyatï, 1926, 34 pp., 2000 cop. [Tur 2 Arab; NN] 1979

History

'Abdu-'s Sattar, Qazi. *Tekimlarïnïng orosh qisä kitabi: Jengnamä*... St. Petersburg: Tipografiia Imperatorskoi Akademii Nauk, 1914, xx and 82 and 55 and 0157 pp., n.c. [Tur 1 Arab; MH, NNC] 1980

Kudryafskï, D. *Qadïm zamanda adamlar naḥïl duryanlar äkän.* Tashkent: Turkistan Ḥukomätining Kitab Basdïrojï Divankhanasï, 1924, v and 167 pp., 5000 cop. [Tur 1 Arab; DLC, NN] 1981

Lilinä, Z. *Linindä adamlïq sipatlarï.* Tashkent: Orta Aziya Dävlät Näshriyatï, 1924, 23 pp., 10000 cop. [Tur 2 Arab; NN] 1982

Trotskï, L. *Länin yoq!... Yoqdir indi länin!* Tashkent: Orta Aziya Dävlät Näshriyatï, 1924, 6 pp., 10000 cop. [Tur 2 Arab; NN] 1983

Law

Türkmenistaan S.Sh.J. qaanuunï (qonïstituutsïyaasï). Ashkhabad: n.p., 1928, 58 pp., 1000 cop. [Tur 3 Lat; DLC] 1984

Türkmenistan soviet sotsialistik respublikasïnïng konstitutsiyasï: Esasi kanunï. Ashkhabad: Türkmenpartneshr, 1938, 30 pp., 9000 cop. [Tur 3 Lat; DLC] 1985

Social Organization

Bädän tärbiyäsi. Tashkent: Hämmät Orsiyät Doyïb Frafsayozlar Maslaḥatïnïng Orta Asiyada Bolan Byorosïnïng Näshriyatï, 1927, 14 pp., 500 cop. [Tur 2 Arab; DLC, NN] 1986

Batraqlarïng häm chopanlarïng mänghäghatlarï oba ḥojolïq vä toqoy ishchilär oyoshmasï nakhïla hämaya ïdya. Tashkent: Oba Hojolïq Näshriyatï, 1927, 34 pp., 1000 cop. [Tur 2 Arab; DLC] 1987

Grämyatskï, M. *Tabighatda dirilik ochin goräsh.* Moscow: SSSR Khalqlarïnïng Doyïb Näshriyatï, 1926, 64 pp., 2000 cop. [Tur 2 Arab; NN] 1988

Kärpinski, V. *Zähmätkäsh dayḥanlar yolbashchïsï.* Ashkhabad: Torkmänistan Dävlät Näshriyatï, 1926, 16 pp., 5000 cop. [Tur 2 Arab; DLC, NN] 1989

Language

Aliyiv, A.; Bööriyif, K. *Orïscha–Türkmenche sözlik*. Ashkhabad: Devlet Neshriyatï, 1929, 452 pp., 20000 cop. [Tur 3 Lat; MH] 1990
Bogdanova, M. I. *Ijtimagi-sïyasi terminlering ruscha–türkmenche qïsga sözlügi*. Ashkhabad: Türkmendövletneshr, 1937, 107 pp., 10000 cop. [Tur 3 Lat; MH] 1991

Literature

Basïr. *Soltan sanjar mazï*. 3 gorïnïsh, 6 chïqïshda. Ashkhabad: Turkmänistan Dävlät Näshriyatï, 1926, 50 pp., 1000 cop. [Tur 2 Arab; DLC, NN] 1992
Basïr, Astïrḥanlï. *Dängsizlik: Dort chiqïshda oyin kitabï*. Ashkhabad: Turkmänistan Dävlät Näshriyatï, 1927, 50 pp., 1080 cop. [Tur 2 Arab; NN] 1993
Borï oghlï, Ali. *Berinji may bayramï*. Ashkhabad: Turkmänistan Dävlät Näshriyatï, 1926, 23 pp., 5000 cop. [Tur 2 Arab; NN] 1994
Farrïq, O. *Maydaja artäkilär: Chalïshïrma*. Ashkhabad: Turkmänistan Dävlät Näshriyatï, 1926, 16 pp., 5000 cop. [Tur 2 Arab; DLC, NN] 1995
Gäldiyif, M. *Maqal vä matallar yighindisi: Babalar sozi*. Ashkhabad: Torkmänistan Däolät Näshriyatï, 1925, 56 pp., 5000 cop. [Tur 2 Arab; NN] 1996
Garrïev, Baymukhammet. *Shakhïrlar sesi: Vatan ve gakhrïmanchïlïk khakïndakï ëserlering yïgïndïsï*. Ashkhabad: Birleshen Türkmendövletneshir, 1944, 150 pp., 10000 cop. [Tur 4 Cyr; DLC] 1997
Kärbabayïf, B. *Makhtïmqulï qoshghelarï*. Ashkhabad: Turkmänistan Dävlät Näshriyatï, 1926, 562 pp., 5000 cop. [Tur 2 Arab; DLC, NN] 1998
Kerbabayïv, B. *Kolkhozlar durmïshïndan yazuv beyanï haqïqat*. Ashkhabad: Türkmenistan Dövlet Neshriyatï, 1932, 195 pp., n.c. [Tur 3 Lat; NNC] 1999
"Naoaiy," Emir Ali Shir. *Moḥakimäto'l loghatäyin*. Ashkhabad: Turkmänistan Dävlät Näshriyatï, 1925, 90 pp., 5000 cop. [Tur 2 Arab; NN] 2000

Qiz bäro. Och pärdädä oaqï'a bir aghelda. Moscow: SSSR Ḥalqlarïnïng Doyïb Näshriyatï, 1928, 31 pp., 1500 cop. [Tur 2 Arab; NN] 2001

Qulmoḥammädof, Abdulḥäkim. *Umit yalqïmlarï.* Ghoshghïlar. Ashkhabad: Torkmänistan Dävlät Näshriyatï, 1926, 27 pp., 5000 cop. [Tur 2 Arab; DLC, NN) 2002

Säydi. *Torkmäning aylï ghoshghïlarïndan säydining ghoshghïlarï.* Ashkhabad: Torkmänistan Dävlät Näshriyatï, 1926, 46 pp., 5000 cop. [Tur 2 Arab; DLC, NN] 2003

Turkmän ärtäkiläri. Poltoratsk: Torkmänistan Dävlät Näshriyatï, 1926, 16 pp., 10000 cop. [Tur 2 Arab; DLC] 2004

Zälili. *Ghoshghïlarï.* Ashkhabad: Torkmänistan Dävlät Näshriyatï, 1926, 57 pp., 4000 cop. [Tur 2 Arab; NN] 2005

UYGHUR Social Sciences

Education

Mohämmädi, Abdülhäy. *Oyghorchä yeziq yollïrï.* Moscow: SSSR Ällirining Märkäz Näshreyatï, 1926, 31 pp., 2000 cop. [Uygh 2 Arab; NN] 2006

UYGHUR Humanities

Literature

Änsäri (ed.). *Tang nurlïrï: Uyghur yash shaïrlïrï äsärlirining toplamï.* Tashkent–Samarkand: Öznäshr, 1930, 132 pp., 3000 cop. [Uygh 3 Lat; DLC] 2007

Pantusov, N. N. *Taranchinskiia piesni.* St. Petersburg: Tipografiia Imperatorskoi Akademii Nauk, 1890, iv and 154 pp., n.c. [Uygh 1 Arab; MH] 2008

Pantusov, Nikolai. *Yetti ṣu vilayetidaki taranchilarning arasida nikalay pantuṣif yarib alghan chorchaklar.* Kazan: Tipo-Litografiia Imperatorskago Universiteta, 1909, 220 and 165 pp., n.c. [Uygh 1 Arab; MH] 2009

UZBEK General (including periodicals)

Älängä (Samarkand) 1928: 1–11; 1929: 2–10; 1930: 2–4 [Uz 3 Lat; DLC] 2010

al-Islah (Tashkent) 1915: 12, 14, 16, 19, 22–24; 1916: 1–2, 4, 6–9, 11–13, 15. [Uz 1 Arab; NNC*] 2011

Bilim ochaghi (Tashkent) 1922: 1; 1923: 2/3. [Uz 2 Arab; NN] 2012

Ekin kämpäniyäsi (Samarkand) 1930: 6. [Uz 3 Lat; DLC] 2013

Ilmii fikr (Samarkand–Tashkent) 1930: 1. [Uz 3 Lat; DLC] 2014

Ishchi mükhbirlär vä häy'ät tähririyälärning ishläri. Samarkand–Tashkent: Öznäshr, 1929, 48 pp., 2000 cop. [Uz 3 Lat; NN] 2015

Kammunist jornali (Samarkand–Tashkent) 1926: 11 [DLC]; 1927: 1–3 [DLC, NN]; 4–7; 1928: 1–10; 1929: 3–4, 6–10; 1930: 1–7, 10/11; 1939: 7–8, 11 [DLC] [Uz 2 Arab, 3 Lat] 2016

Khodasizlar (Samarkand) 1928: 3–4, 6–8; 1929: 4–10; 1930: 1–6, 9–10. [Uz 2 Arab, 3 Lat; DLC] 2017

Ma'arif vä oqoghochi: Balalar bölimi (Tashkent) 1927: 1–3; 1928: 10–13; n.d.: 6–9. [Uz 2 Arab, 3 Lat; DLC] 2018

Ma'arif vä oqotghochi (Tashkent) 1927: 5–8 DLC, [NN]; 9–11; 1928: 1–11; 1929: 2–12; 1930: 1–3 1931: 1–6 [DLC]. [Uz 2 Arab, 3 Lat] 2019

Mäshräb (Samarkand) 1924: 4. [Uz 2 Arab; NN] 2020

Mihnät (Samarkand) 1927: 1, 4. [Uz 2 Arab; NN] 2021

Mukhbirlär yoldashi (Samarkand) 1929: 2, 4; 1930: 1, 3–6. [Uz 2 Arab, 3 Lat; DLC] 2022

Mushtum (Samarkand) 1927: 1–6, 15, 18/19, [NN]; 1929: 21; 1930: 2, 5–6 [DLC]; n.d.: 8, 10, 12 [NN]. [Uz 2 Arab, 3 Lat] 2023

Özb. K. F. Märkäzqomining akhbarati (Samarkand) 1929: 1. [Uz 3 Lat; DLC] 2024

OzSSR saghliqni saqlash khalq kommissariatining rasmiy byulleteni (Tashkent) 1935: 3/4. [Uz 3 Lat; DLC] 2025

Ozbekistan kasaba soyuzlari sovetining byulleteni (Tashkent) 1935: 21/22 [DLC]; 1936: 4–10 [NNC]. [Uz 3 Lat] 2026

Ozbekstan qishlaq khojalik byulleteni (Tashkent) 1939: 7–8. [Uz 3 Lat; DLC] 2027

---

*Microfilm

Ozbĭkistan ĭjtima'i shoralar jomhorĭyäti ishchi vä dihqan ḥokomätining qanon vä boyroqlarĭning yighindisi (Tashkent) Part I. 1925: 1–25, 28–30, 33, 36–46, 50–53, 55–57, 59–60; 1926: 9–10, 13, 15–23, 27–39; 1927: 41–42, 1–11, 17–28, 30, 33–34, 38, 41–43, 45 [DLC]; 1930: 1–3 [MH], 4–5 [DLC, MH], 6–7 [MH], 8 [DLC, MH], 9–15 [MH], 16–17 [DLC, MH], 18 [MH], 19–37 [DLC, MH], 38 [MH], 39–40 [DLC, MH], 41–42 [MH], 43 [DLC, MH], 44–45 [MH], 46 [DLC, MH], 47–48 [MH], 49 [DLC, MH], 50–52, 54–55 [DLC]; 1931: 1 [DLC, MH], 2 [DLC], 3 [DLC, MH], 5 [DLC], 6–10 [DLC, MH], 11 [DLC] 12–14 [DLC, MH], 15, 17 [DLC], 18–22 [DLC, MH], 23–25 [DLC], 26–31 [DLC, MH], 32, 35–37, 39, 41–44 [MH]; 1932: 1–8, 10–13, 15–16, 18–19, 22–42, 44–45; 1933: 1–2, 4–5, 7–16, 18–25, 27–29A, 30–37; 1934: 1–37; 1936: 1–44; 1937: 1–20, 22, 25 [MH]. Part II. 1926: 1–14; 1927: 1–2, 7–11, 14, 17; 1929: 12 [DLC]; 1930: 1–3 [MH], 4–10 [DLC, MH]; 1931: 2; 1933: 3 [MH]. [Uz 2 Arab, 3 Lat] 2028

Ozbĭkstan malĭyä jornali (Samarkand) 1927: 1. [Uz 2 Arab; NN] 2029

Ozbĭkstandaghi khatin-qiz qoloblarĭda ishläsh: Byollĭtĭn (Samarkand–Tashkent) 1927: 1–2. [Uz 2 Arab; DLC, NN] 2030

Pakhta üchün küräsh (Tashkent) 1934: 1–12; [NN] 1935: 1–9; 1936: 1–4 [DLC, NN], 5–8 [DLC]. [Uz 3 Lat] 2031

Qishlaq khojalĭghi turmushi (Tashkent) 1927: 1 [DLC, NN], 4–8 [DLC], 9 [DLC, NN], 10–12; 1928: 1–10 [DLC]. [Uz 2 Arab] 2032

Qïzïl qalam mäjmü'äsi (Samarkand–Tashkent) 1929: II. [Uz 3 Lat; NN] 2033

Sä'id, Nä'im. *Mukhbirlar yoldashi.* Tashkent–Samarkand: Oz. Däolät Näshrĭyati, 1927, 89 pp., 3000 cop. [Uz 2 Arab; DLC, NN] 2034

Sä'id, Zĭya. *Ozbek vaqtli mätbo'ati tä'rikhigä materiyallar, 1870–1927.* Samarkand–Tashkent: Oz. Däolät Näshrĭyati, 1927, 180 pp., 3500 cop. [Uz 2 Arab; NN] 2035

Yängi qishlaq (Samarkand) 1929: 2–9, 11–12; 1930: 3–5. [Uz 2 Arab; DLC] 2036

Yängi yol (Tashkent) 1927: 1–2 [NN], 5–8 [DLC], 9 [DLC, NN], 12; 1928: 1–10; 1929: 2–4, 6–7, 9; 1930: 1, 5–7, 11/12 [DLC]. [Uz 2 Arab, 3 Lat] 2037

Yash küch (Tashkent) 1929: 1/3. [Uz 3 Lat; DLC] 2038

Yïr yüzi (Tashkent) 1927: 20 [NN], 22–27 [DLC], 28/29 [NN], 30 [DLC, NN]; 1928: 1–19; 1929: 8, 11, 16–19, 22/23; 1930: 1, 7–12, 19/20 [DLC]. [Uz 2 Arab, 3 Lat] 2039

UZBEK Social Sciences

Economics

Akhonbabayif. *Rayonlashdïrishdan dïhqan khojalïqïgha kïlädirgän faydalar.* Samarkand: Oz. Däolät Näshrïyati, 1926, 16 pp., 5000 cop. [Uz 2 Arab; DLC] 2040

Amanat muamalasi yuzasidan davlat mihnat amanat kassalariga qollanma: Instruksiya. n.p.: "Qzil Ozbekistan" Nashriyatining Basmakhanasi, n.d., 39 pp., 2000 cop. [Uz 3 Lat; DLC] 2041

Balashof, N. *Orta asiyaning iqtïsadi joghrafïyäsi.* Tashkent: Oz. Däolät Näshriyati, 1926, 138 pp., 7000 cop. [Uz 2 Arab; DLC] 2042

Bartold. *Turkistanning sugharïlish tä'rïkhi.* Tashkent: Oz. Däolät Näshrïyati, 1926, xviii and 271 pp., 8000 cop. [Uz 2 Arab; DLC] 2043

Bïkhovski. *Sïghortä sandoghi toghrïsïda.* Samarkand: "Miḥnät Mäs'äläläri" Näshrïyatïning Ozbïkstan Bolimchäsi, 1926, 60 pp., 2000 cop. [Uz 2 Arab; NN] 2044

Bïktemir; Abiz. *I.Sh.J.I.ning iqtïsadi jughrafiyäsi.* Tashkent: Orta Asya Kammonïstlar Darilfinoni Näshriyati, 1928, 556 pp., 5000 cop. [Uz 2 Arab; CStH] 2045

1936 nchi yilda kolkhozchilar budjeti. Tashkent: SSSR Davlat Planining Khalq Khojaligini Hsabga Alish Markaziy Idarasi, 1936, 15 pp., n.c. [Uz 3 Lat; DLC] 2046

1936-nchi yilda SSSR-ning qishlaq sovetlarida bashlanghich uchot yurutish yuzasidan instruksiya. Tashkent: SSSR Davlat Plani Khalq Khojaligini Hsabga Alish Markaziy Idarasi, 1936, 56 pp., 2500 cop. [Uz 3 Lat; DLC] 2047

1932 nchi yïlnïng köntröl raqamlarï haqïdaghï mä'rüzä boyïncha ÖzÏShCh Shoralar M.Ï.Q.ning IV nchi chaqïrïsh 2 nchi sessiyäsining qararï. Tashkent: Märkäzi Ïjraqom Näshri, 1932, 14 pp., 500 cop. [Uz 3 Lat; DLC] 2048

Birläshgän qishlaq khojalighi salighi. Tashkent: Oz. Khälq Maliyä Kämisärligining Näshri, 1928, vi and 234 pp., 5053 cop. [Uz 2 Arab; DLC] 2049

Birläshgän qishlaq khojaliq salighi toghrïsïda dästoril'ämäl. I. Samarkand: Oz. Khalq Malïyä Kämisärligi, 1930, 111 pp., 3000 cop. [Uz 2 Arab; DLC] 205◀

Birläshkän qishlaq khojaliq salighi toghrisïda dästoril'ämäl. II. Samarkand: Oz. Khälq Malïyä Kämïsärliki, 1930, 66 pp., 3000 cop. [Uz 2 Arab; DLC] 205.

Bornash, 'A. *Ozbekstanda 1930/31inchi yil uchun birläshgän qishlaq khojaliq salighi.* Tashkent: I.Sh.J.I. Dävlät Maliyä Näshriyatining Orta-Asiya Shu'bäsi, 1930, 55 pp., 15000 cop. [Uz 2 Arab; DLC] 205.

Chayanif, A. *Qisqacha käpïrätsïyä därsligi.* Samarkand: Oz.I.Sh.J. Qishlaq Khojälïgi Bankäsïning Näshri, 1927, 71 pp., 2000 cop. [Uz 2 Arab; DLC, NN] 205.

Chïrqashïnïqof, I. I. *Dokan kämïsïyäsi nïmädir.* Samarkand: Oz. Däolät Näshriyati, 1926, 35 pp., 3047 cop. [Uz 2 Arab; DLC] 205

Däolät säna'ät salïghi toghrïsïda nïzamnamä vä dästoril'ämäl. Tashkent: Oz. Däolät Näshrïyati, 1927, 178 pp., 2053 cop. [Uz 2 Arab; DLC] 205

Dästoril'ämäl Oz.I.Sh. jomhorïyätïdä 1927–28 nchi yildä sov saloghini otkazish tärtibi häqïdä. Samarkand: Oz.I.Sh.J. Khalq Malïyä Kamïsarïyätïning Näshrïyati, 1927, 24 pp., 450 cop. [Uz 2 Arab; DLC] 205◀

Davïdof, Ä. *Qoqan qishlaq kïnti.* Tashkent: Oz. Dävlät Näshrïyati, 1927, 197 pp., 553 cop. [Uz 2 Arab; DLC, NN] 205

Dävlät sïghortä ïdaräsïdä 'omrni sïghortä qïldirish. Tashkent: Oz. Dävlät Näshrïyati, 1926, 66 pp., 10000 cop. [Uz 2 Arab; DLC] 205

Dïhqan-shäkhsi sïghortä qa'ïdäläri. Samarkand: Oz. Dävlät Näshri, 1927, 16 pp., 500 cop. [Uz 2 Arab; DLC] 205◀

Fäyzi, Hadi. *Industiriyäläshdirish häm ishchi-diyqan ittifaqi.* Moscow–Samarkand: Oz. Dävlät Näshriyati, 1927, 45 pp., 5000 cop. [Uz 2 Arab; NN] 206

Firstof. *Ozbekistan kochmä qumlari vä ulargha qarshi kuräsh.* Samarkand: Oz.I.Sh.J. Yer Ishläri Khälq Kämïsärligi, 1928, 37 pp., 2530 cop. [Uz 2 Arab; CStH] 206

Fomitski, V. *Yakhshi häm yaman käpirätif toghrisida.* Moscow: Shora Ittifaqi Khalqlarining Näshriyati, 1929, 46 pp., 3000 cop. [Uz 2 Arab; NN] 206

Ĭkramif, Äkmäl. *Yĭr islaḥatĭning yäkunläri oä uni mustäḥkämläshdä kelgusi nämällär.* Tashkent: Oz. Dävlät Näshrĭyati, 1927, 79 pp., 4000 cop. [Uz 2 Arab; DLC] 2063

Instruksiya: Davlat ichki ikkinchi beshyillik zayomi. Tashkent: OzSSR DMAK va DK Idarasĭ, 1936, 18 pp., 12000 cop. [Uz 3 Lat; DLC] 2064

Ishchi vä khizmätkarlärning ʿomrĭni groh tärtĭbiyä sĭghortä qĭldirishning shärtlari. Tashkent: Oz. Däolät Näshrĭyati, 1926, 30 pp., 5000 cop. [Uz 2 Arab; DLC] 2065

Ishmĭt. *Qärz shĭrkätĭni qanday qĭlib qurush vä achish keräk.* Tashkent: Oz. Däolät Näshrĭyati, 1927, 45 pp., 5053 cop. [Uz 2 Arab; DLC] 2066

Istipänif, V. *Mämläkätimizning baylighi.* Samarkand–Moscow: Oz. Däolät Näshrĭyati, 1927, 63 pp., 6000 cop. [Uz 2 Arab; NN] 2067

Itkin, A. *Özbekistanda käpirätsiyä qanday qĭlĭb ösdi.* Samarkand: Özbekistan Dävlät Näshrïyatï, 1929, 63 pp., 3000 cop. [Uz 3 Lat; DLC, NN] 2068

Kämbäghäl vä orta ḥal diyqanlargha qarz berish vä undan toghri faydalanish. Samarkand: Oz.I.Sh.J. Yer Ishläri Khalq Komisärligi, 1930, 30 pp., 15000 cop. [Uz 2 Arab; NN] 2069

Käperätsiyä israfchilari bilän qanday kuräshmäk keräk? Moscow: Shora Ittifaqi Khalqlarining Märkäz Näshriyati, 1928, 30 pp., 10000 cop. [Uz 2 Arab; NN] 2070

Kharraben, J. *Yer yüzining tarïykhïy-iqtïsadïy jughrafïyasï.* Samarkand–Tashkent: Öznäshr, 1929, 138 pp., 6000 cop. [Uz 3 Lat; DLC] 2071

Kharrabĭn, J. *Yer yuzining jughrafĭyäsi.* Tashkent–Samarkand: Oz. Däolät Näshriyati, 1926, vi and 138 pp., 7000 cop. [Uz 2 Arab; DLC] 2072

Khojalïq khïsabïgha köchish toghrïsïdaghï sanaat karkhanalarïgha aïd matïrïallarnïng toplamï. Samarkand: Oz.Ĭ.Sh.J. Khalq Alïy Khojalïq Shorasï, 1930, 48 and 50 pp., 500 cop. [Uz 3 Lat; DLC] 2073

Khojaliq tuzĭlĭshĭmiz häm äppäzĭtsĭyä. Tashkent: Oznäshr, 1928, 69 pp., 2000 cop. [Uz 2 Arab; DLC] 2074

Khojayif, Fäyzollä. *Ozbekstanning iqtĭsadi tuzolĭshĭdä kĭlgusi ämällär.* Tashkent: Oz. Däolät Näshrĭyati, 1926, 56 pp., 3000 cop. [Uz 2 Arab; DLC] 2075

Lapïydus. *Sïyasïy ïqtïsad.* I. Samarkand–Tashkent: Özbekistan Dävlät Näshriyati, 1929, 224 pp., 5000 cop. [Uz 3 Lat; DLC] 2076

Lenin, N. *Käperätsiyä toghrisida.* Moscow–Samarkand: Oz. Däolät Näshriyati, 1927, 18 pp., 5000 cop. [Uz 2 Arab; NN] 2077

Lï'ontiyef. *Sïyasi iqtïsad bashlanghichlari.* Tashkent: Oz. Dävlät Näshrïyati, 1926, 180 pp., 7000 cop. [Uz 2 Arab; DLC] 2078

Mäkäröv, Ä. F. *Pakhta ekinini qachan vä qanday sugharïsh keräk.* Moscow: OGIZ Näshriyatï, 1931, 34 pp., 17000 cop. [Uz 3 Lat; NN] 2079

Matveyïnko, A. *Sugharïsh toghrïsïda pakhtakarnïng nimä bilishi keräk.* Tashkent: NIKhI Näshrïyatï, 1931, 14 pp., 40000 cop. [Uz 3 Lat; NN] 2080

Mihnätni saqlash babïda käsäbä sayozlarïnïng ishläri. Tashkent: Bütün Ïttïfaq Käsäbä Sayozlarïnïng Märkäzii Shuvrasï Orta-Asya Byurasï. Tährirat-Näshriyat Shü'bäsi, 1930, 26 pp., 1000 cop. [Uz 3 Lat; DLC] 2081

Mïlonif, Yo. *Bizning käsäbä sayuzlarïmizning qay khildä ishläshläri lazim.* n.p.: Orta-Asya Byurasi, 1926, 49 pp., 3000 cop. [Uz 2 Arab; DLC] 2082

Mïrkolif, A. V. (Glïbof). *Qishlaq-khojaliq shirkätläridä krïdït ishi.* Samarkand: Oz.I.Sh.J. Qishlaq Khojaliq Bankäsining Näshri, n.d., 54 pp., 3000 cop. [Uz 2 Arab; DLC, NN] 2083

Molotov, V. M. *SSSR khalq khojaligi rvajlanishining uchinchi beshyillik plani.* Tashkent: OzK(b)PMK Partiya Nashriyati, 1939, 93 pp., 20000 cop. [Uz 3 Lat; DLC] 2084

Molotov, V. M. *SSSR khalq khojaligini rvajlantirishning uchinchi besh yillik plani.* Tashkent: OzK(b)PMK Partiya Nashriyati, 1939, 35 pp., 50000 cop. [Uz 3 Lat; DLC] 2085

Oz.I.Sh.J. tashkänt okroghïni rayonlashtïrishgha tïkishli matïryallar. Tashkent: Tashoïlayät Rayonlashtïrish Kämïsïyäsi Näshrïyati, 1927, 43 pp., 400 cop. [Uz 2 Arab; DLC] 2086

Oz käpirätifning ostafini bilish nimä uchun keräk. Moscow: Shora Ittifaqi Khalqlarining Märkäz Nishriyati, 1929, 48 pp., 3000 cop. [Uz 2 Arab; NN] 2087

Ozbekstan ijtïma'i shoralar jumhorïyäti qishlaq khojaliq bankäsining nïzamnamäsi. Samarkand: Oz. Qishlaq Khojaliq Bankäsi, 1927, 18 pp., 1000 cop. [Uz 2 Arab; DLC] 2088

Ozbekstan ijtïma'i shoralar jumhorïyätïning rayonlashdirïlishi.

Samarkand: Oz.I.Sh.J. Märkäz Ijraqomi vä Khalq Kämisärläri
Näshri, 1927, 40 pp., 1500 cop. [Uz 2 Arab; DLC]   2089
*Ozbekstan jomhurïyätïdä 1926–27 nchi yilgi qishlaq khojalighï
saloghï.* Samarkand: Oz. Dävlät Näshrïyati, 1928, 28 pp.,
10000 cop. [Uz 2 Arab; DLC]   2090
Ozbekstandä mïḥnät vä ijtïmaʿi sïghortä. Tashkent: Oz. Däolät
Näshrïyatïning Birinchi Mätbäʿäsi, 1926, 236 pp., 1047 cop.
[Uz 2 Arab; DLC]   2091
Ozbekstanda pakhta ishläri. Tashkent: Oz. Dävlät Näshrïyati, 1927,
55 pp., 1553 cop. [Uz 2 Arab; DLC]   2092
*Ozbekstanda yer tuzush ishläri häm SSSR märkäzi ijraqomining
manefesti.* Samarkand–Tashkent: Oznäshr, 1929, 24 pp., 3000
cop. [Uz 2 Arab; NN]   2093
Ozbekstanda yïr mäs'äläsi. Tashkent: Oz. Dävlät Näshrïyati, 1927,
52 pp., 1553 cop. [Uz 2 Arab; DLC]   2094
Ozbekstanning ishläb chïqarish kochläri. Samarkand: Oz.I.Sh.J.
Märkäz Ijraqomi, 1927, 46 pp., 1500 cop. [Uz 2 Arab; DLC]   2095
Pavïlïvä. *Charvachiliq shirkätining aʿzasi nimälärni bilish keräk.*
Samarkand: Oz.I.Sh.J. Yïr Ishläri Khalq Komïsärligi, 1930,
24 pp., 15000 cop. [Uz 2 Arab; DLC]   2096
Perevod va akkreditiv muamalarï yuzasidan qollanma. Tashkent:
OzSSR Davlat Mihnat Amanat Kassalari va Davlat Krediti
Idarasining Nashri, 1936, 64 pp., 1000 cop. [Uz 3 Lat; DLC]   2097
Qishlaq khojaliq qärz pakhtakarchïlïk shïrkätïning nïzamnamäsi.
Samarkand: Oz. Qishlaq Ïttïfaqïning Näshri, 1925, 25 and 17
pp., 5000 cop. [Uz 2 Arab; NN]   2098
Qishlaq matlubat käpirätsïyäsi ḥaqida suḥbätlär. 2 nchi bolum.
Samarkand–Tashkent: Oznäshr, 1929, 95 pp., 3000 cop.
[Uz 2 Arab; NN]   2099
*Qishlaq shuralarïda hïsabgha alïsh, hïsabat vä ish yürgizish toghrïsïda
dästürülʿämäl.* Moscow: SSSR Ishchi-Dïyqan Nazaratï Khalq
Komisärligining Ïdara Qïlïsh Tekhnikäsi Institütining Näshri,
1930, 47 pp., 3500 cop. [Uz 3 Lat; NN]   2100
Rozenfeld, A. *Käsäbä ḥäräkäti älifbesi.* Samarkand–Tashkent:
Ozbekstan Dävlät Näshriyati, 1928, 46 pp., 1000 cop.
[Uz 2 Arab; DLC]   2101
Sadiqov, S. *Ozbekistanda Sovet Misr pakhtasi.* Tashkent: OzSSR
Davlat Nashriyati, 1939, 80 pp., 3000 cop. [Uz 3 Lat; DLC]   2102

Sämärqänd, tashkänt, vä färghanä vilayätlärĭdä otkäzilgän yer-sov islaḥatining ḥisabati. Tashkent: Yer Ishläri Khälq Kämĭsärliginıng Näshri, 1927, 117 pp., 1053 cop. [Uz 2 Arab; NN] 2103

Shatalif, D. N. *Ozbekstan ijtĭma'i shoralar jumhorĭyäti* shära'ĭti *ĭchĭdä kĭnt bodjäti.* Samarkand: Oz.I.Sh.J. Khalq Malĭyä Kämĭsärlĭgĭning Näshri, 1926, n.pp., 2000 cop. [Uz 2 Arab; DLC] 2104

Shĭflĭr, M. Y. *Dĭhqan khojalighĭgha qärz bĭrish ishi.* Samarkand: Ozbĭkstan Qishlaq Khojaliq Bankäsi, 1927, 22 pp., 5000 cop. [Uz 2 Arab: DLC, NN] 2105

Shoralar ḥukumätining saliq siyasäti. Samarkand–Tashkent: Oznäshr, 1929, 33 pp., 3000 cop. [Uz 2 Arab; NN] 2106

Sĭghortä qĭlish toghrisĭda äsholälär. Tashkent: Oz. Däolät Näshrĭyati, 1926, 40 pp., 5000 cop. [Uz 2 Arab; DLC] 2107

Sovet hakimiyati 20 yil ichida—Statistik toplam. Tashkent: OzSSR Davlat Nashriyati, 1939, 110 pp., 15000 cop. [Uz 3 Lat; DLC] 2108

Tärtĭbnamä vä ongä tä'lĭmat. Tashkent: Oz. Däolät Näshrĭyati, 1926, 16 pp., 5046 cop. [Uz 2 Arab; DLC] 2109

Tĭzĭslär: Ĭfäkchĭlik toghrĭsĭda daklad qĭladirghanlar ochon. n.p.: Uzgiz Tashoblit, n.d., 15 pp., 1030 cop. [Uz 2 Arab; NN] 2110

Tomski, M. P. *Käsäbä oyoshmäläri ishlärĭning yäkoni vä olärning näobätdägi väzĭfäläri.* Tashkent: Oz. Däolät Näshrĭyati, 1927, 186 pp., 5000 cop. [Uz 2 Arab; DLC] 211

Tsĭmmĭrman, Z. Z. *Quyash, shamal, yaghur, orta asyada ärzan otondir.* Samarkand–Tashkent: Ozbĭkstan Däolät Näshrĭyati, 1927, 52 pp., 4000 cop. [Uz 2 Arab; DLC] 211

Uch-nchi dävlät dĭhqan zäyomi. Kokand: n.p., 1927, 7 pp., 200 cop. [Uz 2 Arab; NN] 211

Valfson, M. *S.S.S.R.ning iqtĭsadi qurĭlishlari.* Samarkand: Oz. Dävlät Näshrĭyati, 1926, 167 pp., 10000 cop. [Uz 2 Arab; DLC] 211

Yarashĭvĭch, N. K. *Orta Asya dĭhqan rozgharĭning tuzĭlĭsh.* Tashkent: Oz. Däolät Näshrĭyati, 1927, 128 pp., 5056 cop. [Uz 2 Arab; DLC, NN] 211

Yĭfanif, Z. *Käsäbä sayuzlarĭning mädäni aqartish ishläri.* Tashkent: Orta Asya Käsäbälär Byorosi, 1927, 55 pp., 1000 cop. [Uz 2 Arab; DLC] 211

Economics

Yïfanof, Z. D. *Käsäbälär ittïfaqi nïmä?* Moscow: B.S.M.K.A.Sh. Orta Asïya Boyorasi, 1925, 136 pp., 3000 cop. [Uz 2 Arab; NN] 2117

Za'ozerski, S. *Kochmä qumlar vä ular bilän kuräshish yollari.* Samarkand: Oz.I.Sh.J. Yer Ishläri Khalq Komisärligi, 1930, 24 pp., 5000 cop. [Uz 2 Arab; DLC] 2118

Zelkïna, I. *Yer islaḥati vä dïhqan khatin-qizlar azadlighi.* Tashkent: Oz. Däolät Näshrïyati, 1927, 40 pp., 3000 cop. [Uz 2 Arab; DLC] 2119

Education

ʿAbïdif, Ḥäyrolla. *Oz-ozïdän orgänish yollari.* Tashkent: Orta-Aziya Kammonïstlar Darilfunoni Näshriyati, 1927, v and v and 218 pp., 3000 cop. [Uz 2 Arab; DLC] 2120

Abraztsof. *Kitablar—amma arasïgha.* Samarkand–Tashkent: Öznäshr, 1929, 17 pp., 5000 cop. [Uz 3 Lat; NN] 2121

ʿAdil, M. *Ḥisab mäs'äläläri.* 1inchi kitäb. Tashkent: Oz. Dävlät Näshriyati, 1926 2d ed., 89 pp., 35000 cop. [Uz 2 Arab; DLC] 2122

ʿAdil, M. *Ḥisab mäs'äläläri.* 1inchi kitäb. Tashkent: Oz. Dävlät Näshriyati, 1927 3d ed., 88 pp., 45000 cop. [Uz 2 Arab; DLC] 2123

ʿAdil, M. *Ḥisab mäs'äläläri.* 2nchi kitäb. Tashkent: Oz. Dävlät Näshriyati, 1926 2d ed., 114 pp., n.c. [Uz 2 Arab; DLC] 2124

ʿAdil, M. *Ḥisab mäs'äläläri.* 2nchi kitäb. Tashkent: Oz. Dävlät Näshriyati, 1927 3d ed., 107 pp., 30000 cop. [Uz 2 Arab; DLC] 2125

ʿAdil, M. *Ḥisab mäs'äläläri.* 3inchi kitäb. Tashkent: Oz. Dävlät Näshriyati, 1927 3d ed., 89 pp., 8060 cop. [Uz 2 Arab; DLC] 2126

Alavi, A. *Ozbïk yängi älifbasini tozishdä äsaslär.* Tashkent: Özbekistan Dävlät Näshriiatï, 1927, 24 pp., 5000 cop. [Uz 2 Arab; DLC] 2127

Altinchi sinifning ozbekchä oqosh kïtabi. III. Tashkent: Turkpechat', 1926, iii and 96 pp., 2000 cop. [Uz 2 Arab; DLC] 2128

Ammaviy kutubkhanalarda ktab fondini saqlash toghrisida qollanma. Tashkent: "Oktabr" Kutubkhanasining Metod Kabineti, 1936, 10 pp., 2500 cop. [Uz 3 Lat; DLC] 2129

Aqartish kämïsïyäsi. Tashkent: Orta-Asya Käsäbälär Byurasi, 1927, 16 pp., 1000 cop. [Uz 2 Arab; DLC] 2130

Arbuzïf. *Pedälögiyä mäs'äläläri.* Tashkent–Samarkand: Öznäshr, 1930, 38 pp., 4000 cop. [Uz 3 Lat; DLC] 2131

Ästräb. *Sinamali händäsä.* II–III häm IV bolim. Samarkand–Tashkent: Ozbekstan Dävlät Näshrĭyati, 1927, 208 pp., 10000 cop. [Uz 2 Arab; DLC, NN] 213

Atazhan; Serbov; Alim, Gh. *Qĭzĭl yol: Yängi özbek latin älifbasi orgänish uchun.* Samarkand: Özbekistan Dävlät Näshriyatĭ, 1927, 23 pp., 15000 cop. [Uz 3 Lat; DLC] 213

Balashof, N. I. *Torkistan.* Tashkent: Turkestanskoe Gosudarstvennoe Izdatel'stvo, 1922, 88 pp., 15000 cop. [Uz 1 Arab; NN] 213

Bärishinkivi; Shiverdinä. *Mäktäbgächä tärbiyä.* Samarkand–Tashkent: Oz Däolät Näshriyati, 1927, 69 pp., 2500 cop. [Uz 2 Arab; DLC] 213

Birinchi basqĭch mäktäbining III–IV nchi oquv yĭli vä ösmürlär mäktäbining birinchi oquv yĭlĭ üchün Jughrafĭya pirögrämmäsi. Tashkent: Öznäshr, 1932, 10 pp., 1000 cop. [Uz 3 Lat; DLC] 213

1-nchi basqĭch mäktäblär üchün ĭjtĭmaĭyat prögrämmäsi. Tashkent: Öznäshr, 1932, 14 pp., 1000 cop. [Uz 3 Lat; DLC] 213

Birinchi basqĭch mäktäblär üchün täbi'iyat progrämmäsi. Tashkent: Öznäshr, 1932, 14 pp., 1000 cop. [Uz 3 Lat; DLC] 213

Birinchi basqich mäktäblärining birinchi yili prägrämmäsi. Tashkent: Oznäshr, 1928, 343 pp., 3000 cop. [Uz 2 Arab; DLC] 213

Birinchi basqich mäktäblärining birinchi yili prägrämmäsi. Tashkent–Samarkand: Oznäshr, 1928, 56 pp., 2000 cop. [Uz 2 Arab; DLC] 214

Birläshkän pirägrämmä. Samarkand–Tashkent: Oznäshr, 1927, 22 pp., 2000 cop. [Uz 2 Arab; NN] 214

Chäläsaodalar ochon oqosh kĭtabi. Tashkent: Orta-Asya Däolät Näshrĭyati, 1924, 139 pp., 5000 cop. [Uz 2 Arab; NN] 214

Chäläsäoadlar uchun qira'ät kĭtabi. I. Tashkent: Oz. Däolät Näshrĭyati, 1926, 94 pp., 25000 cop. [Uz 2 Arab; DLC] 214

Gordi, I. *Saoadsizlikni bĭtirochĭning yoldashi.* Tashkent: Oz. Däolät Näshriyati, 1926, 96 pp., 5047 cop. [Uz 2 Arab; DLC] 214

Gordi, I. *Sĭyasi mä'arif ishchĭsĭning yoldashi.* Samarkand: Oz. Bash Sĭyasi Mä'arif Qomĭtäsĭning Näshri, 1926, iv and 222 pp., 8000 cop. [Uz 2 Arab; DLC] 214

Ḥisabat däftäri. Tashkent: Tipografiia "Shkola i Kniga," 192?, 18 pp., 10000 cop. [Uz 2 Arab; NN] 214

Ijtima'iyat ish kitabi. I bolim. Tashkent–Samarkand: Ozbekistan Dävlät Näshriyati, 1929, 216 pp., n.c. [Uz 2 Arab; NN] 214

Ĭlbĭk; Lebkinekht. *Bilim.* Tashkent: Oz Däolät Näshrĭyati, 1926, 119 pp., 50000 cop. [Uz 2 Arab; DLC] 2148

Ĭlbĭk; Lebkinekht. *Bilim.* II bolim. Tashkent: Oz. Dävlät Näshrĭyati, 1926, 168 pp., 35000 cop. [Uz 2 Arab; DLC] 2149

Ĭlbĭk; Lebknekht. *Bilim.* 3nchi bolim. Tashkent: Oz. Däolät Näshrĭyati, 1927, 264 pp., 35000 cop. [Uz 2 Arab; DLC] 2150

Ĭoanof. *Baslanghich jughrafiya.* Samarkand: Oz. Dävlät Näshrĭyati, 1927, 104 pp., 20000 cop. [Uz 2 Arab; DLC] 2151

Islam, I.; Qähhar, 'A.; 'Adil, M. *Ḥisab mäs'äläläri.* Tashkent: Oz. Dävlät Näshrĭyati, 1926, 107 pp., 7000 cop. [Uz 2 Arab; DLC] 2152

Islam, I.; Qähhar, 'A.; 'Adil, M. *Ḥisab mäs'äläläri.* IV. Tashkent: Oz. Däolät Näshrĭyati, 1926, 142 pp., 10000 cop. [Uz 2 Arab; DLC] 2153

Ivänüf, G. I. *Ĭjtïmaïy shora jümhüriyätläri ïttïfaqïnïng qïsqa jughrafïya sabaqlïghï.* Tashkent: Özbekistan Dävlät Näshriyatï, 1929, 196 pp., 12000 cop. [Uz 3 Lat; DLC] 2154

Iyvanuf. *Bashlanghïch jughrafïya.* Birinchi bölim. Samarkand–Tashkent: Özbekistan Dävlät Näshriyati, 1929, 104 pp., 15000 cop. [Uz 3 Lat; NN] 2155

Iyvanuf. *Bashlanghïch jughrafïya.* Üchinchi bölim. Avrupa. Samarkand–Tashkent: Özbekistan Dävlät Näshriyatï, 1929, 223 pp., 7000 cop. [Uz 3 Lat; NN] 2156

Kalkhuzlarda mädäniy maarïf. Samarkand: Öznäshr, 1929, 14 pp., 3000 cop. [Uz 3 Lat; DLC] 2157

Kasanoguva, K. *Fĭzĭkädän bashlanghich musaḥäbälär.* Tashkent: Oz. Däolät Näshrĭyati, 1927/1928, 176 pp., 7000 cop. [Uz 2 Arab; DLC] 2158

Kättälär älifbesini oqotochilargha osovli tä'lĭmati. Samarkand–Tashkent: Oz. Däolät Näshrĭyati, 1928, 23 pp., 2000 cop. [Uz 2 Arab; NN] 2159

Kättälärni oqotishda roḥi äsaslär. Moscow: SSSR Khalqlarĭning Märkäz Näshrĭyati, 1925, 35 pp., 10000 cop. [Uz 2 Arab; NN] 2160

Keller, B. A. *Proletar revolutsiyasi va Sovet zyalilari.* Tashkent: Oz. Dav. Nashr., 1938, 47 pp., 20150 cop. [Uz 3 Lat; DLC] 2161

Kolosif, A. *Qayĭrda oqosh kĭräk?* Moscow: SSSR Khälqlärĭning Märkäz Näshrĭyati, 1924, 55 pp., 3000 cop. [Uz 2 Arab; NN] 2162

Kömmünistlär sïrtqï üniversiteti. Birinchi qurs. Samarkand–Tashkent: Öznäshir, 1929, 158 pp., 3000 cop. [Uz 3 Lat; DLC] 216

Kömmünistlär sïrtqï üniversiteti. Ikkinchi qurs. n.p.: n.p., 1929, n.pp., 3000 cop. [Uz 3 Lat; DLC] 216

Krögliköf, P. *Mäktäbdä ölkäni örgänüv muzakhanasï vä uning ishläri.* Tashkent–Samarkand: Öznäshr, 1929, 40 pp., 4000 cop. [Uz 3 Lat; DLC] 216

Kropiskaya, N. K. *Khälq mä'arifi toghrĭsĭda Lĭnĭnning oäsĭyätläri.* Moscow: SSSR Khälqlarĭning Märkäz Näshrĭyati, 1925, 48 pp., 10000 cop. [Uz 2 Arab; CStH, NN] 216

Länkef. *Hĭsab mäs'äläläri.* Samarkand–Tashkent: Özdävnäshr, 1929, 244 pp., 20000 cop. [Uz 3 Lat; DLC] 216

Lebedĭnsif, K. F. *Jäbr mäs'äläläri.* Samarkand: Oz. Dävlät Näshrĭyati, 1926, 149 pp., 7000 cop. [Uz 2 Arab; DLC] 216

Lebedĭnsif, K. F. *Jäbr mäs'äläläri.* I kitab. Samarkand–Tashkent: Ozbekstan Dävlät Näshrĭyati, 1927, 150 pp., 7000 cop. [Uz 2 Arab; NN) 216

Lĭbĭdĭnsif, K. F. *Jäbr qollanmasi.* Tashkent: Oz. Däolät Näshri, 1927, 192 pp., 6000 cop. [Uz 2 Arab; DLC] 217

Lobĭnsif. *Usul tä'lĭm qollanmalarĭgha matĭryallar toplami.* Samarkand–Tashkent: Ozbĭkstan Däolät Näshrĭyati, 1926, 77 pp., 4000 cop. [Uz 2 Arab; DLC] 217

Mädäniy inqilab vä dĭyqanlar. Tashkent: Öznäshr, 1929, 15 pp., 3000 cop. [Uz 3 Lat; DLC] 217

Mäzhär; Sädrĭtdĭn. *Qolay älĭfba.* Moscow: Buḥara Khälq Mä'arĭf Näzarätĭning Näshri, 1924, 80 pp., 10000 cop. [Uz 2 Arab; CStH, NN] 217

Minglibayif, Ḥäy. *Siyasi iqtisad därsligi.* Tashkent: Orta-Azya Kammonĭstlar Daralfinonĭning Näshriyati, 1927, iii and 220 pp., 6000 cop. [Uz 2 Arab; DLC] 217

Mo'äsäsälär khuzorĭda ärkhĭq matĭryallarĭni tärtibdä saqlashning qisqächä dästorĭl'ämäl. Tashkent: Oz.Ij.Sh.J. Märkäzi Ärkhĭq Ishläri Ĭdaräsining Näshri, 1927, 12 pp., 1000 cop. [Uz 2 Arab; NN] 217

Nĭyazi, Ḥusäyn Khan; Mujaoyr, Zĭya. *Kĭmya därsligi.* Samarkand: Oz. Dävlät Näshrĭyati, 1926, iv and 222 pp., 5000 cop. [Uz 2 Arab; DLC] 217

Övchinniköf. *Karkhanalarda mädäniy ishlär*. Samarkand: Özbek Dävlät Näshriyatï, 1929, 20 pp., 3000 cop. [Uz 3 Lat; NN] 2177

Özbekistan birinchi basqïch mäktäbläri üchün pöletekhnik mihnät progrämmäsi. Tashkent: Öznäshr, 1932, 17 pp., 1000 cop. [Uz 3 Lat; DLC] 2178

Özbekistan shähär vä qïshlaq ösmürlär mäktäbining I–II nchi oquv yïlï prögrämmäsi. Tashkent: Öznäshr, 1931, 55 pp., 5000 cop. [Uz 3 Lat; DLC] 2179

Özbekistan yetti yïllïq fäbrik zovod mäktäbläri (F.Z.S.) üchün oqush prögrämmäsi. Tashkent: Öznäshr, 1931, 42 pp., 4000 cop. [Uz 3 Lat; DLC] 2180

Ozbekstanda mäʿarif ishläri. Tashkent: Oz. Däolät Näshrĭyati, 1927, 92 pp., 1553 cop. [Uz 2 Arab; DLC] 2181

Ozbĭkstan mäʿarif ishchĭläri oyoshmäsi rayon mäḥalqomlärĭning ishlärĭdägi yaqin oazĭfälär: Rayon yĭghinalish oä känfĭrinsyälärĭgä märkäzi ĭdaräning tĭzĭsläri. Samarkand: n.p., 1927, 19 pp., 1000 cop. [Uz 2 Arab; DLC, NN] 2182

Ozbĭkstan shura jumhurĭyätining birlik äsasĭdägi miḥnät mäktäbläri uchun proghramma. Tashkent: Oz. Däolät Näshrĭyati, 1926, 62 pp., 4000 cop. [Uz 2 Arab; DLC] 2183

Perövskiy, Y. Y. *Kömpilekisdäqi mäläkälär*. Samarkand–Tashkent: Öznäshr, 1930, 80 pp., 4000 cop. [Uz 3 Lat; NN] 2184

Piröekt Özbekistan yetti yïllïq fäbrik-zavod vä kölkhoz-yashlar mäktäblärining II-nchi könsentiri üchün oqush prögrämmäsi. Tashkent: Öznäshr, 1932, 12 pp., 500 cop. [Uz 3 Lat; DLC] 2185

Qari-Nĭyazi, T. M. *Händäsädän achiq havada ishlänädirgän ʿämäli ishlär*. Samarkand–Tashkent: Ozbekstan Däolät Näshrĭyatining Näshri, 1927, 36 pp., 10000 cop. [Uz 2 Arab; DLC] 2186

Qishlaq yächĭkälärĭni täshkĭli tozish oä olarning ishläsh tärtĭbi ḥäqĭdä qaʿĭdälär. Tashkent: OzTsKKP(b)ning Näshrĭyati, 1926, 29 pp., 350 cop. [Uz 2 Arab; DLC] 2187

Qishlaqgha mäkhsos kochmä sĭyasi saoad mäktäbi uchun proghramma. Samarkand: Oz. Dävlät Näshrĭyati, 1926, 42 pp., 500 cop. [Uz 2 Arab; DLC] 2188

Qisqa muddätli shähär sĭyasi savad mäktäbi uchun proghramma. Samarkand: Oz. Dävlät Näshriyati, 1926, 29 pp., 1000 cop. [Uz 2 Arab; DLC] 2189

Räḥĭmi, Sh. *Kättälär yoldashi.* Tashkent: Oz. Däolät Näshrĭyati, 1926, 86 pp., 65000 cop. [Uz 2 Arab; DLC] 219

Räḥĭmi, Sh. *Savgha.* Tashkent: Oz. Däolät Näshrĭyati, 1927 8th ed., 48 pp., 35000 cop. [Uz 2 Arab; DLC] 219

Räḥĭmi, Shakirjan. *Ozbek älipbasi.* Tashkent: Torkistan Däolät Näshrĭyati, 1922, 63 pp., n.c. [Uz 2 Arab; NN] 219

Räḥĭmi, Shakirjan. *Saogha.* Tashkent: Oz. Däolät Näshriyati, 1926, 76 pp., 50000 cop. [Uz 2 Arab; DLC] 219

Ramazan, Qayyum; Zünnün, Sharäsül. *Özbek tili ish kitabĭ.* II. Samarkand–Tashkent: Özbekistan Dävlät Näshriyati, 1929, 101 pp., 20000 cop. [Uz 3 Lat; DLC] 219

Ramiz, M. *Oktäbir vä khälq mäʿarĭfi.* Tashkent: Oz. Dävlät Näshrĭyati, 1928, 134 pp., 3560 cop. [Uz 2 Arab; DLC] 219

Rayküf, B. Y.; Ölyanĭnĭskĭ, V. Yu.; Yagüdüvski, K. P. *Pedagogiyä ishidä—tekshirish usulĭ.* Tashkent: Özbek Dävlät Näshriyatĭ, 1929, 74 pp., 4000 cop. [Uz 3 Lat; DLC] 219

Säyfi, Fatiḥ; Elbek. *Ozbekchä oqush.* Birinchi kitab. Tashkent: Turkestanskoe Gosudarstvennoe Izdatel'stvo, 1922, 60 pp., 35000 cop. [Uz 2 Arab; NN] 219

Säyfilmuluk, ʿĬzziddĭn. *Mäktäbdä saghliqni saqlash äsasläri.* Tashkent: Oz. Däolät Näshrĭyati, 1927, 258 pp., 4000 cop. [Uz 2 Arab; DLC] 219

Säyfi-Qazanli, Fatiḥ. *Ozbekchä oqosh.* Ĭkinchi kitab. Tashkent: Torkistan Jimhorĭyänĭng Däolät Näshrĭyati, 1922, 100 pp., 30000 cop. [Uz 2 Arab; NN] 219

Sirtdan oquchilar uchun pedagogika programmasiga metodik korgazma va pedtekhnikumlar programmasi. Tashkent: Maarif Kadrlining Kvalifikatsiyasini Kotarish Instituti, 1936, 85 pp., 1200 cop. [Uz 3 Lat; DLC] 220

Tekhnikum vä bilim yurtlarigha 1928–29 inchi yildä oqochĭlar qabol qilish shärtläri. Tashkent: Oznäshr, 1928, 96 and 20 pp., 1000 cop. [Uz 2 Arab; DLC] 220

Väränets, Ä. M. *Rĭyazĭyat ish kitabĭ.* Tashkent–Samarkand: Özdavnäshr, 1928/1929, 88 pp., 25000 cop. [Uz 3 Lat; DLC] 220

Velichäniskiy, G. S. *Hĭsabchĭlĭq.* 1nchi qĭsĭm. Samarkand–Tashkent: Öznäshir, 1929, 135 pp., 3000 cop. [Uz 3 Lat; NN] 220

Velichäniskiy, G. S. *Hĭsabchĭlĭq.* 2nchi qĭsĭm. Samarkand–Tashkent: Öznäshir, 1930, 136 pp., 3000 cop. [Uz 3 Lat; NN] 220

Education

Ventärgälter. *Täbi'iyätdän 'ämäli ishlär*. Samarkand: Oz. Dävlät Näshriyati, 1927, 66 pp., 20000 cop. [Uz 2 Arab; DLC] 2205

Vĭntärgaltir. *Täbĭ'ĭyatdan 'ämäli ishlär*. II. Tashkent: Oz. Dävlät Näshrĭyati, 1926, 104 pp., 5000 cop. [Uz 2 Arab; DLC] 2206

26 nchi yil oqutghuchi oä tärbĭyächĭlärĭning mäläkä (iqtidar)larin ashĭrish mä'räkäsĭni yäkoni vä kĭlgosĭdägi väzĭfälär. Samarkand: Oz. Khalq Mä'arif Kämĭsärligi, 1927, 26 pp., 1000 cop. [Uz 2 Arab; DLC] 2207

Geography

Balashof, N. I. *Ozbĭkstan oä ungä qoshni jumhorĭyätlär oä hämdä oĭlayätlär*. Tashkent: Oz. Däolät Näshrĭyati, 1926 2d ed., 159 pp., 7000 cop. [Uz 2 Arab; DLC] 2208

Ĭoanof, G. E. *Ijtĭma'i shora jomhorĭyätläri ittifaqining qisqacha joghrafyasi*. Samarkand–Tashkent: Oz. Däolät Näshrĭyati, 1927, 162 pp., 8000 cop. [Uz 2 Arab; DLC, NN] 2209

Karvĭnĭvski, L. N. *Orta-Asyaning täbĭ'i-jughrafi täsvĭri*. Tashkent: Oz. Däolät Näshrĭyati, 1929, 126 pp., 4000 cop. [Uz 2 Arab; DLC] 2210

Government

Asa avĭyakhim (täĭyarä häm kĭmĭyachĭlĭk) S.S.S.R.ni tĭnchlĭk mĭḥnäti häm modafä'äsi uchun bir träkdir. n.p.: OzIHSRning Asa Avĭyakhĭmi, n.d., 12 and 12 pp., 1000 cop. [Uz 2 Arab; NN] 2211

Asa-avyakhim. Samarkand–Tashkent: Oz. Däolät Näshriyati, 1927, 28 pp., 2060 cop. [Uz 2 Arab; DLC] 2212

Batmanif, O. *Qizĭl 'äskär toghrĭsĭda kamsamol mosaḥäbäsi*. Samarkand: Oz.L.I.Itt.Märk.Qomi. Siyasi Aqartish Bolimning Näshri, 1926, 16 pp., 5000 cop. [Uz 2 Arab; DLC] 2213

1927–1928 inchi yilda orta asyadaghi oäkĭlälär yĭghilishlarĭni qaytadan saylaogha matĭryallar. n.p.: "Srĭdaz Knĭgä" Mätbä'äsi, 1928, 53 pp., 1000 cop. [Uz 2 Arab; DLC] 2214

Bizning mämläkätimizni kim idarä qiladir. Samarkand–Tashkent: Oznäshr, 1929, 21 pp., 3000 cop. [Uz 2 Arab; NN] 2215

Botayif. *Siyasät dunyasĭda turkiyä mäs'äläsi.* Samarkand: Oz. Dävlät Näshrĭyati, 1926, 112 pp., 5000 cop. [Uz 2 Arab; DLC] 221

Boton ozbekstan shoralarĭning 2 nchi qoroltayĭgha matĭryallar, 1927: Ozbekstan ijtĭma'i shoralar jomhorĭyäti ḥokomätĭning ishlägän ishläri. Tashkent: Oz.I.Sh.J. Khälq Kämĭsärläri Shorai Äkhbarat Ĭdaräsĭning Näshri, 1927?, 16 pp., 1500 cop. [Uz 2 Arab; NN] 221

Brayda, G. Y. *Millĭyät mäs'äläsi.* Moscow: SSSR Khälqlärĭning Märkäz Näshrĭyati, 1925, 120 pp., 5000 cop. [Uz 2 Arab; CStH, NN] 221

Butun ittĭfaq kämmonĭst(b)lär firqäsi nĭzamnamäsi. Tashkent: Oz. Dävlät Näshrĭyati, 1927, 46 pp., 10000 cop. [Uz 2 Arab; DLC] 221

Butun ittĭfaq kämmonĭstlär firqäsĭning proghrammasi. Samarkand–Tashkent: Oz. Dävlät Näshrĭyati, 1927, 68 pp., 15000 cop. [Uz 2 Arab; DLC] 222

Chĭrnyäyevski, I. *Saylaolar sayĭli.* Tashkent: Oz. Däolät Näshriyati, 1927, 160 pp., 1000 cop. [Uz 2 Arab; DLC] 222

Dĭmanshtäyn. *Milliyät mäs'äläsi.* Moscow: SSSR Khalqlarining Märkäz Näshrĭyati, 1927, 52 pp., 10000 cop. [Uz 2 Arab; NN] 222

Dĭmanshtäyn. *Qachan urushlar bolmaydi?* Moscow: SSSR Khälqlärĭning Märkäz Näshrĭyati, 1924, 67 pp., 4000 cop. [Uz 2 Arab; NN] 222

Dübbinskii, I. *Millii qoshun nimä?* Tashkent: Öznäshr, 1930, 30 pp., 3000 cop. [Uz 3 Lat; DLC] 222

Firqa savadi. 2nchi bolim. Moscow–Samarkand: Oz. Däolät Näshrĭyati, 1928, 272 pp., 6000 cop. [Uz 2 Arab; NN] 222

Firqa tuzilishining tob väzifäläri. Moscow: SSSR Khalqlarining Märkäz Näshriyati, 1927, 228 pp., 10000 cop. [Uz 2 Arab; NN] 222

Gĭrĭns, S. *Vladĭmĭr il'ĭch lĭnĭn ĭfadäsi boyncha karl marks tä'lĭmati.* Tashkent: Oz. Däolät Näshrĭyati, 1926, 56 pp., 3000 cop. [Uz 2 Arab; DLC] 222

Gĭrĭns, S. *Yängi korinishdä—ĭski khatalar.* Tashkent: Oz. Dävlät Näshrĭyati, 1926, 32 pp., 4000 cop. [Uz 2 Arab; DLC] 222

Girishin, M. I. *Lenin yolidan.* Moscow–Samarkand: Oz. Däolät Näshrĭyati, 1928, 360 pp., 6000 cop. [Uz 2 Arab; NN] 222

Girishin, M. I. *Lenin yolidan.* I bolim. Moscow–Samarkand: Oz. Dävlät Näshriyati, 1928, 336 pp., 6000 cop. [Uz 2 Arab; NN] 223

Girüppäviy firqa täshkilatchïlarï. Samarkand–Tashkent: Öznäshir, 1929, 16 pp., 2000 cop. [Uz 3 Lat; DLC] 2231

II nchi basqich kamsamol sïyasi mäktäbläri uchun praghramma. Samarkand: "Sredazkniga," n.d., 16 pp., 300 cop. [Uz 2 Arab; NN] 2232

ʿÏmadi, Ziya. *Firqä shora mäktäbläri häm ulärning tuzilishläri.* Tashkent: Orta–Asya Kammonïstlar Darilfinonïning Näshrïyati, 1926, 162 pp., 2000 cop. [Uz 2 Arab; DLC] 2233

Ishchi dïhqan ittifaqi qanday osdi: Shoralar ittifaqi vä butun dunya inqilabi. Moscow: Kengäsh Ittifaqi Khalqlarining Märkäz Näshriyati, 1927, 270 pp., 5000 cop. [Uz 2 Arab; NN] 2234

Ïski shähärlärdägi oäkïlälär yïghïlishlari ochon pragramma häm matïryallar. Tashkent: Srïd Az Knïgä, 1927, 137 pp., 700 cop. [Uz 2 Arab; DLC] 2235

Istälin. *Khitay inqilabi häm äppäzïtsiyäning khatalari.* Tashkent: Oznäshr, 1927, 64 pp., 2000 cop. [Uz 2 Arab; DLC] 2236

Istanchïnski, A. P. *Sïyasi säoad.* Tashkent: Oz. Däolät Näshrïyati, 1926, ix and 422 pp., 15000 cop. [Uz 2 Arab; DLC] 2237

Kaganovïch, L. M. *Butun ittïfaq kämmonïstlär(b) firqäsi qanday tuzulgän.* Samarkand–Tashkent: Ozbïkstan Dävlät Näshrïyati, 1927, 96 pp., 5000 cop. [Uz 2 Arab; DLC, NN] 2238

Kälesnikif, L. *Kämsämol häm shärq qizi.* Samarkand–Moscow: Oz. Däolät Näshriyati, 1927, 78 pp., 4000 cop. [Uz 2 Arab; NN] 2239

Källiktif. *Qïshlaq shoralarï seksiyälärining ishläri toghrïsïda.* Tashkent: Öznäshr, 1929, 16 pp., 3000 cop. [Uz 3 Lat; DLC] 2240

Kamalof, Shakïr; Mänsorif, Ḥänäfi. *Jahangïrlik däori häm kämmonïzmgä yol.* Tashkent: Oz. Dävlät Näshrïyati, 1926, 118 pp., 1500 cop. [Uz 2 Arab; DLC] 2241

Kammonïstlar mäʿarifi häm uning täjribäläri. Tashkent: Orta-Asya Kammonïstlar Darilfononi Näshrïyati, 1927, 468 pp., 3000 cop. [Uz 2 Arab; DLC] 2242

Kamsamol sïyasi mäktäblärïning 26–27 nchi oqish yilïdägi: 1–2 nchi basqich praghrammasi oä osoli täʿlïm qollanmasi. Samarkand: Oz.L.Y.K.Ï. Märkäz Qomïtäsi Täshtägh Bolïmïning Näshri, 1926, 30 pp., 2000 cop. [Uz 2 Arab; DLC, NN] 2243

Kamsamol yächïkälärïgä täshoïqat tärghïbat täshkïlatlarïgä . . . qollanma. Samarkand: Märkäzi Yashlar Qomïtäsi Täsh-Tär Bolïmïning Näshri, 1926/27, 8 pp., 1000 cop. [Uz 2 Arab; NN] 2244

Käntir, L. M. *Ozbekistanda mäḥälli yähodilär.* Samarkand–Moscow: Oz. Däolät Näshriyati, 1929, 67 pp., 3000 cop. [Uz 2 Arab; NN] 2245

Kaoalĭnkä, B. *Siyasi saoad kĭtabi.* Tashkent: Torkistan Däolät Näshrĭyati, 1923, 134 pp., 5000 cop. [Uz 1 Arab; NN] 2246

Käshshaflarning yazdaghi ishläri. Tashkent: Oz. Däolät Näshriyati, 1926, 48 pp., 3000 cop. [Uz 2 Arab; DLC] 2247

Ke'mrad, S. *Lenĭnchi yash kämmunĭstlär sayozĭning ustafĭni tushuntĭrish.* Moscow: SSSR Khalqlarining Märkäz Näshriyati, 1926, 79 pp., 5000 cop. [Uz 2 Arab; NN] 2248

Khodorof, A.; Pavlovĭch, M. *Khĭtayning istiqlal yolĭda kuräshi.* Samarkand–Tashkent: Oz. Dävlät Näshrĭyati, 1927, v and 112 pp., 4000 cop. [Uz 2 Arab; DLC, NN] 2249

Kĭm oä oning praghrammasi. Tashkent: Oz. Däolät Näshriyati, 1927, 76 pp., 5000 cop. [Uz 2 Arab; DLC] 2250

Kĭsĭlaf. *Ĭski shähärlärdägi 2 basqich kamsamol sĭyasi mäktäbläri ochon sĭyasi oqosh kĭtabi.* I. Samarkand: Oz. Märkäzi Firqä Qomĭtäsining Ghaybat Bolimi, 1926, 42 pp., 3000 cop. [Uz 2 Arab; DLC] 2251

Kĭtaygaradski; Porĭtski. *Märakäsh tonĭs oä jäza'irdä azadliq uchun kuräsh:* Tashkent: Ozbĭkstan Dävlät Näshrĭyati, 1926, iii and 134 pp., 4000 cop. [Uz 2 Arab; DLC] 2252

Kon, F. *Yängi urish khavfi.* Samarkand–Tashkent: Ozbĭkstan Däolät Näshriyati, 1927, 38 pp., 3000 cop. [Uz 2 Arab; DLC] 2253

Kozĭn, O. *Yash käshshaflär lagĭri.* Tashkent: Oz. Mätbä'äsi, 1927, 56 pp., 3000 cop. [Uz 2 Arab; DLC] 2254

Kropskäyä, N. K. *Lĭnĭn bayraghi.* Samarkand–Tashkent: Oz. Dävlät Näshrĭyati, 1927, 23 pp., 5000 cop. [Uz 2 Arab; DLC, NN] 2255

Lenen, N. *1905 yil inqilabi.* Moscow: SSSR Khälqlarĭning Märkäzi Näshrĭyati, 1926, 388 pp., 5000 cop. [Uz 2 Arab; NN] 2256

Lenen, N. *Parĭzh kämmonäsi.* Moscow: SSSR Khälqlarĭning Märkäz Näshrĭyati, 1925, 71 pp., 5000 cop. [Uz 2 Arab; NN] 2257

Lenin, N. *Az bolsa häm saz bolsin.* Moscow–Samarkand: Oz. Dävlät Näshriyati, 1927, 36 pp., 5000 cop. [Uz 2 Arab; NN] 2258

Lenin, V. I. *Birinchi may.* Tashkent: ÖzK(b)P MK Partiya Nashriyati, 1939, 68 pp., 20000 cop. [Uz 3 Lat; DLC] 2259

Lenin, V. I. *Demokratik revolutsiyada sotsial-demokratiyaning ikki taktikasi.* Tashkent: OzK(b)MK Partiya Nashriyati, 1939, 120 pp., 20000 cop. [Uz 3 Lat; DLC] 2260
Lenin, V. I. *RSDRPning II syezdi haqida.* Tashkent: OzK(b)MK Partiya Nashriyati, 1939, 18 pp., 20000 cop. [Uz 3 Lat; DLC] 2261
Lenin, V. I. *Reaksiya va yangi kotarilish davri.* Tashkent: OzK(b)P MK Partiya Nashriyati, 1939, 98 pp., 20000 cop. [Uz 3 Lat; DLC] 2262
Lenin, V. I. *Rus sotsial demokratlarining vazifalari.* Tashkent: OzK(b)P MK Partiya Nashriyati, 1939, 32 pp., 20000 cop. [Uz 3 Lat; DLC] 2263
Lenin, V. I. *Saylanma asarlar.* I. Tashkent: OzK(b)P MK Partiya Nashriyati, 1939, 630 pp., 15000 cop. [Uz 3 Lat; DLC] 2264
Lenin, V. I. *Sotsialistik revolutsiya va millatlarning ozbelgilash huquqi.* Tashkent: OzK(b)P MK Partiya Nashriyati, 1939, 24 pp., 20000 cop. [Uz 3 Lat; DLC] 2265
Lenĭn qashĭno qishlaghida. Tashkent: Ozbekstan Däolät Näshrĭyati, 1927, 20 pp., 2000 cop. [Uz 2 Arab; DLC] 2266
Lĭnĭn, N. *9 yänvär.* Moscow: SSSR Khälqlarĭning Märkäz Näshrĭyati, 1926, 58 pp., 5000 cop. [Uz 2 Arab; CStH, NN] 2267
Lĭnĭn, N. *Millĭyät mäs'äläsĭ.* Samarkand: Oz. Dävlät Näshrĭyati, 1926, 195 pp., 5000 cop. [Uz 2 Arab; DLC] 2268
Lĭnĭn khiristamatiyasi. II bolim. Samarkand: Oznäshr, 1928, 290 pp., 4000 cop. [Uz 2 Arab; DLC] 2269
Manifest diyqanlargha nimä berädi? Samarkand–Tashkent: Oznäshr, 1929, 21 pp., 3000 cop. [Uz 2 Arab; NN] 2270
Mopr nĭmä? Moscow: Mopr Märkäz Kamĭtĭti, 1924, 47 pp., 3000 cop. [Uz 2 Arab; NN] 2271
Narĭmanif, N. *Lĭnĭn oä shärq.* Moscow: SSSR Khälqlärĭning Märkäz Näshrĭyati, 1924, 20 pp., 4000 cop. [Uz 2 Arab; NN] 2272
Nekitin. *Yängi olchävlär.* Tashkent: Oznäshr, 1928, 72 pp., 4000 cop. [Uz 2 Arab; DLC] 2273
Oäkĭlälär uchon lazim bolghan matĭryallar mäjmo'äsi. Moscow: SSSR Khälqlarĭning Märkäz Näshrĭyati, 1925, 214 pp., 3000 cop. [Uz 2 Arab; NN] 2274
Oäsĭlĭyoski; Girĭnĭs. *V. I. Lĭnĭnning fikr oä oäsĭyätläri.* Samarkand–Tashkent: Oz. Däolät Näshriyati, 1926, iv and 120 pp., 5000 cop. [Uz 2 Arab; DLC, NN] 2275

Otpüskägä qaytuchi qïzil äskärining esdäligi—1929 yïl üchün. Samarkand–Tashkent: Öznäshr, 1929, 104 pp., 2500 cop. [Uz 3 Lat; NN] 2276

OzLKSM VII qurultayining rezolutsiyalari—1936/II. Tashkent: Yash Leninchi Gazetasining Nashri, 1936, 32 pp., 10000 cop. [Uz 3 Lat; DLC] 2277

Ozbekstan ijtïma'i shoralar jomhorïyäti ḥokomätïning ishlägän ishläri. Tashkent: Oz.I.Sh.J. Khälq Kämïsärläri Shorasi Äkhbarat Ïdaräsïning Näshri, 1927, 16 pp., 1500 cop. [Uz 2 Arab; DLC] 2278

Ozbekstan 2 nchi shoralar qoroltayi ochon matïryallar, 1927: Ozbekstanda Mä'arif Ishläri. Tashkent: Oz. Khälq Mä'arif Kämïsärlïgïning Näshri, 1927, 92 pp., 1553 cop. [Uz 2 Arab; NN] 2279

Özbekistanda fabzavmestkomlarnï saylavaldï—hïsabat kompaniyasi yäkünläri. Tashkent: Özsovprof Näshri, 1932, 19 and 18 pp., 1000 cop. [Uz 3 Lat; DLC] 2280

Ozbïkstan ijtïma'i shoralar jumhorïyätïndä shura tuzulïshi. Samarkand: OzIShJ Märkäz Ijraqomi oä Khälq Kämïsärläri Shorasi yanïdaghi Äkhbarat Ïdaräsïning Näshri, 1927, 59 pp., 1500 cop.[Uz 2 Arab; DLC] 2281

Papof, N. N. *Shuralar ḥukumätïning milli sïyasäti.* Tashkent–Samarkand: Oz. Dävlät Näshrïyati, 1927, 132 pp., 3000 cop. [Uz 2 Arab; DLC, NN] 2282

Pärtiyäviy-tashkiliy ish mäsäläläri. Tashkent: Ozdävnäshr, 1944, 30 pp., 10000 cop. [Uz 4 Cyr; CStH] 2283

Qaraqalpaq ASSR aliy sovetining birinchi sessiyasi. Tortkol–Tashkent: QQASSR Aliy Sovetining Nashri, 1939, 87 pp., 1500 cop. [Uz 3 Lat; DLC] 2284

Qïzil burchäk. Tashkent: Orta-Asya Käsäbälär Byurasi, 1927, 8 pp., 1000 cop. [Uz 2 Arab; DLC] 2285

"*Qïzil chaykhanä.*" Tashkent: Orta Asya Käsäbälär Byurasi, 1927, 27 pp., 1000 cop. [Uz 2 Arab; DLC, NN] 2286

RSDRP(b) qurultayi. Tashkent: OzK(b)P MK Partiya Nashriyati, 1939, 96 pp., 20000 cop. [Uz 3 Lat; DLC] 2287

Rïs, F. *Mopr nïmädir.* Tashkent: Oz. Däolät Näshrïyati, 1926, 15 pp., 5000 cop. [Uz 2 Arab; DLC] 2288

SSSR aliy sovetining oninchi sessiyäsi: Stenogräfiyä hisabati. n.p.: SSSR Aliy Soveti Näshri, 1944, 340 pp., n.c. [Uz 4 Cyr; DLC] 2289

Sakalof, I. *ʿÄskäri khizmätkächä taĭyarlanochĭning oz saghlĭghi toghrĭsĭda nĭmälärni bĭlĭsh keräk.* Samarkand: Qizil Ay Jämʿiyäti, 1927, 60 pp., 10053 cop. [Uz 2 Arab; DLC] 2290

Shähär saylaochĭlari tamanĭdan ozlärĭning shoralardaghi oäkĭllärĭgä bĭrilgän yol-yoroq. Samarkand: Oz. Kämmonĭst(b) Firqäsi, 1927, 36 pp., 2000 cop. [Uz 2 Arab; DLC, NN] 2291

Shärq oä mopr: Bäynälmĭläl inqĭlab koräshchĭlärĭgä yardam (*Mopr*). Tashkent: Oz. Däolät Näshrĭyati, 1926, 50 pp., 20000 cop. [Uz 2 Arab; DLC] 2292

Shelgin, V. N. *Kämmünistlik akhlaqïnï tarbiyä qïlïsh toghrïsïda.* Samarkand–Tashkent: Özbek Dävlät Näshriyatï, 1929. 73 pp., 4000 cop. [Uz 3 Lat; NN] 2293

Shoralargha qaytadan saylaolar toghrĭsĭda täshoĭqatchi oä mäʿrozächĭlär ochon matĭryallar. Samarkand: Oz.I.Sh.J. Märkäzi Ĭjraqomi Näshri, 1926, 35 pp., n.c. [Uz 2 Arab; DLC] 2294

Sĭyasi oqosh kĭtabi. Samarkand: Oz. Dävlät Näshrĭyati, 1926, 130 pp., 3053 cop. [Uz. 2 Arab; DLC] 2295

Sorin, Ĭ. *1-may bayrami.* Samarkand–Moscow: Oz. Däolät Näshriyati, 1927, 66 pp., 5000 cop. [Uz 2 Arab; NN] 2296

Stalin, I. *Yana partiyamizdagi sotsial-demokratik aghmachiliq toghrisida.* Tashkent: OzK(b)P MK Partiya Nashriyati, 1938, 74 pp., 20000 cop. [Uz 3 Lat; DLC] 2297

Tashkänt oĭlayätining 2nchi näobä ijraʾĭyä qomĭtäsĭning bergan ḥĭsabi, 1925–26. Tashkent: Oz. Däolät Näshrĭyati, 1927, 222 pp., 1060 cop. [Uz 2 Arab; DLC, NN] 2298

Ṭomski. *Oktäbr inqilabi ishchilärgä nimä berdi?* Moscow: Shora Ittifaqi Khalqlarining Märkäz Näshriyati, 1928, 52 pp., 3000 cop. [Uz 2 Arab; NN] 2299

Topchilikning muväqqät urush nizamnamäsi—sänaĭʿ (*tekhnikä*) *bolimi.* Tashkent: Tagh Topining Maddi Bolimi, n.d., 272 pp., 500 cop. [Uz 2 Arab; DLC] 2300

Topĭkof, B. *Afrĭqa chollärĭdä yashlar.* Moscow: SSSR Khalqlarining Märkäz Näshrĭyati, 1925, 132 pp., 7000 cop. [Uz 2 Arab; NN] 2301

Traynin, I. *SSSR khalqlarining bradarlik hamkarligi.* Tashkent: OzK(b)P MK Partiya Nashriyati, 1939, 71 pp., 20000 cop. [Uz 3 Lat; DLC] 2302

VKP(b) ustaviga kiritildigan ozgartishlar. Tashkent: OzK(b)P MK Partiya Nashriyati, 1939, 21 pp., 50000 cop. [Uz 3 Lat; DLC] 2303
Vätänning chäqirighigä jävab. Tashkent: Ozdävnäshr, 1943/1944, 130 pp., 10000 cop. [Uz 4 Cyr; DLC] 2304
Virgänski, V. *Qishlaq kamsamollari ochon siyasi oqosh kitabi*. III bolim. Moscow: SSSR Khälqlarĭning Märkäz Näshriyati, 1927, 69 pp., 8000 cop. [Uz 2 Arab; NN] 2305
Virgänski, V. *Qishlaq kamsamollari uchun siyasi oqush kitabi*. II bolim. Moscow: SSSR Khälqlarining Märkäz Näshrĭyati, 1927, 80 pp., 8000 cop. [Uz 2 Arab; NN] 2306
Yaraslavski, I. *Yängi appazĭtsiya vä tratskĭzm*. Tashkent–Samarkand: Oz Däolät Näshrĭyati, 1927, 146 pp., 4000 cop. [Uz 2 Arab; DLC, NN] 2307
Yash käshshaflär ĭsdäligi. Tashkent: Oz. Däolät Näshrĭyati, 1926, 109 pp., 5000 cop. [Uz 2 Arab; DLC] 2308
Zämayski, P. *Lenĭngä khät*. Moscow: SSSR Khalqlarining Märkäz Näshriyati, 1926, 20 pp., 4000 cop. [Uz 2 Arab; NN] 2309
Zorin, V. *Gharb pi'onerläri arasida 54 kun*. Samarkand: Oznäshr, 1928, 88 pp., 3000 cop. [Uz 2 Arab; DLC] 2310

History

Abo'lghazi Bahadir Khan. *Shajara-i turk*. 2 vols. St. Petersburg: Imprimerie de l'Academie Imperiale des Sciences, 1871, I 386 pp., II 393 pp., n.c. [Uz 1 Arab; MH] 2311
Abo'lghazi Bahadir Khan. *Shajarä-i turk*. Kazan: Ex Universitatis Imperialis Typographeo, 1825, 183 pp., n.c. [Uz 1 Arab; MH, NN] 2312
Ä-n, Ärk. *Änglĭyä, fränsĭyä oä gĭrmanĭyädä ishchĭlär ḥäräkäti tärĭkhi*. Tashkent: Oz. Däolät Näshrĭyati, 1926, 321 pp., 5000 cop. [Uz 2 Arab; DLC] 2313
Atabek oghli, Fazil bek. *Dukchi eshan oaqi'äsi: Färghanädä istibdad jälladläri*. Tä'rĭkhi räsmlär bĭlän. Samarkand–Tashkent: Ozbekstan Däolät Näshrĭyati, 1927, 88 pp., 6000 cop. [Uz 2 Arab; DLC] 2314
⟨Babir, Zahiriddin Muḥammad⟩ *Babir namä*. Kazan: n.p., 1857, iv and 508 pp., n.c. [Uz 1 Arab; MH] 2315

Bartold, V. *Torkistan tarïkhi.* Moscow: Bukhara Khälq Mäʻarïf Näzarätïning Näshri, 1924, 101 pp., 3000 cop. [Uz 2 Arab; NN] 2316
Bartold, V. V. *Qisqacha islam mädänïyäti tä'rïkhi.* Tashkent–Samarkand: Ozbekstan Dävlät Näshrïyati, 1927, 78 pp., 4000 cop. [Uz 2 Arab; NN] 2317
Grïmyätski, M. *Täbïʻätdä tiriklik uchon koräsh.* Moscow: Märkäzi Shärq häm Ghärb Näshrïyati, 1924, 64 pp., 3000 cop. [Uz 2 Arab; CStH, NN] 2318
ʻÏmadi, Ziya. *Ängliyä tä'rïkhi.* Tashkent: Orta Asya Kamonïstlar Darilfonuni Näshrïyati, 1928, 471 pp., 3000 cop. [Uz 2 Arab; DLC] 2319
Kodräfski, D. *Burunghi adamlar qanday kun korär ïdïlär.* Tashkent–Samarkand: Oz. Dävlät Näshrïyati, 1927, 121 pp., 3000 cop. [Uz 2 Arab; DLC, NN] 2320
Lïpïshiynski, P. N. *Oladïmïr ïlya oghli lïnïn qamaq häm surgundä.* Moscow: SSSR Khälqlärïning Märkäz Näshrïyati, 1925, 16 pp., 10000 cop. [Uz 2 Arab; CStH, NN] 2321
Mishulin, A. V. (ed.). *Qädimgi dun'ya tärikhi.* Tashkent: OzSSR Dävlät Näshriyati, 1945, 292 pp., 15000 cop. [Uz 4 Cyr; DLC] 2322
Moravïyski, S. (V. Lapokhif). *Orta asyadaghi inqïlabi ḥäräkät toghrïsïda tä'rïkhi parchalar.* Tashkent: Oz. Dävlät Näshrïyati, 1926/1927, 90 pp., 5000 cop. [Uz 2 Arab; DLC, NN] 2323
Muḥämmädjan oghli, Mo'minjan. *Turmish orïnishläri: Bir mullä bächchäning ḥatïrä däftäri.* 1- oä 2nchi bolim. Tashkent: Oz. Dävlät Näshrïyati, 1926, 345 pp., 5100 cop. [Uz 2 Arab; DLC, NN] 2324
Oambiri, Gïrman. *Bukhara yakhod maora'alnahir tarïkhi.* Moscow: Bokhara Khälq Mäʻarïf Näzarätïning Näshri, 1924, 295 pp., 3000 cop. [Uz 2 Arab; NN] 2325
Pakrofski, M. *Qisqacha ros tä'rïkhi.* Tashkent: Oz. Däolät Näshrïyati, 1927, vii and 304 pp., 10000 cop. [Uz 2 Arab; DLC] 2326
Papof, N. N. *Butun ittïfaq kammunïst(b)lär firqäsïning tä'rïkhi.* Tashkent: Oz. Däolät Näshrïyati, 1927, vi and 510 pp., 7000 cop. [Uz 2 Arab; DLC] 2327
Papof, N. N. *Bütün ïttïfaq kämmünist (bälshivik)lär fïrqasïnïng tarïkhï.* Samarkand–Tashkent: Özb. Dävlät Näshriyatï, 1929, 405 pp., 4000 cop. [Uz 3 Lat; NN] 2328

Qizil sharq maqalalar vä esdäliklär toplami. I. Samarkand: Oznäshr, 1929, 161 pp., 3000 cop. [Uz 2 Arab; DLC] 2329
Rämzĭn, K. (comp.). *Orta asyadä ozgärish, rasim oä täsoĭratlarda.* n.p.: Sakoning Näshrĭyati, 1928, 258 pp., 5000 cop. [Uz 2 Arab; NN] 2330
Razanif, A. N.; Soravtsĭf, V. I. *Shärq ʿilmi häy'ät tä'rĭkhi.* Tashkent: Oz. Däolät Näshrĭyati, 1927, 41 pp., 4000 cop. [Uz 2 Arab; DLC] 2331
Rĭd, Jon. *Yĭr yuzini titrätkän on kun.* Tashkent: Oz. Jomhorĭyätĭning Bash Sĭyasi Mäʿarifi, 1926, 416 pp., 3000 cop. [Uz 2 Arab; DLC] 2332
Saliḥ, Muḥammad. *Shaybani namä.* St. Petersburg: Elektro-Pechatnia A. M. Boraganskago, 1904/1908, xv and 14 and 220 pp., n.c. [Uz 1 Arab; MH] 2333
Saylĭyif, Bolat. *Orta asya tarĭkhi.* Samarkand–Tashkent: Oz. Däolät Näshriyati, 1926, 120 pp., 4000 cop. [Uz 2 Arab; DLC] 2334
"*VKP(b) tarikhining qisqa qursi*" chiqarilishi munasabati blan *partiya propagandasi ishining qoyilishi haqida.* Tashkent: OzK(b)P MK Partiya Nashriyati, 1939, 35 pp., 50000 cop. [Uz 3 Lat; DLC] 2335
Yaraslavski, Yim. *Butun ittĭfaq kammonĭst(b) firqäsĭning qisqacha tä'rĭkhi.* Birinchi bolim. Tashkent: Orta Asya Kammonĭstlar Darilfinunĭning Näshriyati, 1927, 245 pp., 6000 cop. [Uz 2 Arab; DLC, NN] 2336
Zekis; Nekänorĭf; Mitskivech (comps.). *Fĭrqa tarĭkhĭ: Lävhälärgä ĭzahat.* Samarkand–Tashkent: Öznäshr, 1929, 172 pp., 3000 cop. [Uz 3 Lat; CStH, NN] 2337

Law

Bashpakhtaqom mekhanichiskii ishkhanasĭnĭng köllektiv shärtnamasĭ, 1931-inchi yĭl üchün. Tashkent: n.p., 1931, 89 pp., 3000 cop. [Uz 3 Lat; DLC] 2338
Bĭrĭzĭn, S. M. *Jäza ḥuqoqi toghrĭsĭda ʿomomi mäʿlomat khulasäläri.* 1inchi qĭsm. Samarkand: Ozbĭkstan ʿÄdlĭyä Khaiq Kämĭsärligĭning "Ḥuqoqi Näshrĭyati," 1927, 61 pp., 1000 cop. [Uz 2 Arab; DLC, NN] 2339

Bĭrĭzĭn, S. M. *Jäza ḥuqoqi toghrĭsĭda ʿumomi mäʿlomat khulasäläri.* III qism. Samarkand: Ozbĭkstan ʿÄdlĭyä Khälq Kämĭslärlĭgĭning Ḥuqoqi Näshrĭyati, 1927, 63 pp., n.c. [Uz 2 Arab; DLC] 2340

Bĭrĭzĭn, S. M. *Jäza ḥuqoqi toghrĭsĭda ʿumomi mäʿlomat khulasäläri.* ʿUmomi qism. Samarkand: Ozbĭkstan ʿÄdlĭyä Khälq Kämsärligĭning "Ḥuqoqi Näshrĭyati," 1927, 56 pp., 1000 cop. [Uz 2 Arab; DLC] 2341

Dälvig, B. N. *Jĭnayät muḥakämäsi toghrĭsĭda ʿumomi mäʿlomat khulasäläri.* Samarkand: Oz.I.Sh.J. Khälq Kämĭsärläri Shorasĭning Ishlär Mudĭrĭyäti ḥuzorĭdaghi "Ḥuqoqi Näshrĭyati," 1927, 127 pp., 1000 cop. [Uz 2 Arab; DLC, NN] 2342

Ishchi dïyqan qïzïl qoshunïnïng härbii khïzmatchïlarï vä härbii mäjbürläri vä ularnïng aïlalarï üchün yengilliklär toghrïsïdaghï qanunlar mäjmüäsi. Tashkent: Öznäshr. Härbii Bölüm, 1931, 90 pp., 5000 cop. [Uz 3 Lat; DLC] 2343

Kölkhozchïlarnïng vä kölkhozchï khatun-qïzlarnïng jamaat öz-ara yardam kässäsining nïzamnamasï vä täkhminii ustafï. Tashkent: ÖzÏShCh KhKSh LShIÄRI Müdiriyätining Näshri, n.d., 20 pp., 7000 cop. [Uz 3 Lat; DLC] 2344

Krĭlĭnku, N.V. *Shora sodi qanday tuzulgän oä qanday ishläydir.* Samarkand: Oz.I.Sh.J. ʿÄdlĭyä Khälq Kämĭsärligĭning Ḥuqoqi Näshrĭyati, 1926, 34 pp., 3000 cop. [Uz 2 Arab; DLC] 2345

Lagovyĭr, N. *Shora prakororlar häy'äti oä oning dĭhqanlar ochon ähimiyäti.* Samarkand: Oz. Khälq ʿÄdlĭyä Kämĭsärlikĭning Ḥoqoqi Näshrĭyati, 1926, 27 pp., 3000 cop. [Uz 2 Arab; DLC] 2346

Maktab haqida partiya va hukumat qararlari. Tashkent: OzSSR Oquv-Pedagogik Davlat Nashriyati, 1938, 123 pp., 10000 cop. [Uz 3 Lat; DLC] 2347

Nämünävii köllektiv shartnama: 1932 nchi yïl üchün. Tashkent: VTsSPS Orta-Asïya Byurosïnïng Tährirat vä Näshriyat Bölimi, 1932, 61 pp., 5000 cop. [Uz 3 Lat; DLC] 2348

Öz.Ï.Sh.J. ämäldägi mehnät qanunlarï. Tashkent: Dävlät Mehnät Näshriyatï. Orta-Asïya Shü'bäsi, 1930, 822 pp., 2000 cop. [Uz 3 Lat; DLC] 2349

Öz.Ï.Sh.J. ïdaralarï vä märkäzii müässäsälärining dästüril'ämäl qaïda vä nïzamnamalarïnïng tädrjii toplamï. I, II, III, IV vä V qïsïmlar. Tashkent: Özbekistan Dävlät Näshriyatï, 1931, 420 pp., 2000 cop. [Uz 3 Lat; DLC] 2350

ÖzÏShJ khalq kämissärläri shorasïnïng ishläri müdiriyäti. Özbekistan ïjtïmaïï shora jümhüriyätining jïnayat mühakämä qanunlarï mäjmüäsi. Tashkent: Özbekistan Dävlät Näshrïyatï, 1931, 48 pp., 2000 cop. [Uz 3 Lat; DLC] 2351

Özbekistan ïjtïmaïï shora jümhüriyätining ämäldägi qanunlarïnïng muntazam yïghïndïsï. Birinchi qïsïm. Tashkent–Samarkand: Özbekistan Dävlät Näshriatï, 1930, 380 pp., 3000 cop. [Uz 3 Lat; DLC] 2352

Özbekistan ïjtïmaïï shora jümhüriyätining ämäldägi qanunlarïnïng—muntazam–yïghïndïsï: Älifbe-äshïya körgäzgichi. Tashkent: Özbekistan Dävlät Näshriyatï, 1930, 52 pp., 3000 cop. [Uz 3 Lat; DLC] 2353

Özbekistan ïjtïmaïï shora jümhüriyätining gräzhdänlik muhakämä qanunlarï mäjmüäsi. Tashkent: Öz.Ï.Sh.J.Kh.K.Sh. Ishläri Mudïrïyatïnïng Näshri, 1931, 106 pp., 3000 cop. [Uz 3 Lat; DLC] 2354

Özbekistan ïjtïmaïï shora jümhüriyätining gräzhdänlik qanunlarï mäjmüäsi. Tashkent: Öz.Ï.Sh.J.Kh.K.Sh. Ishläri Müdiriyätining Näshri, 1931, 109 pp., 3000 cop. [Uz 3 Lat; DLC] 2355

Ozbekistan sovet sotsiälistik respublikäsining konstitutsiyäsi: Äsasiy kanun. Tashkent: Ozbekstan Dävlät Näshriyati, 1941, 30 pp., 20000 cop. [Uz 4 Cyr; DLC] 2356

Ozbekstan sovet sotsialistik respublikasi amaldagi qanunlarining sistematik yighindisi. I. Tashkent: OzSSR Khalq Komisarlari Soveti Ishlar Mudirligining Nashri, 1939, 530 pp., 4000 cop. [Uz 3 Lat; DLC] 2357

Ozbekstan sovet sotsialistik respublikasi amaldagi qanunlarining sistematik yighindisi. II. Tashkent: OzSSR Khalq Komisarlari Soveti Ishlar Mudirligining Nashri, 1938, 469 pp., 4000 cop. [Uz 3 Lat; DLC] 2358

Ozbĭkstan ujtĭmaʿi shora jomhorĭyätĭning qanon äsasi (kanstĭtotsĭyä)si. Samarkand: Oz.I.Sh.J. Märkäzi Ijraqom oä Khälq Kämĭsärlär Shorasi yanĭdaghi Äkhbarat Ĭdaräsĭning Näshri, 1927, 36 pp., 1500 cop. [Uz 2 Arab; DLC] 2359

Ozbĭkstan ijtĭmaʿi shoralar jomhorĭyätĭning grazhdanliq—moḥakämä

qanonlari mäjmoʿäsi. Samarkand: Ozbїkstan I.Sh.J.ning Khalq
Kämїsärlär Shorasi, 1927, 68 pp., 250 cop. [Uz 2 Arab; DLC]   2360
Ozbїkstan ijtїmaʿi shoralar jumhorїyätїning sod turo nїzamlari.
Tashkent: Oz.I.Sh.J. Khälq Kämїsärläri Shorasїning Ishlär
Mudїrїyäti ḥuzorїdaghi "Ḥuqoqi Näshrїyat," 1927, 39 pp., n.c.
[Uz 2 Arab; DLC]   2361
Qanon zamїn o ab. Samarkand: Khalq Ziraʿt Kamїsariyati.
Ozbikstan Sh.I.J., 1929, 44 pp., 5000 cop. [Uz 2 Arab; DLC]   2362
Rosiyä ijtїmaʿi qoshma shoralar jumhorїyätїning grazhanliq
qanonlari. Moscow: Khälq ʿÄdlїyä Kämїsarїyati Häyʾätїning
Näshri, 1925, 164 pp., 2000 cop. [Uz 2 Arab; NN]   2363
Vїshnäkof, A. Grazhdanliq ḥuqoqi toghrїsїda ʿumomi mäʿlomat
khulasäläri. 2nchi qism. Samarkand: Oz.I.Sh.I. Khalq
Kämїsärläri Shorasїning Ishlär Mudїrїyäti ḥuzorїdägi "Ḥuqoqi
Näshrїyat," 1927, iv and 134 pp., 1000 cop.
[Uz 2 Arab; DLC, NN]   2364
Vїzga, S. O. (comp.). Ish yurutish nämunä vä shäkilläri. Samarkand:
Oz.I.Sh.J. Kämїsärlär Shorasining Ishlär Modiriyäti ḥozoridägi
"Ḥuqoqi Näshrїyat," 1927, 72 pp., 1000 cop. [Uz 2 Arab; DLC]   2365

Social Organization

Bädän tärbїyäsi. Tashkent: Orta Asya Käsäbälär Byurasi, 1927,
13 pp., 1000 cop. [Uz 2 Arab; DLC]   2366
Dїkshtäyn, S. Kim nїmä bilän yashaydir? Moscow: SSSR
Khälqlärїning Märkäzi Näshrїyati, 1924, 44 pp., n.c.
[Uz 2 Arab; NN]   2367
Grigoriyvä, N. Bala tärbiyäsi—ana väziyfäsi. Samarkand–
Tashkent: Oznäshr, 1929, 20 pp., 1000 cop. [Uz 2 Arab; NN]   2368
Їskorobogätöf, Shukach. Özbekistannїng avchїlїq khojalїghї.
Samarkand–Tashkent: Öznäshr, 1930, 64 pp., 4000 cop.
[Uz 3 Lat; DLC]   2369
Ispiränski, G. N. Balani qanday baqish kїräk. Moscow: SSSR
Khalqlarining Märkäzi Näshriyati, 1925, 50 pp., 5000 cop.
[Uz 2 Arab; NN]   2370
Läogor, A. Kunbatish vä kunchїqishda yashlar ḥäräkäti. Samarkand–
Tashkent: Oz. Däolät Näshriyati, 1927, 106 pp., 3000 cop.
[Uz 2 Arab; DLC]   2371

M. D. *Ana vä balaning saghlighi qanday saqlanadi?* Samarkand–Moscow: Oz. Dävlät Näshriyati, 1927, 36 pp., 3000 cop. [Uz 2 Arab; NN] 2372

Mirkhojayif, Ḥ. *"Pakhta kuni" dihqanlar ḥäyiti.* Tashkent: Öznäshr, 1929, 72 pp., 5000 cop. [Uz 2 Arab; DLC] 2373

Obcheshkuf. *Ichkilikkä qarshï.* Samarkand–Tashkent: Öznäshr, 1930, 20 pp., 4000 cop. [Uz 3 Lat; NN] 2374

Orta ḥal dĭhqan kim? Samarkand–Tashkent: Oznäshr, 1929, 22 pp., 3000 cop. [Uz 2 Arab; NN] 2375

Ozbekstan ijtĭmaʿi shoralar jumhorĭyätining khälq salighĭni saqlash ishläri. Samarkand: Oz.I.Sh.J. Märkäz Ijraqomi, 1927, 40 pp., 1500 cop. [Uz 2 Arab; DLC] 2376

Qishlaq oäkĭlälär yĭghlishlarĭning 1926–1927 yil uchun praghrami oä matĭryallari. n.p.: Oz. Kämmonĭstlär Firqäsi Märkäzi Qomĭtäsi ḥuzurĭdägi Ishchi Dĭhqan Khaton-Qizlar Bolimi Näshri, 1927, 60 pp., 600 cop. [Uz 2 Arab; DLC] 2377

Qolĭsif, Al. *Khitay dehqanlarining turmushi.* Samarkand–Tashkent: Ozbĭkstan Däolät Näshrĭyati, 1926, 19 pp., 5000 cop. [Uz 2 Arab; DLC] 2378

SSSRdä shähär häm qishlaq. Moscow: SSSR Khalqlarining Märkäz Näshriyati, 1927, 95 pp., 5000 cop. [Uz 2 Arab; NN] 2379

Sayuz qoshchi qanday ishläsh keräk. Samarkand–Tashkent: Oznäshr, 1929, 27 pp., 2000 cop. [Uz 2 Arab; NN] 2380

Setkin, Klara. *Leninning butun dunya ayallariga vasiyatlari.* Tashkent: OzK(b)P MK Partiya Nashriyati, 1939, 40 pp., n.c. [Uz 3 Lat; DLC] 2381

Sigäl, B. S. *Jinsi mäsʾälä.* Samarkand–Tashkent: Oznäshr, 1929, 76 pp., 3000 cop. [Uz 2 Arab; NN] 2382

Skoräbagatof. *Ozbekstan avchĭsining esdälik däftäri.* Samarkand: Oz.I.Sh.J. Yĭr Ishläri Khälq Kämĭsärliki, 1927, 51 pp., 5053 cop. [Uz 2 Arab; CStH, DLC, NN] 2383

Tashkĭnt oĭlayäti saghliqni saqlash ĭdaräsining ana häm bala saghlighĭni saqlash bolimi. Tashkent: Uzgosizdat, n.d., 5 pp., 4000 cop. [Uz 2 Arab; DLC] 2384

Volfson, M. B. *Ijtimaʿiiat parchalari.* Moscow: SSSR Khälqlarĭning Märkäz Näshrĭyati, 1925, 116 pp., 6000 cop. [Uz 2 Arab; NN] 2385

Yash käshshflärning bädän tärbiyäsi. Samarkand: Kamsamol Märkäzi Näshri, n.d., 30 pp., 3000 cop. [Uz 2 Arab; DLC] 2386

Zi̊li̊nski, I. A. *Khatinlar azadli̊ghi yoli̊da.* Tashkent: Oz. Dävlät Näshri̊yati, 1927, 43 pp., 1000 cop. [Uz 2 Arab; DLC] 2387

UZBEK Humanities

Language

1921 yil yänvärdä bolghan birinchi olkä ozbek til vä imla qoroltayiyning chiqarghan qararlari. Tashkent: İski Shähär Musulman Basmakhanäsi, 1922, 51 pp., 1000 cop [Uz 2 Arab; NNC*] 2388

Fi̊trät. *Näḥv.* Tashkent: Oz. Däolät Näshri̊yati, 1926 2d ed., 52 pp., 5000 cop. [Uz 2 Arab; DLC] 2389

Fi̊trät. *Näḥv.* Samarkand: Oz. Däolät Näshri̊yati, 1927 3d ed., 54 pp., 7000 cop. [Uz 2 Arab; DLC] 2390

Fi̊trät. *Särf.* Tashkent: Oz. Däolät Näshri̊yati, 1926, 59 pp., 6000 cop. [Uz 2 Arab; DLC] 2391

Fi̊trät. *Särf.* Samarkand: Oz. Dävlät Näshriyäti, 1927 5th ed., ii and 62 pp., 10000 cop. [Uz 2 Arab; DLC] 2392

Ḥäsän, M. *Ozbekchä si̊yasi-ijti̊ma'i loghat.* Tashkent: Oz. Däolät Näshri̊yati, 1926, 87 pp., 15000 cop. [Uz 2 Arab; DLC] 2393

Kalliktif. *Ozbekchä til sabaqlighi.* I. Tashkent: Oz. Däolät Näshriyati, 1926 3d ed., 82 pp., 25000 cop. [Uz 2 Arab; DLC] 2394

Källiktif. *Ozbekchä til sabaqlighi.* I. Tashkent: Oz. Däolät Näshri̊yati, 1927 4th ed., 70 pp., 35000 cop. [Uz 2 Arab; DLC] 2395

Kalliktif. *Ozbekchä til sabaqli̊ghi.* II. Tashkent: Oz. Däolät Näshri̊yati, 1926 3d ed., 118 pp., 10000 cop. [Uz 2 Arab; DLC] 2396

Källiktif. *Ozbekchä til sabaqlighi.* II. Tashkent: Oz. Däolät Näshri̊yati, 1927 4th ed., 90 pp., 10000 cop. [Uz 2 Arab; DLC] 2397

Kalliktif. *Ozbekchä til sabaqlighi.* III. Tashkent: Oz. Däolät Näshri̊yati, 1926 3d ed., 106 pp., 10000 cop. [Uz 2 Arab; DLC] 2398

Kalliktif. *Ozbekchä til sabaqlighi.* IV. Tashkent: Oz. Däolät Näshri̊yati, 1926, 100 pp., 7000 cop. [Uz 2 Arab; DLC] 2399

Lapin, S. A. *Karmannyi russko–uzbekskii slovar'.* Samarkand: Samarkandskii Oblastnyi Statisticheskii Komitet, 1899, 63 pp., n.c. [Special Cyr; NN] 2400

---

* Microfilm

Lapin, S. A. *Karmannyi russko–uzbekskii slovar' i prilozhenie: kratkaia grammatika uzbekskago iazyka.* Samarkand: Tipografiia Shtaba Voisk Samarkandskoi Oblasti, 1895, 106 and 56 pp., n.c. [Special Cyr; NN] 2401

Lapin, S. A. *Karmannyi russko–uzbekskii slovar' (4000 slov) s prilozheniem kratkoi grammatiki uzbekskago iazyka.* Samarkand: Izd. Samarkandskago Statisticheskago Komiteta, 1899, 109 and 63 pp., n.c. [Special Cyr; MH] 2402

Pantusov, N. "K izucheniiu sartskago nariechiia tiurkskago iazyka. Prilozheniia: Kubla bashi," *Uchenija zapiski.* (Kazan: Universitet) No. 66 (Sept.–Dec. 1899), pp. 1–23. [Uz 1 Arab; NN] 2403

Qari-Niyaziy, T. N.; Borovkov, A. K. *Ruschä–ozbekchä lughät.* Tashkent: OzFÄN Näshriyati, 1942, 536 pp., 10000 cop. [Uz 4 Cyr; NN, NNC] 2404

Ruscha–özbekchä tola sözlik. Jild II, P-Yä. Tashkent–Kazan: Özdävnäshr, 1934, 1094 pp., 10000 cop. [Uz 3 Lat; NNC] 2405

Starchevskii, A. *Sputnik russkago cheloveka v Srednei-Azii.* St. Petersburg: A. Transhel', 1878, 803 pp., n.c. [Special Cyr; CtY] 2406

Veliaminof-Zernof, V. de. *Dictionnaire Djaghataï-Turc.* St. Petersburg: Imprimerie de l'Académie Impériale des Sciences, 1869, 27 and 425 pp., n.c. [Uz 1 Arab; MH, NN] 2407

Literature

ʿÄbbasif, Ḥaji Agha. *Ozgärish älängäläri.* Tashkent–Samarkand: Oz. Dävlät Näshriyati, 1927, 44 pp., 1000 cop. [Uz 2 Arab; DLC] 2408

ʿAbid Jan ibn Muḥammad Qabil Akhond Namangani. *Tuḥfät al-ʿabidin va-ʾanis al-ʿashiqin.* Tashkent: Turkestanskii Kur'er, 1917, 160 pp., n.c. [Uz 1 Arab, Taj 1 Arab; NN] 2409

Älisher Navaiy. *Khämsä.* Qisqartib basmaga tayyarlavchi: S. Äyniy. Tashkent: Oquvpednashr, 1940, 452 pp., 10000 cop. [Uz 3 Lat; NNC] 2410

ʿÄlïyif, Mirza Agha. *Uyerdä unaqa, buyerdä bunaqa.* Tashkent: Oz. Dävlät Näshrïyati, 1927, 23 pp., 1000 cop. [Uz 2 Arab; DLC] 2411

Anqabay. *Khäbär, mäqalä, shiʿr vä ḥikayä yazish yollari.* Samarkand–Tashkent: Ozbïkstan Däolät Näshrïyati, 1927, 76 pp., 5000 cop. [Uz 2 Arab: DLC] 2412

Äreshin, P. *Yängi damla: Oruslar turmishindan hikäyä.* Samarkand: Kengäsh Ittifaqi Khalqlarining Märkäz Näshriyati vä Ozbekstan Dävlät Näshrïyati, 1927, 20 pp., 4000 cop. [Uz 2 Arab; CStH, NN] 2413

Arïf'iy, Ïsma'ïl (comp.). *Tapïshmaqlar: Termä.* Samarkand–Tashkent: Özbekistan Dävlät Näshriyatï, 1929, 20 pp., 3000 cop. [Uz 3 Lat; NN] 2414

Atajan; Serböt; Läskeviskiy; Rähim (comps.) *Yänghi turmush.* Tashkent: Özbekistan Dävlät Näshriyati, 1929, vii and 295 pp., 15000 cop. [Uz 3 Lat; DLC] 2415

Aybek. *Toygholar.* Tashkent: Oz. Däolät Näshrïyati, 1926, 60 pp., 5100 cop. [Uz 2 Arab; NN] 2416

Babir padishah. *Majmo'ä-i ash'ar-i babir padishah.* Ed., A. Samoilovich. Petrograd: Ilyas Mirza Borghaniskinïng Maṭb'äsi, 1917, 34 and 90 pp., n.c. [Uz 1 Arab; NNC] 2417

Baqïyif, S. *Käpïrätsïyä faydaliq närsä.* Tashkent: Oz. Däolät Näshrïyati, 1927, 24 pp., 1000 cop. [Uz 2 Arab; DLC] 2418

Bäshir, Zärif. *Aghilkhanada.* Ḥikäyächä. Samarkand–Tashkent: Oz. Däolät Näshriyati, 1927, 20 pp., 4000 cop. [Uz 2 Arab; NN] 2419

Bäshir, Zärif. *Ipäk koyläk.* Samarkand: Oz. Dävlät Näshriyati, 1927, 48 pp., 4000 cop. [Uz 2 Arab; DLC] 2420

Bäshir, Zärif. *Turghunbayning tumarlari.* Samarkand–Tashkent: Oznäshr, 1927, 18 pp., 4000 cop. [Uz 2 Arab; NN] 2421

Batu. *Tolqïn tavïshlarï.* Shiir toplamïdan II bölim. Samarkand: Özbek Dävlät Näshriyatï, 1929, 48 pp., 3000 cop. [Uz 3 Lat; NN] 2422

Bektagiyif, Rostäm. *Yonis äraväkäsh.* Moscow–Samarkand: Oz. Däolät Näshriyati, 1927, 76 pp., 4000 cop. [Uz 2 Arab; NN] 2423

Bïrinchi may. Tashkent: Oz. Däolät Näshriyati, 1927, 30 pp., 1000 cop. [Uz 2 Arab; DLC] 2424

Cholpan. *Oyghanish.* Shi'rlär toplami. Tashkent: Torkistan Jomhorïyatïning Däolät Näshrïyati, 1922, 40 pp., n.c. [Uz 2 Arab; NN] 2425

Cholpan. *Yarqin ay.* Tashkent: Oz. Dävlät Näshrïyati, 1926, 172 pp., 3000 cop. [Uz 2 Arab; DLC] 2426

Elbek. *Ḥäyvanlar.* Samarkand–Tashkent: Oz. Däolät Näshrïyati, 1926, 16 pp., 10000 cop. [Uz 2 Arab; DLC, NN] 2427

Elbek. *Kozgi.* Tashkent: Oz. Däolät Näshrïyati, 1926 2d ed., 72 pp., 3000 cop. [Uz 2 Arab; NN] 2428
Elbek. *Mehnät küyläri.* Shiirlär toplamï. 6nchï bölim. Tashkent: Öznäshr, 1930, 49 pp., 4000 cop. [Uz 3 Lat; DLC] 2429
Elbek. *Sezgilär.* Tashkent: Oz. Dävlät Näshrïyati, 1927, 50 pp., 3000 cop. [Uz 2 Arab; DLC] 2430
Fättah, Temur. *Yäpraqlär.* Tashkent: Ozdävnäshr, 1945, 108 pp., 5000 cop. [Uz 4 Cyr; DLC] 2431
Fïtrat. *Äbul fäyz khan. Bukhara olkäsining tarikhidan.* Bïsh pärdälik fajïʿä. Moscow: SSSR Khalqlarining Märkäz Näshriyati, 1924, 92 pp., 5000 cop. [Uz 2 Arab; NN] 2432
Fïträt. *Ädäbïyat qaʿidalari.* Tashkent: Oz. Dävlät Näshrïyati, 1926, 122 pp., 3000 cop. [Uz 2 Arab; DLC] 2433
Fïträt. *Arslan.* 5 pärdälik dramma. Samarkand: Oz. Dävlät Näshriyati, 1926, 119 pp., 4000 cop. [Uz 2 Arab; DLC] 2434
Fïṭrät. *Bïdil.* Bir mäjlisdä. Moscow: Millat Ishläri Kämïsärligi Qashïda "Markazi Sharq Nashriyati," 1924, 54 pp., 5000 cop. [Uz 2 Arab; NN] 2435
Fiträt. *Eng eski turk ädäbiyati nämunäläri.* Tashkent: Oz. Däolät Näshrïyati, 1927, 124 pp., 5000 cop. [Uz 2 Arab; DLC] 2436
Fiṭrat. *Qiyamät.* Khäyali ḥikayä, Moscow: Markaz Sharq Nashriyati, 1923, 28 pp., 5000 cop. [Uz 2 Arab; NN] 2437
Gelisheviskiy, Ä. *Yun-lï: Khïtay ishchiläri turmïshïdan.* Samarkand–Tashkent: Öznäshr, 1929, 45 pp., 3000 cop. [Uz 3 Lat: NN] 2438
Ghäyräti. *Erk tavushi.* Shiʿrlär toplami. Birinchi bolim. Samarkand–Tashkent: Oz. Däolät Näshrïyati, 1927, 39 pp., 3000 cop. [Uz 2 Arab; CStH, DLC, NN] 2439
Ghayratiy. *Qutulïsh.* Hikäyä. Tashkent: Öznäshr, 1928, 45 pp., 3000 cop. [Uz 3 Lat; DLC] 2440
Ḥäqvïrdïyif, ʿA. *Khanning sevgïsi.* Tashkent: Oz. Däolät Näshrïyati, 1927, 20 pp., 2000 cop. [Uz 2 Arab: DLC] 2441
Ḥäqvïrdïyif, ʿA. *Millätchïlär: Jädïdlik daorïdan alinghan.* Tashkent: Oz. Dävlät Näshrïyati, 1927, 28 pp., 1000 cop. [Uz 2 Arab; DLC] 2442
⟨Ḥaziniy⟩. *Bayaẓ-i ḥazini.* Tashkent: G. Kh. Aridzhanov, 1914, 238 pp., n.c. [Uz 1 Arab; NN] 2443
Ismaʿilzadä, Mirza Kälan. *8 inchi mart azadlighi.* Tashkent: Oz. Dävlät Näshrïyati, 1927, 48 pp., 3000 cop. [Uz 2 Arab; DLC] 2444

Lahuti. *Krĭmil.* Tashkent: Ozpaligraf Tirestining Birinchi
Mätbäʿäsi, 1929, 31 pp., 3500 cop. [Uz 2 Arab; DLC] 2445
Mäʿarif yolĭda. Tashkent: Oz. Dävlät Näshrĭyati, 1927, 22 pp.,
1000 cop. [Uz 2 Arab; DLC] 2446
Mäjĭdif, Äsʿäd. *Lĭnĭn yolĭdä.* Samarkand–Tashkent: Oz. Däolät
Näshriyati, 1927, 26 pp., 2000 cop. [Uz 2 Arab; DLC, NN] 2447
Majmuʿä-i nur namä. Tashkent: n.p., 1917, 128 pp., n.c.
[Uz 1 Arab; NN] 2448
Mohämmäd, ʿÄbdoräḥman. *Näsäb qurbani.* Tort pärdälik mozĭkä
dramä. Moscow: Oz. Bash Säyasi Mäʿarĭf Qomĭtätĭning Näshri,
1925, 42 pp., 5000 cop. [Uz 2 Arab; NN] 2449
Mordivinkin. *Dehqan bilän bälshävek, borjuvay bilan genäräl
toghrisida.* Samarkand–Moscow: Oz Däolät Nashriyati, 1927,
32 pp., 4000 cop. [Uz 2 Arab; NN] 2450
Niyazi, Ḥamza Ḥakĭm zadä. *Yangghi saʿadat: Milli roman.* n.p.:
n.p., 1915, 46 pp., n.c. [Uz 1 Arab; NNC*] 2451
Oktäbr golläri. Tashkent: Oz. Däolät Näshriyati, 1927, 50 pp., 2000
cop. [Uz 2 Arab; DLC, NN] 2452
Orazmäḥämmädif, M. *Bizdä häm ulärdä.* Tashkent: Oz. Däolät
Näshrĭyati, 1927, 44 pp., 1000 cop. [Uz 2 Arab; DLC] 2453
Qadĭri, ʿÄbdolla (Jolqonbay). *Miḥrabdan chayan: Khudayarkhan oä
munshĭläri ḥäyatĭdan täʾrĭkhi roman.* Samarkand–Tashkent:
Oznäshr, 1929. 345 pp., 7000 cop. [Uz 2 Arab; NN] 2454
Qadĭri, ʿÄbdolla. *Otkän kunlär.* Birinchi bolim. Tashkent–
Samarkand: Ozbĭkstan Dävlät Näshrĭyati, 1926 2d ed., 128 pp.,
5000 cop. [Uz 2 Arab; DLC, NN] 2455
Qishlaq käperätifi. Samarkand–Tashkent: Oz. Dävlät Näshriyati,
1927, 19 pp., 4000 cop. [Uz 2 Arab; NN] 2456
Räfĭq. *Balaqor.* Namangan: Nämängän Mäḥälli Khojälĭk Mätbäsi,
1926, 16 pp., n.c. [Uz 2 Arab; DLC, NN] 2457
Räḥimi, N. *Qizil yapraqlar.* Shĭʿrlär toplami. Samarkand–Tash-
kent: Oz. Däolät Näshrĭyati 1927, 43 pp., 3000 cop.
[Uz 2 Arab; DLC, NN] 2458
Robĭrts, Charlĭz. *Bir kozlik ata ghaz oä ĭpäk qanatlar.* Moscow:
SSSR Khalqlarining Märkäz Näshriyati, 1925, 40 pp., 4000 cop.
[Uz 2 Arab; NN] 2459

---

*Microfilm

Robirts, Charliz. *Tuyuqsan bir dostlik oä tingiz balasi.* Moscow: SSSR Khalqlarining Märkäz Näshriyati, 1925, 30 pp., n.c. [Uz 2 Arab; NN] 2460

Rozi, Sher 'Äli (comp.). *Ozbäk maqallari.* Moscow: SSSR Khälqlarining Märkäz Näshriyati, 1926, 52 pp., 4000 cop. [Uz 2 Arab; NN] 2461

Sä'dii, Tashpolat. *Köngül tashqinlarï.* She'rlär toplamï. Tashkent: Öznäshir, 1930, 62 pp., 3000 cop. [Uz 3 Lat; DLC] 2462

Sä'id, Ziya; Mo'minjan. *Qanli kun.* Samarkand–Tashkent: Oz. Däolät Näshriyati, 1926, 66 pp., 3000 cop. [Uz 2 Arab; DLC] 2463

Säyfullinä, Laläkhan. *Ichkäri: Ozbik khatin qizlari tormushidan alingan sachma shi'rlär.* Samarkand–Tashkent: Oz Däolät Näshriyati, 1927, 68 pp., 3000 cop. [Uz 2 Arab; DLC, NN] 2464

Sharafiddinov, A. *Älisher Navaiy: Zamani, hayati, ijadiyati va olumi.* Tashkent: OzSSR FANlar Komiteti Nashiriyati, 1939, 70 pp., 10000 cop. [Uz 3 Lat; DLC] 2465

Shanli Leningräd. She'r, hikayä vä ocherklär toplämi. Tashkent: OzSSR Dävlät Näshriyati, 1942, n.pp., n.c. [Uz 4 Cyr; DLC] 2466

Shaykhzadä. *Geniäl shair: Navaiy ijadining bä'zi mäsäläläri.* Tashkent: Ozädäbiynäshr, 1941, 82 pp., 10000 cop. [Uz 4 Cyr; DLC] 2467

Sinariyä. Tashkent: Oz. Däolät Kina Idaräsi, 1926, 31 pp., 3000 cop. [Uz 2 Arab; DLC] 2468

Siräfimovich. *Khatin-khalach qishlaghi: Oroslar tormishdan ḥikayä.* Samarkand–Moscow: Oz. Dävlät Näshriyati, 1927, 20 pp., 4000 cop. [Uz 2 Arab; NN] 2469

Siräfimövich, A. *Muzliqda.* Hikäyä. Samarkand–Tashkent: Öznäshir, 1929, 27 pp., 3000 cop. [Uz 2 Arab; DLC] 2470

Soläyman, 'A.; Zahiri, 'A. *Ädäbiyat parchalari.* Tashkent: Oz. Däolät Näshriyati, 1926, 224 pp., 5100 cop. [Uz 2 Arab; NN] 2471

Tisur-Miyolin, G. *Ashnalar ḥikäyäsi.* Tashkent–Samarkand: Oz. Däolät Näshriyati, 1928, 47 pp., 3000 cop. [Uz 2 Arab; DLC] 2472

Tülkilär. Samarkand–Tashkent: Öznäshr, 1929, 117 pp., 3000 cop. [Uz 3 Lat; NN] 2473

Välidüf, A. *Azadliq yolida.* Moscow-Samarkand: Özbek Dävlät Näshriyatï, 1930, 112 pp., 5000 cop. [Uz 3 Lat; NN] 2474

Veselovskii, N. (ed.). *Oros lashkarining turkistanda tarikh 1269–1282 senälärdä qilghan futuḥatlari.* St. Petersburg: Parovaia

Skoropechatnia P. O. Iablonskago, 1894, iv and 82 and 125 pp., n.c. [Uz 1 Arab, Kaz 1 Arab; MH] 2475

Yäkävlef, Ä. *Oktäbr*. Ḥikäyä. Samarkand–Moscow: Oz. Däolät Näshriyati, 1927, 40 pp., 4000 cop. [Uz 2 Arab; NN] 2476

Yassavi, Khoja Aḥmad. *Divan-i ḥikmät*. n.p.: n.p., n.d., 78 pp., n.c. [Uz 1 Arab; NN] 2477

Yonis, Ghazi. *Islamïyat oyi*. Pajï'ä 4 pärdädä. Tashkent: Torkistan Däolät Näshrïyati, 1922, 54 pp., n.c. [Uz 1 Arab; NN] 2478

Yonis, Ghazi. *Savadsizliq bälasi*. Tashkent: Oz. Dävlät Näshrïyati, 1926, 42 pp., 5100 cop. [Uz 2 Arab; DLC] 2479

Yonis, Ghazi. *Tapilghan närsä*. Bir pärdälik kulgu. Tashkent: Torkistan Jomhorïyätïning Däolät Näshrïyati, 1921, 20 pp., 10000 cop. [Uz 2 Arab; NN] 2480

Yoqsul; Sherif (comps.). *Intilish*. Termä shi'rlär toplamï. Tashkent–Samarkand: Öznäshr, 1930, 189 pp., 5000 cop. [Uz 3 Lat; NN] 2481

Yunis, Ghazi. *Hay shärq!* Tashkent: Oz. Däolät Näshriyati, 1926, 25 pp., 3100 cop. [Uz 2 Arab; DLC] 2482

Yunis, Ghazi. *Savadsizliq qanday yaman*. Tashkent: Oz. Däolät Näshrïyati, 1926, 32 pp., 3100 cop. [Uz 2 Arab; DLC] 2483

Yunusof, G. *Tulki, khoraz oä mushuk mäsäli*. Tashkent: Oz. Dävlät Näshrïyati, 1927, 17 pp., 10000 cop. [Uz 2 Arab; DLC] 2484

Zäpäri, Ghulam. *Balalar dunyasi*. Tashkent: Oz. Däolät Näshriyati, 1926, 19 pp., 5000 cop. [Uz 2 Arab; DLC] 2485

Zäpäri, Ghulam. *Kuylik tamashalar*. I. Tashkent: Oz. Däolät Näshriyati, 1926, 12 pp., 5000 cop. [Uz 2 Arab; DLC] 2486

Zäpäri, Gulam. *Kuylik tamashaliqlar*. II. Samarkand: Oz. Dävlät Näshrïyati, 1926, 15 pp., 5000 cop. [Uz 2 Arab; DLC] 2487

Zäpäri, Gulam. *Tätimbay ata*. Samarkand: Oz Dävlät Näshrïyati, 1926, 16 pp., 5000 cop. [Uz 2 Arab; DLC] 2488

Zärt, Y. *Dovänä*. Samarkand–Moscow: Oz. Dävlät Näshriyati, 1927, 30 pp., 4000 cop. [Uz 2 Arab; NN] 2489

Zärt, Y. *Kohi mäläk*. Samarkand–Moscow: Oz. Däolät Näshriyati, 1927, 19 pp., 4000 cop. [Uz 2 Arab; NN] 2490

Zärt, Yilinä. *Qimmät*. Samarkand–Moscow: Oz. Dävlät Nashriyati, 1927, 28 pp., 4000 cop. [Uz 2 Arab; NN] 2491

Zärtä, Yilinä. *Mirab*. Ḥikayä. Samarkand–Moscow: Oz. Däolät Näshriyati, 1927, 24 pp., 4000 cop. [Uz 2 Arab; NN] 2492

Zolin (Fränj). "*Lina*" *jälladlärigä sod*. Tashkent: Oz. Dävlät Näshriyati, 1926, 55 pp., 3100 cop. [Uz 2 Arab; DLC] 249

Music

Fiträt. *Ozbik eski zaman muzikasi oä uning tä'rikhi*. Samarkand–Tashkent: n.p., 1927, n.pp., n.c. [Uz 2 Arab; DLC] 249

Mirönof, N. *Musiqa näzäriyäsige addi qisqacha därslik*. Samarkand: "Öznäshr," 1929, 50 pp., 2000 cop. [Uz 3 Lat; DLC] 249

Philosophy and Religion

Adamzat aghizasining tirikligi toghrisida fän vä din qarashlari. Samarkand–Tashkent: Oznäshr, 1929, 114 pp., 3000 cop. [Uz 2 Arab; NN] 249

Ḥariri, Muḥammad. *Muṣayyib namä*. Tashkent: Litografiia Br. Portsevykh, 1900/1901, 231 pp., n.c. [Uz 1 Arab; MH] 24

Khudasizlar togäräkläri uchun därslik. II. Samarkand–Tashkent: Ozbek Dävlät Näshriyati, 1929, 130 pp., 5000 cop. [Uz 2 Arab; DLC] 249

Lenin, V. I. *Din toghrisida*. Tashkent: OzSSR Davlat Nashriyati, 1939, 40 pp., 10000 cop. [Uz 3 Lat; DLC] 24

⟨Rabghuzi⟩. *Qiṣaṣ al-anbiya'*. Tashkent: Tip.-Lit. Br. Portsevykh, 1900, 528 pp., n.c. [Uz 1 Arab; MH] 25

Ramiz, Männan. *Khayaldan ḥäqiqätgä*. Tashkent: Oz. Däolät Näshriyati, 1928, 75 pp., 3000 cop. [Uz 2 Arab; DLC] 25

Timiryazev, K. A. *Charlz Darvin va uning ta'limati*. Tashkent: OzSSR Davlat Oquv-Pedagogik Nashriyati, 1939, 344 pp., 3000 cop. [Uz 3 Lat; DLC] 25

Yusif päyghämbär 'aliyä al-islamning tä'bir kitabi. Kazan: Tipolitografiia Imperatorskago Universiteta, 1901, 39 pp., n.c. [Uz 1 Arab; NN] 25

VOLGA TATAR General (including periodicals)

Auïl ḥüjalïghï-ürman ïshchïlärï prafsayüzï tatarstan bülïgïnïng qärar, sirkülär, anglatü häm bïldïrülär byüllitini (Kazan) 1928: 1; 1929: 8–10; 1930: 3/4. [Tata 2 Arab, 3 Lat; NN] 2503

Auïl yäshläri (Kazan) 1927: 6, 9, 11; 1929: 1–2, 4–5, 8, 10, 12; 1930: 1. [Tata 2 Arab, 3 Lat; NN] 2504

Azad ḥatïn (Kazan) 1927: 13, 17, 18; 1928: 3–4, 8–9, 13/14, 18–21; 1929: 5, 7–9, 13, 17/18; 1930: 4. [Tata 2 Arab, 3 Lat; NN] 2505

Azad sibir (Novosibirsk) ⟨1927⟩: 40(387). [Tata 2 Arab; NN] 2506

1927 nchï yïlghï kitab ïsmaïgïnä ikinchï östämä. n.p.: Kooperativnoe Iz-vo "Nashriiat," n.p.: n.d., 6 pp., 1500 cop. [Tata 2 Arab; NN] 2507

Bezneng yül (Kazan) 1925: 1–2; 1927: 9; 1928: 3, 5, 8; 1929: 3–5, 11–12. [Tata 2 Arab, 3 Lat; NN] 2508

Blmne zavot öchen köräsh (Kazan) 1930: 2. [Tata 3 Lat; NN] 2509

Chayan (Kazan) 1927: 6/7, 9; 1928: 5, 7; 1929: 5–6; 1930: 7. [Tata 2 Arab, 3 Lat; NN] 2510

al-Din va'l-Adab (Kazan) 1906: 1–12; 1907: 13–14, 1–12; 1908: 13/14, 1–7. [Tata 1 Arab; NN] 2511

Fän häm din (Moscow) 1927: 19, 24/25; 1928: 2–3, 10, 16–17; 1929: 16–20, 22; 1930: 2, 4, 6, 18–20. [Tata 2 Arab, 3 Lat; NN] 2512

Igenchï (n.p.) 1927: 18–22, 24; 1928: 1/2. [Tata 2 Arab; NN] 2513

⟨by 1929 title changed to⟩ *Kümäk khujalïq* (Kazan) 1929: 14–16, 21–22, 24; 1930: 3–4, 7–8, 10, 15–16, 19. [Tata 2 Arab, 3 Lat; NN] 2514

Jitäkji (Kazan) 1927: 12–14; 1929: 3. [Tata 2 Arab, 3 Lat; NN] 2515

Kichkïnä ibdäshlär (Moscow) 1925: 1 (9); 1927: 11 (43); 1928: 2–3. [Tata 2 Arab; NN] 2516

Kitap letopise (Kazan) 1939: 1/2. [Tat 3 Lat; DLC] 2517

Kristiyan zhurnalï (Penza) 1927: 10 (22); 1928: 1 (23). [Tata 2 Arab; NN] 2518

Kümäk khujalïq, see number 2514.

Mägharif (Kazan) 1928: 1–3, 9; 1929: 4–5; 1930: 2, 5–7. [Tata 2 Arab, 3 Lat; NN] 2519

Mäqharif eshchese (Moscow) 1929: 5, 7/8; 1930: 3, 7/8. [Tata 3 Lat; NN] 2520

Mirat—(Kozgï) (St. Petersburg–Kazan) 1900: 1–6; 1902: 7–11; 1903: 12–18; 1908: 19–21; 1909: 22. [Tata 1 Arab; NN*] 2521

---

* Microfilm

"*Näshriyat*" *ka'üpirativïnïng kitab ïskladïnda häm magazininda här vaqt satïlatörghan kitablar isïmlïgï.* Moscow: n.p., 1925, 27 pp., 2000 cop. [Tata 2 Arab; NN] 252

Qazan üzäk ïshchïlär kapiratifïnïng infarmatsiyä biyüllitinï (Kazan) 1927–28: 4. [Tata 2 Arab; NN] 252

Qzïl Tatarstan (Kazan) 1928: 111 (2780), 152 (2821), 165 (2834). [Tata 3 Lat; CStH] 252

Qzïl yül: Tatarstan. 4nchi kitabqa qüshïmta. Kazan: Tatarstan Dävlät Näshriyatï, 1929, 134 pp., 12000 cop. [Tata 2 Arab; NN] 252

Rabsel'korlarnïng III nche Ural Ölkä kingäshmäse rezalütsiä häm qärarlarï. Sverdlovsk: n.p., 1930, 30 pp., 5000 cop. [Tata 3 Lat; NN] 252

Shäpy agay: "*Kammünist*" *gäzitäsïnïng qüshmtasï bülib aygha bïr märtäbä chïghatörghan gäzitä* (Sverdlovsk) 1925: 1 (2). [Tata 2 Arab; NN] 252

Shora (Orenburg) 1913: 2–4, 6, 13, 15, 17, 21, 23; 1915: 21; 1916: 3. [Tata 1 Arab; NNC]. 1908: 2–8, 10–13, 15, 17–24; 1909: 2–23; 1910: 1–24; 1911: 1–24; 1912: 5–11, 13–14, 18–19, 24; 1913: 3; 1914: 1–24; 1915: 1–19, 21–24; 1916: 1, 6–8, 12; 1917: 1–24. [Tata 1 Arab; NNC*] 252

Sovet ädäbiyätï (Kazan) 1944: 2–5, 7–9 [DLC]; 1945: 12 [CStH]. [Tata 4 Cyr] 252

Tahirïva, S. *Ghilmi bibliyagrafiya.* Kazan: Tatar Mädäniyätï Yörtï Basmasï, 1928, 101 pp., 2000 cop. [Tata 2 Arab; NN] 253

Tahirïva, S. *Ghilmi bibliyagrafiya—1925 yïlda chïqqan tatarcha äsärlär öchön.* Kazan: Tatar Mädäniyäte Yorto Basmasï, 1929, 101 pp., 2000 cop. [Tata 2 Arab, 3 Lat; DLC] 253

Tamashachï (Kazan) 1929: 3. [Tata 2 Arab; NN] 253

Tatar dävlät akadimiyä tiyatïrï mäjmüghä-programma (Kazan) 1928: 3. [Tata 2 Arab; NN] 253

Tatar kalindarï: 1925 miladi häm 1343/4 hijri yïllar öchin. Kazan: Tatarstan Matbüghat häm Näshriyat Kambinatï Näshrï, 1924, 165 pp., 3000 cop. [Tata 2 Arab; NN] 253

Tatar sotsial sovitlar jömhüriäte eshche-krästiännär khökümäteneng zakon-boyrqlar jïïntïghï (Kazan) 1930: 7 [NN], 25–26, 28 [DLC]. [Tata 3 Lat] 253

* Microfilm

Tatarstan (Kazan) 1929: 3. [Tata 3 Lat; NN] 2536

Tatarstan jömhüriyäti ïshchï häm igïnchïlär ḥükümätïnïng zakün häm böyrïqlar mäjmüghäsï (Kazan) 1925: 32, 34, 36–49; 1926: 1–46; 1927: 1–56, 58–60; 1928: 2–4, 6–47; 1929: 5–10, 13–20, 22, 26–27; 1930: 6–16, 18–23; 1935: 2–7, 15; 1937: 2. [Tata 2 Arab, 3 Lat; MH] 2537

Tatarstan üzäk bashqarma yanndaghï Tatarstan däülät näshriatï "Tatizdat" nïng kitaplar ismnege (Kazan) 1930: 9. [Tata 3 Lat; NN] 2538

Tatsayüz ḥäbärchisi (Kazan) 1928: IV 5, V, 1/2; 1930: 1, 5–7. [Tata 2 Arab, 3 Lat; NN] 2539

Üktäbr balasï (n.p.) 1929: 1, 3. [Tata 3 Lat; NN] 2540

Üqüchi säḥifäsi (Kazan) 1929: 1; 1930: 4. [Tata 2 Arab, 3 Lat; NN] 2541

Üralda mägharif (Sverdlovsk) 1928: 3; 1930: 2(13). [Tata 2 Arab, 3 Lat; NN] 2542

"Yalchï" gäziteneng yllïq podpischiklarïna istälek-kalindar. Kazan: n.p., 1930, 32 pp., 3300 cop. [Tata 3 Lat; NN] 2543

"Yanga kitab": Näshriyat kapiratifï shirkätïnïng kitablar isïmlïgï 1927–1928 nchï yïllargha. Kazan: Kooperativnogo Izdatel'skogo T-va "Yänga Kitab," 1927, 32 pp., 2000 cop. [Tata 2 Arab; NN] 2544

Yängalif (n.p.) 1927: 11; 1928: 6/7, 11, 13/14, 16, 23/24; 1929: 1, 5/6, 9, 12–13, 15, 17, 19/20, 22; 1930: 3. [Tata 3 Lat; NN] 2545

Yäsh ishchï (Moscow) 1927: 8, 10; 1928: 1, 3. [Tata 2 Arab; NN] 2546

Yäsh pidaguk (Kazan) 1929: 7. [Tata 3 Lat; NN] 2547

VOLGA TATAR Social Sciences

Economics

Äbübäkirif, F. *1929–30 nchï yïlnïng birläshtïrïlgän auïl ḥüjalïghï salïmï türïnda palazhiniyä häm anï ütkärü türïnda qüllanma: Instrüksiyä.* Kazan: Tatarstan Maliyä Ḥalq Kamisariyatï Näshïrï, 1929, 266 pp., 1300 cop. [Tata 2 Arab; NN] 2548

Äḥmädif, Äḥäd. *S.S.S.R. ikanümikasï (iqtisadï halï).* Moscow: SSSR Ḥalqlarï Üzäk Näshriyatï, 1924, 87 pp., 4000 cop. [Tata 2 Arab; NN] 2549

Äḥmädif, Äḥät. *S.S.S.R. iqtisadï säyäsätïning töp sïzïqlarï.* Moscow: "Näshriya" Ka'üpirativï Mätbäghäsï, 1926, 29 pp., 5000 cop. [Tata 2 Arab; NN] 255

Äḥmitif, Äḥmit. *S.S.S.R.nïng iqtisadï sayasatï.* Moscow: Näshriyat Mätbäghäsï, 1926, 117 pp., 4000 cop. [Tata 2 Arab; CStH] 255

Ananin, V.; Dmitriyif, S. *Fabrik-zavüdlarda.* Moscow: SSSR Ḥalqlarïnïng Uzäk Näshriyatï, 1927, 292 pp., 6000 cop. [Tata 2 Arab; NN] 255

Arski, R. *Ural (Uralnïng ṭabighi baylïqlarï häm sanäghät ïshlärï ḥaqïnda).* Kazan: R.V.Ü., 1921, 70 pp., 10000 cop. [Tata 1 Arab; NN] 255

Auïl ḥüjalïghï kapiratifï süt tavarishstvasïnïng üstafï. Moscow: Sintr'izdat häm Sayüzlar Sayüzïnïng Millätlär Byürasï Näshrï, 1929, 44 pp., 1000 cop. [Tata 2 Arab; NN] 255

Barisif, I. G. *Rusiyänïng iqtisadï jüghrafiyäsi.* Moscow: Märkäz Shärq Näshriyatï, 1924, 200 pp., 5000 cop. [Tata 2 Arab; NN] 255

Bayimbitif, Ghilmdar. *Sayasi iqtisad.* Kazan: Shärq Kammünistlarï Märkäz Byürasïnïng Näshriyatï, 1921, 328 pp., 10000 cop. [Tata 1 Arab; NN] 255

"*Bish yïllïq—dürt yïlda*" *zayümï abligatsiyälärïnä almashtïrünï ütkärü tärtibï häm shartlarï.* Kazan: n.p., 1930, 7 pp., n.c. [Tata 2 Arab; NN] 255

5 yïllïq 4 yïlda zayümï auïl jirlärindä taratünïng tärtibi häm shartlarï. Kazan: Tatarstan Finans Ḥalq Kamisariyatï Näshirï, 1930, 62 pp., 6500 cop. [Tata 2 Arab; NN] 255

"*Bish yllïq—dürt ylda*" *zayumïn chgharu, taratu häm bashqa zayum obligatsiälärenä almashtïru shartlarï.* Kazan: Tatpoligraf, 1930, 4 pp., 5000 cop. [Tata 3 Lat; NN] 255

Bödäyli, Mäḥmüd; Kazaköf, Isḥaq. *Ilnï indüstriyäläshdïrü öchin yaḥshï yüllar kiräk.* Kazan: "Tat'aftayül," 1929, 28 pp., 3000 cop. [Tata 2 Arab; NN] 256

Büharin, N. *Dünya ḥüjalïghï häm impiriyalizm.* Kazan: Tatarstan Matbüghat häm Näshriyat Kambinatï Näshrï, 1924, 219 pp., 5000 cop. [Tata 2 Arab; NN] 256

D. S. *Özlksez esh atnasï.* Moscow: SSSR Khalqlarïnïng Üzäk Näshriatï, 1930, 62 pp., 6000 cop. [Tata 3 Lat; NN] 256

Fäḥri, Sh. *Kapiratsiyä häm yäshlär.* Kazan: "Tatsayüz" Basmasï, 1928, 48 pp., 1500 cop. [Tata 2 Arab; NN] 256

Famitski, V. *Patribitl jämghiyätïnïng säüdä ishï.* n.p.: Basdïrüchïsï
Tatsayüz, 1929, 25 pp., 1500 cop. [Tata 2 Arab; NN] 2564
Fäyzüllin, S. *Ka'üpiratsiyä ïshläri.* Moscow: SSSR Ḥalqlarï Üzäk
Näshriyatï, 1924, 71 pp., 4000 cop. [Tata 2 Arab; NN] 2565
Ghümrnï ïstraḥaü itü. Kazan: Däülät Ïstraḥaüïnïng Tatarstan
Kantürï "Tan'straḥ," 1928, 30 pp., 2000 cop. [Tata 2 Arab; NN] 2566
Gladün. *S.S.S.R.nï indüstriyäläshtürü häm auïl ḥüjalïghï-ürman
ïshchïläri.* Kazan: Auïl Ḥüjalïghï-Ürman Ïshchïläri Sayüzïnïng
Tatarstan Büligï, 1930, 104 pp., 2500 cop. [Tata 2 Arab; NN] 2567
Güröf, P. Ya. *Birlashdirilgän auïl kön körüshï salmi türindaghï
dikrit: Süal häm jävablï.* Moscow: Märkäz Shärq Näshriyatï,
1923, 120 pp., 5000 cop. [Tata 2 Arab; CStH, NN] 2568
Güsif, V. *Bezning ḥüjalïq bish yïldan söng nichek bölachaq.* Moscow:
SSSR Ḥalqlarïnïng Üzäk Näshriyatï. 1929, 28 pp., 5000 cop.
[Tata 2 Arab; NN] 2569
Ilnï indüstriyäläshdirügä 500 milyön söm. Moscow: SSSR
Ḥalqlarïnïng Üzäk Näshriyatï, n.d., 40 pp., 20000 cop.
[Tata 2 Arab; NN] 2570
*Indüstriyä zayömï häm krästiyän ḥujalïghï nïghïtü zayömï
abligatsiyälärïn "bish yïllïqnï dürt yïllïqda" zayömï
äbligatsiyälärïnä almash zayömï abligatsiyälärïnä almashdïrü
türinda.* Kazan:SSSR Finans Ḥalq Kamisariyatï Kridit, 1930,
46 pp., 8000 cop. [Tata 2 Arab; NN] 2571
Isḥaqïf, Väli. *Tatarstan jömhüriyätï ḥalq ḥüjalïghïnïng häm
kültüra tözïlïshïnïng 4 yïllïq pirispiktif planïndan töb mamintlar.*
Kazan: Tatarstan Dävlät Plan Kamisiyäsï Basmasï, 1928, 69 pp.,
2500 cop. [Tata 2 Arab; NN] 2572
Izirski, P. *Yazghï chächü kampaniäsnda potribitel kopiratsiäse.*
Moscow: Sintrizdat, 1930, 48 pp., 30000 cop. [Tata 3 Lat; NN] 2573
Kaganovich, A. S. *Daülät zayumnarï.* Moscow: Sintrizdat, 1929,
47 pp., 4000 cop. [Tata 3 Lat; NN] 2574
Kalḥüzlar türinda yalghan häm döreslek. Saratov: SSSR Märkäz
Näshriyätïnïng Tübän Idel Bülegi, 1930, 53 pp., 3000 cop.
[Tata 2 Arab; NN] 2575
Kapiratsiyälärdaghï tüzdïrüchïlar blän nichek köräshirgä. Moscow:
SSSR Ḥalqlarïnïng Üzäk Näshriyatï, 1928, 29 pp., 16000 cop.
[Tata 2 Arab; NN] 2576
Kaütsky, K. *Karl marksnïng iqtisadï täghlimatï.* Moscow: Märkäzi

"Shärq Näshriyatï," 1923, 264 pp., 8000 cop. [Tata 2 Arab; CStH, NN] 2577

Kazaküf, Isḥaq. *Tatarstan baylïghï*. Kazan: Tatarstan Dävlät Näshriyatï Basmasï, 1927, 71 pp., 5000 cop. [Tata 2 Arab; NN] 2578

Khismatullin. *Tatarstanda 5 yïl, III-IV nchï uqu ylï öchen*. Kazan: Tatizdat, 1930, 32 pp., 10000 cop. [Tata 3 Lat; NN] 2579

Khismatullin, Kh. *SSSRda bish yïl IV nche uqu ylï öchen*. Kazan: Tatizdat, 1930, 40 pp., 10000 cop. [Tata 3 Lat; NN] 2580

Kindief. *Kolkhozlar tözeleshndäge möhim burchlar*. Moscow: Sintrizdat, 1930, 47 pp., 50000 cop. [Tata 3 Lat; NN] 2581

Kolkhozlar khäräkäte häm auïl khujalïghïn kütärü. Kazan: Tatizdat, 1930, 21 pp., 5000 cop. [Tata 3 Lat; NN] 2582

Kolkhozlar öchen l'gotalar turnda. Kazan: n.p., 1930, 29 pp., 5000 cop. [Tata 3 Lat; NN] 2583

Kolkhozlargha häm ayrïm khujalïqlargha jingllklär turnda. Sverdlovsk: "Sotsializm Yulï" Redaksiäse häm Uralkoopkhlebsoyuz Näshre, 1930, 12 pp., 5000 cop. [Tata 3 Lat; NN] 2584

Kümäk kilshmä. Kazan: n.p., 1930, 68 pp., 3000 cop. [Tata 3 Lat; NN] 2585

Lokshin, Ë. *Sovetlar soyuzï-kuätle industrial' derzhava*. Kazan: Tatgosizdat, 1945, 64 pp., 10185 cop. [Tata 4 Cyr; DLC] 2586

Mishchiräküf, N. L. *Savit rüsiyäsindä ka'üpiratsiyä*. Moscow: Tsentral'noe Vostochnoe Izdatel'stvo pri N.K.N., 1923, 84 pp., 3000 cop. [Tata 2 Arab; NN] 2587

Molotov. *Kolkhozlar khäräkäte turnda*. Moscow: Sintrizdat, 1930, 34 pp., n.c. [Tata 3 Lat; NN] 2588

Pirifirküvich, M. S. *Chit illärgä chïgarïb satü öchin nindi närsälär ḥäzirlärgä kiräk*. Moscow: "Näshriyat" Kapiratifï, 1928, 67 pp., 3000 cop. [Tata 2 Arab; NN] 2589

Prafsayüzlarnïng bötïn sayüz külämindägï VIIInchï isyizïnïng rizälütsiyäläri. Kazan: Tatarstan Prafsayüzlar Savitï Basmasï, 1929, 83 pp., 1000 cop. [Tata 2 Arab; NN] 2590

Qazan üz ara bürch birïshü öyishmasïnïng 1926nchï yïl birinchï üktäbrdän 1927nchï yïl birinchï üktäbrgä qädär ïshlägän ïshlärï ḥaqinda kingäsh (savit) ḥay'ätïnïng öyishmanïng 5nchï ghadï ghömümi jiyilïshïna maghrüzasï. Kazan: n.p., 1927, 19 pp., 300 cop. [Tata 2 Arab; NN] 2591

Qazan üzäk ïshchïlär kapiratifïnïng 1926–27 yïl atchütï. Kazan: Izdatel'stvo Gazety "Krasnaia Tatariia," 1928, 32 pp., 200 cop. [Tata 2 Arab; NN] 2592

SSSR finans khalïq komisariatï tarafnnan 1929 yïl 14/X, 4/XI, häm 14/XI raslanghan khalq khujalïghïnïng jämäghätläshterlghän siktor molkätlären majbüri strakhau itü qaghidäsenä instruksiä. Kazan: Bastïruchïsï Tatstrakh, 1930, 27 pp., 1000 cop. [Tata 3 Lat; NN] 2593

S.S.S.R.nïng qïsqacha iqtisadi jäghrafiyäsi. Moscow: "Näshriyat" Ka'üpirativï Mätbäghäsï, 1926, 87 pp., 5000 cop. [Tata 2 Arab; NN] 2594

Sarabyanïf, V. *Yanga iqtisadi säyasät*. Kazan: Tatarstan Dävlät Näshriyatï Basmasï, 1926, 54 pp., 10000 cop. [Tata 2 Arab; NN] 2595

Singavatïf, I. A. *Patribitl jämghiyätlärïnïng aqchalarï nindi sümalardan jiyïla häm närsälärgä tötïla*. Kazan: "Tatsayüz," 1928, 51 pp., 1500 cop. [Tata 2 Arab; NN] 2596

Smirnof, I. M. *Auïl khujalïghï kolliktifïnïng proizvodstva planï (skhima)*. Kazan: Tatizdat, 1930, 63 pp., 4000 cop. [Tata 3 Lat; NN] 2597

Stalin. *SSSRda agrar säyasät mäs'äläläre*. Moscow: SSSR Khalqlarïnïng Üzäk Näshriatï, 1930, 39 pp., 50000 cop. [Tata 3 Lat; NN] 2598

Tahirif, M. *Üktäbr rivälütsiyäsï tatarlargha närsä birdï?* Kazan: Tatarstan Üzäk Kämisiyäsï Näshrï, 1928, 82 pp., 3000 cop. [Tata 2 Arab; NN] 2599

Tatarstan dävlät fündï jirlärinä küchïrü türinda qaghidälär. Kazan: n.p., n.d., 7 pp., 1000 cop. [Tata 2 Arab; NN] 2600

Tatarstan jömhüriyätï auïl ḥüjalïghï yangadan tözü häm algha jibärünïng töb börchlärï. Kazan: Tatarstan Jir Ïshlärï Ḥalq Kamisariyatï Basmasï, 1929, 156 pp., 3000 cop. [Tata 2 Arab; NN] 2601

Tatarstan jömhüriyätï külämindä 1930–31 nchï yïlghï auïl ḥüjalïghï salïmï buïncha salm kartchïkalarïn tötdirü öchïn instrüksiyä. Kazan: Tatarstan Finans Ḥalq Kamisariyatï Nashïrï, 1930, 24 pp., 2800 cop. [Tata 2 Arab; NN] 2602

Tatarstan khisap escheläre brläshmäse eshlärenеng khisabï (ORU). Kazan: n.p., 1930, 5 pp., n.c. [Tata 3 Lat; NN] 2603

Tatarstan mitalislar profsoyuzï blän Tatarstan mitaltrisï arasnda

1930-nchï ylgha tözlgen kümäk kilshmä. Kazan: n.p., 1930, 31 pp., 5000 cop. [Tata 3 Lat; NN] 260

Tatarstan potribitel kopiratsiäse 1928–29 ylda. Kazan: Tatsoyuz, 1930, 62 pp., 800 cop. [Tata 3 Lat; NN] 260

Tiksherü komisiäläre häm alarnïng auïldaghï eshe. Kazan: Tatarstan Finans Khalïq Komisariatï Basmasï, 1930, 58 pp., 1200 cop. [Tata 3 Lat; NN] 260

Vasilyiva, K. *Tübängï kapiratiflarda üyränchik ḥatïnqïzlar.* Kazan: Basdïrüchïsï Tatasayüz, 1928, 50 pp., 1000 cop. [Tata 2 Arab; NN] 260

Education

Agapïf, S.; Kaminitski, V.; Kashchinkü, B.; Sakalüf, S. *Yäsh jäghrafiyächï.* Moscow: SSSR Ḥalqlarïnïng Üzäk Näshriyatï, 1928, 180 pp., 7000 cop. [Tata 2 Arab; NN] 260

Äḥmädif, F.; Välid, Gh.; Sattarïf, Sh. *Ïsh häm bilïm.* Öchïnchï üqü kitabï. Moscow: "Näshriyat" Ka'üpirativï Mätbäghäsï, 1926, 248 pp., 30000 cop. [Tata 2 Arab; CStH] 260

Alparov, Gïybad. *Saylanma khezmätlär.* Kazan: Tatgosizdat, 1945, 329 pp., 5185 cop. [Tata 4 Cyr; DLC] 261

Aqbülat, H. Ḥ. *Üqü öyï häm qïzl pöchmaqlarda kötïbḥanä ïshlärï.* Moscow: SSSR Ḥalqlarïnïng Üzäk Näshriyatï, 1928, 60 pp., 3000 cop. [Tata 2 Arab; NN] 261

Aqilat, Gh. *Kötïbḥanänïng üqüchïlarïn öyränü.* Moscow: SSSR Ḥalqlarnïng Üzäk Näshriyatï, 1928, 29 pp., 3000 cop. [Tata 2 Arab; NN] 261

Arïslan, M. *Eshchelär älifbasï: Zurlar öchön.* Moscow: SSSR Khalïqlarïnïng Üzäk Näshriyatï, 1928, 79 pp., 35000 cop. [Tata 3 Lat; NN] 261

Arslanïf, M.; Möḥämmädïf, M. *Ishchïlär älifbasï.* 1nchï bülek. Moscow: SSSR Ḥalqlarïnïng Üzäk Näshriyatï, 1928, 72 pp., 8000 cop. [Tata 2 Arab; NN] 261

Atnaghulof, Salakh. *Uqïtu programnarïbïz häm tärbiä mitodlarïbïz.* Kazan: Tatizdat, 1930, 42 pp., 3200 cop. [Tata 3 Lat; NN] 261

Auïl mäktöplärene nadanlïqnï btrü öchen shulay uq mäghlämät alïr öchen zurlargha proghramma. n.p.: Astpoligraf, n.d., 16 pp., 150 cop. [Tata 3 Lat; NN] 261

I-nche basqïch jäyäüle ghäskäri blem tügäräklärеneng programï. Kazan: Tatarstan Asoaviakhim Sovitï Basmasï, 1930, 52 pp., 1500 cop. [Tata 3 Lat; NN] 2617

Bikchäntäy, Ir'üghlï. *Balalarnï öyränü mitidlarï.* Kazan: Tatarstan Dävlät Näshriyatï, 1929, 126 pp., 3000 cop. [Tata 2 Arab; NN] 2618

Bikchäntäy, Irüghlü. *Qïsqacha pidalügiyä.* Moscow: SSSR Ḥalqlarïnïng Üzäk Näshriyatï, 1925, 208 pp., 3000 cop. [Tata 2 Arab; CStH] 2619

"*Bïtsïn nadanlïq.*" "Bitsïn nadanlïq" yächäykälärï öchin qüllanma. Kazan: Tatarstan Dävlät Näshriyatï Basmasï, 1927, 60 pp., 3000 cop. [Tata 2 Arab; NN] 2620

Brnche basqïch mäktäplärneng I–II–III-nche yllar programïna krtlgän ridaksiä üzgärshläre häm 4-nche yïl öchen program proyktï. Kazan: Tatarstan Mägharif Khalïq Komisariatï Basmasï, 1929, 47 pp., 3000 cop. [Tata 3 Lat; NN] 2621

Brnchi mitüd ḥatï Moscow: "Näshriyat" Ka'üpirativi, 1926, 43 pp., 3000 cop. [Tata 2 Arab; NN] 2622

Brnchï tïl-ädäbiyat känfirinsiyäsï matiriyallarï. Kazan: Tatar Mädäniyätï Yörtïnïng Basmasï, 1927, 199 pp., 3500 cop. [Tata 2 Arab; NN] 2623

Distanïf, Gh.; Burnash, V. *Yanga yul: Az blmne zurlar öchen esh kitabï.* Kazan: Tatizdat, 1929, 61 pp., 2000 cop. [Tata 3 Lat; NN] 2624

F. T. *Kitab düstlarï tügäräklärin öyishdïrü.* Moscow: "Näshriyat" Ka'üpirativï Mätbäghäsï, 1926, 48 pp., 5000 cop. [Tata 2 Arab; NN] 2625

Faleev, G. I.; Perïshkin, A. V. *Fizika: Tulï bulmagan urta häm urta mäktäpneng 6–7 nchï klasslarï öchen däreslek.* Kazan: Tatgosizdat, 1945, 217 pp., 20185 cop. [Tata 4 Cyr; DLC] 2626

Fazlülla, M. *Tatarstandaghï tatar mäktäblärin yangalïqläshtïrü türïnda.* Instrüksiyä ḥatï no. 4. Kazan: Izdanie Akademicheskogo Tsentra Narkomprosa TSSR, 1928, 40 pp., 3000 cop. [Tata 2 Arab; NN] 2627

Fazlulla, M.; Khismätüllin, Kh. *Döres yazu künegüläre.* Kazan: Tatizdat, 1930, 38 pp., 5000 cop. [Tata 3 Lat; NN] 2628

Ghüni, Shähid. *Chojïq qïra'ät kitabï maktab ibtida'iänïng bernchi senäsindä alifba tamamïnda uqutmaq ichün yazïldï.* Kazan: Magharïf Kutubkhanäsi, 1913, 32 pp., n.c. [Tata 1 Arab; CLU] 2629

Grumïf, V.; Karachunskï, V. *Izbach yardämchïsï*. Kazan: Tatarstan Jömhüriätï Dävlät Ḥizmät Saqlïq Kassïsï Basmasï, 1929, 24 pp., 5000 cop. [Tata 2 Arab; NN] 2630

Ḥabib, Ghäbdlḥay; Möbaräkshin, Fazl. "*Yangalif*" *häm yäshlär*. Kazan: Basïb Taratüchïsï "Yangalif" Jämghiyätï, 1927, 23 pp., 2000 cop. [Tata 2 Arab; NN] 2631

Ḥämidulla, Fazïlghan; Ḥabib, Gh. *Tabighät ikskürsiyälärï*. Kazan: Tatarstan Matbüghat–Näshriyat Kambinatï Basmasï, 1925, 116 pp., 3000 cop. [Tata 2 Arab; CStH] 2632

Ḥayri, Q.; Nighmäti, Gh.; Mänsürif, B. *Ïsh häm belem*. Moscow: "Näshriyat" Ka'üpirativï Mätbäghäsï, 1926, 188 pp., 40000 cop. [Tata 2 Arab; CStH] 2633

Ḥayri, Q.; Sattarïf, Sh. *Ish häm belem*. Moscow: "Nashriyat" Ka'üpirativï Mätbäghäsï, 1926, 72 pp., 20000 cop. [Tata 2 Arab; CStH] 2634

Ḥayri, Q.; Sattarïf, Sh. *Ïsh häm belem*. Moscow: "Näshriyät" Ka'üpirativï Mätbäghäsï, 1926, 123 pp., 20000 cop. [Tata 2 Arab; CStH] 2635

Ḥayri, Q.; Sattarïf, Sh. "*Ïsh häm belem*" *alifbasï büincha üqïtü öchin qüllanma*. Moscow: "Näshriyät" Ka'üpirativï Mätbäghäsï, 1926, 31 pp., 5000 cop. [Tata 2 Arab; NN] 2636

Ibrahimif, Ghali; Mansür, Ḥ. *Savit maktäbï*. II. Moscow: SSSR Ḥalqlarïnïng Üzäk Näshriyätï, 1928, 216 pp., 15000 cop. [Tata 2 Arab; NN] 2637

Ibrahimïf, Ghäli; Mansür, Kh. *Savit mäktäbe*. II. Berenche basqïch avïl mäktäpläreneng ikenche uku yïlï öchön esh kitabï. Moscow: SSSR Khalïqlarïnïng Üzäk Näshriyatï, 1928, 159 pp., 30000 cop. [Tata 3 Lat; NN] 2638

Ibrahimof, Gh.; Mansurof, Kh. *Sovit mäktäbe*. II kitab, I bülek. Moscow: SSSR Khalqlarïnïng Üzäk Näshriätï, 1930, 72 pp., 25000 cop. [Tata 3 Lat; NN] 2639

Ibrahimof, Gh.; Mansurof, Kh. *Sovit mäktäbe*. II kitap, II bülek. Moscow: SSSR Khalqlarïnïng Üzäk Näshriatï, 1930, 197 pp., 25000 cop. [Tata 3 Lat; NN] 2640

Ibrahimof, Ghäli; Mansur, Kh. *Savit mäktäbe*. II. Brnche basqïch auïl mäktäpläreneng iknche uqu ylï öchen esh kitabï. Moscow: SSSR Khalqlarïnïng Üzäk Näshriätï, 1929, 183 pp., 40000 cop. [Tata 3 Lat; NN] 2641

Istalin, I. *Shärq ḥalqlarï ünivirsititïnïng säyasï bürchlärï*. Moscow: SSSR Ḥalqlarïnïng Üzäk Näshriyätï, 1925, 32 pp., 10000 cop. [Tata 2 Arab; NN] 2642

Kalliktif. *Yanga il*. Brïnche basqïch mäktäplärneng 3nche uqu ylï öchen tabighiattan esh kitabï. Kazan: Tatizdat, 1930, 192 pp., 20000 cop. [Tata 3 Lat; NN] 2643

Kalliktif. *Yanga il*. Dürtnche uqu ylï öchen töp esh kitabï. Kazan: "Tatizdat," 1930, 336 pp., 20000 cop. [Tata 3 Lat; NN] 2644

Kalliktif. *Yanga il*. 2nche uqu ylï öchen matimatikadan esh kitabï. Kazan: Tatizdat, 1930, 120 pp., 30000 cop. [Tata 3 Lat; NN] 2645

Kalliktif. *Yanga il*. 2nche uqu ylï öchen töp esh kitabï. Kazan: "Tatizdat," 1930, 184 pp., 30000 cop. [Tata 3 Lat; NN] 2646

Karimi, Fatiḥ. *Ijtimaghï tärbiyä: Balalïq yäshindä*. Kazan: Tatarstan Matbüghat häm Näshriyät Kambinatï Näshrï, 1924, 56 pp., 3000 cop. [Tata 2 Arab; NN] 2647

Kiselev. *Geometriyä. Urta mäktäpneng 9–10 klasslarï öchen*. 2nchï kisäk. Kazan: Tatgosizdat, 1945, 115 pp., 10185 cop. [Tata 4 Cyr; DLC] 2648

Kolliktif. *Yanga il*. 2nche uqu ylï öchen töp esh kitabï. Kazan: Tatizdat, 1931, 148 pp., 55000 cop. [Tata 3 Lat; NN] 2649

Kolliktif. *Yanga il*. 3nchï uku yelï öchïn matimatikadan esh kitabï. Kazan: Tatizdat, 1931, 121 pp., 35000 cop. [Tata 3 Lat; NN] 2650

Krüpskaya, N. *Närsägä häm nichek öyranänirgä*. Moscow: SSSR Ḥalqlarïnïng Üzäk Näshriyatï, 1926, 139 pp., 5000 cop. [Tata 2 Arab; NN] 2651

Küchmä kütbḥänälär. Moscow: "Näshriyat" Ka'üpirativï, 1926, 56 pp., 5000 cop. [Tata 2 Arab; NN] 2652

Kürsätmälï händäsä. Kazan: Tatarstan Matbüghat häm Näshriyat Kambinatï Näshrï, 1924, 190 pp., 10000 cop. [Tata 2 Arab; NN] 2653

Likpunktlarda uquchïlar häm uqïtuchïlar öchen kirak bulghan kitaplar ismnege. n.p.: n.p., n.d., 13 pp., 10000 cop. [Tata 2 Arab, 3 Lat; NN] 2654

Mansür, Börhan. *Üqü öylärïnïng bürchlarï*. Moscow: "Näshriyat Ka'üpirativï" Mätbäghäsï, 1925, 33 pp., 5000 cop. [Tata 2 Arab; NN] 2655

Mansürif, Gh. *Yanga auïl*. Moscow: SSSR Ḥalqlarïnïng Üzäk Näshriyatï, 1928, 222 pp., 15000 cop. [Tata 2 Arab; NN] 2656

Maqsüd, Ghäyas. *Qïsqacha jäbr därslärï.* Kazan: Tatarstan Matbüghat häm Näshriyat Kambinatï Näshrï, 1924, 244 pp., 5000 cop. [Tata 2 Arab; NN] 265

Maqṣüdi, Aḥmid Hadi. *Mughallïm avval.* Kazan: Tipo-Litografiia Imperatorskago Universiteta, 1898, 64 pp., n.c. [Tata 1 Arab; NN] 265

Mäktäp eshen proykt mitodï blän oyshtïru. Kazan: Tatizdat, 1930, 82 pp., 3000 cop. [Tata 3 Lat; NN] 265

Möhämmädif, M.; Arslanif, M.; Shamif, Äfzal. *Üqi yaza belemävni bitirüchilärgä yüldash.* Moscow: SSSR Ḥalqlarïnïng Üzäk Näshriyatï, 1926, 175 pp., 2000 cop. [Tata 2 Arab; CStH] 266

Möhämmädif, Märdghäläm; Arslanïf, Miftaḥ. *Krästiyanlär öchin "yanga auïl" älifbasï.* Moscow: SSSR Ḥalqlarïnïng Üzäk Näshriyatï, 1927, 68 pp., 38000 cop. [Tata 2 Arab; CStH] 266

Möḥitdinif, Nasiḥ. *Mäktäbdä jïns tärbiyäsï mäs'ällärï.* Kazan: Tatarstan Mägharïf Ḥalq Kamisariyatï Basmasï, 1928, 100 pp., 4000 cop. [Tata 2 Arab; NN] 266

Möshtäri, Ḥämid. *Jäbr.* Bïrnchï kisäk. Kazan: Tatarstan Mätbüghat häm Näshriyat Kambinatï Näshrï, 1925, 227 pp., 3000 cop. [Tata 2 Arab; CStH] 266

Mühämmädif, Märdghaläm. *Mäktäbdä sälämätlik.* Moscow: "Nashriyat" Ka'üpirativï, 1926, 80 pp., 5000 cop. [Tata 2 Arab; NN] 266

Nadiyif, N.; Asmanïf, N. *Mäktäbdä dissiplina mäs'äläläri.* Kazan: Tatarstan Mägharif Ḥalq Kamisariyatï Basmasï, 1928, 104 pp., 4000 cop. [Tata 2 Arab; NN] 266

Nävshirvanïf, Zinät. *Tatar-bashqord tilïndä yanga älifba.* Moscow: SSSR Khalqlarïnïng Märkäz Näshriyatï, n.d., 19 pp., 2000 cop. [Tata 2 Arab, 3 Lat; NN] 266

Nighmät, S.; Yafay, R. *Tulï khisap kurïsï.* Kazan: Yangalif, 1929, v and 430 pp., 5000 cop. [Tata 3 Lat; NN] 266

Nughaiybik, Gh. *Yanga älifba.* Kazan: "Yangalif" Jämghiyate, 1928 3d ed., 36 pp., 10000 cop. [Tata 3 Lat; NN] 266

Nughaiybik, Gh.; Fazlulla, M. *Alifba: Balalar öchön.* Kazan: "Yangalif," 1928, 83 pp., 100000 cop. [Tata 3 Lat; NN] 266

III nche Ural ölkä yangalif konfirinsiäsenen qärarlarï (29–31 avghus 30 yïl). Sverdlovsk: Ölkä Yangalif Komitetï Basmasï, 1930, 55 pp., 1000 cop. [Tata 3 Lat; NN] 267

Oktäbr älifbasï. Sverdlovsk: n.p., n.d., 13 pp., n.c. [Tata 2 Arab, 3 Lat; NN] 2671

Pidagüglarnïng belemlärïn kütärü institütïnïng tatar bülïgï infarmatsiyä ḥatï. Kazan: n.p., 1929, 4 pp., 4000 cop. [Tata 2 Arab; NN] 2672

Pirilman, Ya. I. *Matimatika öchïn üqü kitabï: Keshï—tabighat—tiḥnika.* Kazan: Tatarstan Matbüghat-Näshriyat Kambinatï Basmasï, 1925, 183 pp., 10000 cop. [Tata 2 Arab; CStH] 2673

Polänski, M. *Kul'turalï kolkhozgha.* Moscow: Sintrizdat, 1930, 52 pp., 15000 cop. [Tata 3 Lat; NN] 2674

Potemkin, M. P.; Terekhov, P. G. *Geografiyä: Zürlar mäktäbe öchen dareslek.* Kazan: Tatgosizdat, 1940, 120 pp., 30000 cop. [Tata 4 Cyr; DLC] 2675

Qazan vuzlarïna häm rabfaklarïna qabul itü shartlarï häm snau programmarï. Kazan: Tatarstan Magharif Khalq Komisariatïnïng Ghilmi Uzäge, 1930, 58 pp., 25000 cop. [Tata 3 Lat; NN] 2676

Qïzïl yul. Ikenche kitap. Kazan: "Tatizdat," 1929, 36 pp., n.c. [Tata 3 Lat; NN] 2677

Qïzïl yül: Balalar älifbasï. Kazan: Tatarstan Matbüghat-Näshriyat Kambinatï Basmasï, 1925, 88 pp., 100000 cop. [Tata 2 Arab; CStH] 2678

Qïzïl yul: Balalar älifbasï. Kazan: "Tatizdat," 1929, 16 pp., n.c. [Tata 3 Lat; NN] 2679

Qorbanghäliyef, M.; Ghäzizef, R. *Urïslar öchön tatar tele däreslege: II-nche kisäk, II-nche basqïch mäktäplärneng 6-nchï giruppilarï öchön.* Kazan: "Tatizdat," 1929, 88 pp., 7000 cop. [Tata 3 Lat; NN] 2680

Qorbanghäliyef, M.; Ghäzizef, R. *Urïslar öchön tatar tele däreslege: Berenche kisäk, II-nche basqïch mäktäplärneng 5-nche yilï öchön.* Kazan: "Tatizdat," 1929, 80 pp., 5000 cop. [Tata 3 Lat; NN] 2681

Qörbanghäliyif, M.; Bädigh, Ḥüja. *Rüs mäktäblärï öchin tatar tïlï därslïgï.* Bernchï kitab. Kazan: Tatarstan Matbüghat-Nashriyat Kambinatï Basmasï, 1925, 162 pp., 5000 cop. [Tata 2 Arab; CStH] 2682

Qörbanghäliyif, M.; Baghdanïf, Gh. *Matimatikï därslärï.* II.

Kazan: Tatarstan Dävlät Näshriyatï Basmasï, 1928, 149 pp., 10000 cop. [Tata 2 Arab; NN] 2683

Qörbanghäliyif, M.; Baghdanïf, Gh. *Matimatikï därslärï, berenchï basqïch mäktäblärïnïng: Berïnchï yïlïnda üqïtü öchin.* Kazan: Tatarstan Dävlät Näshriyatï Basmasï, 1925, 177 pp., 15000 cop. [Tata 2 Arab; CStH] 2684

Qörbanghäliyif, M.; Baghdanïf, Gh. *Matimatikï därslärï, berenchï basqïch mäktäblärïnïng: Ikïnchï yïlïnda üqïtü öchin.* Kazan: Tatarstan Dävlät Näshriyatï Basmasï, 1925, 149 pp., 25000 cop. [Tata 2 Arab; CStH] 2685

Qörbanghäliyif, M.; Baghdanïf, Gh. *Matimatikï därslïgï.* 3nchï kisäk. Kazan: Tatarstan Dävlät Näshriyatï, 1929, 79 pp., 15000 cop. [Tata 2 Arab; NN] 2686

Qörbanghäliyif, M.; Baghdanïf, Gh. *Riyaziyat därsliklärï.* I. Kazan: Tatarstan Matbüghat häm Näshriyat Kambinatï Näshrï, 1924, 140 pp., 2000 cop. [Tata 2 Arab; NN] 2687

Qörbanghäliyif, M.; Baghdanïf, Gh. *Riyaziyat därsliklärï.* III. Kazan: Tatarstan Matbüghat häm Näshriyat Kambinatï Näshrï, 1924, 95 pp., 10000 cop. [Tata 2 Arab; NN] 2688

Qörbanghäliyif, M.; Baghdanïf, Gh. *Riyaziyat därslikärï.* IV. Kazan: Tatarstan Matbüghat häm Näshriyat Kambinatï Näshrï, 1924, 108 pp., 10000 cop. [Tata 2 Arab; NN] 2689

Qörbanghäliyif, M.; Ghäzizif, R. *Rüslargha tatar tïlï öyrätü öchin qüllanma häm därslik.* Kazan: Tatarstan Dävlät Näshriyatï Basmasï, 1925, 135 pp., 5000 cop. [Tata 2 Arab; CStH] 2690

Qorbanghäliyif, M.; Säyfi, F. *Tabighi jäghrafiya därslïgï.* Kazan: Matbüghat häm Näshriyat Ishlärï Kambinatïnïng "Sharq" Mätbäghäsï, 1923, 135 pp., 25000 cop. [Tata 2 Arab; NN] 2691

Qörbanghäliyif, Möḥitdin; Isḥaqïf, Ḥasan. *Yavrüpa illärï jäghrafiyä därslïgï.* Kazan: Tatarstan Dävlät Näshriyatï Basmasï. 1925, 172 pp., 10000 cop. [Tata 2 Arab; CStH] 2692

Qörbanghaliyif, Saliḥ. *Kimiya: Ikïnchï basqïch mäktäblär, ïshchï fakültitlarï, kürslar häm üzlikdän öyränir öchin qüllanma.* Kazan: Tatarstan Matbüghat–Näshriyat Kambinatï, 1926, 360 pp., 5000 cop. [Tata 2 Arab; CStH] 2693

Qzïl yül. Ikncht kitab. Kazan: Tatarstan Dävlät Näshriyatï Basmasï, 1928, 138 pp., 20000 cop. [Tata 2 Arab; NN] 2694

Qzïl yül: Balalar älifbasï. Kazan: Tatarstan Dävlät Näshriyatï Basmasï, 1928, 96 pp., 30000 cop. [Tata 2 Arab; NN] 2695

Qzïl yül. I nchï basqïch mäktäblärnïng I nchï üqü yïlï öchin. Berenchï kitab. Kazan: Tatarstan Dävlät Näshriyatï Basmasï, 1925, 232 pp., 40000 cop. [Tata 2 Arab; CStH] 2696

Qzïl yül: I nchï basqïch mäktäblärnïng I nchï üqü yïlï öchin. Ikenchï kitab. Kazan: Tatarstan Dävlät Näshriyatï Basmasï, 1925, 312 pp., 30000 cop. [Tata 2 Arab; CStH] 2697

Qzïl yül: I nchï basqïch mäktäblärnïng I nchï üqü yïlï öchin. Öchïnchï kitab. Kazan: Tatarstan Dävlät Näshriyatï Basmasï, 1925, 400 pp., 25000 cop. [Tata 2 Arab; CStH] 2698

"Qzïl yül" ismindägï älifba büincha Üqïtü öchin mitüdikä ḥatï. Kazan: Tatarstan Matbüghat–Näshriyat Kambinatï Basmasï, 1925, 12 pp., 3000 cop. [Tata 2 Arab; CStH] 2699

R.S.F.S.R. häm T.S.S.R. mäghärïf khalïq komisariatlarï: Diagram häm kartagramnar tözüneng äsasläre. Kazan: Izdanie Tat. Org. Instituta PKP pri Narkomprose RSFSR i TSSR, 1929, 20 pp., 3000 cop. [Tata 3 Lat; NN] 2700

R.S.F.S.R. häm T.S.S.R. mägharif khalïq komisariatlarï pidagoglarnïng blmnären kutärü institutïneng tatar bülege: Chittä torïp uqïtu siktoru khalïq khujalïghïnïng biologia nigzläre. Kazan: Izd.Tat. Org. Instituta P.K.R. pri NKP RSFSR i TSSR, 1929, 20 pp., 3000 cop. [Tata 3 Lat; NN] 2701

RSFSR häm TSSR Mägharif khalïq komisariatlarï: Pidologiä, 8 nche sabaq. Kazan: Izdanie Tat. Otd. I.P.K.P. pri NKP RSFSR i TSSR, 1929, 23 pp., 3000 cop. [Tata 3 Lat; NN] 2702

RSFSR häm TSSR Mägharif khalïq kamisaryatlarï. Pidaguglarnïng belemnären kütärü inestitutïnïng Tatar bülege: Chittä torop uqïtu siktïrï. Khalïq khujalïghïnïng fizike-tikhnik nigezläre. Kazan: Izdanie Tat. Otd. Instituta Povysheniia Kvalifikatsii Pedagogov, 1929, 27 pp., 3000 cop. [Tata 3 Lat; NN] 2703

RSFSR Tatarïstan Mägharif khalïq kamisariyatï. Pidaguglarnïng belemnären kütärü inestitutïnïng Tatar bülege: Pidalogiye, 5 nche sabaq. Arganizäm konestïtutsiyäse. Kazan: Izdanie Otd. Instituta Povysheniia Kval. Pedagoga, 1929, 17 pp., 3000 cop. [Tata 3 Lat; NN] 2704

Räkhmätullin, I.; Bïykof, P. *Tatarstanda ghomumi mäjbüri*

bashlanghïch uqu. Kazan: Tatizdat, 1930, 32 pp., 3000 cop. [Tata 3 Lat; NN] 270

Rïbkin, N. *Geometrik mäsïälälär jïentïgï.* 2nche kisäk-stereometriyä. Kazan: Tatgosizdat, 1945, 96 pp., 10000 cop. [Tata 4 Cyr; DLC] 270

Rïbkin, N. *Geometrik mäsïälälär jïentïgï-planimetriyä.* Kazan: Tatgosizdat, 1945, 121 pp., 15000 cop. [Tata 4 Cyr; DLC] 270

Rüs maktablärndä häm vaqtlï kürslarda Tatar tïlï öyrätü öchin janlï söyläshü tïlï sabaqlarï. Berïnchï kitab. Kazan: Tatarstan Matbüghat häm Näshriyat Kambinatï Näshrï, 1923, 198 pp., 3000 cop. [Tata 2 Arab; NN] 270

Saghalüf, S. N.; Bilavin, A. F.; Üvarïf, P. P.; Kaminitski, V. A. *Mäktäblär öchin jäghrafiyä atlasï.* Moscow: SSSR Ḥalqlarïnïng Üzäk Näshriyatï, 1928, 21 pp., 6000 cop. [Tata 2 Arab; NN] 270

Säghid, Kärim; Äḥmädiyif, Ghabdülla. *Zö'alügiyä.* I. Kazan: Tatarstan Matbüghat häm Näshriyat Kambinatï Näshrï, 1924, 404 pp., 10000 cop. [Tata 2 Arab; NN] 271

Saliḥiyä, Zöhrä. *Mäktäbkä qädär tärbiyä: Qüllanma.* Kazan: Tatarstan Matbüghat–Näshriyat Kambinatï Basmasï, 1925, 46 pp., 3000 cop. [Tata 2 Arab; CStH] 271

Salikhov, M. *Yanga taṣnif qiyinghan üzi üzini üyratküch tatarlarghä ruschä, ruslarghä tatarchä süylashürghä häm üqürghä.* Kazan: Tip. Imp. Universiteta (Izd. A. A. Dubrovina), 1893, 54 pp., n.c. [Tata 1 Arab; MH] 271

Sättarif, Shärif. *Qzïl armiyst älifbasï.* Moscow: SSSR Ḥalqlarïnïng Üzäk Näshriyatï, 1925, 64 pp., 5000 cop. [Tata 2 Arab; CStH] 271

Sattarof, Shärif. *Qzïl armies älifbasï.* Moscow: SSSR Khalqlarïnïng Üzäk Näshriyatï, 1930, 103 pp., 25000 cop. [Tata 3 Lat; NN] 271

Sattarof, Shärif. *Qzïl ärmies: "Qzïl armies" älifbasnnan song brnche esh kitabï.* Moscow: SSSR Khalqlarïnïng Üzäk Näshriatï, 1929, 200 pp., 10000 cop. [Tata 3 Lat; NN] 271

Shabad. *Mäktäbkä qädär tärbiyä närsä häm ülni öchin kiräk.* Moscow: "Näshriyat" Kapiratifï, 1928, 24 pp., 3000 cop. [Tata 2 Arab; NN] 271

Shabanov, Kh.; Nigmatullin, Sh. *Tatar tele däreslege.* 3nche kisäk. Kazan: Tatgosizdat, 1945, 77 pp., 35000 cop. [Tata 4 Cyr; DLC] 271

Shänasi, Ghabdülla. *Fizika därslïgï.* Kazan: Tatarstan Mätbüghat häm Näshriyat Kambinatï Näshrï, 1924 4th ed., 167 pp., 5000 cop. [Tata 2 Arab; NN] 2718

Shänasi, Ghabdülla. *Fizika därslïgï.* Iknchï bülim. Kazan: Tatarstan Matbüghat häm Näshriyat Kambinatï Näshrï, 1924, 81 pp., 5000 cop. [Tata 2 Arab; NN] 2719

Shanasi, Ghabdülla. *Fizika därslïgï.* I. Kazan: Tatarstan Dävlät Näshriyatï Basmasï, 1925, 132 pp., 10000 cop. [Tata 2 Arab; CStH] 2720

Shanasï, Ghabdülla. *Fizika därslïgï: Yaqtïlïq.* III. Kazan: Tatarstan Dävlät Näshriyatï Basmasï, 1925, 43 pp., 5000 cop. [Tata 2 Arab; CStH] 2721

Shäräf, Gh.; Aliksiyif, I. A. *Yanga auïl.* II. Kazan: Tatarstan Dävlät Näshriyatï, Basmasï, 1928, 100 pp., 15000 cop. [Tata 2 Arab; NN] 2722

Sokalof, I. N. *Igen ungïshïn kütärü köräshndä mäktäp häm uqïtuchï.* Kazan: Pidagoglarnïng Blmnären Kütärü Institutïnïng Tatar Bülege Basmasï, 1929, 46 pp., 5000 cop. [Tata 3 Lat; NN] 2723

T.S.S.J. Mägharif khalq komisariatï: Kolkhozlarda balalar mäydanï öyshtïru turnda mitod khatï. Kazan: Tatar Pidagoglarïnïng Blmnären Kütärü Institutï Basmasï, 1930, 29 pp., 3000 cop. [Tata 3 Lat; NN] 2724

Tahir, S. *Kasmagrafiyä därslïgï.* Kazan: Tatarstan Dävlät Näshriyatï Basmasï, 1928, 157 pp., 5000 cop. [Tata 2 Arab; NN] 2725

Tahirif, R.; Ḥäbibüllina, Z. *Linin häm kötibḫanä.* Kazan: Tatarstan Dävlät Näshriyatï, 1928, 32 pp., 3000 cop. [Tata 2 Arab; NN] 2726

Tashmökhämmät. *Fätkhulla khäzrät.* Kazan: n.p., 1928, 110 pp., 5000 cop. [Tata 3 Lat; NN] 2727

Tatar älifbäsï. Kazan: Tatarstan Matbüghat häm Näshriyat Kambinatï Näshrï, 1924, 63 pp., 10000 cop. [Tata 2 Arab; NN] 2728

"*Tatarïstannï öyränü jämghiyäte*"*neng ustafï.* Kazan Tatarïstannï Öyränü Jämghiyäte," 1929, 12 pp., 1000 cop [Tata 3 Lat; NN] 2729

Tetyürev, V. A. *Tabigatï beleme.* I. Kazan: Tatgosizdat, 1945, 104 pp., 25000 cop. [Tata 4 Cyr; DLC] 2730

Timerbulat, Gh. *Savit mäktäbe.* I. Moscow: SSSR Khalïqlarïnïng Üzäk Näshriyatï, 1928, 112 pp., 38000 cop. [Tata 3 Lat; NN] 2731

Timerbulat, Gh. *Savit mäktäbe: Älifba.* Moscow: SSSR Khalïqlarïnïng Üzäk Näshriyatï, 1928, 94 pp., 38000 cop. [Tata 3 Lat; NN] 2732
Timerbülat, Gh. *Savit mäktäbï.* I. Moscow: SSSR Ḥalqlarïnïng Özäk Näshriyatï, 1928, 142 pp., 8000 cop. [Tata 2 Arab; NN] 2733
Timerbülat, Gh. *Savit mäktäbï: Älifba.* Moscow: SSSR Ḥalqlarïnïng Üzäk Näshriyatï, 1928, 108 pp., 15000 cop. [Tata 2 Arab; NN] 2734
Timrbulat, Gh. *Sovit mäktäbe.* I. Moscow: SSSR Khalqarïnïng Üzäk Näshriatï, 1929, 126 pp., 50000 cop. [Tata 3 Lat; NN] 2735
Tsuzmer, M. Yä. *Zoölogiyä.* VI khäm VII klasslarï öchen. Kazan: Tatgosizdat, 1945, 254 pp., 30185 cop. [Tata 4 Cyr; DLC] 2736
Unlï vaqlanmalarnï, qabatlav bülü häm pïrasintlar. Kazan: Tatarïstan Devlet Näshriatï, 1929, 67 pp., 15000 cop. [Tata 3 Lat; NN] 2737
Uqïy-yaza blmäüche zurlarnï uqïtu öchen program. Kazan: n.p., 1929, 56 pp., 10000 cop. [Tata 3 Lat; NN] 2738
Üqü kitablarï. Kazan: Tatarstan Matbüghat häm Näshriyat Kambinatï Näshrï, 1924, 115 pp., 25000 cop. [Tata 2 Arab; NN] 2739
Uqu öyläre, kötpkhanälär kul'tura yortlarïna häm qzïl pochmaqlarnïng böyek öktyäbr rivolütsiäseneng 13 yllïq bäyrämenä qatnashularï turnda mitodika khatï. Kazan: Tatpoligraf, 1930, 3 pp., 700 cop. [Tata 3 Lat; NN] 2740
Üqüchïlar blän ürmangha chïghïb yörü. Kazan: Tatarstan Matbüghat häm Näshriyat Kambinatï Näshrï, 1924, 31 pp., 3000 cop. [Tata 2 Arab; NN] 2741
Ürta idel ölkä mägharif büligïnïng mitid savitï qarshïndaghï tatar mitid kamisiyäsïnïng I nchï ḥatï: I–II basqïch savit mäktäbläri, likpünktlar, auïl üqü öylärï häm mäktäbkächä tärbiyä yürtlarïnda yangalïq blän ish alïb barü turïnda. Samara: Ürta Idel Ülkä Mägharif Bülïgï, 1929, 16 pp., 1000 cop. [Tata 2 Arab; NN] 2742
Ustaf. Kazan: Tatarïstan Yangalif Jämghiyäte "Yangalif," 1928, 30 pp., 5000 cop. [Tata 3 Lat; NN] 2743
Üzlegengnän belem alu mitïtlarï. Kazan: Pidaguglarnïng Belemnären Kütärü Inestitutïnïng Tatar Bülege Basmasï, 1929, 30 pp., 3000 cop. [Tata 3 Lat; NN] 2744
Vagapov, A. A. *Üzi üzidän üyrangüch tatlar uruschä uruslar tatarchä suylashurga ön öchönchi mrtbä baṣlïldï.* Kazan: Tipo-Litografiia

Imperatorskago Universiteta, 1899, 64 pp., n.c. [Tata 1 Arab; MH] 2745

Välit, Gh.; Arslan, M. *Eshchelär älïfbasï: Zurlar öchen.* Moscow: SSSR Khalqarïnïng Üzäk Näshriatï, 1930, 88 pp., 30000 cop. [Tata 3 Lat; NN] 2746

Yangalif öch aylïghïna qarata qullanma matiriallar. Kazan: Tatizdat, 1929, 36 pp., 10000 cop. [Tata 3 Lat; NN] 2747

Yangï mäktäb: Tatarcha älifba. Ufa: Bashknigä, 1927, 76 pp., 10000 cop. [Tata 2 Arab; NN] 2748

Yösüpif, Farisi. *Mäktäb akvariyümï.* Kazan: Tatarstan Dävlät Näshriyatï Basmasï, 1926, 40 pp., 3000 cop. [Tata 2 Arab; CStH] 2749

Yüsef, Nurïy. *Berenche basqïch esh mäktäpläre öchön matimatika sabaqlarï: Berenche uqu yïlï.* Moscow: SSSR Khalïqlarïnïng Üzäk Näshriyatï, 1929, 102 pp., 30000 cop. [Tata 3 Lat; NN] 2750

Yüsif, Nüri. *Matimatika därslärï.* Moscow: "Näshriyat" Kapiratifï, 1928, 141 pp., 7000 cop. [Tata 2 Arab; NN] 2751

Yüsüpif, Farisi. *Mäktäblärdä girbarilar häm üsmlikär kalliksiyälärï tözü yüllarï.* Kazan: Tatarstan Dävlät Näshriyatï Basmasï, 1925, 24 pp., 3000 cop. [Tata 2 Arab; CStH] 2752

Yüsüpif, Nüri. *Matimatika därslärï.* Moscow: "Nashriyat" Ka'üpirativï Mätbäghäsï, 1926, 119 pp., 30000 cop. [Tata 2 Arab; CStH] 2753

Zäyni, Kh.; Iskhaqov, F.; Burnash, V. *Krästiän älifbasï.* Moscow: Sintrizdat, 1930, 80 pp., 500000 cop. [Tata 3 Lat; NN] 2754

Geography

Äḥmäd, S. *Jäghrafiyä mitüdikasï.* Kazan: Tatarstan Matbüghat häm Näshriyat Kambinatï Näshrï, 1924, 39 pp., 3000 cop. [Tata 2 Arab; NN] 2755

Äḥmäd, S. *Tatarstannïng tabighi jäghrafiyäsï.* Kazan: Tatarstan Dävlät Näshriyatï Basmasï, 1925, 56 pp., 10000 cop. [Tata 2 Arab; CStH] 2756

Barkov, A. S.; Polovinkin, A. A. *Fizik geografiyä.* Kazan: Tatgosizdat, 1945, 137 pp., 30185 cop. [Tata 4 Cyr; DLC] 2757

Ḥarrabin, J. *Bötïn dönyanïng tariḥi-iqtisadi jäghrafiyäsï.* Kazan: Tatarstan Matbüghat–Näshriyat Kambinatï Basmasï, 1925, 188 pp., 10000 cop. [Tata 2 Arab; CStH] 2758

Isḥaqïf, Ḥ. *S.S.J.S. (Satsiyal savit jömhüriyätlärï sayüzï)nïng qïsqacha jäghrafiyäsï.* Kazan: Tatarstan Dävlät Näshriyatï Basmasï, 1928 2d ed., 183 pp., 10000 cop. [Tata 2 Arab; NN] 2759

Isḥaqïf, Ḥ. *S.S.J.S.nïng qïsqacha jäghrafiyäsï.* Kazan: Tatarstan Dävlät Näshriyatï Basmasï, 1925, 184 pp., 15000 cop. [Tata 2 Arab; CStH] 2760

Säyfi, Fatih-Qazanlï. *Yavrüpadan tïsh illär jäghrafiyäsï.* Kazan: Tatarstan Dävlät Näshriyatï Basmasï, 1925, 96 pp., 10000 cop. [Tata 2 Arab; CStH] 2761

Government

A. B. *Süghishqa süghish.* Moscow: SSSR Ḥalqlarïnïng Üzäk Näshriyatï, 1929, 68 pp., 5000 cop. [Tata 2 Arab; NN] 2762

Abezgaüz, G.; Prütasïf, A. *Partiyanï tanü.* Bernchï bülek. Moscow: SSSR Ḥalqlarïnïng Üzäk Näshriyatï, 1927, 315 pp., 10000 cop. [Tata 2 Arab; NN] 2763

Abezgaüz, G.; Prütasïf, A. *Partiyanï tanü.* 2nchï bülek. Moscow: SSSR Ḥalqlarïnïng Üzäk Näshriyatï, 1927, 347 pp., 10000 cop. [Tata 2 Arab; NN] 2764

Abu ʿlghanïf, Khalil. *Üṣül-i jadidkä qarashï berïnchi adïm.* Kazan: "Ürnäk" Mäṭbäghäsi, 1911, viii and 32 pp., n.c. [Tata 1 Arab; NNC*] 2765

Adaratski, V. *Lininizmnïng töb nigezlärï.* Kazan: Tatarstan Matbüghat häm Näshriyat Kambinatï Näshrï, 1925, 55 pp., 3000 cop. [Tata 2 Arab; NN] 2766

Aftanümiyälï tatarstan satsiyal sävitlär jömhüriyätïnïng ḥalq kamisarlarï sävitï türïnda palazhiniyä. Kazan: Üzäk Bashqarma häm Ḥalq Kamisarlarï Sävitï Basmasï, 1928, 10 pp., 250 cop. [Tata 2 Arab; NN] 2767

Ähli, Ḥ. *Qïzïl ärmiyä häm üktäbir.* Kazan: Tatarstan Dävlät Näshriyatï, 1928, 32 pp., 3000 cop. [Tata 2 Arab; NN] 2768

Äḥmädif, F. *Savitlar sayüzïnïng tüzilishï.* Moscow: "Näshriyat" Kaʾüpirativi, 1926, 49 pp., 5000 cop. [Tata 2 Arab; NN] 2769

---

* Microfilm

Ämirḥan, Mäḥmüd. *Yaqïn-ürta shärq vä yavrüpa impiriyalizmï.* Kazan: Tatarstan Matbüghat häm Näshriyat Kambinatï Näshrï, 1923, 112 pp., 3000 cop. [Tata 2 Arab; NN] 2770

Appazitsiyä türïnda ibdäsh büḥarin dakladï häm bïrläshkän plinüm qararï. Kazan: Tatarstan Dävlät Näshriyatï Basmasï, 1927, 48 pp., 1500 cop. [Tata 2 Arab; NN] 2771

Äspirantski, M. *Alar sönggḥï märtäbä jingildïlär: Kamsamüllar türmïshïndan.* Moscow: "Näshriyat" Ka'üpirativï Mätbäghäsï, 1926, 48 pp., 5000 cop. [Tata 2 Arab; NN] 2772

Atnaghülïf, Ṣälaḥ. *Shärq ḥatïn-qïzlarï häm ijtimaghï rivalütsiyä.* Kazan: Izdanie Biuro Komnarvostoka pri TsKRKP(b), 1921, 87 pp., 10000 cop. [Tata 2 Arab; NN] 2773

Auïl kamsamüllarï arasïnda ïshläü qüllanmalarï jiyïntïghï. Moscow: SSSR Ḥalqlarïnïng Üzäk Näshriyatï, 1925, 84 pp., 5000 cop. [Tata 2 Arab; NN] 2774

Auïl kamsamüllarïnïng säyasï belemi. Moscow: SSSR Ḥalqlarïnïng Üzäk Näshriyatï, 1925, 64 pp., 5000 cop. [Tata 2 Arab; NN] 2775

Auïl sävitlärï yanïnda häm kalḥüzlarda tözilgän ḥökümät bürch häm saqlïq kassasï ïshlärïnä bülïshlïq kämisiyälärï öchin qüllanma. Kazan: n.p., 1930, 6 pp., 5000 cop. [Tata 2 Arab; NN] 2776

Auïllarda säyasï belem mäktäbläri öchin pragramma. I kitab. Moscow: SSSR Ḥalqlarinïng Üzäk Näshriyatï, 1925, 48 pp., 6000 cop. [Tata 2 Arab; NN] 2777

Avinavitski, Ya. L. *Süghïshïrgha tilämibïz, lakin süghïshqa ḥäzirbiz.* Moscow: SSSR Ḥalqlarïnïng Üzäk Näshriyatï, 1927, 30 pp., 5000 cop. [Tata 2 Arab; NN] 2778

I häm II nchi basqïch kamsamül mäktäbläri vä auïldaghï kamsamül säyasi tügäräkläri öchin prügrammalar. Moscow: "Näshriyat" Ka'üpirativi, 1926, 56 pp., 3000 cop. [Tata 2 Arab; NN] 2779

1918 nche elda Kazannï ak interventlardan azat itü. Kazan: Tatgosizdat, 1940, 90 pp., 5150 cop. [Tata 4 Cyr; DLC] 2780

Birdniküf, A.; Svitlüf, F. *Kammünistlar partiyäsïnä kïrüchï här ber ïshchï närsä belirgä tiyish?* Kazan: Tatarstan Matbüghat häm Näshriyat Kambinatï Näshrï, 1924, 75 pp., 5000 cop. [Tata 2 Arab; NN] 2781

Bish yïl ichindä. Kazan: Tip. im. "Kamil' Iakub," 1925, 288 pp., n.c. [Tata 2 Arab; MH] 2782

Bödäyli, M. *Kammünistnïng bernchï älifbasï.* Kazan: Tatarstan Matbüghat häm Näshriyat Kambinatï Näshri, 1924, 88 pp., 5000 cop. [Tata 2 Arab; NN] 2783

Bödäyli, Mäḥmüd. *Tübän yächäykälärgä baghïshlab karl mark häm fridrid änglis tarafïndan yazïlghan kammünistlar manifistï.* Kazan: Tatarstan Matbüghat häm Näshriyat Kambinatï Näshrï, 1924, 127 pp., 5000 cop. [Tata 2 Arab; NN] 2784

Börnash, Fätḥi. *Müpr (rivalyütsiyä köräshchïlärïnä bäynälmiläl yardäm öyishmasï).* Kazan: Tatarstan Matbüghat häm Näshriyat Kambinatï Näshrï, 1924, 50 pp., 5000 cop. [Tata 2 Arab; NN] 2785

Büdzhitläre bulghan rayon bashqarma komititläre häm auïl sovitläreneng hisap yörtü häm otchut birüläre turnda instruksiä. Kazan: Tatarstan Finans Khalïq Komisariatï Näshere, 1929, 44 pp., 1500 cop. [Tata 3 Lat; NN] 2786

Buḥarin, N. *Impiriyalizm diktatürasïndan pralitariyat diktatürasinä.* Moscow: Izdanie Tsent. Biuro Komörganizatsii Narodov Vostoka Pri TsK RKP(b), n.d., 79 pp., n.c. [Tata 2 Arab; NN] 2787

Büḥarin, N. *Satsiyalizmgha yül häm ïshchï-krästiyän sayüzï.* Moscow: SSSR Ḥalqlarïnïng Märkäz Näshriyatï, 1927, 136 pp., 6000 cop. [Tata 2 Arab; CStH, NN] 2788

Büḥarin, N. *V.L.K.S.M. ïshï türïnda.* Moscow: SSSR Ḥalqlarïnïng Üzäk Näshriyatï, 1926, 95 pp., 6000 cop. [Tata 2 Arab; NN] 2789

Büḥarin, N.; Priyabrazhinski. *Kammünizm älifbasï.* Kazan: Tatarstan Matbüghat häm Näshriyat Kambinatï Näshrï, 1924, 141 pp., 8000 cop. [Tata 2 Arab; NN] 2790

Bükharin, N. *Kammünist (balshivik)lar praghrammasï.* Moscow: Izd. Tsentr. Biuro Komorganizatsii Narodov Vostoka, 1920, 129 pp., n.c. [Tata 1 Arab; NN] 2791

Butun rusiyä musulmanlarining 1917 nchi yildä 1–11 maydä mäskäudä bulghan ʿumumi isiyizdining prutaqullari. Petrograd: "Amanat" Shirkati Maṭbaʿäsi, 1917, 470 pp., n.c. [Tata 1 Arab; NNC*] 279

Chichirin, Giyürgi. *Yäshlär intrnatsiyanalï tariḥïndan parchalar.* Moscow: SSSR Ḥalqlarïnïng Üzäk Näshriyatï, 1925, 176 pp., 5000 cop. [Tata 2 Arab; NN] 279

*Microfilm

Dimanshtäyn. *Bötin dönya süghïshïnïng ün illïghï.* Moscow: SSSR Ḥalqlarïnïng Üzäk Näshriyatï, 1924, 60 pp., 3000 cop. [Tata 2 Arab; NN] 2793

Dimanshtäyn, S. *XV ïsiyizd häm anïng qararlarï.* Moscow: SSSR Ḥalqlarïnïng Üzäk Näshriyatï, 1928, 118 pp., 3000 cop. [Tata 2 Arab; NN] 2794

Dinisïf, S. A. *Tiksherü kämisiäse paychïnïng khüjalïq küze.* Kazan: Bastïruchïsï Tatsayuz, 1929, 31 pp., 2000 cop. [Tata 3 Lat; NN] 2795

Dmitriyïva, M. *Silsävitlär häm diligatkï.* Kazan: Tatarstan Dävlät Näshriyatï, 1929, 62 pp., 2500 cop. [Tata 2 Arab; NN] 2796

Düblinsgi, I. *Milli ghäskär närsä.* Kazan: Tatarstan Dävlät Näshriyatï, 1928, 40 pp., 3000 cop. [Tata 2 Arab; NN] 2797

Ëngelïs, F. *Lyudvig Feyerbakh häm nemets klassik filosofiyäseneng tämam buluï. Feyerbakh türïnda Marks.* Kazan: Tatgosizdat, 1940, 63 pp., 10000 cop. [Tata 4 Cyr; DLC] 2798

Fäyzüllina, Ḥ. *Üktäbr balalarï: Zäki, Ghäli.* Moscow: SSSR Ḥalqlarïnïng Üzäk Näshriyatï, 1928, 26 pp., 3000 cop. [Tata 2 Arab; NN] 2799

Fedoseev, P. *Vatan sugïshï shartlarïnda VKP(v) tarikhïnïng kïskacha kursïn öyränü.* Kazan: Tatgosizdat, 1943, 64 pp., 5070 cop. [Tata 4 Cyr; NN] 2800

Furmanof, D. *Qzïl disant.* Kazan: Yangalif, 1930, 64 pp., 3000 cop. [Tata 3 Lat; NN] 2801

Ghäli, Ḥäsän. *Sörav-javab kichälärï.* Kazan: Tatarstan Dävlät Näshriyatï, 1928, 27 pp., 3000 cop. [Tata 2 Arab; NN] 2802

Ghäliyif, Gh. *Yaḥshï aparat häm satsiyalizm tözïlïshin yaḥshïrtü öchin.* Kazan: Tatarstan Dävlät Näshriyatï, 1929, 68 pp., 1500 cop. [Tata 2 Arab; NN] 2803

al-Gharabi, Mavlana Abusaghid. *Hindüstan anglitirä büyündüghi altïndä.* Moscow: SSSR Ḥalqlarïnïng Markaz Näshriyatï, 1924, 116 pp., 3000 cop. [Tata 1 Arab; NN] 2804

Ghimran, Z. *Appazitsiyägä qarshï faktlar häm sanlar.* Kazan: Partiyänïng Tatarstan Ölkä Kämititï Näshrï, 1927, 92 pp., 1500 cop. [Tata 2 Arab; NN] 2805

Ghöbäydy, Gh. *Il ïshï.* Kazan: Müprnïng Tatarstan Ölkä Kämititï Basmasï, 1929, 14 pp., 3000 cop. [Tata 2 Arab; NN] 2806

Ghömärïf, Äḥmäd. *Marksizm häm darvinizm: Antün panni—kük*

mäqaläsï büincha. Kazan: Tatarstan Mätbüghat häm Näshriyat Kambinatï Näshrï, 1923, 44 pp., 3000 cop. [Tata 2 Arab; NN] 2807

Grishin, M. I. *Linin yülindan.* I bülek. Moscow: SSSR Ḥalqlarïnïng Üzäk Näshriyatï, 1928, 514 pp., 4000 cop. [Tata 2 Arab; NN] 2808

Grishin, M. I. *Linin yülindan.* II bülek. Moscow: SSSR Ḥalqlarïnïng Üzäk Näshriyatï, 1927, 544 pp., 4000 cop. [Tata 2 Arab; NN] 2809

Grishin, M. I. *Linin yülindan.* II bülek. Moscow: SSSR Ḥalqlarïnïng Uzäk Näshriyatï, 1928, 544 pp., 4000 cop. [Tata 2 Arab; CStH] 2810

Ibrahimïf, Ghalimjan. *Böyök üktäbr rivalyütsiyäsï häm prülitariyat diktatürasï.* Kazan: Tatar-Satsiyal Savitlar Jömhüriyätïnïng Däv̈lät Näshriyatï, 1922, 147 pp., n.c. [Tata 2 Arab; NN] 2811

Il'ich sabaqlarï: Lininizm türinda qïsqacha qüllanma. Moscow: SSSR Ḥalqlarïnïng Üzäk Näshriyatï, 1925, 261 pp., 7000 cop. [Tata 2 Arab; NN] 2812

Istalin. *Auïlgha yöz blän.* Kazan: Tatarstan Dävlät Näshriyatï Basmasï, 1925, 29 pp., 10000 cop. [Tata 2 Arab; NN] 2813

Istalin, I. *Partiyänïng auïldaghi alda türghan ïshläri.* Moscow: SSSR Ḥalqlarïnïng Üzäk Näshriyatï, 1925, 16 pp., 5000 cop. [Tata 2 Arab; NN] 2814

Istalin, I. *Trütskizm yäḥüd lininizm.* Moscow: SSSR Ḥalqlarïnïng Üzäk Näshriyatï, 1925, 68 pp., 5000 cop. [Tata 2 Arab; NN] 2815

Istirlin, S. *Süghïsh vaqïtïnda ḥalq qïzïl armiyägä närsä blän yardäm äyttä ala.* Moscow: Sintr Izdat, 1929, 31 pp., 3000 cop. [Tata 2 Arab; NN] 2816

Istüchka. *Sävitlär kanstitütsiyäsï.* Kazan: Tatarstan Dävlät Näshriyatï, 1928, 102 pp., 3000 cop. [Tata 2 Arab; NN] 2817

Izmailïf, Sh. *R.K.P.gä krüchi ïshchïlär närsä belïrgä tiyshi.* Moscow: SSSR Ḥalqlarï Üzäk Näshriyatï, 1924, 47 pp., 5000 cop. [Tata 2 Arab; NN] 2818

Kaganüvich, L. M. *Rüsiyä kammünist (balshivik)lar partiyäsï nichek tözilgän.* Kazan: Tatarstan Matbüghat häm Näshriyat Kambinatï Näshrï, 1924, 54 pp., 10000 cop. [Tata 2 Arab; NN] 2819

Kaghanovich. *VKP(b) üzäk komititïnïng nuyäber plinumï närsä äytte.* Moscow: SSSR Khalqlarïnïng Üzäk Näshriatï, 1930, 64 pp., 25000 cop. [Tata 3 Lat; NN] 2820

Kammunis internatsiyanalnïng program häm ustafï. Moscow: SSSR Khalïqlarïnïng Üzäk Näshriyatï, 1929, 81 pp., 5000 cop. [Tata 3 Lat; NN] 2821

Kamsamül häm anïng bürchlarï "lininizm älifbasï" na östämä. Moscow: SSSR Ḥalqlarïnïng Üzäk Näshriyatï, 1928, 37 pp., 5000 cop. [Tata 2 Arab; NN] 2822

Kamsamüllarnïng I nchï basqïch säyasi mäktäbï. Moscow: Näshriyat Ka'üpirativï Mätbäghäsï, 1925, 102 pp., 5000 cop. [Tata 2 Arab; NN] 2823

Kavalinkü, P. *Säyasï belïm kitabï.* Moscow: SSSR Ḥalqlarïnïng Üzäk Näshriyatï, 1924 2d ed., 141 pp., 3000 cop. [Tata 2 Arab; CStH, DLC, NN] 2824

Kazaküf, A. *Balshiviklär partiyäsï yalchïlarïnïng faydalarïn nichek yaqlï.* Kazan: Auïl Ḥüjalïghï–Ürman Ishchïlärï Prafsayüzïnïng Tartarstan Bülïgï, 1928, 32 pp., 3000 cop. [Tata 2 Arab; NN] 2825

Kidrïf, I. *Pravliniyä häm tikshïrü kämisiyälärïnä kimlärnï saylargha?* Kazan: Tatsayüz Basmasï, 1929, 16 pp., 2500 cop. [Tata 2 Arab; NN] 2826

Kimrad. *R.L.Y.K.S. üstafï.* Kazan: Tatarstan Dävlät Näshriyatï Basmasï, 1926, 108 pp., 2000 cop. [Tata 2 Arab; NN] 2827

Kirzhinsïf; Liyüntiyif. *Lininizm älifbasï.* Moscow: SSSR Ḥalqlarïnïng Üzäk Näshriyatï, 1928, 575 pp., 10000 cop. [Tata 2 Arab; NN] 2828

Kolkhoz khäräkätndä partiä liniäsen bozulargha qarshï. Moscow: Sintrizdat, 1930, 28 pp., 75000 cop. [Tata 3 Lat; NN] 2829

Komsomolnïng sugïshchan traditsiyäläre. Kazan: Tatgosizdat, 1945, 77 pp., 10185 cop. [Tata 4 Cyr; DLC] 2830

Kontr-rivolütsion Soltanghäliefchelkkä qarshï: Jüntïq. Kazan: "Tatizdat," 1929, 99 pp., 3000 cop. [Tata 3 Lat; NN] 2831

Köräsh yïllarï. Moscow: SSSR Ḥalqlarïnïng Üzäk Näshriyatï, 1927, 131 pp., 4000 cop. [Tata 2 Arab, CStH] 2832

Kosaryof, A. *Böten soyuz—ber bärmä brigada.* Kazan: Tatizdat, 1930, 68 pp., 3000 cop. [Tata 3 Lat; NN] 2833

Krästiyän ïshlärï türïndaghï gharizalarnï häm shikayätlärnï nichek yazargha häm qaya birirgä. Kazan: Tatarstan Yüstitsiyä Ḥalq Kamisariyatï Näshrï, 1929, 172 pp., 2000 cop. [Tata 2 Arab; NN] 2834

Krüpskaya, N. K. *Linin mägharif türindaghï vasiyatlarï*. Moscow: SSSR Ḥalqlarïnïng Üzäk Näshriyatï, 1925, 46 pp., 5000 cop. [Tata 2 Arab; NN] 2835

Küznitsüf, I. *Linin häm kristiyanlar*. Kazan: Tatarstan Matbüghat häm Näshriyat Kambinatï Näshrï, 1924, 56 pp., 5000 cop. [Tata 2 Arab; DLC, NN] 2836

Lenin, V. I. *Närsä ul "khalïk duslarï" häm alar sotsial-demokratlarga karshï nichek sugïshalar*. Kazan: Tatgosizdat, 1941, 219 pp., 5070 cop. [Tata 4 Cyr; DLC] 2837

Lenin, V. I. *Üz-bilgelänü turïndagï diskussiyä yomgaklarï*. Kazan: Tatgosizdat, 1940, 44 pp., 10000 cop. [Tata 4 Cyr; DLC] 2838

Libkniḥt, Karl. *Jiyntiq*. Moscow: SSSR Ḥalqlarïnïng Üzäk Näshriyatï, 1925, 55 pp., 5000 cop. [Tata 2 Arab; CStH, NN] 2839

Linin, N. *1905 yïl*, Moscow: SSSR Ḥalqlarïnïng Üzäk Näshriyatï, 1926, 302 pp., 8000 cop. [Tata 2 Arab; CStH] 2840

Linin, N. *Impirializm*. Moscow: Märkäz Shärq Näshriyatï, 1924, 174 pp., 5000 cop. [Tata 2 Arab; CStH, NN] 2841

Linin, N. *Impiriyalizm kapitalizmnïng ing yanga basqïchï*. Moscow: SSSR Ḥalqlarïnïng Üzäk Näshriyatï, 1926, 180 pp., 5000 cop. [Tata 2 Arab; CStH] 2842

Linin, N. *Karl marks: Marksnïng linin qälämï blän yazïlghan qïsqacha tärjïmä'iy ḥalï häm marksizm täghlimatï*. Kazan: Tatarstan Matbüghat häm Näshriyat Kambinatï Näshrï, 1924, 56 pp., n.c. [Tata 2 Arab; NN] 2843

L'vof, B. *Dozornïng sughïsh khzmäte*. 24 räsem blän. Samara: Tsentral'noe Izdatel'stvo; Sredne-Volzhskoe Kraevoe Otdelenie, 1930, 52 pp., 5000 cop. [Tata 3 Lat; NN] 2844

Mansürïf, Gh. *Tatar pravakatrlarï*. Moscow. SSSR Ḥalqlarïnïng Üzak Näshriyatï, 1927, 76 pp., 3000 cop. [Tata 2 Arab; NN] 2845

Mansürïf, Ghasim. *Berïnchï rivalütsiyä yïllarnda tatarlar*. Moscow: SSSR Ḥalqlarïnïng Üzäk Näshriyatï, 1926, 158 pp., 5000 cop. [Tata 2 Arab; CStH] 2846

Mansürïf, Ghasim. *Kammünistlar partiyäsï häm milliyät mäs'äläsï*. Kazan: Tatarstan Matbüghat häm Näshriyat Kambinatï Näshrï, 1923, 391 pp., 3000 cop. [Tata 2 Arab; NN] 2847

Markïf, Q. *Süghïsh belïmïn öyranü nigä kiräk*. Kazan: Tatarstan Davlät Näshriyatï, 1928, 48 pp., 3000 cop. [Tata 2 Arab; NN] 2848

Marks, K.; Ingils, F. *Kammünistlar partiyäsining manifisti.* Moscow: Sharq Baṣmakhanäsi, 1918, 46 pp., n.c. [Tata 1 Arab; DLC] 2849

Maybirg, B.; Zütsinkï, M. *Bötön dönya eshchelärenеng oyoshmasï.* Moscow: SSSR Khalïqlarïnïng Üzäk Näshriyatï, 1929, 98 pp., 3000 cop. [Tata 3 Lat; NN] 2850

Milli idarädä tatar kaditlarï ni ïshlägänlar. Moscow: Sharq Baṣmakhanäsi, ⟨1918⟩, 56 pp., n.c. [Tata 2 Arab; DLC] 2851

Möbarakshin, F.; Mirsäy. *Yanga auïl tözüdä kamsamüllar.* Kazan: Tatarstan Dävlät Näshriyatï Basmasï, 1928, 54 pp., 3000 cop. [Tata 2 Arab; NN] 2852

Möḥtar, Ghabdülla. *Kammünist balalar qüzghalïshï.* Moscow: SSSR Ḥalqlarï Üzäk Näshriyatï, 1924, 43 pp., 5000 cop. [Tata 2 Arab; NN] 2853

Möḥtar, Ghäbdülla. *Yäsh piyanirlar isdälïgï.* Moscow: "Nashriyat" Ka'üpirativï Mätbäghäsï, 1925, 96 pp., 5000 cop. [Tata 2 Arab; NN] 2854

Müpr närsä? Moscow: Müpr Üzäk Kamititi, 1924, 48 pp., 5000 cop. [Tata 2 Arab; NN] 2855

Müstaqay, Q. *Pra'izvüdstïva kingäshmäläri nichïk ïshlärgä tiyish.* Kazan: Tatarstan Prafisiyanal Sayüzlar Savitï Basmasï, 1928, 175 pp., 2000 cop. [Tata 2 Arab; NN] 2856

Navaküvski, I. S. *Ün yïllïq körash häm tözïlïsh.* Moscow: SSSR Ḥalqlarïnïng Märkäz Näshriyatï, 1927, 163 pp., 4000 cop. [Tata 2 Arab; NN] 2857

Nighmäti, Gh. *Kammünizm türïnda.* Moscow: SSSR Ḥalqlarinïng Üzäk Näshriyatï, 1924, 93 pp., 4000 cop. [Tata 2 Arab; NN] 2858

Nilsen, V. *Kimnïng un yllïghïna nichek khäzrlänrgä.* Moscow: SSSR Khalqlarïnïng Üzäk Näshriatï, 1929, 32 pp., 6000 cop. [Tata 3 Lat; NN] 2859

Öch lüzingï, ïshchï-krästiyän dävlätï mäs'äläsï häm krästiyänlär mäs'äläsï büincha partiyänïng öch töb lüzingïsï türïnda. Kazan: Tatarstan Dävlät Näshriyatï Basmasï, 1928, 46 pp., 3000 cop. [Tata 2 Arab; NN] 2860

Palänski, S. *Linin ibdäshnïng yäshlär türïnda äytkän süzlärï: Tügäräklär öchin matiriyallar.* Moscow: "Näshriyat" Ka'üpirativï Mätbäghäsï, 1926, 40 pp., 5000 cop. [Tata 2 Arab; NN] 2861

Palänski, S. *V.I. lininnïng mägharif türïnda süzlärï.* Moscow: "Näshriyat" Ka'üpirativï Mätbäghäsï, 1926, 23 pp., 3000 cop. [Tata 2 Arab; NN] 2862

Palänski, S. N. *Lininnïng ḥalq mägharifï türïndaghï üylarï.* Moscow: "Näshriyat" Ka'üpirativï Mätbäghäsï, 1925, 31 pp., 5000 cop. [Tata 2 Arab; NN] 2863

Parizh kammünasï: Dakladchilar öchin matiriyal. Kazan: Tatarstan Matbüghat häm Näshriyat Kambinatï Näshrï, 1925, 32 pp., 3000 cop. [Tata 2 Arab; NN] 2864

Parsin, Möḥämmäd. *Yäsh lininchïlär.* Kazan: Tatarstan Matbüghat häm Näshriyat Kambinatï Näshrï, 1924, 45 pp., 5000 cop. [Tata 2 Arab; NN] 2865

Parsin, Möḥämmäd. *Yäshlär intrnatsiyanalï ḥäräkätindän yashlär bäynälmilälinïng ïshtütgard häm birn kanfirinsiyäläri: I nchi häm II nchi bäynälmiläl küngrislar.* Kazan: Tatar Satsial Shüralar Jömhüriyäti Dävlät Näshriyatïnïng Yäshlär Bülekchäsi Näshriyatï, n.d., 63 pp., 5000 cop. [Tata 2 Arab; NN] 2866

Partiyä auïlda ni ïshlärgä tiyish? Kazan: Tatarstan Matbüghat häm Näshriyat Kambinatï Näshrï, 1924, 102 pp., 5000 cop. [Tata 2 Arab; NN] 2867

Pavlüvich, M. P. (M. Viltman). *Ülïm häm hälakät intrnatsiyanalï.* Kazan: Izdanie Tsentr. Biuro Musul'manskikh Kommunisticheskikh Organizatsii RKP(b), n.d., 248 pp., n.c. [Tata 2 Arab; NN] 2868

Pionirlar slyutïnïïg nakazï; pionirlar khäräkäteneng khäle häm burchlarï turnda. Kazan: Tatizdat, 1930, 93 pp., 3000 cop. [Tata 3 Lat; NN] 2869

Qannï aqchalar. Kazan: Tatizdat, 1930, 63 pp., 5000 cop. [Tata 3 Lat; NN] 2870

Qazan shähäri häm yïlgha ariyaghï raiyünï ïshchï häm qïzl ärmiyä dipütatlarï sävitinïng ḥisabïna matiriyallar. Kazan: Shähär Sävitining Näshri, 1929, 69 pp., 150 cop. [Tata 2 Arab; NN] 2871

Qörban, Bari. *Tormïsh blän: Komsomolnïng "yanga" esh tärtipläre.* Kazan: Tatizdat, 1930, 61 pp., 3000 cop. [Tata 3 Lat; NN] 2872

Qzïl ärmiä safndaghï partiä yächäykälärenä instruksiä. Kazan: Tatizdat, 1930, 36 pp., 5000 cop. [Tata 3 Lat; NN] 2873

R.K.P.(b) *tatarstan ölkä kämititïnïng agitprüp bülïgï: Trütskinïng lininizmgä qarshï köräshï.* Kazan: Tatarstan Matbüghat häm Näshriyat Kambinatï Näshrï, 1924, 152 pp., 5000 cop. [Tata 2 Arab; NN]   2874

Radomski. *Brnche may.* Moscow: Sintrizdat, 1930, 37 pp., 12000 cop. [Tata 3 Lat; NN]   2875

Rafäs, M. *Qïzïl armiya türïnda.* Moscow: SSSR Halqlarïnïng Üzäk Näshriyatï, 1924, 62 pp., 3000 cop. [Tata 2 Arab; NN]   2876

Ravinski, L. *Partiyänïng 15 nchï ïsyïzdï türïnda auïl yäshlärï närsä bïlïrgä tiyish.* Moscow: SSSR Halqlarïnïng Üzäk Näshriyatï, 1928, 154 pp., 3000 cop. [Tata 2 Arab; NN]   2877

Razumof. *VKP(b)ning XV nche Tatarstan ölkä konfirinsiäse otchotï.* Kazan; Tatizdat, 1930, 160 pp., 5000 cop. [Tata 3 Lat; NN]   2878

Rizhüf, A. *Yäsh piyanirlar: Jiyntïq.* Moscow: SSSR Halqlarïnïng Üzäk Näshriyatï, 1926, 134 pp., 8000 cop. [Tata 2 Arab; NN]   2879

Rüsiyä kammünistlar partiyäsïnïng XIII nchï ïsyïzdï qärarlarï. Kazan: Tatarstan Matbüghat häm Näshriyat Kambinatï Näshrï, 1924, 176 pp., 3000 cop. [Tata 2 Arab; NN]   2880

SSSR Verkhovnïy sovetïnïng altïnchï sessiyäse: Stenografiyä otchetï. n.p.: SSSR Verkhovnïy Sovetï Basmasï, 1940, 599 pp., 3000 cop. [Tata 4 Cyr; DLC]   2881

SSSR Verkhovnïy sovetïnïng zhidenche sessiyäse: Stenografiyä otchetï. Moscow: SSSR Verkhovnïy Sovetï Basmasï, 1940, 219 pp., 3000 cop. [Tata 4 Cyr; DLC]   2882

Sarabiyanïf, V. *Tarïhi matiriyalizm.* Moscow: SSSR Halqlarïnïng Üzäk Näshriyatï, 1925, 284 pp., 7000 cop. [Tata 2 Arab; CStH]   2883

Sarükin, V. *Böyik üktäbr piyanirlar blän ütïrïsh.* Moscow: SSSR Halqlarïnïng Üzäk Näshriyatï, 1927, 36 pp., 4000 cop. [Tata 2 Arab; NN]   2884

Satsiyal savit rispüblikälärï sayüzïnïng bashqarma kamititï manifistï. Moscow: SSSR Halqlarïnïng Üzäk Näshriyatï, 1927, 31 pp., 4000 cop. [Tata 2 Arab; NN]   2885

Savit vïlasï: Az belemle zurlar öchön. Moscow: SSSR Khalïqlarïnïng Üzäk Näshriyatï, 1929, 70 pp., 6000 cop. [Tata 3 Lat; NN]   2886

Säyasi ütïrïshlarï alïb barüchïlar öchin qüllanma. Moscow: Dävlät Ghäskäri Näshriyat Näshrï, 1926, 463 pp., 4000 cop. [Tata 2 Arab; CStH]   2887

Shähär säyasi belem mäktäbläri öchin pragramma. II kitab. Moscow: SSSR Ḥalqlarining Üzäk Näshriyatï, 1925, 72 pp., 6000 cop. [Tata 2 Arab; NN] 2888

Shahiäkhmitof, Z. *Jingel kavalïriä.* Kazan: Tatizdat, 1930, 106 pp., 3000 cop. [Tata 3 Lat; NN] 2889

Shibayif, I. *IV nchï bötïn sayüz külämindägï savitlar ïsyizdïnïng qärarlarï.* Moscow: SSSR Ḥalqlarïnïng Üzäk Näshriyatï, 1927, 50 pp., 3000 cop. [Tata 2 Arab; NN] 2890

Shibaylü, G. *Auïlda ïshläv türïnda V.K.P.(b) nïng XV nchï ïsyizdï.* Moscow: SSSR Ḥalqlarïnïng Üzäk Näshriyatï, 1928, 64 pp., 4000 cop. [Tata 2 Arab; NN] 2891

Shivilüv, Y. *Auïlda müpr.* Kazan: Müprnïng Tatarstan Ölkä Kamititï Basmasï, 1929, 31 pp., 3000 cop. [Tata 2 Arab; NN] 2892

Sichüf, P. A. *Qïzïl ghäskärnïng köchï närsädä.* Moscow: "Näshriyat" Ka'üpirativï Mätbäghäsï, 1926, 53 pp., 3000 cop. [Tata 2 Arab; NN] 2893

Singalivich, S. P. *Mäktäbdä lininizm.* Kazan: Tatarstan Dävlät Näshriyatï Basmasï, 1926, 115 pp., 4000 cop. [Tata 2 Arab; NN] 2894

Stalin, I. *RKP(b)nïng XIV konferentsiyäseneng ësh yomgaklarïna karata.* Kazan: Tatgosizdat, 1940, 37 pp., 10000 cop. [Tata 4 Cyr; DLC] 2895

Stalin, I. *Sovetlar soyuzïnïng büyek vatan sugïshï turïnda.* Kazan: Tatgosizdat, 1945, 158 pp., 35185 cop. [Tata 4 Cyr; DLC] 2896

Stalin, I. V. *Böyek Oktyabr' sotsialistik revolyutsiyäseneng 27 ellïgï.* Kazan: Tatgosizdat, 1944, 31 pp., 30185 cop. [Tata 4 Cyr; DLC] 2897

T.K.Ü. ïstüdintï T.K.Ü.V.K.P.(b) yachäykäsï ürganï nüyäbr 1927 nchï yïl. n.p.: n.p., 1927, n.pp., 500 cop. [Tata 2 Arab; NN] 2898

Tamishin, M. I.; Kazlüf, F. F. *Partiyanï tanü.* Moscow: SSSR Ḥalqlarïnïng Üzäk Näshriyatï, 1927, 119 pp., 10000 cop. [Tata 2 Arab; NN] 2899

Tatar kommunistlarïnïng chittän torïp uqu univirsitite säyasi iqtisat. Zadania 3. Kazan: n.p., 1930, 32 pp., 1500 cop. [Tata 3 Lat; NN] 2900

Tatarstan jir ïshlärï ḥalq kamsariyatïnïng auïl ḥüjalïghï idaräsï. Kazan: Tatpoligraf, 1929, 8 pp., 5000 cop. [Tata 2 Arab; NN] 2901

Tatarstan S.S. jömhüriyätï ḥökümätï ïshlärïnïng töb yömghaqlarï. Kazan: Tatarstan Ḥalq Kamisarlarï Sävitï Mätbäghäsï, 1929, 133 pp., 500 cop. [Tata 2 Arab; NN] 2902

Tatief, D. *Aviatsiä sughshta.* Samara: Tsintrizdat Urta Idel Kray Bülege, 1930, 50 pp., 5000 cop. [Tata 3 Lat; NN] 2903

Tayshin, M. I.; Kazlüf, F. F. *Partiyänï tanü.* III bülek. Moscow: SSSR Ḥalqlarïnïng Üzäk Näshriyatï, 1927, 286 pp., 10000 cop. [Tata 2 Arab; NN] 2904

Tipief, Sh. *Milliät, milli kul'tura.* Moscow: SSSR Khalqlarïnïng Üzäk Näshriatï, 1929, 90 pp., 5000 cop. [Tata 3 Lat; NN] 2905

Tirigulof, Ibraḥim. *Äträttä sughïsh eshläre.* Kazan: Tatizdat, 1929, 56 pp., 3000 cop. [Tata 3 Lat; NN] 2906

IX. chaqrïlïsh Tatarstan üzak bashqarma komititïnïng II-sissiäse: Qärarlarï. Kazan: Tatizdat, 1932, 67 pp., 5000 cop. [Tata 3 Lat; DLC] 2907

Tümski *Üktäbr rivalyütsiyäsï ïshchïlärgä närsä birdï.* Moscow: SSSR Ḥalqlarïnïng Üzäk Näshriyatï, 1928, 39 pp., 3000 cop. [Tata 2 Arab; CStH, NN] 2908

Ülyanïf-Linin, V. I. *Dävlät häm rivalyütsiyä.* Moscow: SSSR Millätläri Üzäk Näshriyatï, 1924, 192 pp., 5000 cop. [Tata 2 Arab; CStH, NN] 2909

XVI-Tatarstan ölkä partiä konfirinsiäse qärarlarï. Kazan: Tatizdat, 1932, 27 pp., 10000 cop. [Tata 3 Lat; DLC] 2910

Ürazmöḥämmädïf, M. *Beznïng bäyrämlär.* Moscow: SSSR Ḥalqlarïnïng Üzäk Näshriyatï, 1927, 120 pp., 6000 cop. [Tata 2 Arab; NN] 2911

V. I. linin äsarlärï kristiyänlär türïnda. Kazan: Tatarstan Matbüghat-Näshriyat Kambinatï Basmasï, 1925, 27 pp., 10000 cop. [Tata 2 Arab; NN] 2912

V. I. lininnïng satsiyal tärbiyä türïnda. Moscow: "Näshriyat" Ka'üpirativi, 1926, 36 pp., 4000 cop. [Tata 2 Arab; NN] 2913

V.K.P.(b)nïng 15 nchï kanfirinsiyäsï: Mäqalä häm rizalütsiyälär. Moscow: "Näshriyat" Ka'üpirativï Mätbäghäsï, 1926, 120 pp., 4000 cop. [Tata 2 Arab; CStH] 2914

V.K.P.(b) XV nchï ïsyizdïnïng rizalyütsiyä häm qararlarï, 2–19 nchï dikäbïr, 1927 nchï yïl. Moscow: SSSR Ḥalqlarïnïng Üzäk Näshriyatï, 1928, 116 pp., 5000 cop. [Tata 2 Arab; CStH, NN] 2915

V.K.P.(b) üzäk kämititï plinümï tarafïndan chïgharïlghan qararlar, 24 nchï nüyäbïr, 1928 nchï yïl. Kazan: Tatarstan Dävlät Näshriyatï, 1928, 54 pp., 11500 cop. [Tata 2 Arab; NN] 2916

VLKSMning VI konfirinsiä rizolütsiäläre. Moscow: SSSR Khalqlarïnïng Üzäk Nashriatï, 1930, 58 pp., 5000 cop. [Tata 3 Lat; NN] 2917

Valütski. *Ilnï saqlaüda zavüd häm qïrlar nishlärgä tiyish.* Kazan: Bernchï Üqchï Diviziyä Säyasi Bülïgï Qaraüïnda Basïldï, 1929, 28 pp., 3000 cop. [Tata 2 Arab; NN] 2918

Vladimir ilyich linin äsärlärï: bötïn dönya rivalyütsiyäsï häm kamintirn mäs'äläläri. Kazan: Tatarstan Matbüghat-Näshriyat Kambinatï Basmasï, 1925, 32 pp., 10000 cop. [Tata 2 Arab; CStH] 2919

Vladimir ilyich linin äsärlärï: kammünistlar intrnatsiyanalï. Kazan: Tatarstan Dävlät Näshriyatï Basmasï, 1926, 170 pp., 5000 cop. [Tata 2 Arab; CStH] 2920

Vladimir ilyich linin äsärlärï: krästiyänlär häm rivalyütsiyä. Kazan: Tatarstan Matbüghat-Näshriyat Kambinatï Basmasï, 1925, 212 pp., 5000 cop. [Tata 2 Arab; CStH] 2921

Vladimir ilyich linin äsärlärï: krästiyänlär türïnda. Kazan: Tatarstan Matbüghat Näshriyat Kambinatï Basmasï, 1925, 31 pp., 10000 cop. [Tata 2 Arab; CStH] 2922

Vladimir ilyich linin äsärlärï: Linin häm üktäbr. Kazan: Tatarstan Dävlät Näshriyatï, 1928, 84 pp., 3000 cop. [Tata 2 Arab; NN] 2923

Vladimir ilyich linin äsärlärï: partiyä türïnda. Kazan: Tatarstan Matbüghat-Näshriyat Kambinatï Basmasï, 1925, 211 pp., 5000 cop. [Tata 2 Arab; CStH] 2924

Vladimir ilyich linin äsärlärï: partiyä türïnda. Kazan: Tatarstan Matbüghat-Näshriyat Kambinatï Basmasï, 1925, 32 pp., 10000 cop. [Tata 2 Arab; NN] 2925

Vladimir ilyich linin äsärlärï: pralitariyat diktatürasï. Kazan: Tatarstan Matbüghat-Näshriyat Kambinatï Basmasï, 1925, 23 pp., 10000 cop. [Tata 2 Arab; NN] 2926

Vladimir ilyich linin äsärlärï: yäshlär türïnda. Kazan: Tatarstan Matbüghat Näshriyat Kambinatï Basmasï, 1925, 68 pp., 10000 cop. [Tata 2 Arab; NN] 2927

Volkof, I. *Auldaghï massavi eshlär: Auïl sovitlarï rayon häm volïs bashqarma komititläre qarshndaghï komisiä (siksiä)lär turnda bulghan polozhiniälärne populär angnatu.* Kazan: TSSJ Üzäk Bashqarma Komitite Oyshtïru Büleqe Näshre, 1929, 94 pp., 1250 cop. [Tata 3 Lat; NN] 2928

Vülis häm töbäk bashqarma kämititlärinïng ḥisab yörtüläri häm ḥisab birüläri türinda instrüksiyä. Kazan: Tatarstan Maliyä Ḥalq Kamisariyatï Büdzhit Idaräsï Näshïrï, 1928, 51 pp., 1000 cop. [Tata 2 Arab; NN] 2929

Yirmiyif, Q. 1. *Linin häm ïshchïlär sinfi.* 2. *Linin blän öchrashü.* Moscow: "Näshriyat Ka'üpiratifï" nïng Näshrï, 1924, 23 pp., 5000 cop. [Tata 2 Arab; NN] 2930

Yulbashchïga antïbïz. Kazan: Tatgosizdat, 1944, 65 pp., 10000 cop. [Tata 4 Cyr; DLC] 2931

Zäliyif, Kamal. *Üram chatïndan kammünagha.* See under *Literature*, Number 3269. 2932

Zinüvyif. *Linin häm kamintirn.* Kazan: Tatarstan Dävlät Näshriyatï Basmasï, 1926, 60 pp., 10000 cop. [Tata 2 Arab; NN] 2933

Zinüvyif, G. *Ïshchïlär sinfï häm krästiyänlär.* Kazan: Tartarstan Dävlät Näshriyatï Basmasï, 1926, 88 pp., 10000 cop. [Tata 2 Arab; NN] 2934

Zinüvyif, G. *Lininizm nigïzïndä.* Kazan: Tatarstan Matbüghat häm Näshriyat Kambinatï Näshrï, 1924, 54 pp., 5000 cop. [Tata 2 Arab; DLC, NN] 2935

Züin, B. *Qïzïl armiyänïng köchï närsädä.* Moscow: SSSR Ḥalqlarïnïng Üzäk Näshriyatï, 1928, 43 pp., 5000 cop. [Tata 2 Arab; NN] 2936

History

Bädighullin. *Litva.* Kazan: Yangalif, 1929, 32 pp., 3000 cop. [Tata 3 Lat; NN] 2937

Birïn, M. *Adamnïng tabighät blän köräshövï.* Moscow: SSSR Ḥalqlarïnïng Üzäk Näshriyatï, 1926, 159 pp., 6000 cop. [Tata 2 Arab; NN] 2938

Birïn, M. *Adämnïng tabighat blän köräshüvï.* Moscow: SSSR Ḥalqlarïnïng Üzäk Näshriyatï, 1924, 76 pp., 4000 cop. [Tata 2 Arab; NN] 2939

Bish yïl ïchïndä 1920—VI 25 1925. Kazan: n.p., 1925, 288 pp., n.c. [Tata 2 Arab; NN] 2940

Bolghar khärabäläre kürgäzmäse. Kazan: T.M.Y. Basmasï (Tatar Mädäniyäte Yorto), 1929, 50 pp., 350 cop. [Tata 3 Lat; DLC, NN] 2941

Bülatïf, N. P.; Rüdin, A. F. *Tomas alfa äḍisün.* Moscow: "Näshriyat" Ka'üpirativï, 1926, 32 pp., 4000 cop. [Tata 2 Arab; NN] 2942
Fedoseyev, R. *Vatan sugïshï sharlarïnda VKP(b) tarikhïnïn kïskacha kursïn öyrënu.* Kazan: Tatgosizdat, 1943, 63 pp., 5070 cop. [Tata 4 Cyr; NN] 2943
Fridländ, Ts. *Tizis häm planlar ghärbi yavrüpadaghï rivalütsiyä ḥäräkätläri tariḥïndan.* Moscow: SSSR Ḥalqlarïnïng Üzäk Näshriyatï, 1925, 255 pp., 6000 cop. [Tata 2 Arab; NN] 2944
Gerimätski, M. *Tabighät echendä tormosh öchön köräsh.* Moscow: SSSR Khalïqlarïnïng Üzäk Näshriyatï, 1929, 72 pp., 3000 cop. [Tata 3 Lat; NN] 2945
Ghäläv, Mäḥmüd. *Pügach yavï.* Moscow: SSSR Ḥalqlarïnïng Üzäk Näshriyatï, 1924, 143 pp., 3000 cop. [Tata 2 Arab; CStH] 2946
Ghäli, M. *Balalïq künlärimdä, 1914–1923.* Kazan: Tatarstan Matbüghat–Näshriyat Kambinatï Basmasï, 1925, 70 pp., 5000 cop. [Tata 2 Arab; CStH] 2947
Ghäziz, Gh. *Börïnghï bölgharlar.* Kazan: Tatarstan Matbüghat häm Näshriyat, 1924, 27 pp., 5000 cop. [Tata 2 Arab; NN] 2948
Ghäziz, Gh. (Ghöbäydüllin). *Tatar tariḥï.* Kazan: Tatarstan Matbüghat häm Näshriyat Kambinatï Näshrï, 1924, 152 pp., 15000 cop. [Tata 2 Arab; CStH] 2949
Ghäziz, Gh. *Tatarlarnïng kilïb chighüvï häm altïn ürda.* Kazan: Tatarstan Matbüghat häm Näshriyat Kambinatï Näshrï, 1924, 15 pp., 5000 cop. [Tata 2 Arab; NN] 2950
Ghöbäydüllin, Ghäziz. *Tatarlarda sinïflar tariḥï öchïn matiriyallar.* Kazan: Tatarstan Matbüghat–Näshriyat Kambinatï Basmasï, 1925, 73 pp., 5000 cop. [Tata 2 Arab; CStH] 2951
Ghöbäydüllin, Ghäziz. *Tatarlarda sinïflar tariḥï: 17, 18 ghäsr häm 19 ghasïrnïng bashïnda.* Kazan: Tatarstan Matbüghat häm Näshriyat Kambinatï Näshrï, 1925, 60 pp., 3000 cop. [Tata 2 Arab; NN] 2952
Girmaniyä—rivalütsiyä aldïnda. Moscow: Millätlär ïshi Kamisariyatï Yanïndaghï Märkäz Shärq Näshriyatï, 1923, 40 pp., 3000 cop. [Tata 2 Arab; NN] 2953
Khalfiy, Ibrahim Bin Isḥaq. *Aḥval jinkïzḥan vä aqsaqtimir.* Kazan: n.p., A.H.1294/A.D.1822, 1819, 91 and 71 pp., n.c. [Tata 1 Arab; DLC] 2954

Khanisov, G. A. *I. I. Mechnikov: Anïng tormïsh yulï häm gïyl'mi ëshchänlege.* Kazan: Tatgosizdat, 1941, 132 pp., 3075 cop. [Tata 4 Cyr; DLC] 2955

Kildibäk, Hadi. *Daniyä.* Kazan: "Tatizdat," 1929, 52 pp., 3000 cop. [Tata 3 Lat; NN] 2956

Mannir, K. *Finländiä.* Kazan: Tatizdat, 1930, 58 pp., 3000 cop. [Tata 3 Lat; NN] 2957

Nikol'skiy, V. K. *Keshelek dön'yäsïnïng balalïk chorï.* Kazan: Tatgosizdat, 1941, 247 pp., 5000 cop. [Tata 4 Cyr; DLC] 2958

Pakrüfsky, M. *XIX häm XX nchï yözlärdä rüsiyädä rivalyütsiyä ḥäräkätï tariḥï.* Moscow: SSSR Ḥalqlarïnïng Üzäk Näshriyatï, 1928, 424 pp., 3000 cop. [Tata 2 Arab; NN] 2959

Pakrüvsky, M. N. *Rüs kültürasï tariḥï parchalarï.* 1nchï bülïk. Kazan: Tatarstan Matbüghat häm Näshriyat Kambinatï Näshrï, 1924, 308 and 28 pp., 3000 cop. [Tata 2 Arab; NN] 2960

Partiä tarikhï sabaqlarï. Kazan: Tatar Chittän Torïp Öyränü Kom-Vuzï Näshre, 1930–1931, 73 pp., 1500 cop. [Tata 3 Lat; NN] 2961

Piyantküfski. *Fivral rivalütsiyäsï.* Moscow: SSSR Ḥalqlarïnïng Üzäk Näshriyatï, 1927, 149 pp., 6000 cop. [Tata 2 Arab; NN] 2962

Samitïf, Z. *Istüniyä häm anïng ärmiyäsï.* Kazan: Tatarstan Dävlät Näshriyatï, 1928, 16 pp., 3000 cop. [Tata 2 Arab; NN] 2963

Säyfi-Qazanlï, Fatiḥ. *Rüsiyä tariḥï.* Kazan: Tatarstan Matbüghat häm Näshriyat Kambinatï Näshrï, 1924, 288 pp., 15000 cop. [Tata 2 Arab; DLC] 2964

Säyfi-Qazanlï, Fatiḥ. *Rüsiyä tariḥï.* Kazan: Tatarstan Matbüghat–Näshriyat Kambinatï Näshrï, 1925, 263 pp., 15000 cop. [Tata 2 Arab; CStH] 2965

Sayrami, Mullah Müsi bin Mullah Ghaysi . . . *Sayramining ta'lifi ta'rikh-i umniyyä.* Kazan: Kitabkhanä-i Madrasä-i Ghilom, A.H.1323/A.D.1905, 325 pp., n.c. [Tata 1 Arab; DLC] 2966

Shüḥin, Andïry. *Kamsamül tariḥï.* Moscow: SSSR Ḥalqlarïnïng Üzäk Näshriyatï, 1928, 114 pp., 5000 cop. [Tata 2 Arab; NN] 2967

Stalin, I. *Lenin turïnda.* Kazan: Tatgosizdat, 1944, 61 pp., 10185 cop. [Tata 4 Cyr; DLC] 2968

Tatar-Bashqïrd shüralar jumḥüriyati. Moscow: Märkäz Musulman Kamisariyat Näshri, 1918, 59 pp., n.c. [Tata 1 Arab; DLC] 2969

Tatarstannïng un ylï, 1920–1930. Kazan: Tatizdat, 1930, 68 pp., 10000 cop. [Tata 3 Lat; CStH] 2970

Tat'yänin, D. *Sergey Muronovich Kirov Kazanda.* Kazan: Tatgosizdat, 1944, 30 pp., 10185 cop. [Tata 4 Cyr; DLC] 2971

12 yülbashchining bi'ügrafiyäsï. Moscow: SSSR Ḥalqlarï Üzäk Näshriyatï, 1925, 80 pp., 6000 cop. [Tata 2 Arab; CStH, NN] 2972

Ün yïl ichïndä tatar-bashqïrtlar: Mäqalälär jiyntïghï. Moscow: "Näshriyat" Kapiratifï Mätbäghäsï, 1927, 158 pp., 3000 cop. [Tata 2 Arab; NN] 2973

Varabiyüf, N. I. *Qazan tatarlarï.* Kazan: n.p., 1928, 36 pp., 500 cop. [Tata 2 Arab; NN] 2974

Vladimir iliych linin ḥatiräsï. Kazan: Tatarstan Matbüghat häm Näshriyat Kambinatï Näshrï, 1924, 127 pp., 10000 cop. [Tata 2 Arab; NN] 2975

Vlasivich, V. *V.K.P.ning ing qisqa tariḥï.* Moscow: SSSR Ḥalqlarïnïng Üzäk Näshriyatï, 1927, 268 pp., 6000 cop. [Tata 2 Arab; NN] 2976

Yäfimïf, V. L.; Gay, Y. *Patsha samadirzhaviyäsï nijïk ighadï.* Moscow: SSSR Ḥalqlarïnïng Üzäk Näshriyatï, 1928, 55 pp., 4000 cop. [Tata 2 Arab; NN] 2977

Yäroslavskiy, Ye. M. *V. I. Lenin biografiyäse.* Kazan: Tatgosizdat, 1941, 232 pp., 10070 cop. [Tata 4 Cyr; DLC] 2978

Yerikäy, Äkhmät. *Salavat Kärimov.* Kazan: Tatgosizdat, 1943, 70 pp., 10010 cop. [Tata 4 Cyr; DLC] 2979

Zinüviyif, G. *Kammünistlar partiyäsïnïng qïsqacha tariḥï.* Kazan: Tatarstan Matbüghat häm Näshriyat Kambinatï Näshrï, 1924, 24 pp., 5000 cop. [Tata 2 Arab; NN] 2980

Zinüviyif, G. *Rüsiyä kammünist (balshivig)lar partiyäsïnïng tariḥï.* Kazan: Tatarstan Matbüghat häm Näshriyat Kambinatï Näshrï, 1924, 275 pp., 10000 cop. [Tata 2 Arab; NN] 2981

Law

Ḥözmät zakünlarï Moscow: SSSR Millätläri Üzäk Nëshriyatï, 1924, 78 pp., 4000 cop. [Tata 2 Arab; NN] 2982

Nichayif, G. *Tatarstan jömhüriyätindä 1928–29 nchï yïlghï bïrläshdirilgän auïl ḥüjalïghï salïmï.* Kazan: Tatarstan Finans Ḥalq Kamisariyatïnïng Salïmlar Idaräsï Näshirï, 1928, 72 pp., 3000 cop. [Tata 2 Arab; NN] 2983

Law

Qüshayif, Gh. *Nikaḥ häm gha'ilä türïnda savit zakünlarï.* Moscow: "Näshriyat" Kapiratifï, 1928, 36 pp., 3000 cop. [Tata 2 Arab; NN] 2984

Sünmäs *Auïl khujalïghï zakonnarï turnda krästiän ni blrgä tiesh.* Kazan: Tatizdat, 1929, 150 pp., 5000 cop. [Tata 3 Lat; NN] 2985

Tatarstan jir ïshlarï ḥalq kamisariyatïnïng üsmliklärnï saqlav ïstansiyäsï. Kazan: n.p., 1928, 4 pp., 2000 cop. [Tata 2 Arab; NN] 2986

Tatarstannïng ghädliyä jir ïshlärï häm ïchkï ïshlär ḥalq kamisariyatlarïnïng instrüksiyäsï. Kazan: n.p., 1928, 45 pp., 1200 cop. [Tata 2 Arab; NN] 2987

Social Organization

Abrüy. *Tatar ḥatïnqïzlarï azadlïq yülïnda.* Kazan: Tatarstan Ïktäbr Ün Yïllïghïn Üzdïrü Üzäk Kämisiyäsï Näshrï, 1927, 72 pp., 3000 cop. [Tata 2 Arab; NN] 2988

Ädhämöva, S. *Auïl törmïshïndan ber körinish.* Kazan: Tatarstan Matbüghat häm Näshriyat Kambinatï Näshrï, 1924, 16 pp., 5000 cop. [Tata 2 Arab; DLC] 2989

Äḥmitif, Ä.; Nighmäti, Gh. *Könbatïshdaghï sinfi köräshlär tariḥï.* I kisäk. Kazan: Tatarstan Dävlät Näshriyatï Basmasï, 1928, 252 pp., 5000 cop. [Tata 2 Arab; NN] 2990

Arïna, A. *"Bagati plat" auïlï krästiyän ḥatïnqïzlarïndan ürnäk alïghïz!* Kazan: Tatarstan Jir Ishlärï Ḥalq Kamisariyatï Näshriyati, 1928, 36 pp., 3000 cop. [Tata 2 Arab; NN] 2991

Auïl ḥüjalïghï ärtilindä ïchki tärtib qaghidälärï. Kazan: Tat'izdat, 1930, 24 pp., 15000 cop. [Tata 2 Arab; NN] 2992

Auïl ḥüjalïghï ärtilïnï üstafï. Kazan: "Tatizdat," 1930, 16 pp., 40000 cop. [Tata 2 Arab; NN] 2993

Auïl savitï chlinï krästiyän ḥatïnqïzïnïng isdälïgï. Kazan: n.p., 1927, 34 pp., 3000 cop. [Tata 2 Arab; NN] 2994

Aulnï öyränü. Tatar aullarïn monografiä usülï blän öyränü öchen *jntkle qüllanma-proghram.* Kazan: Tatizdat, 1930, 52 pp., 2000 cop. [Tata 3 Lat; NN] 2995

Balalar mäydanchïghï närsä häm anï nichek tözärgä. Moscow:

"Näshriyat" Ka'üpirativï Mätbäghasï, 1926, 24 pp., 5000 cop. [Tata 2 Arab; NN] 2996

Balïqshïlar qüghamïnïng övstabï. Astrakhan: n.p., n.d., 11 pp., 3000 cop. [Tata 2 Arab; NN] 2997

Chit illärdä tau eshcheläre: Matiriallar. Moscow: SSSR Khalqlarïnïng Üzäk Näshriatï, 1930, 59 pp., 3000 cop. [Tata 3 Lat; NN] 2998

Dinmöḥämmädïf, Gh.; Na'il, M. *Auïl yarlïlarï häm batraklar arasïnda ïshläü türïnda.* Moscow: SSSR Ḥalqlarïnïng Üzäk Näshriyatï, 1929, 100 pp., 3000 cop. [Tata 2 Arab; NN] 2999

Dinmöḥämmädïf, Gh.; Tabipïf, Säid. *Üz ara tänqid mäs'äläsï häm beznïng bürïchlarïbïz.* Moscow: SSSR Ḥalqlarïnïng Üzäk Näshriyatï, 1929, 56 pp., 2500 cop. [Tata 2 Arab; NN] 3000

Diyamint, Ḥ. *"Linin pöchmaghï" tözüchïlärgä qüllanma.* Moscow: "Näshriyat" Ka'üpirativi Matbaghasï, 1925, 56 pp., 5000 cop. [Tata 2 Arab; NN] 3001

Fäḥri, Sh. *Auïl yarlïlarï arasïnda ïshläü mäs'äläläri.* Kazan: Tatarstan Dävlät Näshriyatï, 1928, 40 pp., 1500 cop. [Tata 2 Arab; NN] 3002

Falknir, V. N. *Köchlï häm taza büliyq!* Moscow: SSSR Ḥalqlarïnïng Üzäk Näshriyatï, 1926, 140 pp., 10000 cop. [Tata 2 Arab; NN] 3003

Fäyzi, Ḥ. *Töra bïlirgä kiräk.* Kazan: Tatarstan Dävlät Näshriyatï Basmasï, 1927, 56 pp., 3000 cop. [Tata 2 Arab; NN] 3004

Fäyzüllin, S. *Yanga keshï türïnda.* Moscow: SSSR Ḥalqlarïnïng Üzäk Näshriyatï, 1929, 128 pp., 2000 cop. [Tata 2 Arab; NN] 3005

Fazil. *Qïzlar arasïnda nichek ïshlärgä.* Kazan: Tatarstan Dävlät Näshriyatï 1928, 39 pp., 3000 cop. [Tata 2 Arab; NN] 3006

Gäshälina. *Mäktäb yäshïnä qädär bülghan balalargha närsälär häm nichek ashatïrgha.* Moscow: SSSR Ḥalqlarïnïng Üzäk Näshriyatï, 1928, 40 pp., 4000 cop. [Tata 2 Arab; NN] 3007

Gharif, Märdghaläm. *Yäsh balanï nichek ashatïrgha häm anï nichek qarargha.* Moscow: "Näshriyat" Ka'üpirativï Mätbäghäsï, 1926, 31 pp., 4000 cop. [Tata 2 Arab; NN] 3008

Grimätski, M. *Bornghï kshelär jir östndä nichek yäshägännär.* Moscow: Sintrizdat, 1930, 45 pp., 8000 cop. [Tata 3 Lat; NN] 3009

Ishchïlärnïng törü ürïnlarï tözü kapiratifï tavarishstvasïnïng narmalni üstafï. Kazan: Tatzhilsayüz Näshrï, 1926, 17 pp., 1000 cop. [Tata 2 Arab; NN] 3010

Jïrnï jämäghät blän ishläü shirkätlärïnïng üstafï. Birsk: Börï Shähär Savïtï Mätbäghäsï, 1929, 40 pp., 900 cop. [Tata 2 Arab; NN] 3011

Kanükïf, I. A. *Jïr ish ärtilläri häm kammünalar.* Moscow: "Näshriyat" Ka'üpirativi, 1926, 48 pp., 5000 cop. [Tata 2 Arab; NN] 3012

Kärimïvä, Sh. *Ḥatïnqïz pöchmaqlarïnda ishnï nichek alïb barïrgha: Qüllanma.* Kazan: Tatarstan Dävlät Näshriyatï Basmasï, 1928, 40 pp., 3000 cop. [Tata 2 Arab; NN] 3013

Kislanski, S. S. *Tözek krästiyän yörtï.* Kazan: Tatarstan Jir Ishlärï Ḥalq Kamisariyatï, 1927, 45 pp., 3000 cop. [Tata 2 Arab; NN] 3014

Krafchinkö, Yelina. *Kalḥüzlarda krastiyän ḥatïnqïzlarï.* Kazan: Tatarstan Jir Ishlärï Ḥalq Kamisariyatï yanïndaghï "Igïnchï" Näshriyatï, 1929, 90 pp., 3000 cop. [Tata 2 Arab; NN] 3015

Lipilin, I. P. *Savitlar ḥagimiyätï yanga törmïshnï nichek tözi.* Moscow: SSSR Ḥalqlarïnïng Üzäk Näshriyatï, 1926, 291 pp., 10000 cop. [Tata 2 Arab; CStH] 3016

Lipski, I. M. *Analar häm balalarnï saqlaü närsä?* Kazan: Tatarstan Matbüghat–Näshriyat Kambinatï Basmasï, 1925, 36 pp., 5000 cop. [Tata 2 Arab; CStH] 3017

Mäjidïf, Äsghäd. *Böyik tözü chörïnda "ädäbi mantazh."* Kazan: Tsentr. Kabineta Politprosveta Rabotnika TNKP, 1929, 27 pp., 1000 cop. [Tata 2 Arab; NN] 3018

Miller. *Tormïsh tügäräkläre.* Moscow: Sintrizdat, 1930, 117 pp., 5000 cop. [Tata 3 Lat; NN] 3019

Minglïkäy, S. *Balalar öchin jïrlï üyinlar.* Kazan: Tatarstan Matbüghat–Näshriyat Kambinatï Basmasï, 1925, 48 pp., 5000 cop. [Tata 2 Arab; CStH] 3020

Mobaräkshin. *Yäsh udarniklar.* Moscow: Sintrizdat, 1930, 23 pp., 8000 cop. [Tata 3 Lat; NN] 3021

Möbaräkshin, F. *Bezning chörda yäshlärgä sinfi tärbiyä ishlärï.* Moscow: SSSR Ḥalqlarïning Üzäk Näshriyatï, 1929, 51 pp., 2500 cop. [Tata 2 Arab; NN] 3022

Möḥämmädif, Märdghaläm. *Tämäkï tartü irlik tügil.* Moscow:

SSSR Ḥalqlarïnïng Üzäk Näshriyatï, 1928, 16 pp., 5000 cop. [Tata 2 Arab; NN] 3023

Müstafina, Z. *Krästiyän ḥatïnqïzï häm gha'ilä: A. Kaligina ibdäsh kitabï büincha yazïldï.* Kazan: Tatarstan Dävlät Näshriyatï Basmasï, 1927, 48 pp., 3000 cop. [Tata 2 Arab; NN] 3024

Popof, P. *Yäsh astronom.* Moscow: SSSR Khalqlarïnïng Üzäk Näshriyatï, 1929, 93 pp., 5000 cop. [Tata 3 Lat; NN] 3025

Rähim, Ghäli. *Ghäbdöräshid babaynïng ayülarï, jlan mögïzï.* Kazan: Tatar Satsiyal Shüralar Jömhüriyätïnïng Dävlät Näshriyatï, 1922, 24 pp., 20000 cop. [Tata 2 Arab; NN] 3026

Rämzi, Sh. *Ghärbdä yäshlär ḥäräkätï.* Kazan: Tatarstan Matbüghat häm Näshriyat Kambinatï Näshrï, 1924, 168 pp., 3000 cop. [Tata 2 Arab; NN] 3027

Savit äghzalarï—ishchï krästiyän ḥatïnqïzlarnïng berïnchï bötïn tatarstan isyizdï matiriyallarï. Kazan: T.J.Ü.B. Kamititï Öyishdïrü Bülïgïnïng Basmasï, 1928, 32 pp., 3000 cop. [Tata 2 Arab; NN] 3028

Säyfi, Abruy̆. *Sotsializm tözegändä khatïn-qzlar häm 8 nche Mart.* Kazan: Tatizdat, 1930, 48 pp., 3000 cop. [Tata 3 Lat; NN] 3029

Shamkin, Ḥäkim. *Piyanirlar aträdindä tän tärbiyäsï.* Kazan: Tatarstan Dävlät Näshriyatï Basmasï, 1927, 32 pp., 3000 cop. [Tata 2 Arab; NN] 3030

Shäräfitdinïf, S.; Nighmäti, Gh.; Möḥämmädïf, M. *Jämghiyätnï öyränü.* Kazan: Tatarstan Dävlät Näshriyatï Basmasï, 1928, 118 pp., 5000 cop. [Tata 2 Arab; NN] 3031

Sïynfi köräshlär häm khälq ara eshchelär khäräkäte tarikhï. Kazan: Kommunislar Univrisititïnïng Basmasï, 1931, 82 pp., 1500 cop. [Tata 3 Lat; NN] 3032

Uennar-balalar ploshchadkasï tärbiyäsenä yärdämlek. Kazan: Tatgosizdat, 1945, 13 pp., 3185 cop. [Tata 4 Cyr; DLC] 3033

Välitïva, Qoyash. *Balalar baqchasïnda nichek eshlärgä.* Moscow: SSSR Khalïqlarïnïng Üzäk Näshriyatï, 1929, 46 pp., 2000 cop. [Tata 3 Lat; NN] 3034

Yäsh igïnchï. 1nchï kisäk. Moscow: SSSR Ḥalqlarïnïng Üzäk Näshriyatï, 1928, 262 pp., 6000 cop. [Tata 2 Arab; CStH, NN] 3035

Yäsh igïnchï. II kisäk, *Yört ḥayüanlarï* Moscow: SSSR Ḥalqlarïnïng Üzäk Näshriyatï, 1928, 199 pp., 6000 cop. [Tata 2 Arab; NN] 3036

Social Organization

Yäsh tabighätchïlär tügärägin nichek öyishtirïrgha. Kazan: Tatar Pidagügiyä Jämghiyätï Basmasï, 1929, 31 pp., 500 cop. [Tata 2 Arab; NN] 3037

Yäümi, Mirza. *Shakhmat.* Kazan: Yangalif, 1929, 60 pp., 3000 cop. [Tata 3 Lat; NN] 3038

Yenikiyif, Ḥ. I. *Kün ishindä prafisiyanal zararlïlïqlar häm avïrülar.* Kazan: Tatarstan Dävlät Näshriyatï, 1929, 63 pp., 3000 cop. [Tata 2 Arab; NN] 3039

Zakir, Gh. *Yäshlär häm kültüra mäs'äläläri.* Moscow: SSSR Ḥalqlarïnïng Üzäk Näshriyatï, 1928, 51 pp., 3000 cop. [Tata 2 Arab; NN] 3040

Zalatnitski, V. N. *Analargha kingäshlär.* Kazan: Tatarstan Matbüghat–Näshriyat Kambinatï Basmasï, 1925, 23 pp., 5000 cop. [Tata 2 Arab; CStH] 3041

Zäyni, Ḥäbib. *Kalliksiyalar tözär öchin qüllanma.* Moscow: "Näshriyat" Ka'üpirativi Mätbäghäsï, 1926, 67 pp., 5000 cop. [Tata 2 Arab; NN] 3042

VOLGA TATAR Humanities

Art and Architecture

Dämin, Bari. *Üqü öylärïndä sïnlï sänghät ishï.* Kazan: Tatarstan Dävlät Näshriyatï Basmasï, 1928, 55 pp., 3000 cop. [Tata 2 Arab; NN] 3043

Ghözäyrïf, M. *Üz qülïbïz blän.* Moscow: SSSR Ḥalqlarïnïng Üzäk Näshriyatï, 1928, 68 pp., 5000 cop. [Tata 2 Arab; NN] 3044

⟨1.⟩ *Imdäsh,* 2 pp.; ⟨2.⟩ *Ankita,* 2 pp. Kazan: Tsentral'nyi Muzei Tatrespübliki, 1929, 500 cop. [Tata 2 Arab; NN] 3045

⟨1.⟩ *Iptäsh.* ⟨2.⟩ *Ankita, muzïï shäreq gulyäzmälär.* Kazan: Tatar Üzäk Müzie, 1929, 4 pp., n.c. [Tata 3 Lat; NN] 3046

Rämzi, Sh. *Auïl üqü yörtlarï häm matür sänghät tügäräkläri.* Moscow: SSSR Ḥalqlarïnïng Üzäk Näshriyatï, 1929, 69 pp., 2500 cop. [Tata 2 Arab; NN] 3047

Räsem-iskülptüra blän kürsätlgän böyik ün il. Moscow: SSSR Ḥalqlarïnïng Üzäk Näshriyatï, 1927, 25 pp., 3000 cop. [Tata 2 Arab; CStH] 3048

Language

Alparïf, Ghibad. *Tatar grammatikasï.* Kazan: Tatarstan Dävlät Näshriyatï Basmasï, 1926, 164 pp., 3000 cop. [Tata 2 Arab; CStH] 3049

Alparïf Ghibad. *Tatar tïlïnïng imla süzlïgï.* Kazan: Tatarstan Dävlät Näshriyatï Basmasï, 1927, 138 pp., 8000 cop. [Tata 2 Arab; NN] 3050

Bigiyif, Müsi Äfändi. *Ḥalq naẓarinä ber nechä mäs'älä.* Kazan: Nashri Maḥämmädghälim Äfändi Maqṣüdïf, 1912, 93 pp., n.c. [Tata 1 Arab; CLU] 3051

Ghäli, M. *Gäzit üqüchïlar öchin ksä süzlïgï.* Kazan: Tat'izdat Basmasï, 1928, 203 pp., 3000 cop. [Tata 2 Arab; NN] 3052

Ghämäli tïl sabaqlarï. Ikenchï kitab. Kazan: Tatarstan Matbüghat häm Näshriyat Kambinatï Näshrï, 1924, 95 pp., 25000 cop. [Tata 2 Arab; NN] 3053

Kalliktif. *Yanga il: III nchï uqu ylï öchin tel künegülärnnän esh kitabï.* Kazan: Tatizdat, 1930, 128 pp., 20000 cop. [Tata 3 Lat; NN] 3054

Katanov, N. Th. "*Materialy k izucheniiu Kazansko-tatarskago nariechiia.*" Kazan: Tipo-Litografiia Imperatorskago Universiteta, 1898, 168 and 113 pp., n.c. [Tata 1 Arab; MH] 3055

Kratkii russko–tatarskii slovar' voennykh terminov. Moscow: Shtab R.K.K.A., 1926, 176 pp., 5000 cop. [Tata 2 Arab; NN] 3056

Nasyri-i-l-Kazani, Abul'-Kaium-in-Abdu-N-Nasyri-N. *Rus ḥuruf hejasi üzrä müretteb lughat kitabï.* Kazan: Knigoprodavets Shamsutdinov, 1904, 264 pp., n.c. [Tata 1 Arab; MH] 3057

Nekliudov, E. *Slovar'-samouchitel'; 1500 tatarskikh slov.* Kazan: Tip. Imp. Universiteta, 1894, 88 pp., n.c. [Tata 1 Arab; MH] 3058

Nügaybik; Ëmirkhan; Korban; Fäyzullin (comps.). *Ruscha–Tatarcha süzlek.* Kazan: Tatgosizdat, 1941 2d ed., 750 pp., 40000 cop. [Tata 4 Cyr; NN, NNC] 3059

Nughaybik; Ämirkhan; Qorban; Fäyzullin. *Ruscha–Tatarcha süzlek.* Kazan: Tatgosizdat, 1938, 667 pp., 10000 cop. [Tata 3 Lat; NNC] 3060

Ostroumov, N. P. *Slovar' tatarsko–russkii.* Kazan: Imperatorskii Universitet, 1892, 244 pp., n.c. [Special Cyr; NN] 3061

Language

Räḥim, Ghäli. *Bernchï törkalügiyä qöriltayï häm anïng tikshirgän mäs'äläläri.* Kazan: Tatarstan Ḥalq Mägharïf Kamisariyatï Basmasï, 1926, 95 pp., 1500 cop. [Tata 2 Arab; NN] 3062

Ramazanov, Sh.; Khismatullin, Kh. *Tatar tele grammatikasi.* 1nchï kisäk fonetika häm morfologiyä. Kazan: Tatgosizdat, 1944, 215 pp., 20185 cop. [Tata 4 Cyr; DLC] 3063

Ruscha–Tatarcha avïl khujalïghï terminnarï süzlege. Kazan: Tatgosizdat, Avïl Khujalïghï Ädäbiatï Sektorï, 1939, 175 pp., 3000 cop. [Tata 3 Lat; NNC] 3064

Säyfüllin, G. *Orfografik künegülär jïyentïgï.* Kazan: Tatgosizdat, 1945, 150 pp., 5185 cop. [Tata 4 Cyr; DLC] 3065

Literature

Absalamov, G. *Bakhet koyäshï.* Khikëyälër. Kazan: Tatgosizdat, 1941, 181 pp., 5000 cop. [Tata 4 Cyr; NN] 3066

Ädäbi yardäm mäjmüghäsï. Kazan: "Tatarstan Matbaghasï," 1922, 240 pp., 5000 cop. [Tata 2 Arab; CStH, NN] 3067

Ädäbi yardäm mäjmüghäsï. Kazan: T.S.Sh.J. 2nchï Nümirlï Dävlät Basmaḥanäsïndä Ishländï, 1922, 130 pp., 10000 cop. [Tata 2 Arab; CStH, NN] 3068

Ädhämöva, S. *Auïl törmïshïndan ber kürïnïsh.* Kazan: Tatarstan Matbüghat häm Näshriyat Kambinatï Näshrï, 1924, 16 pp., 5000 cop. [Tata 2 Arab; NN] 3069

Agiyif, Fäḥrl'islam. *Ḥikayälär jiyntighï.* Moscow: "Nashriyat" Ka'üpirativï, 1926, 60 pp., 4000 cop. [Tata 2 Arab; NN] 3070

Alf saḥar vä saḥar yäghni mengdä ber saḥar. 3 vols. Kazan: Tipo-Litografiia Imperatorskago Universiteta, 1903, I 203 pp., II 262 pp., III 228 pp., n.c. [Tata 1 Arab; MH; DLC (vols. 1 & 2)] 3071

Almay, F. *Parizh kammünasï.* 2 pärdädä, 3 kürinïshdä. Moscow: "Näshriyat" Ka'üpirativï Matbaghasï, 1925, 18 pp., 5000 cop. [Tata 2 Arab; NN] 3072

Ämirḥan, Fatiḥ. *Tigizsizlär, tatar qïzï, ḥalq qïzlarï.* Kazan: Tatarstan Matbüghat–Näshriyat Kambinatï Basmasï, 1925, 92 pp., 3000 cop. [Tata 2 Arab; NN] 3073

Ämiri, Kärim. *Ish östindä.* Kazan: Tatarstan Matbüghat–Näshriyat Kambinatï Basmasï, 1925, 99 pp., 5000 cop. [Tata 2 Arab; CStH] 3074

Ämiri, Kärim. *Pechän bazarï.* Kamidiyä 4 pärdädä. Kazan: Tatarstan Matbüghat–Näshriyat Kambinatï Basmasï, 1925, 76 pp., 3000 cop. [Tata 2 Arab; CStH, NN] 3075

Ämiri, Kärim. *Pralitariyat mönglarï.* Moscow: "Näshriyat" Ka'üpirativï Mätbäghäsï, 1926, 23 pp., 5000 cop. [Tata 2 Arab; NN] 3076

Ämiri, Kärim. *Qazan qïzï.* 4 pärdädä kämidiyä. Kazan: Tatarstan Dävlät Näshriyatï, 1928, 56 pp., 3000 cop. [Tata 2 Arab; NN] 3077

Ämiri, Kärim. *Ural balasï.* Khikäyä. Kazan: "Yangalif," 1930, 94 pp., 3000 cop. [Tata 3 Lat; NN] 3078

Ämiri, Kärim. *Zavüd mäktäbïndä: Balalar ḥikäyäsï.* Kazan: Tatarstan Matbüghat–Näshriyat Kambinatï Basmasï, 1925, 32 pp., 5000 cop. [Tata 2 Arab; CStH] 3079

Appakova, Darjiyä. *Dürt äkiyät.* Kazan: Tatgosizdat, 1945, 30 pp., 10185 cop. [Tata 4 Cyr; DLC] 3080

Äpsälämov, G. *Tön'yäk balkïshï:* Jïentïk. Kazan: Tatgosizdat, 1944, 143 pp., 5000 cop. [Tata 4 Cyr; DLC] 3081

Aqikitzadä, Müsa. *Ḥisametdin mnlla: Milli rüman yaki ḥikayä.* Kazan: Tatarstan Matbüghat–Näshriyat Kambinatï Basmasï, 1925, 56 pp., 3000 cop. [Tata 2 Arab; CStH] 3082

Ärinbürg, I. *Chïn kammünar.* Kazan: Tatarstan Matbüghat häm Näshriyat Kambinatï Näshrï, 1924, 23 pp., 5000 cop. [Tata 2 Arab; NN] 3083

Äsghäd, F. *Törmish qöchaghïnda ḥikayälär häm näserlär.* Kazan: Tatarstan Matbüghat–Näshriyat Kambinatï Basmasï, 1925, 36 pp., 3000 cop. [Tata 2 Arab; NN] 3084

Aydarski, Ghäziz. *Auïl tiyatri: Auïl dram tügäräklärï öchin.* Moscow: "Näshriyat" Mätbäghäsï, 1926, 51 pp., 5000 cop. [Tata 2 Arab; NN] 3085

Ayu belän babay: Tatar khalïk äkiyäte. Kazan: Tatgosizdat, 1944, 6 pp., 15185 cop. [Tata 4 Cyr; DLC] 3086

Azamat, A. S. *Qaf tav artïnda.* Kazan: "Yangalif," 1928, 56 pp., 3000 cop. [Tata 3 Lat; NN] 3087

Babich, Shäiḥzadä. *Shighïrlär mäjmüghäsï.* Kazan: Tatarstan Savitlar Jömhüriyätïnïng Dävlät Näshriyatï, 1922, 163 pp., 7000 cop. [Tata 2 Arab; CStH, NN] 3088

Bakirïf, Ghösman. *Berïnchï jingü: Mäktablär häm kamsamüllar öchin säḥnä äsärï.* Kazan: Tatarstan Dävlät Näshriyatï, 1928, 32 pp., 3000 cop. [Tata 2 Arab; NN] 3089

Bakirof, Gh. *Uraq öste: Balalar öchen khikäyälär jüntïghï.* Kazan: Tatizdat, 1930, 39 pp., 5000 cop. [Tata 3 Lat; NN] 3090

Baqïrküz. *Ït fälsäfäsï.* Kölkï ḥikäyälär. Kazan: Tatarstan Dävlät Näshriyat "Tat'izdat" Basmasï, 1927, 33 pp., 3000 cop. [Tata 2 Arab; NN] 3091

Baqiyif, S. *Ka'üpiratsiyä faidalï arganizatsiyä.* 2 pärdädä. Kazan: Tatarstan Matbüghat-Näshriyat Kambinatï Basmasï, 1925, 16 pp., 3000 cop. [Tata 2 Arab; NN] 3092

Bayanïf, N. *Jimerelgän akuplar: Payima, shighïrlar jiyïntïghï.* Kazan: n.p., 1928, 16 pp., 3000 cop. [Tata 3 Lat; NN] 3093

Baychürina, Zahirä. *Shighïrlär mäjmüghäsï.* Kazan: "Tatpichät" Näshrï, 1923, 44 pp., 2000 cop. [Tata 2 Arab; NN] 3094

Bayimbitïf, Gh. *Asïlghan.* Öch pärdälik piyäsä. Kazan: Tatarstan Matbüghat Näshriyat Kambinatï Näshrï, 1924, 110 pp., 2000 cop. [Tata 2 Arab; NN] 3095

Bayimbitïf, Gh. *Patsha töshirälär.* Moscow: "Näshriyat Ka'üpiratifï"nïng Näshrï, 1924, 36 pp., 5000 cop. [Tata 2 Arab; NN] 3096

Bayrün. *Shil'ün tötqöni.* Paima. Ufa: n.p., 1924 2d ed., 30 pp., 2000 cop. [Tata 2 Arab; NN] 3097

Bazhov, P. *Nemetslar turïnda khikäyätlär.* Kazan: Tatgosizdat, 1945, 59 pp., 10185 cop. [Tata 4 Cyr; DLC] 3098

Bigiyïf, Möhämmäd Zaher märḥüm Aḥünd Mülla Jarülla üghli. *Gönahö käba'ir.* Kazan: Tatarstan Matbüghat-Nashriyat Kambinatï Basmasï, 1925, 64 pp., 3000 cop. [Tata 2 Arab; NN] 3099

Biz Salkü, P. *Häläkät.* Rüman. Kazan: Dävlätnïng Altïnchï Nümirlï "Kamil Yaqüb" ismïndägï Mätbäghäsï, 1923, 140 pp., 3000 cop. [Tata 2 Arab; NN] 3100

Bluk, A. *Un ikäv.* Kazan: n.p., 1928, 25 pp., 2000 cop. [Tata 3 Lat; NN] 3101

Borhan, Safa; Nighmäti, Gh.; Ämirkhan, Fatikh. *Tashqïn: Ädäbi khristamatiä.* 1nche kisäk. Kazan: Yangalif, 1930 2d ed., 196 pp., 5000 cop. [Tata 3 Lat; NN] 3102

Börnash, F. *Öjmaḥ qöshï.* Äkiyät-piyäsä, bish pärdädä. Kazan: Tatarstan Satsiyal Savitlar Jömhüriyätïnïng Dävlät Näshriyatï, 1922, 75 pp., 4000 cop. [Tata 2 Arab; NN] 3103

Bülat. *Qaz: Ḥikäyälär ädäbi barchalar jiyntïghï*. Kazan: Tatarstan Dävlät Näshriyatï Basmasï, 1928, 48 pp., 3000 cop. [Tata 2 Arab; NN] 3104

Bürnash, F. *Köräsh jïrlarï*. Kazan: Tatarstan Dävlät Näshriyatï, 1923, 236 pp., 2000 cop. [Tata 2 Arab; NN] 3105

Bürnash, Fätḥi. *Kämali qart*. Piyäsä 4 pärdädä, 7 kürinishdä. Moscow: SSSR Ḥalqlarïnïng Üzäk Näshriyatï, 1926, 127 pp., 5000 cop. [Tata 2 Arab; CStH] 3106

Bürnash, Fätḥi. *Shighir, pa'imalarï jiyntïghï*. Kazan: Tatarstan Mätbüghat–Näshriyat Kambinatï Basmasï, 1925, 79 pp., n.c. [Tata 2 Arab; CStH] 3107

Burnash, Fätkhi. *Khätirä apa: Auïl tormoshonnan*. Piyïssï, 5 pärdädä. Moscow: SSSR Khalïqlarïnïng Üzäk Näshriyatï, 1929, 59 pp., 3000 cop. [Tata 3 Lat; NN] 3108

Chenäkäy. *Yïllar ïskripkäsindä jïrlar*. Moscow: SSSR Ḥalqlarïnïng Üzäk Näshriyatï, 1929, 59 pp., 1500 cop. [Tata 2 Arab; NN] 3109

Dämin, Gh. *Kapiratr ḥäyläsï*. Öch pärdädä piyäsä. Kazan: Tatarstan Dävlät Näshriyatï, 1928, 44 pp., 3000 cop. [Tata 2 Arab; NN] 3110

Dävlät. *Priyüt balasï: Balalar ädäbiyatï*. Kazan: Tatarstan Matbüghat häm Näshriyat Kambinatï Näshrï, 1924, 16 pp., 5000 cop. [Tata 2 Arab; NN] 3111

Fätḥi, Dimiyan. *Taliyan*. Kazan: "Tatizdat," 1929, 32 pp., 3000 cop. [Tata 2 Arab; NN] 3112

Fäyz, M. Ḥäydär. *Asïl yar*. Piyssä 5 pärdä, 6 kartinada. n.p.: Tatarstan Matbüghat häm Näshriyat Kambinatï Näshrï, 1924, 94 pp., 2000 cop. [Tata 2 Arab; NN] 3113

Fäyz, M. Häydär. *Auïl bäyrämï*. Ikï pärdälï piyissä. Kazan: Tatarstan Matbüghat häm Näshriyat Kambinatï Näshrï, 1924, 58 pp., 2000 cop. [Tata 2 Arab; NN] 3114

Fäyzi, Mir Ḥäydär. *Ghaliyä banü*. Dramma dürt pärdädä. Kazan: Tatar Satsiyal Savitlar Jümhöriyätinïng Dävlät Näshriyatï, 1922, 76 pp., 5000 cop. [Tata 2 Arab; NN] 3115

Fridman, David. *Mäḥäbbät närsä?* (*Mindil marans*). Kechkenä rüman. Kazan: "Yanga kitab" Näshriyat Kapiratifï Basmasï, 1927, 72 pp., 4000 cop. [Tata 2 Arab; NN] 3116

Furmanof, D. *Chapayef*. Kazan: Tatgosizdat. Matür Ädäbiat Sektorï, 1937, 438 pp., 10130 cop. [Tata 3 Lat; NN] 3117

G. Tukay. Akademik basma. I tom. Kazan: Tatarstan Däulät Izdatel'stvosï. Matur Ädäbiyät Sektori, 1943, 470 pp., 9070 cop. [Tata 4 Cyr; NN] 3118

Galeev, Garif. *Zirekle jirendä*. Khikäyälär. Kazan: Tatgosizdat, 1941, 230 pp., 10070 cop. [Tata 4 Cyr; DLC] 3119

Gäliev, Garif. *Shäm yäktisï: Khikäyälär jïentïgï*. Kazan: Tatgosizdat, 1944, 111 pp., 5185 cop. [Tata 4 Cyr; DLC] 3120

Garaditski, S. *Qara shähär*. Kinü rüman. Kazan: Tatarstan Matbüghat häm Näshriyat Kambinatï Näshrï, 1924, 126 pp., 3000 cop. [Tata 2 Arab; NN] 3121

Gäräy. *Isdäliklär*. Moscow: SSSR Ḥalqlarïnïng Üzäk Näshriyatï, 1929, 36 pp., 3000 cop. [Tata 2 Arab; NN] 3122

Gäräyshina, Sh. *Tabighat qöchaghïnda*. n.p.: Bashknigä, 1928, 23 pp., 2000 cop. [Tata 2 Arab; NN] 3123

Ghäfüri, M. *Ḥäzer ansat ül—Ïlïk qiyn idï: Balalar öchin*. Moscow: SSSR Ḥalqlarïnïng Üzäk Näshriyatï, 1927, 32 pp., 5000 cop. [Tata 2 Arab; NN] 3124

Ghäfüri, Mäjid. *Ishchi*. Pa'ima. Kazan: Tatar Satsiyal Shüralar Jömhüriyätïnïng Dävlät Näshriyatï, 1921, 48 pp., 2000 cop. [Tata 2 Arab; NN] 3125

Ghäfüri, Mäjid. *Qïzïl bayraq*. Kazan: Tatar Satsiyal Shüralar Jömhüriyätïnïng Dävlät Näshriyatï, 1922, 29 pp., 5000 cop. [Tata 2 Arab; NN] 3126

Ghäli, A. *Yögänsizlär*. Ḥikayä. Kazan: Tatarstan Dävlät Näshriyatï, 1928, 114 pp., 3000 cop. [Tata 2 Arab; NN] 3127

Ghäli, M. *Qala keshïlärï büldiq*. Kazan: Tatarstan Dävlät Näshriyatï Basmasï, 1928, 30 pp., 4000 cop. [Tata 2 Arab; NN] 3128

Ghäliyif, Ghömär, *Küban büylarïnda: Ḥikäyälär jiyntïghï*. Kazan: Tatarstan Dävlät Näshriyatï Basmasï, 1927, 80 pp., 3000 cop. [Tata 2 Arab; NN] 3129

Ghäynan, Qadir. *Üsäbiz*. Kazan: Tatarstan Matbüghat–Näshriyat Kambinatï Basmasï, 1925, 36 pp., 4000 cop. [Tata 2 Arab; CStH] 3130

Ghäziz, Gh. *Pügachev yavï: Rüssiyädä ḥalq rivalyütsiyälärï tariḥindan*. Kazan: Tatarstan Matbüghat häm Näshriyat Kambinatï Näshrï, 1924, 19 pp., 5000 cop. [Tata 2 Arab; NN] 3131

Ghömär, Gharif. *Ber qïzïl galstüknïng kürgänlärï: Balalar ädäbiyätï*. Moscow: SSSR Ḥalqlarïnïng Üzäk Näshriyatï, 1927, 31 pp., 2500 cop. [Tata 2 Arab; NN] 3132

Ghömärïf, Äḥmäd. *Könlär könindä.* Öch pärdädä, dürt kürinïshdä. Kazan: Tatarstan Matbüghat-Näshriyat Kambinatï Basmasï, 1925, 44 pp., 3000 cop. [Tata 2 Arab; NN] 313

Ghösmanïf, Sh. "*Il qïzï.*" Ḥikäyä. Kazan: Tatpichät Idäräsïnïng "Kamil Yaqüb" ismïndägï Mätbäghäsï, 1923, 56 pp., 2000 cop. [Tata 2 Arab; NN] 313

Ghösmanïf, Shamil. *Qïzïl bayraq astïnda.* Ḥikayä. Kazan: Tatarstan Matbüghat häm Näshriyat Kambinatï Näshrï, 1925, 79 pp., 3000 cop. [Tata 2 Arab; CStH, NN] 313

Ghösmanïf, Shamil. *Shamsaldin bay.* Kazan: Tatarstan Matbüghat häm Näshriyat Kambinatï Näshrï, 1924, 43 pp., 5000 cop. [Tata 2 Arab; NN] 313

Ghösmanïf, Yüsïf. *Linin babaynï iskä alghanda.* Moscow: "Näshriyat" Ka'üpirativï Mätbäghäsï, 1926, 80 pp., 5000 cop. [Tata 2 Arab; NN] 313

Ghümar, Gh. *Bektimïr nichek ïshchï büldï?* Ḥikayä. Kazan: Tatarstan Matbüghat-Näshriyat Kambinatï Basmasï, 1925, 23 pp., 5000 cop. [Tata 2 Arab; CStH] 313

Ghüsmanïf, Shamil. *Pamirdan radiyü: Ḥiyaldaghï ḥikayä.* Moscow: "Nashriyat" Ka'üpirativï Mätbäghäsï, 1926, 88 pp., 7000 cop. [Tata 2 Arab; CStH] 313

Gïyzzät, Taji. *Jïrlar.* Kazan: Tatgosizdat, 1945, 75 pp., 10185 cop. [Tata 4 Cyr; DLC] 314

Gïyzzätullina, R. *Ädäbiyät: 5nche klasslar öchen däreslek—khrestomatiyä.* Kazan: Tatgosizdat, 1945, 214 pp., 40185 cop. [Tata 4 Cyr; DLC] 314

Gobäy, Garif. *Öch börket.* Ike kartinalï piesa. Kazan: Tatgosizdat, 1941, 40 pp., 3075 cop. [Tata 4 Cyr; NN] 314

Gorbatov, B. *Buysïnmas keshelär: Taras gailäse.* Kazan: Tatgosizdat, 1944, 138 pp., 5185 cop. [Tata 4 Cyr; DLC] 314

Gor'ki, M. *Ana.* Kazan: Tatgoszidat. Matur Ädäbiat Sektorï, 1937, 446 pp., 10120 cop. [Tata 3 Lat; NN] 314

Gor'ki, M. *Bala chaq.* Kazan: Tatgoszidat, 1936, 263, pp. 10000 cop. [Tata 3 Lat; NN] 314

Gor'ki, Maksim. *Khikäyälär.* Kazan: Tatgoszidat Matür Ädäbiat Sectorï, 1935, 447 pp., 10000 cop. [Tata 3 Lat; NN] 314

Gor'ki, Maksim. *Malaylïqta.* Kazan: Tatgosizdat. Matur Ädäbiat Sektorï, 1935, 385 pp., 7000 cop. [Tata 3 Lat; NN] 314

Gor'kiy. M. *Ädäbiyät turïnda: Mäkalär häm rech'lär*. Kazan: Tatgosizdat, 1941, 238 pp., 5070 cop. [Tata 4 Cyr; DLC] 3148

⟨Gor'kiy, M.⟩ *Gor'kiy fashizmga karshi*. Kazan: Tatgosizdat, 1945, 78 pp., 10185 cop. [Tata 4 Cyr; DLC] 3149

Gosman, Kh. *Ut sïzïgïnda: Jïentïk*. Kazan: Tatgosizdat, 1945, 71 pp., 5185 cop. [Tata 4 Cyr; DLC] 3150

Güriyvich, Ts. S. *Ïspartak; säyasï häm tariḥi rüman*. Moscow: SSSR Millätläri Üzäk Näshriyatï, 1924, 126 pp., 4000 cop. [Tata 2 Arab; NN] 3151

Ḥäbib, Ghäbdülla. *Auïl ḥikäyäläri*. Kazan: "Ignchï" Näshriyatï, 1929, 64 pp., 3000 cop. [Tata 2 Arab; NN] 3152

Ḥäbib, Ghäbdülla. *Mïraü batïr: Köyläb yazïlghan balalar ḥikäyäsï*. Kazan: Tatarstan Dävlät Näshriyatï, 1928, 28 pp., 5000 cop. [Tata 2 Arab; NN] 3153

Hadï, Zakir. *Jihansha ḥäzrät, mäghsüm*. Kazan: Tatarstan Matbüghat–Näshriyat Kambinatï Basmasï, 1925, 95 pp., 3000 cop. [Tata 2 Arab; CStH] 3154

Ḥäyri, Ghaynan. *Chabata*. Moscow: "Näshriyat" Kapiratifï Mätbaghäsï, 1928, 38 pp., 3000 cop. [Tata 2 Arab; NN] 3155

Ibrahimïf, Ghalimjan. *Prülitariyat ädäbiyatï*. Moscow: "Näshriyat" Ka'üpirativï Näshrï, 1924, 74 pp., 5000 cop. [Tata 2 Arab; NN] 3156

Ibrahimïf, Ghalimjan. *Qart yalchï*. Kazan: Tatarstan Mätbüghat–Näshriyat Kambinatï Basmasï, 1925, 24 pp., 5000 cop. [Tata 2 Arab; CStH] 3157

Ibrahimïf, Ghalimjan. *Qazaq qïzï*. Moscow: SSSR Ḥalqlarïnïng Üzäk Näshriyatï, 1924, 135 pp., 5000 cop. [Tata 2 Arab; NN] 3158

Ibrahimïf, Ghalimjan. *Qïzïl chächäklär ḥikäyäsï*. Kazan: Tatar Satsiyal Savitlar Jömhüriyätïnïng Dävlät Näshriyatï, 1922, 148 pp., 3000 cop. [Tata 2 Arab; NN] 3159

Ibrahimïf, Ghalimjan. *Tirän tamïrlar: Tüghrï süz*. Kazan: Tatarstan Dävlät Näshriyatï, 1928, 198 pp., 5000 cop. [Tata 2 Arab; NN, NNC] 3160

Idelle, Gaziz. *Gafiyät Nig"mätullïn*. Kazan: Tatgosizdat, 1943, 45 pp., 10070 cop. [Tata 4 Cyr; DLC] 3161

Ikenche Belorüssiyä frontïnïng Tatar sügïshchïlarïnnan Tatar khalqïna khat. Kazan: Tatgosizdat, 1945, 38 pp., 10185 cop. [Tata 4 Cyr; DLC] 3162

Iliyasïf, Gh. *Fantan.* Ḥikäyälär-näserlär. Moscow: SSSR Ḥalqlarïnïng Üzäk Näshriyatï, 1927, 107 pp., 4000 cop. [Tata 2 Arab; NN] 3163

Illish, Bila. *Nikalay shüghay.* Moscow: SSSR Ḥalqlarïnïng Üzäk Näshriyatï, 1926, 84 pp., 3000 cop. [Tata 2 Arab; NN] 3164

Iskhaq, Ä. *Tash uramnar jïrï.* Moscow: SSSR Khalqlarïnïng Üzäk Näshriyatï, 1929, 42 pp., 3000 cop. [Tata 3 Lat; NN] 3165

Izansïz qrlar jrï: Shighrlar, khikäyälär bäyläme. Moscow: SSSR Khalqlarïnïng Üzäk Näshriatï, 1930, 46 pp., 6000 cop. [Tata 3 Lat; NN] 3166

Kä. Ka. Y. *Im-öm.* Ikï pärdälik insinirüfka. Moscow: "Näshriyat" Ka'üpirativi Mätbäghäsï, 1926, 43 pp., 5000 cop. [Tata 2 Arab; NN] 3167

Kamal, G. *Saylanma äsärlär.* Kazan: Tatgosizdat, 1942, 388 pp., 3070 cop. [Tata 4 Cyr; DLC] 3168

Kamal, Gh. *Büläk öchön.* Kämidiyä 1 pärdädä. Kazan: n.p., 1928, 15 pp., 3000 cop. [Tata 3 Lat; NN] 3169

Kämal, Gh. *Diklamatsiyälär.* Kazan: Shärq Kammünistlarï Märkäz Byürasinïng Näshri, 1921, 153 pp., 1000 cop. [Tata 2 Arab; NN] 3170

Kamal, Sh. *Aqcharlaqlar.* Kazan: "Tatpoligraf," 1928, 56 pp., 3000 cop. [Tata 3 Lat; NN] 3171

Kamal, Sh. *Äsärlär.* I-nche tom. Kazan: Tatgosizdat. Matur Ädäbiyät Sektori, 1941, 419 pp., 7035 cop. [Tata 4 Cyr; NNC] 3171

Kamal, Shärif. *Aqcharlaqlar: Ïshchïlär törmishïndan ḥikayä.* Kazan: Tatarstan Matbüghat–Näshriyat Kambinatï Basmasï, 1925, 91 pp., 3000 cop. [Tata 2 Arab; NN] 3172

Kärim, Fatikh. *Yäzgï töndä, khikäyä.* Kazan: Tatgosizdat, 1945, 109 pp., 10185 cop. [Tata 4 Cyr; DLC] 3173

Kärim, Kh. *Yïrtïlghan perikaz.* Khikäyä. Kazan: Yangalif, 1929, 72 pp., 5000 cop. [Tata 3 Lat; NN] 3174

Kärimi, Fatiḥ. *Äsärlärï:* "Saliḥ babaynïng öylänüvï," "Shäkert blän ïstüdint," "Jihangir mäḥdüm," "Ghayash ḥälfä." Kazan: Tatarstan Matbüghat–Näshriyat Kambinatï Basmasï, 1925, 84 pp., 4000 cop. [Tata 2 Arab; CStH] 3175

Kashshaf, Gazi. *Kalëm masterlarï.* Kazan: Tatgosizdat. Matur Ädäbiyät Sektorï, 1940, 117 pp., 10000 cop. [Tata 4 Cyr; NN] 3176

Katayef, Val. *Aqcha tuzdïruchïlar* (*rastratchiklar*). Kazan: Yangalif, 1930, 71 pp., 5000 cop. [Tata 3 Lat; NN] 3177

Khösni, Fattïykh. *Usallar*. Bügnge tormsh dramasï 4 pärdädä. Kazan: Tatizdat, 1929, 36 pp., 4000 cop. [Tata 3 Lat; NN] 3178

Kirzhintsïf, V. *Ijadi tiyatr*. Kazan: Jömhüriyätnïng Säyasï Idaräsi qarshïndaghï Shärq Shöghbäsi Näshri, 1921, 86 pp., 5000 cop. [Tata 2 Arab; NN] 3179

Krïlov, I. A. *Mäsällär*. Kazan: Tatgosizdat, 1944, 64 pp., 10185 cop. [Tata 4 Cyr; DLC] 3180

Kutuy, Gadel'. *Röstäm majaralarï*. Khïyälïy roman. Kazan: Tatgosizdat, 1945, 71 pp., 5185 cop. [Tata 4 Cyr; DLC] 3181

Libedinski, Yü. *Atna*. Moscow: SSSR Ḥalqlarïnïng Üzäk Näshriyatï, 1926, 134 pp., 3000 cop. [Tata 2 Arab; NN] 3182

Linin. *Näfis-ädäbi jiyntïq; ïshchï-krästiyän yazüchïlarïn berläshdirgän "üktäbr kümägï" ridaksiyäsindä*. Kazan: Tatarstan Matbüghat häm Näshriyat Kambinatï Näshrï, 1924, 62 pp., 3000 cop. [Tata 2 Arab; NN] 3183

Lündïn, Dzhik. *Chinagü*. Ḥikäyä. Kazan: "Yanga Kitab" Näshriyat Kapiratifï Basmasï, 1928, 30 pp., 4000 cop. [Tata 2 Arab; NN] 3184

Lündön, Dzhik. *Ser*. Ḥikäyä. Moscow: "Näshriyat" Ka'öpirativï Näshrï, 1925, 24 pp., 5000 cop. [Tata 2 Arab; NN] 3185

M.S.; M.T. *Yulavchï baqa: 2-nche sïynïf balalarï öchön*. Kazan: "Tatizdat," 1929, 20 pp., 3000 cop. [Tata 3 Lat; NN] 3186

Mähdi, M. *Yanga diklamatïr*. Moscow: "Näshriyat" Ka'üpirativï Mätbäghäsï, 1926, 108 pp., 5000 cop. [Tata 2 Arab; NN] 3187

Mäḥmüd, Shäräf. *Ghäskär: Dürt pärdälik 36 kürinïshdä iskï häm qzïl ghäskärilär törmïshïndan alïb yazïlghan tariḥi piyäsä*. Kazan: Tatarstan Matbüghat–Näshriyat Kambinatï Basmasï, 1925, 79 pp., 3000 cop. [Tata 2 Arab; NN] 3188

Mäjidïf, A.; Agiyif, A. *Jiyntïq*. Moscow: SSSR Ḥalqlarïnïng Üzäk Näshriyatï, 1925, 96 pp., 5000 cop. [Tata 2 Arab; CStH] 3189

Mäjidïf, Äsghäd. *Bäyräm bülägi: Ïshchi rayünlar häm auïllar öchen pyisalar, insinirüfkälar jiyntïghï*. Moscow: "Näshriyat" Kapiratifï, 1927, 80 pp., 3000 cop. [Tata 2 Arab; NN] 3190

Mäjidïf, Äsghäd. *Par-chiläk: Auïl törmïshïndan 3 pärdälk pyissä*. Moscow: SSSR Ḥalqlarïnïng Üzäk Näshriyatï. 1928, 114 pp., 3000 cop. [Tata 2 Arab; NN] 3191

Männafov, Kh. *Kochigar.* Ḥikäyä. Kazan: Tatizdat, 1930, 35 pp., 3000 cop. [Tata 3 Lat; NN] 3192

Mannür, Sh. *Taygha töbindän.* Kazan: Tatarstan Dävlät Näshriyatï, 1928, 80 pp., 3000 cop. [Tata 2 Arab; NN] 3193

Maqsüd, M. *Beznïng chächäklär.* Kazan: Tatarstan Matbüghat-Näshriyat Kambinatï Basmasï, 1925, 82 pp., 5000 cop. [Tata 2 Arab; CStH] 3194

Maqsut, Mäkhmüt. *Qanlï bojralar.* Khikäyälär. Kazan: "Tatizdat," 1929, 48 pp., 3000 cop. [Tata 3 Lat; NN] 3195

Mayäkovskiy, V. *Shigïrlär.* Kazan: Tatgosizdat, 1941, 76 pp., 6000 cop. [Tata 4 Cyr; DLC] 3196

Mödärris, Shäräf. *Frontovik Tatarlar.* Ocherklar. Kazan: Tatgosizdat, 1944, 126 pp., 5185 cop. [Tata 4 Cyr; DLC] 3197

Möḥtar, Gh. *Linin babay türïnda.* Moscow: SSSR Ḥalqlarï Üzäk Näshriyatï, 1925, 41 pp., 5000 cop. [Tata 2 Arab; CStH, NN] 3198

Mörtazin, V.; Chenäkäy, T. *Tatar tiyatïrï tariḥindan.* Moscow: SSSR Ḥalqlarïnïng Üzäk Näshriyatï, 1926, 106 pp., 5000 cop. [Tata 2 Arab; NN] 3199

Näjmi, Kavi. *Färidä.* Kazan: Tatgosizdat, 1944, 116 pp., 6185 cop. [Tata 4 Cyr; DLC] 3200

Näjmi, Qävi. *Öyirmälär: Ḥikayälär-shighirlär jintïghï.* Kazan: Tatarstan Mätbüghat häm Näshriyat Kambinatïnïng Basmasï, 1924, 127 pp., 3000 cop. [Tata 2 Arab; CStH] 3201

Näjmi, Qävi. *Tashtüghaygha qaytmibiz.* Kazan: Tatarstan Dävlät Näshriyatï Basmasï, 1928, 95 pp., 3000 cop. [Tata 2 Arab; NN] 3202

Nasiri, I. *Vagünda:* Ḥikäyä. Moscow: SSSR Ḥalqlarïnïng Üzäk Näshriyatï, 1929, 67 pp., 4000 cop. [Tata 2 Arab; CStH] 3203

Nasiri, Qäyyüm. *Mäjmüghäsi.* Kazan: T.S.S.J. Dävlät Näshriyatï, 1922, 160 pp., 2000 cop. [Tata 2 Arab; CStH] 3204

Nasyrov, A. K.; Poliakov, P. A. *Skazki kazanskikh Tatar.* Kazan: Tipo-Litografiia Imperatorskago Kazanskago Universiteta, 1900, 112 pp., n.c. [Special Cyr; MH] 3205

Növikof-Priböy, A. S. *Sikrtmäler.* Kazan: Yangalif, 1929, 68 pp., 3000 cop. [Tata 3 Lat; NN] 3206

Nurïy, Zäki. *Shigïr'lär.* Kazan: Tatgozisdat, 1945, 63 pp., 5185 cop. [Tata 4 Cyr; DLC] 3207

Ocherk literaturnoi deiatel'nosti Kazanskikh tatar-Mokhammedan za 1880–1895 gg. Sochinenie Nikolaia Ashmarina. Lazarevskii institut Vostochnykh iazykov; trudy po Vostokovedeniiu. vyp. IV. Moscow: Tipografiia Varvary Gattsuk., 1901, 58 pp., n.c. [Tata 1 Arab; Special Cyr; NN] 3208

Qäyyüm nasïrïnïng möngarchï basïlmaghan äsärläri. Kazan: Tatarstan Dävlät Näshriyatï Basmasï, 1926, 133 pp., 1000 cop. [Tata 2 Arab; NN] 3209

Qïrïq vezir qiṣäsi. Kazan: Qazan Univirsititinïng Ṭabgh, 1900, 160 pp., n.c. [Tata 1 Arab; MH] 3210

Qïrïymïf, Mansur. *Nänilär büläge: Balalar öchön.* Moscow: SSSR Khalïqlarïnïng Üzäk Näshriyatï, 1929, 42 pp., 3000 cop. [Tata 3 Lat; NN] 3211

"Qïzïl yïrchï." *Yanga yïrlär.* Moscow: SSSR Ḥalqlarïnïng Üzäk Näshriyatï, 1929, 19 pp., 2000 cop. [Tata 2 Arab; NN] 3212

Qöl Äḥmidïf, Ghäfür. *Mäjmüghäsï.* Moscow: SSSR Ḥalqlarïnïng Üzäk Näshriyatï, 1925, 152 pp., 5000 cop. [Tata 2 Arab; CStH] 3213

Qol'äkhmitef, Ghafur. *Ike fiker:* Piyïssa 3 pärdädä. Kazan: Yangalif, 1929, 27 pp., 3000 cop. [Tata 3 Lat; NN] 3214

Qrimïf, M. *Qïzïl bädavam.* Moscow: "Näshriyat" Mätbaghasï, 1925, 24 pp., 5000 cop. [Tata 2 Arab; NN] 3215

Qrimïf, Mansür. *Chükich jïrlarï.* Moscow: SSSR Ḥalqlarïnïng Üzäk Näshriyatï, 1925, 24 pp., 5000 cop. [Tata 2 Arab; NN] 3216

Qrimïf, Mansür. *Ḥikäyälär bäylämï.* Moscow: SSSR Ḥalqlarïnïng Üzäk Näshriyatï, 1928, 74 pp., 3000 cop. [Tata 2 Arab; NN] 3217

Qrimïf, Mansür. *Ïsh irtäsï: Shighirlär jiyntïghï.* Kazan: Tatarstan Dävlät Näshriyatï, 1929, 32 pp., 3000 cop. [Tata 2 Arab; NN] 3218

Qrimïf, Mansür. *Kamsamül jïrlarï.* Moscow: "Näshriyat" Ka'öpirativï Matbaghasï, 1925, 31 pp., 5000 cop. [Tata 2 Arab; NN] 3219

Qüdash, Säyfi. *Bayarlar bar chaqda: Balalar ädäbiyatï.* Kazan: Tatarstan Dävlät Näshriyatï, 1928, 48 pp., 3000 cop. [Tata 2 Arab; NN] 3220

Qütüy, Gh. *Könlär yögergändä.* Kazan: Tatarstan Matbüghat häm Näshriyat Kambinatï Näshrï, 1924, 56 pp., 3000 cop. [Tata 2 Arab; NN] 3221

Qütüy, Gh. *Qaynar könlär: Ḥikäyä, shigir häm pa'imalar jiyntïghï.* Kazan: Tatarstan Dävlät Näshriyatï Basmasï, 1927, 48 pp., 3000 cop. [Tata 2 Arab; NN] 3222

Räḥim, Ghäli. *Idïl.* Ḥikayä. Kazan: "Tatpichät" Näshrï, 1923, 127 pp., 3000 cop. [Tata 2 Arab; CStH] 3223

Räḥim, Ghäli; Ghaziz, Gh. *Tatar ädäbiyatï tariḥï.* Bïrïnchï jild. Kazan: Tatarstan Matbüghat häm Näshriyat Kambinatï Näshrï, 1924, 171 pp., 5000 cop. [Tata 2 Arab; NN] 3224

Räḥim, Ghäli; Ghäziz, Gh. *Tatar ädäbiyatï tariḥï: Fiyüdalizm dävrï.* Kazan: Tatarstan Matbüghat häm Näshriyat Kambinatï Näshrï, 1925, 313 pp., 5000 cop. [Tata 2 Arab; CStH] 3225

Ramanïf, Pantiläyman. *Rätsiz ḥalq.* Ḥikäyälär. Kazan: Näshriyat Kapiratifï Basmasï, 1928, 40 pp., 4000 cop. [Tata 2 Arab; NN] 3226

Säädi, Ghäbdöraḥman. *Tatar ädäbiyatï tariḥï.* Kazan: Tatarstan Dävlät Näshriyatï Basmasï, 1926, 300 pp., 6000 cop. [Tata 1 Arab; NNC*] 3227

Sadrï, Jälal. *Ḥikäyälär bäylämï.* Kazan: Tatarstan Dävlät Näshriyatï Basmasï, 1928, 50 pp., 3000 cop. [Tata 2 Arab; NN] 3228

Samitïf, Zakir (ed.). *Qïzïl ärmiyä yïrlarï.* Kazan: Tatarstan Dävlät Näshriyatï Basmasï, 1928, 36 pp., 3000 cop. [Tata 2 Arab; NN] 3229

Säyfi, Fatiḥ. *Düshmanlar.* Dramma dürt pärdädä. Kazan: Törk Ḥalqlarï Kammünistlarïnïng Märkäz Byüra Näshriyatï, 1921 99 pp., n.c. [Tata 2 Arab; NN] 3230

Säyfi, Fatiḥ. *Krüshniklar, zimagür, dvür öyindä.* Ḥikayälär. Kazan: Tatarstan Matbüghat–Näshriyat Kambinatï Basmasï, 1925, 64 pp., 5000 cop. [Tata 2 Arab; NN] 3231

Shähärtdinïf, Sh. *Il'ichkä ḥat.* Moscow: SSSR Ḥalqlarïnïng Üzäk Näshriyatï, 1928, 35 pp., 4000 cop. [Tata 2 Arab; NN] 3232

Shamïf, Äfzal. *Dülqïnlar arasïnda.* Moscow: SSSR Ḥalqlarïnïng Üzäk Näshriyatï, 1927, 118 pp., 3000 cop. [Tata 2 Arab; CStH, NN] 3233

Shamïf, Äfzal. *Ïshpana.* Hikäyälär törkïmï. Kazan: Tatarstan Dävlät Näshriyatï Basmasï, 1927, 32 pp., 3000 cop. [Tata 2 Arab; NN] 3234

Shamïf, Äfzal. *No. 175 paravüz.* Kazan: Tatarstan Dävlät Näshriyatï Basmasï, 1926, 64 pp., 3000 cop. [Tata 2 Arab; CStH] 3235

Shamïf, Äfzal. *Rävfä.* Khikäyä. Moscow: SSSR Khalqlarïnïng Üzäk Näsheriyatï, 1929, 43 pp., 4000 cop. [Tata 3 Lat; NN] 3236

* Microfilm

Sirin. *Qïsh*. Kazan: Tatizdat, 1929, n.pp., 3000 cop. [Tata 3 Lat; NN] 3237

Tagiyif, Rüstämbik. *Arbakäsh yünïs*. Moscow: SSSR Ḥalqlarïnïng Üzäk Näshriyatï, 1928, 74 pp., 4000 cop. [Tata 2 Arab; NN] 3238

Tahir, Äfzal. *Ach häm yalanghachlar*. Bïr pärdälik pyisa. Moscow: Märkäz Shärq häm Ghärb Näshriyatï, 1924, 18 pp., 2000 cop. [Tata 2 Arab; NN] 3239

Tahir, Äfzal. *Kiyäü häm käläsh*. Pyisä, bïr pärdädä. Moscow: SSSR Millätläri Üzäk Näshriyatï, 1924, 26 pp., 3000 cop. [Tata 2 Arab; NN] 3240

Tahir, Äfzal. *Üyindan üyimaq*. Kölki, iki pärdälik. Moscow: Märkäz Shärq häm Ghärb Näshriyatï, 1924, 24 pp., 2000 cop. [Tata 2 Arab; NN] 3241

Tahirïf, Äfzal. *Äträgälämlär*. Ḥikäyä. Moscow: SSSR Ḥalqlarïnïng Üzäk Näshriyatï, 1927, 108 pp., 5000 cop. [Tata 2 Arab; NN] 3242

Tahirïf, Äfzal. *Köräsh yïllarï*. Moscow: SSSR Ḥalqlarïnïng Üzäk Näshriyatï, 1927, 131 pp., 4000 cop. [Tata 2 Arab; NN] 3243

Taqtash. *Tavfiqli mächi*. Kazan: Tatarstan Dävlät Näshriyatï, 1928, n.pp., 4000 cop. [Tata 2 Arab; NN] 3244

Taqtash, H. *Daüldan süng*. Kazan: Tatarstan Matbüghat–Näshriyat Kambinatï Basmasï, 1925, 80 pp., 3000 cop. [Tata 2 Arab; NN] 3245

Taqtash, H. *Jir üllarï tragidiyasï*. 6 kürinishdä. Kazan: "Tatarstan" Matbaghasï, 1923, 102 pp., 2000 cop. [Tata 2 Arab; NN] 3246

Taqtash, Hadi. *Qara börïnnïng düstï: Balalar ḥikäyäsï*. Moscow: SSSR Ḥalqlarïnïng Üzak Näshriyatï, 1927, 23 pp., 3000 cop. [Tata 2 Arab; NN] 3247

Tinchürin, K. *Süngän yöldïzlar*. Müziklï köchlï dramma. Kazan: Tatarstan Matbüghat–Näshriyat Kambinatï Basmasï, 1925, 82 pp., 5000 cop. [Tata 2 Arab; CStH] 3248

Tinchürin, K. *Zar: Bäni adäm fajighäsï*. Altï pärdädä. Kazan: Tatarstan Matbüghat häm Näshriyat Kambinatï Näshrï, 1924, 144 pp., 2000 cop. [Tata 2 Arab; CStH, NN] 3249

Tläshef, Gh. *Partizan*. Poima. Kazan: Tatizdat, 1930, 46 pp., 3000 cop. [Tata 3 Lat; NN] 3250

Tufan, Kh. *Paima, lirika.* I kisäk. Kazan: Yangalif, 1929, 88 pp., 3000 cop. [Tata 3 Lat; NN] 3251

Tülümbayski, Ghümir. *Bez üskändä.* Kazan: Tatarstan Matbüghat-Näshriyat Kambinatï Basmasï, 1925, 112 pp., 5000 cop. [Tata 2 Arab; CStH] 3252

Tülümbayski, Ghümir. *Chitän büyï.* Ḥikäyälär. Kazan: Tatarstan Dävlät Näshriyatï, 1929, 80 pp., 3000 cop. [Tata 2 Arab; NN] 3253

Tülümbayski, Ghümir. *Kechkenä chaqlarda: Jintiq.* Kazan: Tatarstan Matbüghat-Näshriyat Kambinatï Basmasï, 1925, 23 pp., 5000 cop. [Tata 2 Arab; CStH] 3254

Tülümbayski, Ghümir. *Qïzïl armiyädän qaytqach.* Ḥikayä. Kazan: Tatarstan Matbüghat-Näshriyat Kambinatï Basmasï, 1925, 32 pp., 10000 cop. [Tata 2 Arab; CStH] 3255

Tüqay. *Äsärlärï.* Kazan: Tatarstan Matbüghat-Näshriyat Kambinatï Basmasï, 1925, 43 pp., 5000 cop. [Tata 2 Arab; CStH] 3256

Tüqay, Ghabdülla. *Shürälï.* Kazan: Mätbüghat häm Näshriyat Ïshlärï Kambinatïnïng "Sharq" Mätbäghäsï, 1923, 10 pp., 3000 cop. [Tata 2 Arab; NN] 3257

Üksizlär. Kazan: Tatarstan Matbüghat häm Näshriyat Kambinatï Näshrï, 1924, 16 pp., 5000 cop. [Tata 2 Arab; NN] 3258

Üktabr chächäklärï: Piyänirlar piyäsäsï. Öch pärdädä. Kazan: Tatarstan Matbüghat-Näshriyat Kambinatï Basmasï, 1925, 36 pp., 3000 cop. [Tata 2 Arab; NN] 3259

Üral bülägi. Sverdlovsk: n.p., 1929, 32 pp., 5000 cop. [Tata 2 Arab; NN] 3260

Urayskiy, Sakhab. *Yäz tangïnda.* Kazan: Tatgosizdat, 1945, 87 pp., 5185 cop. [Tata 4 Cyr; DLC] 3261

Üsmanïf, Shamil. *Bay qïzï.* Piyäsa 4 pärdädä. Kazan: Qazanda "Tatpichät" Idaräsïnïng "Sharq" Mätbäghäsï, 1923, 63 pp., 3000 cop. [Tata 2 Arab; NN] 3262

Vagnir, Yu. *Üsemleklärnïng tereklïkï häm tözïlïshï türïnda bashlanghïch belem.* Kazan: Tatarstan Dävlät Näshriyatï Basmasï, 1926, 68 pp., 6000 cop. [Tata 2 Arab; CStH] 3263

Väli, Kh. *Tatar shigher tözeleshe* (*mitrikä*). 1nchï kisäk. Kazan: Yangalif, 1929, 133 pp., 3000 cop. [Tata 3 Lat; NN] 3264

Valin. *Yäsh piyanirlarnïng üyïn häm jïrlarï.* Moscow: SSSR Ḥalqlarïnïng Üzäk Näshriyatï, 1927, 148 pp., 8000 cop. [Tata 2 Arab; CStH, NN] 3265

Yerikäy, Äkhmät. *Khalkïma.* Kazan: Tatgosizdat, 1945, 110 pp., 5000 cop. [Tata 4 Cyr; DLC] 3266

Yunüs, A. (comp.). *Bezneng yäsh'lär.* Shigïr'lär, khikäyälär, ocherklar. Kazan: Tatgosizdat, 1944, 99 pp., 5000 cop. [Tata 4 Cyr; DLC] 3267

Yunus, Äkhmät. *Bez kaytïrbïz.* Shigïr'lär. Kazan: Tatgosizdat, 1944, 64 pp., 3000 cop. [Tata 4 Cyr; DLC] 3268

Zäliyif, Kamal. *Üram chatïndan kammünagha.* Moscow: "Näshriyat" Kapiratifï, 1928, 47 pp., 3000 cop. [Tata 2 Arab; CStH, NN] 3269

Philosophy and Religion

Altï barmaq kitabï. Kazan: Tipografiia Imperatorskago Universiteta, 1899, 535 pp., n.c. [Tata 1 Arab; NN] 3270

Börhan, Safa. *Alla ismï blän.* Kazan: Tatarstan Dävlät Näshriyatï, 1929, 72 pp., 3000 cop. [Tata 2 Arab; NN] 3271

Bulat. *Allasïz kölü.* Ufa: Bashgiz, 1930, 93 pp., 5000 cop. [Tata 3 Lat; NN] 3272

Cheghtay, A. *Din ḥörafatlarï.* Moscow: SSSR Ḥalqlarïnïng Üzäk Näshriyatï, 1929, 80 pp., 3000 cop. [Tata 2 Arab; NN] 3273

Cheghtay, A. *Dini qörbanlar.* 3nchï bülek. Moscow: SSSR Ḥalqlarïnïng Üzäk Näshriyatï, 1927, 76 pp., 5000 cop. [Tata 2 Arab; CStH, NN] 3274

Chghtay, A. *Dinnär khorafatlar.* Moscow: Sintrizdat, 1930, 82 pp., 6000 cop. [Tata 3 Lat; NN] 3275

Chïn den knyägyäse . . . den simbolï, Khoday imanï un boyorok, tugïz bakhetlek turïsïnda. Kazan: Pravoslavnoe Missionerskoe Obshchestvo, Tipografiia M. A. Chirkovoi, 1893 3d ed., 80 pp., n.c. [Special Cyr; MH] 3276

Dährilär tügäräklärï öchin pragram häm mitüd kürgäzmälär. Moscow: SSSR Ḥalqlarïnïng Üzäk Näshriyatï, 1928, 47 pp., n.c. [Tata 2 Arab; NN] 3277

Davuding zabularï . . . Astrakhan: Yüḥna Mitshildan Baṣildï, 1818, 150 pp., n.c. [Tata 1 Arab; NNJ] 3278

Faza'il al-suhur. Kazan: n.p., A.H.1302/A.D.1884, 62 pp., n.c. [Tata 1 Arab; DLC] 3279

Ḥaji Düsmayl ibn Qachqimbay. *Iman risaläsi.* Kazan: Maṭbagh-i Karimiyä, 1902, 18 pp., n.c. [Tata 1 Arab; CLU] 3280

Ḥüjäyif, M. *Dinlär tariḥï.* 1nchï kisäk. Kazan: Tatarstan Dävlät Näshriyatï Basmasï, 1928, 94 pp., 3000 cop. [Tata 2 Arab; NN] 3281

Kalliktif. *Dähri tügäräklär öchin därslik.* Moscow: SSSR Ḥalqlarïnïng Üzäk Näshriyatï, 1928, 311 pp., 4000 cop. [Tata 2 Arab; NN] 3282

Kildibäk, Hadi. *Islam häm ḥatïnqïzlar.* Kazan: Tatarstan Dävlät Näshriyatï Basmasï, 1928, 59 pp., 3000 cop. [Tata 2 Arab; NN] 3283

Mämläkät ghilmi shürasïnïng (GUSnïng) 4 nchï mitüd ḥatï. Moscow: "Nashriyat" Ka'üpirativi, 1926, 34 pp., 4000 cop. [Tata 2 Arab; NN] 3284

Müsining avval kitabï . . . Avvaldä allah kükliriy viriy . . . ⟨Astrakhan: n.p., 1825⟩, 216 and 268 pp., n.c. [Tata 1 Arab; NNJ] 3285

Nävshirvan, Zinät. *Ḥilafätnïng ülüvi.* Moscow: Märkäz Shärq Näshriyati, 1924, 70 pp., 3000 cop. [Tata 2 Arab; NN] 3286

Psaltyr' na tserkovno-slavianskom i tatarskom iazykakh. n.p.: Pravoslavnoe Missionerskoe Obshchestvo, 1893, iv and 496 pp., n.c. [Special Cyr; MH] 3287

Rämzi, Sh. *Säyasi aghartü üchrizhdiniyälärindä dinsïzlär ïshïn alïb barü türïnda.* Moscow: SSSR Ḥalqlarïnïng Üzäk Näshriyatï, 1929, 43 pp., 2000 cop. [Tata 2 Arab; NN] 3288

S.S.S.R.dägï dährilär sayüzïnïng üstafï häm dingä qarshï köräsh yïllarï. Moscow: SSSR Ḥalqlarïnïng Üzäk Näshriyatï, 1927, 21 pp., 5000 cop. [Tata 2 Arab; NN] 3289

Säyfi, Fatiḥ. *Din blän nichek köräshirgä.* Kazan: Tatarstan Matbüghat häm Näshriyat Kambinatï Näshrï, 1924, 28 pp., 5000 cop. [Tata 2 Arab; NN] 3290

Sayfi, Fatiḥ. *Dinnï dävlätdän ayïrü.* Kazan: Tatarstan Matbüghat häm Näshriyat Kambinatï Näshrï, 1924, 35 pp., 5000 cop. [Tata 2 Arab; NN] 3291

Säyfi, Fatiḥ. *Tatar dinï: Tatarnïng iske, yanga dinlärï, bölarnïng sinfi-iqtisadi ḥällärgä mönasäbätï ḥaqïnda ḥalq öchin yazïlghan.* Kazan: Tatarstan Matbüghat häm Näshriyatï Kambinatï Näshrï, 1924, 50 pp., 5000 cop. [Tata 2 Arab; NN] 3292 al-Sharighät, Ghubaydullah bin Mas'üd ibn Taj. *Tärjemä-i mükhṭasir al-viqayät.* Kazan: Shams'aldin Ḥüsäynif Virthäsi, 1914, 419 pp., n.c. [Tata 1 Arab; NN] 3293

Sughshchan allaszlar soyuzïnïng böten SSSR külämndäge iknche syïzïnïng rizolütsiäläre. Moscow: Sintrizdat, 1930, 94 pp., 5000 cop. [Tata 3 Lat; NN] 3294

Sviatoe evangelie Gospoda nashego Iisusa Khrista. Kazan: Pravoslavnoe Missionerskago Obshchestvo, 1898 2d ed., 511 pp., n.c. [Special Cyr; NNC] 3295

Tatar, bashqort krästiyänlärï dähri tügäräklärï öchin därs praghrammasï. Moscow: SSSR Ḥalqlarïnïng Üzäk Näshriyatï, n.d., 35 pp., 25000 cop. [Tata 2 Arab; NN] 3296

Telyäklyär: Chasoslov na tatarskom iazykie. n.p.: Pravoslavnoe Missionerskoe Obshchestvo, Tipografiia M. A. Chirkovoi, 1893, n.pp., n.c. [Special Cyr; MH] 3297

Yalchghïl ughlï, Tajaldin. *Risalä-i ghazizä: sharḥ-i thebat al-ghajizin.* Kazan: Qazan Ünivirsititïnïng Aryanskoy nam Ṭabgh Khanäsi, 1850, 440 pp., n.c. [Tata 1 Arab; CLU] 3298

YAKUT General (including periodicals)

Cholbon (Yakutsk) 1927: 3–7; 1928: 4/5, 11/12. [Yak 2 Lat; NN] 3299

Jokuuskay aptanïamnay sebieskey sessieliiskey öröspüü bülüke ülehitin gamnachchịtịn, baahị nayịn bịrabịị talịstịbatị tahaar bịt uuruularịn jahayịịlarịn qomuyuuta (n.p.) 1926: 12. [Yak 2 Lat; NN] 3300

Kïhïl illïk (Yakutsk) 1930: 1. [Yak 3 Lat; NN] 3301

"*Sassïarda*" (Yakutsk) 1927: July. [Yak 2 Lat; NN] 3302

YAKUT Social Sciences

Economics

Kepereessiye uönna qomsomuöl sessieliismeghe tirierder suöikepereessiüe buolar. Moscow: SSÖS Kinige Becheettiir Kiin Sire, 1927, 14 pp., 4000 cop. [Yak 2 Lat; NN] 3303

Laappị kemiissiyete dien tuquy, kiniege qaydaq ülelenillere. Moscow: SSÖS Näruöttarịn Kinige Becheettiir Kiin Sire Bïanna Kiin Seyuus Tahaarịịlara, 1928, 40 pp., 2000 cop. [Yak 2 Lat; NN] 3304

Lienin keppereessiye tuhunan tugu diebitey: Sessieliismeghe tirierder suöl keppereessiüe. Moscow: SSÖS Noruottarịn Kinige Becheettiir Kiin Sire, 1927, 15 pp., 4000 cop. [Yak 2 Lat; NN] 3305

Qapïaratịịp laappịtịn ongähuta-teriltete. Moscow: SSÖS Näruöttarịn Kinige Becheettiir Kiin Sire Bïanna Kiin Seyuus Tahaarịịlara, 1928, 24 pp., 1000 cop. [Yak 2 Lat; CStH, NN] 3306

Qolquos tuhugar. Yakutsk: Saqa Sudaarïstïbata Kinige Tahaarar Kïttïgastaaq Uopsastïbata, 1930, 70 pp., 4100 cop. [Yak 3 Lat; NN] 3307

Tïa jadangịlarịgar qasaayịstịba kömöltötün sayịnnarar küühürder jahallar tustarịnan ASBSÖ noruodunay qamịssairdarịn sebiete uurbut uuraafa. Yakutsk: n.p., 1929, 12 pp., 1000 cop. [Yak 2 Lat; NN] 3308

Education

Donskuöy, Semen. *Uöreq küühe: Uöreqteeq jon eppit sehennere.* Moscow: SSSR Omugun Ologhun Becheettiir Kiing Sir Saqalịị Salaata, 1924, 54 pp., 2000 cop. [Yak 2 Lat; NN] 3309

Künde (Ö. Ö. Uybanïap). *Bihigi tịlbịt kịramaatịka ikkis suöla saqa tịla ularịyarịn teleriyerin uöreghe.* Moscow: SSÖS Noruöttarịn Kinige Becheettiir Kiin Sire, 1926, 94 pp., 5000 cop. [Yak 2 Lat; NN] 3310

Künde (Öl. Uybanïap); Biniigin, Öl. *Sanga oloq: Ulaqan jon uorener buukubaardara.* Moscow: Uoreghe Suöghu Uöreqtiir Arassịịya Kemitiete, 1927, 72 pp., 5000 cop. [Yak 2 Lat; NN] 3311

Künde (Öl. Uybaniap); Biniigin, Öl. *Sanga oloq: Ulaqan jon uörener buukubairdara üsüshün becheettenen taqsịịta.* Moscow: Uöreghe Suöghu Uöreqtiir Arassịịya Kemitiete, 1929, 72 pp., 5000 cop. [Yak 2 Lat; NN] 3312

Künde (Uybanïap); Kuobelep, Suösun. *Ulaqan jon aasar kinigelere.* Moscow: SSÖS Kinige Becheettiir Kiin Sire, 1926, 99 pp., 5000 cop. [Yak 2 Lat; NN] 3313

Langkïap, A. B. *Aqsaan uöreghin kinigete.* Uöreq ikkis sịlịgar. Moscow: SSÖS-n Kinige Becheettiir Kiin Sire, 1925, 99 pp., 5000 cop. [Yak 2 Lat; NN] 3314

Langkïap, A. B. *Aqsaan uöreghin kinigete.* Uöreq mangnaygị jịlịgar. Moscow: SSÖS-n Kinige Becheettiir Kiin Sire, 1925, 112 pp., 5000 cop. [Yak 2 Lat; CStH, NN] 3315

Sebieskey uluus: Kịra uöreqteeq jon oskuölalarịgar aaghar kinige. Moscow: SSÖS Noruötarịn Kinige Becheettiir Sire, 1928, v and 192 pp., 3500 cop. [Yak 2 Lat; NN] 3316

Government

Amuöhap, M. K. *S.A.S.S.O. keskilin ongohuuta: Bütün saqa sirin sebietterin 5-s siyiehiger brabịịtalịstịba ongorbut ochchuöta.* Yakutsk: Jokuuskay Kuorat, 1927, 67 pp., 1000 cop. [Yak 2 Lat; NN] 3317

Arassịịya qommuppustarịn baartịyatịn (bassabịịk) ustaaba. Moscow: SSSR Omugun Ologhun Becheettiir Kiing Sir Saqalị Halaata, 1924, 32 pp., 2000 cop. [Yak 2 Lat; CStH, NN] 3318

Bütün saqa sirin sebietterin 6-s siyiehe uurbut uuruuta. Yakutsk: Saqa Sudaarịstịbata Kinige Tahaarar Sire, 1929, 65 pp., 3500 cop. [Yak 2 Lat; NN] 3319

Lienin, B. Ị. *Qomsomuöl kihite qaytaq buöluöqtaaghịy.* Yakutsk: Saqa Sudaarịst Kinige Tahaarar Sire, 1927, 23 pp., 2000 cop. [Yak 2 Lat; NN] 3320

Sebietter maassabay ülelere. Yakutsk: Saqa Sudaarïstïbata Kinige Tahaarar Kïttïgastaaq Uopsastïbata, 1930, 42 pp., 3000 cop. [Yak 3 Lat; NN] 3321

History

Kuybïsheva, Yelena. *Valerian Kuybïshev: Siëstirëtin akhtïïta.* Moscow–Leningrad: OGhO Literaturëtin Izdatel'stvëtë, 1940, 80 pp., 15000 cop. [Yak 4 Cyr; DLC] 3322

12 kihi ologhung kerseene. n.p.: Tsentral'noe Izdatel'stvo Narodov SSSR, n.d., 77 pp., 2000 cop. [Yak 2 Lat; NN] 3323

Social Organization

Bayaarap, Ö. S. (A. F. Boiarov). *Saqa ologhun bïhïïtïn chebdigidii.* Yakutsk: Jokuuskay Kuörat, 1927, 51 pp., 1100 cop. [Yak 2 Lat; NN] 3324

Iyelerge sübe ama: Nirey oghonu ogholuur, ahatar, beyeni qaytaq tuttar tuhunan. Yakutsk: Ịraas Oloq Tahaarịịta, 1927, 47 pp., 4000 cop. [Yak 2 Lat; NN] 3325

Kuöbelep, S. *Beye beyeghe kömölöhör uöbsastuöba: Qamnachchuot soyuuha.* Moscow: Kuörakka SSÖS-n Kinige Becheettiir Kiin Sire, 1924, 70 pp., 2000 cop. [Yak 2 Lat; CStH, NN] 3326

Ogholooq jaqtarga anammịd ịyịị kerdii. Moscow: SSÖS-n Kinige Becheettiir Kiin Sirin, 1924, 35 pp., 2000 cop. [Yak 2 Lat; CStH, NN] 3327

Qormieklep, A. B. *Jaqtar beyetin tuhunan tugu bilien soebüy.* Yakutsk: Gosudarstvennoe Izdatel'stvo, 1927, 26 pp., 1500 cop. [Yak 2 Lat; NN] 3328

Selieskey, E. B. *Emiydeeq ogholorgutun qarịstaang.* Yakutsk: Saqa Sudäärịsịịbata Kiniige Tahaarar Sire, 1929, 41 pp., 2000 cop. [Yak 2 Lat; NN] 3329

YAKUT Humanities

Language

Pekarskii, Ed. K. *Slovar' iakutskago iazyka.* 3 vols. St. Petersburg: Imperatorskaia Akademiia Nauk, 1912–1923, viii and 3858 pp., 750 cop. [Yak 1 Cyr, 2 Lat; NN] 3330

Popov, I. N. ... *Saqalïï nyuchchalïï tïljït.* Yakutsk: Saqa Kinigetin Becheete, 1931, 228 pp., 10000 cop. [Yak 3 Lat; NN] 3331

Literature

Boppuop, Biikter. *Qoroghor kirgieley: Öksökülegh ölöksöy.* Moscow: SSÖS-n Kinige Becheettiir Kiin Sire, 1925, 31 pp., 2000 cop. [Yak 2 Lat; CStH, NN] 3332

Künde. *Ol jịllar.* Dịraama. Yakutsk: Saqa Sudarịst Kinige Tahaarar Sire, 1928, 96 pp., 1500 cop. [Yak 2 Lat; NN] 3333

Nosturuoyap, Nukulay. *Kepseetter.* Yakutsk: Saqa Sudaarịst Kinige Tahaarar Sire, 1929, 65 pp., 2000 cop. [Yak 2 Lat; NN] 3334

Nosturuoyap, Nukulay. *Kuhaghan tịịn: Öröbölüüssüye innineeghi oloqton ịlịllịbịt 4 tögülleeq kemiediye.* Yakutsk: Saqa Sud. Kinige Tahaarar Sire, 1927, 36 pp., 1000 cop. [Yak 2 Lat; NN] 3335

Öröbölüüsüye inniger mökküheechilerge kömölöhör barị doydu ürdünen terilte (MUÖPR). Yakutsk: Saqa Sudaarịst Kinige Tahaarar Sire, 1928, 15 pp., 500 cop. [Yak 2 Lat; NN] 3336

Oyunuskay, B. Ö. *Ịrïa qohoon.* Yakutsk: Saqa Sudaarịst Kinige Tahaarar Sire, 1927, 65 pp., 2000 cop. [Yak 2 Lat; NN] 3337

Soppuruonap, A. U. *Manchaarị.* n.p.: SSÖS Kinige Becheettiir Kiin Sire, 1926, 88 pp., 2000 cop. [Yak 2 Lat; NN] 3338

Philosophy and Religion

Donuskoy, Semen. *Tangara uöreghe hịmịya.* Moscow: SSSR Omugun Ologhun Becheettiir Kiin Sir Saqalịï Halaata, 1924, 70 pp., 2000 cop. [Yak 2 Lat; CStH, NN] 3339

Sviashchennoe evangelie. n.p.: n.p., 1858, n.pp., n.c. [Yak 1 Cyr; DLC] 3340

Sviatoe evangelie na iakutskom iazykie. Kazan: Pravoslavnoe Missionerskoe Obshchestvo, 1898, 273 pp., n.c. [Yak 1 Cyr; MH] 3341

TRANSLITERATION TABLES

TRANSLITERATION TABLES FOR WRITING SYSTEMS OF THE SOVIET EAST

The nationalities of the Soviet East command attention today more than ever before among persons concerned with developments in the USSR or the greater Middle East. This new focus upon the Soviet East increasingly demands that thorough research utilize and cite the many publications issued in indigenous languages—Tajik, Uzbek, and others—of the Soviet East. The major research libraries of the United States which regularly receive books, newspapers, and periodicals from the Soviet East endeavor to organize such collections in a fashion that will contribute to this new direction in scholarship. The general lack of established methods for representing modern Soviet Eastern languages in English-language publications and catalogs, however, cannot help but handicap the work of both writers and librarians, exerting a totally restrictive influence upon the advancement of Soviet Eastern studies in America.

To forward the efforts of all those who analyze publications from the Soviet East, therefore, the following series of transliteration tables has been prepared. The application of most of these has been demonstrated in the previous section, where they provide equivalents for the authors' names, titles of publications, and publishers' designations making up the bulk of the Bibliographical Directory to Publications from the Soviet East. Only languages found in that bibliography are represented here by the transliteration system.

The function of transliteration can be described as dual. It allows the representation of foreign words in published research and, equally important, it makes possible the alphabetical arrangement of names and titles of foreign works, a process absolutely basic to systematic scholarship and cataloging. The method followed here in organizing the system of transliteration provides distinct equivalents in the Roman alphabet used to write English, not necessarily phonetic correspondences, for every letter in each alphabet of the indigenous languages printed or lithographed in the Soviet East. To a reasonable degree the rationale behind this approach calls for selecting letters which will convert words transliterated through the system into *easily recognizable* and typewritable form. Consequently, the tables do not everywhere employ the same Roman letter in place of a particular symbol recurring in the writing of separate foreign languages or their different alphabets. This flexibility is an acknowledgement that the orthographies effective among Soviet Eastern nationalities often vary widely in the assignment of characters to sounds from language to language and at various times. To illustrate, in the Uzbek transliteration [Uz 4 Cyr] (see the headings on the following tables), *o* is rendered as *a*, but in Volga Tatar [Tata 4 Cyr] *o* equals *o*. This deviation occurs because [Uz 4 Cyr] also assigns *ў* as the representative of *o*, and *a* equals *ä*.

A plethora of modified characters like Uzbek *ў* occurs in the three principal writing systems which have been employed in the Soviet East. If the standard Arabic–Persian alphabet in that area can be said to have possessed 35 letters, the Cyrillic 32, and the "Latin" (the Soviet term for Roman) 26, a canvass of the following transliteration tables discloses that the aggregate of modified characters added to the usual Arabic alphabet numbers 16, to the Cyrillic 42 (many more variants than original letters), and to the Roman 16 (more than half of the total comprising the original alphabet). In concert with the other factors already seen to be working against selection of a rigid allotment of symbols to sounds in transliteration, the existence of these many modifications argues strongly for sensitivity to language differences in transliterating. But there is also a limit to which peculiarities reflected in the assignment of characters to sounds in transliteration can be comfortably accommodated without converting a transliteration system into a virtual transcription. This limit consists of a transitional band rather than a thin line, because it can be drawn mainly through observance of applicable conventions employed in dealing with

Eastern languages and writing systems, conventions which must at the same time be borrowed only if they are appropriate to the English-language adaptation of the Roman alphabet. Custom is honored, for example, in rendering Arabic *ha* as *ḥ* or Arabic *ʿayn* as ʿ in Azeri [Az 1 & 2 Arab]. The highly literate Volga Tatars, who exploited the Arabic alphabet in a great deal of their publishing, gave this Arabic letter (*ʿayn*) the function of standing for *ghayn*. That letter is ordinarily denoted in the Arabic alphabet by another character, which the Volga Tatars have discarded. To insist upon overruling local practice in this case in order to follow outside conventions of transliteration would obviously produce equivalents which are not easily recognized (Volga Tatar *Ghalimjan* becomes under the old tradition *ʿAlimjan*). Clearly, following convention would throw off completely the expected alphabetization in English of these transliterated names, with consequent disruption in the order, not only of authors' names, but publication titles entered in catalogs, indexes, and bibliographies.

The chosen transliteration method allows a given letter to serve alternative functions for various alphabets in the same or different languages. As a result, transliterations may reflect the distinctiveness of each language graphically to some extent, aiding the recognition of equivalents. From the standpoint of a scholar or bibliographer there is no necessity to ignore the convenience of quick identification in transliteration in order to follow slavishly a principle of "a single Roman transliteration for each foreign character" throughout all Soviet Eastern alphabets. In contrast to that mechanistic device, the method followed herein creates what may be called a responsive transliteration system which takes each language and alphabet as a unit with its own personality. Social scientists, librarians, and humanists who choose this middle way in transliteration will avoid the extremes of obligatory 1 to 1 correspondences on one side and strict linguistic transcription on another.

Beyond the goal of facilitating research through establishing a system of transliteration for Soviet Eastern languages, the aim in constructing the following tables includes recording the precise alphabetical order on specified dates in which each set of symbols was actually used, together with indicating some of the changes in that order; supplying all the letters of each alphabet in the form adopted locally, showing the many modifications of symbols; displaying the major changes in the choice of writing systems while reporting the timing of those innovations; and citing published sources from which information regarding these alphabets and writing systems can be obtained.

An occasional alphabet reproduced here falls short of fulfilling the above aims. For lack of an explicit source some have been reconstructed from written texts rather than drawn from an alphabetical chart or listing. These exceptions, whose order may be somewhat at odds with the sequence adopted locally, are specified in footnotes to the tables.

Some alphabets presented in the tables amalgamate in themselves slight variations introduced at different times. This happens for example, in [Az 5 Cyr], where *j* (which is rendered as *y*) replaced *й* (which also equals *y*) years after the Cyrillic alphabet had first become obligatory for the Azerbayjan SSR. Both letters, of course, are included in [Az 5 Cyr]. Another sort of amalgamation occurs in the Yakut tables. [Yak 1 Cyr] and [Yak 2 Lat] each combines more than one alphabet's characters because several alphabets sponsored by diverse agencies or groups coexisted. This technique in the tables does not supply a replica of every early Yakut alphabet. The same process has been followed with Ossetic for the same reason. In each instance the separate alphabets can be examined in the references cited. Alphabets contrived by the Russian Orthodox Missionary Society have served particularly the Yakuts, Chuvash, and Kreshen Tatars. These alphabets have appeared infrequently in the Bibliographical Directory, where they are referred to as [Special Cyr]. No transliteration tables have been especially designed to process them, since the books' titles are usually written in the Russian language. This practice is analogous to the habit of Karaim publishers, who customarily titled their books in Hebrew.

To the confusion of generations of Soviet Eastern schoolchildren, as well as scholars outside the USSR, the order of alphabets in that region of the Soviet Union has been remarkably unstable. Kazakh perhaps exposes this difficulty as well as any alphabet (see [Kaz 5 Cyr]). Experienced readers will remember also that many times in the history of the USSR an officially discarded nationality alphabet continued in force long after the government decreed an end to its tenure. Soviet Azerbayjan, the second of the Soviet Easterners to adopt the Roman alphabet formally (1922), had not completely relinquished Arabic for domestic consumption until late 1928.

Arabic, Armenian, Cyrillic, Georgian, Hebrew, and Roman writing systems have been utilized in publishing by the Iranian and Turkic nationalities of the Czarist or Soviet East at one time or another. All except Armenian, applied to Kurd, are reproduced here in the tables which follow. Although linguists in Russia and elsewhere have elaborated phonetic transcriptions for study of most, if not all, of these twenty-six languages,[1] and transliteration tables have occasionally appeared in the United States for certain of the alphabets,[2] no comparable set of transliteration tables in English intended especially for use by social scientists, librarians, and humanists in treating published materials from the beginning of publishing in the territory of the Soviet East up to the present has previously become available.[3] Nevertheless, it is not the pur-

---

[1]The Imperial Russian Academy of Sciences gave extensive attention to transcription systems for many of these languages; see also *Philologiae Turcicae Fundamenta*, Vol. I (Wiesbaden: Aquis Mattiacis Apud Franciscum Steiner, 1959); János Eckmann, "Alphabet and Transcription," *Chagatay Manual* (Bloomington: Indiana University Publications, Uralic and Altaic Series, Vol. 60, 1966), pp. 25–27.

[2]John R. Krueger, *Chuvash Manual* and *Yakut Manual* (Bloomington: Indiana University Publications, Uralic and Altaic Series, Vol. 7 and vol. 21, 1961 and 1962); *Transliteration Tables for Non-Slavic Cyrillic-Alphabet Languages* (Washington: Library of Congress, n.d.), 7 pp.; *Transliteration of Non-Slavic Languages Written in the Russian Alphabet* (Washington: Library of Congress, n.d.), 27 pp.; *Transliteration of Turkic–Cyrillic Letters* (New York: New York Public Library, Slavonic Division, 1967), 1 p.; Edward Allworth, *Uzbek Literary Politics* (The Hague: Mouton, 1964), p. 253.

[3]R. S. Giliarevskii and N. V. Krylova, "Transliteratsiia bibliograficheskikh opisanii na iazykakh narodov SSSR latinskimi bukvami," *Sovetskaia bibliografiia*, No. 5 (1960), pp. 37–44; *Study on the Transliteration of the Alphabets of Non-Slavic Languages Using Cyrillic Characters* (Budapest: Hungarian Office for Standardization, 1967), 3, 6, and 14 pp. of tables; "List of Transliterations," *The Encyclopaedia of Islam* I (Leiden: E. J. Brill, 1960 2d ed.), p. xiii.

pose of this effort to thrust the system upon any potential user. It is offered as a tried, workable transliteration scheme to be adopted or improved upon as may seem fit. In either event, let us hope that this step will encourage the absorption of Soviet Eastern publications expeditiously into the general body of research materials contributing to scholarship and entered in library catalogs.

Users of the transliteration system will notice that throughout the tables, as well as the foregoing Bibliographical Directory, the undotted capital *I*, following American and English usage, stands as the equivalent of the dotted small letter *i*. This is true of the transliterations as well as the Roman alphabets of the Soviet East, which also accepted the same practice. No single-dotted capital *İ* will be found, therefore in the transliterations, but double-dotted small *ï* matches its capital *Ï* in both tables and bibliography.

Russian words included in the above Iranian- or Turkic-language titles, when printed with conventional Russian spelling, usually come through the transliteration of recent Cyrillic alphabets in their Russian form [Russ Cyr]. Non-Russian grammatical endings affixed to such words undergo transliteration via appropriate tables for the Soviet Eastern alphabets shown below. For examples of this technique, see Nos. 2881 and 2882 (Volga Tatar), or No. 2356 (Uzbek). Because Soviet practice calls for each nationality except the Russian to employ, in effect, two Cyrillic alphabets simultaneously—the Iranian or Turkic plus the Russian—the transliteration system must, of necessity, reflect this.

ALTAY [Alt 1 Cyr]

*ca. 1924–1928**

Alphabet	*Transliteration*
А а	a
Б б	b
В в	v
Г г	g
Д д	d
ДЬ дь	j
Е е	ye† e‡
Ж ж	zh
З з	z
И и	i
Й й	y
J j	j
К к	k
Л л	l
М м	m
Н н	n
Ҥ ҥ	ng
О о	o
Ӧ ӧ	ö
П п	p
Р р	r
С с	s
Т т	t
У у	u
Ӱ ӱ	ü
Ф ф	f
Х х	kh
Ц ц	ts
Ч ч	ch
Ш ш	sh
Ы ы	ï̡
Э э	ë
Ю ю	yu
Я я	ya

**Kul'tura i pis'mennost' Vostoka*, IV (1929), 190; and reconstructed from texts represented in this bibliography, the majority of which are printed in this alphabet. Publications designated as Altay or Oyrot are subsumed under this heading.

† initially

‡ elsewhere

ALTAY [Alt 2 Lat]

*1929–1937**

Alphabet	*Transliteration*	*Alphabet*	*Transliteration*
A a	a	X x	kh
B в	b	Y y	ü
C c	ch	Z z	z
Ç ç	j	Ƶ ƶ	zh
D d	d	Ь ь	ï
E e	e		
F f	f		
G g	g		
I i	i		
J j	y		
K k	k		
L l	l		
M m	m		
N n	n		
Ꞑ ꞑ	ng		
O o	o		
Ɵ ɵ	ö		
P p	p		
R r	r		
S s	s		
Ş ş	sh		
T t	t		
U u	u		
V v	v		

* N. A. Kalanakov, *Ömölik joktuga arga. Jaan ulustïng üüreneten tangmaligï* (Moscow: SSSR-de Jatkan Jüzün Jüür Uklu Albatïga Bichik Chigarïp Bazïbjasatkan Tsentrizdat, 1930 dilï), p. 62; N. Nurmakov, ed., *Alfavit oktiabria: Itogi vvedeniia novogo alfavita sredi narodov RSFSR* (Moscow–Leningrad: Tsentral'nyi Komitet Novogo Alfavita pri Prezidiume VTsIK, 1934), end sheet; *Kul'tura i pis'mennost' Vostoka*, IV (1929), 188, 190.

ALTAY [Alt 3 Cyr]

*1937–**

Alphabet	*Transliteration*	*Alphabet*	*Transliteration*
А а	a	У у	u
Б б	b	Ӱ ӱ	ü
В в	v	Ф ф	f
Г г	g	Х х	kh
Д д	d	Ц ц	ts
J j	j	Ч ч	ch
Е е	ye†	Ш ш	sh
	e‡	Щ щ	shch
Ё ё	yo	Ъ ъ	”
Ж ж	zh	Ы ы	ï
З з	z	Ь ь	’
И и	i	Э э	ë
Й й	y	Ю ю	yu
К к	k	Я я	ya
Л л	l		
М м	m		
Н н	n		
Ҥ ҥ	ng		
О о	o		
Ӧ ӧ	ö		
П п	p		
Р р	r		
С с	s		
Т т	t		

* R. S. Giliarevskii and V. S. Grivnin, *Opredelitel' iazykov mira po pis'mennostiam* (Moscow: Izdatel'stvo Vostochnoi Literatury, 1961), p. 55; N. A. Baskakov and T. M. Toshchakova, *Oyrot–orus sözlik* (Moscow: Gosudarstvennoe Izdatel'stvo Inostrannykh i Natsional'nykh Slovarei, 1947).

† initially

‡ elsewhere

AZERI [Az 1 & 2 Arab]

*–1922; 1922–1928/29**

Alphabet	*Transliteration*
ا	a
ه	ä
ب	b
پ	p
ت	t
ث	th
ج	j
چ	ch
ح	ḥ
خ	kh
د	d
ذ	dh
ر	r
ز	z
ژ	zh
س	s
ش	sh
ص	ṣ
ض	z̲
ط	ṭ
ظ	ẓ
ع	ʿ
غ	gh
ف	f
ق	q
ک	k
ڭ	ñ
گ	g
ل	l
م	m
ن	n
ه	h
و	v; o/ö, u/ü
ی	y; i/ï
ء	ʾ

* Lazar Budagov, *Prakticheskoe rukovodstvo turetsko-tatarskago Aderbidzhanskago nariechĭia* (Moscow: Universitetskaia Tipografĭia, 1859), p. 2; Sultan Majid Ghani-zadä, *Lughat-i turki vä rusi* (Baku: Tipografĭia Pervago Tipografskago Tovarishchestva, 1904); alphabet for 1928/29 reconstructed from R. Akhundov, *Ruscha–Turqchä lugät*, 2 vols. (Baku: Azärnäshr, 1928). The Azeri Arabic alphabet for 1922–1929 underwent little, if any, modification or reform because a Roman alphabet (see [Az 3 Lat]) already had been officially adopted. Most publishing continued in the Arabic, however.

AZERI [Az 3 Lat]

*1922–1928**

Alphabet	*Transliteration*
A a	a
B b	b
C c	j
Ç ç	ch
D d	d
E e	e
Ə ə	ä
F f	f
G g	g
H h	h
I i	i
I̡ ı̡	ï
J j	y
K k	k
L l	l
M m	m
N n	n
N̡ n̡	ng
O o	o
Ɵ ɵ	ö
P p	p
Q q	q
Ƣ ƣ	gh
R r	r
S s	s
T t	t
U u	u
V v	v
X x	kh
Y y	ü
Z z	z
Ƶ ƶ	zh
Ʒ ʒ	sh

* H. A. Sanïlï, *Turq älifbasï* (Baku: Azärnäshr, 1927/28), pp. 37–38.

AZERI [Az 4 Lat]

*1928–1939**

Alphabet	*Transliteration*
A a	a
B ь	b
C c	j
Ç ç	ch
D d	d
E e	e
Ə ə	ä
F f	f
G g	g
H h	h
I i	i
J j	y
K k	k
L l	l
M m	m
N n	n
Ꞑ ꞑ	ng
O o	o
P p	p
Q q	q
Ƣ ƣ	gh
R r	r
S s	s
Ş ş	sh
T t	t
U u	u
V v	v
X x	kh
Y y	ü
Z z	z
Ƶ ƶ	zh
Ь ь	ï
’	’
Ɵ ɵ	ö

* N. Nurmakov, ed., *Alfavit Oktiabria: Itogi vvedeniia novogo alfavita sredi narodov RSFSR* (Moscow–Leningrad: Tsentral'nyi Komitet Novogo Alfavita pri Prezidiume VTsIK, 1934), end sheet; note that the order of this alphabet had been changed by 1939, with *gh* following *g*, *ï* after *i*, *ö* after *o*, *ü* after *u*; *ng* was dropped and ’ added at the end. After 1934, *c* represented the sound *ch*, and *ç* represented the sound *j*, a reversal of earlier practice. H. Hüseynov, *Azärbayjancha–ruscha lüghät* (Baku: SSR Elmlär Aqademiyasï Az. Filialïnïn Näshriyyatï 1939).

AZERI [Az 5 Cyr]

*1940–**

Alphabet	*Transliteration*
А а	a
Б б	b
В в	v
Г г	g
Ғ ғ	gh
Д д	d
Е е	ye† e‡
Ә ә	ä
Ж ж	zh
З з	z
И и	i
Й й / J j	y††
К к	k
Ҝ ҝ	q
Л л	l
М м	m
Н н	n
О о	o
Ө ө	ö
П п	p
Р р	r
С с	s
Т т	t

Alphabet	*Transliteration*
У у	u
Ү ү	ü
Ф ф	f
Х х	kh
Һ һ	h
Ц ц	ts
Ч ч	ch
Ҹ ҹ	j
Ш ш	sh
Ы ы	ï
Э э	ë
Ю ю	yu
Я я	ya

* H. Hüseinov, ed., *Azärbayjanja-Rusja lüghät* (Baku: SSRI Elmlär Akademiyasï Azärbayjan Filialïnïn Näshriyyatï, 1941).

† initially

‡ elsewhere

†† J replaced Й in 1959

BASHKIR [Bash 1 Arab]

*–ca. 1923**

Alphabet	*Transliteration*	*Alphabet*	*Transliteration*
آ	a	ک	k
ب	b	گ	g
پ	p	ڭ	ng
ت	t	ل	l
ث	th	م	m
ج	j	ن	n
چ	ch	و	v ; o/ö ; u/ü
ح	ḥ	ه	h
خ	kh	ی	y ; i/ï
د	d	ە	e
ذ	dh	ء	ʾ
ر	r		
ز	z		
ژ	zh		
س	s		
ش	sh		
ص	ṣ		
ض	z̲		
ط	ṭ		
ظ	ẓ		
ع	ʿ		
غ	gh		
ف	f		
ق	q		

* K. Nasyrov, *Kratkaia tatarskaia grammatika izlozhennaia v primierakh* (Kazan: v Universitetskoi Tipografīi, 1860), p. 1.

BASHKIR [Bash 2 Arab]

*ca. 1924–1927**

Alphabet	*Transliteration*	*Alphabet*	*Transliteration*
ا	a	ن	n
ە	e	ئُوٗ,	o
ب	b	ئُوٗ	ö
پ	p	ئو,	u
ت	t	ئو	ü
ث	th	و	v
ج	j	ھ	h
چ	ch	ى/ئيـ	i
ح	ḥ	ىٗ	ï
د	d	يـ	y†
ذ	dh		
ر	r		
ز	z		
ژ	zh		
س	s		
ش	sh		
ع	gh		
ف	f		
ق	q		
ک	k		
ڭ	ng		
گ	g		
ل	l		
م	m		

* A. Saadi, "Bashkirskaia literatura," *Literaturnaia entsiklopediia*, I (n.p.: Izdatel'stvo Kommunisticheskoi Akademii, 1929), 375; Z. Shakiref, Sh. Churayïf, *Ghämäli Bashqort tele däreslege* (Ufa: Üdhäk Bashqort Yangï Älep Kämitäte häm "Bashkenäge" Näshere, 1928), p. 64.

† initially and with vowels

BASHKIR [Bash 3 Lat]
*1927–1940**

Alphabet	*Transliteration*	*Alphabet*	*Transliteration*
A a	a	S s	s
B ʙ	b	Ş ş	sh
C c	ch	T t	t
Ç ç	j	Ƀ ƀ	th
D d	d	U u	u
Đ đ	dh	V v	v
E e	e	X x	kh
Ə ə	ä	Y y	ü
F f	f	Z z	z
G g	g	Ƶ ƶ	zh
Ƣ ƣ	gh	Ь ь	ï
H h	h	Ьj ьj	ïy
I i	i		
J j	y		
K k	k		
Q q	q		
L l	l		
M m	m		
N n	n		
Ꞑ ꞑ	ng		
O o	o		
Ɵ ɵ	ö		
P p	p		
R r	r		

* Z. Shakiref and Sh. Churayïf, *Ghämäli Bashqort tele däreslege* (Ufa: Üdhäk Bashqort Yangï Älep Kamitäte häm "Bashkenäge" Näshere, 1928), p. 64.

BASHKIR [Bash 4 Cyr]

*1940–**

Alphabet	*Transliteration*	*Alphabet*	*Transliteration*
А а	a	С с	s
Б б	b	Ҫ ҫ	th
В в	v	Т т	t
Ғ ғ	g	У у	u
Г г	gh	Ү ү	ü
Д д	d	Ф ф	f
Ҙ ҙ	dh	Х х	kh
Е е	ye†	Һ һ	h
	e‡	Ц ц	ts
Ё ё	yo	Ч ч	ch
Ж ж	zh	Ш ш	sh
З з	z	Щ щ	shch
И и	i	Ъ ъ	”
Й й	y	Ы ы	ï
К к	k	Ь ь	'
Ҡ ҡ	q	Э э	ë
Л л	l	Ә ә	ä
М м	m	Ю ю	yu
Н н	n	Я я	ya
Ң ң	ng		
О о	o		
Ө ө	ö		
П п	p		
Р р	r		

* *Bashqortsa–russa hüdhlek* (Moscow: Sit häm Milli Teldärdhäge Hüdhlektär Däülät Izdatel'stvohï, 1958), p. 16.

† initially

‡ elsewhere

CHUVASH [Chu 1 Cyr]

*ca. 1871–1937**

Alphabet	*Transliteration*	*Alphabet*	*Transliteration*
А а	a	Ç ç	s'
Ӓӓ/Ӑӑ	ä	Т т	t
Б б	b	Т̆ т̆	t'
В в	v	Ꚋ ꚋ	tch
Г г	g	У у	u
Д д	d	Ӱ ӱ	ü
Е е	e	Ф ф	f
Ӗ ӗ	ë	Х х	kh
Ж ж	zh	Ц ц	ts
З з	z	Ч ч	ch
И и	i	Ш ш	sh
Й й	y	Щ щ	shch
İ і	ĭ	Ъ ъ	"
К к	k	Ы ы	ï
Л л	l	Ь ь	'
Ԓ ԓ/Ӆ ӆ	l'	Ю ю	yŭ
М м	m	Я я	yă
Н н	n		
Ԋ ԋ	n'		
Ҥ ҥ/Ӊ ӊ	ng		
О о	o		
П п	p		
Р р	r		
Р́ р́	r'		
С с	s		

* Ashmarin, *Materialy dlia izsledovaniia chuvashkago iazyka* (Kazan: Tipo-litografiia Imperatorskago Universiteta, 1898), pp. xxxiii–xxxiv; on Chuvash, and other title pages, often the publisher is given in Russian. In such cases, the transliteration will be shown according to [Russ Cyr].

CHUVASH [Chu 2 Cyr]

*1938–**

Alphabet	*Transliteration*
А а	a
Ă ă	ä
Б б	b
В в	v
Г г	g
Д д	d
Е е	ye† e‡
Ё ё	yo
Ĕ ĕ	ĕ
Ж ж	zh
З з	z
И и	i
Й й	y
К к	k
Л л	l
М м	m
Н н	n
О о	o
П п	p
Р р	r
С с	s
Ç ç	s'
Т т	t
У у	u
Ÿ ÿ	ü
Ф ф	f
Х х	kh
Ц ц	ts
Ч ч	ch
Ш ш	sh
Щ щ	shch
Ъ ъ	''
Ы ы	ï
Ь ь	'
Э э	ë
Ю ю	yŭ
Я я	yă

* M. Ia. Sirotkina, ed., *Chävashlavïräsla slovar'* (Moscow: Yüt S'ĕrshïv Tata Natsi Slovarĕsen Patshaläkh Izdatel'stvi, 1961), p. 18; John R. Krueger, *Chuvash Manual* (Bloomington: Indiana University Publications, Uralic and Altaic Series, vol. 7, 1961), pp. 61–62.

† initially

‡ elsewhere

CRIMEAN TATAR [Crim 1 Arab]

*–ca. 1923**

Alphabet	*Transliteration*	*Alphabet*	*Transliteration*
ا	a	ك	k
ب	b	گ	g
پ	p	ل	l
ت	t	م	m
ث	th	ن	n
ج	j	و	o/u
چ	ch	ه	h
ح	ḥ	ى	i/ï
خ	kh	ء	ʾ
د	d		
ذ	dh		
ر	r		
ز	z		
ژ	zh		
س	s		
ش	sh		
ص	ṣ		
ض	z̲		
ط	ṭ		
ظ	ẓ		
ع	ʿ		
غ	gh		
ف	f		
ق	q		

* L. M. Lazarev, *Turetsko-tatarsko–russkii slovar'—nariechĭi osmanskago, krymskago i kavkazskago* (Moscow: Lazarevskii Institut Vostochnykh Iazykov, 1864), pp. 1–2.

CRIMEAN TATAR [Crim 2 Arab]
*ca. 1924–1928**

Alphabet	*Transliteration*	*Alphabet*	*Transliteration*
ا	a	ن	n
أ	ë	و	v; o/ö, u/ü
ب	b	ە	e
پ	p	ھ	h
ت	t	ي	y; i/ï
ج	j		
چ	ch		
ح	ḥ		
خ	kh		
د	d		
ر	r		
ز	z		
ژ	zh		
س	s		
ش	sh		
ع	ʿ		
غ	gh		
ف	f		
ق	q		
ک	k		
گ	g		
ڭ	ng		
ل	l		
م	m		

* *Köz aydïn* No. 9 (Simferopol: Qrïm Merkezi Yanï Elifba Qomitesi, Jan. 15, 1928), p. 8.

CRIMEAN TATAR [Crim 3 Lat]
*ca. 1928–1938**

Alphabet	*Transliteration*	*Alphabet*	*Transliteration*
A a	a	R r	r
B ʙ	b	T t	t
C c	ch	U u	u
Ç ç	j	V v	v
D d	d	Y y	ü
E e	e	X x	kh
F f	f	Z z	z
G g	g	Ƶ ƶ	zh
H h	h		
I i	i		
J j	y		
Ь ь	ï		
K k	k		
Q q	q		
Ƣ ƣ	gh		
L l	l		
M m	m		
N n	n		
Ꞑ ꞑ	ng		
O o	o		
Ɵ ɵ	ö		
P p	p		
S s	s		
Ş ş	sh		

* *Köz aydïn* No. 9 (Simferopol: Qrïm Merkezi Yanï Elifba Qomitesi, Jan. 15, 1928), p. 8; N. Nurmakov, ed., *Alfavit oktiabria. Itogi vvedeniia novogo alfavita sredi narodov RSFSR* (Moscow–Leningrad: Tsentral'nyi Komitet Novogo Alfavita pri Prezidiume VTsIK, 1934), pp. 124–33 and end sheet.

CRIMEAN TATAR [Crim 4 Cyr]

*1938–**

Alphabet	*Transliteration*
А а	a
Б б	b
В в	v
Г г	g
ГЪ гъ	gh
Д д	d
ДЖ дж	j
Е е	ye† e‡
Ё ё	yo
Ж ж	zh
З з	z
И и	i
Й й	y
К к	k
КЪ къ	q
Л л	l
ЛЬ ль	l'
М м	m
Н н	n
НЪ нъ	ng
О о	o
П п	p
Р р	r
С с	s
Т т	t
У у	u
Ф ф	f
Х х	kh
Ц ц	ts
Ч ч	ch
Ш ш	sh
Ъ ъ	(see КЪ, ЛЪ, НЪ)
Ы ы	ï
Ь ь	'
Э э	ë
Ю ю	yu
Я я	ya

*Gerhard Doerfer, "Das Krimtatarische," *Philologiae Turcicae Fundamenta*, Vol. I (Wiesbaden: F. Steiner, 1959), I, 374; also, reconstructed from A. V. Shestakov, *SSSR tarikhï qïsqa kurs* (Krïm ASSR Devlet Neshriyatï, 1938); K. M. Musaev, *Alfavity iazykov narodov SSSR* (Moscow: Izdatel'stvo "Nauka," 1965), p. 32.

† initially

‡ elsewhere

KARACHAY–BALKAR [Kar–Bal 1 Arab]

*1916–ca. 1924**

Alphabet	*Transliteration*
ا	a
ب	b
پ	p
ت	t
ج	j
چ	ch
خ	kh
د	d
ر	r
ز	z
ژ	zh
س	s
ش	sh
غ	gh
ف	f
ق	q
ک	k
گ	g
ڭ	ng
ل	l
م	m
ن	n
ه	h
و	u/ü

Alphabet	*Transliteration*
و̂/ۋ	v
و̄	o
و̆	ö
ە	e
ی	y; i
ىٕ	ï
ۛ	ĭ

* "Karachaevskaia literatura," *Literaturnaia entsiklopediia* (n.p.: Izdatel'stvo Kommunisticheskoi Akademii, 1931), V, 118; Khasanov, "Knigoizdatel'skoe delo i literatura na severnom Kavkaze," *Knigonosha* No. 28 (July 19, 1924), p. 5.

KARACHAY–BALKAR [Kar–Bal 2 Lat]

*ca. 1924–1937**

Alphabet	*Transliteration*	*Alphabet*	*Transliteration*
A a	a	T t	t
B b	b	U u	u
C c	ch	V v	v
Ç ç		X x	kh
D d	d	Y y	ü
E e	e	Z z	z
F f	f	Ƶ ƶ	zh
G g	g	Ь ь	ï
Ƣ ƣ	gh		
H h	h		
I i	i		
J j	y		
K k	k		
L l	l		
M m	m		
N n	n		
Ꞑ ꞑ	ng		
O o	o		
Ɵ ɵ	ö		
P p	p		
Q q	q		
R r	r		
S s	s		
Ş ş/Š š	sh		

* Umar Alilanï, *Jangngï qarachay-malqar elible* (Kislovodsk: Oblastnoe Karachaevskoe Izdatel'stvo, 1929), p. 34.

KARACHAY–BALKAR [Kar–Bal 3 Cyr]

*ca. 1938–**

Alphabet	*Transliteration*
А а	a
Б б	b
В в	v
Г г	g
ГЪ гъ	gh
Д д	d
Е е	ye† e‡
Ё ё	yo
Ж ж	zh
ДЖ дж	j
З з	z
И и	i
Й й	y
К к	k
КЪ къ	q
Л л	l
М м	m
Н н	n
НГ нг	ng§
НЪ нъ	ng‖
О о	o
П п	p
Р р	r
С с	s
Т т	t
У у	u
У́ у́	ü‖
Ф ф	f
Х х	kh
Ц ц	ts
Ч ч	ch
Ш ш	sh
Щ щ	shch
Ъ ъ	”
Ы ы	ï
Ь ь	’
Э э	ë
Ю ю	yu
Я я	ya

* K. M. Musaev, *Alfavity iazykov narodov SSSR* (Moscow: Izdatel'stvo "Nauka," 1965), p. 32; R. S. Giliarevskii and V. S. Grivnin, *Opredelitel' iazykov mira po pis'mennostiam* (Moscow: Izdatel'stvo Vostochnoi Literatury, 1961), pp. 56–57.

†initially

‡ elsewhere

§ Balkar only

‖ Karachay only

KARAIM [Karai 1 Heb]

*–ca. 1930**

Alphabet	*Transliteration*	*Alphabet*	*Transliteration*
א	a	מ (ם)	m
ב	v	נ (ן)	n
בּ	b	ס	s
ב׳	b̈	ע	ʿ
ב̄	ŭ	פ (ף)	f
ג	gh	פּ (ףּ)	p
גּ	g	פּ׳	p̈
ג̄	g̈	פּ̄	f̈
ג׳	j	צ (ץ)	ch
נּ⃛	ng	ק	q
ד	dh	ק⃛	q̈
דּ	d	ק̄	x
ה	h	ר	r
ו	o	שׁ	sh
ו̈	ö	שׂ	ṣ
ו⃛	w	ת	t
ז	z	תּ	th
ח	ḥ		
ט	ṭ		
י	y		
י̄	i		
י⃛	ï		
כ (ך)	kh		
כּ (ך)	k		
כ̄	k̈		
כ׳	ḳ̈		
ל	l		

* Reconstructed from Karaim publications listed in the bibliography and K. M. Musaev, *Grammatika karaimskogo iazyka: Fonetika i morfologiia* (Moscow: Izdatel'stvo "Nauka," 1964), pp. 34–36.

KARAIM [Karai 2 Lat]

*ca. 1910–ca. 1927**

Alphabet	*Transliteration*	*Alphabet*	*Transliteration*
A a	a	Ü ü	ü
B b	b	W w	v
CH ch	kh	Y y	ï
CZ cz	ch	Z z	z
D d	d		
DŻ dż	j		
E e	e		
F f	f		
G g	g		
H h	h		
I i	i		
J j	y		
K k	k		
L l	l		
M m	m		
N n	n		
O o	o		
Ö ö	ö		
P p	p		
R r	r		
S s	s		
SZ sz	sh		
T t	t		
U u	u		

* K. M. Musaev, *Grammatika karaimskogo iazyka. Fonetika i morfologiia* (Moscow: Izdatel'stvo "Nauka," 1964), pp. 29, 34–35; A. Mardkowicz, *Karay sez bitigi* (Lutsk: Drukarnia Richtera, 1935), p. 6. The Karaims in Lithuania and the Ukraine do not have their own Cyrillic alphabet at present. Ananiasz Zajączkowski, *Karaims in Poland: History, Language, Folklore, Science* (The Hague–Paris: Państwowe Wydawnictwo Naukowe, 1961), p. 42.

KARAIM [Karai 3 Lat]
*ca. 1928–1940**

Alphabet	*Transliteration*	*Alphabet*	*Transliteration*
A a	a	T t	t
B b	b	U u	u
C c	ch	V v	v
Ç ç	j	X x	kh
D d	d	Y y	ü
E e	e	Z z	z
F f	f	Ƶ ƶ	zh
G g	g	Ь ь	ï
Ƣ ƣ	gh		
H h	h		
I i	i		
J j	y		
K k	k		
L l	l		
M m	m		
N n	n		
Ꞑ ꞑ	ng		
O o	o		
Ɵ ɵ	ö		
P p	p		
Q q	q		
R r	r		
S s	s		
Ş ş	sh		

* N. Nurmakov, ed., *Alfavit oktiabria: Itogi vvedeniia novogo alfavita sredi narodov RSFSR* (Moscow–Leningrad: Tsentral'nyi Komitet Novogo Alfavita pri Prezidiume VTsIK, 1934), p. 157, end sheet. The Krymchaks (Crimean Jews) employed the same Roman alphabet as the Karaims, beginning in 1928, though the two Turkic languages were not identical.

KARAKALPAK [Kar 1 Arab]

*–ca. 1923**

Alphabet	*Transliteration*	*Alphabet*	*Transliteration*
ء	ʾ	ق	q
آ	a	ک	k
ب	b	گ	g
پ	p	ڭ	ng
ت	t	ل	l
ث	th	م	m
ج	j	ن	n
چ	ch	و	v; o/ö, u/ü
ح	ḥ	ھ	h
خ	kh	ە	ä
د	d	ی	y; e, i/ï
ذ	dh		
ر	r		
ز	z		
ژ	zh		
س	s		
ش	sh		
ص	ṣ		
ض	z̲		
ط	ṭ		
ظ	ẓ		
ع	ʿ		
غ	gh		
ف	f		

* Karakalpak was written in the Kazakh or Volga Tatar alphabets in this period; see [Kaz 1 Arab] and [Tata 1 Arab], below.

KARAKALPAK [Kar 2 Arab]

*1924–1928**

Alphabet	*Transliteration*	*Alphabet*	*Transliteration*
ا	a	ۇ	u/ü
ە	ä	ۋ	v
ب	b	ھ	h
پ	p	ى	i
ت	t	ي	y
ج	j		
چ	ch		
خ	kh		
د	d		
ر	r		
ز	z		
ژ	zh		
س	s		
ش	sh		
غ	gh		
ف	f		
ق	q		
ک	k		
ڭ	ng		
گ	g		
ل	l		
م	m		
ن	n		
و	o/ö		

---

* N. A. Baskakov, *Karakalpakskii iazyk*, Vol. II, part I (Moscow: Izdatel'stvo Akademii Nauk SSSR, 1952), pp. 128–29.

KARAKALPAK [Kar 3 Lat]

*1928–1940**

Alphabet	*Transliteration*	*Alphabet*	*Transliteration*
A a	a	Ş ş	sh
B в	b	T t	t
C c	ch	U u	u
Ç ç	j	V v	v
D d	d	X x	kh
E e	e	Y y	ü
Ə ə	ä	Z z	z
F f	f	Ƶ ƶ	zh
G g	g	Ь ь	ï
Ƣ ƣ	gh		
H h	h		
I i	i†		
J j	y‡		
K k	k		
L l	l		
M m	m		
N n	n		
Ꞑ ꞑ	ng		
O o	o		
Ө ө	ö		
P p	p		
Q q	q		
R r	r		
S s	s		

* N. A. Baskakov, *Karakalpakskii iazyk* vol. II, part I (Moscow: Izdatel'stvo Akademiia Nauk SSSR, 1952), pp. 128–29; N. A. Baskakov, *Qaraqalpaqsha-russha sözlik* (Moscow: Shet Til häm Milliy Sözlik Mämleket Baspasï, 1958), pp. 794–95.

† 1938–1940: y

‡ 1938–1940: i

KARAKALPAK [Kar 4 Cyr]

*1940–**

Alphabet	*Transliteration*	*Alphabet*	*Transliteration*
А а	a	С с	s
Ә ә	ä	Т т	t
Б б	b	У у	u
В в	v	Ү ү	ü
Г г	g	Ў ў	w
Ғ ғ	gh	Ф ф	f
Д д	d	Х х	kh
Е е	ye† e‡	Ҳ ҳ	h
Ё ё	ya	Ц ц	ts
Ж ж	j zh§	Ч ч	ch
		Ш ш	sh
		Щ щ	shch
З з	z	Ъ ъ	”
И и	i	Ы ы	ï
Й й	y	Ь ь	’
К к	k	Э э	ë
Қ қ	q	Ю ю	yu
Л л	l	Я я	yä
М м	m		
Н н	n		
Ң ң	ng		
О о	o		
Ө ө	ö		
П п	p		
Р р	r		

* N. A. Baskakov, *Qaraqalpaqsha–russha sözlik* (Moscow: Shet Til häm Milliy Sözlik Mämleket Baspasï, 1958), p. 14.

† initially

‡ elsewhere

§ in foreign words

KAZAKH [Kaz 1 Arab]
*–ca. 1922**

Alphabet	*Transliteration*	*Alphabet*	*Transliteration*
ء	ʾ	ق	q
آ	a	ک	k
ب	b	گ	g
پ	p	ڭ	ng
ت	t	ل	l
ث	th	م	m
ج	j	ن	n
چ	ch	و	v; o/ö, u/ü
ح	ḥ	ھ	h
خ	kh	ە	e
د	d	ی	y; i/ï
ذ	dh		
ر	r		
ز	z		
ژ	zh		
س	s		
ش	sh		
ص	ṣ		
ض	ẕ		
ط	ṭ		
ظ	ẓ		
ع	ʿ		
غ	gh		
ف	f		

* Kh. Makhmudov and Gh. Mŭsabaev, *Qazaqsha–orïssha sözdïk* (Alma Ata: Qazaq SSR Ghïlïm Akademiyäsïnïng Baspasï, 1954), p. 520.

KAZAKH [Kaz 2 Arab]

*ca. 1923–1927**

Alphabet	*Transliteration*	*Alphabet*	*Transliteration*
آ	a	ې	e
ب	b	ء	ʾ
پ	p	ىٔ	ĭ
ت	t		
ج	j		
چ	ch		
د	d		
ر	r		
ز	z		
س	s		
ش	sh		
غ	gh		
ق	q		
ک	k		
گ	g		
ڭ	ng		
ل	l		
م	m		
ن	n		
و	o/ö		
ۇ	u/ü		
ۋ	v		
ە	ä		
ى	i/ï		

* "Kazakhskii iazyk," *Literaturnaia entsiklopediia*, V (n.p.: Izdatel'stvo Kommunisticheskoi Akademii, 1931), 23; Äbdiragman and Ghabiyt, *Qïzïl äsker älipbesi* (Kzil Orda: Qazaqstan Baspasï, 1929), p. 117; Kh. Makhmudov and Gh. Mŭsabaev, *Qazaqsha–orïssha sözdïk* (Alma Ata: Qazaq SSR Ghïlïm Akademiyäsïnïng Baspasï, 1954), p. 521; Nazïr Toräqul, *Janga alïb-bi nägä käräk?* (Moscow: Säbät Odaghïndaghï Khalqdardïng Kindik Basbasï, 1924), p. 84.

KAZAKH [Kaz 3 Arab]

*ca. 1927–1929**

Alphabet	*Transliteration*	*Alphabet*	*Transliteration*
ا	a	ئۇ	ü
ب	b	ە	e
پ	p	ى	ï
ت	t	ئى	i
ج	j	ي	y
ح	ḥ	ء	ʾ
د	d	ھ	h
ر	r		
ز	z		
س	s		
ش	sh		
ع	gh		
ف	f		
ق	q		
ک	k		
گ	g		
ڭ	ng		
ل	l		
م	m		
ن	n		
و	o		
ئو	ö		
ۇ	u		
ۋ/ۆ	v		

* "Kazakhskii iazyk," *Literaturnaia entsiklopediia*, V (n.p.: Izdatel'stvo Kommunisticheskoi Akademii, 1931), 23; Äbdiragman and Ghabiyt, *Qïzïl asker älipbesi* (Kzil Orda: Qazaqstan Baspasï, 1929), p. 117; Kh. Makhmudov and Gh. Mŭsabaev, *Qazaqsha–orïssha sözdik* (Alma Ata: Qazaq SSR Ghïlïm Akademiyäsïnïng Baspasï, 1954), p. 521.

KAZAKH [Kaz 4 Lat]

*1928–1940**

Alphabet	Transliteration	Alphabet	Transliteration
A a	a	V v	v
B в	b	Y y	ü
C c	sh	Z z	z
Ç ç	j	Ь ь	ï
D d	d		
E e	e		
Ə ə	ä		
G g	g		
Ƣ ƣ	gh		
H h	h		
I i	i		
J j	y		
K k	k		
L l	l		
M m	m		
N n	n		
Ꞑ ꞑ	ng		
O o	o		
Ɵ ɵ	ö		
P p	p		
R r	r		
S s	s		
T t	t		
U u	u		

* "Kazakhskii iazyk," *Literaturnaia entsiklopediia*, V (n.p.: Izdatel'stvo Kommunisticheskoi Akademii, 1931), 23; Äbdiragman and Ghabiyt, *Qïzïl äsker älipbesi* (Kzil Orda: Qazaqstan Baspasï, 1929), p. 117.

KAZAKH [Kaz 5 Cyr]

*1940–**

Alphabet	*Transliteration*
А а	a
Ә ә	ä
Б б	b
В в	v
Г г	g
Ғ ғ	gh
Д д	d
Е е	e
Ё ё	ya
Ж ж	j zh†
З з	z
И и	i
Й й	y
К к	k
Қ қ	q
Л л	l
М м	m
Н н	n
Ң ң	ng
О о	o
Ө ө	ö
П п	p
Р р	r
С с	s
Т т	t
У у	u
Ұ ұ	ŭ
Ү ү	ü
Ф ф	f
Х х	kh
Һ һ	h
Ш ш	sh
Щ щ	shch
Ъ ъ	”
Ы ы	ï
І і	ĭ
Ь ь	’
Э э	ë
Ц ц	ts
Ч ч	ch
Ю ю	yu
Я я	yä

* Gh. Begaliev, Kh. Makhmudov, and Gh. Mŭsabaev, *Qazaqsha–orïssha shaghïn sözdĭk* (Alma Ata: Qazaq SSR Ghïlïm Akademiyäsï. Tĭl Jäne Ädebiet Institutï, 1959), p. 5; Boris N. Shnitnikov, *Kazakh–English Dictionary* (London: Mouton, 1966), p. 9. The order of letters in this alphabet has changed significantly between 1940 and 1959, like many others. In 1954, these letters fell at the end of the alphabet: *ĭ, q, ng, gh, ü, ŭ, ö, ä, h.*

† in foreign words

KHAKASS [Khak 1 Cyr]

*ca. 1924–1929**

Alphabet	*Transliteration*	*Alphabet*	*Transliteration*
А а	a	Э э	e
Б б	b	Һ һ	gh†
Г г	g	I i	ĭ
Д д	d	Я я	yă
З з	z		
И и	i		
К к	k		
Л л	l		
М м	m		
Н н	n		
О о	o		
П п	p		
Р р	r		
С с	s		
Т т	t		
У у	u		
Х х	kh		
Ч ч	ch		
Ы ы	ï		
J j	j		
Ӱ ӱ	ü		
Ӧ ӧ	ö		
Ң ң	ng		
Й й	y		

* K. Togïshev, *Khakasstïng ing pastap ügrener pichi* (Moscow: Tsentrizdat Narodov SSSR, 1926), p. 24; N. A. Baskakov and A. I. Inkizhekova-Grekul *Khakassko-russkii slovar'* (Moscow: Gosizdat Inostrannykh i Natsional'nykh Slovarei, 1953), pp. 368–69.

† 1927–1929.

KHAKASS [Khak 2 Lat]
*ca. 1929–1939**

Alphabet	*Transliteration*	*Alphabet*	*Transliteration*
A a	a	U u	u
B ʙ	b	V v	v
C c	ch	X x	kh
Ç ç	j	Y y	ü
D d	d	Z z	z
Ə ə	ä	Ƶ ƶ	zh
E e	e†	Ь ь	ï
F f	f	Ļ ļ	ĭ
G g	g		
Ƣ ƣ	gh		
I i	i		
J j	y		
K k	k		
L l	l		
M m	m		
N n	n		
Ꞑ ꞑ	ng		
O o	o		
Ө ө	ö		
P p	p		
R r	r		
S s	s		
Ş ş	sh		
T t	t		

*K. Samrin, *Naa chol: Khakas bukvarï* (Moscow: SSRS Chonïnïng Santïr Izdalälïstïvazï, 1930); N. A. Baskakov and A. I. Inkizhekova-Grekul, *Khakassko-russkii slovar'* (Moscow: Gosizdat Inostrannykh i Natsional'nykh Slovarei, 1953), pp. 368–69.

† introduced 1936 for same sound as *ə*

KHAKASS [Khak 3 Cyr]

*ca. 1939–**

Alphabet	*Transliteration*	*Alphabet*	*Transliteration*
А а	a	Ӱ ӱ	ü
Б б	b	Ф ф	f
В в	v	Х х	kh
Г г	g	Ц ц	ts
Ғ ғ	gh†	Ч ч	ch
Д д	d	Ҷ ҷ	j†
Е е	e	Ш ш	sh
Ж ж	zh	Щ щ	shch
З з	z	Ъ ъ	”
И и	i	Ы ы	ï
İ i	ĭ	Ь ь	'
Й й	y	Э э	ë
К к	k	Ю ю	yu
Л л	l	Я я	ya
М м	m		
Н н	n		
НЪ нъ	ng		
О о	o		
Ӧ ӧ	ö		
П п	p		
Р р	r		
С с	s		
Т т	t		
У у	u		

* N. A. Baskakov and A. I. Inkizhekova-Grekul, *Khakassko-russkii slovar'* (Moscow: Gosizdat Inostrannykh i Natsional'nykh Slovarei, 1953), pp. 368–69.

† 1946

KIRGIZ [Kir 1 Arab]
*–1927**

Alphabet	*Transliteration*	*Alphabet*	*Transliteration*
ا	a	ى	i/ï
ب	b	ي	y
پ	p	ء	'
ت	t		
ج	j		
ح	ḥ		
چ	ch		
د	d		
ر	r		
ز	z		
س	s		
ش	sh		
ع	gh		
ق	q		
ک	k		
گ	g		
ڭ	ng		
ل	l		
م	m		
ن	n		
و	o/ö		
ۇ	u/ü		
ۋ	v		
ه	e		

* "Kirgizskii iazyk," *Literaturnaia entsiklopediia*, V (n.p.: Izdatel'stvo Kommunisticheskoi Akademii, 1931), 213; *Bïzdïn jangi alïpbee* (Frunze: Qïrgïzïstandïn Basma Soz Taratuu Mekemesi, 1927), p. 6; Kirgiz publications issued before ca. 1922 employed the Kazakh or Tatar alphabets. See [Kaz 1 Arab].

KIRGIZ [Kir 2 Lat]
*1927–1940**

Alphabet	*Transliteration*
A a	a
B ʙ	b
C c	ch
Ç ç	j
D d	d
E e	e
F f	f
G g	g
Ƣ ƣ	gh
I i	i
J j	y
K k	k
L l	l
M m	m
Ꞑ ꞑ	n
N n	ng
O o	o
Ɵ ɵ	ö
P p	p
Q q	q
R r	r
S s	s
Ş ş	sh
T t	t
U u	u
V v	v
X x	kh
Y y	ü
Z z	z
Ƶ ƶ	zh
Ь ь	ï

* "Kirgizskii iazyk," *Literaturnaia entsiklopediia*, V (n.p.: Izdatel'stvo Kommunisticheskoi Akademii, 1931), 213; K. K. Yudakhin, *Kïrgïzcha–oruscha sözdük* (Moscow: Izdatel'stvo Inostrannykh i Natsional'nykh Slovarei, 1940), p. 10.

KIRGIZ [Kir 3 Cyr]

*1940–**

Alphabet	*Transliteration*	*Alphabet*	*Transliteration*
А а	a	Ф ф	f
Б б	b	Х х	kh
В в	v	Ц ц	ts
Г г	g	Ч ч	ch
Д д	d	Ш ш	sh
Е е	e	Щ щ	shch
Ё ё	yö	Ъ ъ	’’
Ж ж	j	Ы ы	ï
З з	z	Ь ь	'
И и	i	Э э	ë
Й й	y	Ю ю	yu
К к	k	Я я	ya
Л л	l		
М м	m		
Н н	n		
Ң ң	ng		
О о	o		
Ӧ ӧ	ö		
П п	p		
Р р	r		
С с	s		
Т т	t		
У у	u		
Ү ү	ü		

* K. K. Yudakhin, comp., *Kïrgïzcha–oruscha sözdük* (Moscow: "Sovetskaia Entsiklopediia" Basmasï, 1965), p. 16.

KRESHEN TATAR [Kresh 1 Cyr]

*1862–ca. 1928**

Alphabet	*Transliteration*	*Alphabet*	*Transliteration*
А а	a	Ф ф	f
Ӓ ӓ	ä	Х х	kh
Б б	b	Ч ч	ch
В в	v	Ш ш	sh
Г г	g	Ы ы	ï
Д д	d	Ь ь	'
Е е	e	Э э	ë
Ж ж	j	Ю ю	yu
З з	z	Я я	yä
И и	i		
Й й	y		
К к	k		
Л л	l		
М м	m		
Н н	n		
Ң ң	ng		
О о	o		
Ӧ ӧ	ö		
П п	p		
Р р	r		
С с	s		
Т т	t		
У у	u		
Ӳ ӳ	ü		

---

* Reconstructed from titles included in this bibliography and A. N. Grigor'ev, *Kryäshennyär arasïnda "Yängalif" myäsyälyäse* (Kazan: Izdatel'stvo "Ianalif," 1927), p. 23; Nikolai Il'minskii, *Iz perepiski po voprosu o primienenīi russkago alfavita k inorodcheskim iazykam* (Kazan: Tipografīia Imperatorskago Universiteta, 1883), p. 11.

KRESHEN TATAR [Kresh 2 Arab]

*1922–1928**

Alphabet	*Transliteration*	*Alphabet*	*Transliteration*
ا	a	ئۇ	ö
ئه	ä	ئو,	u
ب	b	ئو	ü
پ	p	و/ۋ	v
ت	t	ه	h
ج	j	ئيـ	i
چ	ch	ئيـ,	ï
ح	kh	ئيـ,	ïy
د	d	ئۀ	e
ر	r	ى	y
ز	z		
ژ	zh		
س	s		
ش	sh		
ع	gh		
ف	f		
ق	q		
ك	k		
گ	g		
ڭ	ng		
ل	l		
م	m		
ن	n		
ئۇ,	o		

* A. N. Grigor'ev, *Kryäshennyär arasïnda "Yängalif" myäsyälyäse* (Kazan: Izdatel'stvo "Ianalif," 1927), pp. 3–4, 23; *Stenograficheskii otchet tret'ego plenuma vsesoiuznogo tsentral'nogo komiteta novogo tiurkskogo alfavita, zasedavshego v g. Kazani ot 18-go po 23-e dekabria 1928g.* (Kazan: Izdanie Vsesoiuznogo Tsentral'nogo Komiteta Novogo Tiurkskogo Alfavita, 1928), pp. 173, 185. Kreshen Tatar books had also been printed in Arabic between 1847 and 1861, but in an unmodified alphabet (see [Tata 1 Arab]); see also Nikolai Il'minskii, *Iz perepiski po voprosu o primienenii russkago alfavita k inorodcheskim iazykam* (Kazan: Tipografiia Imperatorskago Universiteta, 1883), p. 11.

KRESHEN TATAR [Kresh 3 Lat]

*ca. 1928–1937**

Alphabet	*Transliteration*	*Alphabet*	*Transliteration*
A a	a	Ş ş	sh
B ʙ	b	T t	t
C c	ch	U u	u
Ç ç	j	V v	v
D d	d	X x	kh
E e	e	Y y	ü
Ə ə	ä	Z z	z
F f	f	Ƶ ƶ	zh
G g	g	Ь ь	ï
Ƣ ƣ	ʾ	ЬJ ьj	ïy
H h	h		
I i	i		
J j	y		
K k	k		
L l	l		
M m	m		
N n	n		
Ꞑ ꞑ	ng		
O o	o		
Ɵ ɵ	ö		
P p	p		
Q q	q		
R r	r		
S s	s		

* A. N. Grigor'ev, *Kryäshennyär arasïnda "Yängalif" myäsyälyäse* (Kazan: Izdatel'stvo "Ianalif," 1927), p. 23; Alexandre Bennigsen and Chantal Quelquejay, *The Evolution of the Muslim Nationalities of the USSR and their Linguistic Problems* (London: Central Asian Research Centre, 1961), p. 18. Although the Kreshen Tatars adopted the Romanized alphabet in 1927, no publications using it have been found in the United States. It is possible that they were not given permission to make the change and continued employing the Cyrillic. Their separate linguistic status ended in 1937.

KRYMCHAK [*see* Karai]

KUMYK [Kum 1 Arab]

*ca. 1912–ca. 1923**

Alphabet	*Transliteration*	*Alphabet*	*Transliteration*
ا	a	ق	q
ە	ä	ک	k
ب	b	ڭ	ng
پ	p	گ	g
ت	t	ل	l
ث	th	م	m
ج	j	ن	n
چ	ch	ه	h
ح	ḥ	و	o/u
خ	kh	ی	y; i/ï
د	d	ء	ʾ
ذ	dh		
ر	r		
ز	z		
ژ	zh		
س	s		
ش	sh		
ص	ṣ		
ض	z̲		
ط	ṭ		
ظ	ẓ		
ع	ʿ		
غ	gh		
ف	f		

* Chobanzadä, *Qumuq dili vä ädäbiyyatï tädqiqläri* (Baku: Adhärbayjanï Tädqiq vä Tätäbbüʿ Jämʿiyyat Näshriyatï, 1926), pp. 29–35; Khasanov, "Knigoizdatel'skoe delo i literatura na severnom Kavkaze," *Knigonosha* No. 28 (July 19, 1924), p. 5.

KUMYK [Kum 2 Arab]

*ca. 1923–1927**

Alphabet	*Transliteration*	*Alphabet*	*Transliteration*
ا	a	ە	ä
ب	b	ى	y; i/ï
پ	p	ﻫ	h
ت	t		
ج	j		
چ	ch		
خ	kh		
د	d		
ر	r		
ز	z		
ژ	zh		
س	s		
ش	sh		
غ	gh		
ق	q		
ک	k		
گ	g		
ل	l		
م	m		
ن	n		
ڭ	ng		
و	v; u/ü		
و̄	o		
ۊ	ö		

* Mahammad Dibirof, *Qumuq alifba* Makhachkala: Daghïstan Yanghï Alifba Qomitetinï Nashriyyati, 1928), p. 27; N. A., "Kumykskii iazyk," *Literaturnaia entsiklopediia*, V (n.p.: Izdatel'stvo Kommunisticheskoi Akademii, 1931), 730.

KUMYK [Kum 3 Lat]

*ca. 1927–1937**

Alphabet	*Transliteration*	*Alphabet*	*Transliteration*
A a	a	Ş ş	sh
B b	b	T t	t
C c	ch	U u	u
Ç ç	j	V v	v
D d	d	X x	kh
E e	e	Y y	ü
Ə ə	ä	Z z	z
F f	f	Ƶ ƶ	zh
G g	g	Ь ь	ï
Ƣ ƣ	gh		
H h	h		
I i	i		
J j	y		
K k	k		
L l	l		
M m	m		
N n	n		
Ꞑ ꞑ	ng		
O o	o		
Ɵ ɵ	ö		
P p	p		
Q q	q		
R r	r		
S s	s		

* Mahammad Dibirof, *Qumuq alifba* Makhachkala: Daghïstan Yanghï Alifba Qomitetinï Nashriyyatï, 1928), p. 27.

KUMYK [Kum 4 Cyr]

*ca. 1938–**

Alphabet	*Transliteration*	*Alphabet*	*Transliteration*
А а	a	Р р	r
Б б	b	С с	s
В в	v	Т т	t
Г г	g	У у	u
ГЪ гъ	gh	УЬ уь	ü
ГЬ гь	h	Ф ф	f
Д д	d	Х х	kh
Е е	ye†	Ц ц	ts
	e‡	Ч ч	ch
Ё ё	yo	Ш ш	sh
Ж ж	j	Щ щ	shch
	zh§	Ъ ъ	”
З з	z	Ы ы	ï
И и	i	Ь ь	'
Й й	y	Э э	ë
К к	k	Ю ю	yu
КЪ къ	q	Я я	ya
Л л	l		
М м	m		
Н н	n		
НГ нг	ng		
О о	o		
ОЬ оь	ö		
П п	p		

* R. S. Giliarevskii and V. S. Grivnin, *Opredelitel' iazykov mira po pis'mennostiam* (Moscow: Izdatel'stvo Vostochnoi Literatury, 1961), p. 50.

† initially

‡ elsewhere

§ in foreign words

KURD [Kur 1 Arab]
*–1927**

Alphabet	*Transliteration*	*Alphabet*	*Transliteration*
آ	a	ک	k
ب	b	گ	g
پ	p	ل	l
ت	t	م	m
ث	th	ن	n
ج	j	ئو	o/ö;u
چ	ch	ڤ	v
ح	ḥ	و	w
خ	kh	ھ	h
د	d	ه	ä
ذ	dh	ی	y; i/ï
ر	r		
ز	z		
ژ	zh		
س	s		
ش	sh		
ص	ṣ		
ض	ẕ		
ط	ṭ		
ظ	ẓ		
ع	äʿ		
غ	gh		
ف	f		
ق	q		

* Peter Lerch, *Forschungen über die Kurden und die iranischen Nordchaldäer* (St. Petersburg: Gedruckt auf Verfügung der Kaiserlichen Akademie der Wissenschaften, 1858), p. 31; K. K. Kurdoev, *Grammatika kurdskogo iazyka (Kurmandzhi): Fonetika, morfologiia* (Moscow: Izdatel'stvo Akademiia Nauk SSSR, 1957), pp. 12–13, 14. Kurdish was written also in an adaptation of the Armenian alphabet from 1920 to 1927. Neither the alphabet employed nor a specimen of the text printed in that alphabet has become available for purposes of this study.

KURD [Kur 2 Lat]

*1927–1945**

Alphabet	*Transliteration*	*Alphabet*	*Transliteration*
A a	a	Ɵ ɵ	ö
B в	b	P p	p
C c	ch	Ꝑ ꝑ/Ᵽ ᵽ	p'
Ꞓ ꞓ	ch'	R r	r
Ç ç	j	S s	s
D d	d	Ş ş	sh
E e	e	T t	t
Ə ə	ä	Ţ ţ	t'
Ə' ə'	äʿ	U u	u
F f	f	Y y	ü
G g	g	V v	v
Ƣ ƣ	gh	W w	w
H h	h	X x	kh
Ħ ħ	ḥ	Z z	z
I i	i	Ƶ ƶ	zh
Ь ь	ï		
J j	y		
K k	k		
Ķ ķ	k'		
Q q	q		
L l	l		
M m	m		
N n	n		
O o	o		

* K. K. Kurdoev, *Grammatika kurdskogo iazyka* (*Kurmandzhi*). *Fonetika. Morfologiia* (Moscow: Izdatel'stvo Akademii Nauk SSSR, 1957), pp. 12–13; N. Nurmakov, ed., *Alfavit oktiabria: Itogi vvedeniia novogo alfavita sredi narodov RSFSR* (Moscow–Leningrad: Tsentral'nyi Komitet Novogo Alfavita pri Prezidiume VTsIK, 1934), end sheet; *Kul'tura i pis'mennost' Vostoka*, IV (1929), 188–89.

KURD [Kur 3 Lat]

*ca. 1960**

Alphabet	*Transliteration*	*Alphabet*	*Transliteration*
A a	a	R r	r
B b	b	S s	s
C c	j	Ş ş	sh
Ç ç	ch	T t	t
D d	d	U u	u
E e	ä	Û û	ü
E' e'	ä'	V v	v
F f	f	W w	w
G g	g	Y y	y
H h	h	Z z	z
Ḧ ḧ	ḥ		
X x	kh		
Ẍ ẍ	gh		
Î î	i		
Ê ê	e		
I i	ï		
J j	zh		
K k	k̇		
Q q	q		
L l	l		
M m	m		
N n	n		
O o	o		
P p	p		

* Q. Kurdo, comp., *Färhänga Kurdi-Rüsi* (Moscow: Näshirkhana Däwläte ya Färhänged Zimane Miläted Därävä Ǚ Ye Sovetistane, 1960), p. 36. This alphabet was used mainly outside the USSR in 1960.

KURD [Kur 4 Cyr]

*1945–**

Alphabet	*Transliteration*	*Alphabet*	*Transliteration*
А а	a	Ф ф	f
Б б	b	Х х	kh
В в	v	Ч ч	ch
Г г	g	Ч' ч'	ch'
Г' г'	g'	Ш ш	sh
Д д	d	Щ щ	j
Е е	e	Ь ь	ï
Ж ж	zh	Э э	ë
З з	z	һ һ	h
И и	i	һ' һ'	h'
Й й	y	Q q	q
К к	k	W w	w
К' к'	k'	Ә ә	ä
Л л	l		
М м	m		
Н н	n		
О о	o		
Ö ö	ö		
П п	p		
П' п'	p'		
С с	s		
Т т	t		
Т' т'	t'		
У у	u		

* K. M. Musaev, *Alfavity iazykov narodov SSSR* (Moscow: Izdatel'stvo "Nauka," 1965), pp. 26–28; N. A. Baskakov, ed., *Osnovnye protsessy vnutristrukturnogo razvitiia iranskikh i iberiisko-kavkazskikh iazykov* (Moscow: Izdatel'stvo "Nauka," 1969), pp. 159–62.

NAGAYBAK [Nag 1 Cyr]

*1923–ca. 1937**

Alphabet	*Transliteration*
А а	a
Б б	b
В в	v
Г г	g
Д д	d
Е е	e
Ж ж	j
З з	z
И и	i
Й й	y
К к	k
Л л	l
М м	m
Н н	n
О о	o
П п	p
Р р	r
С с	s
Т т	t
У у	u
Ф ф	f
Х х	kh
Ч ч	ch
Ш ш	sh
Ы ы	ï
Ь ь	'
Э э	ë
Ю ю	yu
Я я	yä† ä‡

* Reconstructed from the title included in this bibliography; Alexandre Bennigsen and Chantal Quelquejay, *The Evolution of the Muslim Nationalities of the USSR and their Linguistic Problems* (London: Central Asian Research Centre, 1961), p. 18. The Nagaybaks—like the Kreshen Tatars extremely close to the Volga Tatars linguistically—apparently never employed the Roman alphabet, for neither small group appears in comprehensive charts or references concerning the Turkic nationalities which adopted the new Romanized (uniformalized) Turkic alphabet. Nagaybak ceased to function as a separate printed language ca. 1937.

† initially

‡ elsewhere

NOGHAY [Nogh 1 Arab]

*–ca. 1923**

Alphabet	*Transliteration*	*Alphabet*	*Transliteration*
ا	a	ك	k
ب	b	ک	g
پ	p	ل	l
ت	t	م	m
ث	th	ن	n
ج	j	نك	ng
چ	ch	و	o/u
ح	ḥ	ه	h
خ	kh	ى	y; i/ï
د	d	ء	ʾ
ذ	dh		
ر	r		
ز	z		
ژ	zh		
س	s		
ش	sh		
ص	ṣ		
ض	z̲		
ط	ṭ		
ظ	ẓ		
ع	ʿ		
غ	gh		
ف	f		
ق	q		

* Noghay had been written for centuries before 1923 in the Arabic alphabet of the Astrakhan Tatars and was published as early as 1825 in religious books. See [Tata 1 Arab].

NOGHAY [Nogh 2 Arab]

*ca. 1923–1928**

Alphabet	*Transliteration*	*Alphabet*	*Transliteration*
ا	a	و	v
ئه	ä	ى	i
ب	b	ىٔ	ï
پ	p	ي	y†
ت	t	؞	e‡
ج	j		
د	d		
ر	r		
ز	z		
س	s		
ش	sh		
ع	gh		
ف	f		
ق	q		
ک	k		
گ	g		
ڭ	ng		
ل	l		
م	m		
ن	n		
ئو,	o		
ئو	ö		
ئۇ,	u		
ئۇ	ü		

* Äliy Ibräyimip, *Üykönner ushun Noghay elippesi* (Moscow: SSSR Orta Basbasï, 1929).

† initial and final position or with vowels

‡ between consonants

NOGHAY [Nogh 3 Lat]

*ca. 1928–1937**

Alphabet	*Transliteration*	*Alphabet*	*Transliteration*
A a	a	U u	u
B в	b	X x	kh†
Ç ç	j	Y y	ü
D d	d	J j	y
E e	e	Ь ь	ï
Ə ə	ä	Z z	z
F f	f†	Ƶ ƶ	zh†
G g	g	V v	v
Ƣ ƣ	gh‡		
H h	h†		
I i	i		
K k	k		
L l	l		
M m	m		
N n	n		
Ꞑ ꞑ	ng		
O o	o		
Ө ө	ö		
P p	p		
Q q	q		
R r	r		
S s	s		
Ş ş	sh		
T t	t		

* Äliy Ibräyimip, *Üykönner ushun Noghay elippesi* (Moscow: SSSR Orta Basbasï, 1929); N. Nurmakov, ed., *Alfavit oktiabria. Itogi vvedeniia novogo alfavita sredi narodov RSFSR* (Moscow–Leningrad: Tsentral'nyi Komitet Novogo Alfavita pri Prezidiume VTsIK, 1934), end sheet.

† added after 1929

‡ dropped by 1934

NOGHAY [Nogh 4 Cyr]

*ca. 1938–**

Alphabet	*Transliteration*	*Alphabet*	*Transliteration*
А а	a	У у	u
Б б	b	УЬ уь	ü
В в	v	Ф ф	f
Г г	g	Х х	kh
Д д	d	Ц ц	ts
Е е	ye† e‡	Ч ч	ch
Ё ё	yo	Ш ш	sh
Ж ж	j zh	Щ щ	shch
З з	z	Ъ ъ	”§
И и	i	Ы ы	ï
Й й	y	Ь ь	ʼ
К к	k	Э э	ë
Л л	l	Ю ю	yu
М м	m	Я я	ya
Н н	n		
НЪ нъ	ng		
О о	o		
ОЬ оь	ö		
П п	p		
Р р	r		
С с	s		
Т т	t		

* N. A. Baskakov, *Nogaysha–orïssha sözlik* (Moscow: Inostrannyi Em Natsional'nyi Sözliklerding Gosudarstvennyi Izdatel'stvosï, 1963), p. 18.

† initially

‡ elsewhere

§ not transliterated thus with *Н, О, У*

OSSETIC [Oss 1 Cyr]

*1846–1923**

Alphabet	*Transliteration*	*Alphabet*	*Transliteration*
А а	a	Ш ш	sh
Б б	b	Т т	t
В в	v	Т̓ т̓ /Тҕ тҕ	th
Г г	g	У у	u
Ҕ ҕ	h	Ў ў /W w	w
Д д	d	Ѵ ѵ	ü
Æ æ	ä	Ф ф	f
Е е	e	Х х	x
З з	z	Ц ц	ts
Ж ж	zh	Ҵ ҵ /Ц̓ ц̓	ṭs
Дз дз	dz	Ч ч	ch
ДЖ дж	j	Ҹ ҹ /Ч̓ ч̓	c
J j	y		
К к	k		
К̓ к̓ /Қ қ	kh		
Q q	q		
Л л	l		
М м	m		
Н н	n		
О о	o		
П п	p		
П̓ п̓ /Пҕ пҕ	ph		
Р р	r		
С с	s		

* B. Älbortü, *Iron füstü damühätä* (Dzäujüqäu: n.p., 1929), pp. 15–17; V. Abaev, "Osetinskii iazyk," *Literaturnaia entsiklopediia,* VIII (Moscow: Gosudarstvennoe Slovarno-Entsiklopedicheskoe Izdatel'stvo "Sovetskaia Entsiklopediia," 1934), 338.

OSSETIC [Oss 2 Georg]

*-ca. 1923, 1937-**

Alphabet	*Transliteration*	*Alphabet*	*Transliteration*
ა	a	ჰ	ḥ
ბ	b	ღ	h
გ	g	ქ	k
დ	d	ფ	p
ე	e	თ	th
ვ	v	ყ	q
ზ	z	ძ	dz
ი	i	ჯ	j
კ	kh	წ	ṭs
ლ	l	ჭ	c
მ	m	ჲ	ǰ
ნ	n	ჳ̂	ü
ო	o	ჶ	f
პ	ph		
ჟ	zh		
რ	r		
ს	s		
ტ	t		
უ	u		
შ	sh		
ჩ	ch		
ც	ts		
ხ	x		

* B. Älbortü, *Iron füstü damühätä* (Dzäujüqäu: n.p., 1929), pp. 15–17; V. Abaev, "Osetinskii iazyk," *Literaturnaia entsiklopediia*, VIII (Moscow: Gosudarstvennoe Slovarno-Entsiklopedicheskoe Izdatel'stvo "Sovetskaia Entsiklopediia," 1934), 338.

OSSETIC [Oss 3 Lat]

*ca. 1924–1937**

Alphabet	*Transliteration*	*Alphabet*	*Transliteration*
A a	a	U u	u
Æ æ	ä	V v	v
B b	b	X x	kh
C c	ts	Y y	ü
Č č	ch	Z z	z
D d	d	Ƶ ƶ	zh
DZ dz	dz		
DŽ dž	j		
E e	e		
F f	f		
G g	g		
H h	h		
I i	i		
J j	y		
K k	k		
L l	l		
M m	m		
N n	n		
O o	o		
P p	p		
Q q	q		
R r	r		
S s	s		
T t	t		

* N. Nurmakov, ed., *Alfavit oktiabria. Itogi vvedeniia novogo alfavita sredi narodov RSFSR* (Moscow–Leningrad: Tsentral'nyi Komitet Novogo Alfavita pri Prezidiume VTsIK, 1934), end sheet; V. Abaev, "Osetinskii iazyk," *Literaturnaia entsiklopediia*, VIII (Moscow: Gosudarstvennoe Slovarno-Entsiklopedicheskoe Izdatel'stvo "Sovetskaia Entsiklopediia," 1934), 338; *Kul'tura i pis'mennost' Vostoka*, I, (1928), 107.

OSSETIC [Oss 4 Cyr]

*ca. 1937–**

Alphabet	*Transliteration*
А а	a
Æ æ	ä
Б б	b
В в	v
Г г	g
ГЪ гъ	h
Д д	d
ДЖ дж	j
ДЗ дз	dz
Е е	e
Ё ё	yo
Ж ж	zh
З з	z
И и	i
Й й	y
К к	k
КЪ къ	kh
Л л	l
М м	m
Н н	n
О о	o
П п	p
ПЪ пъ	ph
Р р	r
С с	s
Т т	t
ТЪ тъ	th
У у	u
Ф ф	f
Х х	x
ХЪ хъ	q
Ц ц	ts
ЦЪ цъ	ṭ
Ч ч	ch
ЧЪ чъ	c
Ш ш	sh
Щ щ	shch
Ъ ъ	”†
Ы ы	ï
Ь ь	’
Э э	ë
Ю ю	yu
Я я	ya

* A. M. Kasatï, ed., *Iron-uïrïssag dzïrduat* (Moscow: Fäsaräynag Ämä Natsion Dzïrduättï Paddzaxadon Rauahdad, 1952), p. 10.

† in Russian words

SHOR [Shor 1 Cyr]

*–1931**

Alphabet	Transliteration	Alphabet	Transliteration
А а	a	Ю ю	yu
Б б	b	Я я	ya
Г г	g	Ы ы	ï
Д д	d	ь	'
Ж ж	j		
З з	z		
И и	i		
Й й	y		
К к	k		
Л л	l		
М м	m		
Н н	n		
Ҥ ҥ	ng		
О о	o		
Ӧ ӧ	ö		
П п	p		
Р р	r		
С с	s		
Т т	t		
У у	u		
Ӱ ӱ	ü		
Ч ч	ch		
Ш ш	sh		
Э э	e		

* Ya. Tel'gerekov and A. Totïshev, *Karashkïdan shïgar: Shorlardïng pashtapkï urgencheng bukvar'ï* (Moscow: Tsentral'noe Izdatel'stvo Narodov SSSR, 1927), p. 24.

SHOR [Shor 2 Lat]

*1931–ca. 1937**

Alphabet	*Transliteration*	*Alphabet*	*Transliteration*
A a	a	Y y	ü
B в	b	Z z	z
C c	ch	Ƶ ƶ	zh
D d	d	Ь ь	ï
Ə ə	ä	Ꞁ ꞁ	ĭ
F f	f		
G g	g		
I i	i		
J j	y		
K k	k		
L l	l		
M m	m		
N n	n		
Ꞑ ꞑ	ng		
O o	o		
P p	p		
Q q	q		
Ƣ ƣ	gh		
R r	r		
S s	s		
Ş ş	sh		
T t	t		
U u	u		
V v	v		

---

* N. Nurmakov, ed., *Alfavit oktiabria: Itogi novogo alfavita sredi narodov RSFSR* (Moscow–Leningrad: Tsentral'nyi Komitet Novogo Alfavita pri Prezidiume VTsIK, 1934), p. 157, end sheet. Shor at present has no Cyrillic alphabet of its own, but uses the Altay Cyrillic [Alt 3 Cyr]; see K. M. Musaev, *Alfavity iazykov narodov SSSR* (Moscow: Izdatel'stvo "Nauka," 1965), p. 29.

TAJIK [Taj 1 & 2 Arab]

*–1928**

Alphabet	*Transliteration*
ا	a, e, i, u
آ	ā
ب	b
پ	p
ت	t
ث	th
ج	j
چ	ch
ح	ḥ
خ	kh
د	d
ذ	dh
ر	r
ز	z
ژ	zh
س	s
ش	sh
ص	ṣ
ض	z̲
ط	ṭ
ظ	ẓ
ع	ʻ
غ	gh
ف	f
ق	q
ک	k
گ	g
ل	l
م	m
ن	n
و	v; o, ū
ه	h
ی	y; i/ī
ء	ʼ

* M.V. Rahimī and L.V. Uspenskaia, eds., *Lughati tojikī–rusī* (Moscow: Nashriyoti Davlatii Lughathoi Khorijī va Millī, 1954), p. 572.

TAJIK [Taj 3 Lat]

*ca. 1927–1940**

Alphabet	*Transliteration*	*Alphabet*	*Transliteration*
A a	a	U u	u
Ə ə	ä	Ů ů	ü†
B ʙ	b	V v	v
C c	ch	X x	kh
Ç ç	j	Z z	z
D d	d	Ƶ ƶ	zh
E e	e	Ī ī / I̧ i̧	ī
F f	f	Ū ū	ū
G g	g	'	ʾ
Ƣ ƣ	gh		
H h	h		
I i	i		
J j	y		
K k	k		
L l	l		
M m	m		
N n	n		
O o	o		
P p	p		
Q q	q		
R r	r		
S s	s		
Ş ş	sh		
T t	t		

* Ia. I. Kalontarov, "Razvitie tadzhikskoi pis'mennosti za gody sovetskoi vlasti," *Izvestiia Akademii Nauk tadzhikskoi SSR*, Otdelenie obshchestvennykh nauk. No. 15 (1957), pp. 150–55.

† dropped in 1930

TAJIK [Taj 4 Cyr]

*1940–**

Alphabet	*Transliteration*
А а	a
Б б	b
В в	v
Г г	g
Д д	d
Е е	ye† e‡
Ё ё	yo
Ж ж	zh
З з	z
И и	i
Й й	y
К к	k
Л л	l
М м	m
Н н	n
О о	o
П п	p
Р р	r
С с	s
Т т	t
У у	u
Ф ф	f
Х х	kh
Ц ц	ts
Ч ч	ch
Ш ш	sh
Щ щ	shch
Ъ ъ	”
Ь ь	’
Ы ы	ï
Э э	ë
Ю ю	yu
Я я	ya
Ғ ғ	gh
Ӣ ӣ	ī
Қ қ	q
Ӯ ӯ	ū
Ҳ ҳ	h
Ҷ ҷ	j

* M.V. Rahimī and L.V. Uspenskaia, eds., *Lughati tojikī–rusī* (Moscow: Nashriyoti Davlatii Lughathoi Khorijī va Millī, 1954), p. 6.

† initially

‡ elsewhere

TAT [Tat 1 Heb]

*–1929**

Alphabet	*Transliteration*	*Alphabet*	*Transliteration*
אַ	a	ק	gh
א	ä	ר	r
אָ	o	ש	sh
ב	v	ת	t
בּ	b		
ג	g		
ג׳	j		
ד	d		
ה	h		
ו	u/ü		
ז	z		
ז׳	ch		
ח	ḥ		
אי י	i		
איי	y		
כ	kh		
כּ	k		
ל	l		
מ	m		
נ	n		
ס	s		
ע	h'		
פ	f		
פּ	p		

* *Kul'tura i pis'mennost' Vostoka*, IV (1929), 192; *Ibid.*, VI (1930), 129.

TAT [Tat 2 Lat]

*1929–ca. 1940**

Alphabet	*Transliteration*
A a	a
B в	b
C c	ch
Ç ç	j
D d	d
Ə ə	ä
F f	f
G g	g
Ƣ ƣ	gh
H h	h
Ħ ħ	ḥ
Ḩ ḩ	h'
I i	i
J j	y
K k	k
L l	l
M m	m
N n	n
O o	o
P p	p
R r	r
S s	s
Ş ş	sh
T t	t
Ţ ţ	t'
U u	u
V v	v
X x	kh
Y y	ü
Z z	z

* *Kul'tura i pis'mennost' Vostoka,* V (1929), 201; N. Nurmakov, ed., *Alfavit Oktiabria: Itogi vvedeniia novogo alfavita sredi narodov RSFSR* (Moscow–Leningrad: Tsentral'nyi Komitet Novogo Alfavita pri Prezidiuma VTsIK, 1934), end sheet. Although the Tats are said to possess no Cyrillic alphabet at present, books in Tat continue to be published occasionally; see K. M. Musaev, *Alfavity iazykov narodov SSSR* (Moscow: Izdatel'stvo "Nauka," 1965), p. 23; Edward Allworth "La rivalité entre le Russe et les langues orientales dans les territoires asiatiques de l'U.R.S.S.," *Cahiers du Monde Russe et Soviétique* Vol. VII, No. 4 (1966), p. 548.

TURKMEN [Tur 1 Arab]

*–ca. 1923**

Alphabet	*Transliteration*
ء	ʾ
آ	a
ب	b
پ	p
ت	t
ث	th
ج	j
چ	ch
ح	ḥ
خ	kh
د	d
ذ	dh
ر	r
ز	z
ژ	zh
س	s
ش	sh
ص	ṣ
ض	ẕ
ط	ṭ
ظ	ẓ
ع	ʿ
غ	gh
ف	f

Alphabet	*Transliteration*
ق	q
ک	k
گ	g
ڭ	ng
ل	l
م	m
ن	n
و	v; o/ö, u/ü
ﻫ	h
ه	ä
ی	y; e, i/ï

* Turkmen was written in an alphabet similar to Azeri and in Azeri script prior to 1923. See [Azeri 1 & 2 Arab]; Lazar Budagov, *Sravnitel'nyi slovar' turetsko-tatarskikh nariechĭi so vkliucheniem upotrebitel'nieshikh slov arabskikh i persidskikh i s perevodom na russkii iazyk* (St. Petersburg: Tipografĭia Imperatorskoi Akademii Nauk, 1869) I, x.

TURKMEN [Tur 2 Arab]
*ca. 1923–1927**

Alphabet	*Transliteration*
آ/ا	a
ب	b
پ	p
ت	t
ج	j
چ	ch
ح	ḥ
خ	kh
د	d
ر	r
ز	z
ژ	zh
س	s
ش	sh
غ	gh
ف	f
ق	q
ک	k
گ	g
ڭ	ng
ل	l
م	m
ن	n
و	o

Alphabet	*Transliteration*
ۇ	u
ۋ	v
ھ	h
ە	ä
ي	y; i/ï
ې	e
ء	ʾ

* M. Gäldiyif and Gh. Alparï, *Elipbi* (Ashkhabad–Poltoratsk: Turkmänstan Dävlät Näshriyatï, 1926), p. 47.

TURKMEN [Tur 3 Lat]

*1927–1940**

Alphabet	*Transliteration*	*Alphabet*	*Transliteration*
A a	a	Ş ş	sh
B ʙ	b	T t	t
C c	ch	U u	u
Ç ç	j	V v	v
D d	d	X x	kh
E e	e	Y y	ü
Ə ə	ä	Z z	z
F f	f	Ƶ ƶ	zh
G g	g	Ь ь	ï
Ƣ ƣ	gh†	'	ʾ
H h	h		
I i	i		
J j	y		
K k	k		
L ʟ/l	l		
M m	m		
N n	n		
Ꞑ ꞑ	ng		
O o	o		
Θ ɵ	ö		
P p	p		
Q q	q†		
R r	r		
S s	s		

* A. Sh. Karakhanov, *Grammatika turkmenskogo iazyka*. Chast' pervaia. Morfologiia (Moscow–Tashkent: Ob"edinenie Gosudarstvennykh Izdatel'stv. Sredneaziatskoe Otdelenie, 1931), pp. 5–6; A. Potseluevskii, *Fonetika turkmenskogo iazyka* (Ashkhabad: Turkmengosizdat, 1936), p. 54.

† dropped, beginning in 1934

TURKMEN [Tur 4 Cyr]

*1940–**

Alphabet	*Transliteration*	*Alphabet*	*Transliteration*
А а	a	У у	u
Б б	b	Ү ү	ü
В в	v	Ф ф	f
Г г	g	Х х	kh
Д д	d	Ц ц	ts
Е е	ye† e‡	Ч ч	ch
		Ш ш	sh
Ё ё	yo	Щ щ	shch
Ж ж	zh	Ъ ъ	’’
Җ җ	j	Ы ы	ï
З з	z	Ь ь	'
И и	i	Э э	ë
Й й	y	Ә ә	ä
К к	k	Ю ю	yu
Л л	l	Я я	ya
М м	m		
Н н	n		
Ң ң	ng		
О о	o		
Ө ө	ö		
П п	p		
Р р	r		
С с	s		
Т т	t		

* M. Ya. Khamzaev, ed., *Türkmen dilining sözlügi* (Ashkhabad: Türkmenistan SSR Ïlïmlar Akademiyasïnïng Neshriyatï, 1962), p. 10.

† initially

‡ elsewhere

UYGHUR [Uygh 1 Arab]

*–ca. 1923**

Alphabet	*Transliteration*	*Alphabet*	*Transliteration*
آ	a	ک	k
ب	b	گ	g
پ	p	ڭ	ng
ت	t	ل	l
ث	th	م	m
ج	j	ن	n
چ	ch	و	v; o/ö, u/ü
ح	ḥ	ه	h
خ	kh	ە	ä
د	d	ي	y; e, i/ï
ذ	dh	ء	ʾ
ر	r		
ز	z		
ژ	zh		
س	s		
ش	sh		
ص	ṣ		
ض	z̲		
ط	ṭ		
ظ	ẓ		
ع	ʿ		
غ	gh		
ف	f		
ق	q		

* Robert Barkley Shaw, *A Sketch of the Turki Language as Spoken in Eastern Turkistan (Kashghar and Yarkand) together with a Collection of Extracts*, Part I (Lahore: Printed Under the Authority of the Government of India . . . at the Central Jail Press, 1875), pp. 1–5; V. M. Nasilov, *Grammatika uigurskogo iazyka* (Moscow: Izdanie Moskovskogo Instituta Vostokovedeniia, 1940), p. 17.

UYGHUR [Uygh 2 Arab]

*ca. 1924–1928**

Alphabet	*Transliteration*	*Alphabet*	*Transliteration*
ا	a	و	o
ب	b	ۈ	u
ن	n	ۇ	ü
ت	t	ۋ	v
ﻴ	e	ﻡ	m
ﻳ/ى	y†	ﮬ	h
پ	p	ە	ä
س	s		
ش	sh		
ر	r		
ز	z		
ژ	zh		
د	d		
ج	j		
چ	ch		
خ	kh		
ل	l		
ک	k		
گ	g		
ڭ	ng		
ﺌ	i/ï		
ى	i‡		
غ	gh		
ق	q		

* Abdulhäy Mohämmädi, *Oyghorchä yeziq yollïrï* (Moscow: SSSR Ällirining Märkäz Näshreyatï, 1926), p. 15.

† before and after vowels

‡ final after consonants

UYGHUR [Uygh 3 Lat]

*ca. 1928–1947**

Alphabet	*Transliteration*	*Alphabet*	*Transliteration*
A a	a	U u	u
B в	b	V v	v
C c	ch	X x	kh
Ç ç	j	Y y	ü
D d	d	Z z	z
E e	e	Ƶ ƶ	zh
Ə ə	ä	Ɵ ɵ	ö
G g	g	Ь ь	ï
H h	h		
I i̡	i		
J j	y		
K k	k		
L l	l		
M m	m		
N n	n		
N̡ n̡	ng		
O o	o		
P p	p		
Q q	q		
Ƣ ƣ	gh		
R r	r		
S s	s		
Ş ş	sh		
T t	t		

* N. Nurmakov, ed., *Alfavit oktiabria: Itogo vvedeniia novogo alfavita sredi narodov RSFSR* (Moscow–Leningrad: Tsentral'nyi Komitet Novogo Alfavita pri Prezidiume VTsIK, 1934), end sheet; V.M.Nasilov, *Grammatika uigurskogo iazyka* (Moscow: Izdanie Moskovskogo Instituta Vostokovedeniia, 1940), p. 17.

UYGHUR [Uygh 4 Cyr]
*1947–**

Alphabet	*Transliteration*	*Alphabet*	*Transliteration*
А а	a	Ц ц	ts
Б б	b	Ч ч	ch
В в	v	Ш ш	sh
Г г	g	Щ щ	shch
Д д	d	Ь ь	'
Е е	ye† / e‡	Ы ы	ï
		Ъ ъ	"
Ё ё	ya	Э э	ë
Ж ж	zh	Ю ю	yu
З з	z	Я я	yä
И и	i	Қ қ	q
Й й	y	Ң ң	ng
К к	k	Ғ ғ	gh
Л л	l	Ү ү	ü
М м	m	Ө ө	ö
Н н	n	Җ җ	j
О о	o	Ә ә	ä
П п	p	Һ һ	h
Р р	r		
С с	s		
Т т	t		
У у	u		
Ф ф	f		
Х х	kh		

* Sh. Kibirov and Yu. Tsunvazo, eds., *Uyghurchä–ruschä lughät* (Alma Ata: Qazaqstan Pänlär Akademiyäsining Näshriyäti, 1961), pp. 6, 290.

† initially

‡ elsewhere

UZBEK [Uz 1 Arab]

*–ca. 1923**

Alphabet	*Transliteration*
ء	ʾ
آ	a
ب	b
پ	p
ت	t
ث	th
ج	j
چ	ch
ح	ḥ
خ	kh
د	d
ذ	dh
ر	r
ز	z
ژ	zh
س	s
ش	sh
ص	ṣ
ض	ẕ
ط	ṭ
ظ	ẓ
ع	ʿ
غ	gh
ف	f
ق	q
ک	k
گ	g
ڭ	ng
ل	l
م	m
ن	n
و	v; o/ö, u/ü
ھ	h
ه	ä
ی	y; e, i/ï

* P. Shämsiev and S. Ibrahimov, comps., *Ozbek klässik ädäbiyati äsärläri uchun qisqächa lughat* (Tashkent: Ozbekistan SSR Fänlär Äkädemiyäsi Näshriyati, 1953), p. 7 f.; S. F. Äkabirov, Z. M. Mä''rufov, Ä. T. Khojäkhanov and A. K. Borovkov, eds., *Ozbekchä–ruschä lughät* (Moscow: Kharijiy vä Milliy Lughätlär Dävlät Näshriyati, 1959), p. 733.

UZBEK [Uz 2 Arab]
*ca. 1923–ca. 1927**

Alphabet	*Transliteration*	*Alphabet*	*Transliteration*
ا	a	ف	f
ه	ä	ق	q
ب	b	ک	k
پ	p	گ	g
ت	t	ڭ	ng
ث	th	ل	l
ج	j	م	m
چ	ch	ن	n
ح	ḥ	ۋ/ۋ	v
خ	kh	و	o
د	d	ۇ	u
ذ	dh	ه	h
ر	r	ي	y
ز	z	ې	e
ژ	zh	عي	ï
س	s	ئ/ى	i†
ش	sh		
ص	ṣ		
ض	z̲		
ط	ṭ		
ظ	ẓ		
ء	ʾ		
ع	ʿ		
غ	gh		

* Q. Yudakhin, *Ozbek–rus lughati*, (Tashkent: Izdanie Akts O-va "Sredazkniga," 1927), p. x; E. D. Polivanov, *Vvedenie v izuchenie uzbekskogo iazyka* (Tashkent: Turkpechat', 1925), pp. 30–34; Edward Allworth, *Uzbek Literary Politics* (The Hague: Mouton, 1964), p. 253.

† closed syllable

UZBEK [Uz 3 Lat]

*1927–1940**

Alphabet	*Transliteration*	*Alphabet*	*Transliteration*
A a	a	Ş ş	sh
B в	b	T t	t
C c	ch	U u	u
Ç ç	j	V v	v
D d	d	X x	kh
E e	e	Y y	ü†
Ə ə	ä†	Z z	z
F f	f	Ƶ ƶ	zh
G g	g	Ь ь	ï†
Ƣ ƣ	gh	ʿ	ʿ
H h	h	ʾ	ʾ
I i	i		
J j	y		
K k	k		
L l	l		
M m	m		
N n	n		
Ꞑ ꞑ	ng		
O o	o		
Ɵ ɵ	ö†		
P p	p		
Q q	q		
R r	r		
S s	s		

* Ümär Ähmädjanov and Burhan Ilyazov, *Özbekchä-ruscha lughat* (Tashkent: Öznäshr, 1931), p. 6; R. S. Giliarevskii and V. S. Grivnin, *Opredelitel' iazykov mira po pis'mennostiam* (Moscow: Izdatel'stvo Vostochnoi Literatury, 1961), p. 58; Edward Allworth, *Uzbek Literary Politics* (The Hague: Mouton, 1964), p. 253.

† letter dropped, 1935–

UZBEK [Uz 4 Cyr]

*1940–**

Alphabet	*Transliteration*	*Alphabet*	*Transliteration*
А а	ä	Х х	kh
Б б	b	Ц ц	ts
В в	v	Ч ч	ch
Г г	g	Ш ш	sh
Д д	d	Ъ ъ	’’
Е е	ye† e‡	Ь ь	'
		Э э	ë
Ё ё	ya	Ю ю	yu
Ж ж	j zh§	Я я	yä
		Ў ў	o
З з	z	Қ қ	q
И и	i	Ғ ғ	gh
Й й	y	Ҳ ҳ	h
К к	k	Щ щ	shch
Л л	l	Ы ы	ï
М м	m		
Н н	n		
О о	a		
П п	p		
Р р	r		
С с	s		
Т т	t		
У у	u		
Ф ф	f		

* S. F. Äkabirov, Z. M. Mä’’rufov, Ä. T. Khojäkhanov, and A. K. Borovkov, eds., *Ozbekchä–ruschä lughät* (Moscow: Kharijiy vä Milliy Lughätlär Dävlät Näshriyati, 1959), p. 17; Edward Allworth, *Uzbek Literary Politics* (The Hague: Mouton, 1964), pp. 176, 253.

† initially

‡ elsewhere

§ in foreign words

VOLGA TATAR [Tata 1 Arab]

*–ca. 1920**

Alphabet	*Transliteration*	*Alphabet*	*Transliteration*
ا	a	ك	k
ب	b	گ	g
پ	p	ل	l
ت	t	م	m
ث	th	ن	n
ج	j	نگ	ng
چ	ch	و	v; o/u
ح	ḥ	ه	h
خ	kh	ى	y; i/ï
د	d	ء	ʾ
ذ	dh		
ر	r		
ز	z		
ژ	zh		
س	s		
ش	sh		
ص	ṣ		
ض	ẕ		
ط	ṭ		
ظ	ẓ		
ع	ʿ		
غ	gh		
ف	f		
ق	q		

* K. Nasyrov, *Kratkaia tatarskaia grammatika izlozhennaia v primierakh* (Kazan: v Universitetskoi Tipografīi, 1860), p. 1.

VOLGA TATAR [Tata 2 Arab]

*ca. 1920–1927**

Alphabet	*Transliteration*	*Alphabet*	*Transliteration*
ا	a	ن	n
ئه	ä	ئۇ,	o
ب	b	ئۇ	ö
پ	p	ئو,	u
ت	t	ئو	ü
ث	th	ۋ/و	v
ج	j	ه	h
چ	ch	ئیـ	i
ح	ḥ	ئـ,	ï
د	d	ی/یـ	y
ذ	dh	ء	ʾ
ر	r		
ز	z		
ژ	zh		
س	s		
ش	sh		
ع	gh		
ف	f		
ق	q		
ک	k		
گ	g		
ڭ	ng		
ل	l		
م	m		

*A. Seid-zade, "Tatarstan bol'she ne oplot Arabizma," in A. Nurmakov, ed., *Alfavit oktiabria. Itogi vvedeniia novogo alfavita sredi narodov RSFSR* (Moscow–Leningrad: Tsentral'nyi Komitet Novogo Alfavita pri Prezidiume VTsIK, 1934), p. 36; Kh. Kurbatov, *Tatar teleneng alfavit häm orfografiya tarikhï* (Kazan: Tatarstan Kitap Näshriyatï, 1960), pp. 26, 49.

VOLGA TATAR [Tata 3 Lat]

*ca. 1927–1937**

Alphabet	*Transliteration*	*Alphabet*	*Transliteration*
A a	a	Ş ş	sh
B в	b	T t	t
C c	ch	U u	u
Ç ç	j	V v	v
D d	d	X x	kh
E e	e	Y y	ü
Ə ə	ä	Z z	z
F f	f	Ƶ ƶ	zh
G g	g	Ь ь	ï
Ƣ ƣ	gh	Ьj ьj	ïy
H h	h	'	'
I i	i		
J j	y		
K k	k		
Q q	q		
L l	l		
M m	m		
N n	n		
Ꞑ ꞑ	ng		
O o	o		
Ɵ ɵ	ö		
P p	p		
R r	r		
S s	s		

* Gh. Khäbib and F. Möbaräkshin, '*Yangalif*' *häm yäshlär* (Kazan: Basïp Taratuchïsï 'Yangalif' Jämghiyäte, 1927).

VOLGA TATAR [Tata 4 Cyr]

*1938–**

Alphabet	*Transliteration*	*Alphabet*	*Transliteration*
А а	a	Ц ц	ts
Б б	b	Ч ч	ch
В в	v	Ш ш	sh
Г г	g	Щ щ	shch
Д д	d	Ъ ъ	”
Е е	ye† e‡	Ы ы	ï
		Ь ь	'
Ё ё	ya	Э э	ë
Ж ж	zh	Ю ю	yu/yü
З з	z	Я я	yä
И и	i	Ә ә	ä
Й й	y	Ө ө	ö
К к	k	Ү ү	ü
Л л	l	Җ җ	j
М м	m	Ң ң	ng
Н н	n	Һ һ	h
О о	o		
П п	p		
Р р	r		
С с	s		
Т т	t		
У у	u		
Ф ф	f		
Х х	kh		

**Tatarcha–ruscha süzlek* (Moscow: “Sovetskaia Entsiklopediia” Näshriyätï, 1966), pp. 15, 819–21.

† initially

‡ elsewhere

YAKUT [Yak 1 Cyr]

*19th century**

Alphabet	*Transliteration*
А а	a
Б б	b
В в	v
Г г	g
Ҕ ҕ	gh
Д д	d
Џ џ	j
ДҞ дҟ	dzh
Е е	ye
И и	i
І і	ĭ
Й й	ÿ
Ɉ ɉ	y
J j	y̱
К к	k
Л̓ л̓	l
Л л	l'
М м	m
Н н	n
Ң ң	ng
Н̆ н̆	nğ
Н̇ н̇	ny
О о	o
Ö ö	ö
Ё ё	ö̱
П п	p
Р р	r
С с	s
Т т	t
У у	u
Ӱ ӱ	ü
Х х	kh
Ч ч	ch
Ы ы	ï
Ä ä	ä
УО уо	uo
ӰÖ ӱö	üö
Ю́ ю	yu
ЮЁ юё	yö

* L. N. Kharitonov, *Sovremennyi iakutskii iazyk* (Yakutsk: Gosizdat Iakutskoi ASSR, 1947), pp. 304–5. Of the several variations employed in the nineteenth century, this is basically a synthesis of the alphabets devised by Böhtlingk and the Kazan Orientalists, 1851 and 1898.

YAKUT [Yak 2 Lat]

*ca. 1917–1928**

Alphabet	*Transliteration*
A a	a
B b	b
C c	ch
D d	d
E e	e
G g	g
ʃ ʃ	gh
H h	h
I i	i
J j	y
ɟ̇	ÿ
K k	k
Л л	l
ʎ ʎ	l'
L	ḷ
l	ḻ
M m	m
N n	n
Ŋ ŋ	ng
Ɲ ɲ	ny
Ɔ ɔ	o
Œ œ	ö
P p	p
Q q	q

Alphabet	*Transliteration*
R r	r
S s	s
T t	t
U u	u
Y y	ü
З з	j
Ы ы	ï
Ш ш	ḯ
Ҍ ҍ	ïa
Ꙓ ꙓ	ie
W̓ w̓	uo
Ю ю	üo
w̓ w̓	uö

* L. N. Kharitonov, *Sovremennyi iakutskii iazyk* (Yakutsk: Gosizdat Iakutskoi ASSR, 1947), pp. 304–5. The main variants employed in the two versions of a Latinized Yakut alphabet in this period occurred in the representation of diphthongs in the final 5 letters, above. A Yakut, Novgorodov, devised or adapted special letters, whereas the government in 1924 attempted to present the diphthongs graphically.

YAKUT [Yak 3 Lat]

*ca. 1929–1939**

Alphabet	*Transliteration*	*Alphabet*	*Transliteration*
A a	a	Ş ş	sh†
B в	b	T t	t
C c	ch	U u	u
Ç ç	j	V v	v†
D d	d	Y y	ü
E e	e	Z z	z†
Ɔ ɔ	ä†	Ƶ ƶ	zh†
F f	f†	Ь ь	ï
G g	g		
Ƣ ƣ	gh		
H h	h		
I i	i		
J j	y		
K k	k		
L l	l		
M m	m		
N n	n		
Ŋ ŋ	ng		
O o	o		
Ɵ ɵ	ö		
P p	p		
Q q	q		
R r	r		
S s	s		

* L. N. Kharitonov, *Sovremennyi iakutskii iazyk* (Yakutsk: Gosizdat Iakutskoi ASSR, 1947), pp. 304–5; N. Nurmakov, ed., *Alfavit oktiabria: Itogi vvedeniia novogo alfavita sredi narodov RSFSR* (Moscow–Leningrad): Tsentral'nyi Komitet Novogo Alfavita pri Prezidiume VTsIK, 1934), p. 140.

† omitted from 1930 alphabet

YAKUT [Yak 4 Cyr]

*1939–**

Alphabet	*Transliteration*
А а	a
Б б	b
В в	v
Г г	g
Ҕ ҕ	gh
Д д	d
ДЬ дь	j
Е е	ye† e‡
Ж ж	zh
З з	z
И и	i
Й й	y
К к	k
Л л	l
М м	m
Н н	n
Ҥ ҥ	ng
НЬ нь	ny
О о	o
Ө ө	ö
П п	p
Р р	r
С с	s
Т т	t
У у	u
Ф ф	f
Х х	kh
Ц ц	ts
Ч ч	ch
Ш ш	sh
Щ щ	shch
Ъ ъ	”
Ы ы	ï
Ь ь	'
Э э	ë
Ю ю	yu
Я я	ya
h	h
i	ĭ
Y	ü

* L. N. Kharitonov, *Sovremennyi iakutskii iazyk* (Yakutsk: Gosizdat Iakutskoi ASSR, 1947), pp. 304–5; K. M. Musaev, *Alfavity iazykov narodov* SSSR, 1965), pp. 33–35; John R. Krueger, *Yakut Manual* (Bloomington: Indiana University Publications, Uralic and Altaic Series, vol. 21, 1962), pp. 45–46.

† initially

‡ elsewhere

RUSSIAN [Russ Cyr   ]*

Alphabet	Transliteration	Alphabet	Transliteration
А а	a	Ц ц	ts
Б б	b	Ч ч	ch
В в	v	Ш ш	sh
Г г	g	Щ щ	shch
Д д	d	Ъ ъ	”
Е е	e	Ы ы	y
Ё ё	ë	Ь ь	'
Ж ж	zh	Ѣ ѣ	ie
З з	z	Э э	ė
И и	i	Ю ю	iu
І і	ĭ	Я я `	ia
Й й	i	Ѳ ѳ	th
К к	k	Ѵ ѵ	ÿ
Л л	l		
М м	m		
Н н	n		
О о	o		
П п	p		
Р р	r		
С с	s		
Т т	t		
У у	u		
Ф ф	f		
Х х	kh		

* Equivalents shown for the contemporary alphabet are those recommended by the Russian Institute at Columbia University. Transliteration of the symbols now out of use has also been provided for. This table is added for the purpose of furnishing a key to the transliteration of publishers' names, which often appear in the Bibliographical Directory in Russian. A few titles also employ Russian.

INDEX

References to entries in the Bibliographical Directory show entry numbers, followed by abbreviated names of Soviet Eastern languages (see "Entries in the Directory and Index," pp. 22–23). References to material in the Foreword, opening section, and Transliteration Tables give page numbers *in italics*. The many variants in the spelling of the same personal names have resulted from an extremely unstable orthography employed by different nationalities. Wherever these variants appear close to each other in the index they have not been cross-referenced. All main entries are alphabeted letter by letter without regard to diacritical marks. Index prepared by Kathryn W. Sewny.

Index

Basïr, Astïrḥanlï, 1993 Tur
Baṭïrmurza, 'Abdal'aẓïm, 1788 Kum
Batmanif, O., 2213 Uz
Battles, 1980 Tur
Batu, 2422 Uz
Bauer, O., 248 Az
Bayaarap, Ö.S., 3324 Yak
Bayalinov, K., 1736 Kir
Bayanïf, N., 3093 Tata
Bayburtli, Yaḥya'aji, 1089 Crim
Baychürina, Zahirä, 3094 Tata
Baydïlda olï, Abdïraqman, 1348, 1398 Kaz
Bayghoja ulï, Saypolla, 1575 Kaz
Bayimbitïf, Gh., 3095–96 Tata
Bayimbitif, Ghilmdar, 2556 Tata
Bayïsh, Tahir, 677 Bash
Bayrashevski, 'Umer, 1090 Crim
Bayrün, 3097 Tata
Bäyseyit ulï, Qana-bek, 1620 Kaz
Baytorsïn olï, Ahmet, 1551 Kaz
Baytorsïn olï, Aqïmet, 1552–53 Kaz
Baytursïn olï, Aqïmet, 1349 Kaz
Baytursïn ulï, Aqïmet, 1350–51 Kaz
Baytursïn ulï, Aqmet, 1554 Kaz
Baytursunïf, A., 1352, 1555–56 Kaz
Bayzaq olï, Ïysa, 1576 Kaz
Bazhov, P., 3098 Tata
Begäli uli, 1353 Kaz
Begeulov, A., 1219 Kar-Bal
Begi, M., 1241, 1251 Karai
Bekirof, 'A. Zeki, 1133 Crim
Bekirof, 'Üsman, 1155 Crim
Bektagiyif, Rostäm, 2423 Uz
Belavin, A.F., 180 Az
Belayef, Y.M., 1091 Crim
Berdniykof, A., 1399 Kaz
Beren, M., 1156 Crim
Bereshegin, G., 1696 Kir
Bereshshegin, 1400 Kaz
Bereshshegin, G., 1401 Kaz
Bereza, G., 1354 Kaz
Berezansky, L., 1281 Kaz
Berg, M., 1092 Crim
Berg, M.F., 140–41 Az
Besenebïskiy, A.Y., 1528 Kaz
Beyimbet, 1577–78 Kaz
Beymbet, 1579 Kaz
Bianki, Bitali, 1225 Kar-Bal
Bianki, Vitaliy, 1157 Crim
Bible, 1045 Chu; 1815 Nog; 3285 Tata; 3340 Yak; Old Testament selections, 1237, 1250 Karai
Bibliographical Directory: arrangement, *pp. 22–23*; dates and number of titles *pp. 8–9, 10 (table), 11, 12–15 (table), 18 (table), 19, 20–21*; description of, *pp. 7–9, 11, 12–15 (table), 15–23*; entries, *pp. 22–23*; purpose, *pp. vii, 7*; sequel to, *p. 8*; translations from other languages, *pp. 7–8*
Bibliographies, 29 Az; 801 Chu; 1066 Crim; 1268–70, 1275, 1595 Kaz; 1817 Oss; 1925, 1928 Tur; 2035 Uz; 2507, 2522, 2530–31, 2538, 2544, 2654 Tata; periodicals, 31–32, 64 Az; 2517 Tata
Bigiyïf, Möhämmäd Zaher märḥüm Aḥünd Mülla Jarülla üghli, 3099 Tata
Bigiyif, Müsi Äfändi, 3051 Tata
Bikat, 1582 Kaz
Bikbulat, M., 660 Bash
Bikchäntäy, Ir'üghlï, 2618 Tata
Bikchäntäy, Irüghlü, 2619 Tata
Bïkhovski, 2044 Uz
Bïkhovski, N.I., 1529 Kaz
Bikhovsqi, N.I., 361 Az
Bïktemir, 2045 Uz
Bilal, M., 681 Bash
Bilavin, A.F., 2709 Tata
Bilbay, N., 659 Bash
Biniigin, Öl., 3311–12 Yak
Binyadof, 142 Az
Biographies, 271, 331, 461 Az; 742, 744 Bash; 943–46, 995 Chu; 1126, 1128, 1131 Crim; 1218 Kar-Bal; 1408, 1462, 1495, 1501–2, 1504, 1506–7, 1583 Kaz; 1722 Kir; 1750 Kresh; 1777 Kum; 1805, 1807 Kur; 1886, 1888 Taj; 1982–83 Tur; 2321, 2333, 2465 Uz; 2942, 2955, 2968, 2972, 2975,

Edison, Thomas Alva, 2942 Tata
Education: algebra, study of, 159 Az; 2168–70 Uz; 2663 Tata; arithmetic, study of, 130 Az; 1353, 1356–57, 1365–77 Kaz; 1680, 1684 Kir; 1866 Taj; 1942 Tur; 2122–26 Uz; 3314–15 Yak; associations, 2729 Tata; astronomy, study of, 2180 Uz; 3025 Tata; botany, study of, 684 Bash; 1869 Taj; 2205–6 Uz; chemistry, study of, 147, 168, 178 Az; 1103 Crim; 2176, 2180 Uz; 2693 Tata; conferences, 1368, 1378 Kaz; 1762 Kum; 2181, 2279 Uz; cosmography, study of, 2725 Tata; economics of, 2579–80 Tata; field trips, 2741 Tata; geology, study of, 164 Az; 1634 Kaz; geometry, study of, 132, 171 Az; 2132, 2186 Uz; 2648, 2653, 2706–7 Tata; goals, 1381 Kaz; groups, 2829 Tata; laws re, 2347 Uz; mathematics, study of, 7 Alt; 140–41, 149, 157 Az; 678 Bash; 1092, 1095, 1100–2 Crim; 1204–5 Kar-Bal; 1757 Kum; 1801a Kur; 1860–61 Taj; 1950 Tur; 2152–53, 2167, 2202 Uz; 2645, 2650, 2667, 2673, 2683–89, 2737, 2750–51, 2753 Tata; medicine, study of, 2664 Tata; natural history, study of, 1083–87, 1091, 1097, 1114 Crim; 2730 Tata; periodicals, 39, 49–51, 55, 61, 75 Az; 629, 639, 641, 645 Bash; 794–95 Chu; 1059, 1061 Crim; 1259, 1273, 1275 Kaz; 1659 Kir; 1752 Kum; 1795 Kur; 1851 Taj; 2010, 2012, 2018–19, 2038 Uz; 2511, 2519–20, 2525, 2536, 2541–42, 2545, 2547 Tata; physics, study of, 135–39 Az; 853 Chu; 1798 Kur; 1958–59, 1961 Tur; 2158, 2180 Uz; 2626, 2718–21 Tata; physiology, study of, 1960 Tur; planning, 1381 Kaz; policy, 2195 Uz; programs, 2141 Uz; 2615 Tata; propaganda for, 2446 Uz; rural program, 1952 Tur; science study, 677 Bash; 1083, 1087 Crim; periodical, 633 Bash; publications, *p. 9*; self-teaching methods, 2744 Tata; statistics, 2108 Uz; workshops, 2177 Uz; zoology, study of, 2205–6 Uz; 2710, 2736 Tata; *see also* Adult education; Elementary education; Pedagogy; Political education; Primary education; School workbooks; Universities
Education Commission, 1677 Kir
Education entries, 3–7 Alt; 126–83 Az; 676–98 Bash; 829–55 Chu; 1083–1114 Crim; 1202–6 Kar-Bal; 1342–89 Kaz; 1644–46 Khak; 1677–91 Kir; 1749 Kresh; 1757–66 Kum; 1797–1803 Kur; 1810 Nogh; 1819–23 Oss; 1851 Shor; 1859–69 Taj; 1942–61 Tur; 2006 Uygh; 2120–2207 Uz; 2608–2754 Tata; 3309–16 Yak; dates and number of, *pp. 11, 12–15* (*table*), *17, 18* (*table*); description of, *pp. 16–17*; *see also* 101, 225, 269, 292, 366, 373, 375, 377, 395, 425, 487, 568, 576, 609–10 Az; 759 Bash; 861, 968, 979–80, 1054 Chu; 1060, 1072, 1074 Crim; 1327, 1338, 1528, 1551–54, 1556, 1579 Kaz; 1692, 1735 Kir; 1974 Tur; 2053, 2108, 2116, 2232–33, 2237, 2242–43, 2285–86, 2295, 2368, 2394–99, 2412–13, 2446, 2459–60, 2479, 2483, 2495 Uz; 2579–80, 2777, 2835, 2862–63, 2886, 2888, 2894, 2898, 2900, 2913, 3025, 3033–34, 3040, 3043, 3045–47, 3050, 3053–54, 3065, 3079, 3102, 3141, 3263, 3284, 3288 Tata
Efimov, M., 855 Chu
Ekhlin, N., 863 Chu

Farming, dictionary, 3064 Tata
Farms, 364, 380, 384 Az; 1080 Crim; 1328, 1342, 1523–24, 1547 Kaz; 1856 Taj; 2172 Uz; 3012 Tata; households, 3014 Tata; income, 117 Az; laws re, 1778 Kum; 2985 Tata
Farrïq, O., 1995 Tur
Farük, A., 451 Az
Fasting, 1200 Crim
Fateyëva, A., 956 Chu
Fatherless children, 1518 Kaz
Fäthi, Dimiyan, 3112 Tata
Fättah, Temur, 2431 Uz
Fäyz, M. Ḥäydär, 3113–14 Tata
Fäyzi, Ḥ., 3004 Tata
Fäyzi, Hadi, 2060 Uz
Fäyzi, Mir Ḥäydär, 3115 Tata
Fäyzullin, 3059–60 Tata
Fäyzüllin, S., 2565, 3005 Tata
Fäyzüllina, Ḥ., 2799 Tata
Fazil, 3006 Tata
Fazil bek, 2314 Uz
Fazlülla, M., 2627–28, 2669 Tata
Fedoseev, P., 2800 Tata
Fedoseyev, R., 2943 Tata
Feḥritdinïf, Gh., 741 Bash
Feḥrtdinïf, Gh., 699 Bash
Feliche, Art., 1128 Crim
Ferdovsi, 1904 Taj
Feridun Bek Kochärli, 452 Az
Ferskhofen, 1162 Crim
Fevzi, Ä., 453–54 Az
Field trips, 2741 Tata
Fikret, Tevfiq, 455 Az
Filippof, S., 147 Az
Finance, 674 Bash; 1672 Kir; 2041, 2046, 2066, 2097 Uz; 2593, 2603, 2606 Tata; periodical, 2029 Uz
Financial aid for people, 651 Bash
Financing, 1411 Kaz
Finland: army, 216 Az; history, 2957 Tata
Firdausi, *see* Ferdovsi
Firkovits, 'Abraham, 1234 Karai
Firkovits, Moshe ben Ya'aqob, 1243 Karai
Firkovits, Ya'aqob ben Abraham, 1244 Karai
Firstof, 2061 Uz
Fisheries, 1289, 1526 Kaz
Fishermen, 2997 Tata
Fĭträt, 2389–92, 2432–37, 2494 Uz
Five-year plan, 101, 110, 121, 187 Az; 661, 675 Bash; 1069–70, 1077 Crim; 2064, 2084–85 Uz; 2557–59, 2569, 2571–72 Tata
Flörova, E.A., 1114 Crim
Folk literature, 1180a Crim; 1581, 1601, 1615 Kaz; 1656 Khak; 1899 Taj; 1996 Tur; 2009 Uygh; 3171, 3208 Tata
Folklore, 491, 608 Az; 766, 775, 783 Bash; 985 Chu; 1228 Kar-Bal; 1902 Taj
Folk poetry, 434–35, 443, 490, 492, 516 Az; 1567, 1580, 1582, 1584, 1586, 1600, 1606, 1608, 1611–12, 1617–18 Kaz; 1741 Kir; 1814 Nogh
Folk riddles, 491 Az; 775, 783 Bash; 1594 Kaz; 1996 Tur
Folk sayings, 608 Az; 766, 775 Bash; 985 Chu; 1240 Karai; 1573 Kaz; 1996 Tur; 2461 Uz
Folk tales, 624 Az; 1180 Crim; 1226 Kar-Bal; 1238–40, 1247 Karai; 1637 Kaz; 2403 Uz; 3086, 3171 Tata
Fomitski, V., 1932 Tur; 2062 Uz; *see also* Famitski; Pomiytski olï
Food preparation, 1068 Crim
Foreign competition, 84 Az
Foreign policy, 2791a Tata
Foreign states, 206 Az
Foreign trade, 2589 Tata
Foresters Union, 1987 Tur; *see also* Farmers and Foresters Union
Forestry: periodical, 2503 Tata; rules, 950 Chu
Forests, 3308 Yak
Fradkin, G.A., 1094 Crim
Fränj, 2493 Uz

Hanukkah, 1238 Karai
Ḥaqverdiyof, Ä., 466 Az
Ḥaqverdof, 467 Az
Ḥaqverdof, 'Abdalrahimbek, 468 Az
Ḥaqvĭrdĭyif, 'A., 2441–42 Uz
Ḥarĭri, Muḥammad, 2497 Uz
Ḥarrabin, J., 2758 Tata
Harte, Bret, *see* Bret-Gart
Harvard University, *p. 22*
Ḥasan, 'A. Ḥaji, 1104 Crim
Ḥäsän, M., 2393 Uz
Ḥasan, 'Ŭmer, Ḥaji, 1096 Crim
Ḥäyri, Ghaynon, 3155 Tata
Ḥayri, Q., 2633–36 Tata
Ḥaziniy, 2443 Uz
Health, 363 Az; 2290 Uz; periodical, 1257 Kaz; study of, 2664 Tata; *see also* Hygiene; Public health
Health insurance, 649 Bash
Heaven, 604 Az
Hebrew alphabet, *p. 299, 321, 365*
Hebrew language, *p. 298*
Hebrew Union College, Cincinnati, *pp. 15, 22*
Ḥikmät, Isma'il, 610 Az
Ḥikmät, Naẓim, 469 Az
Hiqmät, Ismayĭl, 609 Az
Hiravī, Nāẓim, 1905 Taj
Historical geography, 2071 Uz; 2758 Tata
History: archives, 288 Az; of astronomy, 2331 Uz; Marxist interpretation of, 969 Chu; 2883 Tata; periodicals, 62, 64 Az; 628 Bash; 1266, 1275 Kaz; 2012, 2014, 2019 Uz
History entries, 327–37 Az; 740–44 Bash; 939–49 Chu; 1125–32 Crim; 1218 Kar-Bal; 1233 Karai; 1254–55 Kar; 1501–11 Kaz; 1722–23 Kir; 1750 Kresh; 1777 Kum; 1805–7 Kur; 1886–90 Taj; 1980–83 Tur; 2311–37 Uz; 2937–81 Tata; 3322–23 Yak; dates and number of, *pp. 11, 12–15* (*table*), *17, 18,* (*table*); *see also* 238, 244, 271, 306, 333–34, 370, 461 Az; 859, 864, 866, 881, 927, 936, 960, 969, 995, 1032 Chu; 1287, 1396, 1408, 1437, 1439, 1462, 1495, 1583–84 Kaz; 1732 Kir; 1781a Kum; 1816 Oss; 2035, 2043, 2057, 2071–72, 2465 Uz; 2758, 2780, 2782, 2791a–92, 2800, 2846, 2883, 2990, 3032, 3122, 3145, 3147 Tata
Hobbies, 3025, 3042 Tata
Holy War, 2314 Uz
Home industry, 806, Chu
Home study, 165, 168, 425 Az; 864 Chu; 2120, 2162–64, 2200 Uz; 2900 Tata
Hoover Institution for War, Revolution and Peace, The, *p. 22*
Hoshim, Rahim, 1862 Taj
Housing, 1550 Kaz; 1732 Kir
Housing cooperatives, 3010 Tata
Hugo, *see* Hugho; Küko
Hugho, V., 470 Az
Ḥüjäyif, M., 3281 Tata
Humanities entries: divisions of, *p. 16*; number of, *p. 17*; *see also specific disciplines, e.g.* Language entries
Humor, 528, 573, 581, 600 Az; 3091 Tata; periodicals, 35, 53–54, 69 Az; 640 Bash; 793, 796 Chu; 2020, 2023 Uz; 2510, 2527 Tata
Hunting, 2369 Uz; 3026 Tata
Husäynof, T., 329 Az
Huseynof, T., 330 Az
Huseynov, H., 420–23 Az
Hüseynov, Heydär, 471 Az
Hygiene, 163 Az; 1355, 1372 Kaz; 1653 Khak; schools, 2199 Uz; *see also* Health; Public health
Hymns, 1233 Karai

I (letter), *p. 300*
Iakovlev, 2582 Tata
Ibn Sina, 1886 Taj
Ibragimov, G., 2874 Tata
Ibrahim Bin Isḥag Khalfii, 2954 Tata

Ibrahimif, Ghali, 2637–38 Tata
Ibrahimïf, Ghalimjan, 2811, 3156–60 Tata
Ibrahimof, 'Alïmjan, 472 Az
Ibrahimof, 'Ali Sättär, 42 Az
Ibrahimof, Gh., 2639–40 Tata
Ibrahimof, Ghäli, 2641 Tata
Ibrayimif, Ghäli, 1811 Nogh
Ibräyimip, Äliy, 1810 Nogh
Idelle, Gaziz, 3161 Tata
Ignatyef, V., 1097 Crim
Ĭkramif, Äkmäl, 2063 Uz
Ĭlbĭk, 2148–50 Uz
Il'in, M., 1068 Crim
Iliyasïf, Gh., 3163 Tata
Illish, Bila, 3164 Tata
Illiteracy, *see* Literacy
Il'minskii, N., 1558 Kaz; 2315 Uz
Il oglï, 1965 Tur
Ilyas, Ä., 473 Az
'Ĭmadi, Ziya, 2233, 2319 Uz
Imambay, ulï, Sh., 1621 Kaz
Imperialism, 242 Az; 2561, 2770, 2841–42 Tata; economic, 2241 Uz; 2787 Tata
Imperial Russian Academy of Sciences, *p. 299n*
India, 993 Chu; 2804 Tata; history, 1887 Taj
Industrial investment, 2570 Tata
Industrial planning conference, 1319 Kaz
Industry, 79, 81, 120–22 Az; 664 Bash; 1281, 1304, 1322, 1325 Kaz; 1855 Taj; 2055, 2060, 2073, 2095 Uz; 2552, 2560, 2567, 2585 Tata; conference, 120 Az; inspection, 2795 Tata; periodical, 1264 Kaz
Ingils, F., 2849 Tata
Innokentĭy, 1050 Chu
Ĭnsertof, 1417 Kaz
Inspection: for government, 1773 Kum; for industry and business, 2795 Tata
Insurance, 348 Az; 825 Chu; 1309, 1312 Kaz; 2044, 2058–59, 2065, 2107, 2109 Uz
Intellectuals, 163 Az; 1368, 1378 Kaz; 2161, 2181–82 Uz
Internationalism, 2234, 2271, 2288 Uz
International relations, 9 Alt; 84, 150, 198–99, 201–3, 207, 231–32, 249, 254–55, 258, 274, 279, 354, 616–17 Az; 879, 903, 909 Chu; 1146 Crim; 1453 Kaz; 1707, 1712 Kir; 1770 Kum; 2292, 2301 Uz; 2642, 2770, 2785, 2806, 2850, 2855, 2859, 2868, 2892 Tata; 3336 Yak
Invalids, 1518 Kaz
Ĭoanof, 2151 Uz
Ĭoanof, G.E., 2209 Uz
Ioganson, O., 1051 Chu
Ioganson, P., 1809 Nag
Ipchi, 'Umer, 1169–70 Crim
Iran, 305 Az
Iranian languages: publications: *pp. 6, 8, 10* (*table*); in U.S. libraries, *pp. 8, 11*
Iranian nationalities, *pp. 21, 299*
Irkütov, A., 475 Az
Irrigation, 88, 94, 96 Az; 1306, 1341 Kaz; 1668 Kir; 1933, 1938 Tur; 2043, 2079–80 Uz
Isaev, I.V., 834 Chu
Isakuf, B., 720 Bash
Isatay, 1584 Kaz
Isayef, S.I., 1114 Crim
Isḥaqïf, Ḥ., 2759–60 Tata
Isḥaqïf, Ḥasan, 2692 Tata
Isḥaqïf, Väli, 2572 Tata
Ishemghol, Bulat, 711 Bash
Ishemghulïf, Bulat, 787 Bash
Ishimghöl, 709, 740 Bash; *see also* Iyshïmghül
Ishimghöl, B., 710 Bash
Ishimghöl, Bülat, 712–13, 749 Bash
Ishmidt, V., 670 Bash
Ishmĭt, 2066 Uz
Iskhaq, Ä., 3165 Tata
Iskhaqov, F., 2754 Tata
Ĭskorobogätöf, Shukach, 2369 Uz
Islam, 616–17 Az; 787 Bash; 2317,

Social organization: ancient, 3009 Tata; classes, 3032, 3292 Tata; groups, 3019 Tata; medicine, 2372 Uz; modernization of, 1522 Kaz; new society, 1549 Kaz; periodicals, 28, 34, 40, 58, 63, 65–67, 71–73 Az; 639 Bash; 795, 805 Chu; 1059, 1061, 1067 Crim; 2018, 2025, 2030, 2032, 2037–39 Uz; 2505, 2508, 2515, 2521, 2528, 2540, 2546 Tata; urban and rural, 239, 367 Az; veterinarians, 1517 Kaz; *see also* Poor, the

Social Organization entries: 16–17 Alt; 358–411 Az; 749–56 Bash; 953–77 Chu; 1136–50 Crim; 1219-24 Kar-Bal; 1522–49 Kaz; 1649–53 Khak; 1727–31 Kir; 1781–86 Kum; 1813 Nogh; 1832–37 Oss; 1893–96 Taj; 1923 Tat; 1986–89 Tur; 2366–87 Uz; 2988–3042 Tata; 3324–29 Yak; dates and number of, *pp. 12–15* (*table*), *17*, *18* (*table*); description of, *pp. 16–17*; *see also* 4, 20 Alt; 47, 68, 144, 167, 172, 189, 200, 233–35, 239–40, 250, 255, 262, 265, 269, 273, 275–76, 289, 291, 294–97, 318–19, 332, 337, 347, 349, 454, 612 Az; 647, 681, 705–6, 717–19, 730, 738, 777, 788 Bash; 797, 813, 815, 837–38, 861, 863, 867, 869–70, 872–74, 889, 891, 898–99, 904, 913, 915, 917, 919, 922, 930–33, 937, 1037, 1051, 1055 Chu; 1060, 1065, 1082, 1090, 1094, 1099, 1113, 1117, 1121–23, 1170, 1185 Crim; 1208–9 Kar-Bal; 1291, 1299, 1372, 1393–95, 1409, 1418–19, 1429, 1438–39, 1444, 1448, 1451, 1460, 1464, 1467, 1476, 1478, 1484, 1488, 1491, 1496, 1518, 1568, 1570, 1593 Kaz; 1647, 1657 Khak; 1670, 1695, 1697, 1699, 1705–6, 1713–14, 1719, 1742 Kir; 1776 Kum; 1796, 1799–99a, Kur; 1809 Nag; 1811 Nogh; 1828, 1831 Oss; 1964, 1970, 1976–78, 1981, 1988–89, 2001 Tur; 2060, 2069, 2119, 2185, 2187, 2198, 2213, 2232, 2234–35, 2239, 2243–44, 2247–48, 2250–51, 2254, 2266, 2270, 2274, 2277, 2293, 2295, 2299, 2301, 2305–6, 2308, 2310, 2324, 2344, 2444, 2464, 2469 Uz; 2563, 2606, 2611, 2625, 2631, 2661–62, 2722, 2730, 2746, 2754, 2772–76, 2789, 2792, 2796, 2799, 2811, 2813–14, 2822, 2825, 2827, 2830, 2834, 2836 2852–54, 2861, 2865–67, 2869, 2872, 2877, 2879, 2884, 2892, 2899, 2912, 2917, 2922, 2927–28, 2934, 2947, 3073, 3219, 3265, 3269, 3283, 3296 Tata; 3303, 3320 Yak

Social Sciences entries: divisions of, *p. 16*; number of, *p. 17*; *see also under specific disciplines, e.g.*, Economics entries

Social security, 109, 361 Az; 652 Bash; 813 Chu; 1304 Kaz; 1670 Kir; 2091 Uz

Social studies, 2137, 2147 Uz; 2913 Tata

Social theory, 3031 Tata

Sociology, 373 Az; 2385 Uz; 3031 Tata

Sokalof, I.N., 2723 Tata

Sokhārīvā, 1869 Taj

Sokolof, S., 1097 Crim

Sokolov, S., 829 Chu

Sokolov, S.N., 180 Az

Soläyman, ʻA., 2471 Uz

Solts, A.A., 1882 Taj

Songs, 480 Az; 769 Bash; 1003–4, 1013, 1019, 1043 Chu; 1178 Crim; 1229 Kar-Bal; 1233, 1246 Karai; 1569 Kaz; 2003, 2005 Tur; 2008 Uygh; 2107, 2475 Uz; 3076, 3140, 3165, 3212, 3216, 3219, 3229, 3265 Tata; Tatar, 780 Bash